For our teachers at SOAS,
Richard Rathbone and Andrew D. Ro

CONTENTS

PART III   RELIGION AND BELIEF

PART IV   SOCIETY AND ECONOMY

PART V   ARTS AND THE MEDIA

List of Contributors

Jean Allman teaches African history at Washington University, where she is the J. H. Hexter Professor in the Humanities and chairs the History Department. She is the author of *The Quills of the Porcupine: Asante Nationalism in an Emergent Ghana* (Madison: University of Wisconsin Press, 1993); '*I Will Not Eat Stone*': A Women's *History of Colonial Asante* (Portsmouth, NH: Heinemann, 2000), with Victoria Tashjian; *Tongnaab: The History of a West African God* (Bloomington, Ind.: Indiana University Press, 2005), with John Parker; and has edited several collections, including *Fashioning Africa: Power and the Politics of Dress* (Bloomington, Ind.: Indiana University Press, 2004). She co-edits the New African Histories book series at Ohio University Press and for six years co-edited the *Journal of Women's History*.

Nicolas Argenti is senior lecturer in anthropology at Brunel University. Since the early 1990s, he has worked in Cameroon on questions regarding youth, childhood, political power, and collective memory. He is the author of *The Intestines of the State: Youth, Violence and Belated Histories in the Cameroon Grassfields* (Chicago: University of Chicago Press, 2007) and the co-editor of three collections on youth in Africa, on slavery, and on memories of political violence. He has recently started a new research project on collective memories of political violence in the Aegean island of Chios.

Robert M. Baum (Ph.D., Yale University) is an associate professor of Religious Studies at the University of Missouri. He is the author of numerous articles on Diola religion, African religions, indigenous religions, and the comparative study of prophetic movements. His best known work is *Shrines of the Slave Trade: Diola Religion and Society in Precolonial Senegambia* (New York: Oxford University Press, 1999), which received the American Academy of Religion's Award for the best first book in the history of religions. He is currently completing a book on the history of Diola prophetic movements and is working on a continent-wide history of African religions.

James R. Brennan is Assistant Professor of African History at the University of Illinois at Urbana-Champaign and a research associate at the School of Oriental and African Studies, University of London, where he previously taught. His work focuses on urbanization, political thought, media, and opposition politics in eastern Africa and the Indian Ocean. He is author of numerous articles and book chapters, as well as *Taifa: Making Nation and Race in Urban Tanzania* (Athens, O.: Ohio University Press, 2012). He is currently researching a political biography of Oscar Kambona, who was the main rival to Tanzania's first president, Julius Nyerere.

Barbara M. Cooper is Professor of History at Rutgers University. She earned her Ph.D. at Boston University. Her work explores gender, religion, and family life over the long twentieth century. Recent publications include *Evangelical Christians in the Muslim Sahel* (Bloomington, Ind.: Indiana University Press, 2006), which won the Herskovits Award in 2007. She is a co-editor of the *Journal of African History* and is currently writing a history of motherhood and fertility in Niger.

Shane Doyle was educated at Cambridge and the School of Oriental and African Studies, University of London. Currently Senior Lecturer in African History at the University of Leeds, he was previously a British Academy Post-Doctoral Fellow at the Cambridge Group for the History of Population and Social Structure and before that Assistant Director of the British Institute in Eastern Africa. His current research on the history of sexuality and demographic change in East Africa has been funded by the Arts and Humanities Research Council, the British Academy, and the Economic and Social Research Council, and will be published as *Before HIV: Sexuality, Fertility, and Mortality in East Africa, 1900–1980* (Oxford: OUP, forthcoming).

Deborah Durham is Professor of Anthropology at Sweet Briar College, Virginia. She has conducted field research in Botswana on Herero people living in the context of democratic liberalism and, from the 1980s, on youth and youth organizations. She co-edited, with Jennifer Cole, *Generations and Globalization: Youth, Age, and Family in the New World Economy* (Bloomington, Ind.: Indiana University Press, 2007) and *Figuring the Future: Globalization and the Temporalities of Children and Youth* (Santa Fe: SAR Press, 2008), and is the author of many articles on youth, cultural identity, and democratic liberalism.

Veit Erlmann is an anthropologist and ethnomusicologist and the Endowed Chair of Music History at the University of Texas at Austin. He held previous appointments at the University of Chicago, the University of Natal, the University of the Witwatersrand, and the Free University of Berlin. He has won numerous prizes, including the Alan P. Merriam award for the best English monograph in ethnomusicology, the Arnold Rubin Outstanding Publication Award of the Arts Council of the African Studies Association, and the Mercator Prize of the German Research Foundation DFG. He has published widely on music and popular culture in South Africa, including *African Stars: Studies in Black South African Performance* (Chicago: University of Chicago Press, 1991), *Nightsong: Performance, Power, and Practice in South Africa* (Chicago: University of Chicago Press, 1996), and *Music, Modernity and the Global Imagination: South Africa and the West*. His most recent publication is *Reason and Resonance: A History of Modern Aurality* (New York: Zone Books, 2010). Currently he is working on a book on intellectual property in the South African music industry.

Sean Hanretta received his Ph.D. in African History from the University of Wisconsin-Madison and is currently Associate Professor of History at Stanford University. His work focuses on the intellectual and cultural history of West Africa and includes *Islam and Social*

Change in French West Africa: History of an Emancipatory Community (Cambridge: CUP, 2009) and articles in the *Journal of African History*, *Comparative Studies in Society and History*, and *Past and Present*. His current research focuses on Muslim weddings and funerals in Ghana and the history of higher education in West Africa.

Walter Hawthorne is Professor of African History at Michigan State University. He is the author of *Planting Rice and Harvesting Slaves: Transformations along the Guinea-Bissau Coast 1400–1900* (Portsmouth, NH: Heinemann, 2003) and *From Africa to Brazil: Culture, Identity, and an Atlantic Slave Trade, 1600–1830* (Cambridge: CUP, 2010).

Nancy Rose Hunt, Professor of History at the University of Michigan, Ann Arbor, regularly teaches a course called 'Health and Illness in African Worlds'. She has published essays on breastfeeding, nursing, abortion, letter writing, bicycles, and comics. *A Colonial Lexicon: Of Birth Ritual, Medicalization, and Mobility in the Congo* (Durham, NC: Duke University Press, 1999) received the Herskovits Prize in 2000. *A Nervous State: Violence, Remedies, and Reverie* (Durham, NC: Duke University Press, forthcoming) analyses the securitization of therapeutic insurgency and the medicalization of infertility in a region of the Belgian Congo.

Morten Jerven has a Ph.D. in economic history from London School of Economics and works as Assistant Professor at the School for International Studies at Simon Fraser University. He has published widely on national income accounting, African development statistics, and how these pertain to the debates on African economic performance both currently and over the long term.

Pier M. Larson is Professor of African and Indian Ocean History at the Johns Hopkins University. He grew up in southern Madagascar. His most recent book, *Ocean of Letters: Language and Creolization in an Indian Ocean Diaspora* (Cambridge: CUP, 2009) examines the dispersion of Malagasy in the islands of the western Indian Ocean between 1640 and 1850 through colonial linguistic projects in their language. He is currently working on a history of literacy in nineteenth-century Madagascar and on the biography of a mixed-race family in the islands of France's Indian Ocean empire between 1750 and 1850.

Sidney Littlefield Kasfir, Professor Emeritus of African Art History at Emory University, Atlanta, conducts research in Kenya and Uganda, and formerly in Nigeria. Her most recent publications include *Central Nigeria Unmasked: Arts of the Benue River Valley* (Los Angeles: UCLA Fowler Museum, 2011), edited with Marla Berns and Richard Fardon, and *African Art and Agency in the Workshop* (Bloomington, Ind.: Indiana University Press, 2012), edited with Till Förster.

David Maxwell is Dixie Professor of Ecclesiastical History at the University of Cambridge and Fellow of Emmanuel College. He was editor of the *Journal of Religion in Africa* and is the author of *Christians and Chiefs in Zimbabwe: A Social History of* *the Hwesa People, c.1870s–1990s* (Edinburgh: Edinburgh University Press, 1999) and *African Gifts of the Spirit: Pentecostalism and the Rise of a Zimbabwean Transnational Religious Movement* (Oxford: James Currey, 2006). He is currently researching the missionary and African Christian contribution to colonial science in Belgian Congo.

James C. McCann is Professor of History at Boston University. His publications include *Stirring the Pot: African Cuisines and Global Change, 1500–2000* (Athens, O.: Ohio University Press, 2009), *Maize and Grace: Africa's Encounter with a New World Crop* (Cambridge, Mass.: Harvard University Press, 2005), *Green Land, Brown Land, Black Land: An Environmental History of Africa, 1500–1990* (Portsmouth, NH: Heinemann, 1999), and *People of the Plow: An Agricultural History of Ethiopia, 1800–1990* (Madison, Wis.: University of Wisconsin Press, 1995).

Marie Miran-Guyon is lecturer in African history and the anthropology of religion at the École des Hautes Études en Sciences Sociales (EHESS), Centre d'Études africaines (CEAf), Paris. She specializes in the anthropology of Islam in Côte d'Ivoire and in other regions of the Gulf of Guinea coast. She is the author of *Islam, histoire et modernité en Côte d'Ivoire* (Paris: Karthala, 2006) and has a forthcoming book titled *Patrie des dieux: Religion, nationalisme et citoyenneté en Côte d'Ivoire* (Paris: Karthala; Abidjan: CERAP), the English translation of which will be published by Ohio University Press.

Stephanie Newell has published widely on West African literatures, West African cultural history, and African popular literatures. Her books include *Ghanaian Popular Fiction: 'Thrilling Discoveries in Conjugal Life'* (Oxford: James Currey, 2000), *Literary Culture in Colonial Ghana* (Manchester: MUP, 2002), *West African Literatures: Ways of Reading* (2006), *The Forger's Tale: The Search for 'Odeziaku'* (Athens, O.: Ohio University Press, 2006), and the forthcoming *A History of Anonymity in Colonial West African Newspapers*.

Emily Lynn Osborn is an assistant professor of history at the University of Chicago. Her first book focuses on statecraft, households, and gender in precolonial and colonial West Africa; she has also published on colonial economies and colonial intermediaries in French West Africa. Her current research focuses on the post-Second World War history of West African artisans who recycle aluminum to make everyday objects.

John Parker teaches African history at the School of Oriental and African Studies, University of London. He is the author of *Making the Town: Ga State and Society in Early Colonial Accra* (Portsmouth, NH: Heinemann, 2000); *Tongnaab: The History of a West African God* (Bloomington, Ind.: Indiana University Press, 2005), with Jean Allman; and *African History: A Very Short Introduction* (Oxford: OUP, 2007), with Richard Rathbone.

Richard Reid is Professor of the History of Africa at the School of Oriental and African Studies, University of London. Previously he taught at Durham University and at the University of Asmara in Eritrea. His work on the history of warfare and military organization in Africa has resulted most recently in *Frontiers of Violence: Genealogies of Conflict since c.1800* (Oxford: OUP, 2011) and *Warfare in African History* (New York: CUP, 2012). He is currently working on historical consciousness and culture in Uganda.

Richard Roberts is the Frances and Charles Field Professor in History, professor of African history, and former director of the Center for African Studies, Stanford University. He has published numerous articles and eleven books, including *Trafficking in the Wake of Slavery: Law and the Experience of Women and Children* (Athens, O.: Ohio University Press, 2012), edited with Benjamin Lawrance; *Domestic Violence and the Law in Colonial and Postcolonial Africa* (Athens, O.: Ohio University Press, 2010), edited with Emily Burrill and Elizabeth Thornberry; *Muslim Family Law in Sub-Saharan Africa: Colonial Legacies and Postcolonial Challenges* (Amsterdam: Amsterdam University Press, 2010), edited with Shamil Jeppie and Ebrahim Moosa; *Litigants and Households: African Disputes and Colonial Courts in the French Soudan, 1895–1912* (Portsmouth, NH: Heinemann, 2005); *Two Worlds of Cotton: Colonialism and the Regional Economy of the French Soudan, 1800–1946* (Stanford, Calif.: Stanford University Press, 1996); and *Law in Colonial Africa* (Portsmouth, NH: Heinemann, 1991), edited with Kristin Mann.

Heather J. Sharkey is an associate professor in the Department of Near Eastern Languages and Civilizations at the University of Pennsylvania. She is the author of *Living with Colonialism: Nationalism and Culture in the Anglo-Egyptian Sudan* (Berkeley, Calif.: University of California Press, 2003) and *American Evangelicals in Egypt: Missionary Encounters in an Age of Empire* (Princeton: PUP, 2008). With Mehmet Ali Doğan, she edited *American Missionaries and the Modern Middle East: Foundational Encounters* (Salt Lake City: University of Utah Press, 2011). She is currently writing a history of the social and cultural interactions of Muslims, Christians, and Jews in the Islamic Middle East and North Africa.

Carol Summers is Professor of History and International Studies at the University of Richmond. She is the author of *Colonial Lessons: Africans' Education in Southern Rhodesia, 1918–1935* (Portsmouth, NH: Heinemann, 2002) and *From Civilization to Segregation: Social Ideals and Social Control in Southern Rhodesia, 1890–1934* (1994), as well as articles on the history of education and schooling in colonial Zimbabwe and on various aspects of political culture in colonial Uganda.

Jean-Louis Triaud is Professor Emeritus in African History, Université de Provence, and member of the Centre d'Études des Mondes Africains (CEMAF-CNRS). His publications are concerned with the history of Islam and Muslim societies, mainly during the colonial era, and include *Bayân mâ waqa'a d'al-Hâjj 'Umar al-Fûtî* (Paris: CNRS, 1983), with Sidi Mohamed Mahibou; *La Légende noire de la Sanûsiyya: Une confrérie musulmane saharienne sous le regard français (1840–1930)* (1995); *Le Temps des marabouts: Itinéraires et strategies islamiiques en Afrique occidentale française, 1880–1960* (Paris: Karthala,

1997), edited with David Robinson; *Histoire d'Afrique: Les Enjeux de mémoire* (Paris, 1999), edited with Jean-Pierre Chrétien; and *La Tijâniyya: Une confrérie musulmane à la conquête de l'Afrique* (Paris: Karthala, 2000), edited with David Robinson.

Richard Waller took his undergraduate and doctoral degrees at Cambridge. He has conducted fieldwork in Kenya and taught at the University of Malawi. He currently teaches in the Department of History at Bucknell University in Pennsylvania. His area of interest covers East Africa in the nineteenth and twentieth centuries and he has written on Maasai history, ecology, and economy, the development of the Kenya colonial livestock industry, youth in the colonial period, and aspects of crime and the law in colonial Kenya. He is currently collaborating with a colleague on a collection of studies of crime and the law.

Justin Willis teaches history at Durham University. He has also worked for the British Institute in Eastern Africa based in Nairobi. His research is concerned with authority, ethnicity, and the nature of legitimacy in eastern Africa since the nineteenth century.

MAPS

....

Physical Africa.

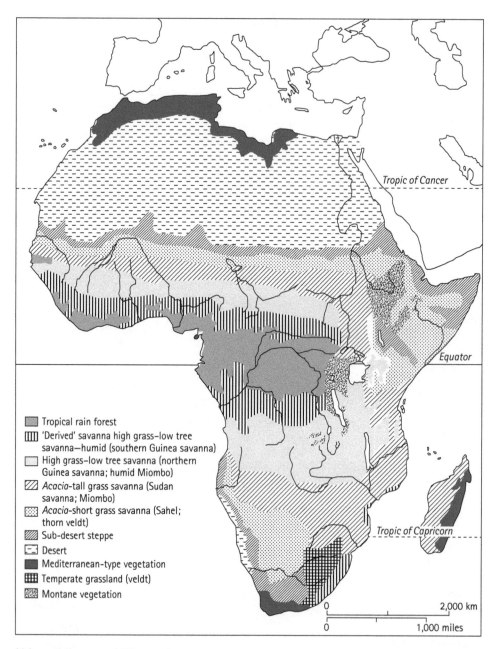

Tropic of Cancer

Equator

Tropic of Capricorn

Tropical rain forest

'Derived' savanna high grass–low tree savanna—humid (southern Guinea savanna)

High grass–low tree savanna (northern Guinea savanna; humid Miombo)

Acacia-tall grass savanna (Sudan savanna; Miombo)

Acacia-short grass savanna (Sahel; thorn veldt)

Sub-desert steppe

Desert

Mediterranean-type vegetation

Temperate grassland (veldt)

Montane vegetation

0   2,000 km

0   1,000 miles

Main vegetation zones of Africa.

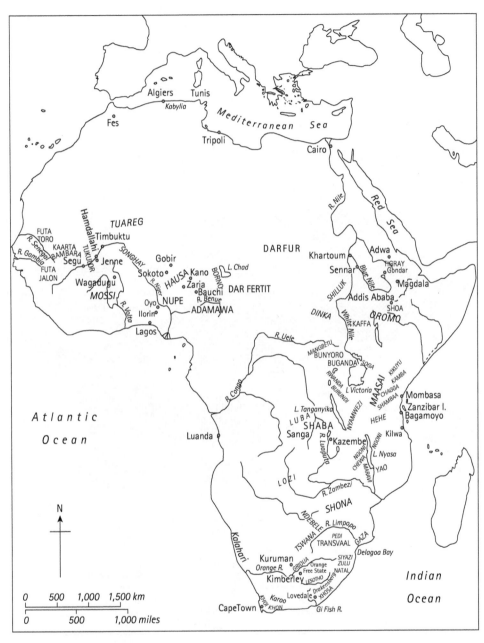

Africa in the nineteenth century: key peoples and places.

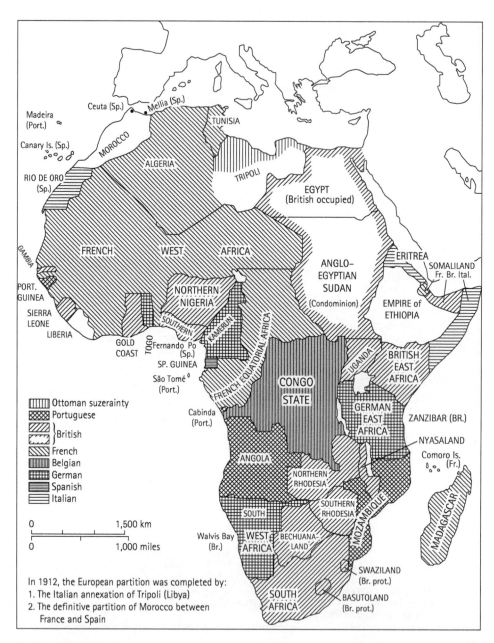

Madeira (Port.)
Ceuta (Sp.)
Mellia (Sp.)
TUNISIA
Canary Is. (Sp.)
MOROCCO
ALGERIA
RIO DE ORO (Sp.)
TRIPOLI
EGYPT (British occupied)
GAMBIA
FRENCH   WEST   AFRICA
ANGLO-EGYPTIAN SUDAN
ERITREA
SOMALILAND Fr. Br. Ital.
PORT. GUINEA
NORTHERN NIGERIA
(Condominion)
EMPIRE of ETHIOPIA
SIERRA LEONE
LIBERIA
SOUTHERN
KAMERUN
GOLD COAST
TOGO
Fernando Po (Sp.)
SP. GUINEA
São Tomé (Port.)
FRENCH EQUATORIAL AFRICA
UGANDA
BRITISH EAST AFRICA
CONGO STATE
GERMAN EAST AFRICA
ZANZIBAR (BR.)
Cabinda (Port.)
NYASALAND
Comoro Is. (Fr.)
ANGOLA
NORTHERN RHODESIA
SOUTHERN RHODESIA
MOZAMBIQUE
MADAGASCAR
SOUTH WEST AFRICA
BECHUANA-LAND
Walvis Bay (Br.)
SWAZILAND (Br. prot.)
SOUTH AFRICA
BASUTOLAND (Br. prot.)

[ ] Ottoman suzerainty
[ ] Portuguese
[ ] } British
[ ] French
[ ] Belgian
[ ] German
[ ] Spanish
[ ] Italian

0 ————— 1,500 km
0 ————— 1,000 miles

In 1912, the European partition was completed by:
1. The Italian annexation of Tripoli (Libya)
2. The definitive partition of Morocco between France and Spain

Partition: Africa c.1902

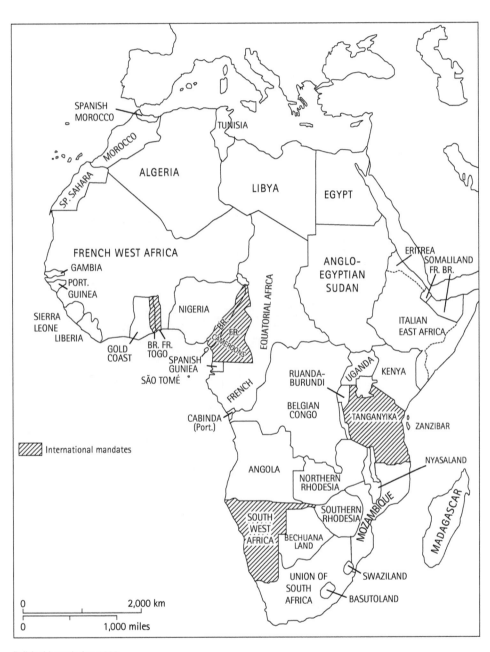

Political boundaries, 1939.

Present-day political boundaries.

INTRODUCTION

AFRICAN HISTORIES

Past, Present, and Future

RICHARD REID AND JOHN PARKER

ONE hundred years ago, in 1912, the European powers came to an agreement that resulted in the declaration of a French protectorate over Morocco, a diplomatic move that effectively brought the colonial partition of Africa to a close. In the same year, at the other end of the continent, a group of elite Africans met in the city of Bloemfontein and agreed to form the South African Native National Congress 'for the purpose of creating national unity and defending our rights and privileges'.[1] Fifty years later, the continent was in the throes of decolonization. As Jean Allman reminds us, 1960 was portrayed in the world's media as the 'Year of Africa'.[2] The end of empire had gathered pace over the course of the previous decade: Libya became independent in 1951, Sudan, Tunisia, and Morocco in 1956, Ghana in 1957, and Guinea in 1958. It was 1960, however, that witnessed the most dramatic dismantling of colonial rule, as the continent's most populous territory, Nigeria, the vast domains of French West and Equatorial Africa, and the Belgian Congo, Somalia, and the island of Madagascar all achieved independence. Not that this was the end of the process: elsewhere, wars of liberation continued—in the Portuguese colonies and Zimbabwe into the 1970s—and it would not be until 1994 that the African National Congress, as the South African Native National Congress came to be known, came to power and brought an end to white minority rule in southern Africa. Standing as we now do a century on from the first of these tumultuous events, and half a century on from the other, it seems an apposite moment to survey the modern history of Africa.

This is not to say that Africa's recent history should necessarily be framed by the beginning and end of European colonial domination. It *is* often periodized in that way, but as many of the following chapters indicate, historians are increasingly concerned to challenge and complicate that logic by exploring processes of continuity and change that transcend the precolonial and colonial eras and extend in turn to the time of renewed sovereignty from the 1960s. Neither is it to suggest that such a political narrative represents the core trajectory of African historical change. As our contributors also demonstrate, intertwined with political transformations are a whole range of alternative social, economic, cultural, and intellectual processes that often follow their own meandering paths. Indeed, the standard configuration of Africa's twentieth century into colonial and postcolonial periods is under threat from those who argue that 1940 or 1990 might actually be seen to have been more profound turning-points than that landmark year of 1960.[3] While we are loath to venture any precise definition of the notoriously slippery concept of 'modernity', our notion of modern African history in this volume covers the nineteenth and twentieth centuries, and extends back in the broad themes considered in Part I several centuries further. Its thematic organization therefore seeks to reflect current directions in the historiography—even if one of those directions, as we discuss below, is a certain neglect of Africa's 'precolonial' period.

Scholarly suspicion of neat watersheds is therefore justified and we are right to interrogate them. In terms of the writing of history, however, one turning-point is clear, and that is that at the same time as anti-colonial nationalism took shape in the decades after the Second World War, so too did the study of the African past begin to emerge as an object of serious academic endeavour. African history, then, made a relatively belated appearance as a recognized part of the broader discipline—and that was a recognition that has had to be struggled for. As a 'field' in its own right it is no older than independent Africa and over the past half-century its fortunes can be seen to have fluctuated in tandem with its object of study: a period of youthful excitement and high expectation giving way to one of anxiety and pessimism, which has in turn been succeeded by a return to cautious optimism. Without wanting to push the metaphor of a life journey too far, African history as an academic discipline might be said to have attained something of the gravitas of middle age; its position in the academy, at least, is now secure. Like the seventeen new nation-states that emerged in the year 1960, the field's premier scholarly journal, the *Journal of African History*, also celebrated its half-century in 2010. In short, we are now as distant from the era of decolonization and of the scholarship which eagerly attended it as the pioneering historians of that generation were from the European partition of the continent in the 1890s and 1900s. Meanwhile, another generation has passed since the end of the Cold War and the last twenty years have witnessed dramatic change across the continent—more change, arguably, than in the previous three decades of independence. There is ample justification to pause and take stock of what progress has been made in the task of reconstructing modern African history, the current state of the field, and potentially fruitful directions for the future.

AFRICA AND THE AFRICANS: UNITY AND DIVERSITY

Before considering the notion of modern Africa, we need to consider that of Africa itself. To what extent do entire continents represent valid categories of historical analysis? Given the sheer size of Africa and its extraordinary diversity in terms of ecology, culture, language, religious faith, and national entities, this is not an easy question to answer. Most historians do not study 'Africa'; rather, they tend to conduct research on particular peoples, localities, states, or, at best, regions. Indeed, the continent's regions—commonly identified by the cardinal points of the compass, between which lies a vaguely defined Central Africa—have considerable purchase in academic scholarship. This is reflected most obviously in the convention of capitalization (although 'southern Africa' tends to be used in order to avoid confusion with the nation of South Africa). It is also apparent in academic job advertisements, which often specify a specialist in the history of, say, East Africa or West Africa. Even within these five broad regions (and a sixth, North-East Africa or 'the Horn', is also often hived off, due largely to the distinctive cultural and historical traditions of the Ethiopian highlands), the historian is confronted with dizzying cultural complexity.[4] Africa's linguistic heritage is particularly daunting: Nigeria, which remains the continent's most populous nation, alone has over three hundred languages, while the Democratic Republic of Congo has a total of twenty-four 'major' languages, that is, with over half a million speakers. Intersecting with indigenous vernaculars is the widespread use of Arabic in North Africa, Sudan, and Mauritania and of the languages of the continent's principal European colonizers: English, French, and Portuguese.[5]

Africa's complex colonial legacy has certainly added to its cultural diversity. African state-builders had themselves forged centralized political structures throughout the ages, succeeding to various degrees in co-opting or coercing rural populations often stubbornly defensive of their own institutions and independence. The nineteenth century witnessed an increase in militarized state-building, ranging from the ephemeral and crudely predatory to the creation of expansive, sophisticated, and deeply rooted entities such as the Sokoto Caliphate in the region of present-day northern Nigeria and southern Niger. But with only one exception, that of imperial Ethiopia, these indigenous political projects ultimately lost out to increasingly determined and better equipped European rivals. Between the 1880s and 1912, a total of seven European powers—Britain, France, Portugal, Belgium, Germany, Italy, and Spain—partitioned almost the entire continent between themselves. France also acquired the huge Indian Ocean island of Madagascar, conventionally considered as an integral off-shore component of the African continent. The colonial map underwent some reorganization following the First World War, when Germany's possessions were confiscated and divided amongst the victorious allies (including self-governing South Africa), technically as 'mandates' of the League of Nations. It was from these colonial empires (and from the indigenous imperial system of Ethiopia) that, in the course of the past half-century, Africa's fifty-four independent nation-states have emerged, the fifty-fourth, South Sudan, only in 2011.

Beyond these multiple layers of diversity, Africa's continental integrity has in recent decades also come under scrutiny as part of the general wariness towards received categories and narratives characteristic of the postmodern or post-imperial juncture. Just as history has been seen to be in need of rescue from the stranglehold of the nation-state, so too has the notion of distinctive continental historical trajectories begun to dissolve in the face of a growing concern on the part of scholars with fluidity, hybridity, and the transregional networks connecting the local to the global.[6] Neither is this an issue simply for historians: in *The Myth of Continents*, Martin W. Lewis and Kären E. Wigen mount a thought-provoking challenge to the 'metageography' that has long divided the world's landmass into discrete units, including the lingering assumption that equates those units with particular cultural or even 'racial' traits.[7] With regard to Africa, Lewis and Wigen argue that there is sound reason for that part of the continent south of the Sahara desert to be considered a distinct geographical zone from that to the north. Historically, North Africa can indeed be seen to be as much a part of the Mediterranean world, of south-western Asia, or of the Middle East—itself a relatively recently coined concept— as it is a part of Africa. It is, however, at least that—although it is striking how recently the continent's historians have begun to get to grips with reconstructing the lineaments of trans-Saharan connectivity.[8]

Originally, the continent's Mediterranean littoral *was* 'Africa', the name given by the Romans to the imperial province created after their defeat of Carthage in 146 BC and which in turn became the Arabic *Ifriqiya* following the Arab conquest of North Africa in the seventh century AD. Like the earlier Greek words, Egypt, Libya, and Ethiopia (the latter from *aithiops*, 'burnt-faced'), as well as the Greek-derived Berber (from *barbaroi*, 'barbarian'), these were terms for places and peoples coined by others. Configured by classical and then Islamic geographical schemes into latitudinal zones which equated climate with culture, such terms acquired vague 'racial' connotations well before a European racial hierarchy was forged in the crucibles of the Atlantic slave trade and nineteenth-century imperial expansion. For Muslim geographers, these ancient schemes were overlain with faith. Following the conversion of most of its indigenous Egyptian and Berber inhabitants, North Africa became an integral part of the *Dar al-Islam*, the abode of Islam, while the *bilad as-Sudan*, 'the lands of the blacks' on the southern fringes of the Sahara desert, was part of the *Dar al-Kufr*, the realm of unbelief. Yet it would be Portuguese mariners, the bearers of a rival militant faith, whose voyages in the course of the second half of the fifteenth century would bring the contours of the entire continent into purview. The transformation in the global economy initiated by Iberian conquest in the Americas and expansion into the Indian Ocean, it can be argued, provided the context for the idea of Africa as it came to be recognized in the modern world.

At the heart of this transformation was the Atlantic slave trade, which between the late fifteenth and the mid-nineteenth centuries resulted in the forced migration of over twelve million African captives to the Americas. African slaves had previously been transported across the Sahara to the Mediterranean world and into the Middle East and Indian Ocean, trades which continued and which together probably resulted in a similar number of removals as that across the Atlantic.[9] Yet it was Atlantic slavery, grounded in a garbled ideology of faith, culture, and race but driven by the ruthless economic self-interest of both European and African slave merchants, that can be seen further to have reinforced the perception of Africa as a 'paradigm of difference'. In the view of Congolese philosopher V. Y. Mudimbe, the idea of Africa was therefore first invented by non-Africans, serving as a prism through which Europeans refracted images of exotic others and of themselves.[10] In his introduction to a companion volume in this series, Jose C. Moya comes to a similar conclusion with regard to the 'invention' of Latin America. Moya identifies a number of factors that have served to unite the disparate geographical and ethno-historical zones of the Americas south of the Rio Grande: their shared multiracial legacy, Iberian colonialism, and their centrality to the rise of globalization and modernity—but argues that the idea of Latin America too was constructed as a paradigm of difference in relation to the 'Anglo' realm to its north.[11] Indeed, given the fact that three-quarters of all migrants to the Americas before 1820 originated from Africa, the forging of their respective continental identities can be seen to have been closely intertwined.

As Mudimbe and others have gone on to argue, the nineteenth-century age of abolitionism saw diasporic Africans in Europe and the Americas begin to appropriate this idea of Africa. Just as Latin American creole elites sought to assert their claim to 'our America', so too did black American intellectuals lay claim to an African homeland. For the latter, it was their very removal and distance from the continent that enabled them to perceive it as a whole. In doing so, they also appropriated European ideas of race: in the view of these pioneering pan-Africanist thinkers, Africa was the homeland of a distinctive people, 'the Negro race', in need of urgent redemption from the evils of slavery on both sides of the Atlantic. For some, that redemption would come principally through Christianity; for others, through freedom and full citizenship in the Americas and self-determination in Africa. Aspirations to racial unity, dignity, and self-determination, however, were swept aside by the rising tide of European imperialism at the end of the century. The ideology of pan-Africanism would survive as a tool of resistance to racial domination across the black Atlantic, but it would be the shared experience of colonial rule that consolidated for many the idea of Africa and of being African.

Rather than simply being taken for granted, it is therefore important that the idea of Africa be seen as historically constituted and contingent. This is not to say that the question of what exactly does constitute the continent and its history is settled. While the ideology of racial difference has largely been consigned to the imperial past, the notion which equates sub-Saharan or 'black' Africa with what is distinctive or essential about the continent's history lingers on. Indeed, it is to be found to some extent in this volume, many chapters of which consider their respective themes with only passing reference to North Africa. This is in part due to entrenched regional specialization and the linguistic skills necessary to support it: Africanist historians often need to work in a number of European and African languages and few feel confident about extending research agendas to the largely Arabic-speaking northern reaches of the continent without a knowledge of that language. The subtitle of the best known single-volume history of Africa, John Iliffe's *Africans: The History of a Continent*, is a clear assertion of that work's inclusive, trans-Saharan ethos. Yet the tendency to read 'Africa' as meaning essentially sub-Saharan Africa remains.[12]

Then there is the question of the African diaspora. Iliffe's history of Africans may include those peoples on both sides of the Sahara, but it does not extend far beyond the shores of the continent itself. Yet as we have seen, the idea of Africa and its diaspora were in many ways mutually constituted, and pioneering efforts to assert a role for black people in human history such as W. E. B. Du Bois's *The Negro* (1915) often set out to consider both. With the rise of anti-colonial nationalism and the decline of pan-Africanism as a political project after the Second World War, the vision of a unified diasporic identity faded somewhat from view—it is notable that Du Bois produced an updated edition of his original work in 1946 retitled *The World and Africa*. The emergence of African history in universities and the rise of academic area studies from the 1960s served further to focus attention on the continent itself. In recent decades, however, the diaspora has re-emerged as an integral component of African history. This has in part been a result of the same epistemological shift from solidity to fluidity noted above—including the rise of more inclusive oceanic ecumenes as units of historical analysis. Indeed, the remit of diaspora studies is extending rapidly from an established focus on the North Atlantic to Afro-Latin America, the Middle East, and the Indian Ocean world. As recent research on diasporic communities in these regions demonstrates, the creative imagining and reimagining of the idea of Africa is far from over.[13]

Modern Africa and African Modernities

Any project of historical analysis is by definition about periodization. How is the passage of time to be ordered? At what points do the myriad events and processes of human existence converge in such a way as to constitute a juncture marking the end of one distinctive era and the start of another? Historians across the ages have wrestled with these questions. Yet they are perhaps of particular concern today to those whose principal interests lie in reconstructing the past of Africa, Asia, and other parts of the non-European world, for the simple reason that the established periodization of human history—at its most fundamental, from ancient to medieval to modern—is one based largely on the experience of Europe. What has been called the 'problem of Europe' arose from the tendency on the part of historians, from the emergence of the professionalized discipline in the mid-nineteenth century, to universalize not only this temporal framework but also the categories on which it was based. An important part of substituting an older Europe-centred (or, more pejoratively, 'Eurocentric') vision of the past with an inclusive 'world history' is, in the words of Jerry H. Bentley, to challenge and to complicate 'the distinctly European valence of terms like state and nation, culture and civilization, tradition and modernity, trade, labor, slavery, feudalism, capitalism, and others that have become workhorses of professional historical scholarship'.[14]

The project of African history has played a crucial role in this ongoing decentring of the wider discipline. And 'project' is an appropriate term, for it can be seen to have arisen in the decades after the Second World War from the same imperative to overthrow established racialized hierarchies that drove forward the processes of decolonization and national liberation. Despite initial resistance on the part of some leading European historians who doubted whether the African past could ever truly be recovered—or, in some unfortunate cases, was even worth recovering—there can be few today who would argue that the lived experience of Africans is not as worthy of sustained research as that of similarly large chunks of humanity long excluded from the historical mainstream: women, say, or ordinary working people everywhere. A variety of methodological and epistemological strategies, from bold experiments with the use of oral history to 'provincializing Europe' and 'Africanizing knowledge', have been mobilized with considerable success in an effort to transcend the old tendency to refract all historical experience through a European prism.[15] In his much-admired examination of the birth of the modern world, C. A. Bayly has argued persuasively that European modernity must be seen as just one element of—and as constituted by—a multicentric global history.[16]

For historians of Africa, however, the problem of Europe has not quite been solved. It is not just that Bayly clearly struggled to incorporate sub-Saharan Africa into his globalizing world, or that the birth of the modern era is still widely seen to have been determined by reference to Europe—whether that is dated to 1492, 1789, or any point in between.[17] It is also that European imperialism in Africa has foisted upon the continent a tripartite historical periodization (precolonial, colonial, and postcolonial) that in many ways has served to underscore the equation between colonial conquest and the coming of modernity. Like their counterparts in South Asia, historians and anthropologists of Africa have in recent years worked hard to identify indigenous expressions and appropriations of modernity.[18] Yet a working definition of 'modern Africa' remains elusive: such an era has been seen variously to begin with the Columbian exchange and the rise of the Atlantic slave trade, with the beginning of the end of that trade in 1807, with European partition, and even with the end of colonial rule.[19] To understand this, it is necessary briefly to consider the trajectory of the field of African history from its belated emergence in the terminal phase of European colonial rule.

It is not the case, as is sometimes suggested, that there was no interest in African history before the 1950s. African states and societies, of course, had their own vision of the past and their own ways of remembering it. Moreover, the 'invention' of Africa by others extended to a fascination with the residual traces of ancient kingdoms and the putative origins of existing ones, especially once Europeans began venturing into the interior of the continent from the late eighteenth century. James Bruce's *Travels to Discover the Source of the Nile* (1790), for example, included material on the history of Ethiopia culled from his purported reading of ancient manuscripts and from conversations with local informants, while the slave-trader Archibald Dalzel's *History of Dahomy* (1793) sought to counter abolitionist sentiments by expounding on the inherent savagery of this West African kingdom.[20] Napoleon's invasion of Egypt in 1798 and the subsequent publication of the massive *Description de l'Egypt* (1809–28) was a key moment, marking the start of the enduring allure of the ancient kingdom and giving rise to various theories of cultural diffusion and of 'degraded' forms of pharaonic statecraft in sub-Saharan Africa.[21] By the age of Victorian exploration, the search for the past was part of a broader imperative to measure, to map, to accumulate knowledge, and to impose epistemological order on the 'primitive' cultures of the world.[22] As the era of exploration shaded into that of conquest and partition, European intruders continued to seek out aristocratic elites and to differentiate the kingdoms they ruled over from the mass of lesser developed 'tribes'. Some kind of historical evolution was at least implicit in the colonial discovery of indigenous political hierarchy—although that knowledge was now sought for the primary purpose of either co-option or coercion.[23] By the late nineteenth century, pioneering African scholars were themselves beginning to write the history of their own people, most famously Samuel Johnson, whose *History of the Yorubas* (completed in 1897) represented the first and greatest instalment of a vigorous local historiography in both English and the vernacular Yoruba language of south-western Nigeria.[24]

Even in those parts of sub-Saharan Africa where states had emerged, however, European conquerors tended to perceive the social landscape in terms of primordial tribal groups. That these non-literate, apparently 'primitive' tribal peoples possessed little in the way of historical consciousness and therefore lay beyond the realm of history itself was part and parcel of the legitimizing ideology of colonial rule.[25] This was harder to claim for North Africa, where Arabic-language records and a visible architectural heritage spoke to the rise and fall of empires and dynasties. Indeed, scholar-administrators in French-ruled Algeria were publishing material on North African history and on Islam as early as the 1850s, a tradition that by the turn of the twentieth century had begun to be extended to France's newly conquered Sudanic empire in West Africa.[26] Yet the dominant colonial social science north and south of the Sahara was anthropology. Taking shape in the late Victorian era but coming into its own during the high tide of European empire between the wars, anthropology had a complex relationship with colonial power. To some extent it can be seen to have been complicit with the project of colonial domination: a tool with which to compile useful knowledge, to divide and to rule—and which in turn served to reinforce the perception of tribal identity on the part of European rulers and of Africans themselves. By the 1930s, however, a new generation of professional, university-trained anthropologists was discovering the extraordinary sophistication of African social structures hitherto seen simply as primitive, while in the following decade their attention began to turn away from 'traditional' tribal life and towards the dynamic social situations of the continent's rapidly growing towns and cities.[27] As ethnographic fieldwork was supplemented by historical research after the war, the two disciplines developed in close dialogue. The recognition by historians of the importance of local forms of knowledge and by anthropologists of temporal change means, as many of the following chapters show, that this trans-disciplinary intellectual conversation continues.

If anthropology in the first half of the twentieth century can in some ways be considered a colonial science, then history was very much associated with the new era of self-determination. Building a future of renewed sovereignty, in other words, involved rebuilding the past.[28] The little that had been written before the 1950s about the continent's past was mostly in the genre of imperial history, concerned first and foremost with the activities—whether heroic or malign—of European colonizers. The self-appointed task of the pioneering generation of scholars in the continent's new universities and abroad was to shake off the legacy of this colonialist worldview by recovering an authentically African history. Associated with the University of Ibadan in Nigeria and later the University of Dar es Salaam in Tanzania, this first, so-called nationalist phase of African historiography was largely concerned with precolonial statecraft and trade, and with resistance to European conquest.[29] Much has been made of the imperative to identify a 'usable past' of indigenous achievement, but this should not be exaggerated: the emphasis on the precolonial was likely to have been determined as much by an urgency to establish African history as a legitimate branch of the academic discipline as by a conscious desire to provide a model for contemporary nation-building. Much too has been made of the decline of nationalist historiography and the rise of a more pessimistic and Marxist-orientated economic history in the 1970s, as the heady optimism of the era of decolonization evaporated in the face of economic downturn and political authoritarianism.[30] That historiographical imperatives are shaped by present realities is of course a commonplace observation: as the postwar emergence of the Third World forced the history of ex-colonized peoples into the Eurocentric academy, so too did the rise of feminism propel the historical experience of women to centre-stage. Yet the turn to historical materialism was short-lived—while the continent's crisis continued. Subsequent shifts towards social history and, more recently, intellectual and cultural history can be seen to have been fashioned by a combination of factors: changes within Africa itself, the evolution of the broader discipline, and the growing availability of documentary sources. These developments have been accompanied by a quite striking temporal reorientation: it would not be an exaggeration to say the overwhelming bulk of historical research over the past two decades has been on the period of colonial rule.

This intensive engagement with the colonial period has greatly enriched our understanding of modern Africa. It has also made a significant contribution to a comparative understanding of the politics, economics, and cultures of colonialism. Whereas the history of European empire was once about what Europeans did—or was at best a simple dichotomy between the alien colonizer and the indigenous colonized—it is now very much focused on the agency of Africans and Asians and their role in the making of the modern world.[31] For sub-Saharan African in particular, recovering the deeper past has been dependent on a mere scattering of written accounts together with whatever evidence can be culled from archaeology, linguistics, and the careful extrapolation of oral traditions and ethnographic observation. In contrast, the dramatic expansion of written sources with the coming of colonial rule and the spread of literacy has enabled historians of Africa to do what those of other regions (including the literate cultures of colonial Asia) have long taken for granted: to reconstruct the intimate lives and interior worlds of individuals and of social groups in all their complexity and contradictions.[32] Rather than stand to one side while their colleagues have reaped rich rewards from the methods of social history, micro-history, history from below, or the 'cultural turn', Africa's historians have unsurprisingly gravitated towards the twentieth-century documentary archive on which these enterprises are so dependent.

If this has come at a cost, then it is a tendency towards a 'foreshortening' of African history.[33] There is a danger here, for the implication seems to be that the precolonial past is less interesting and less relevant, to the extent that those who work even on a period as late as the nineteenth century can feel themselves to belong to a small and endangered group. One important exception is research into the slave trades and slavery. This has remained robust, both because it so important and because it is better documented than many other aspects of the precolonial past. Yet there is a sense across the discipline that anything much before 1900 tells us little about where Africa is today. This prevailing 'presentism' threatens to inhibit our comprehension of the continent's historical trajectories over the longer term, as well as further cementing the modern to the colonial. Just as we are witnessing the rise of so-called 'big history', Africanists find themselves more and more clustered in one century.[34] The challenge remains to extend the range of insights that historians have recently developed into the colonial period to the deeper past—as well as forward into the second half of the twentieth century.

If our designation of modern Africa therefore bears no precise analytical weight, it does at least attempt to 'decentre' the colonial by extending its remit to the nineteenth century and, to some extent, before. Many of the historical processes that unfolded in the twentieth century may be seen to have roots in the continent's turbulent nineteenth century, thereby undermining the notion that European conquest represented a rupture after which nothing would ever be the same again.[35] Likewise, continuity rather than rupture now dominates the transition from colony to 'postcolony'. With the passing of time and the opening of archives, historical research is now moving steadily into the era of African decolonization and independence, allowing a reconsideration of processes once left for political scientists and anthropologists. Amongst current developments in the field, re-examining that mid-century transition and writing histories of contemporary Africa loom large.[36] Whether the end of the Cold War and the 'neoliberal moment' has indeed marked the end of the Africa's postcolonial period will be a question for the next generation of historians.

CHALLENGES AND POSSIBILITIES

From the outset, historians facing the task of reconstructing the African past were confronted with a particularly challenging set of problems. These ranged from the relative dearth of written evidence for much of the continent to scepticism on the part of other branches of the discipline and on to the pressing need to establish viable academic departments and research institutions in what were poor and in some cases unstable new nations. That so much was achieved in so short a time, and from so low a base, is testament to the extraordinary efforts on the part of the pioneering generations of scholars both in Africa and beyond. Consider, for example, the prolific publication output in the 1960s and 1970s of the so-called 'Dar es Salaam school': the group of African, European, and American historians working in the newly established university in Tanzania's capital. Despite government commitment to the development of tertiary education, it should be remembered that Tanzania was one of the world's poorest countries—and by the latter decade, getting distinctly poorer. Historians of Europe or of North America whose copious primary sources are deposited in well-funded and efficiently run archives and libraries in the West often have very little appreciation of the sheer logistical challenges confronting those working on the history of the global South. In the poorest parts of sub-Saharan Africa in particular, simply preserving a fragile documentary record from the ravages of tropical climates, voracious insects, and official indifference is difficult enough. But scholars—particularly those based in the continent itself—have also had to contend with crumbling infrastructure, political conflict, government interference in academic freedom, and sometimes direct threats to physical security.

Some of these challenges have at least in part been overcome. While documentary sources for the African past will never be of the same magnitude and range as those for other continents, necessity has been the mother of invention in terms of innovative methodologies and creative trans-disciplinary dialogue. That African history can be 'done', and done well, has greatly enriched the broader discipline. Yet other challenges remain. One is the struggle to maintain functioning research and teaching programmes in African universities and to preserve or to build links between these institutions and their counterparts beyond the continent. While the teaching, research, and publication of African history remains in robust health in North America and in Europe, within Africa itself the picture is a rather different one. Across much of the continent, history as a subject has been in decline since the 1970s as financial support for the higher education sector has dwindled. Leading institutions such as the universities of Ibadan, Dar es Salaam, and Makerere in Uganda have decayed significantly, as overworked and underpaid academics struggle simply to make ends meet, never mind to conduct new research projects. Many have chosen to practise their craft overseas, particularly in the United States. In recent decades, moreover, there appears to have been a decrease in the level of interest in history—both that of the continent and of the world beyond—among Africa's university students, based on the not unreasonable belief that the humanities are of only limited utility in the search for gainful employment. In an often fiercely competitive job market, students tend to follow the imagined money into degrees in business studies, management, or information technology. Indeed, some history departments have sought to rebrand themselves by adding international relations or development studies to their remit in an effort to attract greater funding and more students. To some degree, this reflects the shifting agendas of African governments: once seen to be an arm of the nation-building project of the 1960s, history has less place in the neoliberal developmental state now so predominant across the continent.

Beyond academic departments, however, competing and often contested visions of the past continue to be formulated. As the recent interest in the intellectual history of modern Africa has begun to demonstrate, the past was envisaged, recounted, and argued over in a variety of ways long before the belated advent of university scholarship, and has been done so since. A further challenge, then, is for professional historians not simply to reconstruct the lineages of these local, 'homespun' histories, but to engage with them as ongoing projects.[37] The cliché that history is written by the powerful and the victorious is just that—and the huge advances that have been made in understanding the lives of colonized peoples in the modern world show, in the long term at least, that it may be quite wrong. Yet the task of rescuing history from the nation-state—of moving beyond received 'statist' narratives in order to unearth submerged and often contrary stories and strategies—is ongoing. Many of the most exciting recent developments in this direction, in both Africa and beyond, have turned on the tension between history and memory. Drawing on groundbreaking works such as Pierre Nora's exploration of France's *lieux de mémoire*, Africanists are increasingly concerned with identifying such sites and streams of popular memory and exploring how they have been fashioned and fought over.[38] The long-standing concern on the part of the continent's anthropologists and then historians with diverse forms of local knowledge suggests that they in turn have much to teach their colleagues elsewhere.

The recognition that local histories, indigenous knowledge, and popular memory often run counter to dominant narratives is emerging as a key concern of historians everywhere. Yet Africa's historians have had to contend with a particularly broad range of divergent discourses, some of which run counter to their own claim to speak to the past based on the recognized methodological rigour of the modern discipline. One such discourse is what has been labelled 'Afrocentrism', a body of work often rooted in older, pan-African visions of racial unity, cultural diffusion, and the central role of pharaonic Egypt in the continent's history.[39] Largely marginal to the mainstream of historical research, this strain of thought nonetheless has some presence in academia and does exert considerable influence over popular perceptions of Africa, particularly in the United States. Indeed, the genre of popular history—intersecting in Africa itself with varieties of local history writing—represents another distinct, and often strikingly divergent, body of literature. Such popular history writing by journalists or independent scholars is sometimes quite good; much of it is certainly highly readable.[40] But it often fails to draw on the huge advances made in academic scholarship on Africa over the last half-century, tending to regurgitate the tired clichés and crude generalizations which have long served to objectify the entire continent. It is these advances that we set out to examine in this volume.

The *Handbook*: Aims and Organization

And so to the specifics of the *Handbook of Modern African History* itself. It should first be stated what this book is not: it is neither a general textbook nor an encyclopedic work of reference. The essays collected here do not aim to supplant either the excellent single-volume surveys now available or the grand multi-volume Cambridge and UNESCO histories of the continent.[41] Those interested in the broad contours of African history need look no further than these valuable resources. Neither does it set out to survey the range of methodological and trans-disciplinary approaches to the study of the continent's past, as has recently been done in John Edward Philips's excellent *Writing African History*.[42] What the book does do, in line with its companion volumes in the series, is to attempt to reflect critically upon the current state of the field of African history. Its aim is to consider the evolution of that field and to set out where, after fifty years of sustained scholarly research, it has arrived. What directions have the study of modern African history travelled in, what are its current concerns, and where might it be going in terms of emerging themes, agendas, and debates?

In order best to achieve these aims, the book is organized thematically rather than around continental or regional narratives. Having raised questions concerning the idea of Africa, the African people, and African history as unified entities, we have in a way answered them by conceding that the continent can, indeed, be considered to be a meaningful category of analysis. The temptation to underscore Africa's diversity by organizing material into a series of regional case-studies was strong—but one we ultimately resisted. The danger there would have been for our contributors to have been forced to reiterate a great deal of detailed narrative readily available elsewhere, at the loss of broader analytical and historiographical reflection. That said, diversity and complexity are embedded within individual thematic essays, emerging by way of the range of regional examples and narrative threads mobilized to support their respective themes.

While in no way pretending to be completely comprehensive, the following chapters do succeed in capturing the range of concerns currently animating the study of modern African history. Many of these research agendas are of course not specific to the African past but are reflective of the trajectory of the discipline as a whole. The decades in which African history was consolidating its academic presence, it should be remembered, was a time of exciting thematic innovation as well as regional expansion for historical research generally. Having effectively to build their field from close to scratch and to overcome the evidential and logistical challenges outlined above, it did in some cases take Africa's historians time to engage with emerging trends elsewhere. Some might argue that this was not necessarily a bad thing: by the time Africanists cottoned on to postmodern 'critical theory' in the 1990s, its most extravagant excesses were mercifully in decline. What emerges from this collection, however, is that they are now engaging on a broad front with the currents that have so dramatically transformed the discipline since the 1960s, from the rise of gender and women's history to that of cities, the arts, religion and belief, crime and punishment, disease and medicine, and environment and demography.

The following twenty-six chapters range freely across Africa's diverse geographical regions. With only a few exceptions, they also trace their respective thematic concerns across the temporal divide separating the continent's precolonial nineteenth century from the colonial and postcolonial twentieth. The five-part structure into which they are ordered does, nevertheless, attempt to impose some degree of overall chronological development. Part I comprises a set of themes that are important for an understanding of the continent's deeper precolonial past, as well as the links between that past and the developments of the last two centuries. The chapters by James C. McCann on ecology and environment, by Shane Doyle on demography and disease, by Pier M. Larson on the slave trades, by Walter Hawthorne on states and statelessness, and by John Parker on the African diaspora all serve to underscore the role of the Columbian exchange and the forging of the Atlantic economy in marking the start of Africa's modern history. Richard Waller on ethnicity and identity and Richard Reid on warfare and the military, too, insist on the importance of a *longue durée* approach to the understanding of these issues, around which so much African history can be written.

Part II is more chronologically circumscribed. Framed by Heather J. Sharkey's examination of the creation of European conquest states and by Jean Allman's re-evaluation of their demise, its focus is the era of colonial encounter from the end of the nineteenth to the mid-twentieth century. Yet both chapters, together with that by Emily Lynn Osborn on work and migration, explore lines of continuity from colony to postcolony, while Justin Willis also looks back to the forms of precolonial political authority in his analysis of the colonial-era creation of 'chiefs of the government'. Richard Roberts draws on a rich comparative literature in his examination of the fundamental role of law, crime, and punishment in the making of colonial Africa.

Parts III, IV, and V are grouped according to a thematic rather than chronological logic. Part III deals with the enormous advances made in recent decades in the task of historicizing religion and belief in Africa. Marie Miran-Guyon and Jean-Louis Triaud on Islam and David Maxwell on Christianity examine the impact of these two world religions, to which the vast majority of the continent's people now adhere. Whereas Africa's religious history was once seen to begin with the process of conversion from 'traditional' belief systems to the global faiths, Robert M. Baum shows that indigenous religions too have a dynamic and recoverable history. Neither is such fundamental transformation a thing of the past: as Sean Hanretta demonstrates in his analysis of new religious movements in postcolonial Africa, religion lies at the very core of the African engagement with modernity.

Part IV brings together a set of concerns central to Africa's social history, which emerged at the forefront of the research agenda in the 1980s and 1990s. Barbara M. Cooper considers the now large and ever-expanding literature on women and gender; John Parker does the same for urban history, and Nancy Rose Hunt for health and healing—the latter dovetailing with Doyle's treatment of modern Africa's disease history. If three decades ago it was the distinctive historical experience of African women that was crying out for sustained research, the same might be said today of the continent's youth. As the proportion of young people in Africa's total population continues to soar, Nicolas Argenti and Deborah Durham argue, generation demands to be brought under the same degree of scrutiny as gender. The same imperative animates Carol Summer's chapter on education and literacy, which, like that by Hunt on systems of healing, hovers on the cusp of established social history and an emergent concern with indigenous knowledge and intellectual production. While the turn to social history had all but overwhelmed the economic history of Africa by the 1990s, Morten Jerven renews the call for historians to draw on the recent advances of economists in developing a new economic history based on long-term growth patterns.

Finally, Part V turns to cultural history. This seems fitting, as African arts, literatures, and other forms of cultural production and transmission are set to emerge as important new directions in historical research. Plastic art and music, in particular, must be counted among Africa's most glorious achievements and their transformations on the continent and in the diaspora demand to be relocated from the margins to the centre of histories of modernity. Sidney Littlefield Kasfir on visual cultures and Veit Erlmann on music consider trends in these two vibrant fields, while Stephanie Newell explores how African literatures, too, not only have a history but are products of—and reflective of—broader historical processes. The volume concludes with James R. Brennan's chapter on communications and media, which explores how media technologies have constituted and transformed Africa's public spheres over the past two centuries.

Notes

1. Quoted in John Iliffe, *Africans: The History of a Continent* (Cambridge: CUP, 2nd edn, 2007), 280.
2. See Ch. 12 by Jean Allman.
3. See e.g. Frederick Cooper, *Africa since 1940: The Past of the Present* (Cambridge: CUP, 2002); James Ferguson, *Global Shadows: Africa in the Neoliberal World Order* (Durham, NC: Duke University Press, 2006); Charles Piot, *Nostalgia for the Future: West Africa after the Cold War* (Chicago: University of Chicago Press, 2010).
4. For an attempt to reconstruct a shared political tradition underlying the cultural complexity of the equatorial forest zone of Central Africa, see Jan Vansina, *Paths in the Rainforests: Toward a History of Political Tradition in Equatorial Africa* (London: James Currey, 1990).
5. Bernd Heine and Derek Nurse, eds, *African Languages: An Introduction* (Cambridge: CUP, 2000).
6. See Prasenjit Duara, *Rescuing History from the Nation: Questioning Narratives of Modern China* (Chicago: University of Chicago Press, 1995).
7. Martin W. Lewis and Kären E. Wigen, *The Myth of Continents: A Critique of Meta-geography* (Berkeley, Calif.: University of California Press, 1997).
8. See Ralph A. Austen, *Trans-Saharan Africa in World History* (New York: OUP, 2010); James McDougall and Judith Scheele, eds, *Saharan Frontiers: Space and Mobility in Northwest Africa* (Bloomington, Ind.: Indiana University Press, 2012).
9. See Ch. 3 by Pier M. Larson.
10. V. Y. Mudimbe, *The Invention of Africa: Gnosis, Philosophy, and the Order of Knowledge* (Bloomington, Ind.: Indiana University Press, 1988), and *The Idea of Africa* (Bloomington, Ind.: Indiana University Press, 1994); from an archaeological perspective, see too Robin Derrincourt, *Inventing Africa: History, Archaeology and Ideas* (London: Pluto Press, 2011).
11. Jose C. Moya, 'Introduction', in *The Oxford Handbook of Latin American History* (New York: OUP, 2011); see too Walter Mignolo, *The Idea of Latin America* (Oxford: OUP, 2005).
12. Compare another much-admired work of synthesis, Frederick Cooper's *Africa since 1940*, which despite its title deals only with sub-Saharan Africa.
13. See Ch. 7 by John Parker.
14. Jerry H. Bentley, 'Introduction: The Task of World History', in *The Oxford Handbook of World History* (Oxford: OUP, 2011), 6.
15. Dipesh Chakrabarty, *Provincializing Europe: Postcolonial Thought and Historical Difference* (Princeton: PUP, 2000); Toyin Falola and Christian Jennings, eds, *Africanizing Knowledge: African Studies Across the Disciplines* (New Brunswick, NJ: Transaction, 2002); Steven Feierman, 'African Histories and the Dissolution of

World Histories', in Robert H. Bates, V. Y. Mudimbe, and Jean O'Barr, eds, *Africa and the Disciplines* (Chicago: University of Chicago Press, 1993).

16. C. A. Bayly, *The Birth of the Modern World, 1780–1914* (Oxford: Blackwell, 2004).

17. See Matthew J. Lauzon, 'Modernity', in Bentley, *Oxford Handbook of World History*.

18. See e.g., Jan-Georg Deutsch, Peter Probst, and Heike Schmidt, *African Modernities: Entangled Meanings in Current Debate* (Oxford: James Currey, 2002).

19. For the latter, see Guy Arnold, *Africa: A Modern History* (London: Atlantic, 2006).

20. James Bruce, *Travels to Discover the Source of the Nile, in the Years 1768, 1769, 1770, 1771, 1772, and 1773*, 5 vols (Edinburgh: G. G. J. & J. Robinson, 1790); A. Dalzel, *A History of Dahomy, an Inland Kingdom of Africa: Compiled from Authentic Memoirs* (London: published by the author, 1793).

21. On how these theories insinuated their way into indigenous visions of the past, see T. C. McCaskie, 'Asante Origins, Egypt, and the Near East: An Idea and its History', in Derek R. Peterson and Giacomo Macola, eds, *Recasting the Past: History Writing and Political Work in Modern Africa* (Athens, O.: Ohio University Press, 2009).

22. Robert A. Stafford, 'Scientific Exploration and Empire', in Andrew Porter, ed., *The Oxford History of the British Empire, iii. The Nineteenth Century* (Oxford: OUP, 1999); George W. Stocking, *Victorian Anthropology* (New York: Free Press, 1987); Michael Adas, *Machines as the Measure of Men: Science, Technology, and Ideologies of Western Dominance* (Ithaca, NY: Cornell University Press, 1989).

23. See Ch. 4 by Walter Hawthorne.

24. Samuel Johnson, *The History of the Yorubas: From the Earliest Times to the Beginning of the British Protectorate* (London: Routledge, 1921).

25. See Ch. 5 by Richard Waller and Ch. 11 by Justin Willis.

26. See Ch. 13 by Marie Miran-Guyon and Jean-Louis Triaud.

27. See Lyn Schumaker, *Africanizing Anthropology: Fieldwork, Networks, and the Making of Cultural Knowledge in Central Africa* (Durham, NC: Duke University Press, 2001).

28. See John Parker and Richard Rathbone, *African History: A Very Short Introduction* (Oxford: OUP, 2007), 114–34.

29. The *zeitgeist* is captured in Terence O. Ranger, ed., *Emerging Themes of African History* (Nairobi: East African Press, 1968).

30. For surveys of these shifts, see Caroline Neale, *Writing 'Independent' History: African Historiography, 1960–1980* (Westport, Conn.: Greenwood, 1985); Bogumil Jewsiewicki and David Newbury, eds, *African Historiographies: What History for Which Africa?* (Beverly Hills, Calif.: Sage, 1986); and Toyin Falola, ed., *African Historiographies: Essays in Honour of Jacob Ade Ajayi* (Harlow: Longman, 1993).

31. See Ch. 8 by Heather J. Sharkey; and also Frederick Cooper, *Colonialism in Question: Theory, Knowledge, History* (Berkeley, Calif.: University of California Press, 2005).

32. See Karin Barber, ed., *Africa's Hidden Histories: Everyday Literacy and Making the Self* (Bloomington, Ind.: Indiana University Press, 2006), and on the ongoing importance of oral history, Luise White, Stephan F. Miescher, and David William Cohen (eds), *African Words, Africa Voices: Critical Practices in Oral History* (Bloomington, Ind.: Indiana University Press, 2001).

33. See Richard J. Reid, 'Past and Presentism: The "Precolonial" and the Foreshortening of African History', *Journal of African History*, 52/2 (2011), and, for a regional discussion, David Schoenbrun, 'Conjuring the Modern in Africa: Durability and Rupture in Histories of Public Healing between the Great Lakes of East Africa', *American Historical Review*, 111/5 (2006).

34. For thoughts, see David Armitage, 'What's the Big Idea? Intellectual History and the *longue dureé*', *Times Literary Supplement*, 21 Sept. 2012. There are, of course, many exceptions: for recent African 'big history', see Christopher Ehret, *An African Classical Age: Eastern and Southern Africa in World History, 1000 B.C. to A.D. 400* (Charlottesville, Va.: University Press of Virginia, 1998), and Jan Vansina, *How Societies are Born: Governance in West Central Africa before 1600* (Charlottesville, Va.: University Press of Virginia, 2004).

35. See Catherine Coquery-Vidrovitch, *Africa and the Africans in the Nineteenth Century*, tr. Mary Baker (Armonk, NY: M. E. Sharp, 2009); Richard J. Reid, *A History of Modern Africa: 1800 to the Present* (Oxford: Blackwell, 2012).

36. Stephen Ellis, 'Writing Histories of Contemporary Africa', *Journal of African History*, 43 (2002).

37. Derek R. Peterson and Giacomo Macola, 'Homespun Historiography and the Academic Profession', in Peterson and Macola, *Recasting the Past*; see too Axel Harniet-Sievers (ed.), *A Place in the World: New Local Histories from Africa and South Asia* (Leiden: Brill, 2002).

38. Pierre Nora, *Rethinking France: Les Lieux de mémoire*, tr. Mary Trouille, 4 vols (Chicago: Chicago University Press, 2001-9); Kerwin Lee Klein, 'On the Emergence of Memory in Historical Discourse', *Representations*, 69, Special Issue: Grounds for Remembering (2000); Mamadou Diawara, Bernard Lategan, and Jörn Rüsen, eds, *Historical Memory in Africa: Dealing with the Past, Reaching for the Future in an Intercultural Context* (New York: Berghahn, 2010).

39. For a vigorous critique, see Stephen Howe, *Afrocentrism: Mythical Pasts and Imagined Homes* (London: Verso, 1998).

40. See e.g. Arnold, *Africa*; Martin Meredith, *The State of Africa: A History of Fifty Years of Independence* (London: Free Press, 2005); and the widely cited Adam Hochschild, *King Leopold's Ghost: A Story of Greed, Terror, and Heroism in Colonial Africa* (Boston: Houghton Mifflin, 1998).

41. *The Cambridge History of Africa*, 8 vols (Cambridge: CUP, 1975–86); *UNESCO General History of Africa*, 8 vols (London: UNESCO, 1981–93).

42. John Edward Philips, ed., *Writing African History* (Rochester, NY: University of Rochester Press, 2005).

BIBLIOGRAPHY

Austen, Ralph A., *Trans-Saharan Africa in World History* (New York: OUP, 2010).

Cooper, Frederick, *Africa since 1940: The Past of the Present* (Cambridge: CUP, 2002).

Bates, Robert H., V.Y. Mudimbe, and Jean O'Barr, eds, *Africa and the Disciplines* (Chicago: University of Chicago Press, 1993).

Bentley, Jerry H., 'Introduction: The Task of World History', in *The Oxford Handbook of World History* (Oxford: OUP, 2011).

Coquery-Vidrovitch, Catherine, *Africa and the Africans in the Nineteenth Century*, tr. Mary Baker (Armonk, NY: M. E. Sharp, 2009).

Ferguson, James, *Global Shadows: Africa in the Neoliberal World Order* (Durham, NC: Duke University Press, 2006).

Iliffe, John, *Africans: The History of a Continent* (Cambridge: CUP, 2nd edn, 2007).

Parker, John, and Richard Rathbone, *African History: A Very Short Introduction* (Oxford: OUP, 2007).

Peterson, Derek R., and Giacomo Macola, eds, *Recasting the Past: History Writing and Political Work in Modern Africa* (Athens, O.: Ohio University Press, 2009).

Philips, John Edward, ed., *Writing African History* (Rochester, NY: University of Rochester Press, 2005).

Reid, Richard J., *A History of Modern Africa: 1800 to the Present* (Oxford: Blackwell, 2012).

PART I

KEY THEMES IN AFRICAN HISTORY

CHAPTER 1

....

ECOLOGY AND ENVIRONMENT

....

JAMES C. MCCANN

In his general history of Africa first published in 1995, John Iliffe describes the continent's people as 'the frontiersmen who have colonized an especially hostile region of the world on behalf of the entire human race. That has been their chief contribution to history'.[1] Iliffe identifies the key themes of African history as the expansion of population, the achievement of human coexistence with nature, and the building of enduring societies. In his description of Africa's physical and climatic conditions, he argues that the environmental challenges faced by humankind were far more hostile that those in either Eurasia or the Americas.

Iliffe's intention was to establish the human struggle against nature as the central text of Africa's prehistory. Yet historians of the modern period must also address the question of Africa's more recent environmental and ecological challenges, shaped by accelerating globalization and, from the late nineteenth to the mid-twentieth centuries, the era of European colonial rule. Africans' early environmental challenges may indeed have been monumental. Yet a key question is whether the modern patterns of Africa's ecology are still distinctive or exceptional in comparison with those of Asia, Europe, or the Americas in the age of imperialism, industrialization, and global economies of trade. Did Africa's colonial experience from the 1870s to the 1960s form a distinctive period in terms of its environmental history? To what extent was the continent's environment shaped by processes that were global rather than purely colonial? This chapter will address these questions by considering the complex interactions between ecological trends and human agency over the past two centuries of African history.

AFRICA'S ENVIRONMENTS

Images of Africa in Western literature and film have often stressed the harsh and unforgiving nature of the environment, in contrast with more benign and insightful portrayals by Africans themselves. At the height of the era of imperialism, Joseph Conrad used the equatorial rainforests of the Congo basin as a backdrop for his reflection on humanity's darker instincts in his novella *Heart of Darkness* (1902). Popular adventure writer Henry Rider Haggard was also fascinated with Africa's landscapes and 'tribal life', as well as playing on European fantasies of Africa's hidden wealth in his best-known novel, *King Solomon's Mines* (1886). Not that imperial dreams of extracting wealth from a forbidding terrain were complete fantasy: over the course of the twentieth century, the gold of South Africa's Witwatersrand, the diamonds of Sierra Leone, Botswana, and elsewhere, and the copper of central Africa all seemed to fulfil Africa's promise of geological endowments awaiting extraction. More recently, the petroleum of Nigeria, Equatorial Guinea, Angola, and Sudan has conveyed an image of vast wealth—but, like that generated by colonial-era mining industries, of wealth accrued by foreign corporations and corrupt oligarchies rather than by Africa's own peoples. In the minds of Europeans and African leaders alike, minerals and oil have been viewed as extractable sources of wealth rather than enduring environmental endowments.

Africans' own images have also invested particular African landscapes and environmental settings with wealth, well-being, and powerful cultural identities. These included the Mande-speaking people's reference to their West African savanna home as the 'Bright Country', Ethiopian emperors' ideas of the dominance of the salubrious Christian highlands over the malarial Muslim lowlands, and ideals of mobility held by pastoral peoples such as the Maasai, Somali, and Fulani. In the latter, seasonal ecological rhythms linked a pastoral sense of selfhood to livestock-based livelihoods that have evolved and adjusted in accordance with economic and political change. These ideas of ecological identity—as pastoralists, farmers, or fisherfolk—were important in shaping the ways that Africans dealt with the challenges of European conquest and rule.[2]

Africa's environmental endowments and landscapes take their underlying form from its geology. Africa is the oldest continent and the largest fragment of what was the land mass of Gondwanaland. Its soils and geomorphology reflect both its great age and more recent volcanic upheavals, as well as the action of water and wind across the land's surface. Altitudes range from the Danakil Depression at 120 metres below sea level near the Red Sea to the highest peak of Mount Kilimanjaro at 5,895 metres elevation. In eastern Africa, geological domes stretching from the Eritrean and Ethiopian highlands to Tanzania split open 750,000 years ago to create the Great Rift Valley. East Africa's Great Lakes formed when the Eastern Rift Dome lifted and fractured the earth's crust to form a line of long, deep basins. While only four per cent of Africa's surface is above 1,500 metres, half of those highlands are in the Eritrean–Ethiopian region, giving the continent a decided tilt from north-east to south-west. Forty per cent of Africa's land has a slope of more than eight degrees, resulting in the natural movement of water and the depositing of soils by rain and river systems, otherwise known as erosion.[3]

Soils too have a history. In many ways, erosion is not so much a recent crisis as a long-standing and inexorable historical process that humans sometimes accelerate or redirect. Soils move, and landscapes exhibit both slow and sudden effects of the actions of water, wind, and agriculture. Africa's soils are in many areas red porous laterite types that easily lose nutrients; other types, such as the black clay 'cotton' soils, are prone to annual waterlogging and require specialized techniques of farming to manage moisture. Yet the continent's soils defy easy categorization: they have distinctive, localized personalities and behave as historical actors in their own right, shaping what farmers can grow from among the crops available to them. Africa's landscapes viewed from the ground or from satellite images reflect at any given moment a snapshot of the historical interactions of geology, botany, zoology, demography, and climate.[4]

CLIMATE AND HISTORY

Beyond the topographic shapes offered by geology, Africa's landscapes reflect changing patterns of climate—the circulation of wind, moisture, and temperature—that mark the continent as distinct from other land masses. In contrast with the temperate zones of Europe, Asia, and North America, where growing seasons and cycles of life respond most directly to fluctuations in temperature, Africa's ecological rhythms are dictated primarily by the distribution of moisture in the form of rainfall. Patterns of rainy and dry seasons, the length of each year's growing season, humidity, and soil moisture all take their cue from the annual rhythms of cyclonic winds, ocean temperature, and the earth's rotation and movement around the sun. Being bisected by the equator, the tilting of half of Africa's land mass towards the sun in summer and away in winter prompts the anticyclonic and trade winds that set the yearly cycle between rainy and dry seasons.

Indeed, Africa's position means that the continent's landscapes have the most distinct separation of wet and dry seasons of any region on earth. The shifting mass of rain-bearing turbulence called the Inter-Tropical Convergence Zone (ITCZ) that gathers around the equator fashions a two-part seasonal pattern that characterizes the entire continent: summer wet and winter dry. This pattern exhibits subtle year-to-year variations in particular places, resulting in short or delayed rains that produce effects on the landscape. Several years of such short or delayed rains along the ITCZ's edges result in drought, historically a common occurrence in the Sahelian region along the southern edge of the Sahara desert and the equivalent grassland areas in southern Africa.

When the ITCZ moves with the season (north from June to September and south from October to May), the onset of the rains have a remarkable effect. Within two weeks, brown, parched landscapes turn green, seeds germinate, and chemical reactions within soils make nutrients available to plants. The rhythms of the ITCZ interact with local geographies to result in moist slopes or rainfall shadows that have local consequences for farmer crop choices, land values, and landscape vegetative textures. At the extremes of the continent at the Cape and along the North African coast, a Mediterranean climate prevails, making possible grape, citrus, and grain production. During more recent periods of history these zones attracted European colonial settlement, making racial conflict a recurrent theme in Algeria and South Africa.

Vegetation, animal life, and human economies in Africa have all adjusted to the repetitive patterns of seasonal climate. Over the course of long-term geological time, some broad trends are discernible: Africa's climate has been more often dry than wet and more often warmer than cooler. During drier periods, expanding desert zones may have connected the Sahara to the Kalahari along an arid corridor passing through a shrunken Central African forest. The biology of mammal species also reflects these shifts: many forest-dwelling species such as hyraxes, squirrels, monkeys, and even elephants show evidence of their struggle to adapt to a new ecology as forest diminished or reappeared over time. Within the last few millennia—the late Holocene era—there have also been wetter periods in what previously were arid zones, including one in which the Sahara was a pastoral grassland that supported cattle, game, and human settlement. That period ended somewhere in the middle of the third millennium BC, when the Sahara's ecology shifted more fully into the desert habitat we know of over the last two millennia.

Scholars of Africa's climate history have used sources such as lake levels, geological stratigraphy, and the archaeology of human settlement to identify ongoing patterns in the period from AD 800 to 1600, when the great Sahelian states of Ghana, Mali, and Songhay flourished and then declined. Historian George Brooks and historical meteorologist Sharon Nicholson offer somewhat contrasting conclusions about climate periods and their effects on political change. Nicholson uses fluctuating lake levels and scarce local records to reconstruct climate epochs, while Brooks seeks to relate climate to changes in political hegemony and patterns of trade.[5] The period 800–1300 was relatively wet, followed by a drier spell in 1300–1450, and again by a wetter period, including the 'Little Ice Age' of 1500–1850, when observers reported snow-capped peaks on Mount Kilimanjaro in Tanzania and Ras Dashan in Ethiopia. Over the course of the twentieth century, Kilimanjaro's ice cap has receded dramatically, while Ras Dashan's has now completely disappeared.

Moisture had a great impact on trade and politics in the West African savannah region. A wetter landscape allowed the expansion of tsetse fly habitat that harboured sleeping sickness, limiting the movement of Mali's famous cavalry, Songhay's camel caravans, and Tuareg raiders. Moister times also moved the forest edges on which blacksmiths depended to forge imperial weapons and tools. Conclusions about the interaction of climate and politics are, of course, subject to ongoing debate as further data emerge from archaeological study of sediments and pollen fragments. Yet it is clear that the overall dynamics of climate provide a fundamental framework for Africa's human history in both the distant and the more recent past.

AFRICA'S ECOLOGIES: LOW BIODIVERSITY AND ENDEMISM

Africa's environmental profile includes particular patterns of biodiversity that reflect longer-term history as well as more recent trends. Many biological endowments are products of geological history that created local microclimates and specialized ecological niches. Examples of such niches include the Usambara Mountains of Tanzania, Ethiopia's Simien Mountains, and the coastal hinterlands of South Africa's Cape of Good Hope.

Africa ranks lower than the world's other tropical and sub-tropical regions in terms of endemism; that is, in the number of endemic species. Tropical regions such as the Amazon basin and South-East Asia have greater numbers of endemic varieties of plants and higher vertebrate species, although Africa has high visibility of particular endangered species such as the black rhino, cheetah, and mountain gorilla. Three-quarters of Africa's species of plants and animals show little evidence of Amazon-like endemism, since their habitats ranges widely across the continent's deserts, savannas, forests, and uplands. The other one-quarter are localized endemic species that evolved within distinctive ecological enclaves or 'centres' of endemism. Among world ecologies, Africa's biodiversity is richest in fresh-water lake fish, with species diversity of cichlids being over 90 per cent in Lakes Malawi and Tanganyika. The areas of highest levels of biodiversity in flora and fauna are in the rainforests of West Africa and the Congo River basin. Recent climate change, human land use, and economic fluctuations have resulted in threats to those specific parts of Africa's biodiversity, most dramatically in the lake fish species where eutrofication and anoxia (increased nutrition loads and lack of oxygen) have sharply reduced species numbers.[6]

In terms of environmental history, however, endemism may be a less important issue than Africa's absorption and adaptation of a genetic stock of domestic animals and food plants that has arrived from global ecological networks. Exchanges of mammal groups began 30 million years ago, when the continent temporarily touched the Eurasian land mass and anthropoid primates (including early humans) and elephants migrated out and ancestors of bovids, horses, rodents, and carnivores made their first entrance onto the African land mass. In the more recent times of the early Holocene epoch, about 7,000 years ago, other migrants to Africa from the north-east arrived via the Nile Valley. These were domesticates of the wild ox, *Bos primigenious*, which mixed with local wild grazers to become Africa's first domestic cattle, *Bos taurus*, a humpless longhorn variety that ranged into the western part of the continent and evolved into several breeds known today, such as the N'Dama, Kuri, and West African shorthorn. The N'Dama was particularly successful in developing resistance to local diseases, including the deadly trypanosomiasis (sleeping sickness). Eastern and southern Africa's bovine ancestors, the humped *Bos indicus,* or zebu, first arrived around 1500 BC and then in large numbers after the seventh century AD. The zebu and its descendent varieties developed a tolerance for arid conditions which allowed local herders and farmers to promote their spread along the entire Sahelian zone and throughout eastern and southern Africa. In the third century AD, another domesticated animal, the camel, made its appearance, introduced by the Romans to North Africa. African peoples in the desert zone, the Sahel, the Horn of Africa, and the Nile Valley quickly mastered camel husbandry and adapted their economic culture around its food and labour potential.

Environmental historian James Webb has pointed out that camels were particularly important for human adaptation to Africa's dry ecologies, enhancing capacity for life in a drier environment in terms of both economic value and human diet. The camel could survive without water or fresh grazing for eight to ten days (twice as long as a donkey), carry 200 kilograms of freight (one-third more than a donkey or ox), and needed fewer men to tend it, thus significantly reducing long-distance transport costs. The milch camel's lactation, moreover, was not dependent upon the availability of fresh pasture, as was the lactation of cattle, sheep, and goats. Milch camels normally lactated for eleven months out of twelve and the camel's ability to turn salty water into sweet milk for almost the entire year allowed desert people to exploit lands which otherwise would have remained too dry for human use.[7]

Imported domesticated plants have also become defining features of Africa's vegetative cover. Wheat and barley arrived early in the north-east to complement endemic food crops there. Bananas arrived from South-East Asia via Indian Ocean trade networks in the first millennium AD, spreading to several areas, including West Africa and the Great Lakes region, where starchy varieties became the primary human food. Human hands induced their spread from Buganda on the northern shore of Lake Victoria to most areas around the northern edge of the lake by the twentieth century. Propagated by cuttings rather than seed, genetic stocks of starchy and sweet bananas diversified rapidly and adjusted to drier conditions and new soils on the western side of the lake around the Kagera River.[8] Varieties of sweet bananas also spread throughout North-East Africa to southern Somalia and warmer areas of north-west Ethiopia; every microclimate and soil type seems to have nurtured its own local type. Until the political crises of the early 1990s, southern Somalia was a major exporter of sweet bananas to European supermarkets and the Gulf.

WEST AFRICA: THE INVENTION OF FOREST FALLOW

Africa's ecology has long been a dynamic force in its history, including the invention of adaptive strategies that allowed increasing food production from challenging environments. One relatively well-documented case was the invention of a fallow cultivation system in the humid forest zone of West Africa. Developed over the course of a few centuries, the 'forest fallow' system presented itself to the first European observers in a fully developed form by the early nineteenth century.[9] The system derives its rhythms and limitations from two seasons of rainfall and a season of dry winds (the harmattan) which blows dry air and dust from the Sahel towards the Gulf of Guinea. West Africa's seasons differ slightly from eastern and southern regions in their seasonality: the heavy rains in forest areas take place between March and early July, with a second, shorter rainy season from September to October allowing farmers the cultivation of a second plot. The farm cycle begins with clearing fields for the primary farm between December and January. Farmers use cutlasses to slash and remove the understory of shrubs and ground cover; they then cut major branches from large trees to open the canopy cover and add leaf debris as a mulch to the soil's surface. With the beginning of the rains in March, farmers place leaf debris, smaller branches, and other vegetation into piles for controlled burning, reducing the weight of the forest biomass to an ash as well as destroying insects and small weeds. Burning also releases phosphorous and singes the leaves and branches of the largest trees, debris from which enhance the layer of mulch while increasing the penetration of sunlight to the forest floor. This process of clearing, burning, and pollarding (the cutting and regeneration of trees), in effect, converts the energy stored above ground in forest vegetation into soil nutrients to sustain food crops.

Farmers learned to interact with the seasons and, from the sixteenth century, to combine the indigenous forest staple, the yam, with new American imports, maize, cassava, and cocoyam. With the first rains of March, they plant yams in mounds near small trees which serve as stakes for the plant's emerging tendrils. Once the rains are fully established, farmers plant maize using minimum tillage techniques to keep mulch and soil moisture in place. Maize thus receives the moisture essential for its early growth and tasseling. Two weeks later, cassava sticks are planted between the germinated maize; cocoyam corms preserved in the soil also begin to sprout. As these crops grow, a dense vegetation emerges, with maize stalks reaching up towards the intense sunlight they require. The leaves of the young cassava and cocoyams closer to the forest floor cool the maize roots and protect the forest soils from rainfall impact and direct sun. West African management of planting time, seed selection, and sequencing of the new crop types reflects an accumulation and dispersal of knowledge over time.

After the October maize harvest, cassava and cocoyams remain in the field, offering shade to suppress weeds and protect the soil. Both crops require at least a year's maturity, but cassava can remain in the ground for as long as two or three years, providing food as the fallow cycle begins. Plantain, a new arrival from Asia by the sixteenth century, may also have been added to this mix of intercropped plants on forest clearings. On a single cleared plot farmers could plant maize in three successive seasons and allow the cassava plants to continue to grow. Maize's capacity to provide a farm's second harvest in a single season offered a strategic boost to local food supply.

Management of fallow land was a learned technique and a crucial aspect of the farming system's resilience. After the maize harvest on the main farm, farmers began managing the succession of regrowth, a process which drew on accumulated knowledge of biodiversity and soil behaviour built up over generations of forest occupation. Farmers on fallow plots deliberately preserved small, pioneer forest species which they knew had nutrient recycling properties. Geographer Kojo Amanor cites eight species of trees and nine shrubs and herbs which local farmers recognized as having soil-enhancing effects. Fallow management was thus not abandonment of old plots, but a careful and conscious selection process that preserved particular species and removed others to allow a sustained production of food. This food supply, in turn, released labour to advance the frontiers of forest settlement and to support development of the art of politics and state-craft.[10] Forest fallow and the incorporation of New World foods after 1500 may well have been a spark to the political and demographic expansion of the forest and forest-edge states such as Asante, Benin, Oyo, and Dahomey.

A significant change in historians' understanding of forest dynamics has come from two scholars who observed contemporary management of forest resources in present-day Guinea, the ecologist James Fairhead and geographer Melissa Leach.[11] The forest fallow system that appeared in the written historical record only in the early nineteenth century (earlier Portuguese observers had never seen it firsthand), Fairhead and Leach argue, was the end result of generations of experimentation and observation, first by hunting and gathering forest dwellers in the early second millennium AD and then as part of an agricultural transformation which drew new labour into the forest to break the logjam of primary forest canopy clearance. The engine that pushed the forest fallow revolution was the arrival of the three New World crops that occupied strategic niches in the forest fallow system: maize, cassava, and, later, cocoa. Maize represented a cultigen offering something new: an early maturing food source that provided carbohydrates by the end of the rains and which required much less labour than yam. Cassava, another New World arrival, complemented maize's early yield and double cropping by being a low-labour crop with the capacity to remain stored in the ground for extended periods. Cassava could tolerate poor soils, drought, and neglect; cassava leaves also provided understory shade below the sun-loving maize leaves as well as a 'relish' in women's cooking repertoire.[12]

NEW WORLD CROPS: COCOA, MAIZE, AND CASSAVA

The economist Polly Hill's classic study of cocoa production in Ghana suggests that farmers began the systematic cultivation of cocoa trees in 'virgin forest' of the eastern region of what was then the British colony of the Gold Coast in the early 1890s.[13] The expansion of fallow cultivation into West Africa's humid zone brought about a change in biodiversity that therefore continued into the nineteenth and twentieth centuries, as the forest economy increasingly became part of a global market. By the mid-nineteenth century, global demand for industrial commodities stimulated the collection and cultivation of nuts of the oil palm, a plant which grew wild but also offered quick results from plantation economies. Collecting palm nuts from the forest with family labour supplemented farm income and linked forest ecology to the expanding world economy. By the 1880s, however, farmer response from West Africa had overwhelmed the palm oil market, as demand collapsed with the arrival of new petroleum lubricants and the entry of Asian producers. It was then that cocoa emerged as a new entry into the forest ecology.

Ghanaian legend recounts that a local blacksmith named Tetteh Quashie established the country's first successful cocoa farm, after bringing seedlings from the island of Fernando Pó in the 1870s. By 1890, cocoa had secured a place within the economy of forest settlement in the Gold Coast, beginning in the east but moving rapidly through the colony as migrant farmers colonized the moister forests to the west. Unlike the oil palm, which produced a commodity for both international markets and local use (as edible oil, palm wine, and distilled spirits), cocoa was a purely cash crop that linked small farms in the forest to the world market. Cocoa production increased from about 500 metric tons in 1900 to 22,631 tons in 1910—by which time the Gold Coast was the world's largest exporter—and to 200,000 tons by 1930.[14]

Vibrant markets, open frontiers, and a ready population of migrant farmers laid the foundation for a new movement of human imprint on forest ecology. Cocoa expansion into forest fallow ecological zones was an example of the overlap of global markets and the growth of colonial economies in West Africa. The ecological dynamics of the cocoa frontier allowed a rapid expansion of a new form of clearance and selection, adding the agronomy of a tree crop to the established food crop forest fallow system. The addition of cocoa mimicked the forest through creation of a shade canopy to control the under-story of weeds and protect the soil humus from direct sunlight. Where farmers intended cocoa seedlings to replace primary forest, clearing was identical to the classic forest fal-low sequence: clearing and burning was followed by three years of maize, yams, and vegetables. Next, cassava, cocoyam, and plantain provided cover for young seedlings and a sequence of food for the five- to seven-year period before cocoa seedlings pro-duced a marketable crop. When mature cocoa trees covered the forest farm the process was complete except for seasonal slashing of weeds and harvest. The farm enterprise could then move onto another forest plot and repeat the process, moving further into the moister forest frontier to the west and drawing migrant labour with it. Migrants who developed cocoa farms on landlords' plots retained the food crops they produced while landlords reaped the longer-term benefits of the cocoa fruits and ownership of a mature cocoa farm.

The cocoa frontier moved progressively into new zones capable of supporting it, creating a new human landscape and a new forest ecology. The construction of a railway from the colonial capital Accra through the heart of the cocoa-growing region in the 1910s, followed by the advent of motorized lorry transport and spread of feeder roads in the 1920s, allowed world markets fully to penetrate the forest biome of the Gold Coast. With transport costs falling and the world market demand rising after the First World War, forest land attained a new economic value.[15] By the 1940s, the ecology and economy of the forest had changed again. Mature cocoa farms in the eastern region began to show signs of crisis in the form of sudden deciduousness of normally evergreen trees and the spread of the devastating swollen shoot disease. In addition to the trees that died directly from the disease, by 1961 the Ghanaian Ministry of Agriculture had destroyed 105 million trees. Farmers also reported increasing dryness of the climate in the eastern zones of cocoa cultivation. With the loss of cocoa trees from disease and fires, many farms reverted to forest fallow food cultivation of maize and cassava mixed with a minor revival of oil palm cultivation. The overall decline in rainfall and spread of disease in the mature cocoa landscapes pushed the forest frontier onto new areas and foreshadowed a new form of human land use on forest ecology. From the mid-nineteenth century, the cultivation of oil palm and then of cocoa had existed in a kind of symbiosis with that of food crops, a relationship that maintained shade cover of forest soils. However, the conversion of old cocoa farms to food production in the post-Second World War period and a political movement to place forests within protective reserves ushered in a new period of landscape history in Ghana's section of the Guinea forest.

Over the last two centuries, changes in Africa's vegetative and human landscapes have moved at a quicker pace. Of all of Africa's exotic imports, maize and cassava have had the most pervasive impact. These two food crops, one a variety of grass and the other a forest tuber, have spread throughout the continent since their introduction in the sixteenth and seventeenth centuries. By the second half of the twentieth century, maize has become the staple food of most of southern and eastern Africa, while in forests of West Africa it was a key ingredient of the forest fallow innovation. Cassava supplemented and sometimes replaced indigenous tubers such as yams, as well as grains such as millet and sorghum, in most of the humid zones of West and Central Africa and has continued its migration into new zones. In some areas of Central Africa, it has expanded its historical presence in local cultivation as a response to economic downturns, political instability, and rainfall fluctuation. Its hardiness and ability to survive in the ground means that it is a safety crop for farmers during troubled times.[16]

Imported non-food crops have also spread quickly over Africa's land surface in the last century as a vegetative version of globalizing economies. Exotic tree species such as eucalyptus, white pine, and black wattle now cover much of southern Africa as plantation crops or as invasive newcomers. Eucalyptus has become the most common tree in the Ethiopian highlands since its introduction only a century ago, its blue-green leaves having become emblematic of human settlement across the region. In South Africa, eucalyptus plantations have become so widespread in areas such as KwaZulu-Natal that they strike some newcomers as natural forest cover. In eastern and southern Africa, imported cash crops such as sisal, pyrethrum, and sugar cane occupy vast monocrop plantations. Indigenous crops such as cowpeas, collard greens, okra, and coffee have also re-entered the continent in varieties developed externally. Some of these owe their presence to world commodity markets that developed over the course of the twentieth century, such as coffee in Kenya, Tanzania, Ethiopia, Côte d'Ivoire, and Rwanda. Meanwhile, rubber trees imported from South-East Asia became an important plantation crop in Liberia and the Belgian Congo.

EAST AFRICA: DISEASE AND THE
SERENGETI LANDSCAPE

Other ecological dynamics played themselves out elsewhere on the continent. That African landscapes change over time should not be in doubt; what new research allows us to see are the complex dynamics of that change. An important example from East Africa illustrates the chronology of change on one of the most publicized pieces of African nature: the Serengeti Plain of northern Tanzania. Holly Dublin, an ecologist who has worked in East Africa since 1981, has examined the botanical and historical records of the Serengeti-Mara ecosystem over the course of the twentieth century. Her research challenges the conventional wisdom that East Africa's savanna woodland ecosystem was a landscape that reflected an unchanging past and a stable future. Dublin argues that, over the course of the twentieth century, the Serengeti-Mara landscape has had distinct vegetative shifts for which there are clear visual and documentary records, including travel narratives by European observers and aerial photographs that allow a quantitative comparison of woody cover for the period from 1950 to 1982.[17] Dublin's research shows that the Serengeti-Mara landscape shifted from an open grassland in the 1880s, to a dense woodland in the 1930s, and then back again by the 1960s, when the Serengeti achieved its international celebrity as a pristine and protected wildlife environment. To account for these changes, Dublin examined the tightly intertwined effects of fire, elephants, and human beings. The evidence from the Serengeti on human agency, however, does not suggest a direct link between human population and deforestation, but rather a complex set of relationships within the biome resulting in landscape change.

In the final decade of the nineteenth century, Maasailand, which included the Serengeti, underwent a set of environmental shocks that affected much of eastern Africa from the Red Sea coast of Eritrea down to the Rift Valley lakes. In September 1890, the deadly livestock viral disease rinderpest arrived on the Serengeti plain, killing as many as 90 per cent of the Maasai's cattle within a few months.[18] Not only cattle but also herd-forming wildlife such as wildebeest and buffalo died in large numbers. Maasai pastoralists who depended on cattle either died or abandoned the region, some becoming *dorobo* (hunters and gatherers) as a strategy to survive. The ecological crisis resulted in other changes in wildlife distribution, included a further reduction of the elephant population due to the expansion of ivory exports into the Indian Ocean from Zanzibar.

By 1900, the combined effects of disease, famine, and expanding ivory markets had left the Serengeti plain devoid of most of its previous fauna, human and otherwise. Travellers to the area in the first decade of the twentieth century described its landscape as 'undulating grasslands, lovely fertile country which seemed almost uninhabited', or 'a broad plain of park-like country, fine grazing land, studded with the occasional yellow-barked *Acacia*'.[19] Others remarked on the peculiar absence of species such as elephants and buffalo. By the early 1930s, these changes in fauna yielded a profound transformation. Hilltop *croton* thickets (*Acacia syal* and other acacia species) had replaced the open grasslands and hunters reported abundant leopard populations (which prefer wooded to grassy settings). Because of the then dominant wooded habitat, the Serengeti also became a prime area for trypanosomiasis. Wildlife that had survived rinderpest developed immunity to it and became primary hosts for trypanosomes carried by the tsetse fly vector. The colonial government's attempts to control tsetse flies failed and anti-tsetse programmes collapsed in the early 1960s after massive forced population relocations that cleared the Serengeti of its human inhabitants and allowed the regrowth of the tsetse's woody habitat.[20]

Landscapes and human settlement patterns could therefore be dramatically transformed as a result of diseases such as rinderpest and sleeping sickness. The latter was the subject of a pioneering and influential study of disease in Africa, the immunologist John Ford's magisterial *The Role of Trypanosomiasis in African History*.[21] Ford's work was an early model in African environmental history, as it connected the sciences of entomology and immunology to historical reconstruction of social, demographic, and political change, especially in East Africa. It inspired a number of more localized studies of the effects of the disease in the woody bush and savanna ecologies of semi-arid East, Central, and West Africa.[22]

The shift of Serengeti woodlands to the open grassland setting of the 1980s and 1990s took place as a historical conjuncture of natural and indirect human forces. Fire has long been an important tool in African range management, hunting, and agriculture, used by local peoples to manage vegetation or promote soil fertility or improve pasture. Unusually high rainfall in the early 1960s resulted in a dramatic increase in grass growth that provided fuel for hot and particularly destructive bush fires. Park authorities also set fires as part of management schemes. Local honey hunters, European travellers, and lightning strikes also accounted for fires within park boundaries. With increased grass growth and wooded areas for fuel, fires in the late 1950s and early 1960s destroyed much of the woody vegetative growth that had dominated outsiders' perceptions of the Serengeti-Mara area since the 1930s. Dublin's research added to this factor the effects of rising human populations at the edge of the Serengeti, which drove elephants and grazing wildlife into the protected reserve areas set aside by colonial rulers. These boundaries of the Serengeti and other game parks such as Maasai Mara in Kenya and Manyara in Tanzania were products of colonial rule that imposed new dynamics on the floral and fauna ecology of the East African savanna.[23]

The increasing density of the elephant population also contributed to the loss of the wooded landscapes. Elephants feed on acacia leaves and bark, and a single hungry elephant can obliterate a 5-metre-high tree in less than fifteen minutes. Fires and the reduction of dense wooded areas also attracted grazers to post-fire pasture and helped push back the woodlands' ecological hegemony. According to Dublin's photographic evidence, between 1950 and 1982 over 95 per cent of the acacia woodland in Serengeti had become grassland. Of this change, 65 per cent took place in the period 1961–7; that is, the years following the highest rainfall. The serendipity of nature and the human intervention to 'protect' the Serengeti thus returned the region from a grassland to a woodland and back again. This dynamism of landscapes included humans as agents, observers, and affected participants.[24]

CHANGING ECOLOGIES AND THE URBAN FOOTPRINT

Changes accumulated over the course of the nineteenth and twentieth centuries have indeed served to transform Africa's diverse landscapes. While colonial conquest and rule represented a profound transformation in the continent's political history, its ecological history has had different trajectories and turning-points in terms of land use, land cover, disease, and demography. The impact of new plants and commodity markets for food crops (such as maize), edible oils (palm and peanut), and fibre (cotton and sisal) underlay colonial rule, but were global economic forces rather than simply colonial ones. For the nineteenth century, prior to the full impact of the Industrial Revolution and colonial rule on Africa, the agents shaping the landscapes would have been familiar: fire, rainfall, geology, seasonal change, and human tools such as ox ploughs, machetes, hoes, and axes. The resulting landscapes would have reflected the sum of local forces, natural and human, climatological and economic.

How do Africa's landscapes present themselves to a traveller of the early twenty-first century? A modern traveller would likely view his or her surroundings from a road—moving quickly in a bus or car—or from above in an aeroplane. On the landscapes themselves, geology and climate would, as in the past, act as conservative rather than dynamic forces in environmental change. Yet it would be clear that changes in human land use and human population itself have wrought the most profound transformations of landscape mosaics over the two centuries. Of the many forces that have shaped the interaction of humans and their physical surroundings, only population has proven to be consistently cumulative in affecting the look of the land. Others have been either episodic, such as the Serengeti's conversion from open grassland to forest woodland and back, or revolutionary, such as the arrival of American food crops. Without the hindsight of history, it would be difficult to predict the condition and form of any particular place.

Even so, major trends in resource use and landscape change have historically depended on economic, social, and political forces that shape where human populations concentrated and how they organized labour and land use. Africa's agricultural fields (whether forest fallow cultivation, swidden, or annual cereal cropping) have greatly expanded their scale over the past two hundred years. Now those fields predominately contain New World food crops rather than Africa's historical mainstays of sorghum, millet, and rice. African forests and woodlots, as often as not, display exotic non-African trees rather than local, slow-growing hardwoods. In open rural spaces new varieties of domestic livestock such as Holstein cattle and white Leghorn chickens dodge cars and trucks on roads that penetrate urban hinterlands like the tendrils of a weed. The human and landscape ecologies of the rural and the urban now overlap with the expansion of market gardening, road construction, water resources, and the halo of peri-urban housing that surrounds towns and cities across the continent. This phenomenon is particularly visible in the use by geographers and historians of satellite imagery displayed in time series over the most recent two decades.[25]

In the postcolonial era from the 1960s, there was a further major trend affecting African environments and perceptions of them: the centralization of political and economic power in urban areas. In the nineteenth century, Africa south of the Sahara was the world's least urbanized area. In 1900, only about 5 per cent of sub-Saharan Africans lived in urban areas, by 1960 only 12 per cent did so, and by 2000 the level of urbanization was still less than half that of Latin America and the Caribbean. Yet, in the last twenty-five years Africa's rate of urban growth has been the fastest in the world. Cities like Dar es Salaam, Maputo, Accra, and Abidjan have begun to approach the levels of Buenos Aires, Mexico City, and Santiago in their dominating percentage of national population.

One of the most important environmental effects of the rapid growth of cities has been what environmental historians call the 'urban footprint', the particular way that cities affect their hinterland. As in other parts of the globe, increasing amounts of African farmland that had once produced food for urban markets is now coming under asphalt and peri-urban housing. The metabolism of big African cities such as Cairo, Lagos, Kinshasa, and Addis Ababa differs substantially from those of the developed world. They absorb energy, water, and food in different ways, putting great strain on seasonal food production and water supplies, while expelling solid and liquid waste in ways that often overwhelm infrastructure. Johannesburg's dependence on the distant Lesotho highlands for power and water offers a dramatic case in point. Beyond these huge primate cities, rapid urbanization has also turned many regional towns from sleepy market and administrative centres into complex urban spaces, which have in turn begun to transform their own hinterlands and wider environmental settings.

Finally, Africa's modern history has witnessed another major trend which will have a substantial impact on the environment: the increasing youth of its population. Globally, there are now more youth (that is, under 25 years of age) than at any point in world history. Africa's population is the youngest of any other world area and its youth is increasingly urban in both experience and in aspirations. By the year 2025, almost half of East Africans and nearly three-quarters of southern Africans will be living in cities. From the perspective of environmental history, this population will be in the process of losing accumulated knowledge about agriculture, land management, and natural resources use that allowed humankind's survival from its early phases of settlement to the more recent past.

Does John Iliffe's depiction of Africans as 'the frontiersmen of mankind' therefore still serve as a guidepost for a survey of the continent's environmental history? Perhaps not, since the context of resource use by humans, including Africans, is increasingly global rather than local. Yet one could equally argue that Africa's people and landscapes may well be harbingers of the longer-range future of the impact of climate change on food production and migration. Small-scale farmers in Africa still protect the historical biodiversity of their seeds, livestock, and landscapes. There will certainly be further clever adaptations and adjustments to global change in the future, but the ultimate effects on Africa's landscapes are difficult to predict.

NOTES

1. John Iliffe, *Africans: The History of a Continent* (Cambridge: CUP, 1995), 1.
2. See e.g. essays on the historical identity of the pastoral Maasai people in Kenya and Tanzania's Rift Valley region in Thomas Spear and Richard Waller, eds, *Being Maasai: Ethnicity and Identity in East Africa* (Athens, O.: Ohio University Press, 1993).
3. Jonathan Kingdon, *Island Africa: The Evolution of Africa's Rare Animals and Plants* (Princeton: PUP, 1989), 11, 146–8.
4. See James C. McCann, *Green Land, Brown Land, Black Land: An Environmental History of Africa, 1800–1990* (Portsmouth, NH: Heinemann, 1999).
5. George Brooks, *Landlords and Strangers: Ecology, Society, and Trade in West Africa, 1000–1630* (Boulder, Colo.: Westview Press, 1993); S. E. Nicholson, 'The Methodology of Historical Climate Reconstruction and its Application to Africa', *Journal of African History*, 20/1 (1979).
6. Les Kaufman, 'Catastrophic Change in Species-Rich Freshwater Ecosystems', *BioScience*, 42/11 (1992), 847.
7. James L. A. Webb, *Desert Frontier: Ecological and Economic Change along the Western Sahel, 1600–1850* (Madison, Wis.: University of Wisconsin Press, 1995), 11.
8. C. C. Wrigley, 'Bananas in Buganda', *Azania*, 24 (1989).
9. The best account is Kojo Amanor, *The New Frontier: Farmer's Response to Land Degradation. A West African Study* (London: Zed Books, 1994).
10. Amanor, *New Frontier*, 173–8.
11. James Fairhead and Melissa Leach, *Misreading the African Landscape: Society and Ecology in a Forest-Savanna Mosaic* (Cambridge: CUP, 1996).
12. See James C. McCann, *Maize and Grace: Africa's Encounter with a New World Crop* (Cambridge, Mass.: Harvard University Press, 2005); on cassava, see McCann, *Green Land*, 119–31.
13. For the pioneering study of Ghana's cocoa economy, see Polly Hill, *The Migrant Cocoa Farmers of Southern Ghana: A Study in Rural Capitalism* (Cambridge: CUP, 1963).
14. James Fairhead and Melissa Leach, *Reframing Deforestation: Global Analyses and Local Realities with Studies in West Africa* (London, 1998), 67.
15. McCann, *Green Land*, 130.
16. On cassava's new role in Central and West Africa, see the optimistic views in Felix I. Nweke, S. C. Dunstan Spencer, and John K. Lynam, eds, *The Cassava Transformation: Africa's Best Kept Secret* (East Lansing, Mich.: Michigan State University Press, 2002).

17. Holly Dublin, 'Dynamics of the Serengeti-Mara Woodlands: An Historical Perspective', *Forest and Conservation History*, 35/4 (1991), 170–8.
18. An excellent analysis of the impact of the rinderpest panzootic and subsequent famine on the Maasai is Richard Waller, 'Emutai: Crisis and Response in Massailand, 1883–1902', in David Anderson and Douglas Johnson, eds, *The Ecology of Survival in Northeast Africa* (Boulder, Colo.: Westview, 1988). This volume includes a number of valuable essays on the ecological crisis of the final decade of the 19th cent.
19. Dublin, 'Dynamics of the Serengeti-Mara Woodlands', 170–8.
20. For analyses of this ecological change, see Richard Waller, 'Tsetse Fly in Western Narok, Kenya', *Journal of African History*, 31 (1990); Kirk Hoppe, *Lords of the Fly: Sleeping Sickness Control in British East Africa, 1900–1960* (Portsmouth, NH: Heinemann, 2003); and James Giblin, *The Politics of Environmental Control in Northeastern Tanzania, 1840–1940* (Philadelphia: University of Pennsylvania Press, 1992).
21. John Ford, *The Role of Trypanosomiasis in African History* (Oxford: OUP, 1971).
22. The most important of these historical studies include Helge Kjekshus, *Ecology Control and Economic Development in East African History* (Athens, O.: Ohio University Press, 1996); and Gregory Maddox, James Giblin, and Isaria Kimambo, eds, *Custodians of the Land: Ecology and Culture in the History of Tanzania* (Athens, O.: Ohio University Press, 1996).
23. For a pioneering and influential collection on the ecology of colonial rule, see David Anderson and Richard Grove, eds, *Conservation in Africa: People, Policies, and Practice* (Cambridge: CUP, 1987), which includes case studies of conservation policy and landscape change in Nigeria, Sierra Leone, Kenya, Tanzania, Ethiopia, Malawi, and South Africa.
24. For an alternative and challenging view of landscape change, see also Michael Mortimer, Mary Tiffen, and Francis Gichuki, *More People, Less Erosion: Environmental Recovery in Kenya, 1939–1990* (London: John Wiley, 1993).
25. A good example of this technique appears in Eric Lambin and Helmut Geist, *Land-Use and Land-Cover Change: Local Processes and Global Impacts* (New York: Springer, 2006).

BIBLIOGRAPHY

Amanor, Kojo, *The New Frontier: Farmers' Response to Land Degradation. A West African Study* (London: Zed Books, 1994).

Anderson, David M., and Richard Grove, eds, *Conservation in Africa: People, Policies and Practice* (Cambridge: CUP, 1987).

Anderson, David M., and Douglas Johnson, eds, *The Ecology of Survival in Northeast Africa* (Boulder: Westview Press, 1988).

Brooks, George, *Landlords and Strangers: Ecology, Society, and Trade in West Africa, 1000–1630* (Boulder, Colo.: Westview Press, 1993).

Dublin, Holly T., 'Dynamics of the Serengeti-Mara Woodlands: An Historical Perspective', *Forest and Conservation History*, 35/4 (1991), 170–8.

Fairhead, James, and Melissa Leach, *Misreading the African Landscape: Society and Ecology in a Forest-Savanna Mosaic* (Cambridge: CUP, 1996).

Giblin, James, *The Politics of Environmental Control in Northeastern Tanzania, 1840–1940* (Philadelphia: University of Pennsylvania Press, 1992).

Iliffe, John, *Africans: The History of a Continent* (Cambridge: CUP, 1995).

McCann, James C., *Green Land, Brown Land, Black Land: An Environmental History of Africa, 1800–2000* (Portsmouth, NH: Heinemann, 1999).

—— *Maize and Grace: Africa's Encounter with a New World Crop* (Cambridge, Mass.: Harvard University Press, 2005).

Maddox, Gregory, James Giblin, and Isiaria Kimambo, *Custodians of the Land: Ecology and Culture in the History of Tanzania* (Athens, O.: Ohio University Press, 1996).

Nweke, Felix I., S. C. Dunstan Spencer, and John K. Lynam, eds, *The Cassava Transformation: Africa's Best Kept Secret* (East Lansing, Mich.: Michigan State University Press, 2002).

Webb, James L., *Desert Frontier: Ecological and Economic Change along the Western Sahel* (Madison, Wis.: University of Wisconsin Press, 1995).

CHAPTER 2

....

DEMOGRAPHY AND DISEASE

....

SHANE DOYLE

THIS chapter will limit its interest in disease to those aspects of ill-health which impact most clearly on population change and leave the more general discussion of illness to be covered in the chapter dealing with health and healing. Again, within the field of demography, it will largely ignore population movement, which will be covered in the chapter on work and migration. Finally, it will deal only briefly with the period before 1800. Still, focusing on the story of changing patterns of birth and death in recent centuries is no narrow task. John Iliffe has described Africa's transition to rapid population growth as the most important development in the continent's modern history.[1] The debate over why and how this transformation in rates of natural increase began remains unresolved. Part of the reason why the sharp increase in growth rates is so significant is because Africa as a continent has historically been characterized by low population densities, a situation which has stimulated highly significant work on issues such as the ability of precolonial societies to adapt to both local environmental change and the impact of the slave trade and long-distance commerce. Moreover, the late nineteenth century witnessed the conquest of most of the continent and the onset of colonial rule, a period associated in most accounts with population decline. The contrast between this long period of demographic setbacks and the onset of Africa's population explosion during the interwar period is remarkable. No other continent has experienced demographic expansion on this scale. Nor have other parts of the world witnessed such a rapid reversal in fertility trends as occurred in countries such as Kenya and Zimbabwe. Nor indeed has the tragic reduction in life expectancy associated with the emergence of AIDS been matched in any other continent in the modern era. Africa's perceived distinctiveness is defined to a large degree by the story of demography and disease. This exceptionalism will be a theme that will recur throughout this chapter, as will discussion of the problems of evidence and the interrelationship between fertility and mortality. But the structure of the chapter will be chronological rather than thematic, because the major debates within African historical demography tend to be confined to particular periods and because its purpose is to help provide context for the later chapters of this book.[2]

PRECOLONIAL POPULATION ESTIMATES AND TRENDS

There is little agreement about the timing and causation of African demographic change after 1900 due to the paucity or poor quality of the statistical resources for much of the modern period. Before 1900, the data are infinitely worse but the debates are no less heated. Yet this lack of consensus is relatively new. Until the 1960s, there was general agreement that the continent's precolonial population had been low and largely stable, limited by violence, slaving, social and economic obstacles to rapid growth such as prolonged breastfeeding and the absence of secure land tenure, and exceptionally high disease loads.[3]

Challenges to this homoeostasis hypothesis, which suggests that Africa's total population numbered around 100 million people between 1500 and 1900, have been based predominantly on a diverse set of re-evaluations of the assumed demographic impact of the slave trade and Africa's integration into the global economic system. Jack Caldwell, on the basis of Philip Curtin's 1969 pioneering census of the Atlantic slave trade, has argued that the demographic cost of slave exports and their attendant violence was less severe than some earlier scholars believed, amounting to an annual loss at a continental level of only one per 1,000. Moreover, he suggests that the removal of some of those exported would have allowed others to survive, in contexts where pressure on resources was relatively intense; that the overwhelmingly male character of the exported population meant that many slaves would never have had the chance to reproduce anyway; and that the demographic losses arising from the slave trade were outweighed by the benefits associated with new food crops, which permitted the cultivation of areas that had previously been unsuitable for agriculture and the achievement of unprecedented densities of settlement. On the basis that African populations must therefore have grown significantly in the centuries before 1900, Caldwell posits 50 million as an estimate of the continent's total population around 1500.[4]

An alternative criticism of the homeostasis hypothesis takes the opposite line to Caldwell's thesis, with scholars such as Joseph Inikori suggesting that Africa's population before the development of the Atlantic slave system was substantially larger than 100 million, and that the slave trade was associated with substantial population decline over the centuries during which it operated.[5] Still another group of scholars has criticized the notion that Africa's population remained stable during the years 1500–1900 by arguing that the period after the ending of the slave trade was characterized by very high levels of mortality. In West Africa the ending of slave exports and the introduction of a new economic system of legitimate commerce resulted in an enormous increase in internal enslavement, fuelled by a remarkable level of firearms imports. On the other side of the continent, similar processes seem to have had even more negative consequences, given the greater degree of isolation formerly experienced by many East African communities. Whether the introduction of long-distance trade was more disruptive than colonial conquest remains a matter of intense debate, but certainly the work of a number of scholars suggests that the nineteenth century was a time of exceptionally severe population loss due to recurrent violence, famine, and epidemic, the latter associated with both newly introduced diseases and outbreaks arising from the disturbance of local systems of environmental management.[6]

Of all the attempts to revise Curtin's estimates of African population loss due to slavery, the *Voyages* database seems to have secured broadest approval. The overall total is little different from that arrived at by Curtin, but it has become clearer how varied the demographic impact of the trade was, so that in areas such as the Bight of Biafra almost as many females as males were exported in the later eighteenth century, and it seems that the exported population was more youthful, and therefore arguably that the loss of reproductive potential was greater, than had earlier been realized.[7]

It should also be noted that Caldwell did not factor into his calculations slave exports across the Sahara, the Red Sea, and the Indian Ocean. The most commonly used synthesis, Paul Lovejoy's *Transformations in Slavery*, estimated that some 11.5 million Africans were exported by these routes. These trades were much longer established than that to the Americas, so that while the drain on population due to the continent's various slave trades lasted longer than is commonly acknowledged, the annual loss through the Sahara and from the east coast seemingly never came close to matching that across the Atlantic. However, the demographic impact of the trade to Asia and the Near East was greater than a simple enumeration indicates, for these markets particularly desired female slaves.[8]

Recent years have also seen an upsurge of new research on Mauritius, Réunion, Iran, Oman, and the Swahili coast which suggests strongly that the scale of exports to the east and north has been significantly underestimated, in large part because it now seems that the trade persisted at a high level for longer than has previously been recognized.[9] Overall, then, it appears that the numbers of Africans exported were larger, and a larger proportion of them were female, than was earlier estimated. It should also be remembered that while the precise proportion of Africans who died between capture and embarkation is unknowable, Joseph Miller's estimate that only 42 per cent of captives survived to make the Atlantic crossing should be taken seriously, given the huge differential that existed between inland and coastal slave prices.[10] Whether the several slave trades caused Africa's population to decline is still unclear, but they must certainly have acted as a major obstacle to growth.

This recent research which emphasizes the severity of the later slave trades reinforces the sense that Africa's demographic situation in the nineteenth century was anything but uniform. There seems to be strong evidence that the populations of North and South Africa were growing relatively rapidly by the second half of the century, primarily due to growing resistance to epidemic disease. The thesis that the spread of American staple crops such as cassava, maize, and sweet potato would have permitted accelerating population growth in tropical Africa may only be true in those ecologically favoured areas such as Rwanda and Burundi that were able to isolate themselves from the excesses of violence and epidemic that dominated the nineteenth century elsewhere. Within East

Africa, a major historiographical debate about the timing of the onset of population decline has seen Juhani Koponen assert that the introduction of capitalist commerce caused a significant increase in conflict and contagion through the nineteenth century, while Helge Kjekshus asserts that it was only the disruption associated with the introduction of colonial rule that fundamentally undermined African societies' capacity to cope with new demographic stresses, coinciding as it did with a prolonged period of drought, the devastating rinderpest panzootic, and new epidemics of sandfleas and sleeping sickness. A series of local studies has lent conclusive support to neither thesis, but it should be noted that in two recent analyses of population decline, in Buganda before the European takeover and in Bunyoro during conquest, emigration as well as excess mortality was key.[11]

Population Growth in the Twentieth Century

Over the course of the twentieth century, the estimated total population of the African continent increased by around 600 per cent, from perhaps 130 million to almost one billion. Growth on such a scale has been achieved by no other continent in recorded history. Moreover, the extraordinary rapidity of this demographic increase contrasts not only with the experience of every other part of the world, but also with Africa's own past. The urgency of the need to explain why it was Africa that provided the accelerant to the world's demographic explosion has naturally led much of the scholarship to seek continent-wide causes of change. This task, though, has proven exceptionally difficult, for three main reasons. The first, as will be shown below, is that a series of local studies have shown that the nature of population change varied sharply from one area to another.

The second is that the quality of demographic data in most parts of Africa was relatively poor before the 1970s.[12] Before the late 1940s, most African censuses were unworthy of the name, being little more than mere population counts. Not infrequently, only taxpayers were counted, the resulting total being adjusted by an unscientifically calculated multiplier to account for women, children, and elderly and infirm males. Censuses, moreover, were inconsistent in the information they gathered and in the techniques of population recording used. The demographer Robert Kuczynski's great *Demographic Survey of the British Colonial Empire* was remarkable for the thoroughness with which it analysed official sources on African demography and for the author's willingness to discuss the various examples of poor practice he uncovered with withering mockery.[13] In a few societies in Africa before the 1950s, census information can be supplemented by vital registration data, but even in those few cases where the requirement to register births, deaths, and marriages was introduced relatively early, colonial reluctance to train local administrators meant that the recording of vital events in countries like Uganda was never as comprehensive as it was in colonial India. Demographic surveys, meanwhile, even though they often covered a significant proportion of particular populations and claimed to have secured a representative sample, were frequently affected by problems of self-selection, as of course were all hospital records.

Although most analyses of data quality from this era have focused on the structural problems of the recording process, some studies have also emphasized that demographic data suffered from Africans' suspicions of the purposes to which such information might be put. While many African societies considered that counting people, especially children, was a hubristic invitation to death to reduce their numbers, other concerns reflected the more novel threat posed by the tendency of the colonial state to seek information about subject societies in order to extract tax and labour from them. As well as this producing widespread evasion, it seems likely that the age structure of African societies was also misrepresented. European condemnation of the marriage of young girls tended to encourage the inflation of female adolescents' ages, while fathers often under-reported their sons' ages so they would not have to pay tax.[14]

The third reason why the challenge of explaining Africa's shift to rapid population growth is still unresolved is that the evidence that does exist by no means tells a coherent story of steady, consistent mortality decline and fertility increase. The impact of colonial rule on demography, as is the case with so many aspects of Africa life under European overrule, was contradictory. This was shown most clearly in the debate about whether it was a reduction in death rates during the colonial era which triggered Africa's demographic expansion. Scholars such as Iliffe and Caldwell suggest that the evidence of population growth which could be detected in a number of sub-Saharan societies from the 1920s can best be explained by the decline in crisis mortality, which they believe was firmly established by this decade. They assert that large-scale mortality during famines became less common primarily due to the development of more sophisticated administrative systems, communications, and markets, and a growing sense, particularly within the British Empire, that famine prevention, prediction, and relief were key measures of good governance. Certainly, no major famine occurred within Britain's African empire after 1927 and elsewhere large-scale death became rare outside of wartime situations. In addition, Iliffe and Caldwell emphasize that in the second and third decades of the twentieth century colonial medical departments also began to make an impact on epidemic diseases such as smallpox and plague through limited vaccination and basic sanitation. They believe that in some countries such as Kenya the smoothing of the peaks in mortality was sufficient in itself to enable population to start growing.

The thesis that it was the imperial model of ordered, developmentalist government that facilitated population growth focuses particularly on the acceleration of population increase evident from the late 1940s, which seemingly was prompted not only by new investment in preventive medicine, the introduction of wonder drugs such as penicillin and chloroquine, and the mass provision of antenatal, maternity, and child welfare clinics, but also by the broader benefits of the later colonial period such as mass education and rising incomes. In a large-scale comparative study, Caldwell demonstrated that the most important single factor in the decline of child mortality in low-income societies after the Second World War was female education, but that it was the synergy between healthcare and educational provision that was especially transformative. Within Nigeria, for example, he found that the gain in life expectancy at birth was 20 per cent when illiterate mothers gained access to adequate health facilities, 33 per cent when women were educated but no health facilities were available, and 87 per cent when both female schooling and medical provision were provided. Scholars have hypothesized that female education reduced child mortality by increasing faith in scientific medicine, helping mothers appreciate the importance of hygiene and sanitation, and increasing the likelihood that medical advice would be sought and followed when children became ill.[15]

This positivist appreciation of the direct and indirect health benefits of imperialism has not been universally shared by all scholars. For some, it harks back to earlier generations of writers about health and healing in Africa, servants of empire or mission who obeyed Kipling's injunction to 'bid the sickness cease'. In the nineteenth century, as Philip Curtin argued in his seminal *The Image of Africa*, colonial conquest was justified in part on the grounds that at last professional medical help would be provided for Africa's uniquely diseased peoples. As colonial rule became firmly established, successive victories over tropical disease were hailed as further evidence of Western beneficence and the technological mastery of the imperial scientist.[16]

Some, more sceptical analyses of colonial healthcare have questioned the effectiveness of colonial medicine, noting, for example, that levels of non-epidemic disease were hardly affected before the 1950s. Colonial doctors have been criticized for fixating on the immediate symptoms of illness by neo-Foucauldian historians who note that patients' understanding of their own illnesses tended to be disregarded and by neo-Marxist scholars who argue that Western practitioners tended to ignore the background causes of disease, such as poverty, poor nutrition, or poor education.[17] The thesis that colonialism if anything contributed to worsening standards of health has been reinforced by a number of local studies which argue that it actually facilitated the spread of disease: labour migration exposed Africans to new disease environments and undermined rural food production; the demands of cash cropping impacted on maternal care of infants; dams and irrigation schemes spread malaria, schistosomiasis, and bilharzia; new roads and railways accelerated the spread of epidemics; and the concentration of population disrupted intricate local systems of environmental management, negatively affecting the disease ecology of rural areas.[18]

To some degree this disagreement about the impact of colonialism on health and mortality can be resolved by careful periodization and by distinguishing between increasing life expectancy and improving health. Colonial medicine may have begun by concentrating its resources on maintaining the health of European officials, their servants, and African soldiers, police, and other key groups. But by the 1950s, going to the clinic was one of the most common points of contact between Africans and the colonial state, and in some areas at least medical interest in African attitudes to disease and in a broader conception of epidemiology increased over time. Yet while epidemics and famines did reduce in frequency and severity, mortality levels did fall overall, and colonial medicine did become more popular, individual Africans may not have enjoyed better day-to-day health. Iliffe has discussed how the decline of famine did not necessarily result in improved nutritional standards, for the adoption of famine-resist-ant crops, wider food markets, and growing labour demands in many cases worsened malnutrition. Whether the decline in epidemics was similarly countered by a worsening of endemic disease is still open to debate.[19]

Disagreements about the overall impact of colonialism on health and longevity have also shaped the debate about the timing and causes of fertility increase. Scholars who are sceptical of colonialism's capacity significantly to reduce levels of morbidity and mortal-ity have argued that Africa's transition to rapid population growth must therefore have been driven by rising birth rates from the interwar period. The key studies which out-line this thesis make four major arguments in their attempt to demonstrate the primacy of rising fertility. First, colonial demands for high taxes created pressure for parents to increase desired family size, as child labour became crucial in a cash-crop economy. Second, colonial labour migration enabled young men to acquire the wealth to marry at an earlier age than had traditionally been the case. Third, colonial economies and legal systems tended to lower female status, thus reducing women's ability to control their fer-tility by traditional birth spacing techniques such as prolonged breastfeeding and post-partum sexual abstinence. Fourth, and perhaps contradictorily, female education also served to reduce birth intervals, as women who had been to school would have been less likely to pay heed to traditions aimed at delaying conception.[20]

Official sources that provide convincing statistical evidence of any increase in fertility in tropical Africa before the late 1940s, however, have not yet been found. By contrast, local surveys suggest that there existed a band of sub-fertility that stretched across equatorial Africa, encompassing much of present-day southern Uganda, north-west Tanzania, South Sudan, Central African Republic, both Congos, Cameroon, and Gabon, where birth rates remained depressed until well after the Second World War. Most studies of this region have tended to identify sexually transmitted diseases (STDs), often associated with marital breakdown due to commercialization, labour migration, or social disruption, as the pre-eminent cause of this enduring pattern. Worsening nutrition as well as long-established factors such as high levels of post-partum infection and prolonged post-partum abstinence also contributed to the sub-fecundity of this region's population. In this broad swathe of middle Africa it seems that fertility increase only began from the late 1940s or 1950s due to the release of the physical limitations on reproduction imposed by diet and disease, with scholars such as Anne Retel-Laurentin and Anatole Romaniuk arguing that sub-fertility reduced primarily in response to improvements in nutrition, the medicalization of childbirth, and the antibiotic treat-ment of STDs.[21]

Continental fertility levels, then, were boosted by these societies' retreat from exceptionalism, but postwar censuses showed that fertility was rising in all parts of the continent. In the absence of data showing rising birth rates before 1945, Iliffe and Caldwell have maintained their position that improved health and longevity were the drivers of Africa's early population growth. They emphasize the role of improving reproductive health in raising birth rates everywhere after the Second World War and otherwise tend to prioritize medical and social over economic causes of increased fertility. They suggest that the durations of post-partum sexual abstinence and lactation only shortened significantly from the 1940s, by which time sustained improvements in child survival rates had convinced mothers that they could risk shortening their birth intervals, and more than a small minority of women had been convinced by Christianity, urbanization, and schooling that traditional methods of birth spacing were associated with immorality and backwardness.[22]

Only new statistical information about fertility levels relating to the period before the Second World War will allow this debate to progress. The most likely sources of such data are the church registers of baptism and marriage, which became common from the early decades of the twentieth century across much of Africa. These registers' recording of life events allow individuals' reproductive histories to be reconstructed, and enables the reconstitution of families by linking parents to the children they baptized over a period of years. The resulting longitudinal datasets permitting the identification of shifts over time in average age at marriage, birth intervals, and family size clearly have great potential significance. The most complete attempt at family reconstitution so far available for Africa, Sarah Walters's work on four large parishes in the region surrounding Mwanza in Tanzania, has produced results which tend not to support the thesis that fertility change drove population growth during the colonial period. Her analysis of 109,000 births, marriages, and deaths shows that mortality for those under five years old was already falling substantially by the 1930s, that birth intervals only began to reduce from the early 1940s, and that marriage age rose steadily from the 1920s. The Total Marital Fertility Rate was stable until around 1940 but then increased by two births per woman in the decade that followed. Walters's findings do push back by several years the date at which statistical evidence clearly indicates that fertility was rising within Africa, but suggest that a decline in marriage age was irrelevant to this development and that mortality decline, at least among children, preceded the fertility increase.

This is, however, only one study, and it must be borne in mind that the accuracy and representativeness of church parish data are imperfect and may have changed over time. It is possible that parishioners were more likely to have been exposed to Western healthcare and education than non-Christians and even that good recorders, the reconstitutable minority of people who remained resident in one parish for decades and participated consistently in church sacraments, may not have been typical of the larger church community. Parish records almost certainly underestimated neo-natal mortality and had nothing to say about sterility, while a church marriage was not necessarily a first marriage. Still, family reconstitution has transformed historical understanding of the trajectory and causation of demographic change in Europe before the era of censuses, so its potential should not be dismissed lightly. Moreover, the hypothesis that rapid population growth in Africa was triggered by economically induced earlier marriage was heavily influenced by Wrigley and Schofield's English reconstitutions. It seems logical to replicate the same methodology in the testing of this translocated theory. For all of its costs and complications, it is likely that further reconstitution work, ideally among highly Christianized communities little affected by migration, will be the source of significant advances in our understanding of colonial-era demographic change.[23]

FERTILITY DECLINE

In most African countries, independence around 1960 was accompanied by an acceleration in the rate of fertility increase. Medicine was one of the chief areas in which postcolonial governments chose to invest, reducing sub-fecundity as well as improving standards of health and increasing life expectancy. One of the most striking aspects of this expansion of medical provision was the rapid increase in popularity of antenatal care and institutionalized delivery. Secondary sterility and pregnancy loss due to mis-carriage and stillbirth declined significantly in areas with especially well-developed medical systems. Even Gabon, whose Total Fertility Rate (TFR) was half that of Rwanda in the 1950s, primarily because one in three Gabonese women was sterile in the late colonial period, moved towards a high fertility regime in the 1960s. Yet, just as it seemed that Africa was about to achieve a degree of demographic uniformity, the first signs of a decline in fertility emerged. The onset of fertility control began first in Egypt and the indigenous population of South Africa in the 1960s, before spreading to the rest of North Africa in the 1970s. By the early 1980s, it was noticeable in southern Nigeria, southern Ghana, Kenya, Botswana, Zimbabwe, and Lesotho, and has spread steadily in the years that followed. The scale of the decline in fertility in these countries is every bit as remarkable as the speed with which fertility was rising a decade or so before. Kenya's TFR was estimated at 8.0 in the late 1970s, the highest national level ever recorded. By 1998, it had fallen to 4.7. The combination of exceptionally high fertility and rapidly declining mortality—under-5 mortality rates in Kenya, for example, halved between 1960 and 1990—meant that sub-Saharan Africa's population was growing at 3.1 per cent per annum by the 1980s, the fastest natural growth rate for any large population in history.

Early explanations for the decline in fertility levels in Africa were influenced by demographic transition theory, which held that birth rates would fall in response to improvements in living standards, life expectancy, and especially infant survival. Where parents could expect that all their children might survive to adulthood, experience elsewhere indicated that they would risk restricting their family size. Researchers at first concentrated on the role of education, urbanization, and women's increasing involve-ment in the workplace in enabling reproductive decision-making to shift from the line-age to the individual.[24] The availability of contraception was also crucial, and while Susan Cotts Watkins has argued convincingly that the remarkable success of family planning policy in Kenya resulted from the degree to which ideas about birth control were trans-lated into locally relevant idioms, the experience of South Africa suggests that where a desire for contraception exists then resistance to an external model of fertility control can be largely overcome, if provision is sufficiently ubiquitous. By 1991, the apartheid state had the highest density of family planning clinics in the world, almost all of which were targeted at non-white communities. Despite these clinics clearly serving the interests of white supremacy, they were nonetheless utilized relatively heavily by black women.[25]

The assumption that fertility decline in Africa would follow the pattern set in other parts of the world has, however, been effectively challenged. The decline in birth rates in many African societies coincided with growing land shortages and the introduction of structural adjustment policies which brought worsening unemployment, urban poverty, and a weakening of state educational and medical systems. The exceptionally negative context within which fertility decline occurred in much of Africa has forced a reassessment of the motivations underlying fertility limitation. Recent studies accordingly have emphasized Africans' desire to maintain rather than enhance their living standards and children's life chances. Moreover, the experience of Kenya, where the TFR fell rapidly during the 1980s and early 1990s but then stalled at a relatively high level of almost five births per woman, has challenged the assumption that demographic transition is a universal and indeed irreversible process. One influential outcome of this rethinking has been Caldwell, Orubuloye, and Caldwell's thesis that contraception would be utilized differently in Africa due to the sustained power of pro-natalism and birth spacing traditions. Rather than being employed as a means of stopping further pregnancies once a desired number of children had been achieved, which is the pattern elsewhere in the world, contraception would be used by Africans as a culturally acceptable substitute for traditional birth spacing techniques. Caldwell predicted therefore that African fertility decline would affect women of all ages and parities.[26] This thesis has been supported by a number of studies, which have shown that the way in which African women use contraception does not tend to change significantly as they get older and their family size increases. Surveys found that women justified the use of contraception on the grounds that it would increase child survival, not simply reduce completed family size.[27]

However, this emphasis on continuity disregards to some degree the evidence that birth spacing in Africa declined substantially from the mid-twentieth century and does not fully explain why fertility levels rose so quickly before falling so sharply. It seems likely both that the first generation of women who abandoned prolonged breastfeeding and post-partum abstinence were aware that their birth intervals would reduce, and that the demographic consequences of these decisions only became fully apparent to the generation that followed. If this process involved a conscious rejection of the past and a decades-long disruption of birth spacing knowledge, then further historical research into the conceptual as well as the economic and social context of this apparent revival of birth spacing tradition would be advantageous.[28] One important recent revision of the thesis that Africa's fertility decline was about spacing rather than stopping behaviour has emerged from the work of scholars who have turned attention increasingly to the apparent frequency with which Africans have understood fertility limitation in terms of postponement of further childbearing until personal or social circumstances improve. Of course, for many women circumstances may never get better, but if the focus is placed on intention rather than reproductive outcome, then such behaviour should not be viewed as 'stopping'. The particular attraction of this theory is that it can help explain emerging patterns of fertility decline in parts of Africa where social indicators were less favourable than demographic transition theory seems to require.[29]

THE DEMOGRAPHIC IMPACT OF HIV/AIDS

The tendency for demographic analysis to increase in sophistication and confidence as the period of study nears the present is shown even more clearly within the literature on HIV/AIDS. There is broad consensus about the scale and shape of the mortality associated with the pandemic. More than fifteen million people in Africa had died due to AIDS by 2010, with perhaps 15 per cent of all deaths in the first decade of the twenty-first century in sub-Saharan Africa being attributed to that disease. By 2002, it was calculated that life expectancy at birth in this region had fallen to 47 years; without AIDS, it was estimated that life expectancy would have been 62 years. This resurgence in high levels of mortality, combined with declining fertility, caused Africa's annual rate of population growth to fall to 2.3 per cent by 2010. Because most new cases arise out of heterosexual intercourse, and because of a high incidence of both early sexual debut and other STDs, which increase the risk of vaginal infection, women make up the majority of people living with HIV in Africa, in marked contrast with other regions of the world. Low levels of income and hygiene are thought to be the primary reasons why mother-to-child infections are also particularly high.

There is again relatively little disagreement about the relationship between HIV and fertility. Scholars have long been aware that many of the societies which have suffered the highest prevalence of HIV were precisely those countries such as Botswana and South Africa which had experienced the fastest declines in fertility. To some degree this simply reflected the fact that HIV transmission and fertility control were associated with similar social indicators, such as high levels of urbanization. But later research identified more direct connections, noting, for example, that injectable contraceptives appear to thin the vaginal wall, making HIV transmission during intercourse significantly more likely.[30] Similarly, while early research on the role of HIV in reducing fertility levels in Africa focused primarily on social factors, such as women delaying marriage, declining widow remarriage, declining extramarital conceptions, increased use of barrier contraception, and the advice which many HIV-positive women received to avoid further conceptions, subsequent research has emphasized the biological impact of HIV on fecundity, through mechanisms such as higher levels of miscarriage, stillbirth, and amenorrhoea due to weight loss. It is now generally accepted that a combination of social and physical/psychological factors is responsible for the fertility of HIV-positive women being 25–40 per cent lower than that of HIV-negative women.[31]

What has prompted more debate is the question of why Africa should have suffered such exceptionally high rates of HIV infection compared with the rest of the world. One major thesis is Iliffe's argument that Africa's epidemic was the worst because it was the first, as the disease had spread into the general population before health authorities appreciated the threat that it posed. Other approaches have tended to focus more on trying to explain how HIV could have emerged as a mass pandemic among a generally heterosexual, non-drug-injecting population, given the relatively low risk of infection during any individual sex act. Controversially, Jack and Pat Caldwell and Pat Quiggan have argued that HIV spread so quickly in Africa due to a social tolerance for high levels of sexual partner exchange, before and outside marriage, because African family life has historically centred on the extension and multiplication of the lineage by maximizing fertility. This thesis has been criticized by a number of scholars who object to African sexual behaviour being described in terms that strengthen stereotypes about African promiscuity and who suggest that this theory underestimates the diversity of sexual behaviour across precolonial Africa, as well as the scale of sexual behavioural change under colonial rule and after independence. Jack Caldwell subsequently refined his approach, emphasizing the particular vulnerability of non-circumcising societies, and the importance of the emergence during the twentieth century of prostitution and sexually transmitted diseases. Yet studies of the emergence of AIDS have demonstrated great variation in the nature and popularity of commercial sex work and in the prevalence of STDs across the continent. Moreover, many researchers have stressed the need to periodize behavioural change more precisely, with a large body of work arguing that the rapidity with which HIV spread across Africa during the 1970s and early 1980s requires particular appreciation of the high levels of violence, economic decline, and urbanization experienced during these years.[32]

A more recent approach which tries to explain why Africa has suffered so severely from HIV has focused on the frequency with which Africans have engaged in sustained, concurrent sexual relationships. Scholars such as Helen Epstein have argued that Africa's characteristically dense networks of interconnected concurrent partnerships tend to facilitate the transmission of HIV more than the serial monogamy which is so common in Western societies, or even serial monogamy combined with occasional high-risk sex. This is because repeated sex with the same multiple partners supposedly maximizes the possibility of transmission, especially given that HIV is highly contagious in the weeks after infection has taken hold. Epstein asserts that Africans do not have more sexual partners over their lifetime than do people in Western societies and that policy has focused overmuch on high-risk groups and practices. This thesis has attracted significant criticism, largely on the basis that the epidemiological model on which it is based has not been fully replicated in real-life situations.[33] The assertion that Africans have fewer sexual partners than Americans and Europeans is also problematic, based as it is on surveys conducted after behavioural change in response to HIV had begun. Earlier studies suggested that a very high number of sexual partners had often been the norm. Moreover, it is likely that future research into the historical development of concurrency will emphasize that its frequency and nature changed over the past century, as socially legitimate extra-marital sex declined in acceptability, polygamy became less stable, and new opportunities for less regularized sexual affairs emerged, generally creating more open, longer-distance sexual networks. Historical evidence also suggests that sexual networks in the decades before HIV became an epidemic commonly linked together relatively stable concurrent relationships with often rather frequent shorter-term encounters between sex workers and barmaids and their customers, but clearly further research on sexual behaviour in the crucial decades of the 1950s, 1960s, and 1970s is required.[34]

CONCLUSION

While research into disease and concepts of health remains one of the most vibrant fields of African historical research, the future of Africanist demographic history is uncertain. When John Iliffe's overview of the continent's history, *Africans*, was first published in 1995, it seemed possible that it would foster greater interest among Africanists in the role of demography as a crucial context and, in some circumstances, as a driver of historical change. Yet, while *Africans* was widely acclaimed, its central thesis failed to convince many scholars. For example, Thomas Spear's review in the *Journal of African History* was admiring of *Africans'* scope and analytical power, but suggested that the significance of demographic change had been exaggerated and that Iliffe's work veered at times towards demographic determinism.[35] Subsequent surveys of African history have certainly not ignored demographic change, but it has resumed its role as bridesmaid rather than bride.

In two review articles, Dennis Cordell has suggested that in fact demographic history has reduced in prominence within African studies since 1990, a trend which the publication of Iliffe's book disguised.[36] Several reasons have been advanced to explain this apparent retreat. Cordell emphasizes above all the impact of the cultural turn within African studies, which marked a profound shift in intellectual interest away from quantitative history of all kinds. The perceived tendencies of demographic historians to create an essentialized version of the past and to seek to override Africa's remarkable cultural diversity by developing and applying universalizing theories has caused the subdiscipline to be viewed with a degree of scepticism by many scholars. An alternative, and in some ways contradictory, explanation for the decline in population history derives from demographers' and demographic historians' ever-increasing statistical sophistication. The growing complexity of the data analysis which underpins demographic research reflected in part a desire to explain the local distinctiveness of patterns of fertility and mortality. However, as demography became more technical, so it divorced itself to a large degree from the arts and other social sciences. Historians of population change, where they apply techniques from pure demography, have at times written in a language which is largely incomprehensible to non-specialists. Moreover, while the statistical skills needed for demographic history have perhaps been over-estimated, there is no doubt that the investment of time and money required for family reconstitution from church registers, for example, is a significant disincentive. In terms of person-hours, entering, refining, linking, and analysing the data recorded over the course of the twentieth century within the baptism, marriage, and burial registers of just one large parish is equivalent to three to four months' work.

Cordell's more recent review was more optimistic than the first, as he noted something of an upsurge in writing about Africa's population history during the first decade of the new millennium. What seemed most impressive about the new scholarship was the sophistication of its critical analysis of the biases within demographic sources in the past and its examination of the ways in which population recording was used in the exercise of state power and in identity construction. Certainly it does seem that this revival of interest in demographic history, loosely defined, was shaped to a large degree by the intellectual interests of social and cultural historians. Perhaps the most interesting recent work on fertility in colonial Africa, that of Nancy Rose Hunt on the Belgian Congo, employs data on birth rates primarily as context for her research into changing attitudes towards and discourse about reproduction.[37] Similarly, a recent special edition of the *Journal of African History* on death in Africa had little to say about mortality levels, focusing rather on the cultural experience of dying. And the most important works of medical history in Africa concentrated on African concepts of health more than an analysis of disease patterns *per se*.[38] Whether this divide between the quantitative and qualitative can be bridged remains to be seen. To some degree the question depends upon historians' ability to adapt the techniques of epidemiologists and demographers. It is, for example, very noticeable that whereas historians of Africa have continued to engage productively with the other social sciences, this has not been true on the whole with regard to demography. Demography's disengagement from history, and indeed the other social sciences, has been reduced by the growing interest in proximate determinants, which has encouraged a more ethnographic approach, by the growth of anthropological demography, where scholars have operated on a smaller scale than was previously common, and by the need both to understand and to explain the HIV pandemic. But still research based on fieldwork is surprisingly uncommon in the major demographic journals. Until this disciplinary divide is bridged more firmly, claims that population change lies at the heart of African history will continue to be met with scepticism.

NOTES

1. John Iliffe, *Africans: The History of a Continent* (Cambridge: CUP, 2nd edn, 2007), 1–5.
2. This chapter builds upon previous attempts to define the state of the literature on African historical demography and disease, such as Christopher Fyfe and David McMaster, eds, *African Historical Demography*, i (Edinburgh: University of Edinburgh, Centre of African Studies, 1977); Dennis Cordell, 'African Historical Demography in the Years since Edinburgh', *History in Africa*, 27 (2000); Steven Feierman, 'Struggles for Control: The Social Roots of Health and Healing in Modern Africa', *African Studies Review*, 28 (1985).
3. Thomas Malthus, *An Essay on Population* (London: J. M. Dent, 1914), i. 89–98; Alexander Carr-Saunders, *World Population: Past Growth and Present Trends* (Oxford: Clarendon, 1936), 35–36.
4. Jack Caldwell, 'The Social Repercussions of Colonial Rule: Demographic Aspects', in Albert Adu Boahen, ed., *UNESCO General History of Africa*, vii (London: UNESCO, 1985), 465–7;

Jack Caldwell and Thomas Schindlmayr, 'Historical Population Estimates: Unravelling the Consensus', *Population and Development Review*, 28 (2002), 196–8; Philip Curtin, *The Atlantic Slave Trade: A Census* (Madison, Wis.: University of Wisconsin Press, 1969).

5. Joseph Inikori, 'Under-Population in Nineteenth-Century West Africa: The Role of the Export Slave Trade', in Fyfe and McMaster, *African Historical Demography*, ii. 297–9.

6. Paul Lovejoy, *Transformations in Slavery: A History of Slavery in Africa* (Cambridge: CUP, 3rd edn, 2011); Juhani Koponen, *People and Production in Late Precolonial Tanzania: History and Structures* (Uppsala: Scandinavian Institute of African Studies, 1988); Helge Kjekshus, *Ecology Control and Economic Development in East African History: The Case of Tanganyika, 1850–1950* (London: Heinemann, 1977).

7. David Eltis and David Richardson, eds, *Extending the Frontiers: Essays on the New Transatlantic Slave Trade Database* (New Haven, Conn.: Yale University Press, 2008); http://slavevoyages.org/tast/index.faces.

8. Lovejoy, *Transformations*, 27, 61, 138.

9. Richard Allen, 'The Constant Demand of the French', *Journal of African History*, 49 (2008), 67; Paul Lovejoy, Behnaz Mirzai, and Ismael Montana, eds, *Slavery, Islam and Diaspora* (Trenton, NJ: Africa World Press, 2009).

10. Joseph Miller, *Way of Death: Merchant Capitalism and the Angolan Slave Trade, 1730–1830* (Madison, Wis.: University of Wisconsin Press, 1988).

11. Jean-Pierre Chrétien, 'Les Années de l'éleusine, du sorgho et du haricot dans l'ancien Burundi: Ecologie et idéologie', *African Economic History*, 7 (1979); Koponen, *People*, ch. 4; Kjekshus, *Ecology*, 24–5; Henri Médard *Le Royaume du Buganda au XIXe siècle: Mutations politiques et religieuses d'un grand État d'Afrique de l'Est* (Paris: Karthala, 2007); Shane Doyle, *Crisis and Decline in Bunyoro: Population and Environment in Western Uganda 1860–1955* (Oxford: James Currey, 2006).

12. Bruce Fetter, 'Decoding and Interpreting African Census Data: Vital Evidence from an Unsavory Witness', *Cahiers d'Études Africaines*, 27 (1987); Bruce Fetter, ed., *Demography from Scanty Evidence: Central Africa in the Colonial Era* (Boulder, Colo.: Lynne Rienner, 1990).

13. Robert Kuczynski, *Demographic Survey of the British Colonial Empire* (Oxford: Institute of International Affairs, 1949), ii. 124.

14. Fetter, 'Decoding'; Jean Stengers, 'Some Methodological Reflections', in Fetter, *Demography*, 27.

15. Iliffe, *Africans*, 252; Caldwell, 'Social Repercussions'.

16. Philip Curtin, *The Image of Africa: British Ideas and Action, 1780–1850* (Madison, Wis.: University of Wisconsin Press, 1965); Gwyn Prins, 'But What was the Disease? The Present State of Health and Healing in African Studies', *Past and Present*, 124 (1989), 162.

17. Megan Vaughan, *Curing their Ills: Colonial Power and African Illness* (Cambridge: Polity, 1991); Meredith Turshen, 'Population Growth and the Deterioration of Health, Mainland Tanzania 1920–1960', in Dennis Cordell and Joel Gregory, eds, *African Population and Capitalism: Historical Perspectives* (Boulder, Colo.: Westview, 1987).

18. Randall Packard, 'The Invention of the "Tropical Worker": Medical Research and the Quest for Central African Labor on the South African Gold Mines, 1903–36', *Journal of African History*, 34 (1993); Allen Isaacman, 'Displaced People, Displaced Energy, and Displaced Memories: The Case of Cahora Bassa, 1970–2004', *International Journal of African Historical Studies*, 38 (2005).

19. John Iliffe, *The African Poor: A History* (Cambridge: CUP, 1987), 160–1.

20. Dennis Cordell, Joel Gregory, and Victor Piché, 'Introduction', in Cordell and Gregory, *African Population*; Gavin Kitching, 'Proto-Industrialisation and Demographic Change: A Thesis and Some Possible African Implications', *Journal of African History*, 24 (1983), 229–30.

21. Gilles Sautter, *De l'Atlantique au fleuve Congo: Une géographie de sous-peuplement*, 2 vols (Paris: Mouton, 1966); Anne Retel-Laurentin, 'Sub-Fertility in Black Africa: The Case of the Nzakara in Central African Republic', in Babatunde Adadevoh, ed., *Subfertility and Infertility in Africa* (Ibadan: Caxton Press, 1974).

22. Caldwell, 'Social Repercussions', 458, 476–80; Iliffe, *Africans*, 240; Hilary Page and Ron Lesthaeghe, eds, *Child-Spacing in Tropical Africa: Traditions and Change* (London: Heinemann, 1981).

23. Sarah Walters, 'Fertility, Mortality and Marriage in Northwest Tanzania, 1920– 1970: A Demographic Study Using Parish Registers', Ph.D. thesis (University of Cambridge, 2008), 189, 205, 232, 243. www.geog.cam.ac.uk/people/walters/phd.pdf. See also Veijo Notkola and Harri Siiskonen, *Fertility, Mortality and Migration in Sub-Saharan Africa: The Case of Ovamboland in North Namibia, 1925–90* (London: Macmillan Press, 2000); and cf. Edward Anthony Wrigley and Roger Schofield, *The Population History of England 1541–1871: A Reconstruction* (Cambridge: CUP, 1981).

24. Cf. Karen Mason, 'Explaining Fertility Transitions', *Demography*, 34 (1997); Susan Greenhalgh, 'The Social Construction of Population Science', *Comparative Studies in Society and History*, 38 (1996).

25. Susan Cotts Watkins, 'Local and Foreign Models of Reproduction in Nyanza Province, Kenya', *Population and Development Review*, 26/4 (2000); Jack Caldwell and Pat Caldwell, 'The South African Fertility Decline', *Population and Development Review*, 19/2 (1993).

26. Deborah Potts and Shula Marks, 'Fertility in Southern Africa: The Quiet Revolution', *Journal of Southern African Studies*, 27/2 (2001); Jack Caldwell, Israel Orubuloye, and Pat Caldwell, 'Fertility Decline in Africa: A New Type of Transition?', *Population and Development Review*, 18/2 (1992); John Bongaarts, Odile Frank, and Ron Lesthaeghe, 'The Proximate Determinants of Fertility in Sub-Saharan Africa', *Population and Development Review*, 10/3 (1984).

27. Caroline Bledsoe, Allan Hill, Umberto d'Alessandro, and Patricia Langerock, 'Constructing Natural Fertility: The Use of Western Contraceptive Technologies in Rural Gambia', *Population and Development Review*, 20 (1994); Jennifer Johnson-Hanks, 'Uncertainty and the Second Space: Modern Birth Timing and the Dilemma of Education', *European Journal of Population*, 20 (2004).

28. Anatole Romaniuk, 'Increase in Natural Fertility during the Early Stages of Modernization: Evidence from an African Case Study, Zaire', *Population Studies*, 34 (1980); Tim Dyson and Mike Murphy 'The Onset of Fertility Transition', *Population and Development Review*, 11 (1985).

29. Victor Agadjanian, 'Fraught with Ambivalence: Reproductive Intentions and Contraceptive Choices in a Sub-Saharan Fertility Transition', *Population Research and Policy Review*, 24/6 (2005); Ian Timaeus and Thomas Moultrie, 'On Postponement and Birth Intervals', *Population and Development Review*, 34/3 (2008).

30. Renee Heffron et al., 'Use of Hormonal Contraceptives and Risk of HIV-1 Transmission: A Prospective Cohort Study', *The Lancet Infectious Diseases*, 12/1 (2012).

31. Massimo Fabiani, Barbara Nattabi, Emingtone O. Ayella, Martin Ogwang, and Silvia Declich, 'Differences in Fertility by HIV Serostatus and Adjusted HIV Prevalence Data

from an Antenatal Clinic in Northern Uganda', *Tropical Medicine and International Health*, 11/2 (2006); Simon Gregson, Basia Zaba, and Susan-Catherine Hunter, 'The Impact of HIV-1 on Fertility in Sub-Saharan Africa: Causes and Consequences', *UN Population Bulletin, Special Issue on 'Completing the Fertility Transition'* (2003). Of course, HIV infection is strongly correlated with infection with other STDs which also independently depress fertility levels.

32. John Iliffe, *The African AIDS Epidemic: A History* (Oxford: James Currey, 2006); Jack Caldwell, Pat Caldwell, and Pat Quiggan, 'The Social Context of AIDS in Sub-Saharan Africa', *Population and Development Review*, 15/2 (1989); Suzette Heald,'The Power of Sex: Some Reflections on the Caldwells', *Africa*, 65 (1995); Jack Caldwell, 'Rethinking the African AIDS Epidemic', *Population and Development Review*, 26/1 (2000); Helen Pickering et al., 'Sexual Behaviour in a Fishing Community on Lake Victoria, Uganda', *Health Transition Review*, 7 (1997).

33. Helen Epstein, *The Invisible Cure: Africa, the West and the Fight Against AIDS* (London: Viking, 2007), 54–79, 159–61, 173–96. For criticism, see Larry Sawers and Eileen Stillwaggon, 'Concurrent Sexual Partnerships Do Not Explain the HIV Epidemics in Africa: A Systematic Review of the Evidence', *Journal of the International AIDS Society* (132010), 34.

34. Shane Doyle, *Before HIV: Sexuality, Fertility and Mortality in East Africa, 1900–1980* (Oxford: OUP, forthcoming); Roy Anderson et al., 'The Spread of HIV-1 in Africa: Sexual Contact Patterns and the Predicted Demographic Impact of AIDS', *Nature*, 352/6336 (1991), 581–9; Christine Obbo, 'HIV Transmission through Social and Geographical Networks in Uganda', *Social Science and Medicine*, 36/1 (1993), 949–55.

35. Thomas Spear, 'Africa's Population History', *Journal of African History*, 37 (1996).

36. Cordell, 'African Historical Demography', and 'African Historical Demography in the Postmodern and Postcolonial Eras', in K. Ittmann, Dennis Cordell, and Gregory Maddox, eds, *The Demographics of Empire: The Colonial Order and the Creation of Knowledge* (Athens, O.: Ohio University Press).

37. See especially Nancy Rose Hunt, *A Colonial Lexicon: Of Birth Ritual, Medicalization, and Mobility in the Congo* (Durham, NC: Duke University Press, 1999)

38. Rebekah Lee and Megan Vaughan, 'Death and Dying in the History of Africa since 1800', *Journal of African History*, 49 (2008); John Janzen, *The Quest for Therapy in Lower Zaire* (Berkeley, Calif.: University of California Press, 1978); Feierman, 'Struggles for Control'.

BIBLIOGRAPHY

Anderson, Roy, et al., 'The Spread of HIV-1 in Africa: Sexual Contact Patterns and the Predicted Demographic Impact of AIDS', *Nature*, 352/6336 (1991).

Caldwell, Jack, 'The Social Repercussions of Colonial Rule: Demographic Aspects', in Albert Adu Boahen, ed., *UNESCO General History of Africa*, vii (London: UNESCO, 1985).

Caldwell, Jack, Israel Orubuloye, and Pat Caldwell, 'Fertility Decline in Africa: A New Type of Transition?', *Population and Development Review*, 18/2 (1992).

Cordell, Dennis, and Joel Gregory, eds, *African Population and Capitalism* (Boulder, Colo.: Westview, 1987).

Feierman, Steven, 'Struggles for Control: The Social Roots of Health and Healing in Modern Africa', *African Studies Review*, 28 (1985).

Fetter, Bruce, ed., *Demography from Scanty Evidence: Central Africa in the Colonial Era* (Boulder, Colo.: Lynne Rienner, 1990).

Hunt, Nancy Rose, *A Colonial Lexicon: Of Birth Ritual, Medicalization, and Mobility in the Congo* (Durham, NC: Duke University Press, 1999).

Iliffe, John, *Africans: The History of a Continent* (Cambridge: Cambridge University Press, 2nd edn, 2007).

Prins, Gwyn, 'But What Was the Disease? The Present State of Health and Healing in African Studies', *Past and Present*, 124 (1989).

Vaughan, Megan, *Curing their Ills: Colonial Power and African Illness* (Cambridge: Polity, 1991).

CHAPTER 3

···

AFRICAN SLAVE TRADES IN GLOBAL PERSPECTIVE

···

PIER M. LARSON

SLAVE trading has been practised extensively in human history and implicated in nearly all territories of the globe. African captives took their place in world history together with Scandinavian thralls, Caucasian harem women in the Middle East, the sacrificial victims of the Aztecs, and the debt bondswomen of South Asia and Indonesia. Africa was one of multiple geographical sources of captives for the Mediterranean in antiquity and the Indian Ocean over the last two thousand years. Africa participated with other parts of the world in the global history of slaving, yet the continent came to play a disproportionate role in the story of human captivity from about AD 1000 following urbanization and economic growth in the Middle East and a corresponding intensification of the trans-Sahara and Indian Ocean slave trades. Between 1500 and 1850, captives poured into the Americas only from Africa and often in annual numbers greater than those of Africa's other trades. The external slave trades of Africa were complemented by and linked to slave trades contained within the continent itself. African slaving was multicentric and consisted of a variety of patterns of forced human migration which originated within the continent and often surpassed its boundaries. Beginning modestly, the African slave trades progressively intensified over two millennia.

Two features of Africa's slave trades account for the continent's disproportionate modern reputation in the history of global slaving. First, the enslavement of Africans commenced early, ended late, and played a key role in global modernity. Africa supplied captives in increasing numbers from the eleventh to the nineteenth century. The trans-Atlantic slave trade ground to a halt only after 1860, nearly a century after the onset of the Industrial Revolution. Slave trades into the Mediterranean and Indian Ocean ended over the following half-century, during the high noon of European colonialism. Slavery within Africa was legally abolished mostly during the course of the twentieth century, and so too were its internal slave trades. Mauritania proclaimed the expiration of captivity as late as 1981; Niger in 2003. Some anthropologists argue that slavery continues surreptitiously in parts of Africa and that labouring captives, especially children, continue to be traded from place to place. An important feature of the continent's past, slaving preserves many resonances in modern Africa.

A second unique characteristic of Africa's slave trades was the geographical diversity of its captive flows. The sub-Saharan regions from which most (not all) African captives hailed sent slaves spinning out in virtually every direction in which there were populations to employ them: to the continent's east, to its north, and to its west. Within the various regions of Africa, slave masters employed captives acquired from elsewhere in the continent, making the internal slave trades much more voluminous than typically assumed. Before the twentieth century, African slaves could be found in numerous places around the globe. This presence offered concrete evidence of Africa's long participation in the very global circuits that world histories often excluded it from. Africa's slave trades were a tragedy for some and a windfall for others. They were also a significant dimension of the continent's global economic and cultural connections.

The unique features of African slavery—massive numbers captured right into the modern era and a supply of bonded labour from sub-Saharan Africa to all regions of the world—have generated an image of the continent as the quintessential source of captives in world history. There is much truth to this popular perception if one reaches no further back than the fifteenth or perhaps even the eleventh century. Because of its multifaceted importance to African history, slave trading has become a subject of abundant research and vigorous debate. Slaving is a historical theme particularly useful for scholars of Africa to think with, from labour historians to anthropologists of religion, proponents of cultural studies, political scientists analysing modern elections, scholars of African development and underdevelopment, and of course to economic historians and scholars of Africa's diasporas. This chapter introduces some of the key issues, evidence, and arguments concerning Africa's slave trades debated by scholars over recent decades. It focuses on slaving as an economic enterprise and the implications of connected commerce in people and goods for thinking critically about Africa's place in world history.

Some historians of Africa and of Africa's diasporas deem scholarship on slaving tiresome, a fad now having run its course. Much, however, remains to be learnt about Africa's slave trades and the patterns of violence, commerce, movement, and cultural connection associated with them. Many young scholars are taking up slaving as their chosen field of research. The mobility and violence of slave trading presages the importance of these same themes in the history of twentieth- and twenty-first-century Africa. It can be argued that African history is a narrative of mobility and circulations, and the conditions surrounding them. For this reason, scholarship on the massive migrations that were slaving is likely to remain a significant subfield within the disciplines of African studies and African diaspora studies for some time to come.

FOUR TRADES: THE ESTIMATES

Establishing the significance of Africa's role in the history of global slaving through quantitative measures is essential to any assessment of the importance of slaving in the continent and the dimensions of Africa's global connections. Didactic pronouncements that quantification of Africa's slave trades obscures personal experiences of enslavement or other dimensions of African history judged more deserving of study are frequently heard but are nonsensical and harmful to intellectual inquiry (as such moralizing statements typically are). Numbers and experience are linked, yet they are not the same thing. As related dimensions of slaving, both merit research and neither invalidates the other. In practical terms, it is impossible to assess the importance of slaving and the significance of experience without basic estimates pertaining to magnitude and pattern. Quantification also invites historians to new fields of inquiry and complicates simplistic notions of experience. For example, whose experiences should historians prioritize: those of captives, of kith and kin left behind, of merchants, of bankers, of insurers, of ship crews, of the citizens of slaving ports, of others affected by or involved in slaving, or of all the preceding? Slaving is about far more than captives' experiences of enslavement, though these are, of course, essential.[1]

Africa can be considered to have supplied captives into four major slave trades, each designated by the geographical area in which it operated: the Indian Ocean, the Mediterranean (or trans-Sahara), the Atlantic, and within sub-Saharan Africa itself. In reality each of Africa's slave trades was far more segmented and complex than suggested by heuristic models of four regions. The trans-Sahara trade, for example, included flows of captives from Senegambia to Morocco, from the central Sudan (Nigeria, Niger, Chad) to Libya and Egypt, a riverine trade along the Nile, and still other segments that crisscrossed the desert diagonally. For the Indian Ocean, captives departed Egypt, Sudan, and Ethiopia for the Arabian Peninsula, from Zanzibar for the Mascarene Islands, from Kilwa for the Persian Gulf, and from Mozambique for the Mascarene Islands and the Atlantic. In the Atlantic trade, captives hailed from different regions along Africa's west coast and arrived at multiple destinations in the Americas, with Brazil and the Caribbean consuming most. Some West African slaves were disembarked at the Cape of Good Hope and in the Mascarene Islands of the western Indian Ocean. The trans-Atlantic slave trade also drew captives from southeast Africa and islands in the Indian Ocean, complicating the notion of slave trades as contained within single oceans. Within sub-Saharan Africa, captives were moved about in an extensive variety of directions. Those that did not depart the continent, probably the majority, were set to a diversity of employments near the coasts and in the interior.

The magnitude of each of Africa's four slave trades is not known with precision. Each is the object of estimation. The internal slave trade of Africa was the oldest and likely the greatest in magnitude. Many African slavers did not write and in any case it was in their interests to keep their business practices secret. Most slaving activities produced few or no documents and none of the trades has left systematic records. Two of the trades, however, generated more documents than the others. In the trans-Sahara system, merchants sometimes produced correspondence in Arabic regarding their commercial enterprises. These records, which begin as early as the seventeenth century but are richest for the nineteenth, supply evidence of how slaving firms in the Sahara functioned. The existence and usefulness of these Saharan documents, some of which are gathered in libraries and in personal collections about the desert, is only now beginning to be recognized. Yet Saharan papers have so far played little role in producing quantitative estimates of the volume of the trans-Sahara slave trade.[2]

Evidence for the volume of trans-Atlantic slaving from Africa is the richest and most complete. The core of this evidence consists of manifests from European and American ships engaged in the slave trade and other tax-related documents produced for administrators of the ports from which those ships departed or put in to trade in Europe and the Americas. Additional records, such as newspaper registers of ship movements and censuses of slaves, have also been put to use. A group of scholars working with documents such as these recently consolidated their data into a single Transatlantic Slave Trade Database (TSTD). The TSTD was originally issued in the form of a compact disc. Now augmented by much new data, it contains information on nearly 35,000 Atlantic slaving voyages and has been made publicly available at www.slavevoyages.org. David Eltis and David Richardson, two leaders in this project, have estimated the TSTD now contains more than 77 per cent of all trans-Atlantic slaving voyages ever undertaken.[3]

The slavevoyages.org data for the Atlantic has proven extremely useful for scholars working on dimensions of the trans-Atlantic slave trade and on slavery about the Atlantic rim more broadly. It has led to a rapid expansion of knowledge about demography, mortality, African agency, gender, ethnicity, culture, and many other issues. Estimates derived from TSTD have been usefully presented in a series of maps in an *Atlas of the Transatlantic Slave Trade*.[4] Since not all slaving voyages are represented in the TSTD, certain assumptions must be made about the completeness of the data to estimate the total volume, distribution of national carriers, departure points in Africa, and arrival ports in the Americas for the trade as a whole. Scholars who go to the slavevoyages.org website most often employ the derived *estimates* rather than the raw *data*. Few, however, understand the assumptions and methods by which the estimates were generated. The estimation methods, which have not been through formal peer review or publication, are complex, and appear arbitrary in some respects.[5] New research on segments of the trans-Atlantic slave trade suggests deficits in the estimating procedure, which depends upon what is already known rather than what remains to be discovered.[6] Estimates posted at slavevoyages.org will likely be revised slightly upwards over time.

Estimates of the Mediterranean, Indian Ocean, and internal African slave trades are far more rudimentary than those for the Atlantic and entail a much greater margin of error. Indian Ocean and trans-Sahara estimates are not derived from shipping documents or from the records of slaving enterprises. They are for the most part established on contemporary observations by individuals, mostly Europeans, of the annual volumes of those slave trades. This is a rudimentary and error-prone method, but the best one yet available. The most frequently cited trade estimates for both the Mediterranean and the Indian Ocean were compiled by Ralph Austen. While certain scholars of the Sahara take a cautious approach to Austen's figures (no one has actually challenged them in print), the Indian Ocean estimates have been the object of a number of suggested revisions. Abdul Sheriff views the estimates before 1750 as too large but would increase the nineteenth-century numbers. Other scholars of East Africa's slave trades claim that Austen's estimates are too low for particular segments of the Indian Ocean commerce. Together, scholarly interventions suggest that Austen's estimates of the Indian Ocean trade will eventually be revised upwards, especially for the eighteenth and nineteenth centuries.[7]

Commencing from the fifteenth century when all trades operated simultaneously, the published estimates for Africa's external trades are compiled in the first three data columns of Table 3.1. Several observations flow from these figures. Over the last five centuries of Africa's external trades, the volume of trans-Atlantic commerce only exceeded the estimated trans-Saharan and Indian Ocean trades in three centuries: the seventeenth, eighteenth, and nineteenth. During the seventeenth century, the trans-Atlantic slave trade was approximately double that of the trans-Sahara and Indian Ocean trades combined; during the eighteenth century it was thrice the volume. In the nineteenth century, however, the trans-Atlantic slave trade only marginally exceeded the combined trans-Sahara and Indian Ocean trades. The trans-Atlantic slave trade surpassed Africa's other external trades during the last three centuries of its operation, but only in the seventeenth and eighteenth centuries was it clearly dominant as a mover of captive Africans.

Estimates in Table 3.1 also suggest that the trans-Sahara slave trade increased steadily in volume between 1401 and 1900. By contrast, the Indian Ocean slave trade remained relatively flat up to the eighteenth century, when it experienced growth due to increased demand in the Arabian Peninsula, Persian Gulf, and Mascarene Islands. The trans-Sahara slave trade consistently exceeded the Indian Ocean trade in volume during the five centuries represented in Table 3.1. This excess, however, was marginal during the eighteenth and nineteenth centuries, when the trans-Sahara and Indian Ocean trades are estimated to have been similar in volume.

Table 3.1 The Four Slave Trades of Sub–Saharan Africa, 1401–1900 (thousands, discrepancies in totals due to rounding)

Century	Atlantic	Sahara	Indian O.	Internal	Total
1401–1500	81	430	200	711	1,422
1501–1600	278	550	200	1,028	2,055
1601–1700	1,876	710	200	2,786	5,571
1701–1800	6,495	715	600	7,810	15,619
1801–1900	3,874	1,205	1,110	6,189	12,377
Total	12,602	3,610	2,310	18,522	37,045

Sources: Atlantic from 1501 (slavevoyages.org); Sahara (Larson, 2007: 134); Indian Ocean (Larson, 2009: 41).

The estimated combined size of Africa's external slave trades during the last five centuries of the commerce is 18.5 million, of which 12.6 million persons, or just over 68 per cent of the total, crossed the Atlantic. The Atlantic dominated external trades in three centuries, but the overall size of Africa's other external slave trades was also considerable, at nearly 6 million persons between 1401 and 1900, half the size of the trans-Atlantic slave trade in the same era. The changing volume of Africa's three external slave trades over the centuries is represented graphically in Figure 3.1.

If we take a much longer view of Africa's external slave trades by beginning in about AD 650 rather than 1401, the combined volume of the trans-Sahara and Indian Ocean slave trades is equal in magnitude to that of the Atlantic slave trade. Africa's oldest external trades operated over a far longer period and at lower annual volumes than did the trans-Atlantic slave trade. This difference was tied to faster rates of economic growth in the Americas versus the Mediterranean and the Indian Ocean between 1500 and 1900.[8]

Why Africa was a net labour provider to the globe over two millennia has not received adequate attention. Slave traders in all of the external trades justified their operations by mobilizing racial theories alleging the inferiority of dark-skinned persons.[9] Scholars know race to have no basis in biology—it is an influential social argument—and they struggle for alternative explanations. It is clear that the existence of Africans both capable of and willing to capture other Africans was crucial to the emergence of the continent as a supplier of slaves. Tropical disease environments in Africa also played a role, conveying immunities to certain African captives, making them desirable labourers who did not sicken and die with comparative ease. A labour theory of value explanation offered by some researchers suggests that workers in Africa were relatively unproductive. Transferring Africans to parts of the globe where their labour could

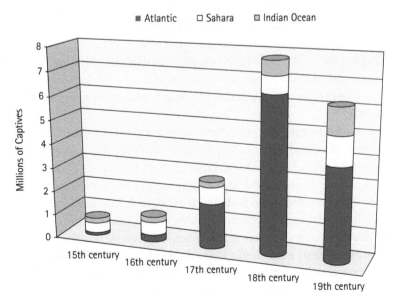

FIGURE 3.1 The external slave trades of sub-Saharan Africa.

be more fecund, even if involuntary, could account for why persons departed that continent over a long interval. Yet other scholars suggest that, in the case of the trans-Atlantic trade, the decision to enslave Africans was not fundamentally an economic one (there were cheaper alternatives, such as enslaving Europeans), but a cultural and intellectual one in that Europeans after the Middle Ages were reluctant to enslave other Europeans but had no objection to capturing Africans.

Racism plays a role in the first and last of these hypotheses. But there are problems with raising any of them to a universal explanation. In the case of the last proposal, the theory works only when considering *European* enslavement of Africans. Yet Africans were enslaved in the southern and eastern Mediterranean, in the Indian Ocean, and throughout Africa by non-Europeans. As for the other theories, some persons outside Africa were also resistant to tropical diseases, and many African captives were not set to productive labour, especially in the Mediterranean and Indian Ocean. Why Africa rather than other continents became a long-term supplier of labour to the world from the fifteenth century begs further inquiry. Answers will not be singular and may require working with complex, interactive models and taking multiple cultural and economic influences into consideration.

An additional lesson emerging from Table 3.1 is that the story of African slaving did not begin and end with the continent's *external* trades. Sub-Saharan Africa's many slave trades were linked to one another. Internal movements of captives within the continent morphed into external trades when captives crossed into the seas or the Sahara Desert. Multiple scholars studying different segments of Africa's external slave trades have demonstrated that not all persons captured within sub-Saharan Africa departed from it. Production of captives for multiple markets was especially characteristic of societies in the African interior at places of intersection between slaving markets. These intersections are an important reason why the continent's slaving history should be set in a global rather than an oceanic framework. Take, for example, the Segu Bambara state of the Middle Niger River of interior West Africa (c.1712–1861). 'The Segu state, unlike its coastal counterparts', writes Richard Roberts, 'managed to avoid dependence on one primary market. Slaves captured by Segu warriors were sent to the Atlantic, the desert, and interior markets. Some were retained locally.'[10]

Persons enslaved in sub-Saharan Africa, as in Segu, were typically 'funnelled' into different slave trades, and half or even more of all those ever enslaved remained at different locations south of the Sahara. Writing about the central Sudan between 1780 and 1850, Paul Lovejoy and David Richardson found that 'a majority, perhaps a large majority, of newly enslaved individuals and their slave descendants stayed within West Africa.'[11] Scholars working on different periods and places in Africa converge on the conclusion that more captives remained in sub-Saharan Africa than departed it and that persons captured in a single place could end up in different parts of the world.[12] Expressing these conclusions in numbers, the column in Table 3.1 labelled 'Internal' provides a very rough estimate of sub-Saharan Africa's internal slave trades between 1401 and 1900 as the sum of its external trades. This estimate is conservative, for it accepts that the internal African trades were equal in volume to the continent's external trades, whereas many researchers claim they were larger.

There are several implications to these order-of-magnitude estimates for the aggregate volume of Africa's four slave trades. If more than 18 million captives departed into Africa's external slave trades between 1401 and 1900, another 18 million or more were enslaved within Africa itself. If the assumption that internal and external trades were roughly equivalent is correct across centuries of slaving activity, then the total volume of Africa's four slave trades would have exceeded 37 million since 1401 and nearly 50 million since their inception some two millennia ago. The total Atlantic share of 12.6 million since 1401 would therefore represent one-third of Africa's slave trades. If all the slave trades *since their inception* are considered, the Atlantic portion falls to one quarter. The comprehensive estimates in Table 3.1 demonstrate that the production, employment, and export of captives in sub-Saharan African history has been a massive undertaking. No other continent produced this number of captives for export and internal employment over such a sustained period nor subjected such a large proportion of its inhabitants to servitude.[13]

Africa, Slaving, and the Oceans

Slaving has typically been considered an activity conducted in oceanic spaces and across the Sahara Desert (often also conceptualized as an ocean). The columns in Table 3.1 are testament to the geographical units that continue to structure research about Africa's commerce, and increasingly, too, about early African history. Of these geographical spaces, the Atlantic has received most attention. Atlantic history, like other oceanic histories, opens up creative avenues of inquiry but at the same time marginalizes Africa as a periphery, a fringe, an origin. The centres of Atlantic history have tended to be on its western side. Oceanic foci make it difficult to synthesize histories of African slaving and fully to assess the role and effects of slaving on the continent, for they divide Africa among them. A more productive and holistic approach for both African and world history would be to recentre histories of slaving on the African continent. A geographical model with Africa at the centre and its captives flowing about both within the continent and in nearly every direction from it places Africa at the centre of its own migratory-economic-social phenomena and offers fresh perspectives on the place of the continent in world history.

Inferences about slaving in Africa based on commerce solely in the trans-Atlantic or any other external sector lead to partial and erroneous conclusions. For example, recent claims from analyses of captives' names that a majority of slaves in certain trans-Atlantic segments were captured relatively close to African coasts, not in the far interior, might lead to an impression that slave trading was mostly a coastal rather than an interior phenomenon. Because the patterns of slaving in Africa resulted from the operation of four slave trades rather than one, however, most African captives were conveyed to and from the continent's interior, not its coasts.

Arrayed along the southern shore of the desert, Sahelian states tended to have hefty populations of captives, as did the Mande-speaking areas, especially those of the middle Niger River. The Senegal River valley, the Futa Jalon highlands, the Asante kingdom, and the Niger River bend were additional regions of concentration. During the nineteenth century, the Sokoto Caliphate boasted a population of some 2 million captives. The Nile River south of the Sahara was another region of interior slave absorption, as was highland Ethiopia. Certain parts of Africa's great lakes supported heavy concentrations of slaves (Buganda, Bunyoro, Busoga, and Buhaya), as did both sides of Lake Tanganyika and the Lualaba River of the Congo forest. The Nyamwezi highland interior of what is now Tanzania (Tabora region) was a major East African centre of captivity, as were both banks of the inland Rufiji River and the regions around Lake Malawi and the inland Zambezi River. The Angolan highlands and points east in southern Central Africa constituted another such region. These interior slave systems, like those at the coast, were fed by Africa's many internal slave trades and are typically invisible in externally oriented histories.

Taking a global and interactive view of sub-Saharan Africa's slave trades is also necessary because of the ways in which persons and commodities in those trades circulated across and through the various oceanic regions of slaving. West African gold was carried north to the Mediterranean together with captives. Much of that gold ended up in Egypt, North Africa's largest economy, from where it travelled on to India and China. Some of it reached southern and Atlantic Europe. Captives who crossed the Sahara Desert often found themselves in parts of the Indian Ocean, such as the Persian Gulf and the Red Sea. American silver was among the bundle of goods exchanged for captives in the Indian Ocean. Slaves from Kilwa, Mozambique, and parts of Madagascar were disembarked in Virginia, Barbados, Rio de la Plata, Haiti, Brazil, and Cuba. South Asian textiles were nearly everywhere key to the Atlantic slave trade. New England cottons purchased slaves and ivory in East Africa during the middle decades of the nineteenth century. Cowrie shells from the Maldive Islands fanned across parts of West Africa, travelling by sea and land in counter-direction to the flow of captives. Books from the Middle East, paper from Europe, and salt from the Sahara were enjoyed in the households of West Africa, arriving across the desert. Captives and ships' crews (not altogether different categories), together with cargoes, often crossed from one ocean to another.

Putting Africa at the centre of the global history of its own slaving systems emphasizes the porous nature of ocean boundaries and allows scholars to set the periphery of every one of these oceanic slave-trading systems—the African interior—into better focus. This is not to say that oceanic history is intrinsically more problematic than continental history. The history of oceans will continue to produce important insights about Africa in interactive regional connection. Histories of the Mediterranean, the Indian Ocean, and the Atlantic were designed to challenge area studies models based on continents but in that function have generated new area studies bounded by land rather than by water. There is nothing intrinsically superior to either oceanic or continental histories. The fact is, historians of Africa and its slave trades must think in nimble terms, embracing area studies that are both continental and oceanic. Recentring analysis to Africa in global histories of slaving, however, allows scholars better to assess the continent's simultaneous participation in multiple commercial systems and to remedy the way in which slaving in the African interior is marginalized by all of them.

SLAVING DEMOGRAPHY

Demography is an essential consideration when assessing linkages among Africa's four slave trades. The trans-Atlantic slave trade carried more males than females (64 versus 36 per cent). A significant minority of the males were boys, not men. This meant that fewer than half of the Africans involuntarily crossing the Atlantic were men (49 per cent). The slim majority of trans-Atlantic captives were therefore women and children. African slaves transited the Atlantic in groups that more resembled families than did free trans-Atlantic migrants, who were overwhelmingly male and mostly men. The demography of trans-Atlantic slaving varied considerably over time and by its various segments, but its overall demographic pattern was distinct among Africa's slave trades in the near-universal preponderance of males among captives.[14]

The domestic slave trade that fed the trans-Atlantic system tended to concentrate female captives in locations near Africa's west coast. Both contemporary accounts and censuses from the eighteenth century suggest larger than normal proportions of girls and women in urban and rural settlements in those coastal areas involved in the trans-Atlantic slave trade. The influx of women towards the littoral represented an internal counterpart to the masculinized external slave trade and allowed seaside populations to maintain themselves and even grow despite the overall drain on sub-Saharan Africa's population. Fertility rates among women near the coasts appear to have remained normal or high even though (or rather because) littoral populations presented abnormal sex and age profiles due to the trade. The specific supplying regions from which most captives hailed experienced the greatest levels of depopulation.

Africa's forced migrations into the Sahara and Indian Ocean also resembled families in that they were composed of varying assortments of boys, girls, women, and men— but in which, with some notable exceptions, females rather than males tended to prevail. Captives crossing the Sahara and departing the Horn of Africa were usually heavily female in composition, whereas the European and indigenous trades of the East African coast south of the Horn, considered together, carried away roughly equal numbers of males and females. Many of these were children.[15] European vessels in the Indian Ocean trade typically carried more males than females. Demographic differences among Africa's various slave trades can be explained by regional African patterns of supply as well as by the exigencies of external demand, making interactive approaches essential to understanding the global demography of African slaving in its various sectors.

Females, for example, constituted the majority of captives in the Indian Ocean trades to the Arabian Peninsula and Persian Gulf, at least to the early nineteenth century. From the mid-nineteenth century, however, the proportion of males carried as slaves towards

Arabia and the Persian Gulf began to increase in parity with females.[16] Flows of East African captives to South Asia throughout the trade and to the Arabian side of the Gulf during the last quarter of the nineteenth century were heavily weighted towards males. Three ships captured by British patrols off the Arab coast of the Gulf between 1872 and 1884 carried human cargoes that were on average 76 per cent male. On two of these vessels for which we have further demographic breakdowns, there were eighty-five men, ninety-two boys, twenty-six women, and twenty-four girls. Not only did males form the majority of captives in this late nineteenth-century segment of the East African trade to the Gulf, children did too.[17]

In the slave trades internal to sub-Saharan Africa a strong preference developed for female captives, though at certain times and places males must have predominated, particularly in areas heavily involved in exporting captives across the Sahara and into the Red Sea or where warfare and capture of opponents played a substantial role in producing slaves. The demography of slaving in the multiple threads of Africa's four trades is best studied segment-by-segment and period-by-period rather than in aggregate by ocean, but only in the trans-Atlantic sector was there consistently a preponderance of males departing the African coast over the entire period of slaving. In other regions, females were in the majority or there was a parity in the gender dimensions of the trades, with minimal exceptions to these rules. The demographic patterns in each of the sectors of African slaving were connected to those of other sectors by patterns of enslavement and markets for captives within Africa. The African interior is where future research should yield important results.

Origins and Destinations

The origins and destinations of African captives have become a staple of the burgeoning field of African diaspora studies. Unfortunately, the study of origins and destinations for Africa's *internal* slave trades has yet to be seriously examined and should become a research priority. Most captives crossing the Sahara Desert were destined for the largest economies of the southern Mediterranean: Egypt, Libya, and Morocco. From North Africa some sub-Saharan captives were conveyed onwards to other Mediterranean and even some Indian Ocean destinations. Cities of the highly urbanized Ottoman Empire from the early sixteenth century were attractive markets for slaves who crossed the Sahara. Not all captives in the Mediterranean and Indian Ocean became urban dwellers, however. Some were discharged at oases in the desert and others were concentrated on small and medium-sized commercial estates at both the northern and southern edges of the desert and also at various locations about the Arabian Peninsula and beyond. Researchers have recently shown that some slaves in the Mediterranean and in parts of the Arabian Peninsula and Persia played a greater role in productive enterprises such as date farming, pearl diving, and opium and cotton production—the resulting commodities of which were headed for world markets—than has previously been recognized. But the majority of captives arriving in North Africa and the Middle East over the centuries were probably absorbed as household servants, elite administrators, and slave soldiers. Service rather than production was the most frequent employment.

The earliest sources of African captives for the Indian Ocean lay in north-east Africa, especially in Sudan and Ethiopia. From about AD 800 slaves were also departing from the East African coast south of the Horn. A 'trickle' of East African captives in the early centuries of the first millennium AD became a 'torrent' by the ninth century, when there is evidence of dense concentrations of East Africans on agricultural estates in southern Mesopotamia. Many of these East African *Zanj* slaves, as they were called, joined in a large-scale revolt against the Abbasid Caliphate in the ninth century, severely weakening Baghdad and its empire. Exports of slaves from East Africa south of the Horn may have slowed for a time after the ninth century, but *Zanj* was a known category of captives about the Indian Ocean as far afield as China. From the sixteenth century, there was an active flow of captives not only from East Africa into the Indian Ocean, but also from Madagascar via the East African Coast. In the second half of the eighteenth century, the volume of the slave trade from Ethiopia and East Africa picked up significantly over previous levels. These involuntary travellers departed primarily from the Horn and points southwards, with Massawa, Lamu, Zanzibar, Kilwa, Mozambique Island, Quelimane, Majunga, and Maintirano (the last two in western Madagascar) as primary ports of embarkation.

Destinations for African captives heading into the Indian Ocean were multiple and changed significantly over time. Shipping in this region demonstrates the deficiency of ocean-bounded histories. Merchants transporting slaves in the Indian Ocean were both indigenous to that region (Africans, Arabs, Indians, Persians) and hailed from further afield in the Mediterranean, Atlantic, and Pacific (Armenians, Jews, Greeks, Romans, Egyptians, Europeans, Chinese). After 1500, shippers from the north-east Atlantic such as the Portuguese, Dutch, English, Danish, and French, joined the Indian Ocean slaving sector. Americans rose to brief prominence during the Napoleonic Wars. Most African captives in this system were absorbed in the western portions of the Indian Ocean, around the rim of the Arabian Sea including the Red Sea, Persian Gulf, western India and the islands of Madagascar, the Comoros, the Seychelles, and the Mascarenes. Some Indian Ocean captives disembarked in the Americas, from New England in the north to Rio de la Plata in the south.

The Arabian Peninsula and lands bordering the Persian Gulf consumed most East African captives entering the Arabian Sea. The ports of Muscat and Sur in Oman played an intermediary role by receiving large numbers of captives from Africa who were 'seasoned' and acquired speaking knowledge of Arabic at places such as the Batinah coast of Oman before transfer to other portions of the Gulf. The French colonial Mascarene Islands, inland Mesopotamia, and portions of South Asia (Gujarat, Bombay, the Deccan, and even Sri Lanka) became significant consumers of African captives in certain defined periods, sending the products of enslaved and free labour into the Atlantic and Mediterranean as well as the Indian Ocean. Only a minority of African slaves reached such distant eastern locations as China and parts of South-East

Asia. In these latter regions, the chief sources of captives were societies of the eastern Indian Ocean itself, especially the Indonesian archipelago. One historian has claimed that 'Black Africans probably formed a minority of slaves traded' in the Indian Ocean.[18] The claim is not accompanied by numbers nor is it supported by historians of slaving in the most densely populated eastern portions of the Indian Ocean. No evidence or estimates currently suggest that any maritime trade in slaves about the Indian Ocean equalled that in captive Africans: some 4 million departing East Africa and its offshore islands between 650 and 1900.

The vast majority of captives departing Africa into the trans-Atlantic slave trade, about 95 per cent, arrived in various parts of Brazil and the Caribbean. Less than 4 per cent landed directly in North America. Captives in the Americas entered a variety of employments, but most were set to productive, profit-seeking enterprises in agriculture and mining, the resulting commodities of which found Atlantic markets, including in Africa. Some slave-produced American staples such as precious metals, cotton, tobacco, sugar, rum, and other spirits travelled as far as Mediterranean and Indian Ocean markets, even China. Household and urban slaves performing the same variety of service functions as those in the Ottoman Empire existed in the Americas but were a minority of slaves there.

When it comes to the departure regions from sub-Saharan Africa for the American slave trade, estimates derived from the TSTD typically divide the African coast into eight segments. These may be simplified to three broad regions of departure: West Africa (the Senegal River to Cameroon), West Central Africa (Loango to Benguela), and the Indian Ocean (Cape Town to Zanzibar, plus the western Indian Ocean Islands). Table 3.2 supplies trans-Atlantic departure estimates for these three broad regions by hundred-year periods. The Atlantic-bound trade from the Indian Ocean comprised less than 5 per cent of that former trade, but directly connected persons and commodities across two oceans. West Central Africa supplied the majority of captives to the Americas in the seventeenth and nineteenth centuries; West Africa did the same during the sixteenth and eighteenth centuries.

When viewed in light of the state of scholarship on Africa and the trans-Atlantic slave trade, the relative prominence of West Central Africa as a region of supply is remarkable. The overwhelming majority of scholarship on the African side of the trade focuses

Table 3.2 Departures for the Americas and Europe from the Coasts of Africa (thousands, discrepancies in totals due to rounding)

Century	West Africa	West Central Africa	Indian Ocean	Total
1501–1600	160	118	0	278
1601–1700	709	1,135	32	1,876
1701–1800	4,058	2,365	71	6,495
1801–1866	1,357	2,077	440	3,874
Total	6,284	5,695	543	12,521
%	50.2	45.5	4.3	

Source: slavevoyages.org estimates.

on West Africa and its coast stretching more than 4,000 kilometres from the Senegal River to Cameroon. Yet nearly as many captives as departed from West Africa embarked for the Americas from only 1,000 kilometres of West Central African coastline. For the comparatively short West Central African littoral through which a disproportionate contingent of captives departed into the Atlantic there is only a modest amount of scholarship on the slave trade.[19]

Two explanations likely account for this unfortunate discrepancy. West Central Africa is today primarily French- and Portuguese-speaking, whereas research on the trans-Atlantic slave trade has been dominated by Anglophone scholars. And Angola, whose coastline covers much of the region, was for some three decades following independence in 1975 torn apart by war and largely off limits to foreign scholars. It is estimated that 1.5 million persons were killed and 4 million displaced during the thirty-year Angolan war—nearly as many persons as ever departed the same region into the trans-Atlantic slave trade over four centuries. With the war at an end, the role of West Central Africa in the trans-Atlantic slave trade is garnering new attention, especially from Portuguese- and Spanish-speaking scholars.[20]

EXPORT COMMODITIES, BOTH HUMAN AND MATERIAL

None of Africa's slave trades operated in commercial isolation. Researchers have often quarantined slave trading as a separate domain of commercial activity so as to avoid treating humans as commodities, as slavers did, and because slaving is so contrary to modern sensibilities. Although certain traders specialized in the movement of captives rather than material commodities, slaves were exchanged between sub-Saharan Africa and other parts of the world, and within sub-Saharan Africa itself, as one component in a spectrum of merchandise. Taking commerce in human beings as a separate theme in world history makes sense (this chapter has done so to this point), but segregation of people and things in African trade risks making Africa too much of an exception in world history rather than part of the commercial norm.

In the trans-Sahara commerce, gold exports from the various mines of the West African forest predominated in value over slaves until some time in the early sixteenth century. Much of the gold crossing the Sahara ended up in Egypt, where the bulk of it departed on ships for the trade of India, linking the forest mines of West Africa to the textile manufactures and spice plantations of South Asia. Human and commodity flows challenge the concept of ocean-contained trades. In the course of the sixteenth century, new European maritime demand at the Atlantic coast diverted up to three-quarters of West Africa's gold exports away from the desert trade and the value of slaves crossing the Sahara came to predominate there, especially as the trans-Sahara slave trade expanded over time. By the nineteenth century, a host of export goods crossing the desert northwards may have displaced both slaves and gold in aggregate value. Scholars disagree on the matter. Some argue that slaves remained the pre-eminent export of sub-Saharan Africa into the desert throughout the nineteenth century; others claim they did not. The export commodities which vied with gold and slaves in the trans-Sahara trade included goat skins, spices, ivory, gum arabic, and ostrich feathers.[21]

The Indian Ocean trade in slaves from Africa's east coast between Delagoa Bay and Suez—a littoral of more than 7,500 kilometres—was likewise part of a multifaceted commerce in a variety of commodities. Ivory departed from most of the extensive East African coast. Lumber in the form of mangrove poles employed in home construction formed a staple export from the central east coast into the Arabian Peninsula, while gold issued into the Indian Ocean from both Nubia and the Zimbabwe highlands. Together with the larger-ticket commodities of gold, ivory, and lumber, a variety of natural products animated the export trades of the region: ambergris, animal skins, rhinoceros horn, turtle shells, food grains, aloe, sesame, gum copal, incense, coconuts, copra, and cloves. These commodities were not all consumed in the Indian Ocean; some entered the Mediterranean and Atlantic.

Slaves may never have surpassed ivory, gold, and other natural products as the export of primary value departing East Africa. In certain times and places, slave exports were clearly dominant, such as in Ethiopia's flow of captives to the Deccan of south-west India between the fifteenth and seventeenth centuries or those of the central East African coast during the ninth century and the early decades of the nineteenth when Mozambique was an important supplier to both the Mascarene Islands and Brazil. Among African exports to the Indian Ocean, Nubian and Zimbabwean gold declined precipitously by 1700 while ivory rose steadily in price and volume. The main markets for East African ivory were India and China, especially the former, where it was exchanged for cloth. Some of this ivory crossed into Atlantic Europe on Portuguese, Dutch, French, British, and American ships. The ever-increasing price of ivory turned the terms of trade decisively in favour of East Africa. Ivory became the main driver of export commerce, not slaves.

In the trans-Atlantic trade, gold dominated by value until about 1700. The Gold Coast exported gold before slaves (hence the name), but in most of Africa the commerce in slaves and in other commodities commenced simultaneously. Both slaves and gold entered the commercial mix at the beginning of Atlantic trading, then, and early on European merchants acquired slaves from the Angolan coast and Benin and discharged them at places like Elmina on the Gold Coast in exchange for gold. In a similar fashion, kola nuts from Sierra Leone even bought slaves in Senegambia for a time. A vigorous coasting trade carried on by African and Eurafrican merchants brought captives and commodities to bulking points on the West African littoral and fed the trans-Atlantic trade of European vessels.

The value of slaves departing West Africa came to exceed that of gold only in the century and a half between about 1700 and the 1840s, with some local exceptions. Along with slaves and gold, a variety of natural products in lesser values were also loaded aboard ships departing West African coasts between the fifteenth and nineteenth centuries. These included ivory, malaguetta pepper, gum arabic, hides, beeswax, lumber, copper, peanuts, and palm oil (the latter two only in the nineteenth century). As in East Africa, the terms of trade moved strongly in favour of West Africans up to the late nineteenth century, accelerating the quantity of European, American, and Asian goods flowing into the continent and enriching certain African entrepreneurs and ruling classes while promoting economic growth and development at points along the coast and in the African interior.

TEXTILES AND SLAVING

A uniting feature of all three of Africa's external slave trades was the status of foreign textiles as import commodities employed to purchase captives. When slave trading is considered only in individual oceans, the role of fabric in *African* commerce does not receive the attention it deserves. In all of Africa's slave trades, including the internal trade, slaves were exchanged for clothing. In the trans-Sahara trade, caravans wending southwards conveyed quantities of Mediterranean-region fabrics, particularly those in colours and patterns not available in West Africa. Some of these textiles were of European manufacture, others hailed from North Africa and the eastern Mediterranean. Textiles formed a significant part of the bundle of goods (including salt, cowries, horses, weapons, glassware, books, and beads) exchanged for captives in and south of the Sahara. The relative share of textiles by value in the southwards trans-Sahara trade is disputed. Some authors find that textiles arriving south of the desert were of secondary value to salt. Others suggest textiles were the primary caravan commodity departing North Africa for points southwards. One explanation for the disagreement lies in the fact that there were different sectors to the trans-Sahara trade, with patterns differing from east to west. Another is that a portion of southbound Mediterranean textiles was exchanged for salt in the Sahara, which was then employed in the savanna to purchase captives. Textiles may have been the commodity of greatest value departing North Africa, but of secondary value among those entering West Africa's Sahel. West African cottons in the white and blue colours typical of the region joined gold, slaves, and other commodities in the northwards crossing to the Mediterranean. Fabrics, then, traversed the Sahara Desert in both directions: in exchange for slaves but also accompanying them—and sometimes carried by them—on their northbound journeys.

In the Indian Ocean trade, South Asian cottons entered East Africa from at least the first century BC. A variety of Indian fabrics have been identified in the archaeological digs at southern Egypt's ancient Red Sea port of Berenike, whose export commodities from the port's origin in Hellenistic times likely included slaves. In the Ethiopian highlands the importation of South Asian textiles in exchange for captives is recorded from at least the fifteenth century AD. Richard Eaton reports that 'African demand for Indian textiles...appears to have been the principal engine behind Ethiopia's slave-extraction process'.[22] Most of the Asian cottons consumed in Ethiopia and in the rest of East Africa (as well as in Atlantic Africa) originated in the manufacturing centres of northwest and southern India. Kutch and Gujarat were important points of production, but the Bombay region, the Coromandel Coast, and even Bengal also supplied cottons to

East Africa. After the Middle East, East Africa represented South Asia's second export market for textiles.

South Asian fabric formed the foremost East African import by value to the nineteenth century, but during the mid-nineteenth century the cotton mills of Massachusetts in the United States supplied fabrics spun from slave-grown and processed American cotton to New England vessels trading at Zanzibar. Very popular in the East African trade, Massachusetts cottons were known as *merikani* and for a brief period between about 1840 and the American Civil War oversold South Asian fabrics in the Zanzibar-based trade. Britain also exported domestically manufactured cloth to East Africa during the nineteenth century, much of it containing American cotton. Textiles were so long dominant as foreign imports to East Africa that for a time during the eighteenth and nineteenth centuries they also functioned as currencies. Foreign fabrics offered consumers a stylistic marker of financial means and international connections. The spread of foreign cottons among consumers in East Africa appears to have been quite broad, moving beyond the mercantile and political elites most often implicated in foreign trade. 'Cloth', concludes Jeremy Prestholdt, 'was at the center of East Africa's global exchanges'.[23] That cloth originated in the far-flung manufacturing centres of disparate oceans.

In the trans-Atlantic slave trade, patterns of textile imports varied dramatically from one part of the west coast of Africa to another. The Gold Coast and the Bight of Biafra represent opposite extremes. The former region displayed a huge appetite for cloth, the latter almost entirely passed up on textile imports. Overall, however, data about imports arriving along Africa's Atlantic coast confirm 'the overwhelming position of textiles as the leading import category'.[24] Creoles in the Cape Verde islands also entered the textile business, producing cotton on slave-worked plantations and fetching weavers from the African mainland to produce cottons with Senegambian, European, and freshly innovated designs that were highly prized by elites along the Upper Guinea Coast. European slavers on that coast also moved West African textiles from one part of the region to another, carrying some of them on to the Americas and to Europe. The coasting trade in African textiles played a significant role in positioning and bulking slaves to board European vessels.

South Asian textiles typically constituted between a third and a half of the value of fabric brought to West Africa on British vessels. West Africans, like their counterparts elsewhere on the continent, were exceedingly choosy as to the design, texture, and even the smell of the textiles they purchased. 'For trading in this river', lectured a Portuguese merchant of the Nunez River along the Upper Guinea Coast during the mid-seventeenth century, 'it is necessary to have cloth and more cloth, and the better the cloth the better the trade'.[25] Africans consumed textiles that matched their sense of taste and style, demanding products manufactured from Massachusetts to Manchester, Marseille, and Calcutta. As in East Africa, certain textile imports came to serve as local currencies. In some places, imports impaired production of West African textiles through price competition. In nearly all regions of sub-Saharan Africa, and in each of Africa's external trades, captives were exchanged for very significant quantities of foreign textiles.

SLAVING AND AFRICA IN WORLD HISTORY

In a recent survey of British Atlantic history, Trevor Bernard cautioned that the 'networks, transatlantic connections, cosmopolitan attitudes, and flux and mobility' that have characterized historical writing on transoceanic studies in recent years 'can be as destructive as they are creative'.[26] In truth, such forces have typically been interpreted as creative in places like the Americas and destructive in Africa. Much of this discrepancy is due to the place of human captives in the external commerce of Africa and the way that historians have chosen to hive off the history of 'the slave trade' as a domain of investigation separate from that of domestic economic and political history or commerce in material goods. Symbolized by Walter Rodney's *How Europe Underdeveloped Africa* (1972), debate about the impact of the slave trades on Africa has tended to focus on the West African coast and to shy away from emphasizing economic growth and development, where they occurred. Within this circumscribed framework, Africa's place in *global* history has been substituted for ocean-oriented perspectives, primarily Atlantic ones, in which Africa lies at the periphery rather than the centre. At the same time, scholars working on quantification of the slave trades or in ways that avoid didactic narratives about the evils of enslavement or the horrific experiences of captives have typically been viewed with suspicion by those whose primary interest is continents.

The impact of Africa's external commerce, most of all, must not be overstated. Sub-Saharan Africa's foreign trade represented a small portion of the total economic output of the continent. It has been estimated that in the eighteenth and nineteenth centuries, the Atlantic trade annually comprised less than 1 per cent of sub-Saharan African economic activity. Figures of similar magnitude characterize the Sahara and the Indian Ocean trades. Slaving in turn represented but a portion of Africa's foreign trade, albeit at times a leading one. The domestic economies of Africa were far more important in a quantitative sense than were Africa's foreign trades, including slaving. 'Africa was becoming less significant to the world economy', Ralph Austen cautions, 'at the same time as it involved itself more closely in international commercial relationships'.[27]

Two avenues of investigation bear promise for the future in these circumstances. The first is for scholars to think broadly about Africa and the world by working in more than one oceanic region and setting the continent at the centre of analysis and the oceans at its periphery—the approach embraced by this chapter. The second is to pay greater attention to the internal economies of Africa, including its internal slave trades. Consider the following: until about 1700, the value of gold among Africa's exports was greater than that of its slaves. The gold exported annually into the Atlantic in this era could easily have fit into a single ship, whereas the *lesser* valued slave trade required thousands of vessels to ferry captives across the water. Value, linkages, and impact are entirely different things. The capture of slaves through war, raids, kidnapping, and other means and their movement from one place to another may not have garnered much foreign trade valuation, but the domestic transformations they wrought were typically tremendous. We need to pay more attention to these internal transformations and their links to the present.

The effects of slaving, moreover, were unevenly distributed about the continent. Large portions of sparsely populated southern Africa did not participate in slave trading. Within those areas of the continent that did, slaving frontiers tended to pass swiftly from one area to the next. Regions where slavery was marginal to the economy, as in the kingdom of Burundi, could be close to places where enslavement was more central to social structures, as in Buganda. The effects of slaving activity are best assessed on the local level. Aggregate assessments typically break down because Africa was integrated in differing ways into various trading systems and economies. What shines clear from histories of slaving is that the continent's engagement with the world has been of long duration and has had varying implications on the home front. A string of recent studies about particular parts of the West African coast during the slave trade has shown the degree to which economic growth, and sometimes development, accompanied external trade. These were in turn premised, at least in part, on enslavement, depopulation, and destruction elsewhere. Both processes tended to promote social stratification—and both require further research attention.[28]

If we do step back to ponder slaving as a whole, we can begin to appreciate how this dimension of Africa's past has influenced its economic, political, and cultural present. In the first instance, the number of individuals affected either first-hand as captives or secondarily as survivors, refugees, and beneficiaries of slaving was extraordinarily large. The participation of many parts of the continent in slaving, from the coasts to the far interior of the Sahel and East-Central Africa, was an impetus for political, economic, cultural, and labour transformations. It was also a precursor to the ubiquitous migrations of the twentieth century and the many disruptions by war that have characterized the postcolonial period. Slaving in Africa was both tragedy and fortune. In an ironic twist, the history of slaving controverts lingering notions of the African continent prior to colonization as little subject to historical dynamics, at once traditional, resistant to change, and limited by the weight of custom and tribe—or as merely a victim of transoceanic economies.

NOTES

1. Pier M. Larson, 'Horrid Journeying: Narratives of Enslavement and the Global African Diaspora', *Journal of World History*, 19/4 (2008).

2. Ghislaine Lydon, *On Trans-Saharan Trails: Islamic Law, Trade Networks, and Cross-Cultural Exchange in Nineteenth-Century Western Africa* (Cambridge: CUP, 2009); Bruce Hall, *A History of Race in Muslim West Africa, 1600–1960* (Cambridge: CUP, 2011).

3. David Eltis and David Richardson, 'A New Assessment of the Transatlantic Slave Trade', in David Eltis and David Richardson, eds, *Extending the Frontiers: Essays on the New Transatlantic Slave Trade Database* (New Haven, Conn.: Yale University Press, 2008), 43.

4. David Eltis and David Richardson, *Atlas of the Transatlantic Slave Trade* (New Haven, Conn.: Yale University Press, 2010).

5. David Eltis and Paul Lachance, 'Estimates of the Size and Direction of Transatlantic Slave Trade' (2010), http://slavevoyages.org/downloads/2010estimates-method.pdf.

6. Toby Green, *The Rise of the Trans-Atlantic Slave Trade in Western Africa, 1300–1589* (Cambridge: CUP, 2012).

7. Ralph Austen, 'The 19th Century Islamic Slave Trade from East Africa (Swahili and Red Sea Coasts): A Tentative Census', *Slavery and Abolition*, 9/3 (1988); Ralph Austen, 'The Mediterranean Islamic Slave Trade out of Africa: A Tentative Census', *Slavery and Abolition*, 13/1 (1992); Abdul Sheriff, 'Slave Trade and Slave Routes of the East African Coast', in Benigna Zimba, Edward Alpers, and Allen Isaacman, eds, *Slave Routes and Oral Tradition in Southeastern Africa* (Maputo: Filsom Entertainment, 2005).

8. Pier M. Larson, 'African Diasporas and the Atlantic', in Jorge Cañizares-Esguerra and Eric Seeman, eds, *The Atlantic in Global History, 1500–2000* (Upper Saddle River, NJ: Pearson Prentice Hall, 2007), table 1, 134.

9. Bruce Hall, *History of Race*; Jonathon Glassman, *War of Words, War of Stones: Racial Thought and Violence in Colonial Zanzibar* (Bloomington, Ind.: Indiana University Press, 2011).

10. Richard Roberts, *Warriors, Merchants and Slaves: The State and the Economy in the Middle Niger Valley, 1700–1914* (Stanford, Calif.: Stanford University Press, 1987), 18.

11. Paul Lovejoy and David Richardson, 'Competing Markets for Male and Female Slaves: Prices in the Interior of West Africa, 1780–1850', *International Journal of African Historical Studies*, 28 (1995), 284.

12. These conclusions are collated in Pier M. Larson, *History and Memory in the Age of Enslavement: Becoming Merina in Highland Madagascar, 1770–1822* (Portsmouth, NH: Heinemann, 2000), 343 n. 44.

13. The population of sub-Saharan Africa has been estimated at 50 million in 1600 and 70 million in 1800: Patrick Manning, *Slavery and African Life: Occidental, Oriental, and African Slave Trades* (Cambridge: CUP, 1990), 170–1.

14. David Eltis and Stanley Engerman, 'Was the Slave Trade Dominated by Men?', *Journal of Interdisciplinary History*, 23/2 (1992), esp. table 1, 241.

15. Manning, *Slavery and African Life*, 22, 36, 49, 52, 73.

16. Abdul Sheriff, 'Localisation and Social Composition of the East African Slave Trade, 1858–1873', in William Gervase Clarence-Smith, ed., *The Economics of the Indian Ocean Slave Trade in the Nineteenth Century* (London: Frank Cass, 1989), 138–42.

17. Pedro Machado, 'A Forgotten Corner of the Indian Ocean: Gujarati Merchants, Portuguese India and the Mozambique Slave-Trade, c.1730–1830', *Slavery and Abolition*, 24/2 (2003), 26; Matthew Hopper, 'Globalization and the Economics of African Slavery in Arabia in the Age of Empire', *Journal of African Development*, 12/1 (2010).

18. Gwyn Campbell, 'Slave Trades and the Indian Ocean World', in John Hawley, ed., *India in Africa and Africa in India: Indian Ocean Cosmopolitans* (Bloomington, Ind.: Indiana University Press, 2008), 21.

19. Two of the most notable contributions are Joseph Miller, *Way of Death: Merchant Capitalism and the Angolan Slave Trade, 1730–1830* (Madison, Wis.: University of Wisconsin Press, 1988) and John Thornton, *Africa and Africans in the Making of the Atlantic World, 1400–1800* (Cambridge: CUP, 2nd edn, 1998).

20. Mariana Candido, 'Slave Trade and New Identities in Benguela, c.1700–1860', *Portuguese Studies Review*, 19/1–2 (2011); Roquinaldo Ferreira, *Cross-Cultural Exchange in the Atlantic World: Angola and Brazil during the Era of the Slave Trade* (Cambridge: CUP, 2012).

21. Ralph Austen, *African Economic History: Internal Development and External Dependency* (London: James Currey, 1987), 34; Ralph Austen and Dennis Cordell, 'Trade, Transportation, and Expanding Economic Networks: Saharan Caravan Commerce

in the Era of European Expansion, 1500–1900', in Alusine Jalloh and Toyin Falola, eds, *Black Business and Economic Power* (Rochester, NY: University of Rochester Press, 2002); Sebastian Prange, '"Trust in God, But Tie your Camel First": The Economic Organization of the Trans-Saharan Slave Trade between the Fourteenth and Nineteenth Centuries', *Journal of Global History*, 1/2 (2006), 221; Ralph Austen, *Trans-Saharan Africa in World History* (New York: OUP, 2010), 27.

22. Richard Eaton, 'The Rise and Fall of Military Slavery in the Deccan, 1450–1650', in Indrani Chatterjee and Richard Eaton, eds, *Slavery and South Asian History* (Bloomington, Ind.: Indiana University Press, 2006), 119.

23. Jeremy Prestholdt, *Domesticating the World: African Consumerism and the Genealogies of Globalization* (Berkeley, Calif.: University of California Press, 2008), 72.

24. David Eltis and Lawrence Jennings, 'Trade between Western Africa and the Atlantic World in the Pre-Colonial Era', *American Historical Review*, 93/4 (1988), 948.

25. George Brooks, *Eurafricans in Western Africa: Commerce, Social Status, Gender, and Religious Observance from the Sixteenth to the Eighteenth Century* (Athens, O.: Ohio University Press, 2003), 115.

26. Trevor Bernard, 'The British Atlantic', in Jack Greene and Philip Morgan, eds, *Atlantic History: A Critical Appraisal* (New York: OUP, 2009), 128.

27. Austen, *African Economic History*, 42, 102; Eltis and Jennings, 'Trade', 955–6.

28. Brooks, *Eurafricans in Western Africa*; Robin Law, *Ouidah: The Social History of a West African Slaving 'Port', 1727–1892* (Oxford: James Currey, 2004); Kristin Mann, *Slavery and the Birth of an African City: Lagos, 1760–1900* (Bloomington, Ind.: Indiana University Press, 2007); Green, *Rise of the Trans-Atlantic Slave Trade*.

Bibliography

Alpers, Edward, *East Africa and the Indian Ocean* (Princeton: Princeton University Press, 2009).

Austen, Ralph, *Trans-Saharan Africa in World History* (New York: Oxford University Press, 2010).

Eltis, David, *The Rise of African Slavery in the Americas* (Cambridge: Cambridge University Press, 2000).

Harms, Robert, and Bernard Freamon, *Slavery and the Slave Trades in the Indian Ocean and Arab Worlds: Global Connections and Disconnections* (New Haven, Conn.: Yale University Press, forthcoming).

Hunwick, John, and Eve Troutt Powell, eds, *The African Diaspora in the Mediterranean Lands of Islam* (Princeton: Princeton University Press, 2002).

Klein, Herbert, *The Atlantic Slave Trade* (Cambridge: Cambridge University Press, 2nd edn, 2010).

Larson, Pier M., *Ocean of Letters: Language and Creolization in an Indian Ocean Diaspora* (Cambridge: Cambridge University Press, 2009).

Lovejoy, Paul, *Transformations in Slavery: A History of Slavery in Africa* (Cambridge: Cambridge University Press, 3rd edn, 2011).

Miller, Joseph, *Way of Death: Merchant Capitalism and the Angolan Slave Trade, 1730–1830* (Madison, Wis.: University of Wisconsin Press, 1988).

Morgan, Philip, 'Africa and the Atlantic, c.1450 to c.1820', in Jack Greene and Philip Morgan, eds, *Atlantic History: A Critical Appraisal* (New York, 2009).

CHAPTER 4

....

STATES AND STATELESSNESS

....

WALTER HAWTHORNE

Based on the nature of their social and political structures, African societies are often divided into two categories: state-based and stateless. Scholars are not in agreement about exactly what distinguishes one category from the other. If they agree about anything, it is that categorization can clarify, but it also obfuscates. There are several reasons for this. First, in Africa, as elsewhere, there is no pure form of a state-based or stateless society. Second, states share much in common with stateless societies. Through both state and stateless social and political structures, Africans have done what peoples everywhere do: organize production, regulate exchange, determine how resources are distributed, resolve disputes, and protect and punish members. Third, African societies have never been fixed and unchanging. As they have transformed to meet local needs, stateless societies have sometimes assumed the form of states and states have sometimes assumed the form of stateless societies. Finally, over time and space, African states have been comprised of a great variety of strikingly different institutions. The same can be said of African stateless societies. Indeed, the creativity of Africans has given rise to an enormous range of approaches to social and political organization.

A survey of scholarly work concerned with the engagement of African states and stateless societies with long-distance trade, with warfare, and with colonization reveals an established and ongoing concern with how local processes and understandings have mediated broader regional and global processes. Africanist historians have demonstrated that events set in motion by European expansion have never constituted the history of Africa. Africans have always shaped their own histories and the nature of the communities in which they lived by working through unique social and political organizations and by adapting them to changing conditions.

DEFINITIONS

....

What generally distinguishes state-based and stateless societies? Looking back to the period before modern African nations emerged in the second half of the twentieth century, state-based societies had entrenched social and political hierarchies and stateless societies did not. States were centralized and stratified organizations that regulated social and economic relations. The number of strata or social classes varied from state to state but at minimum included rulers and ruled. In other words, class distinctions were apparent in state-based societies, members accepting or being forced to concede to elites' claims to a disproportionate share of society's resources. In states, the ruled had tributary obligations to their rulers, remitting to them part of the surpluses from what they produced under terms that were legitimized through a shared ideology of reciprocity. Rulers were expected to protect their followers from harm and to ensure economic and social stability. They were to abide by the accepted 'social contracts' that defined relationships among 'citizens' or members of what can be seen as broad 'moral communities'. In other words, rulers were obliged to act within the parameters of what defined acceptable behaviour and not to exercise power whimsically. Rulers acting illegitimately had to resort to violence to maintain power, lest they be toppled by opposition. Those who ruled did so full time, not often carrying out productive functions. In complex states, the functions of those in government were often highly specialized, multiple office holders performing particular duties.[1]

As the term 'stateless' implies, such societies are often seen as the opposite of states. Stateless societies are also called 'acephalous' (literally 'headless'), 'decentralized', 'non-states', and 'nonmonarchies'. Like 'stateless', these words are oppositional: they define societies based upon what they are not. In stateless societies, political units were often small. In agricultural societies the village or a confederation of villages was the largest political entity; in cattle-keeping or hunter-gather societies it was the clan. Though a range of positions of authority existed within villages, clans, and confederations, no one person or group could be identified as ruler and positions of power were not hereditary, passed from one generation to the next. Often, decisions affecting the whole were thrashed out in face-to-face meetings involving many people—representatives from multiple households or lineages who sat on councils. Across Africa, those representatives were most often people of an advanced age (as opposed to youths), so many stateless societies are also dubbed 'gerontocracies'. They are, too, called 'segmentary societies' because the elders who headed lineage segments represented their familial groups. Lacking social classes, stateless societies were highly egalitarian. That is, wealth was shared much more equally in them than in states and most had strict sanctions against any one person or group accumulating considerably more than others. Individuals or groups with excess riches were seen as immoral; they threatened to transform a society of equals into a society that was hierarchical. At times, particularly influential people emerged—'big men', known for their skills in farming, hunting, combat, or negotiating with spirits. However, no ascriptive authority positions existed. Consensus was most often king. Whereas state-based systems concentrated power narrowly in a single ruler or small group of power brokers, in decentralized systems power was more diffuse. Stateless systems relied on unofficial *leaders*, but they lacked *rulers*.[2]

Scholarship on the history of states and empires in Africa shows that such political structures have long existed across Africa. In modern times, however, most stateless societies have been clustered in particular areas. In West Africa, many stateless societies (including the Igbo, Ibibio, Ijo, and Tiv) are located in a quadrilateral in present-day Nigeria bounded by the Jos Plateau, Forcados Estuary, Cameroon Mountain, and Mambila Plateau. Further to the west, a variety of stateless groups (including the Dagara, Tallensi, Dogon, and Birifor) are situated north of the headwaters of the Volta River and south of the Niger. In the forests of western Côte d'Ivoire, eastern Guinea, and Liberia is another pocket (including the Bete, Kissi, Kru, and Gagu). Stateless societies are also found along the coast of Guinea-Bissau and southern Senegal (the Balanta, Bijago, Diola, and others). In eastern and southern Africa, numerous cattle-keeping societies have stateless orientations (such as the Nuer, Maasai, Luo, Lango, Turkana, and Tonga). Hunter-gatherer groups, such as the Mbuti of the Central Africa's equatorial forests, also have no state structures.[3]

Despite these important concentrations of stateless peoples, Africa's states have long attracted more sustained historical research. In the 1960s, when African history emerged in its own right as an academic field of study in Western universities, scholars went in search of a 'usable past'—proof that Africans had the capacity to rule themselves and that they did not need the paternalistic and exploitative oversight of colonial powers. For this reason, much early scholarship focused on expansive imperial systems, such as the West African trading empires of Ghana, Mali, and Songhay or Great Zimbabwe. As Michael Crowder wrote, historians set out to demonstrate that 'Africa had long been accustomed to centralised states, many of them covering much larger areas than the colonies the Europeans carved out'.[4] If political agendas have shaped historical research, so too have practical considerations. In short, state-based societies offer a denser body of oral and written sources for historical research than do stateless societies. European traders, explorers, and missionaries were attracted to areas dominated by African states. They tended to engage with them and leave written accounts of them to a much greater extent than they did with stateless societies. Moreover, the elites who controlled African states often employed specialists who were trained in the art of remembering historical narratives. Such traditions often lent legitimacy to social inequalities and have been passed down in great detail over time. Stateless societies, in contrast, have more fragmented oral traditions since they have little need to legitimate difference and do not often possess specialists whose role it is to recount histories. This is not to say that the history of stateless societies cannot be written. In recent decades, historians are increasingly turning to the challenge of doing so, by carefully mining written sources, employing linguistic, archaeological, and genetic analysis, and collecting fragmented oral narratives.

HISTORIOGRAPHY AND EARLY STATES

In a chapter published in 1971, Robin Horton made an important statement about the difference between African states and stateless societies. Horton historicized stateless societies, showing how they changed over time by becoming more stratified and complex and morphing into states. In so doing, he provided a forceful critique of a racialized, ethnocentric theory about the origins of states in Africa which had had considerable influence in the first half of the twentieth century. That idea was known as the Hamitic Hypothesis, which purported that black societies in sub-Saharan Africa had never created 'complex' (i.e. state) political organizations. Rather, early African states were seen to have been the product of the influence of non-black outsiders.[5]

Though the hypothesis was contested by the 1970s, the question of how states had formed in early Africa was not yet well articulated. European and Asian models of early state formation were not appropriate in the African context. An African model was needed, and Horton provided one. Focusing on black stateless farming peoples, he argued that they held 'germs from which state organisation and ideology could sprout'. Although lacking in empirical detail, Horton's essay suggested that, under the right conditions, individuals in stateless farming communities could form 'royal lineages' and develop 'ideas of sovereignty—that is, of a defined territory within which all comers are automatically subject to a defined body of law'.[6]

Though most historians agree today that processes internal to Africa were important for early state formation, other aspects of Horton's chapter have been challenged. Particularly influential has been the work of Jan Vansina, who in a watershed publication in 1990 used linguistic analyses to show how some stateless societies became states after developeing high-yielding agricultural practices in equatorial Africa before AD 500. Rather than focusing on early state control of land (Horton's 'defined territory'), Vansina argued that control over people was most important for early and later African states. In stateless areas, successful 'houses' headed by 'big men' sold agricultural surpluses and accumulated wealth. They directed that wealth towards acquiring the ability to conquer and absorb neighbours. With the advent of rules of inheritance, big men's houses became fixed over time at the top of new hierarchical political structures. In these states, kinship continued to be the idiom that described the relationship among group insiders and between king and subject.[7]

Others have revised Horton's thesis by acknowledging the influence of factors external to Africa for early state formation, but doing so in a way that has sought distance from the lingering ghosts of the Hamitic Hypothesis. This is particularly true of scholars who see the impact of external trade as crucial for economic and political stratification. Recent scholarship has argued that foreign influences that came through trade contacts were 'Africanized', elites using wealth from trade to accumulate followers according to local political idioms and creating, as a result, states that had a distinctive African flavour. The emphasis on the 'Africanness' of the Swahili on the East African coast is an important example. As early as the eighth century, a merchant elite emerged as middlemen in the export trade of gold, coral, and ivory from Swahili communities to distant points in the Indian Ocean. Trade connections fostered religious and cultural transformations, Islam becoming the dominant religion in what by the fourteenth century were emerging city-states. Scholars agree that Swahili communities which embraced Islam became part of a larger, literate Indian Ocean community, yet remained essentially African societies.[8]

STATES AND STATELESS SOCIETIES IN THE EARLY MODERN PERIOD

Scholarship on early modern Africa has also been concerned with the effects of foreign influence, especially trade, on states and stateless societies. The consensus is that such influences were 'Africanized' in a variety of ways. Considerable attention has been paid to the impact of the Atlantic slave trade. Philip Curtin laid the foundations for an important debate by arguing in 1975 that the export trade in slaves from Senegambia was not as significant as the export trade in non-slave items. In his estimation, Senegambian states produced slaves for political rather than for economic reasons, meaning that for established ruling elites the advent of the Atlantic slave trade did not usher in a significant break with the past.[9] Though there are some differences in his analysis, John Thornton has buttressed parts of Curtin's thesis, arguing that the slave trade was not 'as critical to the African economy' as some scholars believed and that 'African manufacturing was more than capable of handling competition from preindustrial Europe'. Thornton also stressed the 'agency' of African elites in the period, writing that 'African participation in the slave trade was voluntary and under the control of African decision makers'.[10] An opposing camp comprised of Walter Rodney, Joseph Inikori, Boubacar Barry, and others subscribe to 'underdevelopment' or 'world-system' theories. They have seen the slave trade as inhibiting African political development, sapping the continent of resources, weakening economies, and relegating African elites to subordinate roles in the emergent world trading system. In their conceptualization, the slave trade caused great upheaval on the continent, weakening what had been strong states in earlier periods. The leaders of these states were forced by a dominant Europe to trade people for cheap manufactures.[11]

Another more recent group of scholars has taken a different tack, exploring the internal dynamics of African states and arguing that the production of captives was expensive and dangerous. It required the organization of large numbers of people, each performing specialized tasks. Through these hierarchical structures, wars were waged, the product of which was prisoners. States found ways to hold and feed prisoners and to ship them over long distances. Because slave production necessarily involved violence, the states that were organized around slaving have been dubbed 'predatory' or 'warrior'.

In a rebuke of Curtin's arguments about the impact of the slave trade on Africa, a leading proponent of the 'predatory state thesis', Martin Klein, argued that the slave trade became 'the way the state reproduced itself'.[12] In Klein's view, predatory states became increasingly stratified, typically with 'kings' at their heads, wealthy merchant classes, bureaucracies buttressing elite power, and corps of professional soldiers. African merchants, whose actions were regulated by kings, obtained from Atlantic merchants the items necessary for warfare: firearms, iron weapons, and horses. They also accumulated luxuries such as cloth, beads, and alcohol, which became symbols of wealth and were distributed as largess to warriors and other followers. As in earlier states, such predatory elites used trade items to amass followings of people, meaning that African models of statecraft were quite different from European and Asian ones. Most scholars have argued that predatory states were weak, because when largess did not flow the bonds between elites and their followers frayed and caused states to collapse. Predatory states had the capacity to make war but little ability to transform social realities or to consolidate large areas under lasting political control.[13]

Examples of the workings of such states abound. In the early sixteenth century in West Central Africa, Kongo's kings increased their power by raiding for slaves in the hinterland, trading some to Atlantic merchants and retaining others to increase retinues of followers. To the south in Angola in the same century, the Mbundu kingdom launched attacks on its frontiers, bringing great wealth to the court and offering protection and largess to those within the state. And in the seventeenth century, in what Joseph Miller describes as the Angolan *conquista*, states sought slaves by sending armies against outsiders. In this region, Miller writes, 'increasing stratification manifested itself principally in the spread of enslavement'. Similarly, beginning in the middle of the seventeenth century in the area of present-day Nigeria, elites in the Oyo state fortified their capital and commanded armies to wage war against and enslave neighbours. Elites traded slaves with merchants at coastal ports for cowries, textiles, and weapons. After the Muslim Fulbe established control over the Senegambian region of Futa Jallon in the mid-eighteenth century, they launched jihads against neighbouring pagan countries, capturing people and trading them for weapons and luxuries. Boubacar Barry explains that, once the Fulbe state was consolidated, elites 'made slave trading their exclusive business'. Directly addressing Curtin's thesis, Barry argues that the slave trade caused 'a profound political and social crisis'.[14]

More recent research, however, suggests that the slave trade did not weigh heavily over the whole of Africa. For example, Emily Osborn argues that some states, such as that of Baté in the Milo River Valley in present-day Guinea, did not actively trade slaves and did not become militarized. In the seventeenth and early eighteenth centuries, Baté's elites pursued what Osborn calls 'pacifist strategies' of developing webs of household and kinship connections in order to build and maintain their power. They did so, she argues, for reasons internal to Africa and not because of external stimuli brought about from trade with Atlantic merchants. Baté prospered in a way that may not have been unique in states that have been largely ignored by scholars obsessed with Africa's connections across the ocean.[15]

Another group of scholars has challenged the notion that slave production and state formation went hand in hand. They have done so by examining the strategies of stateless societies. To be sure, some stateless societies disappeared as a result of predation by states seeking captives for exports. Others were incorporated into states as people sought the protection of warrior elites. But my own research into the coastal region of Guinea-Bissau, as well as that by Andrew Hubbell, Robert Baum, and others, has shown that stateless societies often successfully defended themselves from attacks from states, while sometimes themselves participating in slave raiding and trading. Defensive strategies took a number of forms. Some stateless peoples, such as the Samo of present-day Burkina

Faso, built effective defensive walls, while across the Upper Guinea coast people erected palisades known as *tabancas* around villages. Elsewhere, 'live fences' made of prickly bushes or trees kept out invaders. Stateless peoples also located themselves in inaccessible regions. Samo occupied mountainous areas, as did the Kabre of Togo and communities in the Dar al-Kuti region. Similarly, Tallensi, Dogon, Dagara, and Konkomba moved to massifs and outcroppings or to riverbanks. In addition, stateless societies developed a healthy distrust of outsiders. Floup, Balanta, and Bijago killed European and mixed-race traders until they discovered that they could ransom them, and Dagara and Lobi were known for shooting strangers who came into their territories.[16]

If many stateless societies found ways to protect themselves from state-based neighbours, revisionist scholarship has shown that stateless societies also produced slaves. They did so to garner weapons and implements needed for agriculture, animal husbandry, and hunting. For example, when threatened with attacks from the powerful state of Kaabu, the Balanta built fortified settlements near mangrove swamps in Upper Guinea's riverine coastal region. There they developed complex methods for farming rice by fashioning tools from iron obtained by trading slaves at coastal entrepôts. With iron, Balanta also fashioned weapons for both defensive and offensive purposes, notably for the production of tradable captives. Similarly, the neighbouring Diola raided distant communities, nabbing victims, and later ransoming them for cattle, which were an important symbol of wealth. And in the area of present-day southeastern Nigeria, captives flowed from Igbo villages in large volumes beginning in the mid-eighteenth century. There members of the Aro network raided for slaves but also traded for them, exchanging luxuries, salt, and fish for captives with politically decentralized communities.[17]

Recent scholarship focused on stateless societies in the early modern period has therefore revised Horton's positivist model of change by showing that many societies managed to engage in Atlantic commerce, yet the wealth they acquired did not lead to the formation of entrenched groups of elites. In other words, stateless societies that traded slaves did not necessarily morph into states. Those living under stateless conditions ensured the continuation of egalitarianism by strictly enforcing prohibitions against the accumulation of excessive wealth and power. In some places, secret societies were charged with this task, punishing those who appeared poised to elevate themselves over their neighbours. In others, institutional structures were directed at ferreting out suspected 'witches', who were people who attained wealth or fortune above and beyond what others had.[18]

THE NINETEENTH CENTURY

In the course of the first half of the nineteenth century, the Atlantic slave trade was gradually brought to a halt. During the same period, a growing trade in non-slave items forced states and stateless societies to restructure economies, Islam spread in West

Africa, and militarized states rose and expanded in many places. As with scholarship on earlier periods, research into these phenomena has focused on the degree to which external influences (particularly trade and religious ideas) reshaped African states and stateless societies.

The export slave trade reached new heights from some parts of Africa in the first decades of the nineteenth century. Trading was particularly heavy on the coast of West Central Africa south of the equator and from ports of East Africa. In West Africa north of the equator, the slave trade declined after British abolition in 1807. Over the next few decades, African states that had been engaged with the foreign trade in slaves were forced to reorient themselves towards the export of non-slave or 'legitimate' goods, which were increasingly in demand in an industrializing Europe and within Africa itself. Among the most important were kola nuts, palm oil, groundnuts, and wax. Historians have debated the impact of this reorientation on African states, some arguing that states suffered a 'crisis of adaptation' and others that established elites generally adjusted to the transition from the slave trade. This is particularly true of scholarship on the Niger Delta, where there has not been consensus about elites' ability to adapt to shifting patterns of national trade.[19]

Scholars have examined political adaptation (or the lack thereof) elsewhere as well. The Akan kingdom of Asante is one example of a state that made the transition from the trade in slaves to the trade in legitimate goods. Under a centralizing government in the eighteenth century, Asante expanded north and south from its forest heartland in the forest zone of present-day Ghana. Wars and tribute brought captives, who were sold south to coastal merchants or incorporated into the domestic economy. In the early nineteenth century, Asante continued its expansionist tendencies, mounting military campaigns against the neighbouring kingdoms and adding to its wealth in people. As the Atlantic demand for slaves dried up by the 1820s, Asante's elites used 'surplus slaves' internally, moving them to rural areas and directing them towards gold and kola production.[20] On the coast of East Africa in the nineteenth century, the Swahili elite also managed to maintain its hold over society as economies shifted. They too directed rising numbers of slaves to produce a range of 'legitimate' exports, the most important being cloves from the island of Zanzibar. Swahili elites also profited from their middleman position in the trade in ivory, carried from the interior by slave porters.[21]

A contrasting process unfolded in Senegambia, where a more pronounced 'crisis of adaptation' resulted in the establishment of a new elite. There, a class of warriors known as *tyeddo* had dominated the slave trade in the eighteenth and early nineteenth centuries. As the external demand for slaves decreased and was replaced by rising European demand for new foodstuffs, farmers turned to groundnut production. For Senegambians, producing and transporting groundnuts required relatively small capital investment and manpower. Hence, whereas entrance into the market for slaves had been difficult, commoners could enter the groundnut market easily. With money from their crops, they purchased firearms and confronted the region's *tyeddo* warriors, leading to a shift in power relations. Importantly, the embrace of Islam further served to unite commoners. New states headed by Muslims were created where *tyeddo* had once held sway.

As elsewhere, historians have debated whether or not such new states fundamentally transformed social realities, especially in light of the fact that wars producing captives continued throughout the first half of the nineteenth century.[22]

The centrality of Islam to state-building in the eighteenth and nineteenth centuries was also important in the savanna region of West Africa beyond Senegambia. Much scholarship has focused on how the widely dispersed pastoralist Fulbe (or Fulani) forged new states under the banner of Islam, from Futa Jalon in the mid-eighteenth century, to Futa Toro, and on to the great early nineteenth-century jihad which resulted in the formation of the Sokoto Caliphate in present-day northern Nigeria.[23] An initial wave of scholarship saw these jihads in Islamic or ideological terms. Later studies have examined them in terms of particular, local, socio-political contexts. As one scholar notes, Islam is now being treated less as revolutionary and more as 'something available to give further shape and direction to a consciousness already half formed in local conflicts'.[24] As with studies of earlier African states, studies of state formation under the auspices of Islam in later periods have moved from a focus on 'foreign' influences and towards a consideration of the ways that new ideas were shaped in particular African contexts.

Similar processes are apparent in the militarized states controlled by the Kololo, Lozi, Chikunda, Yao, and Nguni that emerged in southern and Central Africa in the nineteenth century. Scholars have depicted these relatively small and inherently unstable states in ways that resemble the warrior states of previous centuries. State power depended on the acquisition of people, some of whom were traded and some of whom were directed towards productive functions such as farming, the harvesting of ivory, and mining of copper. Of these states, the most studied has been that of the Zulu (a northern Nguni group), which launched a series of expansionist wars against neighbours in the early nineteenth century, influencing others to militarize and triggering a widespread cycle of violence and instability throughout the region that became known as the *mfecane*. Reacting against scholarship that saw Zulu militarization as the product of European influences and ingenuity, J. D. Omer-Cooper argued in 1966 that African leaders were responsible for innovations that led to a military, social, and political revolution. Subsequent research has revised Omer-Cooper's thesis by looking at the complex interaction of multiple factors that led to the militarization and the expansion of Nguni states, including escalating competition for grazing grounds caused by population pressure and decreasing rainfall.[25]

In contrast to the growing understanding of nineteenth-century state-building projects, the scholarship on stateless societies is less developed. In West Central Africa, some stateless societies became more hierarchical in response to threats from militarizing states. Others, such as the Ubangi, found organizing opposition to centralizing states to be impossible. Attacked by powerful neighbours, many Ubangi were enslaved, men being sold away and women incorporated into new states as slaves who could expand populations by bearing children and farming. In stateless areas of present-day southern Tanzania, small-scale, stateless societies suffered similarly during the Nguni expansion.[26]

What little research has been conducted on the effects of the rise of legitimate commerce on stateless peoples suggests that they responded without experiencing a pronounced 'crisis of adaptation'. Most appear to have adapted existing, egalitarian social institutions, elders directing youths to produce a shifting range of crops or to step up the production of existing crops. On the Upper Guinea coast, young workers in stateless societies produced large quantities of groundnuts in the nineteenth century, the proceeds from which were distributed widely rather than being concentrated in the hands of a few. Rice cultivation and trade also increased dramatically, as the Floup expanded production in the Casamance region and in northern Guinea-Bissau and the Balanta on the Mansoa and Geba Rivers.[27] Similarly, in south-east Nigeria, stateless Igbo communities eagerly embraced palm oil production. The 'overall tendency', according to David Northup, was for the Igbo 'to seek a balanced distribution of wealth and power...and to avoid centralizing political or economic power'.[28]

STATES AND STATELESS SOCIETIES IN THE ERA OF COLONIAL CONQUEST

By the last quarter of the nineteenth century, the increasing flow of legitimate commodities from Africa contributed to rising competition among rival European powers for control of what they hoped was a resource-rich continent. The ensuing Scramble for Africa was closely shaped by the continent's political landscape. In some places, colonial conquest proceeded by persuading or coercing African leaders to sign treaties and to accept dubious offers of 'protection'; in others, it was the result of military campaigns. In areas dominated by centralized states, the establishment of colonial control tended to be easier than in areas characterized by decentralized societies—despite the fact that many states had organized military hierarchies and stateless societies did not. When 'pacifying' hierarchically structured societies, Europeans found it possible either to co-opt political centres with a combination of threats and gifts or to bring massive military force to bear upon them. But when pacifying stateless areas, Europeans found no political centres to co-opt or attack. Recent scholarship has somewhat complicated this picture, arguing that the binaries of colonizer and colonized as well as domination and resistance should be rethought since they constrain 'the search for precise ways...power is deployed and...engaged, contested, deflected, and appropriated'.[29]

The British conquest of what would become Nigeria provides many contrasts with regard to both European strategies and African responses. The use of superior weaponry in the rapid defeat of the Yoruba state of Ijebu made clear to neighbouring Yoruba kingdoms that direct military opposition to British colonialism was futile. By the end of the 1890s, every important Yoruba ruler had signed treaties with the British. In 1897, a British expeditionary force launched an attack on the kingdom of Benin to the east, which also fell rapidly in the face of modern armaments. A similar scene played out in the emirates of the Sokoto Caliphate to the north. Throughout the region, British Maxim guns, rifles, and cannon won the day, and commanders found it relatively easy to 'cut the heads off' state-based societies.[30] In south-east Nigeria, however, Igbo society had no head. As Elizabeth Isichei notes, the conquest of Igbo territories 'involved peculiar tactical difficulties. Its small polities could be overthrown with relative ease, but their conquest did not necessarily have significant effects. A town was defeated and sacked. It signed a treaty... rebuilt its houses, and continued life as before. And there was still another score of similar towns to conquer, within a twenty-mile radius.'[31] From 1901 to 1917, various Igbo groups engaged in armed clashes with the British. Some of these conflicts involved individual villages resisting colonial interventions and some involved multiple villages taking up arms together.

Similar patterns are apparent in East Africa and Central Africa. When British troops entered the Buganda kingdom, the *kabaka* quickly signed a treaty. However, in decentralized Langi territories things played out quite differently. 'For some twenty years', John Tosh writes, 'the incoming colonial power was violently obstructed by countless clan combinations. It is not immediately obvious, perhaps, that uncoordinated and intermittent resistance of this kind posed serious problems for imperial rule.' Dealing with scattered and sporadic resistance in a stateless area was 'more taxing and more demoralizing' than a full-scale but quickly winnable battle against an army or large rebellious faction.[32] In Southern Rhodesia in the 1890s, a rebellion among the stateless Shona proved much more difficult to subdue than did a rebellion among the more centralized Ndebele. While the British negotiated a quick settlement with Ndebele chiefs, they were forced to resort to 'total war' with scattered and independent Shona settlements, advancing from community to community and destroying dwellings and crops. A similar pattern can be detected in the carving out of King Leopold's Congo Free State: although fierce fighting did occur against established kingdoms such as the Zande, Yaka, and Luba, these states succumbed to military conquest much more quickly than areas occupied by stateless societies such as the Mamvu and Lugbara.[33]

The Portuguese faced a similar problem in what became Guinea-Bissau. They fought few 'pacification' campaigns against the state-based Fula, entering, instead, into negotiations with rulers who signed treaties to avoid attack. However, in stateless areas closer to the coast there were no ruling families with whom to negotiate. Conquest through military action was difficult. Communities were hidden in swampy lowlands, their members were skilled in guerrilla warfare, and they had a long tradition of resisting state aggression. Colonial authorities, then, had to bring every village—one after another—into compliance with Portuguese law. In some places this was not accomplished until the 1930s.[34]

Generally, stateless communities responded to European colonial conquest in much the same way as they had responded to the threat from predatory indigenous states in earlier times. They moved their settlements to remote and more defensible locations, fled when armies arrived, and joined forces with neighbouring villages in order to fend off common enemies. In Maka regions of Cameroon, inaccessible forests hampered incoming German forces. Maka fighters could hide and strike at will before retreating into areas in which colonial troops could not easily manœuvre.[35] Similarly, in Balanta territories of Upper Guinea, Portuguese forces often hacked their way through dense brush to find villages abandoned when they arrived to 'pacify' them. Further, they noted in the early twentieth century how bands of young men from multiple communities came together on numerous occasions to attack their camps. It was much the same in decentralized Baule regions of Côte d'Ivoire, where French attacks on one village raised the ire of people in other villages, who rose up in common cause against imperial armies. As in Balanta regions, Baule marriages often involved women leaving the villages of their birth to settle with husbands in other villages. This created what Timothy Weiskel describes as webs of alliances that stretched through an entire stateless region.[36] In Nigeria, secret societies were used as institutions for drawing together young men from various Igbo villages into a united force that could combat British aggression.

COLONIAL RULE

European powers faced a variety of challenges in administering stateless and state-based regions in their various African territories. Although there were important national differences in the ideologies and practices of colonial rule, all administrations relied to various degrees on local 'chiefs' and other indigenous African intermediaries. In Portuguese Guinea, the established rulers of states were generally allowed to remain in place and were officially recognized as *régulos* or 'chiefs' if they did the bidding (collecting taxes and recruiting labour, especially) of colonial administrators. The British pursued a similar strategy under the policy of indirect rule. As for the French, their colonial system is generally seen as more 'direct' than that of the British, but it too relied increasingly on African chiefs.

Indirect rule was best elaborated in northern Nigeria, where its leading theorist Frederick Lugard encountered a sophisticated Hausa-Fulani government in the Sokoto Empire complete with a complex Islamic judiciary. Applying the policy elsewhere, the British and their indigenous intermediaries devised a variety of arrangements through which existing rulers were recognized as chiefs and allowed to exercise a range of powers. Among the Tiv, Igbo, and other decentralized societies in Nigeria, however, indirect rule could not work since there were no 'traditional' rulers through whom to exercise power. In the face of this problem, the British divided eastern Nigeria into provinces and divisions, each containing hundreds of communities which for governing convenience were grouped into 'native court areas'. Each of these areas was then assigned a chief, whom the British empowered through a 'warrant'. In effect, the British created rulers—the so-called warrant chiefs—where there had been none, enforcing a system of indirect rule through an imposed hierarchical system. Resistance ensued, most notably in the famous Aba Women's War of 1929. This, as well as the earlier Ekumeku movement and later Biafran War, can be seen, G. I. Jones argues, as 'episodes in a continuous struggle between the central government and the local [decentralized] people'.[37]

Contrasts can also be found in the effectiveness of British ruling strategies in state-based and stateless societies in East Africa. As noted above, the British found an existing hierarchically structured system in Buganda that suited, with some alterations, colonial needs. The Bugandan state remained intact and colonial policy was implemented by the *kabaka* and his existing functionaries. However, in Lango, the district that British demarcated to encompass decentralized Langi, colonial administrators created both chiefdoms and chiefs to preside over them. The division of Lango began in 1912; by 1920, there were thirty-seven chiefs ruling over groups of between 2,000 and 6,000 Langi. Responses to the imposition of hierarchy varied greatly: some Langi accepted chiefs who attempted to mediate the demands of the colonial regime; others resisted, moving to other areas outside of chiefly control.[38]

As for the French, their colonial administrative policies were less uniform than those of the British. As Catherine Coquery-Vidrovitch explains, despite their republican desire to suppress existing aristocrats, 'ruling families, already enjoying…authority due to their rank, were more ready to be of service than any other class'.[39] Patterns on the ground were often complex, even within the same regions: French administrators broke up Bur Salum in Senegal into new administrative districts, but in nearby Sine existing rulers were retained until 1963. In Futa Jalon, the office of the *almami* was not recognized, but many of the great ruling families were maintained. Whatever accommodations were made in state-based areas, the strategy of governing through select elite families could not be implemented where rulers had never existed. The French too created rulers for hitherto stateless peoples, handing out the equivalent of 'warrants' to men with no traditional claim to authority over wide-ranging territories. Among the Kissi of Guinea, administrators randomly grouped individual villages together into *cantons* and appointed chiefs to preside over them. In Maka regions of Cameroon, the French forced people to abandon small, politically independent villages and to move to larger ones near roads. Over each large village, colonial administrators appointed a *chef de village* and over them *chefs supérieurs*. Though chiefs tried to 'traditionalize' their new powers, their subjects never thought their rule was legitimate; rather, many chiefs were thought to be excessively cruel in their efforts to enforce the will of the French.[40]

Finding few rulers through whom they could administer coastal Guinea-Bissau, the Portuguese installed in their colony Africans as local-level *régulos* over collections of communities that had been previously politically independent. Africans who had fought in the colonial army were often appointed—even if they were not from the area they were charged with ruling. Hence, Mandinka and Fula were placed over random groupings of Balanta and Floup villages. Balanta resisted by stepping up migrations south from their traditional homelands, refusing to pay taxes and to work on colonial labour projects, and sometimes killing *régulos*. Portuguese rule quickly became violent in the extreme, making colonial Guinea-Bissau, in Joshua Forrest's words, 'a terrorist state'—one in which the only way to maintain order was through the harshest of tactics. Resisters in stateless regions were put in prison, beaten, and in some cases executed, and their property was often seized and cattle killed.[41] It is no wonder that Amilcar Cabral, who led Guinea-Bissau's liberation struggle, found stateless coastal groups among the most enthusiastic participants in his movement. Yet it is in the same region that the independent nation-state has found it difficult to impose control over long-standing local-level social and political organizations. As Forrest writes, 'In Guinea-Bissau, as in other parts of Africa, the various manifestations of rural civil societal authority have preserved their relative autonomy from state-centric forces'.[42]

CONCLUSION

While Forrest detects great continuity in the decentralized stateless regions of Guinea-Bissau from the precolonial to the colonial and on to the postcolonial periods, other historians—particularly those concerned with the dynamics of indigenous states—have seen colonialism as causing a more definitive break with the past.[43] This is an area ripe for further study. But it seems clear that in many parts of the continent, lineages, secret societies, age grades, and other local community structures maintain their own dynamism and relevance beneath—and sometimes beyond—the nation-state. Though neatly categorizing Africa's historical political landscape into one of states and stateless societies is in some ways simplistic, such categorization reveals much about how structures internal to Africa shaped broader historical processes. It has yielded much about the adaptability of societies labelled by some as 'primitive', 'tribal', or 'backward' to changes in regional and global politics and economics. Neither states nor stateless societies have ever been 'frozen in time'. It has long been possible for societies without rulers to maintain the relative equality of their members and to mediate pressures from the outside world. By working through their own unique social and political structures, Africans have shaped their histories and the nature of the communities in which they live. They did so in the era of Atlantic slavery, in the nineteenth-century era of legitimate commerce, in that of colonial rule—and in many ways continue to do so today.

NOTES

1. Walter Hawthorne, *Planting Rice and Harvesting Slaves: Transformations along the Guinea-Bissau Coast 1400–1900* (Portsmouth, NH: Heinemann, 2003), 7–12.
2. Robin Horton, 'Stateless Societies in the History of West Africa', in J. F. A. Ajayi and Michael Crowder, eds, *History of West Africa*, i (Harlow: Longman, 1976).
3. Horton, 'Stateless Societies', 81; John Tosh, *Clan Leaders and Colonial Chiefs: The Political History of an East African Stateless Society, c.1800–1939* (Oxford: Clarendon Press, 1978), 243–4; Colin M. Turnbull, *The Mbuti Pygmies: An Ethnographic Survey* (New York: Holt, Reinhart & Winston, 1983 [1965]). For classic studies of stateless societies, see E. E. Evans-Pritchard, *The Nuer* (Oxford: OUP, 1940); Meyer Fortes, *The Dynamics of Clanship among the Tallensi* (London: OUP, 1945); John Middleton and David Tait, eds, *Tribes without Rulers: Studies in African Segmentary Systems* (London: OUP, 1958).
4. Michael Crowder, *West Africa under Colonial Rule* (London: Hutchinson, 1968), 13.

5. Horton, 'Stateless Societies', 110.

6. Horton, 'Stateless Societies', 112–19.

7. Jan Vansina, *Paths in the Rainforests: Toward a History of Political Tradition in Equatorial Africa* (London: James Currey, 1990), 146–62. Vansina argues for multiple paths for state development in neighbouring savanna regions in his earlier *Kingdoms of the Savanna* (Madison, Wis.: University of Wisconsin Press, 1966).

8. Derek Nurse and Thomas T. Spear, *The Swahili: Reconstructing the History and Language of an African Society, 800–1500* (Philadelphia: University of Pennsylvania Press, 1985); Mark Horton and John Middleton, *The Swahili: The Social Landscape of a Mercantile Society* (Oxford: Blackwell, 2000); for a similar example from West Africa, see Roderick J. McIntosh and Susan Keech McIntosh, 'The Inland Niger Delta Before the Empire of Mali: Evidence from Jenne-Jeno', *Journal of African History*, 22 (1981).

9. Philip D. Curtin, *Economic Change in Precolonial Africa: Senegambia in the Era of the Slave Trade* (Madison, Wis.: University of Wisconsin Press, 1975).

10. John Thornton, *Africa and Africans in the Making of the Atlantic World, 1400–1680* (New York: CUP, 1992), 44, 125; see too David Eltis, *Economic Growth and the Ending of the Transatlantic Slave Trade* (New York: OUP, 1987), 77.

11. Walter Rodney, *How Europe Underdeveloped Africa* (Washington, DC: Howard University Press, 1974); Joseph E. Inikori, 'Ideology versus the Tyranny of Paradigm: Historians and the Impact of the Atlantic Slave Trade on African Societies', *African Economic History*, 22 (1994); Boubacar Barry, *Senegambia and the Atlantic Slave Trade* (Cambridge: CUP, 1998).

12. Martin A. Klein, 'The Impact of the Atlantic Slave Trade on Societies of the Western Sudan', in Joseph E. Inikori and Stanley L. Engerman, eds, *The Atlantic Slave Trade: Effects on Economies, Societies, and Peoples in Africa, the Americas, and Europe* (Durham, NC: Duke University Press 1992), 29.

13. Richard L. Roberts, *Warriors, Merchants, and Slaves: The State and the Economy in the French Soudan, 1900–1946* (Stanford, Calif.: Stanford University Press, 1996), 9; Jeffrey Herbst, *States and Power in Africa: Comparative Lessons in Authority and Control* (Princeton: Princeton University Press, 2000), 11, 41; Nathan Nunn, 'The Long Term Effects of Africa's Slave Trades', *Quarterly Journal of Economics*, 123 (2008); Paul E. Lovejoy, *Transformations in Slavery: A History of Slavery in Africa* (Cambridge: CUP, 1983), 68.

14. Joseph C. Miller, *Way of Death: Merchant Capitalism and the Angolan Slave Trade, 1730–1830* (Madison, Wis.: University of Wisconsin Press, 1988), 140–53; Vansina, *Kingdoms of the Savanna*, 197; Lovejoy, *Transformations in Slavery*, 81; Barry, *Senegambia*, 50, 99–100. For East Africa, see also Pier M. Larson, *History and Memory in an Age of Enslavement: Becoming Merina in Highland Madagascar, 1770–1822* (Portsmouth, NH: Heinemann, 2000), 149.

15. Emily Lynn Osborn, *Our New Husbands are Here: Households, Gender, and Politics in a West African State from the Slave Trade to Colonial Rule* (Athens, O.: Ohio University Press, 2011).

16. On stateless societies as 'the raided', see Patrick Manning, *Slavery and African Life: Occidental, Oriental, and African Slave Trades* (Cambridge: CUP, 1990), 132. On stateless societies defending themselves, Martin A. Klein, 'The Slave Trade and Decentralized Societies', *Journal of African History*, 42 (2001); Andrew Hubbell, 'A View of the Slave Trade from the Margin: Souroudougou in the Late Nineteenth-Century Slave Trade of the Niger Bend', *Journal of African History*, 42 (2001); Chris S. Duval, 'A Maroon

Legacy? Sketching African Contributions to Live Fencing Practices in Early Spanish America', *Singapore Journal of Tropical Geography*, 30 (2009); Hawthorne, *Planting Rice*, 121–3; Robert M. Baum, *Shrines of the Slave Trade: Diola Religion and Society in Pre-Colonial Senegambia* (Oxford: OUP, 1999).

17. Hawthorne, *Planting Rice*, 117–50; Baum, *Shrines of the Slave Trade*, 108–29; G. Ugo Nwokeji, *The Slave Trade and Culture in the Bight of Biafra* (New York: CUP, 2010).

18. Walter Hawthorne, *From Africa to Brazil: Culture, Identity and an Atlantic Slave Trade, 1600 to 1830* (New York: CUP, 2010), 208–47.

19. A. J. Hopkins, *An Economic History of West Africa* (New York: Columbia University Press, 1973), 124; Robin Law, ed., *From Slave Trade to 'Legitimate' Commerce: The Commercial Transition in Nineteenth-Century West Africa* (Cambridge: CUP, 1995).

20. Gareth Austin, 'Between Abolition and *Jihad*: The Asante Response to the Ending of the Atlantic Slave Trade, 1807–1896, in Law, ed., *From Slave Trade*.

21. Frederick Cooper, *Plantation Slavery on the East African Coast* (New Haven, Conn.: Yale University Press, 1977).

22. Martin Klein, 'Slavery, the Slave Trade and Legitimate Commerce in Late Nineteenth Century Africa', *Études d'Histoire Africaine*, 2 (1971).

23. M. Hiskett, 'The Nineteenth-Century *Jihads* in West Africa', in John E. Flint, ed., *Cambridge History of Africa* (Cambridge: CUP, 1976), v; Lovejoy, *Transformations in Slavery*, 184–219.

24. John Lonsdale, 'States and Social Processes in Africa: A Historiographical Survey', *African Studies Review*, 24 (1981), 174.

25. J. D. Omer-Cooper, 'The Nguni Outburst', in Flint, *Cambridge History*; Lance F. Marrow, 'Pre-Mfecane Carry-Overs in Subsequent Ndebele Politics', *The Society of Southern African in the 19th and 20th Centuries*, 3 (1971–2), 85–95; Philip Bonner, *Kings, Commoners, and Concessionaires: The Evolution and Dissolution of the Nineteenth-Century Swazi State* (Cambridge: CUP, 2002).

26. David Birmingham, 'The Forest and the Savanna of Central Africa', and A. C. Unomah and J. B. Webster, 'East Africa: The Expansion of Commerce', both in Flint, *Cambridge History*, 267, 279.

27. Hawthorne, *Planting Rice*, 177–202; Baum, *Shrines of the Slave Trade*.

28. David Northrup, *Trade without Rulers: Pre-Colonial Economic Development in South-Eastern Nigeria* (Oxford: Clarendon Press, 1978), 87, 188.

29. Frederick Cooper, 'Conflict and Connection: Rethinking Colonial African History', *American Historical Review*, 99/5 (1994), 1517.

30. Toyin Falola, *Colonialism and Violence in Nigeria* (Bloomington, Ind.: Indiana University Press, 2009).

31. Elizabeth Isichei, *The Ibo People and the Europeans: The Genesis of a Relationship–to 1906* (London: Faber, 1973), 130.

32. Tosh, *Clan Leaders*, 243–4.

33. Terence O. Ranger, *Revolt in Southern Rhodesia, 1896–97: A Study in African Resistance* (Evanston, IL: Northwestern University Press, 1967), 283; Catherine Coquery-Vidrovitch, 'Western Equatorial Africa', in J. D. Fage and Roland Oliver, eds, *Cambridge History of Africa* (Cambridge: CUP, 1985), vi. 332–3.

34. Malyln Newitt, *Portugal in Africa: The Last Hundred Years* (London: Hurst, 1981), 70; Joshua Forrest, *Lineages of State Fragility: Rural Civil Society in Guinea-Bissau* (Athens, O.: Ohio University Press, 2003).

35. Peter Geschiere, 'Chiefs and Colonial Rule in Cameroon: Inventing Chieftaincy, French and British Style', *Africa*, 63 (1993).

36. Timothy Weiskel, *French Colonial Rule and the Baule Peoples: Resistance and Collaboration, 1889–1911* (Oxford: OUP, 1980), 222.
37. G. I. Jones, 'Review', *International Journal of African Historical Studies*, 6 (1973), 716–18; see too Colin Newbury, 'Accounting for Power in Northern Nigeria', *Journal of African History*, 45 (2004); A. E. Afigbo, *The Warrant Chiefs: Indirect Rule in Southeastern Nigeria, 1891–1929* (Harlow: Longman, 1972).
38. Tosh, *Clan Leaders*, 150–1.
39. Catherine Coquery-Vidrovitch, 'French Black Africa', in A. D. Roberts, ed., *Cambridge History of Africa* (Cambridge: CUP, 1986), vii. 346–351.
40. Peter Geschiere, 'Chiefs and Colonial Rule in Cameroon: Inventing Chieftaincy, French and British Style', *Africa*, 63 (1993).
41. Forrest, *Lineages of State Fragility*, 85–159.
42. Forrest, *Lineages of State Fragility*, 246–7.
43. See e.g. T. C. McCaskie, *State and Society in Pre-Colonial Asante* (Cambridge: CUP, 1995).

BIBLIOGRAPHY

Hawthorne, Walter, *Planting Rice and Harvesting Slaves: Transformations along the Guinea-Bissau Coast 1400–1900* (Portsmouth, NH: Heinemann, 2003).

Herbst, Jeffrey, *States and Power in Africa: Comparative Lessons in Authority and Control* (Princeton: Princeton University Press, 2000).

Horton, Robin, 'Stateless Societies in the History of West Africa', in J. F. A. Ajayi and Michael Crowder, eds, *History of West Africa*, i (London: Longman, 1976).

Klein, Martin A., 'The Impact of the Atlantic Slave Trade on Societies of the Western Sudan', in Joseph E. Inikori and Stanley L. Engerman, eds, *The Atlantic Slave Trade: Effects on Economies, Societies, and Peoples in Africa, the Americas, and Europe* (Durham, NC: Duke University Press, 1992).

Osborn, Emily Lynn, *Our New Husbands are Here: Households, Gender, and Politics in a West African State from the Slave Trade to Colonial Rule* (Athens, O.: Ohio University Press, 2011).

McCaskie, T. C., *State and Society in Pre-Colonial Asante* (Cambridge: Cambridge University Press, 1995).

Tosh, John, *Clan Leaders and Colonial Chiefs: The Political History of an East African Stateless Society, c. 1800–1939* (Oxford: Clarendon Press, 1978).

Vansina, Jan, *Paths in the Rainforests: Toward a History of Political Tradition in Equatorial Africa* (Madison, Wis.: University of Wisconsin Press, 1990).

Wilks, Ivor, *Asante in the Nineteenth Century: The Structure and Evolution of a Political Order* (Cambridge: Cambridge University Press, 1975).

CHAPTER 5

ETHNICITY AND IDENTITY

RICHARD WALLER

MUCH of Africa's history can be written around the question of identity, for creating identities as both descriptive and prescriptive categories and as frames for social action and exploitation has been central to the making of community at every level, from the small-scale and local to the kingdom, the state, and finally the nation, and in any era from the earliest precolonial to the contemporary postcolonial. It is thus very much the historian's concern. Since ethnic identities claim to draw on the past to guide the present and speak to the future, an appreciation of their historical dimension is essential to an understanding of their contemporary use and meaning; and, since representations of those pasts are in part shaped by present ethnic concerns, a grasp of ethnicity in turn brings us to a more subtle understanding and evaluation of the histories we draw on.

Ethnic identity is but one of many possible identities, of varying and changing degrees of salience, held and deployed simultaneously by groups and individuals. Identities overlap, but each defines a different social space, carries a different set of meanings and values, and emphasizes and facilitates a different network of interaction. Since the 1970s, however, ethnicity, with which this chapter is primarily concerned, has come to assume a commanding place in Africanist research. A 'dazzling, ambiguous category', it is slippery and contradictory, difficult to define in any very useful way. 'Strong' constructions are too static, singular, and determinist to capture a fluid reality; weaker versions, while capturing movement, contingency, and ambiguity, are too diffuse to be helpful.[1] Ethnicity is at once 'traditional' and thoroughly modern; apparently fixed and coherent, yet conflicted and constantly redefined; inclusive, creating what some have called 'we-groups', and exclusive, defining 'strangers' as 'other'; an instrument of domination and a defence against it; a means to power and a profoundly moral critique of how power is exercised; a political contrivance and a social foundation.

One helpful way of understanding ethnicity and its relation to other identities is to see it as central to the creation of the individual and collective cognitive maps which order the world and orient people within it. Maps have periodically to be redrawn to take account of changes in the social and political terrain, and they can be built up through overlays, each one of which frames a particular identity or set of variables. Ethnicity is constituted through the combination of several such overlays 'bleeding through'. It can both infuse and be shaped by other identities, as in the emergence of African churches which combined religious and ethnic identification. Looking at ethnicity and identity in this way helps us to see both the flexibility of ethnic identification and the importance of multiple identities. Communities bound together—and connected to others—by sets of overlapping multilateral identities have been common in Africa for a long time. In northern Ghana, for example, boundaries of language, kinship, territory, and allegiance to chiefs and earth shrines rarely coincided, but together created a coherent and meaningful social universe.[2] But flexibility and multiplicity are not the same as vagueness or indeterminacy: people know who they are—or who they aspire to be.

The Colonial History of 'Tribe'

The first systematic attempts to use 'tribe' as a category came with colonial rule. Tribes were assumed to be primordial: fixed, static, bounded, timeless—and often mutually hostile. Membership was ascribed, determined by kin and clan, and denoted by shared language and 'custom'. The idea of tribe was a familiar one and accorded well with a particular evolutionary view of the development of human society. Colonial officials had read their Caesar and Tacitus and were aware that their ancestors too had once been 'tribal'. Africans now were where Europeans had once been, and the mission of colonialism was to help them to progress beyond tribe down the long road to modernity, even perhaps to nationhood. Tribe was not only intellectually convincing, its 'natural' existence seemed to be borne out by observation. Early encounters with African communities were often mediated by guides, interpreters, and auxiliaries who were themselves 'tribesmen' and used the language of tribe and difference to identify those with whom their employers were dealing. Moreover, while Africans did not have histories in a familiar Western sense, they did have myths which spoke to the primordial nature of tribal identity. Observation, however, was misleading. Africans had identities, but not tribes; it would take much effort before the two came into even approximate alignment.[3] Much of the historiography of colonial ethnicity revolves around the explication of this fundamental difference.

If tribe seemed valid as a concept, it was equally so as a principle of rule. Tribes as definable categories helped to make sense of the complex social terrain on which colonial rule was being erected. They placed people in relation to others and determined where they 'belonged', how they were organized, and thus how they might best be ruled and by whom. Hierarchical systems of recognition could be created as different tribes were assigned particular innate qualities of loyalty, industry, bravery, intelligence, and capacity to rule. Ethnic categories thus organized much of what every European 'knew' about Africans and framed their expectations. In British Africa especially, an elaboration of tribe as both concept and principle underpinned the colonial state.

To begin with, tribes were little more than names inscribed on government maps, but the empty spaces were gradually filled in by ethnographic research which fleshed out social organization, elucidated kinship, made 'custom' coherent, and later produced the classic monographs and surveys which introduced tribes to the scholarly world and gave them solidity. The creation of customary law added another element to the construct of tribe, as did local institutions of chiefship.[4] As colonial rule matured, routinized its control, and devolved power to local African subordinates, tribes acquired real resources, particularly in areas under indirect rule. Here, by the 1930s, native authorities controlled local treasuries and courts within an overarching system of tribal government. Moreover, membership of a tribe might determine residence as well as access to resources. Tribes had come to seem not only natural but solid and powerful, worth belonging to and defending.

Half a century of colonial rule transformed tribe, however, and brought other identities into existence. Older views were being challenged by newer concepts of modernity and citizenship. The 'traditional' solidarities and disciplines of tribe had once been seen by both officials and elders as the guarantee of rural stability and order—'detribalized natives', masterless men (and women), were a dangerous anomaly—but those certainties were now being undermined by accelerating economic and social change. In the countryside, economic development and differentiation were threatening to destroy what colonial officials believed to be the essential harmony of traditional communities. In town, where rapidly expanding populations seemed beyond control, the new urban identities and communities that had emerged appeared to be less clearly bounded, cohesive, and tractable than rural tribes.[5]

Yet modernization was both inevitable and necessary if the colonial state was to survive and transform itself after 1945. 'Progressives' were the key to the future. Having once built tribes based on hierarchy and tradition, colonialism now began to construct more modern alternatives based on education, status, and the transformation of both working and family life. The question was how to reconcile the promotion of the new with the selective conservation of the old. Mau Mau, Kenya's multidimensional nightmare, offered a savage warning of what might happen if colonialism lost control over the process of modernization. Contemporary opinion, however, was sharply divided as to what caused it. As John Lonsdale explains, conservatives (not all of whom were white) believed that reform and development had allowed an atavistic tribalism to slip its leash. Progress must, therefore, be reined in and the Kikuyu taught an unforgettable lesson in traditional discipline. Liberals, equally shocked by the violence, believed that it sprang from the trauma of incomplete modernization, the result of too little, not too much, progress. Defeating Mau Mau would involve helping the Kikuyu, and other Africans, to 'cross the river' from tribal past to civic future as fast and as completely as possible.[6]

To find out what was happening to tribe under the pressures of development, colonial states enlisted the help of sociologists. Many of them concentrated their attention on urbanization in southern Africa, reflecting colonial concerns about the long-term consequences of labour migration for the survival of rural community. Their studies laid the groundwork for a tradition of African urban sociology which came to see ethnicity as just one of many factors in the continuous social negotiation of life in town.[7] The assumption that migrants moved between two worlds, one rural and tribal, the other urban and cosmopolitan, still held, despite evidence that the separation between the two was more apparent than real. The concerns and expectations, as well as the remittances, of migrants played a key role in maintaining rural community and identity, suggesting that 'urban' and 'rural' were necessarily part of a single field, especially since workers were denied full acceptance as urban residents. Migrants did not simply switch from one identity to another as they moved; nor was it satisfactory to think of communities as divided between those who embraced and those refused modernity, though such an initial division seemed to fit into the expected trajectory of modernization. Philip Mayer based his study of the processes of urbanization in the South African town of East London on a cultural division between Red Xhosa who remained rural and committed to the maintenance of tradition and School Xhosa who could become 'town-rooted'. Clyde Mitchell's classic study of the *kalela* dance in the compounds of the Northern Rhodesian Copperbelt showed how mine workers created easily recognizable ethnic stereotypes to build solidarity and negotiate difference, but it still separated social interaction in the compounds into different sets of relations, some determined by the workplace, others by rural links.[8] Later, the concept of 'worker consciousness', which assumed that self-identification would eventually be determined by the labour process itself, was equally unable to capture the nuances and contradictions of identity formation. It would be some time before scholars were able to escape the straitjacket of urban/rural and modern/traditional dichotomies created by late colonial and early national hopes and fears to ask questions which took the modernity of ethnicity for granted.[9]

Late colonial officials were not the only ones struggling to fit ethnicity into a new vision of Africa: so too were their African nationalist opponents. For the latter, ethnic mobilization represented a threat to national unity, but also a possible means of achieving independence, for grassroots political activism could use local patriotisms as a lever against colonial rule. Politicians had to make the idea of a nation real to their listeners, and did so by domesticating it in familiar idioms and by linking local concerns to the wider struggle for independence. In that struggle, they hoped, tribe and its divisions would be transcended in the cause of building a nation. But it was difficult to evoke the latter without the former. At least as much intellectual effort went into building local identities as was directed towards constructing a national identity. The apparent weakness of the Kenya African Union, for example, sprang in part from the difficulty of claiming to speak for all while still acknowledging the moral, social, and political autonomy of the communities from which it hoped to draw support.[10] Post-independence attempts to capture community for the state through the promotion and control of official ethnicities were no more persuasive. In Malawi, Chewa villagers saw the nation, in which their language and culture was ostensibly privileged, as no more than a coercive if necessary contrivance and remained sceptical of the regime's ethnic assertions.[11] Identity at the local level was simply too fluid and self-referential to be a reliable prop for an imposed nation. Elsewhere, the belief that the experience of armed struggle, and possibly socialism, might succeed in transcending division and creating national communities where politics and culture had failed proved equally unfounded.

Moulding ethnic constituencies into a national community was not easy. Community had legitimacy, moral and cultural substance, and roots, none of which the nation could yet claim. Where the ethnos might plausibly become a nation in itself, the situation was especially complicated, as the concept of 'ethnic nationalism', an apparent contradiction in terms, suggests. Yoruba politicians were uncertain whether a multiethnic state was what they wanted or whether the 'children of Oduduwa' should stand alone; but if there was to be a 'Nigeria', then Yoruba should take a commanding role in its creation and take their full share of the rewards. In Kenya, Kikuyu considered similar questions of power and leadership, though without a secessionist option. By contrast, Oromo nationalism developed in rejection of an Amhara-dominated Ethiopian state which had denied it expression and self-respect.[12]

The development of ethnic nationalism with its threat of separation, often grounded in a particular reading of the past, could be a defensive as well as opportunistic response to the idea of nation. While colonial rulers could no longer ignore nationalist demands, they could still decide to whom they would listen. As decolonization proceeded, it was vital to be included in negotiations, for once things were settled those who were not were likely to be excluded from power and influence. An alternative for those who feared exclusion was to create a different constituency, one with the power to make itself heard. Ethnic nationalism might provide such a base. In the Gold Coast, the National Liberation Movement, the political vehicle of Asante nationalism, attracted the talents of young Asante (the 'youngmen') who had once been supporters of Nkrumah but saw their fortunes fading with the advent of responsible government. Drawing on the history and legitimacy of the *Asanteman* might give them another voice and a securer place in the new order. Ironically, they were undone by the very tradition to which they appealed, for within it they had no standing and they were thus committed to accepting the direction of their seniors. Ganda nationalism was given a new exclusivity and urgency once it became clear that Britain was intent on devolving power to a unitary state of Uganda without regard for the kingdom's special position. The need to stand united against this particular transfer of power reinvigorated loyalty to the ruler and to one version of what being Ganda meant. Differences were subsumed under the banner of ethnic patriotism and those who urged a wider national allegiance were branded as traitors. Militantly particularistic ethnicity of this sort was, like the nationalist coalition-building it rejected, in part a way of transcending local divisions by positing a single vision of past and future to which all should subscribe and a primary identity to which all must belong.[13]

Underlying nationalists' concern with ethnicity was the fear that colonial rulers might manipulate it against them. 'Divide and Rule' had served colonialism well in the past, and tribes were still to hand. In fact, these fears were generally not realized, if only because territorial nationalism came to appear the simplest and fastest solution to the problems of managing the devolution of power. The British and French generally backed their nationalist partners and used their remaining influence to help their chosen successors fend off challengers. In Rwanda, however, the Belgians, having constructed an overtly ethnicized hierarchy, overturned it at the last and placed the Hutu ruled over the Tutsi rulers, thus adding political exclusion to oppositional ethnicity.

It was during these postwar decades that ethnicity became 'political'; this shaped the way it has been seen since. Ethnicity ran foul of two visions of the postwar future: of economic and social development that would unlock Africa's potential and provide a better living; and of mass nationalism that would deliver Africans from foreign rule and give them equal citizenship in their own states. The first made tribe seem outdated and parochial, for the promise of modernity included the assumption that tribal identities would gradually be replaced by more modern ones. When this failed to happen, tribe was recast as regressive, an obstacle to development. The second saw ethnicity as a political threat: nationalism's evil twin. 'For the nation to live, tribe must die', proclaimed Amilcar Cabral, and though few of his fellow nationalists were quite so categorical, they shared his sense of the opposition between the two.[14] When tribes failed to die, dissolve, or be subsumed by the nation, 'tribalism' became a convenient scapegoat for the failure of the new states to fulfil their promise.

The Historiography of Ethnicity and Identity

The academic study of ethnicity was deeply influenced by the promises and then disappointments of nationalism. Western political and social scientists became increasingly concerned about the survival of the new nation-states whose emergence they had welcomed. Among their concerns were the threats of 'regionalism', easily construed in terms of ethnic nationalism, to territorial integrity and of 'tribalism' to democracy, socialist or liberal, and good government. They had evident grounds for concern, but, as proponents of modernization, their definition of nation was too narrowly territorial or too doctrinaire to allow them to see ethnicity as other than a ghost from a divided past and a threat to a unitary future. Prevailing paradigms of national development based on Western expectations, what Patrick Chabal calls the 'politics of the mirror', did not allow for alternatives that seemed non-national, unplanned, and unprogressive.[15]

Historians followed a similar path. Believing in the need to create new histories for new nations, they emphasized commonalties in the past: state-building and economic growth before colonialism; the distorting effects of colonial rule and underdevelopment; and the common experience of first conquest and resistance and then nationalist mobilization. Historians developed two paradigms: one for resistance and one for nationalism. The first posited a shift from the localism of 'primary resistance', undertaken by single communities under established leadership, to the wider sense of unity found in 'post-pacification resistance', and suggested connections between early resistance and later nationalist movements. The second demonstrated how protest and political awareness gradually acquired momentum and unity as it shifted from elite to mass, from place to place, and from local to central focus.[16] While historians did not ignore ethnicity—indeed, John Iliffe incorporated it into his classic national narrative as a necessary stage of development—they tended to accept it at face value as part of the precolonial past and then of the apparatus of colonial control which was turned against its masters. The idea that ethnicity had a complex history of its own had still to emerge.

With the publication of *Ethnic Groups and Boundaries*, the study of ethnicity took a new turn. Frederic Barth and his contributors focused on the margins of identity and showed how boundaries could be crossed by groups and individuals in search of opportunity and security. They argued that ethnicity was primarily concerned with the creation and management of difference as a way of facilitating and guarding access to resources.[17] By suggesting that ethnic identities could be fluid, instrumental, and situational, the approach offered an escape from the static primordiality of tribe. Barth's lead was taken up by precolonial historians, particularly in East Africa, who began to look at how different identities, shaped by complementary modes of subsistence, enabled groups to control and share access to resources across a range of local ecologies, to structure competition, and to provide for both survival and accumulation. Interlocking and contrasting identities provided an extended and flexible framework for interaction over wide areas. Scholars also began to break down the supposed homogeneity of ethnic communities by examining their constituent parts and showing how different sub-identities, often based on networks of clanship, crossed boundaries and provided pathways from one group to another.[18]

This instrumentalist approach had its limitations, however. It was not much concerned with how identities, as opposed to boundaries, were constructed; nor with what, apart from opportunism, expediency, and patronage, bound communities together. Dealing with the margins, it overlooked the centre. The first limitation was addressed by studies of the 'invention of tradition'.[19] Terence Ranger's original essay was more concerned with the traditions invented by colonial states to structure and civilize their rule and to incorporate Africans through 'models of subservience', but the debate that followed focused attention on the colonial period as the matrix of ethnicity and explored 'invention' as a dialectical process. Ethnic boundary-making had seemed to illuminate precolonial history: the invention of ethnicity was to do the same for the colonial period.

'Europeans believed Africans belonged to tribes; Africans built tribes to belong to'.[20] Both rulers and ruled had an interest in building tribes. In her nuanced study of colonial rule in Central Africa, Karen Fields showed how a search for what Sara Berry has called 'hegemony on a shoestring' led colonial rulers to support what they believed to be legitimate tribal authorities and to engage in discourses about tradition which they could neither fully comprehend nor control. Once they implicitly acknowledged the authority of arguments from tradition, however, they became subject to it. The ethnicities that emerged had official form but local content; African collaborators were as much partners as subordinates in the business of creating legitimacy.[21]

Tribes as units of governance offered access to new political and material resources, especially for those who successfully 'invented' them, but they were more than simply paths to power. As Iliffe pointed out, tribes, like the nations that followed them, were 'attempts to build societies in which men could live well in the modern world'.[22] That world was rapidly changing and so too were definitions of 'living well'. Creating tribes thus involved shoring up and rethinking the moral economies which made life liveable and which were clearly under stress. Peter Ekeh, taking Fields's ideas further, argued that kinship in West Africa was expanded and solidified into ethnicity to fill a void left by the imposition of colonial rule. Until the 1940s, the state rarely intervened in matters of social welfare. 'Tribal' or 'clan' associations, often created by the aggregation of cognate but previously separate kinship units, provided a support network otherwise lacking, especially in towns, and established and attempted to enforce norms of behaviour. Ethnic solidarities were thus propelled by a combination of self-help and socialization. They also attempted to address new questions of accountability. State and society now operated on different principles of morality. Relations between state and community and between communities were governed by the 'institutionalised amorality' of government and law; relations within communities by the intimate morality of family and neighbourhood.[23] The outlawing of self-help made it difficult to impose sanctions on wrong-doers—who might be raiders from outside or witches within—and the state's support for traditional authority freed chiefs from local scrutiny. Defenders and critics were more likely to be seen as law-breakers and 'political agitators' than as honest patriots. Emphasizing kinship and ethnic solidarity was one way of holding rulers to account and of defending oneself against others.

Initially, this new constructivist analysis focused on ethnicity in Southern Africa.[24] Coastal West Africa, with its longer experience of contact with Europe, had already produced its own versions in the writings of an indigenous and diasporic African intelligentsia seeking to build an identity for itself in the face of growing racism and grappling with the problems of finessing Christian modernity and African tradition.[25] Unlike instrumentalism, constructivism concerned itself with how ethnic identities were made as well as with the purposes they served, and linked the two together. It also shifted focus from margin to centre, in two senses: it dealt with the creation of community itself as well as with its relations with others, and it placed ethnogenesis at the heart of the colonial experience. Ethnogenesis required enormous intellectual creativity and labour. A variety of ethnic entrepreneurs and culture-brokers—embattled conservatives, 'progressive traditionalists', mission-educated young men, and simple opportunists—struggled to assert and propagate their own versions of ethnicity, using the newly created languages of Christian literacy to write themselves collectively into existence. To frame and legitimize their ethnic assertions, they turned to a new form of written history, drawing inspiration from the Old Testament as a tribal and providential history to which Europeans apparently attached great weight. In time, these histories acquired authority and added another layer to the mass of selective and competing representations of the past.[26] Historians also examined the broader context, particularly the experience of labour migrancy, tracing the links between rural and urban constructions of identity which had been obscured by the dichotomy between 'townsmen' and 'tribesmen' in late colonial thinking. In looking for ethnicity in town, however, they had to negotiate the rival claims of class and race as prime determinants of collective identity and action.[27]

Attention so far had been focused on men. As Sandra Greene has noted, women had been largely ignored in studies of the construction of ethnicity except as the objects of male concern and control. Leroy Vail thought ethnicity's appeal strongest for men, even though the 'place' of women—and proper gender relations—was a 'central issue' in the formation of ethnic ideologies during the colonial period.[28] There is some truth in this reflection of a patriarchal mind-set, for colonial ethnicity was nothing if not conservative. In town especially, male ethnic assertion was often couched in moral terms and focused through gender: women's public behaviour was a community matter. However, the apparent failure to consider women as active agents in the making and transformation of ethnicity is surprising in view of the attention that has been paid to their struggles to define themselves and fashion their own identities. Greene herself has shown how young Anlo women both accepted and contested their roles as guardians of lineage identity against outsiders through marriage in the nineteenth century and how, in their own interests, they pioneered the adoption of a wider Ewe identification in the twentieth. At a fundamental level, it was women who played the crucial role in determining how, and in some cases which, ethnic identities were domesticated and transmitted: without them ethnicity was not sustainable.[29]

The emphasis on ethnogenesis and writing also tended to obscure the fact that identity is performative as well as declarative. As Jean Allman puts it, 'being Asante' was something you did, not just something you were. Performed identity could be a matter of habitus, the product of quotidian action and knowledge of a sort implicit in earlier ecological approaches to ethnicity, but it could also be enacted, negotiated—and sometimes contested—more formally in ceremonies and rituals. The annual Asante *Odwira* festival represented the unity of the *Asanteman*, reconstituted power, and dramatized the complex relations and understandings that gave meaning to being Asante. As a public performance, it was also open and flexible, capable of responding to changing needs, and to interrogation by participants.[30] *Odwira* ended with Asante's conquest, but elsewhere performance continued under colonialism and, indeed, became the vehicle for the assertion of new identities. In eastern Africa, membership of *beni* dance troupes gave young men the opportunity to demonstrate their modernity in solidarity with their fellows and in competition with others. Here identity was literally on parade. Yet while colonialism opened new avenues for self-expression, it constrained the creativity of popular consciousness. Carefully staged ceremonies, the 'neo-traditionalization' of rulership, became meaningless performances of colonial power rather than communal affirmations of belonging. State surveillance, suspicious of disorder, denied people the opportunity to negotiate status and identity through 'feasts and riot'.[31] It was nationalism which, rather nervously and for a short time, reinvigorated popular performance in pursuit of a different identity.

A decade after 'Invention', Ranger published an autocritique—less widely known than the original—which surveyed the field, voiced doubts about the applicability of the term, and suggested revisions. 'Invention', he now thought, was too authorial a word.

It implied something newly discovered, imposed from above, and possibly contrived. Drawing on Benedict Anderson's influential work on nineteenth-century European nationalisms, Ranger now preferred 'imagination' with its stress on ideas, images, and interaction. Although the historical context was very different, Anderson's 'imagined communities' caught the idea that identity had first to be evoked before being disseminated. The assertion that tribes were merely colonial constructs, although driven partly by concern over the competitive manipulation of ethnicity and the negative use of 'tribe' as an explanation of political conflict in the present, also denied ethnicity any deeper historical roots. Although 'tribe' might be an expedient colonial construction which answered the different needs of rulers and ruled, to be meaningful it had to have resonance, to strike chords in local historical memory. Complete inventions could not work.[32]

Meanwhile, historians had been turning their attention back to the precolonial past. Not all were explicitly concerned with the construction of ethnicity, but their work offered insights into how identities evolved and illuminated the ideas of moral and civic engagement that underpinned them. Earlier work on the creation of boundaries between groups was recast to consider processes of growth on what Igor Kopytoff called the internal frontier. A picture emerged of communities in motion, constantly mutating, growing through the accumulation of power and resources by local leaders who drew others to them and breaking up as followers left to seek their fortunes elsewhere. Charles Ambler's study of communities in eastern Kenya on the eve of colonial conquest brought out the internal dynamism, competitiveness, and the intense parochialism of this world. Ronald Atkinson looked at how polities emerged in northern Uganda through aggregation and then came gradually to adopt a common identity as Acoli, a name first given to them by Sudanese traders with whom they dealt. His study combined the earlier concern with state formation in the precolonial period with a search for the 'long-term roots of ethnicity'. The Isaacmans' study of the Chikunda showed how groups of ex-slaves and others came together and made a place and an identity for themselves on the Zambezi frontier.[33] Historians also engaged more directly with constructivism by examining the antecedents of colonial ethnicity and demonstrating how formerly fluid and very local identities began to expand their range and harden into 'tribe'. Bill Bravman, for example, combining older instrumental and newer constructivist approaches, traced a Taita ethnicity from its origins in the local identities of small communities of drought refugees settled in favourable ecological niches in the Taita Hills of southern Kenya to its emergence as a single identity during the colonial period.[34] But what was the glue that bound communities together; and how could larger identities which transcended the localism of small communities be constructed? Essentially, these were questions about the substance of ethnicity, the second limitation of the instrumental approach.

Lonsdale's reconstruction of Kikuyu moral economy took matters further by directing attention to the internal architecture of identity. If, as he argued, communities are essentially communities of argument, ethnicity might be better understood as continuing discourse, rather than as a discrete cultural and linguistic package. The same approach also addressed relations between communities, the external architecture of identity. The broad themes of argument—power and its proper ends, the bases of authority, and the nature of civic virtue—may be widely shared, but the language and loci of dispute are peculiar to each community. The particular nature and quality of argument thus defines communities internally and differentiates them from others; yet its ubiquity potentially provides common ground between them.[35] In a similar vein, the growing richness, sophistication, and historical depth of the literature on complex states like Asante and Buganda addressed identities that persisted through time and transcended the local. It went further in explicating the core values that gave cohesion and a collective sense of self by asking why people wanted to belong to the state and what, beyond the structures of coercive power, kept their loyalty. Rule in Buganda rested, so Holly Hanson suggests, on 'love', an idea of obligation freely assumed, if forcefully maintained. Asante rulers could be called to account as they were bound by the same sense of civic responsibility as their subjects: all were engaged in the task of building the state. Like the kings of Buganda, they were simultaneously the agents, managers, and guarantors of something larger and more powerful than themselves.[36] The focus on moral economy and accountability encouraged historians to look inside the ethnic box and gave ethnicity ideological substance.

Identity could also be exclusionary, however, an instrument of domination imposed by the strong on the weak. As such it could be contested, appropriated, and subverted by those on whom it had been imposed. The emergent Zulu state consigned some defeated groups to the margins, excluding them from access to resources and calling them *Amalala*. Ngoni chiefdoms established by invasion and assimilation did something similar, creating hierarchies to regulate power based on degrees of 'Ngoni-ness' from 'true Ngoni' who claimed descent from the original core to *sutu* dependants who could rise by demonstrating loyalty and prowess. Later, 'marginals' capitalized on the enforced identity to distance themselves from their overlords and to strike their own bargains with the in-coming colonial state.[37] Frederick Cooper's study of how relations of interdependence between slaves and masters on the East African coast were negotiated shows that identity and its expectations could be more subtly contested by those who were in between, assimilated but yet not fully belonging. Slaves from up-country entered into coastal culture as dependants and inferiors, defined as *Washenzi* ('savages') by masters who were proudly *Wa-Ungwana* ('the civilized'). Assimilating on Swahili terms gave slaves advantages in a paternalistic regime, but they could challenge their imposed status by maintaining practices that marked their foreign origins as *Wa-Nyasa*. When, how, and to what extent slaves accepted assimilation and the inclusions and exclusions it imposed was part of a continual 'skirmishing along the boundaries of mutual expectations'.[38] Categorizing others was a matter of material power, but it could equally convey a moral judgement. Okiek hunter-gatherers were known to their pastoral Maasai neighbours (and then to colonial governments) as *Dorobo* ('stockless') and thus impoverished, greedy, and lacking proper restraint, lazy, and improvident. *Dorobo* was a 'mirror in the forest', a reflection of everything that 'Maasai' was not, but might perhaps become.[39] Exclusion and the expression of unease through ethnic stereotyping had a long history of its own, as did attempts to resist it.

Just as communal solidarities arise out of concerns with moral accountability, they may also emerge from a search for healing. Rulers like the Kilindi in Shambaa performed a vital role in 'healing the land' and maintaining its fertility; the *ituika* ceremony at which one generation of Kikuyu elders handed over power to the next was thought to cleanse the land of sorcery and allow a new start to be made. A belief in the power of healing and renewal was an important part of how Shambaa and Kikuyu understood themselves.[40] Healing was often to be found in collective action. Lemba, a cult of affliction in West Central Africa, created widely ramifying networks of therapy and trust. Neal Kodesh has recently reframed the history of clanship in Buganda by showing how efforts to ensure collective prosperity lay at the heart of early community-building. Nodes of authority emerged around shrines and mediums able to ward off or repair misfortune, and they remained a fixed part of the landscape of power as the kingdom emerged.[41]

Islam and Christianity offered other avenues for healing and moral renewal: both emphasized community and identity, whether as believers or converts. The spread of Islam in nineteenth-century West Africa was in part driven by the formation of communities of belief, often gathered around a charismatic teacher and frequently in conflict with local authority. Christian missionaries also built communities of separation and refuge which adopted identities shaped by belief and belonging. These identities were neither entirely new nor uninflected by the surrounding culture, however. It was black catechists rather than white missionaries who explained Christianity in local terms and mediated the transition between older and newer orders through creative cultural translation. Converts needed to make their own accommodations with a past which was still present, as Ewe did in maintaining a prudent belief in the reality of witchcraft while redefining it in Pentecostal terms.[42] Some went further in arguing that there was no necessary opposition between Christian modernity and cultural tradition. Samuel Johnson wrote his history partly to demonstrate that Christianity was the fulfilment of Yoruba destiny; Kikuyu pamphleteers argued that Christians might actually be better Kikuyu for being Christian.[43] Religious and cultural identities could combine in the making of ethnicity. African preachers and prophets founded their own churches as places 'to feel at home'. Their focus on building communities of faith, revelation, and renewal was couched in local idiom and spoke to local concerns. In western Kenya, the Holy Spirit movement developed its own Luo theology, based in part on a providential Christian interpretation of the sacrificial martyrdom of its founder but fused with older forms of spirituality. It began in an area made tense by bitter inter-ethnic land disputes and spoke to the anxieties of Luo settlers in an unfriendly place.[44] A concern with the spiritual did not, however, imply a disengagement from the political. As in Islam, communities of renewal could be sharply critical of the powers-that-be. Isaiah Shembe's 'theological nationalism' found the Zulu elite morally delinquent and called for a unity based on virtue, not on hereditary kingship.[45] Faith communities also grew in town and, driven by the anxieties of urban living, played a vigorous part in the debate over moral guardianship and the making of ethnic ideology.

IDENTITY IN THE LONG TERM

Uncovering the roots of ethnic identity has enabled historians to gain a much broader and more nuanced sense of ethnicity as a continuous and frequently contested process of becoming and being. The identities and traditions which had once seemed to provide a stable precolonial baseline now appear as merely the most recent in a long series of constructions. But older constructs did not simply disappear: they became latent, dropping below the surface to become part of a thick sediment of ideas on which future attempts to situate self and others might draw. Powerful support for the study of identity in the *longue durée* was provided by Jan Vansina's discovery of an equatorial African tradition of governance, endlessly renewing and reinventing itself as it adapted to change. David Schoenbrun's linguistic study of community formation in the Great Lakes region and Elizabeth MacGonagle's ambitious attempt to demonstrate the evolution and persistence of an Ndau identity in the Mozambique/Zimbabwe border area over 500 years raise the question of whether identity, like governance, can continually reinvent and renew itself.[46]

Vansina believed that the equatorial tradition had been finally destroyed by the material and moral violence of colonial conquest and the imposition of alien concepts of rule; others were not so sure.[47] Nonetheless, the advent of colonial rule, with its unitary sense of belonging and its universalizing view of linear history, did constrain though not destroy the older flexibility, closing down some options, hardening identities, and forcing people to re-evaluate belonging in a new and often defensive way. Identities showed continuity, but they were also shaped by rupture, in response to disorder and to the uncertainties of an unfamiliar and changing world. Kenyatta complained that Kikuyu no longer knew 'what [they] may or may not, ought or ought not, do or believe', and wrote a historical ethnography to remind them.[48] Kikuyu also found that having many different accounts of how they came to be, all internally logical but externally inconsistent, was a serious handicap when it came to arguing with rulers who would listen only to a single coherent 'historical' account. Other communities faced similar problems of explication when faced with government enquiries, especially into land matters, and they too responded by creating simplified and defensive accounts of a complex past. Contests between histories divided people and sharpened ethnic awareness, thus apparently confirming colonial views of primordial loyalties and enmities, but they were part of a much longer process through which identity was negotiated using whatever arenas were available.[49]

The long view requires historians to take account of social memory as another part of that rich sediment in which identity is grounded. Memory is not fixed in a timeless past. It is performative and embodied, and constantly being restated, re-enacted, and reinterpreted, as Rosalind Shaw shows in her study of the continuing production and relevance of memories of the slave trade in Sierra Leone. Thus memory is no more primordial than the ethnicities it informs. It provides a flexible underpinning for identities which are themselves fluid, and it can also be contested. Struggles over memory are often struggles over identity. In Mali, 'national' histories of Samori as a hero of resistance are challenged by local memories of his activities as a slaver and warlord.[50]

Social memory is most obviously accessible to historians through oral tradition which evokes and presents it as a continuous narrative, often in dialogue between teller and listeners and through successive iterations which give traditions their own histories. Such narratives explain where the community 'came from', how it was constituted, and how past experience has made it what it now is. But memory can also be embodied and recalled in other ways. A sense of place is an important part of identity. Shambaa thought of themselves as 'people who live in a particular botanical environment'; Asante's being was rooted in the struggle to hack civilization out of the forest. But landscape is only part of what gives place its significance. It also includes what Pierre Nora calls 'environments of memory' which both embody and evoke the past. Living in and with the landscape situates the community in time as well as space and gives it a particular sense of continuity and identification. Embodied memory is what distinguishes *terroir* as a cultural ideal from territory as a political fact, as Mamadou Diouf notes in a discussion of separatism in the Casamance region of Senegal. Getting to know and 'read' the landscape, encountering the memories it held and becoming part of both it and them, was an essential step towards being a full member of the community.[51] The crucial link between landscape, memory, and identity helps to explain why colonial dispossession posed such an existential threat to community and why it acted as a spur to ethnic assertion. Ranger's study of the Matopo Hills in Zimbabwe deals with struggles over not only the appropriation and proper use of land itself but also how the Matopos should be 'seen' and their meaning and significance understood, for whites too had sites of memory to construct there.[52]

Landscape and healing can be linked through the inscription of 'sacred geographies', as, for example, with the shrine complexes of Central Africa which framed a different sort of regional identity. Bengt Sundkler has suggested that the spiritual maps of the Holy Land, where memory and expectation fuse, created by South African Zionist churches, centred on a New Jerusalem and traced by pilgrimage, were a response to physical dispossession by an alien state. The Bataka movement in Buganda challenged the reorganization of land tenure after 1900 partly in order to defend the alternative landscape of healing and power.[53] Embodied memory and ritual topography have much to tell us about the ways in which identities are understood and enacted, and they demonstrate again how complex and multivalent ethnicity can be.

Despite these new cultural approaches, many political scientists continued to view ethnic mobilization as a threat to democratization or part of the instrumentalization of disorder.[54] Lonsdale now suggested that a distinction could be drawn between 'moral ethnicity' and 'political tribalism'. The one arose from the interior structure of community and reprised arguments about accountability and belonging; the other derived from its externalities and addressed issues of inter-ethnic violence and rival constituencies in national politics. These two aspects of ethnicity were not simply opposed, however. Communities were divided internally as well as externally, demanded accountability from their own as well as others' leaders, and might share parts of a common morality. Recognizing how difficult it is to be 'us', Lonsdale hoped, might make communities more tolerant of 'others'. From this perspective, the state itself might be rethought.[55] Rethinking the state in turn required a reappraisal of both colonial rule and decolonization. Mahmood Mamdani had argued that because colonial regimes ruled through 'decentralised [tribal] despotisms' and because nationalist opposition was constrained to work within that frame, tribe was consolidated, not undermined, at independence. This, however, overestimated the determining power of the colonial state and underestimated the ability of its subjects to forge links which cross-cut tribe and to reshape it for their own purposes. Moreover, both the British and French had considered other ways of devolving power which relied on federation and possibly class, not on nation or tribe. 'Tribalism' and the shape of current conflicts between tribe and nation are not, therefore, historically inevitable, despite their attractiveness as explanatory frameworks. There were and are other possibilities. Historians, whose business it is to be concerned with process and contextualization, are well placed to draw out the implications.[56]

Lonsdale's intervention reminds us that historians have something to say about ethnicity's present as well as its past. Three related developments are of particular interest. One is the re-emergence of latent identities. Some are parochial in scope and purpose, defending land and livelihood through the restatement or recreation of earlier identities which have once again become relevant.[57] Others make larger and more threatening claims, their violent exclusivity a repudiation of an earlier history of ethnic interaction through the assertion of an absolutist primordiality. 'Ethnic cleansing' in Kenya and the ideology of autochthony with its search for 'internal others' in Cameroun and Côte d'Ivoire reflect Lonsdale's 'political tribalism', armed and implacable.[58]

The second lies in the intersection of the local and the global. Ethnic brokers once worked within the confines of the colonial state: their successors now have access to resources and networks unimaginable to those who 'made' the Yoruba a century ago. Marginalized groups in northern Tanzania have positioned themselves within a global discourse of indigeneity in order to make claims on a neo-liberal state; in Kenya, the range of Luo ethnic imagination now stretches from Kisumu to the White House via the virtual 'Little Kisumus' of a world-wide diaspora.[59] The range of actors and interests now involved in the business of making tradition and projecting identity has expanded to include international non-state organizations concerned with 'cultural survival', environmental issues, and local empowerment; transnational business seeking local legitimacy; and tourism entrepreneurs with an interest in marketing the exotic. The search for resources abroad shapes the new discourses of belonging and ethnic distinctiveness at home and encourages a form of 'strategic essentialism' as a way of making ethnicity more widely 'legible'.

Modernity is now invested in tradition. Our third development is the resurgence of 'neo-traditionalism' or 'neo-primordialism', which denies historical process and complexity in order to address both transnational and local constituencies. Discourses of ethnicity continue to address familiar issues of power, identity, and community, but they have now acquired other registers and a wider audience. Struggles over landscape link environmentalist and ethnic concerns: sacred groves can be biological 'hotspots' as well as sites of memory. Founding ancestors and 'culture heroes' can be resurrected and reinterpreted; and their past and its 'traditional culture' can be appropriated, commoditized, and re-enacted at 'heritage sites' and 'cultural villages'.[60]

Contemporary recreations of tradition and ethnicity continue to serve a variety of often conflicting purposes. Like all such constructions, they are interactive not simply imposed, and, in so far as appeals to the past remain central to them, they are of concern to historians. As older approaches yield inevitably diminishing intellectual returns, the new engagement with globalism and contemporary politics may indicate the direction in which the historiography of identity and ethnicity should now go.

Notes

1. Carola Lentz, '"Tribalism" and Ethnicity in Africa: A Review of Four Decades of Anglophone Research', *Cahiers des Sciences Humaines*, 31 (1995), 304; Frederick Cooper and Rogers Brubaker, 'Beyond Identity', *Theory and Society*, 29 (2000).

2. Carola Lentz, 'Contested Identities: The History of Ethnicity in Northwestern Ghana', in Carola Lentz and Paul Nugent, eds, *Ethnicity in Ghana: The Limits of Invention* (Basingstoke: Macmillan, 2000).

3. Jean-Loup Amselle, *Mestizo Logics: Anthropology of Identity in Africa and Elsewhere* (Stanford, Calif.: Stanford University Press, 1998). Officials sometimes complained that Africans did not seem to know to which tribe they 'belonged'.

4. Peter Pels, 'The Anthropology of Colonialism: Culture, History and the Emergence of Western Governmentality', *Annual Review of Anthropology*, 26 (1997); Martin Chanock, *Law, Custom and Social Order: The Colonial Experience in Malawi and Zambia* (Cambridge: CUP, 1985).

5. Sara Berry, *No Condition is Permanent: The Social Dynamics of Agrarian Change in Sub-Saharan Africa* (Madison, Wis.: Wisconsin University Press, 1993), 46–53; Frederick Cooper, 'Urban Space, Industrial Time and Wage Labor in Africa', in Frederick Cooper, ed., *Struggle for the City: Migrant Labor, Capital and the State in Urban Africa* (Beverly Hills, Calif.: Sage Publications, 1983).

6. John Lonsdale, 'Mau Maus of the Mind: Making Mau Mau and Remaking Kenya', *Journal of African History*, 31 (1990).

7. See e.g. Geoffrey Wilson, *An Essay on the Economics of Detribalisation in Northern Rhodesia* (Livingstone: Rhodes-Livingstone Institute, 1941); Abner Cohen, *Custom and Politics in Urban Africa: A Study of Hausa Migrants in Yoruba Towns* (Berkeley, Calif.: University of California Press, 1969).

8. Philip Mayer, *Townsmen or Tribesmen? Conservation and the Process of Urbanization in a South African City* (Cape Town: OUP, 1961); J. Clyde Mitchell, *The Kalela Dance* (Manchester: MUP, 1956).

9. James Ferguson, *Expectations of Modernity: Myths and Meanings of Urban Life on the Zambian Copperbelt* (Berkeley, Calif.: University of California Press, 1999).

10. John Lonsdale, 'KAU's Cultures: Imaginations of Community and Constructions of Leadership in Kenya after the Second World War', *Journal of African Cultural Studies*, 13 (2000).

11. Harri Englund, 'Between God and Kamuzu: The Transition to Multi-Party Politics in Central Malawi', in Richard Werbner and Terence Ranger, eds, *Postcolonial Identities in Africa* (London: Zed Books, 1996).

12. Toyin Falola, 'Ethnicity and Nigerian Politics: The Past in the Yoruba Present', in Bruce Berman, Dickson Eyoh, and Will Kymlicka, eds, *Ethnicity and Democracy in Africa* (Oxford: James Currey, 2004); Cristiana Pugliese, 'Complementary or Contending Nationhoods?', in E. S. Atieno Odhiambo and John Lonsdale, eds, *Mau Mau and Nationhood: Arms, Authority and Narration* (Oxford: James Currey, 2003); Mohammed Hassen, 'The Development of Oromo Nationalism', in Paul Baxter, Jan Hultin, and Alessandro Triulzi, eds, *Being and Becoming Oromo: Historical and Anthropological Enquiries* (Uppsala: Nordiska Afrikainstitutet, 1996).

13. Jean Allman, *The Quills of the Porcupine: Asante Nationalism in an Emergent Ghana* (Madison, Wis.: University of Wisconsin Press, 1993); Ian Hancock, 'Patriotism and Neo-Traditionalism in Buganda: The Kabaka Yekka ("The King Alone") Movement, 1961–1962', *Journal of African History*, 11 (1970).

14. Quoted in Patrick Chabal, 'The Social and Political Thought of Amilcar Cabral: A Reassessment', *Journal of Modern African Studies*, 19 (1981), 44.

15. Patrick Chabal, 'The African Crisis: Context and Interpretation', in Werbner and Ranger, *Postcolonial Identities*.

16. Terence Ranger, 'Connections between "Primary Resistance" Movements and Modern Mass Nationalism in East and Central Africa', *Journal of African History*, 9 (1968); John Iliffe, *A Modern History of Tanganyika* (Cambridge: CUP, 1979).

17. Frederik Barth, ed., *Ethnic Groups and Boundaries: The Social Organisation of Cultural Difference* (London: Allen & Unwin, 1969).

18. e.g. John Lonsdale, 'When did the Gusii (or Any Other Group) Become a "Tribe"?', *Kenya Historical Review*, 5 (1977); Thomas Spear and Richard Waller, eds, *Being Maasai* (London: James Currey, 1993); Gunther Schlee, 'Inter-Ethnic Clan Identities among Cushitic-Speaking Pastoralists', *Africa*, 55 (1985).

19. Terence Ranger, 'The Invention of Tradition in Colonial Africa', in Eric Hobsbawm and Terence Ranger, eds, *The Invention of Tradition* (Cambridge: CUP, 1983).

20. Iliffe, *Modern History of Tanganyika*, 324–5.

21. Karen Fields, *Revival and Rebellion in Colonial Central Africa* (Princeton: PUP, 1985); Berry, *No Condition is Permanent*, ch. 2; Thomas Spear, 'Neo-Traditionalism and the Limits of Invention in British Colonial Africa', *Journal of African History*, 44 (2003), 8–13.

22. Iliffe, *Modern History of Tanganyika*, 324–5.

23. Peter Ekeh, 'Social Anthropology and Two Contrasting Uses of Tribalism in Africa', *Comparative Studies in Society and History*, 32 (1990), 683–5.

24. Leroy Vail, ed., *The Creation of Tribalism in Southern Africa* (London: James Currey, 1989).

25. P. de Moraes Farias and Karen Barber, eds, *Self-Assertion and Brokerage: Early Cultural Nationalism in West Africa* (Birmingham: Centre of West African Studies, 1990); John Peel, *Religious Encounter and the Making of the Yoruba* (Bloomington, Ind.: Indiana University Press, 2000).

26. See John Peel, 'The Cultural Work of Yoruba Ethnogenesis', in Elizabeth Tonkin, Maryon McDonald, and Malcolm Chapman, eds, *History and Ethnicity* (London: Routledge,

1989); chapters by Terence Ranger, Leroy Vail, and Landeg White in Vail, *Creation of Tribalism*; chapters by John Lonsdale, Robin Law, and Terence Ranger in Louise de la Gorgendière, Kenneth King, and Sarah Vaughan, eds, *Ethnicity in Africa: Roots, Meanings and Implications* (Edinburgh: Centre of African Studies, 1996).

27. Patrick Harries, *Work, Culture and Identity: Migrant Laborers in Mozambique and South Africa, c.1860–1910* (Portsmouth, NH: Heinemann, 1994); Kudakwashe Manganga, 'Migrant Labor, Industrial Ethnicity, Urban Violence, and the State in Colonial Zimbabwe', in Michael Mbanaso and Chima Korieh, eds, *Minorities and the State in Africa* (Amherst, Mass.: Cambria Press, 2010). Marxist scholars had argued that ethnicity was a form of false consciousness: Archie Mafeje, 'The Ideology of "Tribalism"', *Journal of Modern African Studies*, 9 (1971).

28. Sandra Greene, 'In the Mix: Women and Ethnicity among the Anlo-Ewe', in Lenz and Nugent, *Ethnicity in Ghana*, 29; Vail, *Creation of Tribalism*, 14–15.

29. Shula Marks, 'Patriotism, Patriarchy and Purity: Natal and the Politics of Zulu Ethnic Consciousness', in Vail, *Creation of Tribalism*; Sandra Greene, *Gender, Ethnicity and Social Change on the Upper Slave Coast* (Portsmouth, NH: Heinemann, 1996); Heidi Gegenbach, *Women as Makers and Tellers of History in Magude, Mozambique* (New York: Columbia University Press, 2005).

30. Jean Allman, 'Be(com)ing Asante, Be(com)ing Akan: Thoughts on Gender, Identity and the Colonial Encounter', in Lenz and Nugent, *Ethnicity in Ghana*, 103–9.

31. Terence Ranger, *Dance and Society in Eastern Africa, 1890–1970: The Beni Ngoma* (London: Heinemann, 1975); Jonathan Glassman, *Feasts and Riot: Revelry, Rebellion and Popular Consciousness on the Swahili Coast, 1856–1888* (Portsmouth, NH: Heinemann, 1995).

32. Terence Ranger, 'The Invention of Tradition Revisited: The Case of Colonial Africa', in Terence Ranger and Olufemi Vaughan, eds, *Legitimacy and the State in Twentieth-Century Africa* (London: Macmillan, 1993); Benedict Anderson, *Imagined Communities: Reflections on the Origin and Spread of Nationalism* (London: Verso, 1983).

33. Igor Kopytoff, 'The Internal African Frontier: The Making of African Political Culture', in Igor Kopytoff, ed., *The African Frontier: The Reproduction of African Traditional Societies* (Bloomington, Ind.: Indiana University Press, 1987); Charles Ambler, *Kenyan Communities in the Age of Imperialism* (New Haven, Conn.: Yale University Press, 1988); Ronald Atkinson, *The Roots of Ethnicity: The Origins of the Acholi of Uganda before 1800* (Philadelphia: University of Pennsylvania Press, 1994); Allen and Barbara Isaacman, *Slavery and Beyond: The Making of Men and Chikunda Ethnic Identities in the Unstable World of South-Central Africa, 1750–1920* (Portsmouth, NH: Heinemann, 2004).

34. Bill Bravman, *Making Ethnic Ways: Communities and their Transformation in Taita, Kenya, 1800–1950* (Portsmouth, NH: Heinemann, 1998).

35. John Lonsdale, 'The Moral Economy of Mau Mau: Wealth, Poverty and Civic Virtue in Kikuyu Political Thought', in Bruce Berman and John Lonsdale, *Unhappy Valley: Conflict in Kenya and Africa* (London: James Currey, 1992).

36. T. C. McCaskie, *State and Society in Pre-Colonial Asante* (Cambridge: CUP, 1995); Holly Hanson, *Landed Obligation: The Practice of Power in Buganda* (Portsmouth, NH: Heinemann, 2003).

37. John Wright and Caroline Hamilton, 'The Making of the Amalala: Ethnicity, Ideology and Relations of Subordination in a Precolonial Context', *South African Historical Journal*, 22 (1990); Heike Schmidt, '(Re)Negotiating Marginality: The Maji Maji War and

its Aftermath in Southwestern Tanzania, ca.1905–1916', *International Journal of African Historical Studies*, 43 (2010).

38. Frederick Cooper, *Plantation Slavery on the East Coast of Africa* (New Haven, Conn.: Yale University Press, 1977), 200.

39. Michael Kenny, 'Mirror in the Forest: Dorobo Hunter-Gatherers as an Image of the Other', *Africa*, 51 (1981).

40. Steven Feierman, *Peasant Intellectuals: Anthropology and History in Tanzania* (Madison, Wis.: University of Wisconsin Press, 1990); Lonsdale, 'Wealth, Poverty and Civic Virtue', 344–6, 369–74.

41. John Janzen, *Lemba, 1650–1930: A Drum of Affliction in Africa and the New World* (New York: Garland, 1982); Neil Kodesh, *Beyond the Royal Gaze: Clanship and Public Healing in Buganda* (Charlottesville, Va.: University of Virginia Press, 2010).

42. Birgit Mayer, *Translating the Devil: Religion and Modernity among the Ewe in Ghana* (Edinburgh: EUP, 1999).

43. Peel, 'Cultural Work', 206–8; John Lonsdale, 'Contests of Time: Kikuyu Historiography Old and New', in Axel Harneit-Sievers, ed., *A Place in the World: New Local Historiographies from Africa and South Asia* (Leiden: Brill, 2002), 239–40.

44. F. Welbourn and B. A. Ogot, *A Place to Feel at Home: A Study of Two Independent Churches in Western Kenya* (London: OUP, 1966); Cynthia Hoehler-Fatton, *Women of Fire and Spirit: History, Faith and Gender in Roho Religion in Western Kenya* (New York: OUP, 1996).

45. Joel Cabrita, 'Isaiah Shembe's Theological Nationalism, 1920s–1935', *Journal of Southern African Studies*, 35 (2009).

46. Jan Vansina, *Paths in the Rainforests: Towards a History of Political Tradition in Equatorial Africa* (Madison, Wis.: Wisconsin University Press, 1990); David Schoenbrun, *A Green Place, A Good Place: Agrarian Change, Gender and Social Identity in the Great Lakes Region to the Fifteenth Century* (Portsmouth, NH: Heinemann, 1998); Elizabeth MacGonagle, *Crafting Identity in Zimbabwe and Mozambique* (Rochester, NY: University of Rochester Press, 2007).

47. Spear, 'Neo-Traditionalism', 6–7; Ranger, 'Invention of Tradition Revisited', 75–8.

48. Jomo Kenyatta, *Facing Mount Kenya* (London: Secker & Warburg, 1938), 251.

49. Derek Peterson and Giacoma Macola, eds, *Recasting the Past: History Writing and Political Work in Modern Africa* (Athens, O.: Ohio University Press, 2009).

50. Rosalind Shaw, *Memories of the Slave Trade: Ritual and the Historical Imagination in Sierra Leone* (Chicago: University of Chicago Press, 2002); Brian Peterson, 'History, Memory and the Legacy of Samori in Southern Mali, c. 1880–1898', *Journal of African History*, 49 (2008).

51. Pierre Nora, 'Between Memory and History: *Les Lieux de Memoire*', *Representations*, 26 (1989), 7–24; Mamadou Diouf, 'Between Ethnic Memories and Colonial Histories in Senegal: The MFDC and the Struggle for Independence in Casamance', in Berman et al., *Ethnicity and Democracy*.

52. Terence Ranger, *Voices from the Rocks: Nature, Culture and History in the Matapos Hills of Zimbabwe* (Oxford: James Currey, 1999).

53. Mathew Schoffeleers, ed., *Guardians of the Land: Essays on Central African Territorial Cults* (Gwelo: Mambo, 1979); Bengt Sundkler, *Zulu Zion* (London: Oxford, 1976); Hanson, *Landed Obligation*, ch. 7.

54. e.g. Berman et al., *Ethnicity and Democracy*, 1–21, 317–23; Patrick Chabal and Jean-Pascal Daloz, *Africa Works: Disorder as Political Instrument* (Oxford: James Currey, 1999), ch. 4.

55. John Lonsdale, 'Moral and Political Argument in Kenya', in Berman et al., *Ethnicity and Democracy*.
56. Mahmood Mamdani, *Citizen and Subject: Contemporary Africa and the Legacy of Late Colonialism* (Princeton: PUP, 1996), chs. 2–3; Spear, 'Neo-Traditionalism', 9; Frederick Cooper, *Africa since 1940: The Past of the Present* (Cambridge: CUP, 2002), chs. 3–4.
57. Lee Cronk, 'From True Dorobo to Mukogodo Maasai: Contested Ethnicity in Kenya', *Ethnology*, 41 (2002); Cheryl Walker, 'Claiming Community: Restitution on the Eastern Shores of Lake St. Lucia', in Benedict Carton, John Laband, and Jabulani Sithole, eds, *Zulu Identities: Being Zulu Past and Present* (New York: Columbia University Press, 2009).
58. Gabrielle Lynch, *I Say to You: Ethnic Politics and the Kalenjin in Kenya* (Chicago: University of Chicago Press, 2011); Peter Geschiere, *The Perils of Belonging: Autochthony, Citizenship, and Exclusion in Africa and Europe* (Chicago: University of Chicago Press, 2009).
59. Dorothy Hodgson, *Being Maasai, Becoming Indigenous: Postcolonial Politics in a Neoliberal World* (Bloomington, Ind.: Indiana University Press, 2011); Mathew Carotenuto and Katherine Luongo, '*Dala* or Diaspora? Obama and the Luo Community of Kenya', *African Affairs*, 108 (2009).
60. Caroline Hamilton, *Terrific Majesty: The Powers of Shaka Zulu and the Limits of Historical Invention* (Cambridge, Mass.: Harvard University Press, 1998); John and Jean Comaroff, *Ethnicity, Inc.* (Chicago: University of Chicago Press, 2009).

Bibliography

Berman, Bruce, Dickson Eyoh, and Will Kymlicka, eds, *Ethnicity and Democracy in Africa* (Oxford: James Currey, 2004).

De la Gorgendiere, Louise, Kenneth King, and Sarah Vaughan, eds, *Ethnicity in Africa: Roots, Meanings and Implications* (Edinburgh: Centre of African Studies, 1996).

Harneit-Sievers, Axel, ed., *A Place in the World: New Local Historiographies from Africa and South Asia* (Leiden: Brill, 2002).

Lentz, Carola, ' "Tribalism" and Ethnicity in Africa: A Review of Four Decades of Anglophone Research', *Cahiers des Sciences Humaines*, 31 (1995).

Lonsdale, John, 'States and Social Processes in Africa: A Historiographical Survey', *African Studies Review*, 24 (1981).

—— 'Moral Ethnicity and Political Tribalism', in Per Kaarsholm and Jan Hultin, eds, *Inventions and Boundaries: Historical Approaches to the Study of Ethnicity and Nationalism* (Roskilde: IDS Roskilde, 1994).

Ranger, Terence, 'The Invention of Tradition Revisited: The Case of Colonial Africa', in Terence Ranger and Olufemi Vaughan, eds, *Legitimacy and the State in Twentieth-Century Africa* (London: Macmillan, 1993).

Spear, Thomas, 'Neo-Traditionalism and the Limits of Invention in British Colonial Africa', *Journal of African History*, 44 (2003), 8–13.

Vail, Leroy, ed., *The Creation of Tribalism in Southern Africa* (London: James Currey, 1989).

Young, Crawford, 'Nationalism, Ethnicity and Class in Africa: A Retrospective', *Cahiers d'Études Africaines*, 23 (1986).

CHAPTER 6

WARFARE AND THE MILITARY

RICHARD REID

WAR: WHAT IS IT GOOD FOR?

THE subject of warfare and the military in African history is a daunting one. A vast topic, it stubbornly resists generalization, while students of organized violence across the continent must contend with seemingly endless regional and local variation, a myriad of typologies, and incomplete historiographical coverage, both temporal and spatial. There are also the prickly issues of popular image and dogged stereotype, which have obscured understanding of the role of war in Africa since the era of the Atlantic slave trade. Yet these challenges must be overcome, especially if we are to understand the topic over the *longue durée*. There is no distinctively 'African' way of war, or at least nothing akin to the much-vaunted 'Western' way of war in the history of the European world; but it is nonetheless possible to identify a number of broad themes as well as distinctively African experiences within particular regional and physical settings and thematic contexts. What is clear, above all, is that warfare and military organization have been of enormous significance in Africa's past, as they continue to be in the continent's present, and that war has been both the product and the driver of much economic, social, and political change. Key themes which have emerged in the literature on organized violence in Africa's deeper past include the struggle to maximize population and harness productive and reproductive labour; the struggle to domesticate hostile physical environments, and to seize control of—or at least gain access to—essential resources; and the role of external trades (including that in slaves) in driving forward new forms of violence and political organization, not least through the arrival of new technologies.

In terms of the modern era, there is enough evidence to suggest that the century between the 1790s and the 1890s might be considered something of a 'golden age' for African political development, albeit a markedly violent one. It was, however, development which was subverted and misunderstood by nineteenth-century Europeans, and another central concern of historians has been the nature and course of the various European invasions of Africa between the 1880s and the 1920s and the resultant wars of imperial violence. Whether we view the period as one of transition, or a turning point in the continent's military history, the era of colonial armies has attracted some interest. Yet a rather larger number of historians, political scientists, and anthropologists have concerned themselves with the decolonizing violence of liberation struggle between the 1950s and the 1980s and the prevalence of the military *coup d'état* for much of the same period. Meanwhile, more recent, post-Cold War and post-'9/11' violence—that involving 'militias' and 'warlords' and apparently crazed and alienated youth and their opportunistic and irreconcilable leaders—has given rise to something of a vibrant intellectual industry since the mid-1990s.

The study of war in contemporary Africa, then—like the incidence of war itself—has increased dramatically in recent years. From a trickle to a relative flood, in the course of the 1990s and 2000s ever more literature has been produced on everything from particular conflicts in Africa to general surveys or collections of essays on the nature of war in the continent. All this is striking, for it was not long ago that the study of war in Africa was very much a minority sport. Between the 1960s and the 1980s, research on the causes and nature of warfare was distinctly unfashionable. For many years scholars were chary of working on warfare, and clearly felt that to highlight the role of violence and the military in Africa's past was to risk association with despairing nineteenth-century missionary writings on the subject—a body of literature which had itself contributed to the cultural environment in which the actual 'scramble' had been possible. The generation of Africanists which took centre stage in the 1960s and 1970s was fundamentally anti-war and associated with the political left; against the backdrop of Vietnam, work on precolonial African warfare was scarce.[1] It was a matter of seeking more nuanced explanations for political malaise in socio-economic processes, nuance which, it seemed, was impossible to achieve through studies of war. Perhaps as important, the European conquest had apparently consigned Africa's earlier military history very firmly to the past—except of course in the minds of a later generation of African nationalists, who sought to link their struggles with those of the late nineteenth and early twentieth centuries.

On one level, of course, the positioning of African military studies outside the fashionable mainstream merely reflected that of military history more broadly. It was long regarded, in Europe as well as in the United States, with some suspicion and indeed contempt by the arbiters of good academic taste until at least the 1980s, since when the discipline has been rehabilitated somewhat—owing at least in part to some clever rebranding. But in the context of African studies, additionally, the tendency of a new generation of Africanists in the 1960s and 1970s was towards socio-economic history from below, denoting a shift away from 'great men' and the kind of politico-military history associated with an older generation. Conventionally defined 'military history'—at least until its reinvention as 'war studies'—was considered a wholly inappropriate means in pursuit of this particular historical end. However, contemporary war has proved impossible to ignore, simply because there has been so much of it. Much of this work signifies a relatively new, and welcome, tendency to regard African wars in ever more nuanced and sophisticated ways; but hardly any of it attempts to make connections between modern conflict and earlier, that is, precolonial, patterns of violence. In his introduction to an anthology of scholarship on precolonial warfare, John Lamphear observes that recent conflicts 'have generated a huge body of writing, greater in volume than the entire corpus of material on pre-colonial Africa'. The vast bulk of the twenty-two contributions to the anthology were published between 1971 and 1992; only three were written or published as recently as the mid- to late 1990s. Although he did not elaborate on the point—which was not, in any case, the purpose of the volume—Lamphear asserted that a 'basic contention of this volume is that pre-colonial conflict was not only important in its own right but was vital in shaping more recent conflicts: without an adequate understanding of previous military aspects, solutions to contemporary conflicts will remain elusive'.[2] This is an echo of the call, made more than thirty years before, by Bethwell Ogot, Ali Mazrui, and Godfrey Uzoigwe, for Africa's military past to be more seriously examined.[3] A handful of scholars over the years answered that call, but in truth it was largely ignored, and certainly in terms of linkages between precolonial and postcolonial eras, the investigation of what we can broadly term 'unfinished business'. Africa's deeper military history has been disconnected from its present.[4]

There is little doubt that at least part of the difficulty lies in the challenges of methodology and in the need to overcome some problematic and persistent mindsets in dealing with African violence—and indeed non-European violence more generally. Students of African war—especially precolonial—must tackle a series of stereotypes and images which have been perpetuated since the era of the slave trade in the seventeenth and eighteenth centuries, images which hardened along with racial attitudes in the nineteenth. In sum, African warfare was seen by European observers as the clearest manifestation of the continent's backwardness, barbarism, and savagery; Africans themselves were held to be wantonly violent and brutal, and little acquainted with what in Europe were regarded as the 'military arts'. Africa, rather, was populated by a multitude of perpetually warring tribes, pursuing their form of what became known in the early twentieth century as 'primitive war'—at once needlessly cruel, tactically and strategically limited, and engendering little of the change and development associated with 'civilized' warfare in Europe. One of the core justifications for the European conquest and partition of Africa in the late nineteenth century was the perceived need to impose a *pax colonia* on the continent, and to eradicate the ceaseless violence which characterized African life and culture.

The sources used for the reconstruction of the history of warfare in Africa can therefore be problematic. Often, we rely on the very European accounts which themselves exaggerated the recurrence of violence in African society, misunderstood the nature of that violence, and dismissed in any case the notion that Africans fought 'proper war' at all. Nonetheless, treated with caution, the descriptions by missionaries and travellers can yield a great deal of information, especially when used alongside African oral traditions and chronicles, and, in some areas, archaeological data. It remains the case that little is known about Africa's military past before the past thousand years or so—and even then, our knowledge is patchy, with early data confined to zones where surviving chronicles are especially detailed (the West African savanna, or the Ethiopian Highlands). Our understanding improves from the seventeenth century onwards, due to the increase in European sources which comes about through trading activity (especially in Atlantic Africa during the slave trade), exploration, and missionary work.

Even so, the fact remains that these same sources implanted in the Western consciousness a set of received wisdoms about the nature of African war which have proven remarkably resilient. Victorian interpretations, in particular, continue to taint modern understanding of African violence.[5] The causes of wars are apparently obscure and the search for them long since abandoned; the wars themselves seem interminable; nihilistic young savages dance menacingly across the pages of broadsheets and news magazines and across television screens, defying logic and modernity and indeed, it appears, humanity itself. Two closely related points are worth noting at this juncture. The first is that in the 1990s there was a tendency to see such violence as representative of a 'new barbarism', into which Africa—in some ahistorical, atavistic manner—had descended, or perhaps reverted to.[6] This was strikingly reminiscent of late nineteenth-and early twentieth-century writing on the nature of Africa's barbaric violence. The second is that a great deal of the interest in modern African war is driven by the search for solutions, not for deeper causes. While the message of Edward Luttwak's notable 1999 article on the inadvisability of 'premature peacekeeping' might be unpalatable to many, the fact remains that outside intervention has frequently proven unhelpful, and certainly intervention which lacks the appropriate level of historical understanding.[7] Countless human tragedies notwithstanding, it is clear that war has frequently been a constructive and developmental phenomenon in African history, and that the modern desire to suppress outbreaks of violence—while doubtless usually well intentioned—betrays a fundamental misapprehension about the role played by violence and militarism in human history more broadly, not just in Africa. Research needs to be carried out on the continent's deeper past if any meaningful level of understanding of modern events is to be achieved.

VIOLENCE IN THE DEEPER PAST

Information on much of the continent before the early second millennium AD is wholly lacking, and only by the middle of the second millennium do we begin to receive a clearer picture across Africa; even then, that picture can remain hazy and we rely on a great deal of intuition and speculation beyond Afro-European zones of interaction. One must look north of the forest for case studies of war in (relative) antiquity. The West African savanna and the Ethiopian Highlands, in particular, offer comparatively rich material and have been the focus of much scholarship in recent decades, albeit from somewhat different perspectives. The grand narrative of Axumite and Ethiopian history is punctuated by outbreaks of prolonged violence both righteous and devastating, and religious and ethnic conflict, all frequently played out through pitched battles and at

the command of celebrated leaders. Above all, it is the story of a political order—that of
Christian and Semitic highlanders—being hammered out, to paraphrase the historian
of Europe's Middle Ages R. A. Brown, on the anvil of war. Indeed, it is arguably the best
example of the process in sub-Saharan African history. A great deal of earlier scholarship privileged the Amhara and the Tigrinya in the tale of early Ethiopia's inexorable
rise against a host of enemies; the other great shapers of the region's history—the Oromo
and the Somali—would have their historiographical day rather later. In the meantime,
the Oromo in particular were, in the eyes of the Amhara, the 'barbarous hordes' *par
excellence*. The Oromo contribution to the Ethiopian way of war needs further examination; but the key point is that the Ethiopian story in the early modern era provides some
of the best material on military organization and the utility of war anywhere in Africa.

In the western savanna, the horse has been the target of much analysis concerned with
the role of cavalry alongside infantry in explaining the peculiar nature—the successes
and the failings—of such great empire-states as Ghana, Mali, Songhay, and Borno. The
ability of horses to function in this environmental zone gave the grasslands south of
the desert a very distinctive military history *vis-à-vis* the forest region. The experience
of expensive, horse-borne military aristocracies, and the state structures they strove
to create, possibly renders comparisons of this zone with the central Asian steppes, for
example, rather more profitable than any with the tsetse-infested tropics to the south. As
with the Ethiopian region, at any rate, the savanna zone offers a wealth of evidence on
the role of war and evolving military culture. Here, cavalry held firm as the pre-eminent
form of military organization until well into the nineteenth century, when the firearm
began to have an impact. This is noteworthy, considering that, at the battle of Tondibi of
1591 between Songhay and Morocco, guns had one of their earliest airings south of the
desert. But their impact was limited, in fact, beyond the initial shock of their appearance.

The vast Atlantic zone of western Africa, from Senegal to Angola, has received
more attention than any other comparable region in Africa. The reasons are not difficult to discern: an intense zone of interaction and observation between Europeans and
Africans, it is comparatively richly, if unevenly, documented from the sixteenth century
onwards, while the Atlantic slave trade itself meant military exchange and innovation,
and, in some places at least, a sharp increase in organized (and some disorganized)
violence. Students of war in the region in the precolonial era now have two fine surveys to hand—by Robert Smith and John Thornton—which remain standard works of
reference, including for those working on other parts of the continent.[8] Indeed, while
Smith was in many respects the pioneer, Thornton was able to produce one of the very
few genuinely *military* histories, drawing on his extensive knowledge of the Portuguese
sources to describe shifting tactical formations in West Central Africa in particular.
Few scholars have been able to match that level of detail or indeed develop the kind
of sophisticated analysis achieved by Thornton, who argued, notably, that the 'military
influence' dynamic was not all one-way traffic. The era of the slave trade itself has been
one of the key periods of interest, hardly surprisingly: Dahomey, Oyo, and Asante, in
particular, have inspired some remarkable work on the nature of warfare and the uses
of violence, as centralized states which were clearly to a greater or lesser extent rooted

in the external slave trade. Much of the debate centred—as essentially it did during the slave trade itself—on whether or to what extent slaves were merely the by-product of wars which these expansionist African states were waging *in any case*, or whether such states, imbued with ever more sophisticated militaristic cultures, were deliberately waging wars for the purpose of capturing slaves for export. In fact, both positions hold true, according to time and place; but it is clear enough, if it is possible to set aside the sheer human tragedy of the era, that the external slave trade frequently drove forward political innovation and led to some remarkably successful, in the loosest and most amoral sense of the term, political organization within the Atlantic zone. This was political dynamism, of course—as all successful military endeavour is—which was at the expense of a host of smaller, less centralized communities on whom the big exporters of slaves preyed. There was destruction and construction in West Central Africa, too. Kongo ripped itself apart in the course of the seventeenth century as warring factions favoured either ever-deeper involvement in the export trade or its rather more careful management. Elsewhere, new and violent societies sprang up. The Imbangala in Angola, notably, had a widespread impact, invading towards the coast from the interior in the course of the seventeenth century and introducing new forms of professional soldiery across the region.

The material culture and hardware of war has long been an interest of Africanists, from armour and the accoutrements of dress more generally, to weapons and fortifications, and what these tell us about tactical formations and organization, and changes in these. Naturally enough, the impact of firearms was a source of fascination early on, leading to a notable series of seminars on the subject at the School of Oriental and African Studies, London, between 1967 and 1970.[9] The upshot was that it is difficult to generalize: the impact of guns varied from place to place, although it *was* clear enough that with a handful of exceptions their impact was fairly minimal before the nineteenth century. African weaponry remained predominant until well into the nineteenth century, and this was clearly much better suited to the conditions of African warfare than imported firearms. Contrary to earlier interpretations, possession of supposedly superior technology was frequently irrelevant, and its role must be understood alongside a range of factors, including climate, environment, deployment, organization, and objective.

As Lamphear has observed, the tendency of older scholarship to focus on 'large imperial states...and on a few great captains' meant that work on African warfare was quickly out of step with the more fashionable 'history-from-below' approach being developed by the early 1980s.[10] Future research on violence in Africa's deeper past will need to take account of such long-term phenomena as environment and geography, climate and demography. War in early African history can only be understood in terms of the physical and demographic contexts within which it is played out: historical underpopulation, difficult terrain, and disease frontiers are only some of the elements which are relevant here. Historians need to consider the logistical challenges in the forest zone owing to lack of draft animals and wheeled transport, the limitations placed on violent state-building exercises, or the very nature of conflict itself—whether 'campaigning' or 'raiding' war, whether 'skulking' way of war or open battle. In sum, scholars need to assess the deeper socio-geographical dynamics at work, and over the longer term, when contemplating what war is for, and how military cultures develop. If this means that the resultant work becomes further removed from 'traditional' military history, then so much the better: war is a multidimensional phenomenon, and it demands a multidimensional approach.

CONFLICT AND CREATIVITY IN THE NINETEENTH CENTURY

There is much to be said for the interpretation of Africa's nineteenth century as something of a 'golden age' of political and cultural dynamism and creativity; it was an undeniably violent era, and in many respects a brutal and traumatic one, but also one in which a remarkable degree of ingenuity flourished, frequently pushed forwards by conflict and itself creating new forms of violence. Elsewhere I have argued that the nineteenth century witnessed a 'military revolution' in Africa.[11] The evidence is certainly impressive, and continent-wide—from Ngoni and Maasai age regimentation, to Nyoro and Yoruba organizational reforms, to jihadist armies and ideological violence, to new states and soldier-kings. The question remains, however, of what that putative revolution actually meant, and, perhaps more importantly, what it *means* for Africa today, as it is this aspect—namely the linking of the contemporary age with nineteenth-century processes—which has been most unfortunately neglected by practitioners in the field. There were new forms of warfare, new levels of professionalism, new structures of command and leadership, and a marked correlation between organized violence and new political and social forms.

In southern Africa, the Zulu under Shaka's remarkable leadership in many ways epitomize the process. Yet in recent years the focus has been not so much on what Shaka actually achieved, but more on the imagery surrounding him and what that imagery has meant to modern South Africa.[12] Even the *mfecane*, long a staple of southern African historiography, came under scrutiny, with questions asked about whether it actually happened at all—or at least in the way that it was supposed to have.[13] Consensus has since been reached that it did indeed happen, even if some earlier interpretations have been modified.[14] More broadly, southern Africa throws up important models of militarism—the Ndebele, the Bemba, and the Sotho all building more effective state structures and military organizations, increasingly underpinned by firearms—which were replicated across Eastern and Central Africa. Ngoni offshoots spread through the area of modern Malawi and Tanzania by the 1850s and 1860s, prompting a further militarization of state and society. As the Eastern African slave trade increased in the course of the nineteenth century, the Nyamwezi and the Yao underwent dramatic changes as traders and soldiers.[15] Among the former, Mirambo's new state of the 1870s and early 1880s was particularly impressive; it had its counterpart in Nyungu-ya-Mawe's Kimbu polity. These states harnessed a generation of aggressive, ambitious, and well-armed youth, the *ruga ruga*, who were alternately bandits and criminals, or young professional soldiers, according to circumstance and the individual observer. Alongside the *ruga ruga* there was militarization of the age-grade regimentation among the Maasai and Turkana, for example, notably similar in form to those of the Zulu.[16] In Katanga, Msiri established a similarly innovative state based on war and commerce, while Tippu Tip's trading-and-raiding 'empire' spread across the eastern Congo basin. All these political organisms shared a violent creativity, and their leaderships were defined by a dynamism which may have been based on diminishing returns—the slave and ivory trades—but which were no less remarkable for that. The focus in the 1960s and 1970s on such innovative state-builders as Shaka and Mirambo was very much in the context of Africa's new-found independence: surely these men were examples of the great captains beloved of nationalists everywhere and so common in European history. It has had unfortunate longer-term implications, however, for with postcolonial disillusion, combined with the shift away from the history of 'big men' and high politics, there was a remarkably swift evaporation of interest in these great leaders of the nineteenth century—except for Shaka, whose potent image, again, continued to enthral.

New military forms and violent innovations were in evidence elsewhere, too. In West Africa, there was the collapse of Oyo, overly dependent on the external slave trade, initiating almost a century of violent conflict between competing Yoruba city-states and warlords.[17] These commanded new armies of professional young soldiers not dissimilar to the *ruga ruga* of East Africa. Dahomey, meanwhile, one of the most successful 'illegal' exporters of slaves, was drawn east into these conflicts, preying on Yoruba communities. North of the forest, in the savanna zone, religious fervour drove the military revolution. Jihads had broken out in Futa Toro and Futa Jalon in the eighteenth century, but the nineteenth century witnessed some of the most remarkable instances of religious violence, leading to the creation of the Sokoto Caliphate and, later, the Tukolor state.[18] Sokoto made use of infantry, at first, and later cavalry; Tukolor was adopting guns in the 1850s, and firearms were finally making an impact on several centuries of cavalry dominance in the savanna region. Rejuvenated Islam across the region fuelled further military innovation as the century developed. Asante, meanwhile, periodically provoked British ire on the Gold Coast, but it proved itself a remarkably robust and successful state in balancing the needs of commerce with military endeavour.[19]

Asante and Dahomey had their roots in the seventeenth century, and their militarisms survived through the nineteenth century. There were other, long-established political traditions which reformed themselves in the nineteenth century, expanded their military horizons, and proved remarkably resilient. In Ethiopia, the first half of the century witnessed a cycle of inter-state warfare which only began to be addressed through an extraordinary reinvention of the Solomonic tradition. Emperors Tewodros, Yohannes, and Menelik embarked on a state-building exercise which was above all the institutionalization of violence and the rendering of that violence rather more efficient.[20] A highly effective indigenous imperialism, highland Ethiopia expanded southwards to incorporate fertile land. Ethiopia has been held up as an example of the 'defensive modernization' evident elsewhere in the continent, especially in North Africa, where the nominally Ottoman provinces and independent Morocco sought to reform their political and military structures in an attempt to ward off the looming European threat. The concept of defensive modernization is debatable; but increasingly guns under-pinned political power, as they did, too, in the kingdom of Bunyoro, where *Mukama* Kabalega instituted military reforms and established regiments of riflemen. These proved essential in the resurgence of Nyoro power. Yet the gun was rather less effec-tive in neighbouring Buganda, where it led to the corruption of military culture at the fractious political centre; but Buganda innovated in other ways, having created a fleet of canoes in its attempt to control Lake Victoria in commercial and military terms in the middle decades of the nineteenth century.[21] Nearby, Rwanda and Burundi held off from engagement with the encroaching outside world, but there is evidence here, too, of political consolidation through military means.[22]

In sum, the evidence points towards a multitude of state-building exercises driven by violence and engendered by military means, new professionalized military corps, and expanded military horizons in terms of culture, technology, and structure. War was driven by the desire to monopolize the benefits of long-distance commerce, and to incorporate local resources; in many societies it brought about social and economic stratification. Across the continent, war drove urbanization—even in eastern Africa, with a long history of dispersed settlement—and new forms of fortification. There were tactical innovations on so many battlefields, and the evidence suggests that everywhere war was being used as policy by other means.

For all these innovations, African states and societies found themselves unable to prevent the conquest of the continent in the last quarter of the nineteenth century. The so-called Scramble for Africa was in reality a multitude of aggressive if ill-planned incursions, and was a subject awarded great importance by a range of scholars in the 1960s and 1970s. For imperial historians, various parts of Africa were only local fron-tiers in a much larger project, and the 'small wars' of colonial expansion only of note either when they (briefly) held that project up, as at Khartoum or Isandlhwana, or when they demonstrated the technological and organizational and moral power of Europe in its pomp. Africanists, naturally, examined the violent encounter from the African side of the field of combat, and considered the reasons behind and nature of the doomed 'primary' resistance which was (so it was believed in the 1960s) followed by a wave of 'secondary' resistance in the 1890s and 1900s. The basic idea was that primary resistance involved defence of sovereignty, and after that was defeated, there was a new generation of more populist, often spiritual leaders which initiated a series of revolts across the continent, more offensive in nature. The Chimurenga in Southern Rhodesia, Maji Maji in German East Africa, the Red Shawls in Madagascar, Bambatha in South Africa: these uprisings and others supposedly exemplified the phenomenon. These were revolts which were also of great interest to nationalist politicians and scholars alike in the 1960s, as they were often interpreted as the first stirrings of modern territorial nationalisms, thus demonstrating linear continuity and progression from the late nineteenth century onwards.[23] The arguments constructed around imperial violence and counter-violence were accompanied by another key piece of received wisdom, namely that Africans either resisted—bravely, but tragically—or they did not, in which case they merely 'collaborated' with Europeans instead.

None of these interpretations allowed much room for nuance, and they were soon being revised, not least because disillusionment with the post-independence nationalist project threw new light on the nature of nationalism itself, while it was increasingly clear that there was more to the European Scramble than met the eye. It relied on African manpower, and was shaped as much by events on the ground as by grand plans being developed in European capitals. It is also clear that there was rarely a straight dichotomy between 'resistance' and 'collaboration'. A great many African states and societies did both, utilizing changing political circumstances to their own advantage. While the colonial order was built on the use of violence or the threat of it, it was very much the product of a vortex of interaction between European and African. Two further broad themes are worth noting, with implications for a 'Western' view of non-Western violence into the twentieth century. The first is the degree to which violence against Africans was racialized; the putative existence of savagery in African culture rendered violence against the 'native' necessary if progress was to be achieved. Second, the supposed total 'defeat' of African militaries hindered understanding of those military systems for decades to come; it seemed that they had been consigned to historical irrelevance. Events later in the twentieth century would prove that view to be a dangerously misguided one indeed.

Warriors in Moderninty

The African warrior in modernity has appeared in many guises, and the image has undergone a series of dramatic transformations between the early twentieth and the early twenty-first centuries. It is difficult to imagine a greater juxtaposition than that between the proud and loyal NCO of the King's African Rifles and the drug-crazed and brutalized child soldier of the Lord's Resistance Army; but this is the kind of range with which we are dealing in considering the man-at-arms in Africa's recent past. While some gloomily journalistic analyses in the late twentieth century might espy a brief period of colonial order and rectitude followed by traumatic collapse, a reversion to the senseless and brutal violence of some dimly perceived precolonial era, in truth the 'long' twentieth century has seen a continual Africanization of imported European military structures and traditions—at best a superficial imposition, in any event—and the resurgence of distinctively African military forms and behaviours in the spheres of the practice and culture of violence.

Just as the Scramble for Africa would hardly have been possible without the African manpower available to European armies, so the colonial order itself rested on locally recruited soldiers. The increasing interest in the colonial era—at the expense, indeed, of the deeper past—and the fashion for reconstructions of the colonial experience was also reflected in studies of the colonial military. While some studies were dedicated to the experience of African troops during the two world wars, especially the Second

World War, this was sporadic, and fairly niche. There was rather greater interest (again, reflecting the concerns of colonial historiography from the early 1980s onward) in the socio-cultural aspects of service in colonial uniform. Thus, work by Echenberg, Parsons, and Killingray and Clayton has been particularly important, for example.[24] There is further work to be done both on how military service interplayed with other aspects of socio-political life during the era of colonial rule, and—perhaps more urgently—its impact on the postcolony. It is clear, for example, that while service in colonial regiments in some territories might have laid the foundations for later national identities— Eritrea may be a case in point—this thesis is emphatically *not* borne out by studies of such unstable and coup-prone territories as Uganda or Nigeria.[25]

Then there was decolonizing violence, in which the armed African appeared as the anti-colonial insurgent; early examples included Algeria and Kenya. Such violence swept across a swathe of southern Africa, from Angola and Mozambique to Zimbabwe and South Africa. It was also a feature in the Horn of Africa, where the imperial Ethiopian government and its Marxist successor were beset by violent regionalisms and ethno-nationalisms. Meanwhile, the politicization of the barracks meant that the military *coup d'état* became common in the course of the 1960s and 1970s.[26] Army rule was welcome at first, both in a number of African states and among interested observers. Soon, however, it came to be regarded as both cause and symptom of the inherent instability of the African postcolonial order, and thus it fascinated a generation of political scientists. 'Legitimate' rebellions against colonial injustice and a politicized officer corps were one thing; but Africa's military affairs became all the more complex and the scene altogether darker as the 1970s progressed. Civil war ripped a number of countries apart—those in Sudan, Nigeria, and Congo were among the bitterest and the earliest—and although to some extent such violence was indeed a product of the failure of the postcolonial order, and thus an indictment of colonial rule itself, much of it was in fact rooted in the conflicts and revolutionary changes of the nineteenth century. Armed struggle took ever more complex forms. It has often been remarked upon that the one typology of war which was comparatively rare was the 'inter-state' kind, familiar in Europe from the seventeenth century onwards. This was an understandable observation in a Eurocentric world, but in fact it missed the point, for the states in question were largely irrelevant to the unfolding military revolution across the continent. Only on rare occasions were nation-states at war with one another—for example, Morocco and Algeria, Uganda and Tanzania, and, more recently, Eritrea and Ethiopia.

The study of guerrilla movements became a particular focus of scholarly interest, and a recent survey by Reno is an excellent introduction.[27] It is notable, however, that much of the most interesting work was done not by historians but by anthropologists and political scientists, many of whom spent extended periods in the field alongside their movements of choice and developed intimate knowledge of their workings. This 'bore-hole' approach was fruitful in many ways; it did, however, often suffer from a failure properly to historicize the violence itself. Nonetheless, historians owe colleagues in other disciplines a great debt in this respect. The same is true of anthropologists working on pastoral peoples, especially in East and North-East Africa, since the 1960s. What anthropological scholarship has sometimes lacked in terms of a temporal dimension, it makes up for in in-depth appreciation of particular ways of violence and the ecological and cultural frameworks within which that violence takes place. Even so, it is clear that the ideal approach is the anthropological-historical one, as exemplified by work done on the Maasai and the Oromo. It is essential that researchers, in exploring particular peoples for whom an earlier documentary record is lacking, do not describe an 'ever thus' scenario from the data gathered during their own fieldwork.

There has been a veritable explosion of writing on modern war. Ethnic and other anti-state insurgencies attracted much attention as the 1990s progressed: thus there were, again, studies of guerrilla movements and of various pastoral and other peripheral groups in arms against one another and larger, state-level actors.[28] Sudan, Sierra Leone, the East African Rift Valley, Liberia, and Congo have received due attention;[29] William Reno's study of 'warlordism' suggested new directions in the study of contemporary conflict;[30] and there were increasingly sophisticated and nuanced collections on the nature and interpretation of African wars.[31] The Horn in particular has attracted more than its fair share of comment and analysis, initially as a result of the Eritrean–Ethiopian war, and later with a concern for the regional repercussions of this mammoth clash.[32] In terms of the latter, the unfolding situation in Somalia remains largely the domain of journalists rather than scholars,[33] but work on Darfur proliferates.[34]

More generally, little attempt has been made to historicize contemporary conflict. In the early 1990s, it was believed that, with the ending of the Cold War, a host of conflagrations across the developing world might be extinguished. An interpretation of world history which was founded on arrogance of proverbial proportions, it was soon proved profoundly erroneous—although it took until September 2001 to bring home the reality. African warfare reminded observers of some vaguely defined primeval dark age; its apparently insoluble conflicts continued to spread, characterized by ever greater levels of shocking brutality. Well meaning but essentially uncomprehending external actors sought to bring warring parties to negotiating tables—often an altogether more complicated business than might have once been the case, as the parties themselves proliferated to a remarkable degree. The war in Darfur was a good example of this, but at least Darfur got talked about in high places, even if inaction was the outcome. Militias engaged in 'LICS' (low intensity conflicts) appeared in ever more bizarre guises, and pursued ever less lucid agendas. While journalists espied a 'new barbarism', scholars examined the collapse of states and considered the motivation behind such violence. Some thought in terms of greed, others of grievance; but in either case it was clear enough that basic poverty and lack of control over key resources was driving a great deal of conflict. What was generally missed in much of this, however, was that this was in many ways economic war which arguably dated to the early nineteenth century—when Africans were increasingly distanced from the benefits of global commerce and denied control over its operation. In a number of respects, it was the latest manifestation of an ongoing military revolution which can be dated, similarly, to the early nineteenth century. Part of the problem, again, has been that much of the work has been undertaken by anthropologists and political scientists rather than historians; for all the excellent work done by both of the former, historians need to start becoming involved in this work to provide a crucial—and frequently absent—temporal dimension.

One defining characteristic of much of the recent literature, then, has been the drive to rationalize the violence unfolding across parts of the continent, to identify and examine particularly salient causal dynamics: thus, ethnicity and *realpolitik* in the enormous conflict that unfolded across the Great Lakes and the eastern Democratic Republic of Congo in the 1990s and 2000s; youth and desperation in the West African forest; the fundamental weakness of the state itself,[35] and its replacement by the warlordism and privatized violence which stepped into the vacuum. In European history, war made states; in modern Africa, it appears to destroy them, but in fact states have commonly been forged through violence throughout Africa's deep past, even while it is clear that innovative alternatives to the war/statehood model proliferate. There were some suggestions, in fact, that West Africa in particular was witnessing something of a reversion on the part of various militias to nineteenth-century tactics and organization. Again, however, two broad questions remain. First, the issue needs to be addressed of whether this was 'old' or 'new' violence, of whether—or to what extent—current patterns of conflict can be considered the continuation of the military revolution begun in the nineteenth century. Although in the day-to-day detail, we encounter sometimes incomprehensible brutality, it may be that in the perennial search for comprehension we need to adjust the conceptual frameworks within which we consider such violence. Over the past two hundred years, Africans have often responded violently to the challenges confronting them; but that process has also been a remarkably creative one, and creativity itself breeds a certain instability. This leads to the second major issue, namely the assumption—implied or otherwise—that war is bad and must be stopped. It is wholly understandable, from a purely humanitarian perspective, that scholarship often reflects the interventionist and preventative agendas of government and non-governmental agencies alike. And it is no doubt desperately unpalatable to many well-meaning and 'right-minded' folk everywhere to suggest an alternative: that war, over the longer term, is not an inherently bad thing and indeed is frequently constructive. So it has proved in Europe, and in Africa in particular places and at particular times; but it is clear that in Africa it may yet have some way to run. Historians must play their part: war must be given a chance.

GIVING WAR A CHANCE: FUTURE DIRECTIONS

Our understanding of warfare and the military in Africa's past has come a long way since the 1960s. There is now a substantial body of literature, both empirical and theoretical, on various dimensions of violence and military organization in Africa's modern history. Studies of nineteenth-century violence and of the 'small wars' of the era of partition are plentiful—although now ageing somewhat, as interest has moved much more firmly into the twentieth century since the 1980s, with the result that some of the standard work on the nineteenth century is now forty years old or more. We now have a considerable corpus of work on the colonial soldier, on the military in African politics, and on anti-colonial insurgency. As for more recent violence, debate continues concerning the motives of disenchanted and apparently nihilistic militias, and our knowledge of such insurgencies becomes deeper and more detailed all the time, our appreciation of their structures and ideologies ever more sophisticated. It will be clear enough that interest in contemporary violence is likely to continue for the foreseeable future; where there is conflict, there are people to study it. However, for all our advances in comprehending particular aspects of African soldiery and warfare in recent decades, the foreshortening of Africa's past and the prevalence of presentist approaches, most clearly manifest in the steady decline of interest in the precolonial past, has hindered deeper comprehension. The role of warfare in African history over the long term still needs systematic examination, and it seems clear that future research will need to move in this direction. The nineteenth century, I would suggest, seems a good place to start; we need, in other words, to award the same level of historical sophistication to African violence as we do to 'Western' warfare, even in the face of the inevitable methodological challenges.

Several themes seem worthy of highlighting. Demography and environment, so important in their own right as sub-fields, have clearly been critical in shaping the patterns and nature of conflict in African history, and more attention needs to be paid to them. Long-term climate change and population movement, as well as population fluctuation, it may be safely assumed, have had an enormous impact on the direction and organization of violence: we have seen this in our own era, and more needs to be done with a view to understanding this in the deep past. Closely connected to these spheres, there is indubitably an intimate relationship between economic and military history. It is certainly a relationship which has lain at the heart of much European history, and while it should go without saying that we need not use Europe as a desirable paradigm, it is the case that European historiography has much to offer Africanists in their search for both answers and (perhaps more importantly) the right questions. While discussions about the role of external trade networks in promoting African violence have been ongoing for a long time, more needs to be done on the relationship between warfare and what we might call 'local' or 'internal' economic systems. In other words, war clearly has its own internal economic logic (and indeed illogic), and this needs to be further explored.

Bringing much of this together is the concept of the frontier in African history, which has real potential in terms of enabling us to think more productively about the provenance and nature of conflict. In a relatively land-rich continent, much violence has been linked to the continual fission and reformation which has characterized a great deal of African socio-political development. Migratory movements, often caused by violence, have led to regional rivalries which in turn spur on conflict. The conflict itself is played out across contested frontier zones, while those frontier zones themselves have been host to new socio-political formations, and ultimately new communities. The notion of the fertile frontier, therefore, needs to be understood as one of the central drivers of change in Africa's past, both violent and otherwise. In this connection, too, greater attention must be paid to the role of violence and militarism in the creation and sustenance of group cohesion and communal identities. 'Ethnicity' and 'identity' have in recent years been the target of much modern Africanist research—notably within an instrumentalist framework, whereby 'ethnicity' is regarded as a comparatively modern phenomenon which is manipulated by various parties in response to heightened competition for resources and access to power within the restricted space of the nation-state. This argument has been, in my view, quite dramatically overstated.[36] We need much more nuanced analysis of the evolution of group cohesion over the longer term and of the role played in that process by both the actual experience of violent conflict and the more abstract cultures of militarism which become so central to the group's view of itself and its place in a given region. In this context, in particular, the ongoing historiographical concern for colonial history and the colonial experience must be tempered; colonialism needs to take its place as merely part (and sometimes not an especially significant part) of a series of experiences which have gone into the 'making' of modern Africa. Again, to study the era of colonial rule in the kind of depth which we have seen in the last quarter of a century or more while neglecting the nineteenth century is to place so many carts before so many horses, and will continue to distort our understanding of the evolution of African violence over the last two centuries. Historians need to be aware, ultimately, of the pitfalls of solution-oriented agendas. We need to be cautious not to privilege such essentially presentist approaches at the expense of historical research. There has been too much focus on conflict resolution at the expense of understanding how they start, and the patterns and forms of organized violence over the long term. Too often wars are prolonged because ill-conceived and ultimately ineffectual 'peace deals' are put in place which do nothing but add new aspects to the conflict itself. In sum, war must be understood over the *longue durée*; and historians need to be aware that war, in Africa as elsewhere, can and has had 'constructive' outcomes as well as deleterious consequences.

Notes

1. J. Thornton, *Warfare in Atlantic Africa 1500–1800* (London: UCL Press, 1999), 3; R. J. Reid, *War in Pre-Colonial Eastern Africa: The Patterns and Meanings of State-Level Conflict in the Nineteenth Century* (Oxford: James Currey, 2007), 9–10; J. Lamphear, 'Introduction', in J. Lamphear, ed., *African Military History* (Aldershot: Ashgate, 2007), pp. xii–xiii.
2. Lamphear, 'Introduction', p. xiv.
3. See B. A. Ogot, ed., *War and Society in Africa* (London: Frank Cass, 1972); A. A. Mazrui, ed., *The Warrior Tradition in Modern Africa* (Leiden: Brill, 1977); G. N. Uzoigwe, 'Pre-Colonial Military Studies in Africa', *Journal of Modern African Studies*, 13/3 (1975); G. N. Uzoigwe, 'The Warrior and the State in Pre-Colonial Africa', in Mazrui, *Warrior Tradition*.
4. I have attempted to address this in *Warfare in African History* (New York: CUP, 2012).
5. R. J. Reid, 'Revisiting Primitive War: Perceptions of Violence and Race in History', *War and Society*, 26/2 (2007); P. Porter, *Military Orientalism: Eastern War through Western Eyes* (London: Hurst, 2009).
6. R. Kaplan, 'The Coming Anarchy', *Atlantic Monthly* (Feb. 1994).

7. E. N. Luttwak, 'Give War a Chance', *Foreign Affairs* (July–Aug. 1999).

8. R. S. Smith, *Warfare and Diplomacy in Pre-Colonial West Africa* (London: James Currey, 2nd edn, 1989); Thornton, *Atlantic Africa*.

9. These led to two special issues of the *Journal of African History* dedicated to the topic, namely 12/2 and 12/4 (1971).

10. Lamphear, 'Introduction', p. xii.

11. Reid, *Warfare in African History*, ch. 5; also 'The Fragile Revolution: Rethinking War and Development in Africa's Violent Nineteenth Century', in E. Akyeampong, R. H. Bates, N. Nunn, and J. Robinson, eds, *African Development in Historical Perspective* (CUP, forthcoming).

12. C. Hamilton, *Terrific Majesty: The Powers of Shaka Zulu and the Limits of Historical Invention* (Cape Town: David Philip, 1998); D. Wylie, *Myth of Iron: Shaka in History* (Scottsville: University of KwaZulu-Natal Press, 2006).

13. J. Cobbing, 'The Mfecane as Alibi: Thoughts on Dithakong and Mbolompo', *Journal of African History*, 29/3 (1988). The standard account is J. D. Omer Cooper, *The Zulu Aftermath: A Nineteenth-Century Revolution in Bantu Africa* (London: Longman, 1966).

14. E. Eldredge, 'Sources of Conflict in Southern Africa, c.1800–30: The "Mfecane" Reconsidered', *Journal of African History*, 33/1 (1992); C. Hamilton, ' "The Character and Objects of Chaka": A Reconsideration of the Making of Shaka as "Mfecane" Motor', *Journal of African History*, 33/1 (1992). More recently, see J. Wright, 'Turbulent Times: Political Transformations in the North and East, 1760s–1830s', in C. Hamilton, Bernard M. Mbenga, and Robert Ross, eds, *The Cambridge History of South Africa, i. From Earliest Times to 1885* (Cambridge: CUP, 2010).

15. N. R. Bennett, *Mirambo of Tanzania, 1840?–1884* (New York: OUP, 1971); E. A. Alpers, *Ivory and Slaves in East Central Africa* (London: Heinemann, 1975); Reid, *War in Pre-Colonial Eastern Africa*.

16. J. Lamphear, 'Brothers in Arms: Military Aspects of East African Age-Class Systems in Historical Perspective', in E. Kurimoto and S. Simonse, eds, *Conflict, Age and Power in North East Africa* (Oxford: James Currey, 1998); T. Spear and R. Waller, eds, *Being Maasai: Ethnicity and Identity in East Africa* (London: James Currey, 1993).

17. R. S. Smith and J. F. Ade Ajayi, *Yoruba Warfare in the Nineteenth Century* (Cambridge: CUP, 1971).

18. R. Roberts, *Warriors, Merchants and Slaves: The State and the Economy in the Middle Niger Valley, 1700–1914* (Stanford, Calif.: Stanford University Press, 1987); J. P. Smaldone, *Warfare in the Sokoto Caliphate: Historical and Sociological Perspectives* (Cambridge: CUP, 1977).

19. I. Wilks, *Asante in the Nineteenth Century: The Structure and Evolution of a Political Order* (Cambridge: CUP, 1975).

20. R. Caulk, 'Firearms and Princely Power in Ethiopia in the Nineteenth Century', *Journal of African History*, 13/4 (1972); S. Rubenson, *The Survival of Ethiopian Independence* (London: Heinemann, 1976); R. J. Reid, *Frontiers of Violence in Northeast Africa: Genealogies of Conflict since c.1800* (Oxford: OUP, 2011).

21. R. J. Reid, *Political Power in Pre-Colonial Buganda: Economy, Society and Warfare in the Nineteenth Century* (Oxford: James Currey, 2002).

22. J. Vansina, *L'Evolution du Royaume Rwanda des origines àa 1900* (Brussels: Belgian Royal Colonial Institute, 1962); J. Vansina, *Antecedents to Modern Rwanda: The Nyiginya Kingdom* (Madison, Wis.: University of Wisconsin Press, 2004).

23. T. O. Ranger, 'Connexions between "Primary Resistance" Movements and Modern Mass Nationalism in East and Central Africa', *Journal of African History*, 9/3–4 (1968).

24. M. Echenberg, *Colonial Conscripts: The* Tirailleurs Senegalais *in French West Africa, 1857–1960* (London: James Currey, 1991); A. Clayton and D. Killingray, *Khaki and Blue: Military and Police in British Colonial Africa* (Athens, O.: Ohio University Center for International Studies, 1989); T. H. Parsons, *The African Rank-and-File: Social Implications of Colonial Military Service in the King's African Rifles, 1902–1964* (Oxford: James Currey, 1999); D. Killingray, *Fighting for Britain: African Soldiers in the Second World War* (Rochester: James Currey, 2010).

25. Uoldelul Chelati, 'Colonialism and the Construction of National Identities: The Case of Eritrea', *Journal of Eastern African Studies*, 1/2 (2007); J. M. Lee, *African Armies and Civil Order* (London: Chatto & Windus, 1969).

26. S. Decalo, *Coups and Army Rule in Africa: Motivations and Constraints* (New Haven, Conn.: Yale University Press, 1990).

27. W. Reno, *Warfare in Independent Africa* (New York: CUP, 2011).

28. Spear and Waller, *Being Maasai*; K. Fukui and J. Markakis, eds, *Ethnicity and Conflict in the Horn of Africa* (London: James Currey, 1994); C. Clapham, ed., *African Guerrillas* (Oxford: James Currey, 1998); Kurimoto and Simonse, *Conflict, Age and Power*. Clapham's volume on guerrilla warfare has recently been followed up by M. Boas and K. C. Dunn, eds, *African Guerrillas: Raging Against the Machine* (Boulder, Colo.: Lynne Rienner, 2007).

29. D. Johnson, *The Root Causes of Sudan's Civil Wars* (Oxford: James Currey, 2003); P. Richards, *Fighting for the Rain Forest: War, Youth and Resources in Sierra Leone* (Oxford: James Currey, 1996); K. Mkutu, *Guns and Governance: Pastoralist Conflict and Small Arms in the North Rift Valley* (Oxford: James Currey, 2008); D. Keen, *Conflict and Collusion in Sierra Leone* (Oxford: James Currey, 2005); S. Ellis, *The Mask of Anarchy: The Destruction of Liberia and the Religious Dimension of an African Civil War* (London: Hurst, 2nd edn, 2007); T. Turner, *The Congo Wars: Conflict, Myth, and Reality* (New York: Zed Books, 2007); G. Prunier, *From Genocide to Continental War: The Congolese Conflict and the Crisis of Contemporary Africa* (London: Hurst, 2009).

30. W. Reno, *Warlord Politics and African States* (Boulder, Colo.: Lynne Rienner, 1998).

31. P. Richards, ed., *No Peace, No War: An Anthropology of Contemporary Armed Conflicts* (Oxford: James Currey, 2005); P. Kaarsholm, ed., *Violence, Political Culture and Development in Africa* (Oxford: James Currey, 2006); B. Derman, R. Odgaard, and E. Sjaastad, eds, *Conflicts over Land and Water in Africa* (Oxford: James Currey, 2007); A. Nhema and P. Tiyembe Zeleza, eds, *The Roots of African Conflicts: The Causes and Costs* (Oxford: James Currey, 2008); A. Nhema and P. Tiyembe Zeleza, eds, *The Resolution of African Conflicts: The Management of Conflict Resolution and Post-Conflict Reconstruction* (Oxford: James Currey, 2008); T. M. Ali and R. O. Matthews, eds, *Civil Wars in Africa: Roots and Resolution* (Montreal: McGill-Queen's University Press, 1999).

32. e.g. P. Gilkes and M. Plaut, *War in the Horn: The Conflict between Eritrea and Ethiopia* (London: Royal Institute of International Affairs, 1999); Tekeste Negash and K. Tronvoll, *Brothers at War: Making Sense of the Eritrean-Ethiopian War* (Oxford: James Currey, 2000); S. Healy, *Lost Opportunities in the Horn of Africa: How Conflicts Connect and Peace Agreements Unravel* (London: Royal Institute of International Affairs, 2008).

33. Work by Ken Menkhaus is an excellent exception: see e.g. 'The Crisis in Somalia: Tragedy in Five Acts', *African Affairs*, 106/424 (2007).

34. Among the best is A. de Waal, ed., *War in Darfur and the Search for Peace* (London: Justice Africa/Global Equity Initiative, Harvard University, 2007); and a recent historical account, M. W. Daly, *Darfur's Sorrow: A History of Destruction and Genocide* (Cambridge: CUP, 2007).

35. e.g. R. H. Bates, *When Things Fell Apart: State Failure in Late-Century Africa* (Cambridge: CUP, 2008); J.-F. Bayart, *The State in Africa: The Politics of the Belly* (Cambridge: Polity, 2009).

36. See also P. Chabal and J.-P. Daloz, *Africa Works: Disorder as Political Instrument* (Oxford: James Currey, 1999), 56 ff.

BIBLIOGRAPHY

Clapham, C., ed., *African Guerrillas* (Oxford: James Currey, 1998).

Decalo, S., *Coups and Army Rule in Africa: Motivations and Constraints* (New Haven, Conn.: Yale University Press, 1990).

Echenberg, M., *Colonial Conscripts: The* Tirailleurs Senegalais *in French West Africa 1857–1960* (London: James Currey, 1991).

Kaarsholm, P., ed., *Violence, Political Culture and Development in Africa* (Oxford: James Currey, 2006).

Lamphear, J., ed., *African Military History* (Aldershot: Ashgate, 2007).

Mazrui, A. A., ed., *The Warrior Tradition in Modern Africa* (Leiden: Brill, 1977).

Nhema, A., and P. Tiyembe Zeleza, eds, *The Roots of African Conflicts: The Causes and Costs* (Oxford: James Currey, 2008).

Nhema, A., and P. Tiyembe Zeleza, eds, *The Resolution of African Conflicts: The Management of Conflict Resolution and Post-Conflict Reconstruction* (Oxford: James Currey, 2008).

Ogot, B. A., ed., *War and Society in Africa* (London: Frank Cass, 1972).

Parsons, T., *The African Rank-and-File: Social Implications of Colonial Military Service in the King's African Rifles, 1902–1964* (Oxford: James Currey, 1999).

Reid, R. J., *Warfare in African History* (New York: CUP, 2012).

Smith, R. S., *Warfare and Diplomacy in Pre-Colonial West Africa* (London: James Currey, 1989).

Thornton, J., *Warfare in Atlantic Africa 1500–1800* (London: UCL Press, 1999).

CHAPTER 7

....

THE AFRICAN DIASPORA

....

JOHN PARKER

No one theme in the study of the African past is currently undergoing such rapid development as that of the relationship between the continent and its diaspora. Less than two decades ago, the diaspora remained largely peripheral to the main thrust of African historical research. For those wrestling with the task of reconstructing the historical complexities of particular societies, states, or regions, it was challenging enough to apply any resulting insights on an Africa-wide basis let alone to extend their analytical gaze beyond the shores of the continent itself. While there was a broad recognition of the role played by African slaves and their descendants in the construction of New World societies, the history of those societies was seen either to be the business of Americanists, Latin Americanists, and Caribbeanists, or to be part of an older, somewhat outmoded tradition of 'vindicationist' pan-Africanism. Likewise, historians of the Americas, even those directly concerned with the experience of African Americans, tended to stick to their side of the Atlantic. As in the Indian Ocean world, where colonial frontiers, nation-states, and then the rise of academic area studies also conspired to obstruct the study of regional comparisons and connections, the focus of African and of African American history remained firmly on their respective hemispheres.

The transformation of this bifurcated historiography since the 1990s has been dramatic. Shifting intellectual trends that accompanied the end of the short twentieth century and the emergence of the neo-liberal world order have impacted broadly upon our view of the African past, but the newly awakened interest in transnational cultural and economic flows, migration, hybridity, nodes of cosmopolitanism, and in the networks connecting the local to the global have had a particular impact upon the diasporic communities that, by their very definition, were forged by these processes and occupied these spaces. The result, in the words of one of a number of synoptic reassessments of the field to appear around the turn of the millennium, has been a 'tidal wave of scholarly, funding, and political interest in the African diaspora'.[1] Yet to extend the metaphor, tidal waves submerge and obscure before receding to reveal a reconfigured landscape—and such has been the case with the outpouring of research on diasporic Africa. The vast geographical and temporal expanse of the field, newly liberated from an established focus on the Anglophone North Atlantic to include Latin America, the Indian

Ocean, the Middle East, and the Mediterranean—plus, it should be noted, the African continent itself—seemed to lend itself to the production of large collected volumes, the individual components of which were endlessly fascinating but from which it was often difficult to discern clear theoretical contours.[2] The past decade, however, has seen those theoretical lineaments take shape. A recent wave of scholarship by historians and historically minded anthropologists has begun to deepen and in some cases radically to transform our understanding of the creation of diasporic cultures and identities, in particular in two of the great outposts of Africa in the Americas, Brazil and Cuba. If the literature on the Middle East and the Indian Ocean has not yet reached anything like this level of production or sophistication, then a challenging agenda has been set by ongoing advances in the study of the black Atlantic.

DEFINITIONS

This is not to argue that a unity of approach has descended over the field. Indeed, differences remain over even the most fundamental definition of what exactly constitutes 'the African diaspora'. Although the term began to gain wide currency only after 1965, when it was introduced by George Shepperson and Joseph E. Harris at a conference of African historians in Tanzania, the idea of a unified black history can be traced to pioneering African American scholars such as W. E. B. Du Bois and Carter G. Woodson and further back to nineteenth-century redemptionist discourse in the United States.[3] As generally understood, the African diaspora is given to refer to those tens of millions of Africans and their descendants forcibly removed from the continent by the various branches of the slave trade, united by a consciousness of a common origin, by the struggle to secure freedom in the face of chattel slavery and subsequent forms of injustice, and, as in the case of other diasporic communities, by ongoing efforts to maintain or to forge links with the African homeland. Problems arise, however, when one begins historically to unpick this package of criteria—as has been the case with recent efforts to extend the study of the African diaspora into the Middle East and Indian Ocean, where the majority of African-descended peoples appear to have little in the way of consciousness of a common origin or sense of ongoing connectedness to Africa.[4]

Such issues arise even with regard to the recognized diasporic heartlands of the Americas. What George Reid Andrews calls Afro-Latin America has both a geographical and a more strictly diasporic meaning: on the one hand, entire multiracial societies based on the historical experience of African slavery; and on the other, African-descended populations of those societies only.[5] But even within the latter, active participation in forms of black cultural expression have varied greatly over space and time. Many Afro-Latin Americans, as Andrews shows, chose to struggle for freedom and citizenship by transcending racial categories through participation in independence armies, Liberal parties, and labour unions, while others did so through the active mobilization of Africanity in maroon communities, mutual aid societies, religious movements, and civil rights movements. Does this make the former necessarily less 'diasporic' than the latter? If reconnection with Africa—'reversing sail', as Michael Gomez puts it—is *the* key attribute of diaspora, does this make Du Bois, who for most of his career actively opposed the return of African Americans to Africa, therefore less representative of diasporic experience than Marcus Garvey? A key breakthrough in terms of historical reconstruction has been that such positions could change over time—in both directions. Just as Du Bois in his twilight years 're-embraced' Africa by migrating to independent Ghana, so too could diasporic cultural forms take on pan-racial characteristics. Such has been the case with religions such as Candomblé in Brazil, once seen as the absolute benchmark for the survival of African tradition in the Americas. In a recent analysis, to which we will return, Stefania Capone questions the uncritical use of the term 'Afro-Brazilian' with regard to Candomblé and other religious movements, arguing that they 'cannot be considered merely as expressions of "Black Brazil," as some authors suggest, because they crossed the color line a long time ago'.[6]

PIONEERS

Some of the most searching recent work on the African diaspora has sought to cast a new light on the intellectual genealogy of the field itself. While this is well enough known with regard to early forms of pan-Africanist thought and scholarship in the United States, the emergence of the study of black cultures in Latin America is only now beginning to be explored. The broad context uniting both halves of the hemisphere was a shared historical trajectory of the nineteenth-century struggle for emancipation from slavery, giving way from the 1880s to an era of dashed hopes and renewed racial oppression, and followed in turn by an afflorescence and valorization of black culture from the 1920s. In Latin America, as in the United States, it was the middle period of renewed repression that provided the impetus, in the opening years of the twentieth century, for the first scholarly engagement with black culture. Two key pioneering figures were the Cuban Fernando Ortiz (1881–1969) and the Brazilian Raymundo Nina Rodrigues (1862–1906). Both turned their attention to African religious practices in, respectively, Havana and Salvador da Bahia, and both, in line with the evolutionary and positivist paradigms of the day, regarded such practices as manifestations of primitiveness and as impediments to the achievement of Cuban and of Brazilian modernity. Ortiz's investigations into the criminal psychology of Havana's ex-slave underclass were prompted by elite fears of African witchcraft, in particular the alleged ritual killing of a white child by black 'wizards', resulting in his landmark 1906 publication *Los negros brujos*, 'The black witches'. Meanwhile, Rodrigues's research into Candomblé, first published in French in 1900 as *L'animisme fétichiste des nègres de Bahia*, was also mobilized by a ruling elite increasingly anxious about the dangerous allure that African culture held for impressionable white inhabitants of Brazil's rapidly growing urban centres.[7]

These initially hostile treatments would, however, be superseded by a more sympathetic engagement with and, in the case of Ortiz, active sponsorship of African cultures. Crucially, pioneering scholars and other local intellectuals can now be seen to have played a key role in the historical evolution of the religions themselves. Rodrigues's subsequent publications were critical of police persecution and drew heavily on information provided by his guide through the world of Afro-Bahian religion, Martiniano Eliseu do Bonfim. A leading diviner of the newly formed Gantois temple (*terreiro*) of the Nagô, or Yoruba, 'nation' of Candomblé, Bonfim would emerge as the dominant figure in the religion in the first half of the twentieth century and, in the words of Capone, as the 'coauthor of the theory of Nagô superiority'.[8] Ortiz too would have a decisive impact upon the affirmation of Africanity in Cuba. By the interwar period, he had transformed himself from a critic into a champion of the various branches of Afro-Cuban religion: La Regla de Ocha (or Santería), Regla de Congo (or Palo Monte), and the once-demonized Abakuá—associated with the *brujería* panic of the early republic. In 1936, he founded the Sociedad de Estudios Afrocubanos, two years later staged the first public concerts of Santería music and dance, and by the 1940s, influenced by the early writings of Melville Herskovits, began to develop his theories of 'transculturation' and syncretism: all key moments in the national embrace of black culture under the banner of 'Afrocubanismo'.[9] By this time, Rodrigues's intellectual heirs Arthur Ramos and Edison Carneiro were also taking up the cause of local African culture. Carneiro was instrumental in staging in 1937 the inaugural Afro-Brazilian Congress and, together with Martiniano Eliseu do Bonfim and the equally famous Mãe Aninha of the Axé Opô Afonjá *terreiro*, in championing the supposed African purity of Nagô Candomblé.

We will return to the theoretical implications of these pioneering Latin American scholarly interventions. What must be noted here is the role played by Melville and Francis Herskovits in first applying such early readings of African religious forms on a hemispheric scale. By the mid-1930s, the Herskovitses had conducted ethnographic fieldwork in maroon communities in Suriname, in rural Haiti, and in Dahomey in West Africa; this research was synthesized in the definitive statement on the survival of African cultures in the Americas, Melville's 1941 *The Myth of the Negro Past*. As is well known, this thesis stood in sharp contrast to that of the sociologist E. Franklin Frazier, who argued instead that the link with an African past was ruptured by the brutal experiences of the Middle Passage and plantation slavery, giving rise—particularly in North America—to a new African *American* or 'Negro' identity. That the famous Herskovits–Frazier debate continues today to be cited as the historiographical or ethnographical starting-point in the introductions to any number of scholarly works attests to its continuing relevance to our understanding of the African diaspora. Indeed, the tension between the polarities of continuity on the one hand and rupture on the other remains, with only some modification, central to the field. As Richard Price, a leading protagonist in this debate, has recently pointed out, the main historical question for most scholars of the diaspora remains a simple one: how did enslaved Africans became African Americans?[10]

Two parallel developments on either side of the Atlantic would, from the 1960s, refashion the approach to this fundamental question: the emergence of a fully fledged African history and the refinement of the original Herskovits–Frazier debate with the formulation of the theory of New World creolization. It is easy to overlook the fact that the study of black cultures in the Americas was pioneered before that of the history of the African continent itself. For those pioneering ethnographers concerned with the Africanness of slave and ex-slave populations in the New World, therefore, it was difficult for 'Africa' to be anything *but* a vague primordial baseline from which to chart subsequent change. C. L. R. James's monumental 1938 study of the Haitian revolution, *The Black Jacobins*, had certainly demonstrated the agency of African slaves in the era of Atlantic revolutions and the overthrow of New World slavery.[11] Yet with so much of the African past a blank, it would take some time for the new historiography to develop enough critical mass fully to engage with older questions of pan-African and diasporic identity.

CONTINUITY VERSUS CREOLIZATION

When that re-engagement came, it would take the form of an assault on the theory of creolization that had emerged from the Herskovits–Frazier debate of the 1930s. A critique both of the Herskovitsian notion of New World African 'survivals' and the Frazerian notion of complete rupture with the past, the creolization model instead argued for the creative rebuilding of cultures and identities by Africans from a diversity of ethnic and linguistic backgrounds. This process was likely already to have been under way in the holds of ships during the Middle Passage, but it was seen to typify the experience of slave plantations and of runaway maroon communities. Indeed, as set out by Sidney Mintz and Richard Price in their 1976 *The Birth of African-American Culture*, it was maroon communities—particularly those of the Suriname forest studied by Price—that emerged as the *locus classicus* of creolization.[12] Whereas Herskovits had presumed that the Saramaka maroons of Suriname were, due to their deep-rural isolation and successful flight from slave plantations, amongst the most purely 'African' of New World populations, Price has sought to demonstrate the opposite: that those very factors provided the conditions for the early reconstruction of a thoroughly creolized culture.[13]

If the explanatory power of the creolization thesis lay in the particular conditions of the Americas, then a new generation of Africanist scholars sought to bring Africa itself back into the picture. A seminal work often cited as signalling the starting-point of this paradigm shift was Robert Farris Thompson's 1983 *Flash of the Spirit*.[14] Art history rather than history, *Flash of the Spirit* traced the continuity in form between Yoruba, Kongo, Dahomean, Mande, and Ejagham visual cultures, on the one hand, and their respective artistic traditions in the Americas, on the other. Although the Yoruba and Dahomean impact upon the visual and philosophical cultures of Brazilian Candomblé, Cuban Santería, and Haitian Vodou was already well attested, that of the Kongo and related Bantu-speaking peoples of West Central Africa and Angola was far less so. In this respect, Thompson's analysis can be seen to have begun the process of reinscribing the enormous contribution made to the black civilizations of the Americas by Africans from West Central Africa—the region that provided more slaves that any other across the four centuries of the trans-Atlantic trade. It also explored the connection, first established by Ortiz, between the Ekpe leopard society of the Ejagham and other Cross River peoples of south-east Nigeria and the Abakuá of Havana. As the leading art historian of Santería David Brown observes, *Flash of the Spirit* was key to the 'revived struggle against the "myth of the Negro past"...which had lost steam until the Civil Rights and black consciousness era'.[15]

In its focus on a range of distinctive artistic traditions, Thompson's book pointed not only towards an analytical shift from creolization back to African origins but also to an emerging concern with trans-Atlantic continuity in particular ethnic and regional identities. This concern was advanced by the appearance ten years later of another key work, John Thornton's *Africa and the Africans in the Making of the Atlantic World*.[16] Some aspects of Thornton's analysis proved controversial: in particular, his portrayal of Africans as active agents rather than primarily as enslaved victims in the opening centuries of the Atlantic commerce and his identification of three broad 'cultural zones', corresponding to the coasts of Upper Guinea, of Lower Guinea, and of West Central Africa from Loango to Angola, that would in turn shape the African impact upon the Americas. Yet the renewed emphasis on black cultural resilience coupled with an ever-increasing understanding of the shifting composition of human cargoes across time and space gave rise to a wave of studies by both Africanist and Americanist historians arguing for the transplantation and survival of particular African ethnicities and cultures in particular American locations.[17] Often highly critical of creolization—one protagonist in the debate recently warned of the 'chilling effect on studies of African ethnicities in the Americas' of Mintz and Price's model—this ongoing analytical trend seeks firmly to establish an Africa-centred perspective to the diaspora.[18]

Yet the notion of new, creolized identities forged in the crucible of slavery and in the ensuing struggle for freedom remained central to a quite distinct historiographical trajectory concerned less with African survivals than with pan-African cultural production and political action. Stretching back to Du Bois, C. L. R. James, and other pioneering scholar-activists, this tradition was reinvigorated by Paul Gilroy's *The Black Atlantic*.[19] Appearing soon after Thornton's *Africa and the Africans*, Gilroy's influential work explored the role of black thinkers, artists, and activists in the creation of a 'counterculture of modernity' in the Atlantic world. Rather than viewing the diaspora essentially in terms of its historical connection to Africa, Gilroy portrays a more fluid, transformative culture shaped by the efforts to overcome racial exclusion from Enlightenment modernity and citizenship. Although rather narrowly focused on Anglophone North America, the Caribbean, and Britain, *The Black Atlantic* served to inject a new theoretical rigour into the study of diasporic political action and expression ranging from the role of seamen and other transient actors in the age of revolution, to nineteenth-century print culture and vindicationist thought, and on to Garveyism, the *négritude* movement, and other forms of twentieth-century nationalism.[20] For some of those concerned with reconstructing the history of what is referred to as 'black internationalism', the insistence on an Africa-centric diaspora is problematic. According to one survey of this literature, 'shifting the discussion from an African-centred approach to questions of black consciousness to the globality of the diaspora-in-the-making allows for a rethinking of how we view Africa and the world, and opens up new avenues for writing a world history from below'.[21] Indeed, the black internationalist approach in its more radical and self-styled insurgent manifestations regards the emergence of African area studies as a deliberate act of Cold War-era 'intellectual segregation' which effectively 'separated and isolated Africa' from the diaspora.[22]

We can see, then, the lineaments of the field of diaspora studies as they have evolved since the foundational Herskovits-Frazier debate and the subsequent emergence of an Africanist historiography. On the one hand, we have the creolization model, a refinement of the Frazier thesis focused on transformations in the New World and associated with ethnographers working on black populations in the Americas. On the other, we have the Herskovitsian argument for the transplantation and resilience of African cultures and identities, developed largely by historians who argue, like Paul Lovejoy, that the study of the diaspora must 'look outwards from Africa'.[23] Running somewhat parallel to this fundamental divide—and in uneasy dialogue with it—is a more radical black internationalist take on the global history of African consciousness and struggle. Yet these approaches are polarities: opposite ends of an analytical spectrum that has, over the past decade, begun to be reconfigured by new theoretical insights, methodologies, and sources. Gilroy's emphasis on circum-Atlantic exchange in *The Black Atlantic* was an early indication of such change. As Richard Price writes of the history of the Saramaka maroons of Suriname, but speaking of the entire field: 'There was ample evidence of both striking African continuities and immense New World creativity'.[24] It is time, he argues, to lay aside the hoary 'creolization versus continuities' debate.

African American Religions

It is perhaps unsurprising that the most notable advances towards this reconciliation have come in the study of those long-recognized strongholds of Africanity in the Americas: the Afro-Cuban, Afro-Brazilian, and, to a somewhat lesser extent, Afro-Haitian religions. As the subtitle of a recent volume surveying these developments suggests, the aim has been to move 'beyond the search for origins' in the study of 'Afro-Atlantic' religions.[25] If the imperative to advance beyond the often single-minded search for African origins reflects a critique of that literature, then the description of such religions as Afro-*Atlantic* rather than Afro-American points to a growing recognition that historical change was not simply confined to creolization in the western hemisphere. We have already seen how emergent scholarly research was part and parcel of this complex history of circum-Atlantic exchanges. Far from being disinterested observers, figures such as Fernando Ortiz and Raymundo Nina Rodrigues in the early twentieth century through to Roger Bastide and Pierre Verger in the 1950s–1960s were thoroughly entangled with the evolution of the pantheons and the practice of Afro-Cuban and Afro-Brazilian religions. What is emerging, in short, is a narrative of transformation rather than one of conservation—with a growing awareness of the agency and creativity of local practitioners and their interlocutors in the invention of tradition.

Stephan Palmié in *Wizards and Scientists* and David Brown in *Santería Enthroned* trace this process with regard to Cuba. While the former is primarily concerned with relocating received notions of Afro-Cuban 'tradition' in the historical construction of Cuban and Atlantic modernity, the latter explores, from the perspectives of art history and visual anthropology, transformations in the institutional, ritual, and iconographic systems of Santería. Both acknowledge the impact of Thompson's canonical *Flash of the Spirit*, but also critique its identification of trans-Atlantic stylistic continuities that serve, misleadingly, to reinforce Ortiz's original ethnic classification of the major Afro-Cuban cults: Regla de Ocha with Yoruba (or, in Cuba, Lucumí); Palo Monte with Kongo/Angola; Regla Arará with the Fon and other Gbe-speakers of the Slave Coast; and Abakuá with the Cross Rivers. Rather than representing bastions of respective cultural purity transplanted wholesale from Africa, these ritual idioms are shown to have emerged from the fusion in the nineteenth century of mutual-aid societies and African ethnic formulations into the *cabildos de nación*. First taking shape in the Havana Bay port town of Regla and mobilizing the reinvented values and iconography of both African and European kingship, these 'miniature neo-African monarchies' would from the 1870s serve as niches for the systemization of esoteric knowledge focused on the dual pantheons of African deities and Catholic saints.[26] As the era of state persecution was succeeded in the 1930s by that of *Afrocubanismo*, the *casa-templos* of Lucumí and its rival ritual registers, Brown and Palmié demonstrate, continued to evolve through the strategic intervention of individual reformers.

A similarly convincing reinterpretation of African American religion has been advanced with regard to Brazil. J. Lorand Matory's *Black Atlantic Religion* and the recent translation of Stefania Capone's *Searching for Africa in Brazil* are the two most significant English-language revisionist works on the history of Candomblé, although it should be noted that Brazilian scholars writing in Portuguese such as Yvonne Maggie and Beatriz Góis Dantas began in the 1970s and 1980s to interrogate the notion of 'Nagô purity'.[27] Beyond Brazil, however, it is Matory who has had the greatest impact on the renewed critique of primordial origins. *Black Atlantic Religion* opens by challenging the established assumption—in an already much-quoted *aperçu*—'that homelands are to their diasporas as the past is to the present'.[28] At the core of the history of Candomblé, Matory argues, is the process of exchange by which diasporas also create their own homelands. The historical context for this dialectical relationship is the uniquely elaborated set of linkages between the coastal urban centres of Brazil and West Africa, beginning with the deportation of rebellious slaves from Salvador to Lagos and other Slave Coast ports in the 1830s and continuing later in the century with the development of commercial ties—including the importation into Brazil of prestigious ritual goods for use by the emergent Candomblé *terreiros*—by 'Jeje' merchants such as Joaquim d'Almeida and Joaquim Francisco Devodê Branco. The result, according to Matory, was an 'Afro-Atlantic diasporic Jeje nation' which straddled Brazil and the Gbe-speaking region of West Africa and which arose in the former alongside similarly reconstructed Nagô (i.e. Yoruba) and Congo (or Angola) cultural identities.[29]

It would be the Nagô 'nation' and its great deities or *orixás*, however, that in the course of the twentieth century would come to dominate Candomblé culture in the city that Mãe Aninha in the 1940s dubbed the 'black Rome', Salvador da Bahia. This was in part due to events in West Africa: internecine conflict in Yorubaland triggered by the collapse of the Oyo Empire in the early nineteenth century fuelled a massive influx of Yoruba-speaking captives into Salvador and the state of Bahia, where by the 1840s up to 69 per cent of slaves were Nagôs. Yet demographic weight alone is not enough to explain the well-documented process of *anagônização*, the 'Yorubaization' of Candomblé. Matory, Capone, and Parés instead point to the strategic assertion of the greater 'African purity' of the Nagô *terreiros* by their leading practitioners, local intellectuals, and scholarly interlocutors. The contingent historical context for this project, as in Cuba, was the shift from state persecution to the valorization of African culture, beginning in Brazil during the regime of the populist president Getúlio Vargas in the 1930s and continuing until Candomblé's official recognition as a legitimate religion—and an integral part of Brazil's patrimony—in the 1970s. Not only did this involve positive efforts by figures such as Mãe Aninha and her successor Mãe Senhora to enhance the prestige of the Ilê Axé Opô Afonjá *terreiro* through the creative adaptation of what Parés calls an 'imagined African orthodoxy', it also saw a struggle against those rival elements of ritual culture deemed to be unorthodox or degenerate: the worship of *caboclos*, the spirits of Brazilian Indians; the leadership of male priests; homosexuality; and *feitiçaria* or 'black magic'. All of these 'adulterated' practices were identified with the Kongo/Angola nation and with the ritual movements associated with it: Macumba and, following its emergence in Rio de Janeiro in the 1930s, Umbanda.

By the era of renewed African sovereignty in the 1960s, the affirmation of the Africanity of Nagô Candomblé in Brazil and of Lucumí Santería in Cuba was feeding into an Atlantic-wide Yoruba cultural renaissance. The international visibility of Yoruba *òrìsà/orichas/orixás* grew with the migration of many Santería practitioners to New York City following the Cuban Revolution, with the rise of the so-called Black American Yoruba Movement and the foundation of Oyotunji village in North Carolina in the early 1970s, and with the inaugural meeting in 1981 of the International Congress of Orisha Tradition and Culture in Ilé-Ifé in Nigeria. In terms of both transnational identity and of scholarship, the Yoruba diaspora has taken shape in a way unmatched by any other ethnic constituency of the global African population, with claims now being made for *òrìsà* devotion as a world religion.[30] Three of the pantheon of Yoruba deities, Ogun, Osun, and Sango, now have scholarly volumes dedicated to their spread, including important historical analysis not just on transformations and encounters in the New World but on those in precolonial West Africa as well.[31] Indeed, scholarly imperatives have in some cases mirrored the contest over the cultural content of Afro-Brazilian religion, with historians seeking to restore a balanced perspective by redirecting attention to the neglected role of West Central Africans, who comprised a clear majority of slaves transported to Brazil.[32]

The third great crucible of African-derived religion in the Americas is, of course, Haiti. Due perhaps in part to the difficulties in conducting sustained research in the strife-torn Caribbean nation in recent decades, the literature on Vodou has been slower to develop than that for Candomblé and Santería.[33] Yet a similar historical trajectory may be discerned, beginning with the emergence of distinct neo-African 'nations', Rada and Petwo, associated with the deities or *lwa* of Dahomey and of Kongo/Angola, respectively. As in Brazil and Cuba, Haiti then experienced a shift from the demonization and criminalization of Vodou practice to its valorization by elite practitioners, local intellectuals associated with the Haitian Bureau d'Ethnologie, and foreign writers such as Maya Deren and Alfred Métraux (although clerical assaults on Vodou continued into the 1940s and reappeared in the 1980s), culminating in the attempted co-option of the religion by the *noiriste* Duvalier regime.[34] Finally, we see the growing internationalization of Vodou with the migration of Haitians to New York City and elsewhere.[35] More work 'beyond the search for origins' in Haiti remains to be done, but recent research accords with that on Brazil and Cuba, Richman concluding that, for Vodou practitioners, 'Guinea' serves as a constructed 'cosmographic metaphor' rather than a primordial place of origin.[36]

Despite its critics, then, it is clear that the creolization model has much analytical life in it yet. All of these major works on the 'classic' Afro-Atlantic religions draw on its theoretical premise, while presenting a serious challenge to those African-centric scholars more concerned with unbroken and unmediated lines of continuity and origin.[37] Their findings also chime with recent research on lesser-known African American cultures, such as the Garifuna or 'Black Caribs' of Honduras and, now, New York City. Paul Johnson shows how Africa, historically *not* a reference on the Honduran coast, has now emerged at the centre of migrant identity: the Garifuna have effectively set about 'joining the religious African diaspora' in the Bronx.[38] The creation of a 'secondary diaspora' through recent transnational urban migration is also the experience of the Saramaka population of Cayenne in French Guyane, one of whom is the subject of Richard Price's *Travels with Tooy*. Price's extraordinary account of the world of the ritual specialist and healer Tooy serves further to reinforce his long-held argument for New World creativity and reinvention. For Tooy today—and, Price argues, for the Saramaka nation-building project as early as the mid-eighteenth century—'Africa and its remembered place names—Komantí, Luángu, Dáome—give each of the powers associated with them, whenever they made the Atlantic crossing, a special cachet of authority and strength.'[39] Particular bundles of rites were and are learnt by an individual 'not because he *was* a Dahomean or Gold Coaster or Kongo "by origin" or by "ethnic identity," but because of particular meanings and uses these rites had taken in contemporary Saramaka life'.[40] Such ritual bundles also included powers encountered in the Suriname forest—like Tooy's personal favourites, the Wénti sea gods—the equivalent of the indigenous *caboclo* spirits, the worship of which has proved so controversial in Brazil. Deep-rural maroon communities like the Saramaka were, of course, very different from those of the cosmopolitan port cities of the Atlantic littoral, and there is no evidence that they engaged in the sort of active dialogue with African homelands portrayed by Matory and others. Yet Price, summing up the revisionist literature, concludes that 'the development of New World cults that claim a specific African origin (or have been identified by anthropologists as having one)...ultimately make sense to practitioners (and now to anthropologists) only as part of distinctive New World systems of oppositions'.[41]

ATLANTIC CREOLES

A second revisionist strand, one also shaped by the more assertive insertion of Africa itself into Atlantic history, seeks to broaden the established understanding of the dynamics of creolization. An important starting-point for this literature was the development by the historian of North American slavery Ira Berlin of the idea of the 'Atlantic creole': typically a member of the earliest, so-called Charter Generation of slaves for whom contact with cosmopolitan Atlantic cultures gave rise to a hybrid identity often *before* arrival in the Americas. This idea has been taken up by Linda Heywood and John Thornton, who suggest that slave cultures in English and Dutch colonies in the first half of the seventeenth century were fashioned by such creoles originating from the West Central African regions of Kongo and Angola. Long-standing engagement in the Christian kingdom of Kongo and in the Portuguese colony of Angola with a raft of European-influenced traits, Heywood and Thornton argue, led to this already creolized culture being transplanted to the Americas, where it would provide a model for later waves of captives, mainly from West Africa, of what Berlin calls the Plantation Generations.[42] Building upon Thornton's earlier argument for the existence in coastal West and West Central Africa of three broad cultural zones, this analysis not only restates the case for the impact on the Americas of these shared cultures, but begins to show how their emergence in Africa itself was also shaped by circum-Atlantic historical change.

It might be argued that the evidence is not enough conclusively to demonstrate either the adherence of captives from Kongo, Angola, and their respective slaving hinterlands to creole lifeways, or the impact of those lifeways on subsequent slave cultures in the Americas. Indeed, Heywood and Thornton concede to Berlin's contention that in some areas of North America, the Charter Generation was overwhelmed by the 'African' Plantation Generation and can only conclude that the homogeneity of the former 'may well have allowed them...to have a substantial impact on the formation of African American culture'.[43] Yet the emergent Atlantic creole thesis does contribute to a more fundamental imperative: that Africa itself must be considered not just as the origin of the diaspora, but as an integral and dynamic part of its history. Matory's reconstruction of the dialogue that shaped both Nagô culture in Brazil and Yoruba culture in Nigeria points in this direction. More recent works such as James Sweet's biography of the eighteenth-century healer Domingos Álvares, who traversed the Atlantic world from Dahomey to Brazil to Portugal, serve to deepen the temporal depth of these entangled histories.[44] The first imperial project that Álvares was drawn into was not that of the Portuguese in Brazil but that of Dahomey on the Slave Coast of West Africa, which sought to hijack local ancestors and *vodun* in the cause of military expansion and rule. New sources mobilized by Sweet such as Portuguese Inquisition records not only allow for the reconstruction of African healing and ritual practice in Brazil, but may also shed light on the evolution of these discourses in Africa itself.

Innovative areas of historical inquiry, both geographic and thematic, are of course dependent not just on new methodological insights but upon the identification and imaginative mobilization of new sources. Three decades after Philip Curtin's ground-breaking census of the Atlantic slave trade acted as a catalyst for the reawakening of diaspora studies, the appearance in 1999 of *The Trans-Atlantic Slave Trade: A Database on CD-ROM* has provided the potential for far more precise analysis of the shifting composition of slave populations in the Americas across space and time. One area where this enhanced data has had an impact is in the recent 'black rice' debate; that is, whether the development of rice cultivation in the Carolina lowlands and other regions of the Americas represented the transfer from Upper Guinea of, in the words of Judith Carney, 'an entire cultural system', on the one hand, or of a new hybrid agricultural system, on the other.[45] African survivals versus creolization may be a hoary debate, but salient it remains—and here we see it extending into the new subfield of agricultural history and Africa's botanical legacy in the Atlantic world.[46] Yet the challenge historians face in recovering individual diasporic voices from often over-generalized 'cultural systems' on both sides of the Atlantic is considerable. A real constraint is the dearth of detailed biographical material: the recently recovered autobiography of Mahommah Gardo Baquaqua is a notable exception, although his account represents the only known narrative by an African enslaved in Brazil.[47]

THE ISLAMIC AND INDIAN OCEAN WORLDS

Such source constraints present just one of a number of challenges for historians of the African diaspora in the Mediterranean, the Middle East, and the Indian Ocean. Given the likelihood that a similar number of Africans were sold into slavery via the trans-Saharan and Indian Ocean trades as those who crossed the Atlantic, the belated extension of diaspora studies into the world of Islam is striking. 'For every gallon of ink that has been spilt on the trans-Atlantic slave trade and its consequences', John Hunwick writes, 'only one very small drop has been spilt on the study of the forced migration of black Africans into the Mediterranean world of Islam and the broader question of slavery within Muslim societies'.[48] Hunwick identifies three main reasons for this: the hesitation on the part of Arab and other Muslim scholars to research the history of slavery; the lack of an active diasporic consciousness on the part of individuals and communities with African ancestry; and linguistic and other constraints facing Western historians in traversing the boundary between African and Middle Eastern studies.[49] There are in turn a host of reasons for the second of these factors, ranging from the role of Islam as the key marker of identity and the concomitant reluctance to acknowledge roots in 'unbelief' to the high proportion of female slaves and the predominance of domestic rather than productive labour. Yet how these factors unfolded in different Muslim societies and shaped the experience of slavery and emancipation is only now beginning to be explored.

Islamic ideologies and processes of assimilation, however, are not the whole story. In those locations where black communities did continue to cohere around African culture, religion emerges as the most obvious form of social solidarity. Spirit possession and healing cults such as *bori*, *zar*, and *tumbura* proved resilient in North Africa and elsewhere, often taking on hybrid forms in dialogue with local Sufi practices and with pre-Islamic beliefs. *Bori* congregations are well attested in early nineteenth-century Tunis, for example, while a hundred years later in Algiers, 'communities of former slaves still organized themselves around religious cult houses that were based on areas of origin: Bornu, Katsina, Zazzau, Bambara, Songhai and Tombo (Dogon)'.[50] Yet it remains unclear whether these ritual communities, with their intriguing similarities to the ethnic nations of Brazil, Cuba, and Haiti, are best characterized as African retentions or creolized inventions. With regard to similar networks of lodges in Istanbul and Izmir, Ehud Toledano suggests the latter, arguing for a process of 'Ottoman cultural creolization' that may have begun not in Anatolia but in the creative fusion of *zar* and *bori* in the Nile valley.[51] As the historiography of Afro-Atlantic cultures moves beyond the search for origins, the nascent study of Africans in the Islamic world would benefit from the further application of its evolving debates.

The idea of the Indian Ocean as a space of connectivity or, as Sugata Bose would have it, an 'interregional arena', is as highly developed as that for the Atlantic.[52] Just as Atlantic history was once limited to its northern reaches, however, that of the Indian Ocean remains dominated by its eponymous subcontinent. There will, of course, never be a 'black Indian Ocean': there is no denying that Africa's contribution to its economy and culture was marginal compared with the Atlantic world, where three out of four of all migrants to the Americas before 1820 were African. Yet the challenge remains to reconstruct the dynamics of diasporic Africa in the Indian Ocean world and by doing so to transform its western rim from a vague periphery into a more integrated part of that interconnected space.[53] As Campbell points out, 'the history of Africans in Asia is overwhelmingly one of integration in which they have shed their African identity'.[54] That may be the case, but recent efforts to promote the Africanness of the so-called Sidis of Gujarat and elsewhere in India by scholars and local intellectuals might be compared with the role of the pioneering Afro-Latin Americanists in the forging of reimagined communities.[55]

Where the study of diasporic culture does have great potential is the islands of the western Indian Ocean, particularly Madagascar and the Mascarene islands of Mauritius and Réunion. Here, rising demand for labour from the eighteenth century and, in the Mascarenes, the development of European plantation colonies led to large concentrations of slaves both from the African mainland and from Madagascar itself. In his recent *Ocean of Letters*, Pier M. Larson reconstructs a history of Malagasy language and identity in a diaspora of slaves, ex-slaves, Christian exiles, and travellers stretching from the 'Big Island' to the Comoros, the Mascarenes, and on to the Cape Colony of South Africa.[56] Larson's innovative work is a suitable point at which to conclude, as not only is it firmly situated in the established debate over creolization in the Americas, it points to ways in which emerging insights from the Indian Ocean might further advance our understanding of the Atlantic. Challenging the established view that Malagasy communities sought—and achieved—rapid cultural integration, Larson mobilizes vernacular texts to demonstrate the importance of a distinct diasporic identity until at least the mid-nineteenth century. Treading a path between the classic models of creolization and African survivals, he argues that, far from being a zero-sum game, hybrid Francophone *créolité* and vernacular Afro-Malagasy identity were closely imbricated with each other. Such inter-oceanic scholarly dialogue augers well for the ongoing advance of this most expansive and in many ways most challenging and disparate theme in the African past.

NOTES

1. Judith Byfield, 'Introduction: Rethinking the African Diaspora', *African Studies Review*, 43/1 (2000), 1; see too Michael A. Gomez, *Reversing Sail: A History of the African Diaspora* (New York: CUP, 2005).

2. See e.g. Isidore Okpewho, Carole Boyce Davies, and Ali A. Mazrui, eds, *The African Diaspora: African Origins and New World Identities* (Bloomington, Ind.: Indiana University Press, 1999).

3. See Kim D. Butler, 'Clio and the Griot: The African Diaspora in the Discipline of History', in Tejumola Olaniyan and James H. Sweet, eds, *The African Diaspora and the Disciplines* (Bloomington, Ind.: Indiana University Press, 2010), 23–5.

4. See Gwyn Campbell, 'Slave Trades and the Indian Ocean World', in John C. Hawley, ed., *India in Africa, Africa in India: Indian Ocean Cosmopolitanisms* (Bloomington, Ind.: Indiana University Press, 2008).

5. George Reid Andrews, *Afro-Latin America, 1800–2000* (New York: OUP, 2004), 6–9.

6. Stefania Capone, *Searching for Africa in Brazil: Power and Tradition in Candomblé* (Durham, NC: Duke University Press, 2010), p. x.

7. Stephan Palmié, *Wizards and Scientists: Explorations in Afro-Cuban Modernity and Tradition* (Durham, NC: Duke University Press, 2002); J. Lorand Matory, *Black Atlantic Religion: Tradition, Transnationalism, and Matriarchy in the Afro-Brazilian Candomblé* (Princeton: PUP, 2005); Capone, *Searching for Africa*, 173–81.

8. Capone, *Searching for Africa*, 178.

9. See Robin D. Moore, *Nationalizing Blackness: Afrocubanismo and Artistic Revolution in Havana, 1920–1940* (Pittsburgh, Pa.: University of Pittsburgh Press, 1997).

10. Richard Price, *Travels with Tooy: History, Memory, and the African American Imagination* (Chicago: University of Chicago Press, 2008), 287.

11. C. L. R. James, *The Black Jacobins: Toussaint L'Ouverture and the San Domingo Revolution* (London: Allison & Busby, 2nd edn, 1980).

12. Sidney W. Mintz and Richard Price, *The Birth of African-American Culture: An Anthropological Perspective* (Boston: Beacon Press, 2nd edn, 1992); for a recent reflection

on the debate, see Richard Price, 'African Diaspora and Anthropology', in Olaniyan and Sweet, *African Diaspora*.

13. Price, *Travels with Tooy*, 307.

14. Robert Farris Thompson, *Flash of the Spirit: African and Afro-American Art and Philosophy* (New York: Vintage Books, 1984).

15. David H. Brown, *Santería Enthroned: Art, Ritual, and Innovation in an Afro-Cuban Religion* (Chicago: University of Chicago Press, 2003), 6. For a superb collection of Thompson's writing on black culture, see Robert Farris Thompson, *Aesthetic of the Cool: Afro-Atlantic Art and Music* (Pittsburgh, Pa.: Periscope Publishing, 2011).

16. John Thornton, *Africa and the Africans in the Making of the Atlantic World, 1400–1680* (Cambridge: CUP, 1992).

17. See e.g. Michael A. Gomez, *Exchanging our Country Marks: The Transformation of African Identities in the Colonial and Antebellum South* (Chapel Hill, NC: University of North Carolina Press, 1998); Paul E. Lovejoy, ed., *Identity in the Shadow of Slavery* (London: Continuum, 2000); Paul E. Lovejoy and David V. Trotman, eds, *Trans-Atlantic Dimensions of Ethnicity in the African Diaspora* (London: Continuum, 2003).

18. Gwendolyn Midlo Hall, *Slavery and African Ethnicities in the Americas: Restoring the Links* (Chapel Hill, NC: University of North Carolina Press, 2005), 49–50.

19. Paul Gilroy, *The Black Atlantic: Modernity and Double Consciousness* (Cambridge, Mass.: Harvard University Press, 1993).

20. See e.g. Peter Linebaugh and Marcus Rediker, *The Many-Headed Hydra: Sailors, Slaves, Commoners, and the Hidden History of the Revolutionary Atlantic* (London: Verso, 2000); James Sidbury, *Becoming African in America: Race and Nation in the Early Black Atlantic* (New York: OUP, 2007); Jane G. Landers, *Atlantic Creoles in the Age of Revolutions* (Cambridge, Mass.: Harvard University Press, 2010).

21. Tiffany Ruby Patterson and Robin D. G. Kelly, 'Unfinished Migrations: Reflections on the African Diaspora and the Making of the Modern World', *African Studies Review*, 43/1 (2000), 26.

22. Michael O. West and William G. Martin, 'Contours of the Black International', in Michael O. West, William G. Martin, and Fanon Che Wilkins, eds, *From Toussaint to Tupac: The Black International since the Age of Revolution* (Chapel Hill, NC: University of North Carolina Press, 2009), 2–3.

23. Paul E. Lovejoy, 'Identifying Enslaved Africans in the Diaspora', in Lovejoy, *Identity in the Shadow of Slavery*, 1.

24. Price, *Travels with Tooy*, 298.

25. Stephan Palmié, ed., *Africas of the Americas: Beyond the Search for Origins in the Study of Afro-Atlantic Religions* (Leiden: Brill, 2008).

26. Brown, *Santería Enthroned*, 35; on Abuaká, see too Stephan Palmié, 'Ecué's Atlantic: An Essay in Methodology', in Palmié, *Africas of the Americas*.

27. The latter's important 1988 work is now available in English translation: Beatriz Góis Dantas, *Nagô Grandma and White Papa: Candomblé and the Creation of Afro-Brazilian Identity* (Chapel Hill, NC: University of North Carolina Press, 2009); see too Luis Nicolau Parés, 'The "Nagôization" Process in Bahian Candomblé', in Toyin Falola and Matt D. Childs, eds, *The Yoruba Diaspora in the Atlantic World* (Bloomington, Ind.: Indiana University Press, 2004); Luis Nicolau Parés, 'Xangô in Afro-Brazilian Religion: "Aristocracy" and "Syncretic" Interactions', in Joel E. Tishken, Tóyìn Fálolá, and Akíntúndé Akínyemí, eds, *Sàngó in Africa and the African Diaspora* (Bloomington, Ind.: Indiana University Press, 2009).

28. Matory, *Black Atlantic Religion*, 3.

29. Matory, *Black Atlantic Religion*, 94–109. On these reverse migrations back to Africa, see José C. Curto and Paul E. Lovejoy, eds, *Enslaving Connections: Changing Cultures of Africa and Brazil during the Era of Slavery* (Amherst, Mass.: Humanity Books, 2004).

30. See Jacob K. Olupona and Terry Ray, eds, *Òrìsà Devotion as World Religion: The Globalization of Yorùbá Religious Culture* (Madison, Wis.: University of Wisconsin Press, 2008).

31. Sandra T. Barnes, ed., *Africa's Ogun: Old World and New* (Bloomington, Ind.: Indiana University Press, 2nd edn, 1997); Joseph M. Murphy and Mei-Mei Sanford, eds, *Òsun across the Waters: A Yoruba Goddess in Africa and the Americas* (Bloomington, Ind.: Indiana University Press, 2001); Tishken et al., *Sàngó*; see too, for its focus on a fourth great òrìsà, Exu, Capone, *Searching for Africa*.

32. See e.g. Linda M. Heywood, ed., *Central Africans and Cultural Transformations in the American Diaspora* (Cambridge: CUP, 2002).

33. But see Donald J. Cosentino, ed., *Sacred Arts of Haitian Vodou* (Los Angeles: UCLA Fowler Museum, 1995).

34. For an important recent work, see Kate Ramsey, *The Spirits and the Law: Vodou and Power in Haiti* (Chicago: University of Chicago Press, 2011).

35. On the last of these processes, see Karen McCarthy Brown, *Mama Lola: A Vodou Priestess in New York* (Berkeley, Calif.: University of California Press, 1991), and Karen E. Richman, *Migration and Vodou* (Gainsville, Fla.: University Press of Florida, 2005).

36. Richman, *Migration and Vodou*, 186.

37. For a recent example of this tendency, which presents a very different picture of Abakuá in Cuba to that of Palmié, see Ivor J. Miller, *Voice of the Leopard: African Secret Societies and Cuba* (Jackson, Miss.: University Press of Mississippi, 2009).

38. Paul Christopher Johnson, 'On Leaving and Joining Africanness through Religion: The "Black Caribs" across Multiple Diasporic Horizons', in Palmié, *Africas of the Americas*; Paul Christopher Johnson, *Diasporic Conversions: Black Carib Religion and the Recovery of Africa* (Berkeley, Calif.: University of California Press, 2007).

39. Price, *Travels with Tooy*, 288–9.

40. Price, *Travels with Tooy*, 297.

41. Price, *Travels with Tooy*, 299.

42. Linda M. Heywood and John K. Thornton, *Central Africans, Atlantic Creoles, and the Foundation of the Americas, 1585–1660* (Cambridge: CUP, 2007), 237.

43. Heywood and Thornton, *Central Africans*, 238 (emphasis added).

44. James H. Sweet, *Domingos Álvares, African Healing and the Intellectual History of the Atlantic World* (Chapel Hill, NC: University of North Carolina Press, 2011); see too Luis Nicolau Parés and Roger Sansi, eds, *Sorcery in the Black Atlantic* (Chicago: University of Chicago Press, 2011).

45. Judith A. Carney, *Black Rice: The African Origins of Rice Cultivation in the Americas* (Cambridge, Mass.: Harvard University Press, 2001). For the most recent counter-argument and a useful summary of the debate, see Walter Hawthorne, *From Africa to Brazil: Culture, Identity, and an Atlantic Slave Trade, 1600–1830* (Cambridge: CUP, 2010).

46. Judith A. Carney and Richard Nicholas Rosomoff, *In the Shadow of Slavery: Africa's Botanical Legacy in the Atlantic World* (Berkeley, Calif.: University of California Press, 2009).

47. Robin Law and Paul E. Lovejoy, eds, *The Biography of Mahommah Gardo Baquaqua: His Passage from Slavery to Freedom in Africa and America* (Princeton: Markus Wiener, 2001).

48. John Hunwick and Eve Troutt Powell, *The African Diaspora in the Mediterranean Lands of Islam* (Princeton: Markus Wiener, 2002), p. ix.

49. Hunwick and Powell, *African Diaspora*, pp. ix–xiii. See also Ehud R. Toledano, *Slavery and Abolition in the Ottoman Middle East* (Seattle: University of Washington Press, 1998), 135–54, and Edward A. Alpers, 'Recollecting Africa: Diasporic Memory in the Indian Ocean World', *African Studies Review*, 43/1 (2000), 83–99.

50. Hunwick and Powell, *African Diaspora*, pp. xxiii–xxiv; see too John Hunwick, 'The Religious Practices of Black Slaves in the Mediterranean Islamic World', and Ismael Musah Montana, 'Ahmad ibn al-Qādī al-Timbuktāwī on the Bori Ceremonies of Tunis', both in Paul E. Lovejoy, ed., *Slavery on the Frontiers of Islam* (Princeton: Markus Wiener, 2004).

51. Ehud R. Toledano, *As if Silent and Absent: Bonds of Enslavement in the Islamic Middle East* (New Haven, Conn.: Yale University Press, 2007), 204–54.

52. Sugata Bose, *A Hundred Horizons: The Indian Ocean in the Age of Global Empire* (Cambridge, Mass.: Harvard University Press, 2006), 6.

53. See Shihan de Silva Jayasuriya and Richard Pankhurst, eds, *The African Diaspora in the Indian Ocean* (Trenton, NJ: Africa World Press, 2003).

54. Campbell, 'Slave Trades', 41.

55. See John McLeod, 'Marriage and Identity among the Sidis of Janjira and Sachin', in Hawley, *India in Africa*.

56. Pier M. Larson, *Ocean of Letters: Language and Creolization in an Indian Ocean Diaspora* (Cambridge: CUP, 2009).

BIBLIOGRAPHY

Andrews, George Reid, *Afro-Latin America, 1800–2000* (New York: OUP, 2004).

Brown, David H., *Santería Enthroned: Art, Ritual, and Innovation in an Afro-Cuban Religion* (Chicago: University of Chicago Press, 2003).

Capone, Stefania, *Searching for Africa in Brazil: Power and Tradition in Candomblé* (Durham, NC: Duke University Press, 2010).

Cosentino, Donald J., ed., *The Sacred Art of Haitian Vodou* (Los Angeles: UCLA Fowler Museum, 1995).

Gomez, Michael A., *Reversing Sail: A History of the African Diaspora* (New York: CUP, 2005).

Larson, Pier M., *Ocean of Letters: Language and Creolization in an Indian Ocean Diaspora* (Cambridge: CUP, 2009).

Matory, J. Lorand, *Black Atlantic Religion: Tradition, Transnationalism, and Matriarchy in the Afro-Brazilian Candomblé* (Princeton: PUP, 2005).

Olaniyan, Tejumola, and James H. Sweet, eds, *The African Diaspora and the Disciplines* (Bloomington, Ind.: Indiana University Press, 2010).

Palmié, Stephan, ed., *Africas of the Americas: Beyond the Search for Origins in the Study of Afro-Atlantic Religions* (Leiden: Brill, 2008).

Price, Richard, *Travels with Tooy: History, Memory, and the African American Imagination* (Chicago: University of Chicago Press, 2008).

Sweet, James H., *Domingos Álvares, African Healing, and the Intellectual History of the Atlantic World* (Chapel Hill, NC: University of North Carolina Press, 2011).

Thompson, Robert Farris, *Aesthetic of the Cool: Afro-Atlantic Art and Music* (Pittsburgh, Pa.: Periscope Publishing, 2011).

PART II

THE COLONIAL
ENCOUNTER

CHAPTER 8

···

AFRICAN COLONIAL STATES

···

HEATHER J. SHARKEY

In February 2005, the National Assembly of France passed a law that asserted 'the positive role of the French presence abroad, especially in North Africa', while directing educators to undertake the 'positive presentation of [French] colonialism' to schoolchildren. A year later, France's president, Jacques Chirac, repealed this law in an effort to defuse what historian Benjamin Stora called the 'dangerous war of memories', which threatened to rupture diplomatic relations between France and its former settler colony, Algeria.[1] If anyone had thought that the history of European imperialism and colonial rule in Africa was decided, then this episode and the public debate it generated quickly dispelled that idea.

Among professional historians too, debates about the nature of colonial rule in Africa have continued to simmer. Writing in 1990 for the UNESCO-sponsored *General History of Africa*, the distinguished Ghanaian historian Adu Boahen argued that 'the colonial rulers had one principal end in view, the ruthless exploitation of the resources of Africa for the sole benefit of colonial powers and their mercantile, mining, and financial companies in the metropolitan countries'. By contrast, Roland Oliver and J. D. Fage, who helped to establish the academic field of African history in Britain, portrayed colonial rule more benignly. Also writing in 1990, they suggested that colonial governments had aimed to 'maintain peace and the rule of law' and, from the 1920s, to fulfil their growing sense of 'moral obligation' to develop African societies.[2] Despite these differences of interpretation, Boahen and Oliver and Fage shared basic assumptions about how colonial states worked. They assumed, first, that Europeans were *colonizers*, that Africans were *colonized*, and that the distinctions between them were clear. They assumed, second, that colonial states formulated and applied policies with a high degree of coherence, so that the theory and practice of rule converged.

Recent scholarship in African history suggests a more complex picture. Many more people—and more *kinds* of people—than previously assumed were involved in shaping colonial states: not only African chiefs and European military men and civilian elites (such as British District Officers and French *commandants de cercle*), but also, for example, African translators, schoolteachers, and tax collectors, as well as European forestry experts, missionaries, and anthropologists. Viewed in this way, the lines between colonized and colonizer look blurrier. Likewise, colonial administration was far more diffuse and less closely coordinated than official discourses of governance suggested, so that colonial states exerted their considerable power in ways that were often arbitrary, variable, and contingent on decisions made by individuals in local settings. In cities such as Paris, Brussels, and London, or Conakry, Léopoldville (Kinshasa), and Khartoum, the ostensible architects of colonial policies had less influence over colonial statecraft, as practised on the ground, than they either wanted or knew. In short, as historians reach deep into the colonial archives of former imperial powers and of African states, they now realize that the day-to-day articulation of colonialism was more complicated than once thought: 'more a multitude of discordant voices than the monotonous drone of imperial hegemony'.[3]

This chapter sketches a history of colonial states in Africa, explaining when and why they emerged, what they did, how they worked, and who made them what they were. At the same time, it aims to explain the historiography of colonial states; that is, the different ways that historians have interpreted their nature, their impact, and their legacies.

THE CREATION OF COLONIAL STATES

During the closing years of the nineteenth century and opening years of the twentieth, seven European countries claimed territories in Africa and devised administrations within them. These were Britain, France, Germany, Belgium (initially through King Leopold's private initiative), Portugal, Spain, and Italy. For decades, historians have described this expansion as the result of a 'new imperialism', which stood in contrast with Europe's 'old' imperialism shaped by maritime trade in the Atlantic and Indian Ocean worlds and which arose from new motives. These included a desire to enhance national prestige, to guarantee access to African raw materials and markets for European industrial goods, and to control strategic concerns such as waterways. For citizens of colonizing countries, African colonial states also offered prospects of employment, adventure, Christian endeavour, and personal gain. Thus, European governments, corporations, missions, and individuals found stakes in the colonial enterprise. Yet Africans seized or created opportunities, too, and in the process pushed the history of colonial states down unexpected paths.

The colonial partition, the so-called Scramble for Africa, is hard to date precisely, but precipitating events included France's occupation of Tunisia in 1881 and Britain's occupation of Egypt in 1882. Otto von Bismarck, chancellor of the newly unified Germany, was concerned about this land grab, but eager also to get a share of the booty. Thus Bismarck called a meeting in Berlin and invited representatives of European states that were vying for African territories. Ultimately, the Berlin Conference of 1884–5 regulated this free-for-all. Contestants agreed to recognize the spheres of influence that some states were already claiming or eyeing, and agreed, too, that countries could only confirm their hold on territories by demonstrating 'effective occupation'; that is, by developing infrastructures for colonial rule. The latter provision changed the nature of European imperialism in Africa. Henceforth, European powers insisted on their right and need to impose strong centralized rule over colonies, and presumed authority to dictate policies and extract taxes within their borders. At the same time, they invoked a 'civilizing mission' to justify their actions, claiming to spread religious values, rational thought, liberty, justice, and other glorious abstractions.

To appreciate the difference between the old and new imperialism in Africa, one can cite Portugal, which claimed a longer history of engagement in the continent than any other party to the Scramble. In 1415, Portugal colonized the enclave of Ceuta (now claimed by Spain, but surrounded by Morocco). It did the same in Guinea (now Guinea-Bissau) in 1446, the Cape Verde Islands in 1462, and the islands of Fernando Pó and Annobón (now part of Equatorial Guinea) in 1472. Portuguese merchants and later chartered companies established trading enclaves along Africa's south-western and south-eastern coasts. This history enabled Portugal, after the Berlin Conference, to stake claims to what became Angola and Mozambique, and to establish ruling infrastructures within their interiors. Likewise, Spanish colonialism in Africa took new turns after the Scramble, as Spanish Guinea (Equatorial Guinea) shows. In 1778, through an exchange with Portugal for land in America, Spain claimed the island of Fernando Pó along with commercial rights to the adjacent coastal enclave of Río Muni. For decades Spain loosely administered this territory from Argentina, in an arrangement that attested to the bonds of empire stretching across the Atlantic. Yet, it was only in 1904 (a full 126 years after Portugal ceded control, and twenty years after the Berlin Conference) that Spain began to coordinate an administration in this territory, and only by 1927 that it began to govern effectively Spanish Guinea's mainland interior.

European technological advances enabled this new imperialism: medicinal quinine (for averting malaria, thereby enabling Europeans to survive in the tropics), rapid-firing rifles and machine guns, steamships, the Suez Canal (opened in 1869), submarine telegraph cables, railways, and macadamized roads (the last allowing for transport of goods by lorry). New image- and text-producing technologies, such as cameras and typewriters (with their potential for carbon copies and mimeographs) became indispensable, too, as they enabled colonial states to record, classify, and publicize, to conduct surveillance and gather intelligence, and to register and enshrine property rights. Innovations continued in the twentieth century, with advances in auditory devices such as radios. Meanwhile, in military technology, Italy introduced aeroplanes as a new tool of empire, dropping hand-held bombs on Arab encampments during its 1911 battle to wrest Libya from the Ottoman Empire. Later other European powers in Africa (such as Britain in the southern Sudan) also engaged in aerial bombardment, in an attempt to 'pacify' people who refused to submit to colonial control.

Italy's invasion of Libya in 1911 presents one conventional end-date for the Scramble for Africa; France's imposition of a military protectorate over Morocco in 1912 another. H. L. Wesseling has recently argued, however, that the French seizure of Morocco was a mere epilogue to the Scramble, and that the Peace of Vereeniging, which ended the South African War of 1899 to 1902, was the real watershed for its closure.[4] The final defeat by British imperial forces of the two independent settler republics established by Afrikaans-speaking agriculturalists or 'Boers' secured British control over all of South Africa and hence mercantile access to the gold mines of the Transvaal. A critical figure in British imperial expansion within southern Africa was the diamond magnate Cecil Rhodes, after whom the two British 'Rhodesias', Northern and Southern (now Zambia and Zimbabwe) were named. The British economist J. A. Hobson (1858–1940), who covered the South African War for the *Manchester Guardian*, was surely thinking of Rhodes when he wrote his brilliant analysis and scathing indictment titled *Imperialism*. 'Finance', wrote Hobson in 1902, 'manipulates the patriotic forces which politicians, soldiers, philanthropists, and traders generate', thereby serving as motors of imperial expansion.[5]

At the opposite, northern extreme of the continent lay the French white settler state of Algeria. As a case study in the history of colonial expansion in Africa, Algeria was also somewhat exceptional, because its initial conquest in 1830 predated the Scramble by some fifty years. Yet in other ways its experiences were emblematic of trends elsewhere in Africa—a point that Frantz Fanon (1925–61), the Martinique-born 'psychopathologist of colonialism' strongly emphasized. Like South Africa, Kenya, and Southern Rhodesia, Algeria became a settler colony, although in this case French authorities welcomed Europeans not only from mainland France but also from Malta, Corsica, Sicily, and mainland Italy. As a settler society, Algeria developed a clear hierarchy of privilege, which recognized European Christians as citizens but subjected the majority Arabic- and Berber-speaking Muslims to a series of harsh penalties, commonly known as the *indigénat*, which France later exported to all its colonies in West and Central Africa. Algeria's harsh colonial system exploded in 1954 into a struggle for liberation that ended with French withdrawal in 1962 and with the 'repatriation' of one million holders of French citizenship (many of whom had never seen, or had no known ancestral connections to France).

Four countries stand out as anomalous cases in this history of African colonial states. The first was Liberia, which had been colonized from the 1820s by African Americans who had been freed from slavery in the United States and who declared independence in 1847 with help from the American Colonization Society. The second was Ethiopia, which retained independence—and its Orthodox Christian monarchy—largely by juggling the demands of competing European players, among whom were influential cadres of merchants and missionaries. However, in 1935–6, Italy—by then under the leadership of Fascist dictator Benito Mussolini—conquered Ethiopia, but held the country for only five years. The third case was South Africa, which emerged in 1910 as a tense union of British- and Afrikaner-dominated regions that applied racial policies empowering 'whites' and restricting the rights of 'natives' or 'blacks', as well as 'coloureds' (mixed heritage people) and people of Indian origin. The fourth was the Anglo-Egyptian Sudan, which from 1898 had a peculiar status as a 'condominium', or shared domain, of Britain and Egypt. Egypt itself had claims to Sudanese territory that dated from a 'Turco-Egyptian' conquest in 1820, although Sudanese Muslim fighters had ousted the Egyptian colonizers in the early 1880s.

The borders that emerged from the Scramble were often arbitrary. Some reflected prior claims, while others were set through the trading of favours. For example, Britain secured parts of northern Nigeria relative to France's Niger in return for recognizing French fishing rights off the Newfoundland coast.[6] In 1911, France agreed to the extension of German Cameroon by giving it two pieces of territory along its southern and eastern fringes; in return, Germany recognized France's free rein in Morocco. Even when officials sought to revise frontiers in light of physical and cultural topographies, the results were sometimes whimsical. In 1913, for example, Britain sent men to tweak the borders of two British-controlled territories, the Sudan and Uganda, with directions to account for the flow of Nile waters and the integrity of African 'tribes'. Captain Kelly, the British officer who came from the Sudan side and who clearly felt a sense of team loyalty, contemplated securing two particular communities of Acholi people for the Sudan because 'their fondness for clothes and such marks of civilisation as brass bands' made them 'progressive' and thus 'worth having'.[7] The most significant reorganization of colonial jurisdiction was the confiscation of Germany's overseas empire following its defeat in the First World War. Its four African colonies, Togo, Cameroon, German East Africa (now Tanzania, Rwanda, and Burundi), and German South-West Africa (Namibia), were apportioned by the League of Nations as 'mandates' under British, French, Belgian, and, in the case of South-West Africa, South African stewardship.

COLONIAL STATES IN THEORY AND PRACTICE

A recurring theme in the history of Africa's colonial states is that they did not emerge, develop, or function in isolation. Frederick Lugard (1858–1945) was one of the most important players in the British Empire during the age of new imperialism. So extensive was his career that his biographer later chronicled it in two hefty volumes subtitled *The Years of Adventure* and *The Years of Authority*.[8] Born in India, Lugard attended the Royal Military Academy at Sandhurst. He went on to serve in campaigns in Afghanistan, the Sudan, Nyasaland (Malawi), and Burma, to represent British commercial interests in exploratory expeditions in eastern and southern Africa, and to hold appointments as Military Administrator of Uganda, High Commissioner of Northern Nigeria, Governor of Hong Kong, and Governor of Nigeria. Lugard's Nigerian years were the most important of his career. Huge, populous, and richly diverse in cultures and terrains, Nigeria provided a laboratory for experiments in 'indirect rule', a method and philosophy of administration that Lugard later described in his famous *The Dual Mandate in British Tropical Africa* (1922).

Indirect rule meant identifying and cultivating local chiefs and other hereditary rulers, and then using them as intermediaries in colonial governance. As described by Lugard, indirect rule worked from the premise that Britain possessed a 'dual mandate' to, on the one hand, colonize territories and extract wealth from them and, on the other, to help backward peoples to progress. Indeed, Lugard held strong views about Africans as 'primitives' and 'child races of the world', 'for whose welfare we are responsible.'[9] A third assumption about indirect rule rested on the romantic, if delusional, premise that Britain could preserve 'authentic' and 'traditional' local cultures while shielding Africans from modern conditions. Along these lines, Lugard wrote with contempt about 'Europeanised Africans'—whom others called 'detribalized blacks'— and stressed the need to avoid making more of them. Through skilful administration, Lugard suggested, it would be possible for Britain to get rich off Africa, reform and save Africans, but stop the clock on change. His writing inspired a generation of British colonial careerists, while his model of indirect rule became Britain's pan-African policy, even if British colonial states applied the idea differently from region to region.

France had its own lofty ideals for colonial rule, at the heart of which was the so-called *mission civilisatrice*, or civilizing mission. Its goal was to propagate the best of French culture along with the rationalist and libertarian values deriving from the Enlightenment and French Revolution. Before 1914 especially, French colonial authorities emphasized a vision of civilization that would 'improve their subjects' standard of living through the rational development, or what the French called the *mise en valeur*, of the colonies' natural and human resources' by, for example, building railroads, improving public hygiene, and promoting justice through the application of law.[10] In contrast with the British, French authorities tended to eliminate chiefs who got in their way and felt little sentimentality about protecting 'tradition'. Also unlike British authorities, who supported or tolerated the policy of Christian missionary schools in using African vernaculars as media for instruction, French colonial authorities promoted French—the proverbial *lingua franca*—consistently throughout their domains. French colonial policy also promoted 'assimilation' (suggesting large-scale adoption of French ways), or in its modified form, 'association' (implying partial acculturation). It also recognized a tiny number of educated Africans who embraced the French language and French ways as *évolués* ('evolved ones'), and granted them a degree of citizenship. In 1936, only 2,000 out of some 14 million French West Africans enjoyed *évolué* status, not including the 80,000 African inhabitants of the four old coastal communes of Senegal, to which France had awarded special privileges in 1848.[11]

In 1925, the distinguished anthropologist Lucien Lévy-Bruhl, whose institute of ethnology at the University of Paris depended on colonial subsidies, explained the importance of rational study to colonial rule. 'When a colony includes peoples with a civilization inferior to, or very different from, our own, competent ethnologists may be just as urgently required as competent engineers, foresters or physicians.' Native populations, he continued, were as critical as natural resources like mines and forests in accounting for a colony's wealth, and required inventories in the form of 'precise, in-depth knowledge of... languages, religions, and social forms.'[12] Although Lévy-Bruhl was writing with French territories in mind, his observations apply equally to those of other European powers in Africa, which emphasized their rationalism as a justification for colonial rule. By encouraging the scholarly analysis of everything from folktales and marriage customs to native flowers and endemic diseases, colonial powers sought to demonstrate mastery to themselves and to others through the production of knowledge.

In this way, too, academic disciplines such as anthropology and tropical medicine became indebted to the colonial states that fostered them during the late nineteenth and early twentieth centuries.

All colonial powers in Africa desired to extract profits from colonies and to keep the costs of administration in check. For Germany, the historian Hans-Ulrich Wehler has argued, money-making was particularly important, as Bismarck hoped that economic success and opportunities abroad would serve as a release valve for rising social pressures at home. German colonies in Africa became 'an integrative force in a recently founded state which lacked stabilising historical traditions and which was unable to conceal its sharp class divisions'.[13] Italy, too, was a newly unified state that hoped to make money in Africa, while exporting surplus population as settlers. For Italy, after the conquest of Libya in 1911–12, the historical romance of African colonization was also critical, since it allowed for the proliferation of nationalist fantasies about reviving the Roman Empire on both shores of the Mediterranean.

In German colonies, the Congo Free State, Portuguese, Spanish, and Italian territories, and some French and British domains, policy-makers hoped to pass costs of administration to private companies in a process that one might describe as the subcontracting of colonial rule. Examples of companies that benefited from such arrangements include the Portuguese Companhia de Moçambique, the German Deutsche Kolonialgesellschaft für Südwest-Afrika, and the Belgian Compagnie du Congo Belge. Companies justified territorial claims and maintained order; in return they gained access to labour and profits. Christian missionaries also featured as proxies in this model of colonial statecraft. Authorities hoped that missionaries would provide welfare services (such as clinics for the sick), open schools to train Africans as workers and colonial servants, and bolster the moral legitimacy of colonialism. In return, the theory went, missionaries gained access to souls.

Yet theory diverged from practice in manifold ways. Financially, colonial states seldom made the profits for which European governments and companies had hoped; that is, profits sufficient to cover the costs of administration and then some. Certain regions had more trading potential than others, depending upon a range of environmental and human factors including the presence of exploitable raw materials, cash crops, and workers. Eventually, France found an accounting trick to offset its costs as well as the regional variations in wealth by making its richest colonies, such as Côte d'Ivoire and Gabon, subsidize the poorest, such as Haute-Volta (Upper Volta, now Burkina Faso) and Oubangui-Chari (Central African Republic). Commercially, big firms were expected to behave in ways that would foster social and economic stability, but companies were often rapacious. This was particularly so in the rainforests of Belgian- and French-ruled equatorial Africa, where in the 1890s and 1900s, so-called concessionary companies hell-bent on the extraction of rubber in order to turn a quick profit inflicted widespread and systematic violence upon village communities. When news of atrocities in the Congo Free State leaked out, the result was the rise of modern international human rights activism in the form of the Congo Reform Association and, in 1908, the handing of King Leopold's personal fiefdom over to the Belgian state.

In terms of governance, *Liberté, égalité, fraternité* may have reigned at home, but in France's African empire despotism was really the king, with the result that colonial law in practice amounted to a kind of 'rule by decree, enacted in often arbitrary and some-times spectacular punishments'.[14] Meanwhile, British rulers did not merely preserve African chiefdoms and customs; in some cases they invented them, or at least assembled them from a jumble of parts, while in other cases African chiefs invented or reinvented themselves.[15] Assessing French colonial practice in light of the high ideals of colonial rhetoric, one historian has concluded that French colonization in the early twentieth century functioned largely as 'an act of state-sanctioned violence'.[16] Yet violence has arguably remained a defining feature of all states in history, not only those that have arisen in colonies. The German sociologist Max Weber (1864–1920) famously defined the state as an 'institutional association of rule' (*Herrschaftsverband*), endowed with a territorial entity, that 'lays claim to the monopoly of *legitimate physical violence*' in the enforcement of its order.[17] Building on Weber, others have defined the state more recently as 'an administrative apparatus where administration means the extraction of resources, control, and coercion, and maintenance of the political, legal, and normative order in society'.[18] The colonial states of Africa certainly claimed monopolies of violence, in the Weberian sense of the term. Colonial states were economic as well as political enterprises, often committed to the extraction of natural resources, to the development of trade, and in the view of critics like Vladimir Lenin (1870–1924), who wrote a famous treatise against imperialism in 1916, to the promotion of private business interests in the form of 'cartels and monopolies'.[19]

Of course, empires are states, too, even if they are often giants in relation to individual colonies. As Jane Burbank and Frederick Cooper have recently noted, empires are highly stratified states, 'self-consciously maintaining the diversity of people they [have] conquered and incorporated'. At the same time, empires are populated by historical actors who are constantly 'pushing and tugging on relationships with those above and below them, changing but only sometimes breaking the lines of authority and power'.[20] Historians are now making similar claims about the tug-and-pull of authority and the diffusion of power within Africa's colonial states.

WORK, CONTROL, AND COERCION

Collecting taxes was a paramount concern of colonial states. So was controlling labour. Colonial rule depended on African labour to build and to maintain infrastructure, from roads, railways, bridges, and telegraph lines to government offices and rest-houses. Colonial sources emphasized the importance of male labour, but in many places women were also involved. Early twentieth-century photographs from the Sudan, for example, show largely female crews engaged in the hard physical labour of digging Nile dams. In response to these needs for 'manpower', colonial states imposed various demands for compulsory labour. These ranged from twelve days a year in French colonies to forty hours a week in the Congo Free State from 1903 to 1908 (subsequently revised to sixty days a year in the Belgian Congo)—although in reality people were often forced to work for longer. Most British colonies ended forced labour in the 1920s, but until then, in what is now Uganda, the demand was so onerous that 'a Ganda peasant might theoretically owe five months' labour a year: one month (in lieu of rent) to his African landlord, one month of local community labour, two months (in lieu of tax) to the state, and one month of compulsory paid (*kasanvu*) labour for the state or (rarely) a private employer'.[21] In the African-American colony of Liberia and in the Portuguese colonies, forced labour remained on the books until the early 1960s. Of course, Europeans were not the first modern imperialists to devise massive and often brutal forced labour schemes in Africa. That distinction goes to Muhammad Ali (1769–1849), the Ottoman governor and dynasty-builder of Egypt, who rounded up vast numbers of Egyptian peasants in the early nineteenth century and forced them to dig irrigation canals, operate textile factories, and fight in his army.

Colonial states also introduced taxes in cash and eliminated earlier currencies. In that part of French Equatorial Africa now containing Chad and the Central African Republic, authorities in 1900 imposed a head tax only on adults—but then defined adults as people over the age of eight.[22] The need for cash to pay taxes compelled many Africans to leave their communities for wage-paying jobs in mostly European-controlled enterprises, such as mines, factories, or, on farms (as in colonies of white settlement such as Kenya). Across the continent, the mobilization of labour by colonial states gave rise to large-scale migrations. As workers found that long distances and meagre incomes kept them from visiting their families, migration in turn led to *de facto* resettlement and urbanization. 'Certainly, by the later 1930s,' wrote one historian with regard to the copper-mining economy of Northern Rhodesia (Zambia), 'it was becoming increasingly difficult to maintain the fiction that Copperbelt workers were essentially rural tribesmen, temporarily working away from their homes.'[23] Equally untenable, given this new urbanization, was the romantic Lugardian idea of preserving 'traditional' African village cultures intact. Some colonial-era labour migrations anticipated postcolonial trends of African migration to Western Europe. Amidst the labour shortages of the First World War, France pressed 300,000 Algerian Muslim males to cross the Mediterranean in order to fill jobs in French factories; by 1939, approximately one in five Algerian men had worked for some time in France.[24]

Mobilizing labour required coercion. After 1905 in the Uele valley of the Belgian Congo, where one company demanded a massive labour supply for extracting and refining gold, 'recruits on their way to the mines were at times linked with ropes around their necks'.[25] In Northern Rhodesia, mining companies and the state used force to round up workers and march them towards the south. Most of these collected workers were men. In some places, such as Swaziland, colonial officials supported efforts of local chiefs as they tried to restrict the labour migration of women—with important consequences for the history of gender relations, family structures, patriarchal authority, and rural–urban connections. The new cash economy also made Africans into buyers of European industrial goods, introducing new cultures of consumerism. In Southern Rhodesia, for example, European manufacturers marketed Lifebuoy-brand soap to African men, in the process revising conceptions of personal hygiene.[26]

What was the difference between using coercion to mobilize labour and using coercion to impose control? The answer was, often, not much. Colonial states relied on an array of coercive bodies, notably armies and police forces, but also on innocuously named 'labour bureaus' (as in Northern Rhodesia) as well as the private militias that some chiefs maintained. Moreover, these coercive bodies sometimes claimed significant autonomy and pursued their own corporate interests relative to other parts of colonial states. Consider the case of German East Africa, where during the 1890s the colonial army was an agent of chaos. The German Foreign Office created a force called the *Schutztruppen*, made up of German army volunteers and African conscripts and charged with promoting security and stability so that German business could prosper. But on the ground in East Africa, German military officers had other ideas: between 1891 and 1897 they fought more than sixty campaigns against local peoples, but only reported the biggest ones back to Berlin. 'Local military commanders', observed one historian, 'often secretly conducted smaller campaigns, of which even the governor was not subsequently fully informed.' To quell opposition, the *Schutztruppen* resorted to burning villages, plundering livestock and food, and adopting 'a strategy of systematic starvation' among civilians. Amidst the instability that they created, military officers created an impression of their own indispensability to the colonial state and thereby engineered 'the militarization of colonial policy' in German East Africa.[27]

In other colonies the lines dividing soldiers (theoretically waging wars or defending territories) from police (theoretically maintaining law and order) were blurry. Consider the colonial police force of the Gold Coast (Ghana): this evolved from an armed frontier force first established in 1865 and modelled on a combination of the Royal Irish Constabulary and Indian and Egyptian paramilitary forces. Authorities recruited 'Hausas', by which they meant Muslim men from the northern interior, and deployed them in various ways, from consolidating the British conquest of the Asante and Northern Territories region in the 1896–1900 period, to breaking strikes and labour disputes, and supervising convict labourers and guarding banks. These 'Hausa' men, who enjoyed opportunities to rise through the ranks, came to wield considerable power, in some places acting as magistrates by judging local criminal and civil cases. As David Killingray notes:

> All too often a uniform seemed a license to loot and extort, and as a result both the Hausa Constabulary and the Fante police were despised and hated by those they affected to police. Preeminently they were hated as unaccountable representatives of an alien colonial power imposing a range of new laws and measures of social control which lacked any semblance of popular consent.[28]

Who did the coercing in African colonial states? Who did the conquering, policing, rounding up, and clamping down? Europeans stood at the top of the hierarchy, but Africans contributed heavily to colonial armed forces as well. The vast majority of soldiers in all colonial armies were Africans, led by small numbers of European officers. Some Africans may have voluntarily joined colonial armies or police forces, but many more were drafted or otherwise coerced into joining; once in, they found opportunities for adventure, steady employment, and the enhancement of social status. Thus, France achieved its conquest of Dahomey in 1892–4 using its West African recruits, the so-called *Tirailleurs Sénégalais* ('Senegalese Riflemen'). The Anglo-Egyptian forces that defeated the Sudan's Mahdist state in 1898 consisted largely of men of Sudanese origin, while the Italian forces that conquered Libya in 1911 consisted largely of Eritreans. During the First World War, Belgians in the Congo sent African soldiers of the Force Publique to invade German East Africa and occupy Ruanda-Urundi (now Rwanda and Burundi). Hundreds of thousands of African soldiers fought in French and British armies during both world wars, serving and dying in campaigns from those of the Western Front in 1914–18 to Burma in the 1940s. As decolonization loomed in the 1950s, France deployed sub-Saharan African troops in Indochina and in Algeria in vain attempts to suppress anti-colonial uprisings.

In 1981, the British imperial historian D. K. Fieldhouse argued that the most important feature of modern colonialism between 1870 and 1945 was 'the fact that colonial powers took full control over the government of the dependent societies within their empires'. While conceding that colonial rule may have rankled Africans at times, Fieldhouse suggested that it was 'historically the lesser of two evils facing most indigenous peoples in the later nineteenth century', with the other possible evil, he implied, having been to leave Africans to themselves.[29] With its claims for prudent administration, firm control, and good intentions, Fieldhouse's description of colonial rule is one that most historians of Africa would argue against. Where Fieldhouse saw cool bureaucracy, systematic law codes, and coherent policies, historians have for some years been more likely to notice the randomness, incoherence, and unpredictable harshness of colonial 'systems'. At the same time, they are now likely to question the broad applicability of Crawford Young's portrayal of the colonial state as *bula matari*, the 'breaker of rocks', a term that Congolese peoples used to describe the brute force of the Congo Free State and its successor regimes. While few historians would query the brutality and venality of the Congo Free State, they are inclined to see the exertion of colonial power generally as somewhat more erratic and uneven.[30]

Indeed, writing in 1988 about Francophone Africa, Patrick Manning emphasized the arbitrary exercise of power as a distinguishing feature of African colonial states. Reflecting on the allure of colonial service, particularly in remote areas removed from firm central oversight, he noted that a

> French man in his twenties, newly out of school, might find himself to be a *commandant de cercle* with complete authority over 200,000 people. He could accept, if he wished, the offers of gifts or women from subjects who sought his good will. Or, for those who refused to pay taxes, he could burn their villages and impose punitive fines in the near-certain knowledge that the governor would back him up.[31]

More recently, Gregory Mann has re-examined the *indigénat*, somewhat misleadingly described in English sources as the French legal 'code'. As Mann shows, the *indigénat* was never codified; it is better seen as a grab bag of sanctions and punishments, operating beyond the realm of courts and providing local *commandants*—and sometimes in rural areas their African *gardes-cercle*—with the option of jailing, fining, or lashing Africans for a host of petty infractions.[32] In Algeria alone, there were thirty-three listed infractions, which included speaking disrespectfully to or about a French official, defaming the French Republic, failing to register a death, refusing to fight forest fires, and avoiding *corvée* (forced) labour.[33]

The arbitrary nature of colonial rule extended into places where, under indirect rule, African authorities heeded ostensible tradition. Illustrating this tendency is an incident that occurred 1936 in the western Sudan involving the court of Ali al-Tom, *nazir* of the Kababish Arabs of Kordofan. One of Ali al-Tom's appointees, a relative, unilaterally divorced a couple so that he himself could wed the beautiful woman. His disregard for Islamic social and legal convention proved too egregious for local Muslims to tolerate, although British officials in Kordofan were inclined to let it stand (much to the displeasure of British legal experts in Khartoum).[34] While this episode illustrates the limits of inventing or revising tradition, it also demonstrates the intricate distribution of authority as well as the efforts of colonial states (involving in this case both Sudanese Muslims and Britons) to maintain power and shield it from challenges.

Examining instances such as these, historians are left to speculate about the consequences of the strong-arm and often arbitrary rule of colonial states for postcolonial African politics. Colonialism bequeathed to postcolonial states an apparatus of government departments (ranging from Post and Telegraphs to Education), military structures, and bureaucratic methods and procedures. But did it also bequeath, through its methods of administration, a governing culture of ruthless tyranny, which included a readiness to allow the unchecked exercise of power?

LOCATIONS OF POWER

In an article published in 1972, Ronald Robinson presented a 'sketch for a theory of collaboration'.[35] British imperial rule was able to function as it did, he argued, because British colonial authorities found local collaborators who were willing to work with and help maintain colonial orders and amass power of their own. Robinson's article became very influential among historians of the British Empire. Yet, appearing at a time when 'the Africanizing of African history was still the central item on the agenda', in Frederick Cooper's words, and when many historians of Africa avoided imperial history as 'white history', identifying some Africans as colonial lackeys conveniently left room for identifying other Africans as heroes.[36] And African heroes, to historians of the 1960s and 1970s, were above all anti-colonial rebels, whether of the peasant-revolter, nationalist-agitator, or guerrilla-insurrectionist variety. To historians of this generation, who were writing soon after decolonization, it was clear who had power in colonial states: white men in pith helmets, white men with guns, and in rural areas that had indirect rule, some black men such as chiefs and emirs.

Here, too, historians' perspectives have changed. For a start, historians today are disinclined to write history in celebratory modes and are sceptical about finding heroes. The picture now looks more complicated. Writing in 2007, John Parker and Richard Rathbone observed:

> The more we discover about colonial rule, the more fragmented, contradictory, and malleable it appears to be, dependent on the active participation of some Africans and full of autonomous spaces within which others pursued their own agendas. No longer are Africans seen as simply "responding" to the imposition of alien rule by either outright "resistance" or self-interested "collaboration".[37]

To this one might add the diffuse nature of colonial policy-making: decisions emanated from various quarters because power rested in multiple and sometimes unexpected places, and many different voices chimed in when issues of policy arose.

Even the *locus* of power was complicated. A scholar writing in 1976 about Northern Rhodesia observed that colonial administration 'did not merely represent the wishes of Britain. Power was filtered through Cape Town', as well as through officials of the British South Africa Company, who made their opinions and priorities well known.[38] In a similar vein, one could argue that Algiers, Brazzaville, and Dakar, and not only Paris, were imperial capitals for French Africa, while Cairo, and not only London, was a centre of power relative to the Sudan and Nile basin. In 2007, Thomas Metcalf made a similar argument about India's centrality to the British Empire *vis-à-vis* the Indian Ocean world from South Africa to Singapore. India, he argued, was a political and cultural capital, from which emanated, for example, distinctive styles of colonial architecture.[39] The presence of small but robust South Asian communities in East Africa and South Africa strengthened these Indian connections.

Among Europeans in colonial Africa, there were the obvious holders of power and authority: administrative authorities, military officers, business executives, big land-owning settlers in places like Kenya and Algeria, and, to a more varying extent, missionaries. Yet, as scholars delve into colonial history through the study of science and technology, health, the environment, and urban planning, a more diverse range of agents are beginning to receive greater attention. Consider, for example, forestry experts. In the early twentieth century, many of these scientist-technicians produced environmental crisis narratives about African deforestation and mismanagement, using these to justify interventions that benefited European settlers or firms. In Benin District of southern Nigeria, British forestry regulations radically transformed farming practices along with notions of land ownership. In 1916, a new forestry ordinance 'prohibited the felling of a long list of tree species except on payment of permit fees in Benin City' and specified fines and imprisonment for infractions. A series of cumulative measures of this sort 'virtually criminalized farming and caused much hardship for the populace, which led to widespread protests and agitation against the ordinance and its strict implementation'.[40] In Algeria, meanwhile, scientists in the forestry service implemented land seizure policies in the name of protecting forests from Muslim Algerians, thereby aiding white wine-makers and other settlers as they expanded their hold on choice farmlands. Officials fined and imprisoned so many Algerians for infractions of forestry regulations that 'some in the military sought to protect the Algerians from the Forest Service and its zealous agents'.[41] Whether in Algeria, Nigeria, or elsewhere, colonial authorities seemed particularly bent on eliminating the farming practice of burning undergrowth before planting. In one region of Northern Rhodesia, local people even dated a particular famine to one District Commissioner's ban on the slash-and-burn technique.[42] Across much of eastern and southern Africa, veterinarians mounted similar interventions into established practices of cattle-keeping, which had a profound impact on many pastoral communities.

Amid such exertions of power, Africans struggled to carve out their own niches of influence. A search of French colonial archives by Emily Osborn unearthed cases in Guinea and Soudan (now Mali) from around 1900 that demonstrated 'the capacity of African colonial employees to influence the knowledge, interpretations, and actions of their French superiors'. One example involved a man named Ousmane Fall who was officially a district interpreter—but in fact a mini-state-builder—who 'had designed and supervised an elaborate colonial "justice" system that employed four other Africans who traveled through the district, hearing cases, and passing down judgments'.[43] Ousmane Fall had also forged certificates claiming colonial authority and taken women as captives, his elaborate scheme only unravelling when stumbled upon by French authorities. His case provides a graphic illustration of colonial dependence on African intermediaries and how such dependence could lead to unexpected mutations in government.

In a series of books and articles, A. H. M. Kirk-Greene, a former British colonial official in northern Nigeria who later became an imperial historian, examined the extreme sparseness of the British presence in African colonies. Officials were so few on the ground that they constituted what he dubbed a 'thin white line', albeit a 'line tipped with steel'. In some ways, Kirk-Greene concluded, British rule in Africa amounted to 'a great-confidence trick, a huge game of white man's bluff'.[44] Yet the British, like the French and other European colonizers, did more than bluff. They had superior technologies to back them up or enable surveillance: aeroplanes, guns, radios, and so on. More importantly, they had large cadres of local men whom they drew into their armies and bureaucracies. Colonial states, once again, rested upon complex structures of power.

'LATE COLONIALSIM' AND THE STATE IN AN ERA OF RAPID CHANGE

Historians sometimes describe the period from the 1930s to 1960s as Africa's era of 'late colonialism'. This term implies something about timing (suggesting the era before independence), but also connotes a shifting mood and purpose in colonial regimes. During these years, regimes faced a spectrum of new challenges. Some were occasioned by the twin global crises of the Great Depression and the Second World War;

others by accelerating population growth, urbanization, and social change across the continent. The dramatic growth of cities was often accompanied by rising urban unrest, as workers and trade union activists began to agitate for improved wages and working conditions. All of this resulted in what has been described as a 'crisis of confidence' or 'loss of faith' in the colonial enterprise. Accompanying the loss of confidence was a sharper interest in the idea of development, as states sought to promote economic growth, expand social welfare, and placate rising African expectations. At the time, the 'fundamental assumption' of colonial states may have been 'that there was still plenty of time'; nevertheless, in retrospect, many of these projects look rushed and haphazard.[45]

A classic example of a late colonial development project that brought rapid change, but which decolonization left hanging, was the 'Zande Scheme'. British officials introduced this scheme in 1946 in the remote south-western corner of the Sudan where sleeping sickness was endemic. Project leaders uprooted 60,000 scattered Zande-speaking people and resettled them in 'elongated village units of 50 families' in an 'agglomeration [that] also facilitate[d] educational arrangements, public health, and medical programs'. The scheme hired Arabic-speaking, northern Sudanese Muslims to supervise the Zande in planting Nigerian palm oil trees and cotton, and in extracting oil and fibre from them. But already, on the eve of decolonization in 1955 (when civil war was poised to erupt), project leaders were acknowledging problems with soil erosion, while they speculated that the scheme needed many more years 'to bring the peasantry to a civilized and prosperous, if not wealthy, state'.[46]

Colonial bureaucracies were also changing. Eager to keep colonial rule cheap, policymakers from the start had been training and hiring African men as petty government employees, who typed and filed papers, surveyed plots of land, taught in government schools, disbursed medicines, counted revenues, and more. In the 1930s, as financial pressure mounted as a result of economic downturn and shrinking revenues, local African professionals became increasingly important to colonial states, while their accretion of responsibility made them more ambitious.[47] By the 1950s, as the political ambitions of urban elites were joined by mounting popular agitation, Britain and France sought to placate rising demands by granting constitutional concessions; the former by expanding or creating local legislatures and the latter by extending African representation in the metropolitan parliament. Between 1945 and 1958, France gradually extended the electoral franchise, resulting in a 'dizzying series' of votes in 'four referenda, two constitutions, three National Assemblies, and three territorial assemblies'.[48]

As the frontier of research moves ever forwards into the second half of the twentieth century, historians of Africa are now devoting increasing attention to the postwar era of late colonialism and decolonization. At the heart of their concerns lies the issue of the nature of the late colonial state and its relationship to independent polities that followed. The question is ultimately about 'what difference the end of empire meant, as well as what kinds of processes continued even as governments changed hands'.[49] That is, to what extent did independence and national liberation simply disguise a process of continuity from autocratic colony to autocratic 'postcolony'?[50] Debates about the legacy of late colonialism also turn on the consequences of the move towards the 'developmental state'. How substantive, lasting, and socially ameliorative were such projects in practice? This much, at least, is clear: colonial states (along with many Christian missions) passed the baton of development and social welfare to multinational and international philanthropic agencies, in a process that anticipated the roles that non-governmental organizations would play in late twentieth- and early twenty-first-century Africa.

CONCLUSION: ON THE AGENDA

As historians of Africa continue to scrutinize the era of colonial rule, they are paying closer attention than in the past to the complex and uneven distribution of power within states, seeking to understand the ways in which diverse peoples—administrative authorities and other European agents, but in particular African historical actors themselves—shaped these states and made them function. They are also seeking to broaden their range of historical sources and approaches to them. This point bears elaboration. A generation ago, historians of colonial states were likely to rely on official reports sent to imperial or colonial headquarters (and now stored in national archives), as well as on correspondence and memoirs from European administrators. These sources tended to reflect the biases of ruling elites and to convey an impression of mastery derived from the gathering of knowledge and 'intelligence'. Historians still read these texts, of course, but are more likely now to read them critically, 'against the grain', while listening for the voices of less powerful people. Now, too, historians are likely to draw upon more diverse types of sources: oral accounts; visual materials such as photographs; and the rich literary and artistic production of Africans, such as poems and songs. Interdisciplinary approaches to history through the lenses of anthropology, art history, environmental studies, and other fields are also opening up new windows.

As a result of the widening frame of sources and methods, the field of 'imperial history' (with its established focus on the interests, policies, and behaviour of European empire-states and their ruling elites) and that of 'African history' (with its focus on the social history of African peoples, including the humblest), have been moving closer to each other. Growing scholarly attention to transnational history and the history of diasporas (including the contemporary history of African migrants living in the former colonizing countries of Europe) has confirmed this trend. Nevertheless, to a large extent, narratives of colonial states have continued to focus almost exclusively on the actions of *men*. One challenge still facing historians is to seek out and explore the history of colonial states as they involved women, as well as the children who were Africa's future.

This study of African colonial states has focused on the discrepancies between the theory and practice of administration, along with the work of collecting taxes, recruiting labour, and maintaining control. It has commented only briefly on the role of colonial states in fostering development and welfare, for example, through vaccination campaigns or public health measures that saved lives, or through establishing schools that opened doors to literacy, learning, and opportunity for African youths. Such welfare-related measures were important, but how many people actually benefited? Only a tiny proportion of school-age Africans in the colonial era, for example, ever got the chance to go to school. Bigger questions loom, too. How can historians assess the evidence for the humanitarian and altruistic deeds of colonial states in light of the evidence for their brutality and rampant, if erratic, aggression? Returning to the debate with which this chapter opened, how can historians reconcile the 'ruthless exploitation' that one eminent historian detected in colonial states with the claims for 'moral obligation' and service that were cited by two of his colleagues? This debate about the intentions and deeds of colonial states shows no signs of abating, so new generations of scholars will need to continue to address it.

NOTES

1. Benjamin Stora, 'Début d'une dangereuse guerre des memoires', *L'Humanité*, 6 (Dec. 2005); see too Michel Laronde, 'Effets d'Histoire: Représenter l'histoire coloniale forclose', *International Journal of Francophone Studies*, 10/1–2 (2007).
2. A. Adu Boahen, ed., *General History of Africa, viii. Africa under Colonial Domination, 1880–1935* (Paris: UNESCO, 1990), 7; Roland Oliver and J. D. Fage, *A Short History of Africa*, 6th edn (London: Penguin, 1990), 184, 197.
3. John Parker and Richard Rathbone, *African History: A Very Short Introduction* (Oxford: OUP, 2007), 67–8.
4. H. L. Wesseling, *The European Colonial Empires, 1815–1919*, tr. Diane Webb (Harlow: Pearson, 2004), 148.
5. J. A. Hobson, *Imperialism: A Study*, 3rd edn (London: George Allen & Unwin, 1938), 59.
6. Ieuan L. Griffiths, *The Atlas of African Affairs*, 2nd edn (London: Routledge, 1994), 51, 108.
7. G. H. Blake, ed., *Imperial Boundary Making: The Diary of Captain Kelly and the Sudan-Uganda Boundary Commission of 1913* (Oxford: OUP, 1997), 21.
8. Margery Perham, *Lugard: The Year of Adventure, 1858–1898*, and *Lugard: The Years of Authority, 1898–1945* (London: Collins, 1956 and 1960).
9. Frederick Lugard, *The Dual Mandate in British Tropical Africa* (London: Frank Cass, 1965), 65, 72.
10. Alice L. Conklin, 'The French Republican Civilizing Mission', in Alice L. Conklin and Ian Christopher Fletcher, eds, *European Imperialism, 1830–1930* (Boston: Houghton Mifflin, 1999), 60–6.
11. Roland Oliver and Anthony Atmore, *Africa since 1800*, 3rd edn (Cambridge: CUP, 1981), 165.
12. Lucien Lévy-Bruhl, 'L'Institut d'Ethnologie de l'Université de Paris', *Revue d'Ethnographie et de Traditions Populaire*, 23–5 (1925), 1–4, cited in Benoît de L'Estoile, 'Rationalizing Colonial Domination? Anthropology and Native Policy in French-Ruled Africa', in Benoît de L'Estoile, Federico Neiburg, and Lygia Sigaud, eds, *Empires, Nations, and Natives: Anthropology and State-Making* (Durham, NC: Duke University Press, 2005).
13. Hans-Ulrich Wehler, 'Industrial Growth and Early German Imperialism', in Roger Owen and Bob Sutcliffe, eds, *Studies in the Theory of Imperialism* (London: Longman, 1977), 84.
14. Gregory Mann, 'What was the *Indigénat*? The "Empire of Law" in French West Africa', *Journal of African History*, 50 (2009), 333.

15. See Eric Hobsbawm and Terence Ranger, eds, *The Invention of Tradition* (Cambridge: CUP, 1983); and Thomas Spear, 'Neo-Traditionalism and the Limits of Invention in British Colonial Africa', *Journal of African History*, 44 (2003).

16. Conklin, 'The French Republican Civilizing Mission', 66.

17. Max Weber, 'The Profession and Vocation of Politics', in Peter Lassman and Ronald Speirs, eds, *Weber: Political Writings* (Cambridge: CUP, 1994), 310–11, 316.

18. Karen Barkey and Sunita Parikh, 'Comparative Perspectives on the State', *Annual Review of Sociology*, 17 (1991), 524.

19. V. I. Lenin, *Imperialism: The Highest Stage of Capitalism*, in *Selected Works* (New York: International Publishers, 1943), v. 24.

20. Jane Burbank and Frederick Cooper, *Empires in World History: Power and the Politics of Difference* (Princeton: PUP, 2010), 2, 14.

21. John Iliffe, *Africans: The History of a Continent,* 2nd edn (Cambridge: CUP, 2007), 203–4.

22. Patrick Manning, *Francophone Sub-Saharan Africa, 1880–1985* (New York: CUP, 1988), 52, 54.

23. L. J. Butler, *Copper Empire: Mining and the Colonial State in Northern Rhodesia, c.1930–1964* (Houndmills: Palgrave Macmillan, 2007), 47, 50.

24. Neil MacMaster, 'Islamophobia in France and the "Algerian Problem"', in Emran Qureshi and Michael A. Sells, eds, *The New Crusades: Constructing the Muslim Enemy* (New York: Columbia University Press, 2003), 291.

25. Manning, *Francophone Sub-Saharan Africa*, 40.

26. Timothy Burke, *Lifebuoy Men, Lux Women: Commodification, Consumption, and Cleanliness in Modern Zimbabwe* (Durham, NC: Duke University Press, 1996).

27. Kirsten Zirkel, 'Military Power in German Colonial Policy: The Schutztruppen and their Leaders in East and South-West Africa, 1888–1918', in David Killingray and David Omissi, eds, *Guardians of Empire: The Armed Forces of the Colonial Powers, c.1700–1964* (Manchester: MUP, 1999), 97.

28. David Killingray, 'Guarding the Extending Frontier: Policing the Gold Coast, 1865–1913', in David M. Anderson and David Killingray, eds, *Policing the Empire: Government, Authority and Control, 1830–1940* (Manchester: MUP, 1991), 119.

29. D. K. Fieldhouse, *Colonialism, 1870–1945: An Introduction* (New York: St Martin's Press, 1981), 11–12, 22–3, 48.

30. Crawford Young, *The African Colonial State in Comparative Perspective* (New Haven, Conn.: Yale University Press, 1994).

31. Manning, *Francophone Sub-Saharan Africa*, 56.

32. Mann, 'What was the *Indigénat?*'

33. John Ruedy, *Modern Algeria: The Origins and Development of a Nation* (Bloomington, Ind.: Indiana University Press, 1992), 89.

34. Justin Willis, 'Hukm: The Creolization of Authority in Condominium Sudan', *Journal of African History*, 46 (2005).

35. Ronald Robinson, 'Non-European Foundations of European Imperialism: A Sketch for a Theory of Collaboration', in Owen and Sutcliffe, *Studies in the Theory of Imperialism*.

36. Frederick Cooper, *Colonialism in Question: Theory, Knowledge, History* (Berkeley, Calif.: University of California Press, 2005), 5, 43.

37. Parker and Rathbone, *African History*, 109.

38. Richard Hall, *Zambia, 1890–1964: The Colonial Period* (London: Longman, 1976), p. vii.

39. Thomas R. Metcalf, *Imperial Connections: India in the Indian Ocean Arena, 1860–1920* (Berkeley, Calif.: University of California Press, 2007).

40. Pauline von Hellermann and Uyilawa Usuanlele, 'The Owner of the Land: The Benin Obas and Colonial Forest Reservation in the Benin Division, Southern Nigeria', *Journal of African History*, 50 (2009).

41. Diana K. Davis, *Resurrecting the Granary of Rome: Environmental History and French Colonial Expansion in North Africa* (Athens, O.: Ohio University Press, 2007), 109, 118, citing Charles-Robert Ageron, *Histoire de l'Algérie contemporaine* (Paris: Presses Universitaires de France, 1979), 208.

42. Hall, *Zambia*, 75.

43. Emily Lynn Osborn, ' "Circle of Iron": African Colonial Employees and the Interpretation of Colonial Rule in French West Africa', *Journal of African History*, 44 (2003), 30, 38, 42.

44. A. H. M. Kirk-Greene, 'The Thin White Line: The Size of the British Colonial Service in Africa', *African Affairs*, 79 (1980), 25, 44.

45. Crawford Young, *Politics in the Congo: Decolonization and Independence* (Princeton: PUP, 1965), 36.

46. William A. Hance, 'The Zande Scheme in the Anglo-Egyptian Sudan', *Economic Geography*, 31/2 (1955), 149–56.

47. Heather J. Sharkey, *Living with Colonialism: Nationalism and Culture in the Anglo-Egyptian Sudan* (Berkeley, Calif.: University of California Press, 2003); Benjamin Lawrance, Emily Lynn Osborn, and Richard Roberts, eds, *Intermediaries, Interpreters, and Clerks: African Employees in the Making of Colonial Africa* (Madison, Wis.: University of Wisconsin Press, 2006).

48. Manning, *Francophone Sub-Saharan Africa*, 140.

49. Frederick Cooper, *Africa since 1940: The Past of the Present* (Cambridge: CUP, 2002), 15.

50. On the continuity of political culture, see Mahmood Mamdani, *Citizen and Subject: Contemporary Africa and the Legacy of Late Colonialism* (Princeton: PUP, 1996); Achille Mbembe, *On the Postcolony* (Berkeley, Calif.: University of California Press, 2001).

BIBLIOGRAPHY

Cooper, Frederick, *Colonialism in Question: Theory, Knowledge, History* (Berkeley, Calif.: University of California Press, 2005).

Coquery-Vidrovitch, Catherine, *African Women: A Modern History* (Boulder, Colo.: Westview Press, 1997).

Davis, Diana K., *Resurrecting the Granary of Rome: Environmental History and French Colonial Expansion in North Africa* (Athens, O.: Ohio University Press, 2007).

Headrick, Daniel R., *Power over Peoples: Technology, Environments, and Western Imperialism, 1400 to the Present* (Princeton: PUP, 2012).

Iliffe, John, *Africans: The History of a Continent*, 2nd edn (Cambridge: CUP, 2007).

Landau, Paul S., and Deborah D. Kaspin, eds, *Images and Empires: Visuality in Colonial and Postcolonial Africa* (Berkeley, Calif.: University of California Press, 2002).

Lawrance, Benjamin, Emily Lynn Osborn, and Richard Roberts, eds, *Intermediaries, Interpreters, and Clerks: African Employees in the Making of Colonial Africa* (Madison, Wes.: University of Wisconsin Press, 2006).

Mamdani, Mahmood, *Citizen and Subject: Contemporary Africa and the Legacy of Late Colonialism* (Princeton: PUP, 1996).

Parker, John, and Richard Rathbone, *African History: A Very Short Introduction* (Oxford: OUP, 2007).

Sharkey, Heather J., *Living with Colonialism: Nationalism and Culture in the Anglo-Egyptian Sudan* (Berkeley, Calif.: University of California Press, 2003).

Thomas, Martin, *Empires of Intelligence: Security Services and Disorder after 1914* (Berkeley, Calif.: University of California Press, 2008).

Wesseling, H. L., *The European Colonial Empires, 1815–1919*, tr. Diane Webb (Harlow: Pearson, 2004).

CHAPTER 9

....

LAW, CRIME, AND PUNISHMENT IN COLONIAL AFRICA

....

RICHARD ROBERTS

In her 1947 preface to Charles Meek's bibliography of colonial law, Margery Perham noted that 'the great importance' of the material 'will be clear to all who have any knowledge of colonial affairs'. The encounter between British rule and colonial subjects has 'produced deep effects' and given rise to 'problems and ambiguities' in need of study. 'It is strange', Perham argued, 'that a people so proud of their achievement in the sphere of law as the British should have given so little serious attention to the wider significance of this side of their imperial responsibilities.'[1] Perham, however, overstated the British lack of interest in colonial law. British anthropologists, often in the employ of colonial states, had been studying African law since at least the 1920s, producing guides to the laws and customs of particular ethnic groups. Such guides were designed to help district officers adjudicate disputes between Africans that landed on their desks. By the early 1950s, British anthropologists had moved from the guidebook to broader anthropological theory of Africans' encounters with the law. Out of these reflections emerged Max Gluckman's famous 1955 statement: 'The Lozi, like all Africans, appear to be very litigious. Almost all Lozi of middle age can recount dispute after dispute in which he has been involved.'[2] This chapter takes seriously the 'deep effects' that the colonial encounter had on law in colonial Africa and how the very 'litigiousness' of Africans reflects both social change and African agency.

THE COLONIAL ENCOUNTER AND LEGAL PLURALISM

....

The long history of human contact and social change introduced new ideas and practices for resolving disputes both between members of different groups and within groups. Except for the most isolated ones, all societies have some form of legal pluralism in which more than one system of normative beliefs and practices coexists.[3] The classic example of colonial legal pluralism was the dual legal system that recognized and separated pre-existing 'native' law from the received law of the metropolis.[4] This model of the law overstates the autonomy of these two legal regimes. More recent approaches, such as Lauren Benton's study of colonial legal regimes, examine the complex and changing character of the encounters between Europeans and indigenous societies between the fifteenth and the nineteenth centuries. During the early phase, Europeans negotiated their legal practices in contexts where several legal regimes coexisted more or less equally. In these multicentric legal systems, individuals engaged in 'rampant boundary crossing' and collective groups engaged in 'jurisdictional jockeying' for legal advantage. Increased interaction between groups led to shared assumptions about the outcomes of transactions and thus cultural convergence around legal concepts and practices. The colonial state was not yet strong enough or sufficiently interested to structure the various legal spheres hierarchically. British practice in India bridged the early and later forms of colonialism and led to the more pronounced form of state-centred legal pluralism in the late nineteenth century, in which the colonial state claimed dominance over other legal regimes.[5] Out of these changes in colonial policy emerged the precursors of the colonial 'invention of tradition'.

Recent research on legal pluralism underscores the need to focus not only on the establishment of formal legal institutions, but also on how litigants used the multiple arenas created by overlapping systems of dispute settlement. The most useful way to think of legal pluralism is as a form of encounter between dynamic, local processes of change in indigenous societies that predated colonial conquest and continued after conquest, and dynamic and changing forms of colonialism.[6] In most of Africa, colonial states were unable to broadcast their power widely throughout the colony.[7] Failure to broadcast power meant that Africans had enhanced abilities to negotiate colonial legal venues or avoid them altogether.

The predominant international legal instrument that furthered late nineteenth-century imperial expansion was the protectorate. The protectorate usually came into being through military conquest or a treaty ceding a certain degree of sovereignty to the superior power. Alfred Kamanda, a Sierra Leonean scholar and one of the few students of the protectorate treaty, argues that 'by reason of its very vagueness and nebulousness, [the protectorate] could be a cloak for many different, and even diametrically opposed, administrations in practice'.[8] British experience with the 'princely states' in India and the French with Algeria provided the model for the protectorate that would guide later colonial encounters. Zanzibar and Northern Nigeria were good examples of British protectorates allowing substantial space for the ruling elite to continue to run its institutions of governance, including legal institutions. At its base, however, the protectorate has its origins in the circumstances that obliged the second party to submit to the protection of the first, most often through force or the threat of force.

The protectorate, whether formally recognized or used as a political and legal blueprint, was characterized by a division between internal and external sovereignty. The colonial administration often took over jurisdiction of capital crimes and others considered threats to public order, while ceding internal sovereignty to 'native authorities', whether long established or recently invented. By separating criminal prosecution from civil litigation, the protectorate thus profoundly changed the nature of the law in practice, relegating all disputes relating to families and personal status to a residual category of family law. The model of the protectorate, which guaranteed legitimacy to the domain of custom, demanded that the institutions of local authority be retained and that natives continue to adjudicate their own disputes. Hence it gave rise to the policy of indirect rule, widely practised in Africa by all colonial powers.[9] Even as it sought to respect native customs, the colonial state retained its authority to determine whether or not customs were 'contrary to civilization' (in the French version) or 'repugnant to justice, equity, and good conscience' (in British parlance). In all societies, law is designed to maintain the social order by creating rules and expectations about human interactions and exchanges. The creation of the protectorate ultimately destabilized these rules and expectations precisely by introducing new rules and expectations in some areas and undermining others, even as it sought to promote stability.

For the purposes of this chapter, we should distinguish between the practice of civil and criminal law, when in fact the two domains overlapped and changed over time. During the early colonial period, for example, African males usually considered adultery a civil offence, subject to claims of damages and thus compensation. Colonial powers, however, understood adultery through the lens of metropolitan legal practice. In many European countries by the late nineteenth century, adultery was a legal category in flux, reflecting changes in divorce, sexuality, and women's legal character. It was usually a criminal offence for which the state imposed fines and prison sentences. Over time, fines replaced prison terms. Africans in the colonial era thus had to negotiate a very different legal landscape in seeking redress for alleged adulterous acts.[10] Similarly, when confronted with waves of married women leaving their husbands' homes in French West Africa, colonial officials began to transform a civil dispute regarding marriage into a criminal one when they punished runaway women with prison sentences.[11]

Colonial states usually reserved for themselves control over criminal acts they regarded as challenging the social order and the authority of the state: rebellion, murder, serious battery, rape, highway robbery, piracy, arson, administrative malfeasance, and issues relating to the slave trade once the colonial states outlawed such practices. In criminal cases, the colonial state prosecuted the cases and called the defendants to come before its courts; in civil disputes, Africans called other Africans before colonial courts with colonial officials acting more like umpires than prosecutors. This distinction between criminal and civil litigation, and between internal and external sovereignty overstates the boundaries between these domains of the law. The existence of appeal procedures—another colonial invention—moved contested judgments up the ladder of courts and thus blurred the boundaries between native, colonial, and metropolitan courts.

Metropolitan legal traditions influenced the practice of law in colonial societies. We need to distinguish common law as applied in colonies influenced by British practice and the civil law tradition applied in colonies influenced by continental European colonial powers. South Africa forms an anomaly in that its legal system developed from its Roman-Dutch legal inheritance, the superimposed British colonial practice, and constructed African customs. Out of South Africa's complicated genealogy, English law became more important precisely because Britain came to dominate the colony.[12] Common law generally refers to the significance of legal precedent developed by judges in the course of adjudicating cases, giving rise to the principle of *stare decisis,* which means that any new case is bound to follow the reasoning of similar disputes. A judge may override precedent if the context of a seemingly similar case has changed sufficiently to warrant a new reasoning. Similarly, common law has been influenced by legislation and regulation so that new legislation trumps precedent unless it contravenes constitutional principles. In common law legal systems, the judge, particularly the appeals judge, plays a prominent role in making the law.

In civil law traditions, in contrast, the law is legislated by the government, usually the national assembly, and takes the form of a code. The judge's role in civil law traditions is to apply the law. Hence, the judge or magistrate is concerned with how well the case or dispute maps onto the existing code. An appeal in the civil law tradition can only proceed if it demonstrates procedural irregularities or raises substantive legal issues not addressed in the code. If an appeal reveals a defect in the law itself, this can only be remedied by new legislation. Both the common law and civil law practices in colonial Africa rested on the need to have either a code or a body of precedent from African indigenous law. Thus, both legal systems in one way or another sought to 'codify' custom. Yet identifying, let alone codifying, custom proved far harder to do than the colonial powers imagined.

The Invention of Tradition, Customary Law, and African Agency

In order to exert some control over the native courts the protectorate created and to deal with appeals into the higher courts dominated by European magistrates, colonial states sought to make legible indigenous law.[13] This process was a key part of what Terence Ranger referred to as the invention of tradition, emerging out of collaboration between indigenous authorities (often male elders who were thought to be custodians of local knowledge) and colonial officials in order to generate handbooks of customary law.[14] Indigenous law became customary law through this process and these handbooks served as guides for colonial magistrates in adjudicating cases and appeals brought to their courts.[15] The production of customary law gave significant power to native informants to reshape gender relations and forms of authority. Male household heads used these opportunities to consolidate their power. Colonial magistrates also shaped customary law according to their perceptions of African societies and African families.

Despite the incentives for elderly male informants to promote a view of custom that served their interests and that resonated with colonial officials' assumptions about African societies, there were limits to how far-ranging inventions could be. Thomas Spear has drawn attention to the crucial role of popular consensus in limiting how far invented custom could stray from established practice. Spear points to the deep continuities of traditions of power and authority and popular debates around them that limited what African political entrepreneurs and colonial officials could promote as custom.[16] Despite these limits, however, the invention of tradition gave rise to what Sara Berry calls 'an era of intensified contestations over custom, power, and property' within colonial courts.[17] One of the central debates was the appropriate level of subservience that wives, junior males, and other dependants owed to household heads. Women and men brought their conflicts before the colonial courts in attempts to gain control over their lives during a period of rapid change in which colonial conquest led to the dissolution of local polities and existing forms of authority. Many of these disputes were efforts to invoke 'moral economies' about the limits on exploitation and were thus efforts to reduce social vulnerabilities and enhance stability through familial and social networks. These struggles did not necessarily challenge the gendered nature of power in the household, however. Social stability remained grounded within patriarchal systems of belonging.[18]

Shari'a, Muslim Family Law, and Qadis

In Muslim communities, the protectorate model recognized the regime of shari'a. Shari'a should be understood as a moral and ethical code regulating both private and public domains of Muslim life. It was derived from human efforts to interpret divine intentions, was drawn from the Qur'an and the prophetic tradition, and was subject to debate and interpretation. Beginning around the tenth century, guilds of scholars increasingly restricted the interpretative scope of shari'a and produced 'schools' of legal thought. The circulation of written Arabic legal texts thus reduced the scope of the invention of tradition, but this did not necessarily limit the debates among Muslims about the meanings and practices of shari'a.[19] Muslim family law and qadis were incorporated into colonial legal systems, although such 'colonizing' of Muslim family law often generated significant disputes over jurisdiction that in turn led officials to control further the application of shari'a. Muslim family law often became one form of customary law among many that native courts applied to Muslim litigants, while qadis often became employees of colonial states when they served as assessors on native courts.[20] It is important to appreciate that not all disputes were brought before colonial courts. Informal dispute resolution remained a prominent feature of all legal systems, and many qadis continued to adjudicate disputes among Muslims outside the formal colonial legal system. The delegated sovereignty of the protectorate also generated policy and legal problems for colonial administrations, especially when custom or shari'a came into conflict with metropolitan legal sensibilities. Thus, the British outlawed corporal punishments sanctioned by shari'a and the French sought to mandate women's consent in marriage.[21] These actions among others contributed to the ongoing debates and struggles over the nature of shari'a that played out in colonial courts.

To assist French officers in supervising the legal work of the qadis in Algeria, the entire Maliki legal code was translated into French in 1854 and later condensed in a new one-volume translation focusing on property and inheritance. This short version would become a staple in the libraries of French district officers and served as the basis of the British translation of the code, which played a similar role in British West Africa. The Maliki school never had a coherent legal code in the French sense; it was instead an 'approach' to the law incorporating common jurisprudential assumptions. However, through this process of selection and translation a reified and condensed version of a broader and messier corpus of judicial commentary and debate emerged to conform to Western categories such as 'family law'. Colonial administrators were under enormous pressure not to spend all their time discovering custom and adjudicating disputes among Africans, the readily available and simplified version of Muslim family law providing them with ready-made templates to apply to individual cases. Qadis often served on native courts as judges or assessors. However, the incorporation of shari'a within a pluralist legal environment and the possibility to appeal were a profound challenge to Muslim jurists and the status of the shari'a within Islamic thought. The provision for appeals rested on the need to assess the evidence and judgment in the original case. It thus put into question the legal standing of the qadi, who was thought to judge cases based on infallible, divine revelation.

There is another side to the story of Muslim family law and legal pluralism in colonial Africa: what impact did shari'a have on African customs? J. N. D. Anderson drew attention to this process when he described how Islamic law has spread through many parts of the continent:

> As a result, the indigenous customary law has been leavened, in certain areas, by Islamic principles and precepts—to a degree which differs widely, of course, from place to place. In certain areas, moreover, it has been virtually displaced by the law of Islam… but nowhere in tropical Africa has the imposition been complete, for traces of customary law survive even in the most rigidly Muslim areas.[22]

The survival of custom in Muslim law is only one side of the complex encounter that is the history of Islamic law in Africa; the other side is the influence of shari'a on African customs.

COLONIAL COURTS AND AFRICAN LAWYERS

Because of the way in which it divided citizens from subjects and the realm of custom from that of metropolitan law, the protectorate clearly shaped the organization of colonial courts. This was, however, a work in progress, changing over time and in relation to the complex application of native policy in various colonies. The notion of a 'bifurcated' legal system that provided separate courts and procedures for citizens relying on metropolitan law and subjects applying custom is highly attractive, but fundamentally misleading.[23] While citizens carefully guarded their prerogatives to bring their disputes to metropolitan courts, subjects constantly jockeyed for the venue they thought would provide the best outcome for their disputes.[24] In our current state of research, we know far too little about how Africans actually used the complex and overlapping sets of colonial courts.

All colonial powers had plans for how the colonial systems of courts were to operate. Most periodically adjusted and reformed these courts in order to make them fit better their changing understandings of African societies, the training of magistrates, and court officials, and in order to prevent abuses of the courts. Colonial powers never got the court system right, in part because they never fully understood African societies and how Africans responded to the changes in their social, economic, and political lives. Colonial courts were therefore always a lagging indicator of social and legal change.

Those colonial powers applying the civil law model—France, Belgium, Germany, Portugal, Italy, and Spain—applied some variant of a hierarchy of courts for African subjects that more or less ran parallel to the courts for citizens. The French colonial legal system has been the best studied.[25] Following a major reorganization of the colonial legal system in 1903, the French imposed a three-tiered system of courts for African subjects: at the base was the village tribunal, led by the village chief and designed to reconcile disputes. The village chief had some powers of 'correction' and could levy small fines. The second tier was the provincial tribunal, presided over by a provincial chief and two other African magistrates or assessors and which heard most of the family law disputes and a body of misdemeanour cases.[26] The provincial tribunal was required to keep a written register of cases, to be approved by district officers, periodically inspected by the attorney-general, and designed to promote consistent punishments and judgments. The third level was the district tribunal, presided over by the French district officer and two African assessors. This heard felony cases and the appeals of judgments from the provincial level. Appeals from the district tribunal and all prison terms exceeding five years (this rule changed periodically) were sent to the *cour d'homologation*, which was part of the colonial appeals court at the government-general, where the procedures were assessed and punishments certified. Lawyers were formally barred from the African courts, although they were permitted in the courts for citizens.

Citizens, including Frenchmen, European nationals, and the *originaires* of Senegal's communes (the original inhabitants and their descendants who were granted French citizenship-like status in 1848), as well as African subjects bringing disputes against citizens, all sought reconciliation with justices of the peace. If not satisfied or if the cases involved misdemeanours, the case went to the tribunal of the first instance; felonies and appeals went to the tribunal of the second instance. All these tribunals were presided over by French magistrates, or the district officer if there was no formally trained magistrate.

Clear and simple on paper, the reality of these courts was far more complex. Many Africans, as I have argued elsewhere, avoided the reconciliation of the village tribunals and brought their domestic disputes before the provincial tribunals.[27] In 1912, these tribunals morphed into subdivisional tribunals, and these changed again periodically up to the 1950s. Most challenging of all for the French native courts, however, was the ambiguity of 'custom' in the absence of codes. Civil law judges ruled on the basis of codes, but although codification was periodically promoted it was never accomplished. Debates over whether or not to codify raised important questions about the changing and adaptive nature of custom. Codification remained unresolved only to be revisited by independent nations as they sought to legislate family codes.

British colonial courts under the common law system were also a work in progress, although more flexible according to different colonial settings. The common law tradition provided a venue for citizens, the Supreme Court, which was also available to African subjects who lived in West African and South African crown colonies. The Supreme Court also served as the highest appeals court in the colony and heard appeals from native courts, thus blurring the boundaries between metropolitan law and African customs.[28] Most British colonies also applied some version of native courts, designed for Africans living within the neatly defined tribal units common to British colonial practice. The jurisdictions of the native courts and the powers reserved for African judges were usually defined by 'warrants'. Native courts were often ranked hierarchically with jurisdiction over simple family law disputes at the lowest level (in Nigeria ranked as D level courts) leading towards higher ranked courts (A level courts) with greater jurisdiction over crimes and appeals from lower courts.[29] Where native authority was well-established, as in Northern Nigeria and Zanzibar, the British recognized the courts of chiefs, emirs, and qadis.[30] Over time, British governors modified the native courts by establishing divisional and district courts.

Native courts technically had jurisdiction over both the territory defined by the district and all natives 'belonging' to that district regardless of their current location, unless they permanently resided in another district. This model assumed a tight symmetry between territory and custom and did not handle well the reality of African social and geographical mobility during the colonial period. The exceptions to this rule were the African employees of colonial governments, who were subject to the provincial courts in which the district officers or 'residents' served as judges. Frederick Lugard, who helped elevate indirect rule to high theory, captured the British ideal:

> In practice, where it is possible to set up a Native Court, that tribunal would deal with most cases of ordinary crimes by natives, and with native civil actions, but crimes against specific laws of the Protectorate, such as those triable under the 'slavery', 'liquor', 'firearms', and 'personation' proclamations, being foreign to native law and custom, would usually be dealt with by the Provincial Courts. The Supreme Court administers strict law; Provincial Courts administer English law modified by native law and custom.[31]

Lugard failed to mention 'Muslim courts' that were broadly within the orbit of native courts, but whose jurisdiction was limited to Muslims. Supervision of native courts fell to district officers, but the 'thin white line' of colonial officials in rural Africa meant that such supervision was uneven and episodic.[32] Abuses of power in the native courts were widespread; that by the warrant chiefs in south-eastern Nigeria contributed to the so-called Aba Women's War of 1929. Elders, clerks, and local officials serving as assessors were often tempted by bribes, especially where custom was not effectively fixed.[33]

Because of the complex nature of common law, lawyers were a central part of the proceedings at colonial Supreme Courts, which also heard appeals based on African customs. Men from the middle-class elite families of West African coastal towns began to be sent to England for legal training from the 1880s, returning to be admitted to what passed for the bars in the Gold Coast and Lagos colonies. These African lawyers played crucial roles in transforming grievances into complaints that could be heard by British judges serving on the colonial high courts; many also played key roles in the development of early 'constitutionalism'.[34] Colonial officials worried about the 'influx' of African lawyers, particularly with regard to land disputes. From the late nineteenth century, the Lagos Supreme Court passed ordinances limiting the roles of African lawyers in court; in Yorubaland, for example, African lawyers were barred from practising in district courts.

With its limited African franchise, the British Cape Colony nurtured indigenous property rights and educational aspirations. British-trained lawyers, including Pixley ka Isaka Seme, were prominent in the founding in 1912 of the South African Native National Congress, which became the African National Congress. Originally from Gujarat, Mohandas K. Gandhi trained as a lawyer in Britain and tested his early skills in law and political mobilization in South Africa. Given the prominence of the rule of law in British colonial ideology, it is not surprising that Africans eager to challenge segregation and racism should be trained in the law: many of the new generation of more radical ANC leaders in the 1950s, including Nelson Mandela and Oliver Tambo, were lawyers. More research on the relationships between legal training and political activism in Africa will certainly yield insights into this neglected area of study.[35]

ANTHROPOLOGY AND THE STUDY OF AFRICAN LAWS AND CUSTOMS

The colonial encounter shaped the study of African laws and customs. Many anthropologists were actually employed by colonial states or served their needs: Margaret Green and Sylvia Leith-Ross, for example, were hired to study Igbo society following the Aba Women's War in part because the British wanted to understand how they failed to anticipate this violent eruption.[36] Pioneering British anthropologists of the interwar period, including R. S. Rattray (who was a trained lawyer), C. K. Meek, and Isaac Schapera, were strongly influenced by ideas of homoeostasis and evolutionism, which were linked to the colonial project of gradual modernization. These anthropologists saw law and custom as central to the maintenance of social stability, producing digests of rule-oriented customs based largely on conversations with male elders. The postwar period introduced a significant break in methods and approach. Max Gluckman led an approach that examined actual disputes and used the evidence to develop theories about how African judges adjudicated them, while A. L. Epstein broke with the established patterns of studying 'bounded' rural societies by examining urban Africans. Epstein used disputes heard in courts to help reconstruct the changing nature of African social life in the rapidly expanding cities of late colonial Africa.[37]

Early French ethnology was largely conducted by scholar-administrators and their African assistants. The most prominent was Maurice Delafosse, who was influenced by Arnold Van Gennep's evolutionism; both played a key role in the founding of the Institut d'Ethnographie in Paris. Delafosse assiduously collected 'customs and laws' from ethnic groups across the Federation of French West Africa, synthesizing his findings into a major statement on what he termed 'Sudanese civilization'.[38] A fascinating part of this production of knowledge was the role of African assistants, many of whom returned to their own communities and produced *coutumiers* or digests of laws and customs.[39] French anthropologists did not, however, play a major role in the development of legal anthropology.

A major shift in the anthropological study of law among colonial and subject peoples came with attention to the dispute as a reflection of core principles of social organization and behaviour. Disputes provided the raw material that scholars used to extract the substance of rules and the meaning of law in societies without formal courts or strong textual traditions. Laura Nader and her students shifted the emphasis from the dispute as a discrete event towards the study of the process of disputing. In their hands, the dispute became a feature of the 'social field' or set of wider social relationships and the process of disputing revealed forms and strategies of conflict management. The dispute was also understood to progress through stages, each providing opportunities for reconciliation. Statistically, very few grievances enter the formal dispute stage, because of social pressures to return the relationship to its 'harmonious' level or to avoid public conflict.[40]

A focus on the processes of conflict resolution, however, tends to efface the often profound asymmetries of power in societies and how these asymmetries skew the options available to disputants. June Starr and Jane Collier have sought to place unequal power relations at the centre of their analysis of law and society, arguing that law and power are mutually reinforcing on cultural and institutional levels as well as in practice.[41] For local courts and judicial personnel, knowing a disputant's social background is highly predictive of the legal outcome. This meant that the aggrieved person of lower status was unlikely to receive satisfaction in disputes with those of higher status. The presence of courts beyond the control of the close-knit community provided litigants with new strategies about where to take their disputes, but also new risks arising from the choices they made. Only those individuals who wished to disrupt or to sever their relationships (or who did not anticipate that this was a likely outcome) would go to colonial or national courts.

The case method has a long history within the field of Anglo-American legal anthropology. Legal anthropologists argue that the cases they use are representative of a wider body of disputes, extracting from them general principles, the value of which stems from the nature of the case observed. Lloyd Fallers proposed a methodological shift from the study of the individual case to what he called 'trouble spots'. Fallers noticed that cases tended to congeal around certain relationships that pointed to systemic conflict stemming from social change:

> Thus societies have their characteristic "trouble spots" out of which disputes sprout like weeds. In societies whose members take their trouble cases to courts of law, those trouble spots shape the docket—give pattern to the traffic of litigation that flows through the courts. Arising from such troubled areas of social life one may expect to find more frequent—and more interesting (from the point of view of an analysis of legal concepts in action)—litigation.[42]

A central part of using court records for social history is to contextualize these trouble spots within wider patterns of social change. Sally Falk Moore has described this method as moving back and forth between the small-scale events documented in the court cases and the large-scale social processes that are not visible through the court records themselves.[43] These examples point to two important issues in the social history of colonial Africa: how and why did Africans bring their disputes to new courts, and what do these disputes tell us about social change? Students of court records must also be attentive to how courts transform disputes into the texts we read.

COURTS AND PROCEDURES IN COLONIAL AFRICA

The establishment of colonial legal systems provided new opportunities for Africans with grievances. New courts coincided with significant transformations set in motion by colonial conquest and rule, altering landscapes of power throughout colonial Africa. These patterns are reminiscent of those described by Bernard Cohn in colonial India, where because courts sought to resolve cases based on clearly defined rights, winners were rewarded and losers punished. Yet, by creating an arena in which judgments were decisive and where courts treated all parties as equal before the law, the new courts became sites where those least entrenched in the social hierarchy could challenge the status quo and occasionally win.[44] Elizabeth Colson found similar patterns among the Tonga of the Gwenbe Valley in Zambia during the thirty-six years she worked in the region. Colson noted that, while the nature of the disputes (the trouble spots) had been more or less constant, the disputants increasingly chose to avoid the reconciliation of the village moots in favour of bringing their disputes before chiefs' courts established by the British. Colson attributed these changes to the tendency for individuals to act on their own initiatives for their own gain, which contributed to the erosion of village elders' authority. Litigants understood that the chiefs' courts were under the authority of the larger colonial state and thus anticipated that the courts' decisions would be enforced.[45]

The creation of multiple legal spheres involving the seepage of metropolitan concepts and procedures into native law often led to changes in the legal character and capacity of individuals. This enabled women, younger adults, and others of low status to confront higher-status men even in courts designed to uphold custom. The transcripts of cases heard in colonial courts contain testimony about wrongs, claims for damages, strained or broken relationships, and requests to the court to act upon those claims. In criminal cases, additional forms of evidence—eyewitness accounts, forensic evidence—were also admitted. But the grievance we read in the transcripts has been altered by the process of transforming the dispute into a court case, by court procedures, by translation, and by the act of transcribing oral testimony as text. As the grievance moves through the naming, blaming, and claiming phases, it is transformed from an inchoate sense of having suffered an injurious act into an articulated claim that can be understood and acted upon by an adjudicating body.

Susan Hirsch has applied linguistic and discourse analysis to Swahili women's disputes brought before the qadi's courts in Mombasa, using both documentary records and her own observations of disputes. By bringing cases before the qadi, the women sought to negotiate marital disputes, thereby refashioning gender relations in the process. Swahili women are supposed to be persevering and subordinate, but by narrating their troubles in court they were transforming gender through speech and attempting to transform their lives through action. Hirsch argues that 'gender is constituted in legal contexts that reproduce and also undermine dominant cultural configurations of gendered subject and gender relations'. The courts thus become 'sites of resistance'—and successful ones, as the judgments tend to favour women.[46]

The transcript of the court appearance is but a shadow of the complex set of interactions that actually took place in the courtroom. James Clifford has reflected on the differences between this stenographic record and what he observed during the 1976 Massachusetts Mashpee Indian land claims case, noting that the trial records omits 'gestures, hesitations, clothing, tone of voice, laughter, irony...sometimes devastating silences'.[47] These omissions are potentially significant because these signs and gestures are often central to the overall effect litigants, witnesses, and lawyers have on the outcome of the trial. Even though Hirsch sought to transcribe the entire disputes, 'the transcription process fails to capture so much of what made these narratives meaningful to the participants at the time and, later, to me as analyst'.[48] As a rule, historians cannot watch and listen to past courtroom encounters. Those working with colonial court records will rarely have access to even the stenographically recorded versions Clifford found so faulty. Most colonial court records are at best summaries of the dispute that were produced by some intermediary, whose control over translation may have been less than perfect. That said, court transcripts—despite taking the form of translated summaries—are rich reservoirs of African lived experience, offering what are often unparalleled insights into social history for periods now beyond the reach of oral testimony.

CRIMES AND PUNISHMENTS

Prisons were rare in Africa during the precolonial period and crimes were primarily victim-focused, with victims or their kin receiving compensation. Some crimes were considered so heinous as to result in execution, enslavement, or expulsion. In a brilliant study of the unintended consequences of the imposition of colonial justice, Colson analysed how the Tonga struggled to deal with the British arrest and imprisonment of a defendant convicted of manslaughter. In the precolonial period, manslaughter required compensation to the kin of the victim; failure to comply called for armed vengeance. British justice undermined both responses: armed violence was prohibited and the imprisonment of the perpetrator robbed the victim's kin of acceptable compensation. Tensions festered until the wives of the two lineages pleaded with their elders to 'invent' a new solution involving formal apologies and negotiated compensation.[49] Colonial practices of crimes and punishment were thus part of ongoing struggles over the meanings of rules and expectations.

Michel Foucault's analysis of the prison as an integral part of the development of European governmentality, surveillance, and control has been enormously productive.[50] Yet importing Foucault into Africa bumps up against the fundamental problem of the colonial state's limited capacity to impose its power over space and time. Few precolonial states had prisons. There is some evidence that more bureaucratized and centralized states may have had prison-like institutions, most likely for political prisoners, while the overseas slave trades generated the need to house captives awaiting shipment in prison-like barracoons or forts.[51] The growth of prisons was associated with the colonial state, appearing as early as 1812 in Sierra Leone and spreading with the development of formal colonies and criminal punishments. Carceral regimes tended to be more developed in white settler societies in Africa, where they were employed as a means of controlling labour and were linked to the elaboration of pass laws and regulations governing conditions of service. Pass laws designed to control the circulation of labour expanded dramatically in South Africa with the advent of the mining industry from 1867 onwards; in Southern Rhodesia and Kenya, laws regulating labour favoured employers and imposed imprisonment for violations. In a 1935 indictment against the abuses of colonial justice, Justice C. Clifton Roberts noted that 'by multiplying the number of offences which an African is able to commit, often unwittingly, the law in Africa is frequently creating criminals'.[52] What criminality meant and to whom is a rich subject that warrants fuller analysis.[53]

Prisons and policing developed with the needs of capital and the capacity of the state. Yet they did not fully institute the capillaries of power so crucial to Foucault's analysis. In French colonial Africa, the most ubiquitous form of punishment stemmed from the *indigénat,* a form of administrative law that emerged in 1887 and gave summary powers of punishment to administrators. In many ways, the *indigénat* reflected the inherent weakness of the colonial state, precisely because perceived challenges to authority were dealt with harshly. It gave officers powers to arrest and imprison Africans for a specified range of petty infractions without the need to present formal cases before judges and without the right of appeal. The *indigénat* was like an accordion: it expanded over time to encompass many more infractions and then shrank as Africans and human rights activists protested the arbitrary nature of the system.[54]

Prisons in Africa expanded dramatically in the post-Second World War era. In South Africa, the National Party's electoral victory in 1948 ushered in a level of investment in surveillance and repression hitherto unprecedented in Africa, the elaboration of Apartheid legislation and the expansion of police and courts resulting in the expanding capacity of the South African state to broadcast its power. One of the results of the widespread African transgression of Apartheid laws was the criminalization of everyday activities and the growth of incarceration as punishment. As Kenya grappled with Mau Mau, the colonial state also invested heavily in prisons and detention camps. In 1940 Kenya had some thirty prisons, most of which were small detention centres linked to the headquarters of district officers; during the height of the emergency in the mid-1950s, the colony housed over 86,000 prisoners in 176 prisons and camps. As prisons expanded, so did punishments—including capital punishment.[55] In the 1950s, punishments in neighbouring Tanganyika were three times as harsh as in the metropole for similar crimes.

Prison was not the only form of punishment for crimes in colonial Africa. Abuses during the Congo Free State era have been widely discussed and involved amputations, hostage taking, the destruction of villages, and whipping. Indeed, whipping was probably the most ubiquitous form of colonial punishment across the continent, although one that diminished over time as exposés forced authorities to rein in abuses. Prisons also became central institutions for the recruitment of forced labour, long a central mechanism in the effort to reform prisoners and inculcate in them the salubrious role of work. In South Africa and throughout colonial Africa, prisons often fed the demand for cheap agricultural labour—despite efforts at reform, including the International Prison Commission of 1929 and the International Labour Office's pressure on the League of Nations to investigate abuses in 1932. Although the late colonial era witnessed significant investment in prisons, especially in settler colonies and when faced with real or perceived threats to authority, little investment was made in reform and probation. A fascinating area of research is the phenomena of reform schools and the nature of juvenile delinquency. The few studies that we have on juvenile delinquency must grapple with the status of the child in African societies and the influences of urbanization and migration on changing the structures of households and of family authority.[56]

Conclusion

Law lay at the heart of the colonial encounter in Africa. Colonial officials used law to promote both the legibility and the stability of African societies. In practice, colonial legal systems promoted conflict by imposing rules and expectations that were not widely shared or deeply embedded in African discourses of political and social authority. The law, however, was only part of wider and intersecting processes of change. Students of colonial law, crime, and punishment need to situate the history of legal systems and litigants' practices within the contexts of these wider transformations. Debates about the meaning of the law, legal statuses, and rights and expectations predated colonialism, were accelerated by the colonial encounter, and persist to this day. Law in colonial societies and how Africans used the law remains an exciting area of research.

NOTES

1. Margery Perham, 'Editor's Preface', in C. K. Meek, *Colonial Law: A Bibliography with Special Reference to Native African Systems of Law and Land Tenure* (London: OUP, 1948), p. v.
2. Max Gluckman, *The Judicial Process among the Barotse of Northern Rhodesia* (Manchester: MUP, 1955), 21.
3. John Griffiths, 'What is Legal Pluralism?', *Journal of Legal Pluralism*, 24 (1986).
4. See Mahmood Mamdani, *Citizen and Subject: Contemporary Africa and the Legacy of Late Colonialism* (Princeton: PUP, 1996), 21–3, 108–28; A. N. Allott, ed., *Judicial and Legal Systems in Africa* (London: Butterworths, 2nd edn, 1970).
5. Lauren Benton, *Law and Colonial Cultures: Legal Regimes in World History, 1400–1900* (Cambridge: CUP, 2002), 3–11.
6. Richard Roberts, *Litigants and Households: African Disputes and Colonial Courts in the French Soudan, 1895–1912* (Portsmouth, NH: Heinemann, 2005); Sally Engle Merry, 'Legal Pluralism', *Law and Society Review*, 22/5 (1988), 879.
7. Jeffrey Herbst, *States and Power in Africa: Comparative Lessons in Authority and Control* (Princeton: PUP, 2000).
8. Alfred M. Kamanda, *A Study of the Legal Status of Protectorates in Public International Law* (Ambilly: Université de Genève, 1961), 97–8.
9. As theorized by Frederick Lugard in *The Dual Mandate in British Tropical Africa* (London: Frank Cass, 1922).
10. Elizabeth Thornberry, 'Sex, Violence, and the Family in South Africa's Eastern Cape', in Emily Burrill, Richard Roberts, and Elizabeth Thornberry, eds, *Domestic Violence and the Law in Colonial and Postcolonial Africa* (Athens, O.: Ohio University Press, 2010).
11. Marie Rodet, 'Continuum of Gendered Violence: The Colonial Invention of Female Desertion as a Customary Criminal Offense, 1900–1947', in Burrill *et al.*, *Domestic Violence*.
12. Jens Meierhenrich, *The Legacies of Law: Long-Run Consequences of Legal Developments in South Africa, 1652–2000* (New York: CUP, 2008), 92–3.
13. June Starr and Jane Collier have suggested that customary law was a colonial invention that needs to be analytically separate from what they term indigenous law: *History and Power in the Study of Law: New Directions in Legal Anthropology* (Ithaca, NY: Cornell University Press, 1989), 8–9.
14. Terence Ranger, 'The Invention of Tradition in Colonial Africa', in Eric Hobsbawm and Terence Ranger, eds, *The Invention of Tradition* (Cambridge: CUP, 1983); see too Martin Chanock, *Law, Custom and Social Order: The Colonial Experience in Malawi and Zambia* (Cambridge: CUP, 1985); Sally Falk Moore, 'Treating Law as Knowledge: Telling Colonial Officers What to Say to Africans about Running "Their Own" Native Courts', *Law and Society Review*, 26/1 (1992);; Jean-Hervé Jézéquel, ' "Collecting Customary Law": Educated Africans, Ethnographic Writings, and Colonial Justice in French West Africa', in Benjamin N. Lawrance, Emily L. Osborn, and Richard L. Roberts, eds, *Intermediaries, Interpreters, and Clerks: Africans in the Making of Modern Africa* (Madison, Wis.: University of Wisconsin Press, 2006).
15. See e.g. Isaac Schapera, *A Handbook of Tswana Law and Custom* (London: OUP, 1938).

16. Thomas Spear, 'Neo-Traditionalism and Limits of Invention of Tradition in British Colonial Africa', *Journal of African History*, 44/1 (2003); see too Carolyn Hamilton, *Terrific Majesty: The Powers of Shaka Zulu and the Limits of Historical Invention* (Cambridge, Mass.: Harvard University Press, 1998).

17. Sara Berry, *No Condition is Permanent: The Social Dynamics of Agrarian Change in Sub-Saharan Africa* (Madison, Wis.: University of Wisconsin Press, 1993), 8.

18. Emily Burrill and Richard Roberts, 'Domestic Violence, Colonial Courts, and the End of Slavery in the French Soudan, 1905–12', in Burrill *et al.*, *Domestic Violence*.

19. See Shamil Jeppie, Ebrahim Moosa, and Richard Roberts, eds, *Muslim Family Law in Sub-Saharan Africa: Colonial Legacies and Postcolonial Challenges* (Amsterdam: AUP, 2010).

20. See e.g. the excellent discussion about the qadis' court of Brava, Italian Somaliland, Alessandra Vianello and Mohamed M. Kassim, eds, *Servants of the Shari'a: The Civil Register of the Qadis' Court of Brava, 1893–1900*, 2 vols (Leiden: Brill, 2006).

21. In French West Africa and Equatorial Africa this was enforced through the 1939 Mandel Decree: Jeanne Maddox Toungara, 'Changing the Meaning of Marriage: Women and Family Law in Côte d'Ivoire', in Gwendolyn Mikell, ed., *African Feminism: The Politics of Survival in Sub-Saharan Africa* (Philadelphia: University of Pennsylvania Press, 1997). On the outlawing of corporal punishment in British colonial Africa, see Steven Pierce, 'Punishment and the Political Body: Flogging and Colonialism in Northern Nigeria', in Steven Pierce and Anupama Rao, eds, *Discipline and the Other Body: Correction, Corporeality, Colonialism* (Durham, NC: Duke University Press, 2007).

22. J. N. D. Anderson, 'The Future of Islamic Law in British Commonwealth Territories in Africa', *Law and Contemporary Problems*, 27/4 (1962), 623.

23. Mamdani, *Subject and Citizen*, promotes this bifurcated model.

24. Michael Crowder discusses the jurisdictional ambiguities that were a ubiquitous feature of colonial law in *The Flogging of Phinehas McIntosh: A Tale of Colonial Folly and Injustice, Bechuanaland 1933* (New Haven, Conn.: Yale University Press, 1988).

25. See esp. Roberts, *Litigants and Households*; on the Italian colonial legal system, see Irma Taddia, *L'Eritrea-colonia 1890–1952: Paesaggi, strutture, uomini del colonialism* (Milan: France Angeli, 1986); on the Belgian Congo, see M. B. Dembour, *Recalling the Belgian Congo: Conversations and Introspections* (Oxford: Berghahn Books, 2000).

26. Ruth Ginio, 'Negotiating Legal Authority in French West Africa: The Colonial Administration and African Assessors', in Lawrance et al., *Intermediaries*.

27. Roberts, *Litigants and Households*.

28. See Kristin Mann, *Slavery and the Birth of an African City: Lagos, 1760–1900* (Bloomington, Ind.: Indiana University Press, 2007), chs 7 and 8.

29. For the operation of these lower level courts in Nigeria, see Paul Bohannan, *Justice and Judgment among the Tiv* (London: OUP, 1957).

30. See e.g. Allan Christelow, *Thus Ruled Emir Abbas: Selected Cases from the Records of the Emir of Kano's Judicial Council* (East Lansing, Mich.: Michigan State University Press, 1994); Elke Stockreiter, 'Child Marriage and Domestic Violence: Islamic and Colonial Discourses on Gender and the Female Status in Zanzibar', in Burrill et al., *Domestic Violence*.

31. Quoted in Margery Perham, *Native Administration in Nigeria* (London: OUP, 1937), 55.

32. Anthony Kirk-Greene, 'The Thin White Line: The Size of the British Colonial Service in Africa', *African Affairs*, 79 (1980).

33. Omoniyi Adewoye, *The Judicial System in Southern Nigeria, 1854–1954* (Atlantic Highlands, NJ: Humanities Press, 1977), 77; see also Maurice Nyamanga Amutabi, 'Power and Influence of African Court Clerks and Translators in Colonial Kenya: The Case of Khwisero Native (African) Court, 1946–1956', in Lawrance et al., *Intermediaries*.

34. See T. O. Elias, *Groundwork of Nigerian Law* (London: Routledge & Kegan Paul, 1954), 351–9; Bjorn Edsman, *Lawyers in Gold Coast Politics, c.1900–1945: From Mensah Sarbah to J. B. Danquah* (Stockholm: Almqvist & Wiksell, 1979).

35. For an example, see Kenneth S. Broun, *Black Lawyers, White Courts: The Soul of South African Law* (Athens, O.: Ohio University Press, 2000).

36. Margaret Mackeson *Ibo Village Affairs, Chiefly with Reference to the Village of Umueke Agbaja* (London: Sidgwick & Jackson, 1947); Sylvia Leith-Ross, *African Women: A Study of the Ibo of Nigeria* (London: Faber, 1939).

37. A. L. Epstein, *Politics in an Urban African Community* (Manchester: MUP, 1958) and *Juridical Techniques and the Judicial Process: A Study in African Customary Law* (Manchester: MUP, 1954).

38. Maurice Delafosse, *Haut-Sénégal-Niger*, 3 vols (Paris: Maisonneuve & Larose, 1972 [orig. 1912]).

39. See Jean-Hervé Jézéquel, ' "Collecting Customary Law": Educated Africans, Ethnographic Writings, and Colonial Justice in French West Africa', in Lawrence et al., *Intermediaries*.

40. Laura Nader, *Harmony Ideology: Justice and Control in a Zapotec Mountain Village* (Stanford, Calif.: Stanford University Press, 1990).

41. Starr and Collier, *History and Power*, 1–3, 6–9.

42. Lloyd Fallers, *Law without Precedent: Legal Ideas in Action in the Courts of Colonial Busoga* (Chicago: University of Chicago Press, 1969), 85–6.

43. Sally Falk Moore, *Social Facts and Fabrications: 'Customary' Law on Kilimanjaro, 1880–1980* (New York: CUP, 1986), 1–12.

44. Bernard Cohn, *Colonialism and its Forms of Knowledge: The British in India* (Princeton: PUP, 1996).

45. Elizabeth Colson, 'The Contentiousness of Disputes', in Pat Kaplan, ed., *Understanding Disputes: The Politics of Argument* (Providence, RI: Berg, 1995), 71–7.

46. Susan F. Hirsch, *Pronouncing and Persevering: Gender and Discourses of Disputing in an African Islamic Court* (Chicago: University of Chicago Press, 1998), 3–4, 136.

47. James Clifford, *The Predicament of Culture: Twentieth Century Ethnography, Literature, and Art* (Cambridge, Mass.: Harvard University Press, 1988), 290.

48. Hirsch, *Pronouncing and Persevering*, 72.

49. Elizabeth Colson, 'Social Control and Vengeance in Plateau Tonga Society', *Africa*, 23/3 (1953).

50. Michel Foucault, *Discipline and Punish: The Birth of the Prison*, tr. Alan Sheridan (New York: Vintage Books, 1995).

51. See the chapters dealing with the precolonial period in Florence Bernault, ed., *Enfermement, prison, et châtiments en Afrique: Du 19e siècle à nos jours* (Paris: Karthala, 1999), 72.

52. C. Clifton Roberts, *Tangled Justice: Some Reasons for a Change of Policy in Africa* (London: Macmillan, 1937), 36.

53. For how crimes can be used to examine wider social trends, see the essays in Burrill et al., *Domestic Violence*.

54. Gregory Mann, 'What was the *Indigénat*? The "Empire of Law" in French West Africa', *Journal of African History*, 50 (2009).
55. David Anderson, *Histories of the Hanged: The Dirty War in Kenya and the End of Empire* (New York: Norton, 2005); Daniel Branch, *Defeating Mau Mau, Creating Kenya: Counterinsurgency, Civil War, and Decolonization* (New York: CUP, 2009).
56. For a useful survey, see Richard Waller, 'Rebellious Youth in Colonial Africa', *Journal of African History*, 47 (2006).

BIBLIOGRAPHY

Adewoye, Omoniyi, *The Judicial System in Southern Nigeria, 1854–1954* (Atlantic Highlands, NJ: Humanities Press, 1977).

Benton, Lauren, *Law and Colonial Cultures: Legal Regimes in World History, 1400–1900* (Cambridge: CUP, 2002).

Burrill, Emily, Richard Roberts, and Elizabeth Thornberry, eds, *Domestic Violence and the Law in Colonial and Postcolonial Africa* (Athens, O.: Ohio University Press, 2010).

Chanock, Martin, *Law, Custom, and Social Order: The Colonial Experience in Malawi and Zambia* (Cambridge: CUP, 1985).

Cohen, David W., and E. S. Atieno-Odhiambo, *Burying SM: The Politics of Knowledge and the Sociology of Power in Africa* (Portsmouth, NH: Heinemann, 1992).

Colson, Elizabeth, 'Social Control and Vengeance in Plateau Tonga Society', *Africa*, 23/3 (1953).

Fallers, Lloyd, *Law without Precedent: Legal Ideas in Action in the Courts of Colonial Busoga* (Chicago: University of Chicago Press, 1969).

Gluckman, Max, *The Judicial Process among the Barotse of Northern Rhodesia* (Manchester: MUP, 1955).

Lawrance, Benjamin N., Emily Lynn Osborn, and Richard L. Roberts, eds, *Intermediaries, Interpreters, and Clerks: Africans in the Making of Modern Africa* (Madison, Wis.: University of Wisconsin Press, 2006).

Mann, Kristin, *Slavery and the Birth of an African City: Lagos, 1760–1900* (Bloomington, Ind.: Indiana University Press, 2007).

—— and Richard Roberts, eds, *Law in Colonial Africa* (Portsmouth, NH: Heinemann, 1991).

Moore, Sally Falk, *Social Facts and Fabrications: 'Customary' Law on Kilimanjaro, 1880–1980* (New York: CUP, 1986).

Ranger, Terence, 'The Invention of Tradition in Colonial Africa', in Eric Hobsbawm and Terence Ranger, eds, *The Invention of Tradition* (Cambridge: CUP, 1983).

Roberts, Richard, *Litigants and Households: African Disputes and Colonial Courts in the French Soudan, 1895–1912* (Portsmouth, NH: Heinemann, 2005).

Shadle, Brett, *'Girl Cases': Marriage and Colonialism in Gusiland, Kenya, 1890–1970* (Portsmouth, NH: Heinemann, 2006).

Spear, Thomas, 'Neo-Traditionalism and Limits of Invention of Tradition in British Colonial Africa', *Journal of African History*, 44/1 (2003).

Starr, June, and Jane Collier, *History and Power in the Study of Law: New Directions in Legal Anthropology* (Ithaca, NY: Cornell University Press, 1989).

CHAPTER 10

....

WORK AND MIGRATION

....

EMILY LYNN OSBORN

THE subjects of work and migration have figured centrally in research on Africa since the early twentieth century. Much of that scholarship has focused on the effects of large-scale transformations, specifically capitalism and industrialization, on patterns of work and migration in the southern reaches of the continent, which became home to extractive mining economies of diamonds, gold, and copper. In the first half of the twentieth century, colonial officials and scholars drew on racial and cultural stereotypes to argue that 'tribal' Africans were ill-suited to waged work and urban life. With the changing political climate of the 1940s and 1950s, modernization theorists proposed a different interpretation, drawing parallels with the process of industrialization in Europe and contending that Africans could indeed adapt to the demands of employment and town life. Since that time, other approaches have emerged. Marxist scholars considered work and employment through the lens of class formation and consciousness. Social historians have exposed the importance of culture and past practice to patterns of work, while other studies have investigated cultures of work and the way that labour has tested and changed political systems.

While the historiography of work and migration in Africa is therefore rich, it is nonetheless riddled with blind spots. The assumption on the part of many studies that work is to be equated with 'modern' industrial and capitalist production has meant that a great deal of research has concentrated on wage labour and the men who carry it out. In effect, the history of work in Africa has often been treated as the history of wage labour. But given that formal waged employment has been more the exception than the rule in the vast majority of the continent for most of the twentieth century, this emphasis has come at the expense of other types of productive activities, such as those carried out by small-scale artisans and entrepreneurs. Until recently, it has also come at the expense of women, who are much less likely than men to obtain waged employment.

This chapter considers the history and the historiography of work and migration, broadly defined, in modern Africa. In so doing, it follows the lead of the literature by placing considerable emphasis on southern Africa, and in particular on South Africa, which in the colonial era became the most industrialized country on the continent as well as home to its most repressive, racialized regime. But it also explores the twentieth-century history of work and migration as they unfolded and have been interpreted elsewhere on the continent.

THE 'PRIMITIVIST' INTERPRETATION

The earliest corpus of writing on migration and labour in Africa concentrated mostly on South Africa where, by 1900, a substantial mining sector had emerged. The discovery of diamonds in 1867 and gold in 1886 drew migrant workers from across southern Africa—and indeed from beyond the continent—who sought to take part in the rush for mineral wealth. From the outset of the boom, white land-owners and speculators united to ban blacks from owning mining claims, but African men nonetheless constituted a vital part of the mining workforce. By 1900, finance capital and imported technologies supplanted the small investors and artisanal miners who had launched the boom. The industrialized mines that replaced them generated a huge demand for cheap African labour and gave rise to the compound mine system, in which African miners signed contracts to work for months at a time during which they lived in tightly controlled enclosures. The demand for labour became critically important to the South African economy and the effort to procure and manage African workers inspired a wealth of writings on 'the labour question'.

The businessmen, colonial officials, and academics of the early twentieth century who analysed the role of Africans in the mining economies promoted what can be called a 'primitivist' interpretation of African labour. At its core, that interpretation proposed that Africans were essentially 'tribal' peoples whose rural roots and backward ways prevented them from managing the demands of European civilization and commerce.[1] Three central tenets anchored the primitivist interpretation of labour. First, the primitivists argued that prior to European contact, Africans lived a static, unchanging existence under environmental conditions that neither inspired nor required innovation. Africans, they posited, were neither capable of, nor interested in progress or in improving their material or cultural condition.[2] Second, the primitivist myth contended that fixed gender norms determined the productive responsibilities of men and women. Men allegedly looked on most manual labour 'with contempt' and they thought that handling 'the hoe and pick' was beneath their dignity.[3] Women consequently cultivated crops while men herded cattle, a division of labour seen to liberate men to work in the mines. Finally, the primitivist interpretation asserted that males migrated and worked only on a temporary basis, for the intractable bonds of tribe and kinship meant that 'the African' could not and would not survive for long in the alien environment of the town or the mine.[4] As a result, so the argument ran, it was neither appropriate nor necessary for the colonial state to extend political or legal rights to Africans living in towns, for to do so would be to intervene with tribal, chiefly authority.

Primitivist thinking made a firm imprint on colonial policies in the early twentieth century. The presumption that Africans were intrinsically rural and tribal peoples who could be directed by chiefs lay at the heart of policies of indirect rule that were used to varying extents by both the British and the French. This idea achieved its most virulent and potent form in South Africa's Apartheid state, which from 1948 designated all Africans to tribal 'homelands' that were ruled by chiefs. The state strictly regulated Africans' mobility and conditions of employment outside these so-called labour reservoirs.

While deeply problematic from the perspective of the twenty-first century, the primitivist interpretation of labour and migration nonetheless presented colonial officials with a handy framework for explaining and managing the profound changes had been taking place on the continent since the late nineteenth century. By the 1940s, the migration of men to the mines had become a dominant feature of the economy of southern Africa. As later studies showed, in some regions it was not uncommon for 80 per cent of all adult men to leave for more than a year at a time to work in the mines.[5] It was, notably, those migratory streams that helped to dissolve the credibility of the primitivist myth. In the postwar era, the rapid growth of African cities provided irrefutable evidence that African urbanization was neither temporary nor transitory. The population of Lagos, for example, went from 99,700 in 1921 to 230,000 in 1950, while that of Dakar ballooned from 30,000 in 1926 to 305,000 in 1953.[6] At the same time—South African being the exception—the experience of the Second World War made crude racial categorizations less palatable and useful to colonial officials.

MODERNIZATION THEORY

The growing body of evidence that Africans could indeed leave behind their agricultural roots, work full time as wage labourers, and reconstitute family and tribal life in urban areas produced an alternative interpretation of African migration, urbanization, and work, that is, modernization theory. Unlike primitivists, modernization theorists saw Africans as active and autonomous agents who could adapt to new working conditions and the demands of urban life. They also believed that industrial-led development was a universal process that took place on a singular pathway, the progress of which in Africa could be measured using the same tools and methodologies as in Europe and elsewhere. In so doing, modernization theorists refuted primitivist claims about the immutability of tribal identity, as they sought to disprove the contention that Africans were ill-equipped to manage the complexities of capitalism and urban life. Proponents of modernization narratives included some French and British colonial officials, as well as an influential group of anthropologists at the Rhodes-Livingstone Institute in Northern Rhodesia who conducted research on the mining regions and urban areas of southern Africa.[7] Their research sought to rethink the role and influence of the tribe in African life. Unlike primitivists, modernists did not regard urbanization and 'detribalization' as synonyms for disintegration and disorder. Max Gluckman, for example, criticized the notion that tribal influence extended, unchanged, into urban areas, arguing that detribalization was not a slow and protracted process but rather an instantaneous occurrence which took place as soon as a migrant 'crosses his tribal boundary to go to town'.[8]

The modernist premise that African migrants could indeed live productive and secure lives in urban areas influenced some significant policy developments on the part of colonial governments. It helped change the way that mining companies in Northern Rhodesia managed their labour in the 1930s, as they moved away from short-term contracts and compound housing systems towards stabilization programmes, which permanently settled miners and their families in urban areas.[9] Modernists also offered a neat solution to a political problem, for they plotted a systematic pathway from Western employment patterns and status hierarchies towards African self-rule. For example, K. A. Busia's study of elites in the Gold Coast indicated that Western education helped to create a class of Africans who specialized in white-collar work and aspired to positions of political leadership.[10] In effect, professional employment laid the foundations for a new social order whose male members would, in time, usher in an era of political independence and autonomy.

The emphasis by modernization theorists on middle-class uplift meant, however, that little attention was paid to the other ways in which African men made their living in town. By and large, modernists gave little credence to small-scale, entrepreneurial productive activities.[11] Modernists seemed to think that such activities would eventually be incorporated into the world of wage labour or, alternatively, evaporate completely with the maturation of capitalist economies. In this regard, modernist studies of women proved more attentive to the diversity of work in urban contexts, in large part because women did not typically engage in regularized, waged work as did men.[12]

Modernization theory nonetheless constitutes an important change in the scholarship on migration and labour. It freed Africans from the determinism of the tribe while making room for other forces, such as Western education and professional employment, to act as causal factors in Africa's changing urban and rural landscapes. Modernists further embraced the idea that Africans could adapt to city life and respond to economic motives and incentives in the same ways as other people in the world. They also recognized that class, as an economic and social condition, could emerge as a basis of association and organization. But unlike later Marxists, modernization theorists identified a Western-educated middle class, not the working class, as key to political and social development, and to Africa's future more generally.

THE MARXIST INTERPRETATION

Wage labour continued to frame the next generation of research devoted to work and migration in Africa. Writing in the 1970s and 1980s, after most African colonies had gained independence, Marxist historians argued that capitalism functioned as the motor of economic, social, and political change on the continent. The Marxist historiography sought to show how capitalism created a self-conscious and politically engaged working class who could mobilize in their own interest against bourgeois owners of the means of production.[13] Those bourgeois capitalists found form in captains of industry, such as mine and factory owners, whose interests were seen to have propelled the operations of the colonial state.

The precise nature of the relationship between capitalism and the colonial state, however, provoked significant debate. Some Marxists claimed that there was virtually no distinction between the colonial state and capitalist prerogatives. In their edited volume on African labour history, Gutkind, Cohen, and Copans asserted that 'all over the continent, the general laws of capitalist development were set in motion by the colonial process'.[14] The reach of capitalism and colonialism left little untouched: colonization introduced capitalist relations of production to the continent and, as a result, 'more and more Africans were wrenched from their previous modes of production and reproduction and constrained to place their labor power at the disposal of alien forces of production'.[15] But other scholars (Marxist and otherwise) disagreed with this rendering of the seamless overlap of capitalism and colonialism. Some argued that capitalist modes of production predated the colonial incursion, while others noted that capitalists and industrialists were not the only ones who made claims on the colonial state. Yet others questioned the assertion that capitalism's encroachment was pervasive, hegemonic, and uncontested. By highlighting in particular the dynamics of production and export in regions outside of South Africa, they argued that other forms of non-capitalist production coexisted with capitalism.[16] Debates about the 'articulation' or 'disarticulation' of capitalism with precapitalist or subsistence economies proliferated within the Marxist literature.

While scholars argued over how, exactly, the colonial state inhered in capitalism, the analytic coupling of these two forces nonetheless enabled Marxists to make a powerful point. They stripped the colonial state of its legitimizing claims and redefined colonialism not as a cultural project that promoted civilization and modernity, but as an economic enterprise propelled by production and profit. Unlike modernization theorists, who tended to see colonialism and capitalism as essentially progressive, Marxists emphasized how those processes coerced, abused, and exploited African peasants and workers.

Yet capitalism emerges in much of the Marxist literature as a monolithic power that often acts in its own right, independently of human action and initiative. It seeks, expropriates, overwhelms, and provokes; it transforms, interpolates, and destroys. It operates as an omnipotent and generative force, the primary trigger of political, economic, and social change. Moreover, the case that the economic prerogatives of an expatriate and white settler bourgeoisie drove people and politics could be sustained more easily in some places than others: finance capital and industrialization played an undeniably powerful role in South Africa, which became home to an industrialized mining economy and a political apparatus, the Apartheid state, which devoted itself to ensuring the availability of cheap black labour. But even there, treating capitalism as the master determinant of social and political processes risked effacing other historical forces that also shaped peoples' position in, and relationship to the world around them. Elsewhere in the continent, where wage labour remained more the exception than the rule, and where colonial governments typically managed large-scale industrialization projects such as railways, it is even more difficult to parse out capitalism's singular influence and prove its linear progression.

While Marxists advanced a very different interpretation of colonialism than that of modernization theorists, the two approaches nonetheless had much in common. Both considered capitalism and colonialism to be transformative, urban centres as dynamic sites of change, and wage labour as critical to forming worker identity; both also assumed an emergence and evolution of social or class hierarchies over time.[17] But the two assigned divergent meanings to those processes because, at core, they viewed sources of change and conflict in fundamentally different ways. Modernists believed that Africa's Western-educated middle class would guide less 'advanced' peoples to a more productive, prosperous, and Westernized future. Impediments to that process, they thought, arose from the past: from tradition and tribe. Marxists, by contrast, did not view bourgeois elites as social and cultural role models whose enlightened and benevolent leadership would improve the lot of the masses. Rather, they emphasized economic processes and the ambition of bourgeois elites to squeeze profit from the workers. For them, conflict came not from the past, but from the present: from material conditions, economic structures, and competing class interests. The terminology employed by each of these interpretive frameworks also tells the tale: where modernists saw 'progress' and 'improvement', Marxists saw 'alienation' and 'exploitation'.

The idea that class position determined interest, behaviour, and action led Marxist historiography to particular topics. A great deal of scholarship focused on the origins and development of class consciousness. Even in the absence of unions or other formal workers' organizations, Marxists sought to demonstrate how workers in factories and mines coalesced into an economic class with a common outlook and agenda. Charles van Onselen takes up this issue in *Chibaro*, a classic study of Southern Rhodesian gold miners.[18] Van Onselen points out that the brutal conditions of compound life—workers lived in prison-like conditions that lacked privacy, basic amenities, and sufficient food rations—did not mean that mine owners achieved full control over mine workers. To the contrary, the stringent conditions of the compounds gave rise to a vibrant culture. Workers' associations, dance groups, burial societies, and mutual aid societies helped African miners contend with the tedium, toil, and dangers of mine life. This collectivity did not necessarily mobilize against mine owners in an attempt to improve their working conditions; efforts by workers to organize and strike for higher wages proved spotty at best. But, van Onselen contends, direct action is not the only measure of worker solidarity and class consciousness found other traceable expressions. Miners, for example, shared knowledge about the various pits and the treatment that they would receive there. This 'market intelligence' exercised a significant effect on labour flows and availability, acting as a check, albeit a weak one, on the mine owners' ongoing quest to squeeze profit from their workers.

The concern that van Onselen showed for establishing a link between class conscious-ness and political action was certainly not unique. In a study of iron ore miners in Sierra Leone, Ibrahim Abdullah argues that miners developed a sense of common identity through their interactions in palm-wine bars and private off-site housing. Those con-nections, as well as the input of former railway workers who had engaged previously in industrial action (yet more evidence of a transcendent working-class conscious-ness), enabled the miners to mobilize and strike in 1935 and 1938.[19] Indeed, it is possible to take a veritable tour of the continent via the historiography on collective action in the immediate post-Second World War period: the Rhodesian rail strike of 1945, the Mombasa strike of 1947, the Gold Coast mineworkers' strikes of 1947, the Zanzibar strike of 1948, and the French West African railway strike of 1947–8. These conflicts raised the political stakes, for Marxists identified them as part of a broader anti-colonial political trajectory. Labour activism, so many of these studies suggest, planted the seeds for nationalist movements. That some of Africa's independence leaders, such as Sékou Touré of Guinea, entered the political playing field through trade unions, helped fortify the contention that worker solidarity could translate into emancipatory political action. Even when direct links between union action and political independence could not be established, some argued that labour movements made the case for independence in a larger, somewhat ineffable moral sense.[20]

The Social History of Work and Migration

While Marxist historiography illuminates the history of working-class consciousness and labour mobilization, other historians investigated different types of productive activities excluded by the focus on waged work.

Social history gained momentum as a field of study in the 1980s and its practition-ers sought to illuminate the lived experience of people, such as women and slaves, who had largely been omitted from mainstream historical narratives. Non-waged systems of production also attracted attention, as historians began to investigate how men and women earned their living by farming, making crafts, and marketing goods and services. The turn towards a social history of work and migration in Africa did not nec-essarily constitute a radical departure from earlier analytical frameworks: some of the studies treated here as social history could be included in the above section, given their materialist bent and concern with class consciousness, while others share common-alities with the modernist interpretation. But what distinguished the new direction of research is that it sought to explore forms of work and mobility that were not captured by the earlier focus on Africa's factories, mines, and railways. These studies further question the progressive stages that undergirded much of the previous scholarship, for they show that transformations in work and production did not necessarily take place in a unidirectional manner, nor could they be explained solely by colonialism and capitalism.

One topic that social historians tackled in a variety of new ways was migration. As has been discussed, various schools of thought posited that capitalism generated altogether new migratory patterns in Africa. In his study of Mozambique, Patrick Harries suggests otherwise. By the nineteenth century, Harries argues, Mozambican men frequently travelled great distances to access new markets and opportunities in hunting and trading. When the mines first opened in South Africa, these footloose men needed little encouragement to go and work in them.[21] Research on other parts of the continent makes a similar point. In West Africa, François Manchuelle established that Soninke peoples in present-day Mali migrated to coastal areas for work and for commerce well before the French colonized their homeland in the late nineteenth century. Manchuelle reveals that internal dynamics are as important as external pressures in explaining the persistence of this system of labour migration during the colonial period.[22] These studies establish that when capitalist enterprises and colonial states sought to make Africans move to work, their demands did not necessarily fall on immobile populations who had never before left their homes, farms, and herds.

Historians and anthropologists interested in agricultural production have further complicated the dividing lines of previous scholarship. The arguments of primitivists, modernization theorists, and Marxists rested on assumptions about the 'backwardness' of Africa's rural economies. Social historians reached very different conclusions about the capacities and dynamism of African agriculture. In her pioneering 1963 study— one that helped lay the foundations for the field of African economic and social history—Polly Hill refuted the conceit that African farmers lacked 'economic foresight' or that they were incapable of accumulating, investing, or expanding their holdings.[23] Hill argued that, from the 1890s, Ghanaian cocoa farmers acted according to capitalist principles of profit motive and market forces, although they did not necessarily deploy 'Western' methods of capital accumulation and management to do so. Cocoa farmers instead drew upon local resources such as established patron–client networks and kinship ties to meet labour demands. Hill thus demonstrated that Ghana's pioneering cocoa farmers did not emerge from a timeless tradition and that the conceptual lines that proliferated in the academic literature, which separated rural from urban and subsistence from capitalist, did little to explain the strategies that farmers used to participate in the cocoa economy.

Hill's careful combination of ethnographic and historical research is a key feature of another important study on agricultural production in West Africa. In her investigation of Yoruba famers in Nigeria, Sara Berry takes up the Marxist paradigm of economic development, which assumes that bourgeois capitalists monopolized the means of production—be it factories, mines, or land—which forced dispossessed proletariats to work for wages, whether for captains of industry or large landholders. Berry argued that this model does not explain the commercialization of the Yoruba agricultural sector. Among the Yoruba, property owners generally held onto their land and wage labour operated as a welcome, although not required, supplement to household income. The

Marxist principle that accumulation required ownership over the means of production and access to capital also did not hold. Farmers who did not necessarily own land or have access to finance capital nonetheless managed to grow cocoa. They did so by drawing on kinship networks and compensating their help with foodstuffs or the promise of future harvests. This system meant that patron-employers 'could expect loyalty and obedience from their workers, but not necessarily efficiency'.[24] Berry goes a long way towards explaining the small-scale processes through which production and accumulation took place in the Nigerian countryside, as well as the incentives and relationships that enabled Yoruba to keep their feet simultaneously in many social and economic worlds.

Slavery and Its Demise

That colonialism and capitalism did not necessarily produce radical transformations or total ruptures is a lesson learnt from research into another system of work in Africa, that of slavery. Historians of slavery bring into focus a large group of people who forcibly performed a wide variety of tasks and jobs. While slavery had been abolished elsewhere in the world by the early twentieth century, in much of Africa it was still widely practised. Many slaves farmed and worked on plantations, producing spices, sugar, and other foodstuffs, while others worked as porters, traders, warriors, ritual specialists, and royal servants. The practice of slavery and slave-trading in Africa had been used by Europeans to justify the late nineteenth-century colonial conquest of the continent. But once conquest gave way to occupation, the colonizers proved reluctant to translate abolitionist rhetoric into policy by actively liberating slaves and promoting 'free labour'. Colonial officials worried that slave departures would cause social upheaval and risk their relations with chiefly elites, upon whom the colonial apparatus of indirect rule delicately rested. The task of abolition was further complicated by the reliance of many colonial states, at least until the Second World War, on forced or conscripted labour. The demands that the French, British, Belgians, and Portuguese made on male populations to work, without compensation, on the construction of roads, railways, and other public works projects, severely undermined the rhetoric and principle of 'free labour'.[25]

The tepid commitment by colonial officials to abolition meant that slavery's demise typically came about because of the initiative of slaves themselves, not because of colonial policies or actions. As a result, in most of Africa, slavery did not end abruptly, but rather underwent an erratic decline from the early 1900 to the 1930s, as slaves abandoned their masters, renegotiated the terms of their continued servitude, or simply died, leaving behind a younger generation who refused to shoulder the obligations of their parents.[26]

While considerable research has been devoted to the end of slavery in the early twentieth century, less attention has been paid to the way that slavery's jagged remnants persist and continue, influencing social relations, political processes, and—importantly for the history of work—professional and educational opportunities and practices. Gregory Mann makes this point in his book on Malian soldiers in French West Africa, observing that contemporary Mali is 'as much a post-slavery society as it is a post-colonial one'.[27] Mann details the strategies that African men used in the colonial era to counteract the stigma of slavery, including name changing and enlisting in the French army. Such investigations are not only important for understanding how the heritage of slavery has been reproduced, combated, and transformed over the twentieth century, but also for understanding the historical antecedents to contemporary slavery and human trafficking, a topic that has garnered considerable attention from non-governmental and international human rights organizations.[28] Various reasons have been used to explain the resurgence of slavery and human trafficking in recent years, and the increased vulnerability of certain groups to these processes in Africa (and elsewhere) has been attributed to poverty, natural disasters, political instability, and neo-liberal economic reforms. What demands more research—and where historians could and should contribute—is in uncovering the connections and disjunctures between present-day coercive labour practices and older forms of slavery. That is, do contemporary forms of human trafficking and slavery bear any social or structural links to earlier practices of pawning, captivity, and sale?

While studies of slavery have done much to illuminate the history of work in Africa, they are not immune from the gender biases that characterize the literature on wage labour. That is to say, research on slavery and its demise has tended to focus largely on men.[29] In part this emphasis can be explained by the visibility of male slaves as a population, as well as by the challenges of absorption and control that they posed. Enslaved men were more likely to work outside the home and thereby gain the attention of colonial officials, travellers, missionaries, and others; they were also more likely to pose a physical threat to their masters and become involved in confrontations and conflicts. By contrast, female slaves tended to work within the households of their masters, where they contributed to the domestic economy through their physical and reproductive labours. The servile status of female slaves, in other words, was often cloaked and complicated by family ties and intimate sexual relationships. What this means, when it comes to colonial archives, is that the voices of male slaves often speak more loudly and clearly than those of women.[30]

WOMEN'S HISTORY

Efforts to overcome the silences of women, slaves and others, in the colonial archive served to foster another genre of social history which is also important to understanding the history of work in Africa, that of women's history. In the 1970s, feminist historians developed a range of new methodologies to uncover the contributions of women to processes of change. Some did so by conducting extensive interviews with individual women, typically non-elites, and the resulting life histories shed light on the labour that women carried out as part of their domestic responsibilities, from preparing food to bearing and raising children and managing relations with co-wives and elders. Women's domestic labour is not necessarily confined to a household or kin group. Research by historians and anthropologists brought attention to women who worked as 'domestics' for other families, often migrating to distant urban areas to do so, while others highlighted how women transform the domestic labour of sex into a source of income and independence.[31] In her pioneering study of prostitution in colonial Nairobi, for example, Luise White drew upon oral interviews and archival evidence to expose domestic labour's transactional forms and processes. There, female sex workers reproduced the 'comforts of home' by offering a range of domestic services to male migrants to the city. Some of those women subsequently invested their earnings in property and became landlords, which increased both their income stream and their customer base.[32]

Of course, women entrepreneurs can also be found in other economic realms, as a visit to marketplaces throughout Africa makes clear. In her ethnographic study of women traders in Ghana, Gracia Clark illuminates the strategies, resources, and associations that women use to conduct business in Kumasi's central market, as well as the challenges that they face in balancing the requirements of commerce with their household duties.[33] Other studies have demonstrated women's historical dominance of various realms of agricultural and craft production, serving to establish that domestic labour constitutes—and should be treated as—'work'. They also show that African women perform many kinds of work both inside and outside the household. Moreover, the various productive activities in which women engage serve as yet another reminder that understanding the nature of work and its history in Africa requires an expansive approach, one that is mindful of labour's intimacies, as well the diverse ways that it can be structured and compensated.[34]

'INFORMALITY', THE PROFESSIONS, AND THE CULTURE OF WORK

Indeed, the many forms that productive activities can take in Africa is further underlined by research on the so-called 'informal sector' of African economies, a term coined by Keith Hart in an influential article on Ghana published in 1973.[35] Since that time, scholars, international organizations, and NGOs have all undertaken various efforts to understand the operations of services and markets that operate outside direct government regulation and taxation. These studies shed light on productive activities that are both highly responsive to and vulnerable to larger economic processes. They also illuminate how a great number of people make their living, not by regularized wages but by making sales, obtaining credit, and engaging in exchanges involving goods, services, and cash.

Where some of this literature goes awry is in its assumption that non-regulated work can be treated as a clearly identifiable 'informal' sector, distinct from the 'formal'. Such sharp delineations obscure the myriad ways in which so-called formality and informality overlap and interpolate one another across the economic spectrum. Also problematic is the description of the work of tailors, mechanics, hairstylists, aluminum casters, and others as 'informal', a term that suggests a degree of haphazardness and arbitrariness that is at odds with the structured systems of organization and apprenticeship that govern many of these activities and services.[36] Some of the research on supposedly informal economic activities is also mistaken in its claim that these activities are relatively new, spawned by neo-liberal reforms and structural adjustment programmes of the 1980s. Such assertions overlook the deep roots of African productive systems and the relationships that contemporary skilled workers and craftsman share with older services and forms of fabrication.[37] Indeed, one of the shortcomings of studies on 'informality' is that they often present snapshots of specific activities and processes, but they do not necessarily locate them within larger trajectories of historical change.

One recent book that avoids many of these pitfalls while also revealing the historicity and highly structured nature of what some might call 'informal' sector work is Trevor Marchand's study of masons in the Malian town of Djenné.[38] Marchand carried out his research by teaming up with some of Djenné's masons and joining their physical labours. He gained entry to their organizational meetings and carried on extended conversations with both masons and their clients. His tactile approach exposes him to the highly developed skill-sets of masons, as well as to the traditions, logics, and daily rhythms of their work. This perspective helps Marchand make the case that ensuring the preservation of Djenné's architectural heritage requires supporting the systems of knowledge that helped to create the city's unique built forms in the first place. This careful attention to practice and to (recent) history provides a lead that other scholars should follow and extend—Marchand neither disassociates masons from the past, nor does he characterize them as static relics of an age-old tradition. Rather, he shows them to be skilled and creative workers whose work is informed by deeply rooted systems of knowledge and production, as well as by new technologies and shifting market demands. This study takes labour seriously, not simply as a class or condition, but as a demanding productive activity that is learnt, executed, repeated, managed, and innovated.

Recent social history has done a good deal to advance our understanding of the diverse forms of work in Africa, as well as the people—men and women, urban and rural, skilled and unskilled—who carry it out. But the emphasis by social historians on the people and activities who live in the lower reaches of the socio-economic order has left another realm, that of Africa's professional middle classes, relatively untouched. Western education and the categories of employment it helped generate were not simply a product of colonization. In the nineteenth century, literate African professionals flourished in Freetown, Sierra Leone, and helped spawn a network of merchants, ministers, lawyers, and doctors who lived up and down the coast of West Africa; in the same era, mission-trained Africans gave rise to an emergent black middle class in South Africa.

By the early twentieth century, formal colonial rule and the repressive racial laws of South Africa narrowed but did not altogether eliminate avenues for Africans to obtain Western education and professional employment. In part, that is because the colonizers needed literate and linguistically proficient employees to staff the colonial bureaucracy. Indeed, recent research has shown that the African men who worked as interpreters, clerks, and scribes exercised considerably more power and influence on the daily operations of the colonial state than their official job titles imply.[39] With independence, the advantages conferred by Western training expanded considerably, as efforts to 'Africanize' industry and government created openings for African personnel to move up the ranks of private sector enterprises and public sector bureaucracies and occupy positions once held by Europeans. By the 1980s, however, structural adjustment programmes shrank governments and political regimes increasingly rewarded loyalty and connections rather than educational achievement. The gains that individuals could achieve through higher education became ever more elusive. This process was made clear by the fate of university students across the continent, who often entered the ranks of the un- and under-employed upon graduation. The history of Africa's professional classes is a complex one that is connected to and illuminative of larger economic and political transformations of the twentieth century. Africa's professionals have long stood at the intersection of competing values, intellectual traditions, and modalities of rule. The way that they managed those intersections over time is a topic that clearly demands more historical analysis.

FUTURE DIRECTIONS

In reflecting upon the present status and future direction of research on work, it is worth considering two important studies that each, in their own way, can be seen as bringing something of a resolution to some of the scholarly questions and debates discussed above. In his monumental comparative study of British and French Africa, Frederick Cooper takes on the question of labour's role in the politics of decolonization and, specifically, the contention that labour movements laid the groundwork for independence.[40] Incorporating the bottom–up techniques and sympathies of the social historian with a careful reading of political economy, Cooper has a number of critical insights about labour and the colonial state. He establishes that African workers were not an undifferentiated mass drawn together by a uniform set of grievances, but rather a diverse group whose shared interests also gave way to arguments and conflict. Disputes and debates also riddled the colonial state, as officials struggled to decide how to manage and control urbanized African men. Ultimately, the lurching steps made towards expanding workers' rights from the 1930s and 1940s—which were balanced by efforts on the part of colonial officials to curtail and co-opt workers' aspirations—reveal that it is a mistake to characterize the colonial state as a unified institution whose officials devoted themselves single-mindedly to exploiting the working class in the interests of capital.

Labour movements, Cooper argues, did indeed play an important role in the road to independence, but not necessarily because of strong ties between trade unions and nationalists. Rather, the link lay in the murkier realm of colonial politics. Union demands and effective strike action helped expose the competing claims that the colonial state made to development, progress, and civilization. In effect, the colonial state could not respond to demands for increased benefits and rights from organized labour—which would put its members on par with metropolitan workers—without dismantling the justification of colonialism and its fundamental distinction between 'subjects' and 'citizens'.

Yet wage labourers—as Cooper freely acknowledges—made up only a small percentage of the overall working population in French and British Africa. Only 1 or 2 per cent of the population worked for wages in the 1930s and 1940s. While these workers and their political legacies are obviously important, it is far from the whole story of work and migration in Africa. It would be fruitful for historians to apply the same sort of rigour that Cooper brings to bear on organized labour in order to explore the histories of the larger numbers of people who supported themselves in other ways, by weaving baskets and repairing cars, by driving taxis and hawking goods, by sewing clothes and recycling rubbish. Such investigations will require different sources and methodologies than those used by Cooper, but they will also infinitely enrich our understanding of work in twentieth-century Africa.

The second study that provides a provocative endpoint to an older body of scholarship is James Ferguson's *Expectations of Modernity*, an anthropological study of miners and retired miners on the Zambian Copperbelt.[41] The men who anchor this study once made their living in a sector that promised steady material rewards (as measured by salary and health and retirement benefits), as well as other, more ineffable returns in terms of cultural cachet and social status. But in the 1970s and 1980s, that pathway to working-class stability and respectability was shattered by structural adjustment programmes and fluctuating global prices of copper. In his analysis of the declining fortunes of Zambian workers, Ferguson dismantles the conceit of modernization theory, which presumed that 'progress', once achieved, would only give way to more advanced stages of development. He demonstrates that workers on the Copperbelt have a clear sense of what it means to be 'modern' and 'developed', with all the attendant cultural forms and material trappings. But for most Zambian workers, that condition remains elusive, a moving target that is ever-distant from their precarious daily lives.

Ferguson's book also points to a more general trend in scholarship about workers, for it makes abundantly clear that unionization and worker solidarity did not bring about radical political transformation, as Marxist historians had once hoped. Indeed, it has become commonplace in recent years to lament the decline of labour history as a distinct field of study. This anxiety emerges from the fact that far fewer scholars today study organized labour than in the 1970s and 1980s. But it also reflects the fact that organized labour is itself on the decline in Africa, as elsewhere in the world. In part that change has come about, as on the Zambian Copperbelt, because global trade agreements and neo-liberal economic policies have changed employment patterns, reduced union membership, and denuded sectors that used to offer employees regularized wages and benefits.[42] So too have political changes altered the landscape of workers' rights and representation, as the push towards multi-party democracies have often fractured and weakened the political clout of unions and workers' organizations. Indeed, job insecurity is more the norm than the exception which, if we widen the lens of analysis beyond organized labour to consider the vast array of ways in which people make their living in Africa, was clearly the case for the majority of Africans during the twentieth century. The instability of economic prospects in many African countries today has also changed migration patterns. Africans are more likely to travel longer distances in search of employment. In the twenty-first century, many African countries have become increasingly dependent upon the productive activities and remittances of their citizens who live abroad in other African countries or in Europe, Asia, and the United States.[43]

At the start of the twenty-first century, it is possible to identify some of the themes in the history of work and migration in Africa that will attract increasing scholarly attention. It is certain that the question of foreign investment on the continent, in particular Chinese interests, will garner more interest. Discussion of Chinese investment will no doubt continue to be informed by some of the terminologies and ideologies that have informed previous scholarship. Some view the Chinese as bearers of much-needed investment and modern technology that will bring African countries the benefits of industrialization and development—a view that echoes with the logic and rationale of the modernization theorists of the 1950s. Others decry Chinese companies and management, labelling them self-interested and exploitative of labour, an interpretation that is reminiscent of subsequent Marxist narratives. Each of these perspectives arguably leaves out as much as it leaves in—and each also overlooks the fact that the workers in Chinese-run factories and mines remain only a small percentage of Africa's working populations.

As this reflection on the evolution of the field suggests, it is imperative to not only trace those transformations that leave a visible and well-documented wake, such as Chinese investment. It is also important to recognize realms of productive activities that have not necessarily made a firm imprint on the colonial or postcolonial archive, to identify structure and history where others see only 'informality', and to pay heed to the ways in which people make their living on the margins, in circumstances that are at once precarious and unpredictable. It is the history of those various forms of work which has been largely undocumented and unwritten but which is, nonetheless, reflective of large portions of the population of the continent.

Notes

1. A note on use of the word 'tribe': from here on, I use the term as do the writers under discussion, without quotation marks.
2. The South African Native Races Committee, *The Natives of South Africa: Their Economic and Social Condition* (London: John Murray, 1901), 2; see also Raymond Leslie Buell, *The Native Problem in Africa* (New York: Macmillan, 1928); Alexander Davis, *The Native Problem in South Africa* (London: Chapman & Hall, 1903).

3. The South African Native Races Committee, *Natives of South Africa*, 3, 85.

4. See e.g. 'A Survey of African Labour', *International Labour Review*, 40/1 (1939), 80–1; Boris Gussman, 'Industrial Efficiency and the Urban African: A Study of Conditions in Southern Rhodesia', *Africa*, 23/2 (1953), 141; and for analysis, Frederick Cooper, *Decolonization and African Society: The Labor Question in French and British Africa* (Cambridge: CUP, 1996), 49 and *passim*.

5. See Isaac Schapera's 1947 study of Bechuanaland (now Botswana), *Migrant Labour and Tribal Life* (London: OUP, 1947), 71 and *passim*.

6. Michael Banton, *West African City: A Study of Tribal Life in Freetown* (London: OUP, 1957), p. xiii.

7. See e.g. Reginald Moore and A. Sandilands, *These African Copper Mines: A Study of the Industrial Revolution in Northern Rodesia [sic], with Principal Reference to the Copper Mining Industry* (London: Livingston Press, 1948), pp. ix, x, 41.

8. Max Gluckman, 'Anthropological Problems Arising from the African Industrial Revolution', in Aiden Southall, ed., *Social Change in Modern Africa* (London: OUP, 1961), 68, 69; see too, Banton, *West African City*; Jean Rouch, *Notes on Migrations into the Gold Coast*, tr. P. E. O. and J. B. Haigham (Paris: Musée de l'homme, 1955); Audrey Richards, *Economic Development and Tribal Change: A Study of Immigrant Labour in Buganda* (Cambridge: W. Heffer & Sons, 1954).

9. Stabilization proponents include R. L. Prain, 'The Stabilization of Labour in the Rhodesian Copper Belt', *African Affairs*, 55/221 (1956), and P. De Briey, 'The Productivity of African Labour', *International Labour Review*, 119 (1955). For analysis, see George Chauncey, 'The Locus of Reproduction: Women's Labour in the Zambian Copperbelt, 1927–1953', *Journal of Southern African Studies*, 7/2 (1981); Charles Perrings, *Black Mineworkers in Central Africa* (New York: Africana, 1979); Harold Wolpe, 'Capitalism and Cheap Labour-Power in South Africa: From Segregation to Apartheid', *Economy and Society*, 1/4 (1972).

10. K. A. Busia, 'The Present Situation and Aspirations of Elites in the Gold Coast', *International Social Science Bulletin*, 8 (1956); see also Paul Mercier, 'Evolution of Senegalese Elites', *International Social Science Bulletin*, 8 (1956); Kenneth Little, 'Social Change and Social Class in the Sierra Leone Protectorate', *American Journal of Sociology*, 54/1 (1948); J. Clyde Mitchell and A. L. Epstein, 'Occupational Prestige and Social Status among Urban Africans in Northern Rhodesia', *Africa*, 29 (1959).

11. For an exception, see Peter Lloyd, 'Craft Organization in Yoruba Towns', *Africa*, 23/1 (1953).

12. Tanya Baker and Mary Bird, 'Urbanisation and the Position of Women', *Sociological Review* (July 1959); see also Banton, *West African City*, 196–212; Kenneth Little, *African Women in Towns: An Aspect of Africa's Social Revolution* (Cambridge: CUP, 1973), 20.

13. For an important survey of much of this scholarship, see Bill Freund, 'Labor and Labor History in Africa: A Review of the Scholarship', *African Studies Review*, 27/2 (1984).

14. Peter C. W. Gutkind, Robin Cohen, and Jean Copans, eds, *African Labor History* (Beverly Hills, Calif.: Sage Publications, 1978), 7.

15. Gutkind et al., *African Labor History*, 8. The South African historiography in particular is replete with claims about the partnership of state and capital.

16. See e.g. Claude Meillassoux, *The Anthropology of Slavery: The Womb of Iron and Gold* (Chicago: University of Chicago Press, 1991); Emmanuel Terray, *Marxism and Primitive Societies: Two Studies* (New York: Monthly Review Press, 1972); and Bruce Berman and John Lonsdale, 'Coping with the Contradictions: The Development of the Colonial

State, 1895–1914', in their *Unhappy Valley: Conflict in Kenya and Africa* (London: James Currey, 1992).

17. Marxist studies of Africa's urban centres are often as much about capital accumulation and working-class politics as they are about the space and dynamics of city living: see e.g. Frederick Cooper, ed., *Struggle for the City: Migrant Labor, Capital, and the State in Urban Africa* (Beverly Hills, Calif.: Sage Publications, 1983).

18. Charles van Onselen, *Chibaro: African Mine Labour in Southern Rhodesia, 1900–1933* (London: Pluto Press, 1976); see also Charles van Onselen, *The Seed is Mine: The Life of Kas Maine, a South African Sharecropper, 1894–1985* (New York: Hill & Wang, 1996), and *Studies in the Social and Economic History of the Witwatersrand, 1886–1914* (Harlow: Longman, 1982).

19. Ibrahima Abdullah, 'Profit versus Social Reproduction: Labor Protests in the Sierra Leonean Iron-Ore Mines, 1933–38', *African Studies Review*, 35/3 (1992).

20. See Richard Sandbrook and Robin Cohen, eds, *The Development of an African Working Class: Studies in Class Formation and Action* (Toronto: University of Toronto Press, 1975), 19.

21. Patrick Harries, *Work, Culture, and Identity: Migrant Laborers in Mozambique and South Africa, c.1860–1910* (Portsmouth, NH: Heinemann, 1993).

22. François Manchuelle, *Willing Migrants: Soninke Labour Diasporas, 1848–1960* (Athens, O.: Ohio University Press, 1997).

23. Polly Hill, *The Migrant Cocoa-Farmers of Southern Ghana: A Study in Rural Capitalism* (Cambridge: CUP, 1963).

24. Sara Berry, *Fathers Work for their Sons: Accumulation, Mobility, and Class Formation in an Extended Yorùbá Community* (Berkeley, Calif.: University of California Press, 1985), 10.

25. See e.g. Babacar Fall, *Le Travaux force en Afrique occidentale française (1900–1945)* (Paris: Karthala, 1993).

26. Martin Klein, *Slavery and Colonial Rule in French West Africa* (Cambridge: CUP, 1998); Richard Roberts, 'The Banamba Slave Exodus of 1905 and the Decline of Slavery in the Western Sudan', *Journal of African History*, 21 (1980).

27. Gregory Mann, *Native Sons: West African Veterans and France in the Twentieth Century* (Durham, NC: Duke University Press, 2006), 6.

28. Siddartha Kara, *Sex Trafficking: Inside the Business of Modern Slavery* (New York: Columbia University Press, 2009); see United Nations Office on Drugs and Crime, *Global Report on Trafficking in Persons* (New York, UN, Feb. 2009), and US State Department, *Trafficking in Persons Report 2012* (Washington, DC: State Dept, 2012).

29. For a recent corrective, see Gwyn Campbell, Suzanne Miers, and Joseph C. Miller, eds, *Women and Slavery, ii. The Modern Atlantic* (Athens, O.: Ohio University Press, 2008).

30. See Joseph Miller, 'Domiciled and Dominated: Slaving as a History of Women', in Campbell et al., *Women and Slavery*, ii. Emily Lynn Osborn, *Our New Husbands are Here: Households, Gender, and Politics in a West African State from the Slave Trade to Colonial Rule* (Athens, O.: Ohio University Press, 2011).

31. Classic life histories are M. G. Smith, *Baba of Karo: A Woman of the Moslem Hausa* (New York: Praeger, 1964), and Sarah Mirza and Margaret Strobel, eds, *Three Swahili Women: Life Histories from Mombasa, Kenya* (Bloomington, Ind.: Indiana University Press, 1989); on domestic work in Africa, see Karen Tranberg Hansen, ed., *African Encounters with Domesticity* (New Brunswick, NJ: Rutgers University Press, 1992).

32. Luise White, *Comforts of Home: Prostitution in Colonial Nairobi* (Chicago: University of Chicago Press, 1990); see too John Chernoff, *Hustling is Not Stealing: Stories of an African Bar Girl* (Chicago: University of Chicago Press, 2003).

33. Gracia Clark, *Onions are my Husband: Survival and Accumulation by West African Market Women* (Bloomington, Ind.: Indiana University Press, 1994).

34. Judith Byfield, *The Bluest Hands: A Social and Economic History of Women Dyers in Abeokuta (Nigeria), 1890–1940* (Portsmouth, NH: Heinemann, 2002); Adria LaViolette, 'Women Craft Specialists in Jenne: The Manipulation of Mande Social Categories', in David C. Conrad and Barbara E. Frank, eds, *Status and Identity in West Africa: Nyamakalaw of Mande* (Bloomington, Ind.: Indiana University Press, 1995); Jean Allman and Victoria Tashjian, *'I Will Not Eat Stone': A Women's History of Colonial Asante* (Portsmouth, NH: Heinemann, 2000).

35. Keith Hart, 'Informal Income Opportunities and Urban Employment in Ghana', *Journal of Modern African Studies*, 11/1 (1973). For an important recent study of the informal economy, see Aili Marie Tripp, *Changing the Rules: The Politics of Liberalization and the Urban Informal Economy in Tanzania* (Berkeley, Calif.: University of California Press, 1997).

36. Frederick Cooper, 'African Labor History', in Jan Lucassen, ed., *Global Labour History: A State of the Art* (Bern: Peter Lang AG, 2006), 111.

37. See e.g. Emily Lynn Osborn, 'Casting Aluminium Cooking Pots: Labour, Migration and Artisan Production in West Africa's Informal Sector, 1945–2005', *African Identities*, 7/3 (2009).

38. Trevor H. J. Marchand, *The Masons of Djenné* (Bloomington, Ind.: Indiana University Press, 2009).

39. See Emily Lynn Osborn, '"Circle of Iron": African Colonial Employees and the Interpretation of Colonial Rule in French West Africa', *Journal of African History*, 44/1 (2003); Benjamin N. Lawrance, Emily Lynn Osborn, and Richard L. Roberts, eds, *Intermediaries, Interpreters, and Clerks: African Employees in the Making of Colonial Africa* (Madison, Wis.: University of Wisconsin Press, 2006).

40. Cooper, *Decolonization*.

41. James Ferguson, *Expectations of Modernity: Myths and Meanings of Urban Life on the Zambian Copperbelt* (Berkeley, Calif.: University of California Press, 1999).

42. For a recent study that effectively brings South African labour history into the post-Apartheid and neo-liberal era, see Franco Barchiesi, *Precarious Liberation: Workers, The State, and Contested Social Citizenship in Postapartheid South Africa* (Albany, NY: SUNY Press, 2011).

43. The literature on this topic is vast. For a start, see David Styan, 'The Security of Africans beyond Borders: Migration, Remittances, and London's Transnational Entrepeneurs', *International Affairs*, 83/6 (2007).

Bibliography

Banton, Michael, *West African City: A Study of Tribal Life in Freetown* (London: OUP, 1957).

Barchiesi, Franco, *Precarious Liberation: Workers, the State, and Contested Social Citizenship in Postapartheid South Africa* (Albany, NY: SUNY Press, 2011).

Berry, Sara, *Fathers Work for their Sons: Accumulation, Mobility, and Class Formation in an Extended Yorùbá Community* (Berkeley, Calif.: University of California Press, 1985).

Clark, Garcia, *Onions are my Husband: Survival and Accumulation by West African Market Women* (Bloomington, Ind.: Indiana University Press, 1994).

Cooper, Frederick, *Decolonization and African Society: The Labor Question in French and British Africa* (Cambridge: CUP, 1996).

Ferguson, James, *Expectations of Modernity: Myths and Meanings of Urban Life on the Zambian Copperbelt* (Berkeley, Calif.: University of California Press, 1999).

Harries, Patrick, *Work, Culture, and Identity: Migrant Laborers in Mozambique and South Africa, c.1860–1910* (Portsmouth, NH: Heinemann, 1993).

Hart, Keith, 'Informal Income Opportunities and Urban Employment in Ghana', *Journal of Modern African Studies,* 11/1 (1973).

Hill, Polly, *The Migrant Cocoa-Farmers of Southern Ghana: A Study in Rural Capitalism* (Cambridge: CUP, 1963).

Marchand, Trevor H. J., *The Masons of Djenné* (Bloomington, Ind.: Indiana University Press, 2009).

Moore, Reginald, and A. Sandilands, *These African Copper Mines: A Study of the Industrial Revolution in Northern Rodesia [sic], with Principal Reference to the Copper Mining Industry* (London: Livingston Press, 1948).

Osborn, Emily Lynn, ' "Circle of Iron": African Colonial Employees and the Interpretation of Colonial Rule in French West Africa', *Journal of African History,* 44/1 (2003).

Van Onselen, Charles, *Chibaro: African Mine Labour in Southern Rhodesia, 1900–1933* (London: Pluto Press, 1976).

White, Luise, *Comforts of Home: Prostitution in Colonial Nairobi* (Chicago: University of Chicago Press, 1990).

CHAPTER 11

....

CHIEFTAINCY

....

JUSTIN WILLIS

> Our Luo system of government was by consent and after consultation between the elders. As I have described, the clan head did not inherit his position but, once he belonged to the right lineage, had to prove his leadership qualities and use them to interpret tribal tradition and weld the agreement of his people. His strength derived from his closeness to the elders and his people. The British changed that. They did not want leaders in whom the people had confidence, but men who could be used for their purposes. When chiefs and headmen came to be selected, men whom the British found in positions of leadership were frequently by-passed, and others installed over them...
>
> Chiefs were no longer the custodians of their peoples' tribal law and custom, they were now civil servants; pensionable, but also subject to instant dismissal by the government. They were the expression of the power of the new government in the village. They could use their position to amass and exercise personal power, something which was previously unheard of among the Luo.[1]

FOR the Kenyan politician Oginga Odinga, the story of chiefs in western Kenya was part of a wider narrative of change, in which precolonial communalism had been swept away by an exploitative individualism driven by the exigencies of colonial rule. His account encapsulates an analysis which has been offered by many academics, as well as radical politicians like Odinga: that Africa's modern history is a story of profound disjuncture, in which colonialism—in its many guises, political, social, and economic—fundamentally transformed the nature of governance. Chieftaincy has been identified as a key site for the multiple inventions of colonial rule, a tool of both exploitative colonial states and of postcolonial autocrats; through its transformation, it has been argued, ordinary people have lost control over those who rule them.

But chieftaincy has also proved resilient. Since the early 1980s, as state structures across much of the continent have shown increasing signs of fragility, chieftaincy has been an increasingly vigorous force in political life in many societies. There is a puzzle here, manifest, for example, in Nigeria, where it has been argued both that colonial indirect rule 'distorted' chieftaincy and that the 'resiliency of indigenous political structures' has meant that the fragile postcolonial state has come to rely on them for local legitimacy.[2] Chieftaincy, vilified as a colonial invention, has also been seen as a manifestation of an enduring African political genius, which confounds teleological assumptions about modern forms of governance: 'in the light of the comparative failure of the African state…chieftaincy has re-emerged as an important vehicle for more or less authentic indigenous political expression.'[3] Even if that celebratory vision of chieftaincy as an inherently 'African' form is not accepted, recent events pose a fundamental question: how is it that chieftaincy, which proved so malleable in the face of colonial state power, has acquired such robust legitimacy in independent Africa?

The development of historical scholarship on chieftaincy suggests that the answer to that question lies in a potent mix of continuity and change, and that understanding these also requires us to 'unpack the assumed dichotomy between African tradition and European modernity'.[4] To speak of 'precolonial chieftaincy' in Africa is to suggest a categorical singularity which did not exist. There were many kinds of political relationships in societies across the continent. Some formed hierarchies; others overlapped in complex and sometimes conflicting patterns. They drew on diverse ideas about community, health, and prosperity, some of which maintained an affective power through the colonial period and beyond it. Colonial states, often confused in their policy aims and usually short of resources, were not as powerfully destructive in all societies as Oginga Odinga argued. But at the same time, colonial rule did change the way in which people talked about authority, in a way which is evidenced by the widespread use today of the phrase 'traditional authority'. The resilience of postcolonial chieftaincy, it may be argued, derives partly from a creative continuity in political culture which is apparent in the diversity and adaptability of ideas about community, leadership, and well-being. But it derives also from a developing relationship with the imaginary but immensely productive distinction between tradition and modernity.

Hierarchy and Heterarchy: Precolonial Authority

Charles Temple, a British colonial administrator and enthusiastic ideologue of the policy of indirect rule, confidently asserted in 1918 that the 'base of all African organization…is rooted in the discipline exerted by the head of the family over his dependents'.[5] For a scholarship on precolonial authority in Africa which emerged very much in the context of colonial rule, the question of why some societies had hierarchical and relatively centralized forms of authority while others did not was a pressing one. Meyer Fortes and E. E. Evans-Pritchard's seminal anthropological collection *African Political Systems* (1940)—with its expressed intent of 'being of interest and use to those who have the task of administering African peoples'—was much concerned with this issue. It included

Evans-Pritchard's study of Nuer society in what is now South Sudan (identified as an example in which ritual authority allowed the management of conflict and the settlement of disputes but gave no political influence) and Fortes's of Tallensi society in what is now northern Ghana (explained as a ritual/political dualism which prevented centralization).[6] Writing in the same collection of the enormous area inhabited by communities speaking Bantu languages, Audrey Richards argued that authority 'is almost invariably based on descent…the chief of the tribe combines executive, ritual and judicial functions…Like the family head, he is a priest of an ancestral cult.'[7] In their introduction, Fortes and Evans-Pritchard suggested the existence of a quintessentially African political system in which the ruler was an 'embodiment of essential values', epitomizing both the community and its 'mystical' ideas of well-being; other anthropological work at the same time argued that importance of the 'supernatural sanctions attached to [the chief's] heredity'.[8] A few years later, precolonial Nyamwezi society, in what is now central Tanzania, was described in similar terms: 'The sacred character of these early chiefs was strongly marked. The chief was essentially the ritual guardian and leader of his chiefdom. There was felt to be an intimate connexion between his person and the well-being of his chiefdom.'[9] There was a consistent concern here: to identify the significant source of ritual authority in society and to understand how an individual came to possess it. In this approach, the elaboration of authority and the development of larger polities could best be explained as the result of a developing hierarchical relationship between different sources of power—notably, between ritual power and the secular power of organized violence.

The argument that precolonial political elaboration was the consequence of an emerging hierarchy between distinct sources of power has subsequently been widely rehearsed. In equatorial Africa, it was argued, 'big men' endlessly competed to accumulate wealth and followers, using the language of kinship as the basis of their authority over a 'house' and then a village. Those political entrepreneurs who brought several such groups together in more elaborate political structures could deploy the language of kinship, but drew also on a developing suite of talents, in warfare, judging cases, and performing or sponsoring rituals which ensured well-being. This was a process driven by innovation and competition; new shrines, rituals, or military skills offered the material for political change and once one community experienced an enlargement of political scale, its neighbours would follow, driven by fear or envy.

Warfare has not been the only factor identified in the elaboration or recasting of authority. Among the Mbundu of modern Angola, authority worked at a lineage level and was derived from the performance of rituals of well-being. Here too, political entrepreneurship led to innovations—mostly associated with the ritual pursuit of community well-being. Most vanished without trace; some allowed the development of a new kind of political organization—though this too came to be expressed in a language of kinship. But the role of new technologies or techniques in the organization of violence in creating more centralized precolonial political forms has been a wider theme. Eighteenth-century Mende leaders in what is now Sierra Leone were lineage heads with local influence, but in the nineteenth century, they were subordinated by war-chiefs. Similar transformations have been suggested for the Krobo of what is now Ghana and for many societies in East Africa. The mastery of violence was also crucial for the big men of precolonial Ibadan, war-chiefs whose position and reputation rested on the ability constantly to generate new supplies of loot to reward their followers. Political elaboration, in this analysis, rested on a hierarchy of innovations: the individual who could master the rain overawed the lineage head, but was in turn subordinated by the warrior-leader.

Increasingly, scholarship has tended to question the notion of hierarchy and whether there was a clear distinction between ritual and political authority. This questioning springs partly from a growing awareness of the fragile, uncertain nature of status and influence in many precolonial African societies. The chronic vulnerability of those who sought to wield authority is exemplified by the chiefs in what is now South Sudan, dubbed by Simon Simonse as 'kings of disaster'.[10] Claiming what was in effect a negative power over well-being, they were in constant danger of being turned from victimizers into victims—if they failed their subjects, they would be murdered. In consequence, they devoted much energy to supplementing their ritual roles with involvement in trade or alliances with other communities. Leadership here rested on the ability to play multiple roles.

This vulnerability may have been particularly intense in precolonial South Sudan, but in other societies too there was multiplicity and competition. Prowess in settling disputes or in leading warriors, control over fertility or disease, relationships with spirits or other ritual powers, skills in dealing with strangers or negotiating deals—all could be the mark of those who possessed some singular degree of authority. It has been argued of Asante society that there was a gendered dualism, with 'chiefs' and 'queen mothers' always associated in complementary roles. This neat parallelism between male and female holders of authority is not so apparent elsewhere, but clearly there was some gendering to the multiplicity of power, with fertility and reproduction more likely to be the domain of women. Some innovations may have been borrowed or copied from neighbouring societies; some were directly linked to new technologies of violence, such as horses or firearms. But all were adapted to local circumstance and this process of adaptation was one of managing and composing knowledge: whether that knowledge related to the interpretation of auguries, to an awareness of precedents in the settlement of disputes, to skill in the use of medicinal herbs, or to an understanding of weather patterns. Authority rested on the ability to manage multiple forms of knowledge, not the possession of some singular and superior form. The corollary of this understanding is that, in any society, there might be multiple and overlapping claims to such knowledge, so that the authority of an individual might be both local and contested: 'Adepts were many and varied…inventing new ways of configuring, storing and using what must have been an ever-shifting spectrum of possibility.'[11]

Even in those societies which did see a very apparent elaboration of political structures, with a single dominant figure, this was not always associated with a hierarchy of forms of power. Faced with the multiplicity of forms of powerful knowledge, the kings or *kabaka*s of Buganda exercised authority more by managing heterarchy than by imposing hierarchy. Like his subjects, the *kabaka* lived in a crowded spiritual world in which there were many different ideas about community and well-being and his palace was a physically and politically complex place. Multiple currencies of knowledge were constantly in circulation and there could be rivalry between individuals who insisted on the value of their knowledge against others. At the same time, for the *kabaka*'s subjects, heterarchy offered alternatives which provided a kind of limit on power: 'heterarchy was a strategy used both to constitute a hierarchical polity and to curb the king's power'.[12]

Buganda may have been unusually complex, but many societies were probably heterarchical to some degree, with people recognizing that there were many kinds of knowledge in circulation. Even in the relatively centralized forest kingdom of Asante, 'individuals who resided in a single village might owe allegiance to several different chiefs and occupy land that belonged to still others'; among the Limba of West Africa, any aspirant leader had to reckon with multiple kinds of powerful knowledge.[13] In such circumstances, possession of any one of these bestowed a degree of authority—because people would turn to those who could reward personal bravery, or ensure well-being, settle disputes, advise on the timing of raids, or wield the language and cultural skills to deal with unfamiliar visitors. Individuals who came to exert an unusual degree of authority were those who could deal in, or with, more than one of these sources of authority. Some took brokerage to a further level—not simply acquiring multiple kinds of knowledge themselves, but also a following which included those who claimed expertise of diverse kinds: 'Leaders had to attract the holders of a knowledge they did not themselves possess.'[14] In precolonial Africa, the creation of political entities which extended beyond the local rested not on one kind of power or the possession of singular authority, but on strategies for dealing in multiple kinds of power. Different kinds of knowledge might, after all, offer different means to address the same problem: was disease the consequence of witchcraft, of ancestral displeasure, or of some other kind of malign spirit? It seems likely that there was a degree of contest between different forms of knowledge, a contest which could make polities unpredictable—because they were based on a constant juggling of forms of knowledge—but also robust in their ability to adapt and incorporate new sources of authority. This competition and uncertainty helps to explain why it is by no means always easy to draw distinctions between societies which had chiefs and those which did not.

Changing economic and political circumstances could create new opportunities and challenges for the management of knowledge. In some parts of nineteenth-century eastern Africa, 'brokers' who supplied trading caravans with food and information turned trade goods into steadily extending influence and growing followings. This allowed these entrepreneurs to accumulate knowledge: learning the language and ways of new trading partners, learning how to handle the technologies and wealth which they brought, recruiting other individuals with specialized knowledge of medicine or of combat. But in other societies in the same region, forms of powerful knowledge remained diffuse. This might be because individuals who possessed one unusual or esoteric form of knowledge, which gave them extensive influence of a particular kind, did not acquire other kinds of knowledge to complement this and turn it into a reliable political authority. Some 'prophets'—possessors of what some have called 'mantic knowledge'—seem to exemplify this. The *laibon*s of the Maasai were a 'political failure', for they were unable to consolidate the brief ascendancy which they achieved in the turbulent years of the late nineteenth century. Among the Nandi of Kenya and the Tonga of what is now Zambia, by contrast, at least some individuals could build prophecy into a repertoire of knowledge which allowed new kinds of centralizing authority to develop, though in each case the process was interrupted by colonial rule.[15]

The analysis of authority in precolonial Africa, then, has undergone significant reinterpretation over the last two decades. In place of a vision of patriarchal power based on kinship and ritual, which might provide building blocks for the elaboration of political hierarchy, historians have increasingly argued for the heterogeneous, overlapping, and multiple nature of influence. With the coming of colonial rule, the engagement between societies characterized by such heterarchy, on the one hand, and colonial officials who imagined a 'chiefly' power which was simple and absolute, on the other, was inevitably complex and troubled.

CHIEFS OF THE GOVERNMENT

European colonial states in Africa were, generally speaking, chronically short of resources. As Charles Temple wrote in 1918, 'if we could have a staff of even one white man to every hundred and fifty natives, direct administration would be perhaps the best'.[16] But this was impossible, and the reality in most territories—particularly in the period up to the 1930s—was a ratio many times this imagined benchmark. 'Indirect rule' was a pragmatic answer to this fundamental weakness. Seeking to understand what he called the 'African acquiescence in colonialism' which allowed these feeble states to impose their will, Terence Ranger identified the importance of 'the invention of tradition', through which a fundamentally coercive system was disguised in the garb of custom.[17] Chieftaincy was at the heart of this, so that the most baleful legacy of colonial rule in Africa was the appointed 'administrative chiefs'. These were 'decentralized despots', in Mahmood Mamdani's phrase—freed from the constraints of custom by the overwhelming coercive support of the state, but outside the systemic restraints which imperial governments placed on the formal structures of colonial rule.[18] The judicial role of the chiefs was central to this; it has been argued that 'customary' courts were the key site for an entirely new accumulation of power by chiefs who benefited from an alliance with colonial officials.

More widely, critics of colonial chiefs, both European and African, have long argued that they were either a complete invention of colonialism—sidelining other, more genuine claimants to local authority—or that they connived to transform established forms of authority reliant on consensus and negotiation into forms which were intrusive, coercive, and acquisitive. The creation of a Kaguru 'paramount chief' in Tanganyika provided 'a handmaiden to imperialist domination as well as a means to power for some opportunistic Kaguru'.[19] Appointed colonial chiefs of the Kikuyu in Kenya were 'creatures of the British administration' who represented the interests of the latter. 'Their authority rested not on reciprocal relationships...but on force.'[20] In Botswana, 'chiefly autocracy [was] intensified and corrupted by British overrule.'[21] These forms were also generally patriarchal, so that women who had possessed forms of influence in precolonial societies were, with only a few exceptions, largely excluded from the new colonial world of 'chieftaincy'. One such exception was among the Mende of Sierra Leone, where some women, like men, were able to transform previous forms of authority into colonial 'chieftaincy'.[22] Faced with forms of authority which were contested, diffuse, and overlapping, colonial officials sought to remodel these and to focus authority in single figures, preferably male, with clear spheres of influence.

This historical analysis of a colonialism which hijacked or invented indigenous authority draws on a rich seam of written evidence from colonial sources. Frederick Lugard's cheerful exhortation to 'build up a tribal authority' and to 'hasten the transition from the patriarchal to the tribal stage' is evidence enough of the conscious desire to create chiefs where none existed.[23] The extravagant language of one key piece of legislation from Sudan nicely evokes both the bombastic flavour of colonial rhetoric on this topic and the linkage to judicial authority and punitive force: 'it has from time immemorial been customary for native sheikhs of nomad tribes to exercise powers of punishment upon their tribesmen and of deciding disputes among them.'[24]

As the use of the term 'sheikh' implies, reliance on local forms of authority was cast in a language of difference. The establishment of a distinctive terminology for these figures, on whom colonial administration relied so heavily, underwrote their imagined separation from the colonial state. In English usage, they were categorized as 'traditional' or 'customary' and the phrase 'native administration' came to be used to describe institutions, sometimes even individuals, as well as practice. Whatever the reality, native administration was supposed to be different to 'Government' (a term which some British officials liked to capitalize to assert its abstract singularity). A descriptive language for the individuals involved was a little more problematic, since their styles and ranges of authority varied so widely. Colonialism brought to Africa a set of words rooted in a European historical imagination of local forms of authority which had been subordinated somewhere along the march of progress: chief, *chef coutumier, hauptlinge, chefe*. Officials—and other European observers—applied these words to individuals who were involved in very varied political relationships. There were some local variations in terminology to express the possibility of hierarchy amongst the individuals recognized by colonial rule, and sometimes local terms or terms derived from earlier colonialisms were adopted: *kabaka, alafin, reth, sheikh, nazir, omda, akida*. Lesser, very local figures might be called headmen; and for a while some Europeans sought to distinguish the most powerful as 'kings', though British official practice turned against such presumption of equality with European monarchs. But, overall, as it transformed these forms of authority, colonialism subjected it to a linguistic and intellectual homogenization and 'chief' became the routine English term for African holders of authority. Like its French, Portuguese, and German counterparts, the term set all such holders of authority together in the imaginary world of custom, in collective contrast to the sphere of state authority.

French colonial officials were generally much less enthusiastic about chiefs than their British counterparts. Historians writing in the 1960s tended to stress the fundamental difference between the approach of British and French officials. Michael Crowder argued that, in contrast with the British, 'the French system of administration deliberately sapped the traditional powers of chiefs', and the pioneering 1970 volume he edited with O. Ikime, *West African Chiefs*, offers this contrast as a central analytical theme.[25] But more recent research suggests that the contrast between the two systems can be overstated. French officials too faced the challenge of asserting control with very limited resources and consequently sought local agents who did not require constant support— as, for example, in the Kaya region of what is now Burkina Faso—while expressing the role of such individuals in a language which evoked the same imaginary distinction between tradition and state that inspired British officials.[26] In some places, the French could even be 'more consistent in supporting "their" chiefs' than were the British.[27]

Despite Mamdani's suggestion that 'the British worked with a single model of authority in pre-colonial Africa...[which] was monarchical, patriarchal and authoritarian', British officials could be ambivalent about chiefs.[28] In practice, some 'chiefs' were too powerful, and others too weak, for colonial tastes. In South Africa, some individuals with substantial influence were sidelined by the British in favour of lesser 'headmen' who would be less dangerous. In some parts of Sudan, colonial chiefs, or the 'dogs of the government' as some abusively called them, had little influence, compromising themselves and the state by their reliance on crude coercion. In other regions of Sudan, more powerful sheikhs and nazirs provided a focus for resentment, becoming a regular target for the ire of their subjects and of an emergent body of aspirant nationalists. With their eyes on the long-term prize of control of the state, these nationalists showed a deep ambivalence to the 'native administration', denouncing chiefs, sheikhs, and nazirs as lackeys of colonialism, yet at the same time distrusting them precisely because they were not entirely reliant on the colonial state. Neither the criticism nor the response were peculiar to Sudan. Across the continent, the misbehaviour of tyrannical chiefs offered ready ammunition to critics like Oginga Odinga. In colonial Ghana, 'the competition for power between Africans... polarized into a long-running battle between what might increasingly be seen as a nationalist elite and the chiefs'.[29]

Such criticisms, and the failings of some chiefs, inspired repeated but often haphazard efforts by the colonial state to reconstitute traditional authority. It also drove colonial attempts to create alternatives to chieftaincy. In the 1930s, the anthropologist Lucy Mair warned British administrators that they had 'altered the basis of the chief's authority in a way which tips the balance of power in his favour', noting too that, for colonial chiefs, 'modern economic conditions create the possibility of abuse which could not in the past have been committed at all'.[30] By the terminal phase of colonial rule in the 1950s, studies of chiefs were set specifically in the context of attempts to make them more 'efficient'. Concerns over accountability and efficiency, and overt displays of popular hostility to some chiefs, inspired the experiments with forms of conciliar government which were increasingly common in British-ruled Africa from the 1920s and which began in the 1940s to morph into late colonialism's brief, confused, but very energetic experiment with elected local government.

If the colonial state's commitment to chieftaincy was not entirely open-ended, neither was it quite so well resourced as some have argued. Colonial states looked for local forms of authority because they lacked the resources to rule directly; so, how could they have possessed the means to maintain chiefs who were entirely reliant on the state for support? There were, in practice, 'limits to invention'. Colonial rule could not sustain chiefs who relied entirely on official support—as the decision to abolish the warrant chiefs of south-eastern Nigeria, perhaps the most egregious example of invented colonial chieftaincy, showed. Asante chiefs acquired considerable power through the colonial belief that their 'stools' had a customary control over land; but this belief, while it may have overstated the linkage between stools and land control, was not a complete invention. In Cameroon, Maka chiefs who relied too much on their knowledge of *les choses des blancs* could not sustain their influence. While studies of central Kenya have emphasized the coercive, invented nature of Kikuyu chieftaincy, they have also suggested that the new chiefs were successful not simply because of the government support, but because they exploited possibilities for accumulation and differentiation which already existed within Kikuyu society.[31] As Tom Spear argues, colonial officials could themselves become 'subject to local discourses of power that they neither fully understood nor controlled'.[32] Elsewhere, repeated efforts to create effective indirect rule through 'tradition' were unsuccessful and left officials in a sort of chronic rage of frustration which found expression through the repeated dismissal of chiefs who had failed to perform. Some of those appointed as chiefs or headmen evidently found themselves profoundly vulnerable: among the Lozi of Northern Rhodesia, both paramount chief and headman reportedly responded to their appointment as chief with the words 'you have killed me'.[33]

An alternative, and perhaps more useful, concept than that of colonial intervention has been that of intermediacy. Colonial chiefs, like some figures in precolonial Africa, have been described as gatekeepers, standing between local society and the state in ways that allowed them to dominate traffic between the two. Chiefs had authority partly because people wanted to maintain the division between these worlds, because they feared the state's ambitions for interference in quotidian social relationships. The idea of a distinct sphere of 'tradition' or 'custom' was a defensive notion deployed by colonial subjects, not simply a colonial imposition. This liminal position, 'between two worlds', was one of moral peril as well as political power—for it made chiefs into creatures of a no-man's land between the laws of the state and the mores of the communities from which they came.

But while the vision of the chief as gatekeeper is a striking metaphor, it risks overstating the actual separation between state and the world of tradition. That separation was not necessarily at all clear: as Lloyd Fallers observed in the 1950s, chiefs operated in a world in which 'African and European social systems have interpenetrated with the result that new social systems embodying diverse and conflicting elements have come into being'.[34] The very nature of colonial rule was that it insinuated itself inexorably into multiple aspects of life. It did so not as an undifferentiated force of modernity, but as a number of changed circumstances: the appearance of new material goods, the commoditization of familiar crops and items, new ways of using old skills, new words, and new meanings for old words.

For those who aspired to status, colonial rule created a need for additional, diverse forms of knowledge—some reasonably familiar, some entirely novel. The linguistic and cultural knowledge to deal with demanding white officials; the knowledge of forms and paper; the knowledge of dates and times: all of these were useful. So too was an ability to manage the languages of Christianity and of Islam, which offered new ways to criticize power but could also give chiefs a novel lexicon with which to argue the rightfulness of their role. But equally important was knowledge of older, enduring ideas about wellbeing and morality, the assertion of that knowledge of the past, and of the techniques of bluff and dissembling. For some, new kinds of knowledge created opportunities, displacing existing ways of dealing with the world. One example was the Yoruba city of Ibadan, where chiefs no longer needed to know how to lead and reward their war-bands, but had instead to concentrate on the 'war of the pen', deploying arguments over the past to establish their claims over their followers and their rights to dispense justice and land.[35] But while individuals who mastered the new kinds of powerful knowledge might acquire a wholly new level of influence, changing the dynamics of authority within communities in dramatic ways, suggestions that previous patterns of authority were entirely destroyed by colonial rule seem overstated.

Such changes may have occurred quickly and on a new scale, but they were not by nature unprecedented. Those who sought to exercise individual authority had always been required to innovate, adapt, and deal with multiple sources of power. And colonial rule did not invalidate all previous forms of knowledge; rather, it gave new value to some, like knowledge of land and history. In other cases, for all the pretensions of colonial health or veterinary services, or of agricultural extension officers, colonialism could not offer the security of health and livelihood which would make alternative shrines or healing practices wholly irrelevant. Colonial chiefs could not simply stand at the point where two worlds met. They had rather to work constantly to manage both, and their principal advantage was not position but a knowledge which was diverse enough to deal with both vaccination campaigns and offerings to ancestors, tax collection, and the rise of new cults or churches.

While the separation between two distinct worlds was an illusory one, it was an illusion that was powerful enough to be manipulated in pursuit of influence and status. The routine characterization of chieftaincy as the core manifestation of tradition, in contrast to the modern state, greatly understated the complexity of the relationship between these multiple forms of knowledge. As a powerful idea, it came to shape the way that those who aspired to authority talked about the possibilities of power and the way that 'their' people understood that role. Chieftaincy became fundamentally implicated in structuring the contrast between tradition and modernity, between African and European, and between custom and the colonial state.

Modern Chiefs

Despised by nationalist politicians, abandoned by late colonial governments in favour of local councils, and often resented by their own subjects, chiefs looked very vulnerable as African states moved towards independence in the 1950s and 1960s. In 1958, Lucy Mair wrote confidently that 'It is quite easy to predict that the chiefs will eventually disappear from the scene'.[36] In some cases, they were indeed entirely abolished by newly independent states: in Tanzania, later in Sudan, Uganda, and elsewhere. In Ghana, Kwame Nkrumah's government systematically sought to reduce the political significance of chieftaincy and to subordinate it to the authority of the modernizing state; here, as across much of the continent, the plans of newly independent states envisaged a rapidly shrinking role for chiefs. When Pierre Alexandre, a colonial administrator turned academic, answered his own rhetorical question: 'Will we then have finished with the whole problem of chieftaincy? We do not think so', his was a lonely voice.[37]

Yet across much of the continent by the 1980s and 1990s, chiefs were returning to play prominent political and administrative roles. In Ghana, 'while chiefs may appear to have lost their power, they actually wield a remarkable degree of influence over the political life of the country'.[38] In several parts of northern Sudan, the 'native authorities' abolished by Gaafar Nimeiri's regime in the 1970s have steadily regained state recognition; in Burkina Faso, Moose chiefs have survived two attempts to abolish them. The democratic transition in South Africa, which many had assumed would see the end of chiefs, led instead to a reaffirmation of their role. And, ironically, even among the Igbo of south-eastern Nigeria—where the ignominious fate of the warrant chiefs provided a graphic illustration of the limits of invention—'traditional rulers' were thriving in the 1980s, having effectively displaced the local government created in the 1950s. It might be noted that one country where officially recognized chiefs have steadily lost status and power is Kenya. There, the children of successful colonial chiefs tended to translate themselves into businessmen and politicians at independence, leaving the descendants of lesser chiefs to be entirely incorporated into the civil service as underpaid petty functionaries without any claim to customary authority.

Why has chieftaincy proved so durable in many cases? Alexandre based his prediction of chiefly longevity on a belief in the enduring power of custom: 'Fifty years of European presence and ten years of training in western democracy are not enough to wipe out all traces of a tradition which goes back several thousand years.'[39] Historians writing with a much clearer sense of the mutability of tradition have nonetheless tended to use the terms 'indigenous' and 'traditional' as synonyms, implying that the revival of chieftaincy is based on the ability to manipulate tradition: 'chiefs have a resource which is not so readily available to commoners: tradition'.[40] This is not because tradition is unchanging; it is rather that there are local patterns of thought and practice surrounding the proper exercise of authority which display considerable continuity over time. As has been suggested of western Cameroon, although it is still the case that 'legitimate authority is based on descent and the ancestors', the importance of chiefs is also very much bound up with current politics.[41]

Like their predecessors, postcolonial chiefs continue to derive power from acting as intermediaries between the spheres of the state and tradition. In some cases, this intermediacy has been given specifically defined legal form, particularly where the management of land has been categorized as at least partly a matter of tradition. In the Asante region of Ghana, for example, Nkrumah's attempts to sideline chiefs crucially failed to include the removal of state recognition of their control over land. But more generally, the distinction between these spheres remains a discursive one, neither clearly set out in legislation nor always readily discernible in lived experience. Indeed, tradition and modernity may be increasingly hard to distinguish in a world of constant technological and cultural innovation, where mobile phones and money, pharmaceuticals and photographs, are very widespread parts of daily life and in which people, words, and images make long and sometimes very rapid journeys.

There is certainly no evidence that modern chiefs restrict themselves to a world of hallowed tradition. Nigerian paramounts cheerfully bestow chieftaincy titles on politicians, while the newly reinvented 'traditional rulers' of the Igbo 'self-confidently borrow cultural elements derived from European, African and Christian origins'.[42] In other countries, too, many chiefs are deeply involved in party politics, professional employment, education, and various kinds of commerce. Carola Lentz's comparative study of three different 'big men' in northern Ghana depicts a chief who drew on multiple sources of power and pursued multiple strategies of accumulation and influence. His strategies, like those of other big men who were not chiefs, combined 'different fields of action' and belie any clear distinction between the spheres of tradition and modernity.[43] Like their precolonial antecedents, modern chiefs draw on multiple kinds of knowledge. Some of these are intensely local: knowledge of family ties, of land use, of boundaries, and of old quarrels. Others are less specific to place but no less valuable: the ability to talk persuasively, the command of several languages, literacy. Others may be esoteric, at least from some perspectives: ritual skills, familiarity with written laws, university qualifications. What is crucial is the ability to operate across the imaginary divide between tradition and modernity, like the Zimbabwean chief who declared 'I have the power of the soil', but was also a Catholic schoolteacher.[44] Yet gender distinctions remain important. For some Ghanaian women, association with traditional authority may be a disadvantage, circumscribing their sphere of action by evoking a customary idea of discrete female spheres of knowledge.

The resilience of modern chieftaincy has been located squarely in the context of the 'abject failure of the developmentalist state' and in the predominance of clientelist, 'ethno-regional' politics.[45] But chieftaincy has also flourished in states which are seen as relatively strong—post-Apartheid South Africa, for example—and arguably it has drawn strength from the patronage and support of the state, rather than thriving on its collapse. It is not so much the weakness of the state in an absolute sense that has given such strength to chieftaincy, but rather the widespread perception that even relatively effective states have failed to meet the expectations of their people. It is this sense of disappointment, frustration, and suspicion which makes the discursive distinction between traditional authority and the state so useful. Tradition, it has been argued, should not be understood simply to mean absolute continuity of practice; rather it 'constitutes a discourse by which people assert present interests in terms of the past'.[46] But it means more than this: it evokes not just the past, but also difference from the state. While twenty-first-century chiefs may show little regard for this notional distinction in practice, they benefit from the powerful tension which continues to exist along the fault line between these two spheres. It allows them to insist that they are distinct from the state and to deny responsibility for its shortcomings and failures: its corruption, inability to provide services and security, and lack of local accountability.

In this respect, the suspicion with which chieftaincy was viewed by nationalist politicians and the hostile rhetoric or bans to which it was subject have served chiefs well. One characteristic of chieftaincy across Africa is that, even though it is entwined with the state, it is seen as somewhat different: 'one of the advantages of chieftaincy since independence has been precisely its distance from the state'.[47] In the new nation of South Sudan, after years of war which saw widespread brutality and extortion by both government and rebel forces, there is a strong suspicion of government and a more generalized distrust of multiple phenomena associated with it: towns, paper, money. Such suspicion does not preclude contact, and actually people's lives constantly cross the moral boundary between rural and urban, and between the economy of money and that of trust. Yet the belief in this distinction encourages a sense that chiefs have a kind of moral authority which government lacks. This almost contradictory quality is widely shared by modern chiefs: that they are perceived to occupy a different moral world from the state, even though they are often deeply complicit in its politics. In the Nigerian city of Abeokuta, the politics of chieftaincy and of the state form an 'organic political system', but 'kingship and chieftaincy exist in opposition to the state only in a very limited sense, namely the basis from which they draw their legitimacy. In this sense "traditional" and "modern" politics remain opposed.'[48] It is this shared characteristic which gives the category 'postcolonial chieftaincy' a coherence which 'precolonial chieftaincy' lacks.

This is not to argue that the ongoing discursive dichotomy between tradition and modernity always produces chiefs. It is important to remember that there are many societies in postcolonial Africa in which they have not flourished. Among the Maka of Cameroon, chiefs have failed to maintain authority because of the popular perception that they were associated with the immoral power of witchcraft. Chiefly power in the Volta Region of Ghana exists only at a local level; the higher echelons of the former colonial chieftaincy system have no influence. In Kenya, where chiefs were largely colonial creations and were turned by the postcolonial state into the pettiest of civil servants, access to the powerful resource of tradition has come rather to lie in the hands of elders (usually men) who claim to be moral custodians, and sometimes political spokesmen, of particular ethnic groups. Their titles, costumes, and presumptions may have little to do with precolonial practice, but they draw evident influence both from a diffuse, gerontocratic model of authority and from their ability to present themselves as distinct from the state—even as they play in its politics. Like 'chiefs' elsewhere in modern Africa, these 'elders' embody the authority which derives from tradition in both its senses: as enduring patterns of speech and practice about authority, and as a discursive resource which gives them a morally advantageous distance from the state and from the multiple, disappointed expectations of modernity.

Notes

1. Oginga Odinga, *Not Yet Uhuru* (London: Heinemann, 1968), 20–2.
2. O. Vaughan, 'Chieftaincy Politics and Communal Ideology in Western Nigeria, 1893–1951', *Journal of African History*, 44 (2003), 301; O. Vaughan, *Nigerian Chiefs: Traditional Power in Modern Politics* (Rochester, NY: University of Rochester Press, 2000), 3.
3. D. Ray and E. A. Van Rouveroy van Nieuwaal, 'The New Relevance of Traditional Authorities in Africa', *Journal of Legal Pluralism*, 37/38 (1996), 7.
4. T. Spear, 'Neo-Traditionalism and the Limits of Invention in British Colonial Africa', *Journal of African History*, 44 (2003), 4.
5. C. Temple, *Native Races and their Rulers* (London: Frank Cass, 2nd edn, 1968 [1918]), 35.
6. M. Fortes and E. E. Evans-Pritchard, eds, *African Political Systems* (London: OUP, 1940), p. vii.
7. A. I. Richards, 'The Political System of the Bemba Tribe of North-Eastern Rhodesia', in Fortes and Evans-Pritchard, *African Political Systems*, 83–4.
8. M. Fortes and E. E. Evans-Pritchard, 'Introduction', in *African Political Systems*.
9. R. G. Abrahams, *The Political Organization of the Nyamwezi* (Cambridge: CUP, 1967), 33.
10. S. Simonse, *Kings of Disaster: Dualism, Centralism and the Scapegoat King in Southeastern Sudan* (Leiden: Brill, 1992).
11. J. Guyer and S. Belinga, 'Wealth in People as Wealth in Knowledge: Accumulation and Composition in Equatorial Africa', *Journal of African History*, 36 (1995), 93; see too B. Stoeltje, 'Asante Queen Mothers: A Study in Female Authority', *Annals of the New York Academy of Sciences*, 810 (1997); L. Brydon, 'Women Chiefs and Power in the Volta Region of Ghana', *Journal of Legal Pluralism*, 37/38 (1996); I. Berger, 'Fertility as Power: Spirit Mediums, Priestesses and the Pre-Colonial State in Interlacustrine East Africa', in D. Anderson and D. Johnson, eds, *Revealing Prophets: Prophecy in East African History* (London: James Currey, 1995); C. Leonardi, 'Knowing Authority: Colonial Governance and Local Community in Equatoria Province, Sudan, 1900–56', Ph.D. thesis (University of Durham, 2005), 81–97.
12. H. Hanson, 'Mapping Conflict: Heterarchy and Accountability in the Ancient Capital of Buganda', *Journal of African History*, 50 (2009), 181.
13. S. Berry, *'Chiefs Know their Boundaries': Essays on Property, Power and the Past in Asante, 1896–1996* (Portsmouth, NH: Heinemann, 2001), 3; R. Finnegan and D. Murray, 'Limba Chiefs', in M. Crowder and O. Ikime, eds, *West African Chiefs: Their Changing Status under Colonial Rule and Independence* (New York: Africana Publishing, 1970); Guyer and Belinga, 'Wealth in People', 109–16.
14. Guyer and Belinga, 'Wealth in People', 113.
15. C. Ambler, *Kenyan Communities in the Age of Imperialism* (New Haven, Conn.: Yale University Press, 1988), 102–5; R. Waller, 'Kidongoi's Kin: Prophecy and Power in Maasailand', in Anderson and Johnson, *Revealing Prophets*; D. Anderson, 'Visions of the Vanquished: Prophets and Colonialism in Kenya's Western Highlands', in

Anderson and Johnson, *Revealing Prophets*; D. O'Brien, 'Chiefs of Rain, Chiefs of Ruling: A Reinterpretation of Pre-colonial Tonga (Zambia) Social and Political Structure', *Africa*, 53 (1983).

16. Temple, *Native Races*, 35.

17. T. Ranger, 'Making Northern Rhodesia Imperial: Variations on a Royal Theme, 1924–38', *African Affairs*, 79 (1980), 349; T. Ranger, 'The Invention of Tradition in Colonial Africa', in E. Hobsbawm and T. Ranger, eds, *The Invention of Tradition* (Cambridge: CUP, 1983).

18. M. Mamdani, *Citizen and Subject: Contemporary Africa and the Legacy of Late Colonialism* (Princeton: PUP, 1996), 37–61.

19. T. Beidelman, 'Chiefship in Ukaguru: The Invention of Ethnicity and Tradition in Kaguru Colonial History', *International Journal of African Historical Studies*, 11 (1978), 227.

20. R. Tignor, 'Colonial Chiefs in Chiefless Societies', *Journal of Modern African Studies*, 9 (1971), 352.

21. S. Gillett, 'The Survival of Chieftaincy in Botswana', *African Affairs*, 72 (1973), 181.

22. L. Day, 'The Evolution of Female Chiefship during the Late Nineteenth-Century Wars of the Mende', *International Journal of African Historical Studies*, 27 (1994).

23. F. D. Lugard, *The Dual Mandate in British Tropical Africa* (London: Frank Cass, 1922), 217.

24. 'The Powers of Nomad Sheikhs Ordinance, 1922', reproduced in A. I. Abushouk and A. Bjorkelo, *The Principles of Native Administration in the Anglo-Egyptian Sudan, 1898–1956* (Omdurman: Abdel Karim Mirghani Cultural Centre, 2004), 219.

25. M. Crowder, 'Indirect Rule: French and British Style', *Africa*, 34 (1964), 201; M. Crowder and O. Ikime, 'Introduction', in Crowder and Ikime, *West African Chiefs*, pp. vii–xxix.

26. J.-B. Ouedraougou, 'The Articulation of the Moose Traditional Chieftaincies, the Modern Political System and the Economic Development of Kaya Region, Burkina Faso', *Journal of Legal Pluralism*, 37/38 (1996).

27. P. Geschiere, 'Chiefs and Colonial Rule in Cameroon: Inventing Chieftaincy, French and British Style', *Africa*, 63 (1993), 153.

28. Mamdani, *Citizen and Subject*, 39.

29. R. Rathbone, *Nkrumah and the Chiefs: The Politics of Chieftaincy in Ghana, 1951–60* (Oxford: James Currey, 2000), 14.

30. L. Mair, 'Chieftainship in Modern Africa', *Africa*, 9 (1936), 311–12.

31. R. Tignor, *The Colonial Transformation of Kenya: The Kamba, Kikuyu and Maasai from 1900 to 1939* (Princeton: PUP, 1976).

32. T. Spear, 'Neo-Traditionalism', 9.

33. M. Gluckman, J. C. Mitchell, and J. A. Barnes, 'The Village Headman in British Central Africa', *Africa*, 19 (1949), 92; see also C. Leonardi, 'Violence, Sacrifice and Chiefship in Central Equatoria, Southern Sudan', *Africa*, 77 (2007).

34. L. Fallers, 'The Predicament of the Modern African Chief: An Instance from Uganda', *American Anthropologist*, 57 (1955), 295.

35. R. Watson, '*Civil Disorder is the Disease of Ibadan': Chieftaincy and Civic Culture in a Yoruba City* (Oxford: James Currey, 2003), 162; see also J. Cabrita, 'Politics and Preaching: Chiefly Converts to the Nazaretha Church, Obedient Subjects and Sermon Performance in South Africa', *Journal of African History*, 51 (2010).

36. L. Mair, 'African Chiefs Today', *Africa*, 28 (1958), 205.

37. P. Alexandre, 'The Problems of Chieftaincies in French-Speaking Africa', in Crowder and Ikime, *West African Chiefs*, 47.

38. P. Nugent, 'An Abandoned Project? The Nuances of Chieftaincy, Development and History in Ghana's Volta Region', *Journal of Legal Pluralism*, 37/38 (1996), 204.

39. Alexandre, 'Problems of Chieftaincies', 47.
40. I. Van Kessel and B. Oomen, '"One Chief, One Vote": The Revival of Traditional Authorities in Post-Apartheid South Africa', *African Affairs*, 96 (1997), 562.
41. M. Goheen, 'Chiefs, Sub-Chiefs and Local Control: Negotiations over Land, Struggles over Meaning', *Africa*, 62 (1992), 400.
42. A. Harneit-Sievers, 'Igbo "Traditional Rule": Chieftaincy and the State in Southern Nigeria', *Africa Spectrum*, 33 (1998), 70; see also Vaughan, 'Chieftaincy Politics in Nigeria', 320.
43. C. Lentz, 'The Chief, the Mine Captain and the Politician: Legitimating Power in Northern Ghana', *Africa*, 68 (1998).
44. D. Maxwell, *Christians and Chiefs in Zimbabwe: A Social History of the Hwesa People, c. 1870s–1990s* (Edinburgh: EUP, 1999), 227.
45. Vaughan, *Nigerian Chiefs*, 212–14; Nugent, 'An Abandoned Project?', 213.
46. Spear, 'Neo-Traditionalism', 6.
47. Nugent, 'An Abandoned Project?', 216; see also J. Comaroff, 'Chiefship in a South African Homeland: A Case Study of the Tshidi Kingdom of Bophutatswana', *Journal of Southern African Studies*, 1 (1974); Maxwell, *Christians and Chiefs*, 5; S. Hawkins, 'Disguising Chiefs and God as History: Questions on the Acephalousness of Lodagaa Politics and Religion', *Africa*, 66 (1996).
48. I. Nolte, 'Chieftaincy and the State in Abacha's Nigeria: Kingship, Political Rivalry and Competing Histories in Abeokuta during the 1990s', *Africa*, 72 (2002), 374, 387.

BIBLIOGRAPHY

Anderson, D., and D. Johnson, eds, *Revealing Prophets: Prophecy in East African History* (London: James Currey, 1995).

Berry, S., *'Chiefs Know their Boundaries': Essays on Property, Power and the Past in Asante, 1896–1996* (Portsmouth, NH: Heinemann, 2001).

Chanock, M., *Law, Custom and Social Order: The Colonial Experience in Malawi and Zambia* (Cambridge: CUP, 1985).

Crowder, M., and O. Ikime, eds, *West African Chiefs: Their Changing Status under Colonial Rule and Independence* (New York: Africana Publishing, 1970).

Fortes, M., and E. E. Evans-Pritchard, eds, *African Political Systems* (London: OUP, 1940).

Leonardi, C., *Dealing with Government in South Sudan: Histories in the Making of Chiefship, Community and State* (Oxford: James Currey, 2013).

Mamdani, M., *Citizen and Subject: Contemporary Africa and the Legacy of Late Colonialism* (Princeton: PUP, 1996).

Oomen, B., *Chiefs in South Africa: Law, Power and Culture in the Post-Apartheid Era* (Oxford: James Currey, 2005).

Richards, A., *East African Chiefs: A Study of Political Development in Some Uganda and Tanganyika Tribes* (London: Faber, 1960).

Temple, C., *Native Races and their Rulers* (London: Frank Cass, 2nd edn, 1968 [1918]).

Vansina, J., *Paths in the Rainforests: Toward a History of Political Tradition in Equatorial Africa* (London: James Currey, 1990).

Vaughan, O., *Nigerian Chiefs: Traditional Power in Modern Politics* (Rochester, NY: University of Rochester Press, 2000).

Watson, R., *'Civil Disorder is the Disease of Ibadan': Chieftaincy and Civic Culture in a Yoruba City* (Oxford: James Currey, 2003).

CHAPTER 12

BETWEEN THE PRESENT AND HISTORY:

African Nationalism and Decolonization

JEAN ALLMAN

> Decolonization, which sets out to change the order of the world, is, obviously, a program of complete disorder. But it cannot come as a result of magical practices, nor of a natural shock, nor of a friendly understanding. Decolonization, as we know, is a historical process: that is to say that it cannot be understood, it cannot become intelligible nor clear to itself except in the exact measure that we can discern the movements which give it historical form and content.[1]

THE year 1960 was the 'Year of Africa', or at least that is what many in the world's media called those heady days of African independence that witnessed seventeen former colonies (of France, Britain, and Belgium) win their freedom from colonial rule in a single year. What began as a trickle—with the Sudan, Tunisia, and Morocco in 1956—gained momentum with Ghana's independence in 1957, followed by that of Guinea in 1958. By 1960, the flags of Britain, France, and Belgium were lowered on vast expanses of African territory. The Portuguese held on to their colonies until 1975 and 'independent' white settler regimes in Southern Rhodesia (now Zimbabwe), Southwest Africa (Namibia), and South Africa clung tenaciously to power (the last until 1994) despite rising international condemnation. But they did so as pariahs. By 1960, the direction of change was clear. As British Prime Minister Harold Macmillan famously announced that year in Cape Town, 'The wind of change is blowing through this continent. Whether we like it or not, this growth of national consciousness is a political fact.'[2]

But in the immediate aftermath of the Second World War, few had a sense of how powerful that wind would be, from what direction it would come, much less what changes it could bring, or what forces might deflect it. How, in only fifteen years, could the political map of the continent undergo such profound transformation? Although a half-century has passed since the Year of Africa, historians are just now beginning to grapple with the question, to explore the multiple, overlapping, and often contradictory political, social, and economic processes that led to the rapid decolonization of the continent in the years after the Second World War. Indeed, until quite recently, the story of Africa's decolonization was left, for the most part, to social scientists, especially to political scientists, who focused their lens on nationalist party mobilization, the transfer of power, modernization, and processes of national integration.

AFRICAN HISTORIANS AND 'NATION TIMES'

In some ways, the fact that historians have only recently come to the topic of decolonization is a simple matter of chronology, endemic to the discipline. Decolonization has fallen within what John Kelly and Martha Kaplan call that 'middle distance between the present and history...Neither generally remembered nor yet well considered, these times pose a challenge to scholarship.'[3] That challenge, of course, was and in some ways continues to be exacerbated by colonial and postcolonial national archives, whose documents have been sealed under 'thirty-' or 'fifty-year rules'. But the neglect of decolonization as a central topic of inquiry is not simply a by-product of the temporal limits of the historian's vision or the temporary inaccessibility of the late colonial archive. Well into the 1970s, the study of precolonial history, especially of African resistance, as Fred Cooper reminds us, was what 'constituted genuine African history, but bringing a similar specificity of inquiry to that which was being resisted risked having one's project labeled as a throwback to imperial history'.[4]

If African historians took some time to get to the story of decolonization, it is not because the discipline was unconcerned with or disconnected from the project of decolonization. To the contrary: the early research agenda of African history was profoundly shaped by the nationalist fervour of the 1950s and 1960s, and from the beginning its aim was to write back against a long tradition of racist, imperialist European scholarship that denied the continent any meaningful, authentic past worthy of the historian's craft. African history, in other words, as a professionalized field of academic inquiry, was born in the cradle of African nationalism and quickly harnessed to its mission. At new universities in Africa and in scattered institutions in the global North, pioneering historians such as Kenneth Onwuka Dike and Jacob Ajayi (of the 'Ibadan School') worked to document the rich histories of precolonial state-building, commerce, and governance on the continent. They were joined by others—such as I. N. Kimambo, A. J. Temu, and Terence Ranger (the 'Dar es Salaam School')—who detailed African resistance to early European encroachment and argued that the seeds of nationalism were planted with the first ('primary') acts of resistance to European encroachment. Nationalism and decolonization thus profoundly shaped the research agendas of Africa's first generation of professional historians, even as those historians worked to reconstruct histories that were focused almost exclusively on the precolonial period.

SOCIAL SCIENTISTS AND THE
'WIND OF CHANGE'

While historians crafted precolonial histories aimed at decolonizing Africa's past and explicating the connections between early resistance and nationalist consciousness, the first sustained scholarly attention to decolonization itself came in the 1950s and was authored primarily by social scientists, who, via country case studies, examined the forces that propelled colonies into nation-states. Those case studies—by David Apter, James S. Coleman, and others—established the basic outline for the metanarrative of decolonization, a story profoundly influenced by modernization theory and closely focused on governments, institutions, and leadership: the educated elite; the emergence of party politics; constitutional development; elections; and negotiations towards the transfer of power and self-rule.

These early accounts of decolonization feature a postwar imperial or global context, riddled with crises and contradictions, and a locally authored anti-colonial or nationalist script. The 'happy ending', as Bill Freund opined in 1984, was always 'national independence'.[5] The story typically begins with the global economic depression of the 1930s, which is characterized as laying bare the hollowness of colonial rhetoric of advancement in the face of massive retrenchment and economic stagnation. The heightened tensions among the European powers and the invasion of Ethiopia by fascist Italy in 1935 are seen as then fuelling the early fires of anti-colonial agitation. But it is the Second World War that figures most prominently as a watershed moment in the metanarrative of decolonization, for its impact both on the global balance of power and on local scripts of nationalist mobilization.

Although military battles were fought only in North Africa and the Horn, the entire continent was profoundly impacted by the 'total war' economy. Hundreds of thousands of African troops fought in the war, some playing a critical role in decisive battles, including those that liberated Ethiopia, Somalia, and Eritrea from Italian occupation. But it was not only African soldiers who were recruited into the war effort. Forced labour pulled many Africans into production of foodstuffs for export and of raw materials in support of imperial war efforts. The end of the war, moreover, witnessed the emergence of a very different global order: the colonial powers were in a weakened state; they were poorer and far less stable. The United States and the Soviet Union were poised to become the new 'super-powers' and neither had a vested interest in buttressing the existing systems of colonial rule. In addition, the United Nations Charter reaffirmed the right of nations to self-determination first outlined in the Atlantic Charter, and shortly after the war ended, European power in Asia began to crumble with the independence of India and Pakistan in 1947 and Ceylon and Burma in 1948. Finally, it was in the immediate postwar context, at the Pan-African Congress of 1945, that future nationalist leaders such as Obafemi Awolowo, Jomo Kenyatta, and Kwame Nkrumah would begin to connect the incipient African struggle against colonial domination to older pan-African movements for freedom and racial justice with roots in North America and the Caribbean.

It is into this global, imperial context that the early authors of the decolonization narrative such as James S. Coleman, Dennis Austin, Robert I. Rotberg, and Ruth Schacter Morgenthau inserted the local script.[6] Those scripts tended to focus on the contradictions of colonial rule, heightened by the depression and the war, and the new kinds of historical actors who were both 'produced' by colonialism and best positioned to challenge it: a mission-educated elite, which would begin to articulate a nationalist vision, narrow though it was, even before the outbreak of the Second World War; peasant producers of cash crops, who were increasingly vulnerable to food shortages, while the prices for their crops rose and then fell, depending on the vicissitudes of the world market; migrant workers, who, through systems of either voluntary or forced migration, spent years away from their rural homes toiling on plantations, in mines, or on public works projects; urban dwellers, who fled to cities, especially during the war, to escape deepening rural poverty, only to find overcrowded slums, with no sanitation or services; wage labourers, who in the rapidly expanding colonial cities, struggled to earn a living wage and to organize in new kinds of associations and trade unions; ex-soldiers, who had fought alongside European soldiers in the war and returned believing that they would be looked after for their service and that the freedom for which they fought would be extended to their own people.

The local script for decolonization, then, became the story of how new social actors forged mass nationalist movements capable of winning national sovereignty from a colonial power at the very same time that those powers sought to undertake a 'second colonial occupation'. By extending social services, infrastructure, and some educational opportunities and by encouraging secondary industry and the development of a small urban working class, colonial governments believed they could pay off their war debts and stabilize their possessions; they were, in other words, digging in for the long haul. But postwar nationalists, as Thomas Hodgkin first argued in 1956, had other plans.[7] For much of the African continent, the story of decolonization from 1945 to 1965 is the story of how a rather narrowly cast elite nationalism, like that of the early African National Congress in South Africa or the National Congress of British West Africa, was transformed by a new breed of nationalist leader, in alliance with workers, peasants, school-leavers, teachers, and veterans, in the wake of the Second World War, into a mass nationalist movement capable—at least in most instances—of forcing European withdrawal.

NKRUMAH'S BLACK STAR AND SÉKOU TOURÉ'S 'NON!'

In many ways, Kwame Nkrumah's Ghana and Sékou Touré's Guinea served to set the stage and outline the plot for the decolonization story. The postwar account of Ghana— the first sub-Saharan country to win independence from colonial rule—usually begins, as it does with Austin's account, with the founding in 1947, by a small number of educated men in the south, of the United Gold Coast Convention, whose aim was to push the British gradually towards independence through a process of modest reforms.[8] Then, enter Kwame Nkrumah. Nkrumah had been studying in the United States and Britain for over a decade and the leadership of the UGCC invited him to return to become their organizing secretary. He accepted the invitation, but quickly came into conflict with the more conservative leadership because he believed it was important to mobilize the masses in the struggle for independence. But while conflict simmered within the UGCC, the masses, as it were, took the lead in early 1948—first with a boycott of European goods and then with demonstrations and riots, in the wake of police firing upon a peaceful demonstration of ex-servicemen who were demanding their pensions and jobs for the future. By 1949, the political momentum had shifted from the more conservative members of the UGCC to Nkrumah and his followers, who then founded their own political party, a mass-based party called the Convention People's Party. From that point on, non-violent protest or Positive Action, as Nkrumah termed it, was the name of the game. By 1951, the colonial government had no choice but to negotiate its way through the devolution of state power. In a 1951 election, the CPP won a resounding victory and Nkrumah became the 'Leader of Government Business'. Through two more general elections in 1954 and 1956, the CPP was able to affirm its leadership role, despite the emergence of regionally and tribally based opposition groups, and stood as the ruling party on 6 March 1957, when the Union Jack was lowered and the Black Star raised.

In contrast with the British, who responded to postwar demands with constitutional plans for the devolution of power to increasingly independent nation-states, France responded with more ambitious plans to assimilate its colonies into a 'greater France', beginning with its new constitution in 1946 which extended voting rights for the French National Assembly to some Africans. In that same year, as Morgenthau recounted in 1964, political party leaders from throughout the twelve territories of French Equatorial and West Africa met in Bamako and formed the Rassemblement Démocratique Africain (RDA), which worked within the framework of union and 'association' to extend citizenship and voting rights.[9] By 1951, the RDA leadership, which included a young Guinean trade unionist, Sékou Touré, was advocating the creation of two strong federations—West and Equatorial—within the French Union, but President de Gaulle had other ideas and pushed for the balkanization of France's African colonies into twelve self-governing, but weaker, states. In an effort to forestall demands for independence, the French government granted the colonies some autonomy in 1956, but the momentum towards independence was strong. Within Guinea, Sékou Touré had moved sharply away from assimilationist strategies and autonomy within a French union by 1951. He built a mass party linked to the RDA, the Parti Démocratique de la Guinée, from a strong trade union foundation and then expanded its base into rural areas by gaining the support of farmers who opposed the rule of French-installed chiefs. When de Gaulle returned to power in 1958, his primary aim was to create some kind of stability in how France ruled its overseas territories. Through a 1958 draft constitution, he offered each of the twelve colonies autonomy within a French Community or immediate independence. The former came with promises of aid, education, and trade; the latter—with nothing. In the September 1958 referendum on the constitution, all of France's African territories voted in favour of de Gaulle's plan, except for Guinea, where an overwhelming majority of voters (94 per cent) said, 'Non!' France immediately withdrew all aid and support and whatever infrastructure it could pack into cargo ships. Guinea became independent, under the leadership of Sékou Touré, on 2 October 1958.

The independence of Ghana and Guinea set the stage for African decolonization in dramatic ways. There appeared to be no turning back. By 1960, the remaining French territories south of the Sahara were granted their independence. Nigeria, the most populous country on the continent, negotiated its way to independence as a federation in the same year. Even in Kenya, where colonial forces fought to uphold white settler domination against armed risings of 'Land and Freedom' armies ('Mau Mau'), the wind of change was blowing by 1960. The Kenya African National Union was founded in that year and the momentum was clearly towards African majority rule and independence, which would follow in 1963.

But perhaps the biggest surprise during the Year of Africa came from the Congo, where the Belgians had done almost nothing to prepare their vast territory for sovereignty. By the late 1950s, they permitted the formation of political parties and local elections, but reforms were minimal. Then after major anti-colonial riots rocked the capital Léopoldville in 1959, Belgium suddenly offered independence in January 1960 and formally withdrew six months later, convinced, perhaps, that a quick independence would mean no real independence at all. Only one political party—Patrice Lumumba's Mouvement National Congolais—had any national reach and, with independence, Lumumba became prime minister. The other political parties were all regionally or ethnically based; the army had no African officers and colonial civil servants immediately packed up and went home. In the end, it was a recipe for disaster and it was not long before the Congo was in full crisis, facing army mutinies and regional secession. Only three months after independence, Joseph Mobutu staged a coup, with Belgian and US support. Fleeing the capital, Lumumba was captured by forces loyal to Mobutu in December. The Year of Africa thus ended with the political disintegration of one of the continent's largest countries and with the arrest of one of its most dynamic young leaders. His subsequent murder, at the hands of secessionists (and, as many would later speculate, with the knowledge, if not approval, of Belgium and the United States) would mark the opening of 1961.

But Whose Dream was it Anyway?

That the grand narrative of decolonization—of Whiggish progress towards independence and modernization—would not stand the test of time was apparent before the ink had even dried on the 1960s social science tracts. In the first instance, the wind of change collided with the obdurate colonialism of the Portuguese, who would fight three wars—in Angola, Guinea Bissau, and Mozambique—for over a decade, before a coup in Portugal in 1974 would oust the dictatorship and bring negotiated settlements in 1975. And wherever nationalist movements confronted entrenched white settler colonialism—in French Algeria (until 1962), Kenya (until 1963), Southern Rhodesia (until 1980), and in South Africa (until 1994), the stakes were higher and the long, bitter struggles waged with arms. The Year of Africa, we should recall, was also the year that sixty-nine peaceful protesters in Sharpeville, South Africa were gunned down by the police for refusing to carry passes.

If the intransigence of some forms of colonialism belied the inevitability of decolonization predicted by Macmillan in 1960, events in the Congo only sharpened questions, already in circulation, about the real meaning of independence for those countries that had already raised their sovereign flags. Did the wind of change actually change anything at all? Or was it only independence of the flag—*uhuru wa bendera* in Swahili—that affirmed forms of neo-colonial power? In many ways, the critique of decolonization unfolded with the very process of decolonization itself, with one of the early and most devastating, on the 'pitfalls of national consciousness', coming from West Indian psychiatrist and revolutionary Frantz Fanon in *The Wretched of the Earth* (1961). In Guinea Bissau, Amilcar Cabral warned in 1964 that decolonization was in the interests of the imperial powers: 'The objective of the imperialist countries was to prevent the enlargement of the socialist camp, liberate the reactionary forces in our countries stifled by colonialism, and enable these forces to ally themselves with the international bourgeoisie.'[10] After the 1966 coup that overthrew him, Nkrumah would come to a critique not very different from Fanon or Cabral: true national liberation, 'the next crucial phase of the Revolution', would require armed struggle.[11]

The revolutionary critique of nationalism and independence that developed alongside the very processes of decolonization in the 1960s and gained momentum in the wake of the Congo crisis, military *coups d'état* in Ghana and Nigeria (1966), the Biafran War (1967–70), and entrenched settler colonialism would also shape the direction of Africanist scholarship—historical and otherwise. By the late 1960s and into the 1970s, 'radical pessimists', as Bill Freund termed them, such as Colin Leys, Bob Fitch, and Mary Oppenheimer would bring new tools—class analysis, dependency theory, neo-Marxist approaches to underdevelopment—to African history writing and to deciphering political economy in a postcolonial context. For those scholars, much of what had been heralded in the 1960s as progressive change, as independence and sovereignty, was nothing but an illusion.[12]

Yet embedded within this radical pessimism was a profound, enduring optimism about the possibility of revolutionary change. Scholars such as John Saul looked first to Tanzania and to Julius Nyerere's African socialism before turning to the armed insurrections of peasants and workers in Angola, Mozambique, Guinea Bissau, and Zimbabwe for the promise of substantive revolutionary change in Africa that could transcend 'independence of the flag' and fulfil Fanon's vision of an entire 'social structure being changed from the bottom up'.[13] Indeed, well into the 1980s, after the revolutionary wars of independence had, in many cases, degenerated into national civil wars fuelled by Cold War hostilities, scholars still looked to the very southern tip of the continent, to Apartheid South Africa—the last bastion of white rule—for a new, alternative 'happy ending'. In the final paragraph of his important survey of contemporary African history published in 1984, Bill Freund typified that revolutionary optimism:

> An Africanist perspective would suggest that a victory for African nationalism in South Africa simply places it at the end of a long trail of victories for nationalism in Africa with South African joining the more than four dozen national entities created in the continent over the last twenty-five years. A Marxist perspective suggests, on the contrary, that revolution in South Africa would bring the working class to the fore and have explosive international consequences, providing Africa with its first industrialized socialist economy and bringing about a storm that would be likely to sweep aside crisis-ridden regimes over half the continent.[14]

Yet in striking ways, the radical tale of decolonization, as it was told after 1966, was no less linear or Whiggish, no less structured by a grand and modernizing metanarrative, than were earlier versions. It still pointed towards a happy ending, but one wrenched from the long arms of neo-colonialism and white settler regimes by the revolutionary forces of national liberation.

COMPLICATING THE METANARRATIVE

Twenty-five years after the Year of Africa, some historians were beginning to ask different kinds of questions about decolonization—questions less directed towards obvious answers or happy endings. Although decolonization was still caught in a kind of dead zone between history and the present, others began to call historians to action with questions such as, 'Whose dream was it anyway?'[15] Indeed, by the 1980s, armed with the new tools of social history and the perspectives opened up by women's history and labour history, Africanist historians began to focus far more attention on the lives of ordinary women and men during the colonial period and follow those stories into the era of nationalist mobilization. They began, in other words, to chip away at the edges of the metanarrative—in both its positivist and pessimist guise—by demonstrating that the authors of nation dreams were not only political parties and their leaders.

Some of the earliest and most powerful challenges were launched from African universities (Nairobi, Dar es Salaam, and Ibadan, in particular),[16] but we should take note that the key sites for the generation of historical knowledge production on Africa were shifting dramatically at this very moment. In the 1960s and early 1970s, the cutting-edge institutions for history-writing were located on the continent—at Ibadan (Nigeria), Dar es Salaam (Tanzania), Dakar (Senegal), and Legon (Ghana). Foreigners who wanted to study African history considered it an enormous privilege to be able to study at African institutions where, as Cooper has written, 'historians...were well organized and conscious of their role in making and writing history'.[17] But the 1980s saw not only new kinds of questions about Africa's pasts, but very serious concerns about its present and its future.[18] The oil shocks of the 1970s, the draconian structural adjustment plans of the 1980s, conflict within and among African states, and increased political repression on many fronts all took a heavy toll on higher education. Budgets were cut, salaries and libraries stagnated, protest was quelled, and the African brain drain accelerated. The impact on historical writing—on the questions asked, the priorities set, and perhaps most importantly, on the organic connections between history-writing and what John Lonsdale termed in 1989 the development of 'effective political language'—was enormous.[19]

The shifts in method and in questions, therefore, that marked the new historiography of the 1980s were often generated from outside African universities (though they encompassed the work of African scholars now working in the global North) and mirrored the turn in North America and in Europe towards questions of historical agency, towards reconstructing the lives of ordinary people, and writing history from the bottom up.[20] Feminist and women's historians, for example, were becoming increasingly interested in exploring the roles of women in colonial Africa—in agricultural labour, in trade, in resistance—and, indeed, it was the field of women's history that wielded some of the earliest and most decisive challenges to the received decolonization narrative.[21] Work such as LaRay Denzer's on West Africa or Susan Geiger's on Tanzania did not just add women to the narrative, it shifted its focus in fundamental ways by demonstrating that women were a central force in constructing and, in TANU's case, performing nationalism through their organizations and their collective memory. Women, in other words, were not simply an audience for the nationalist message and historians needed to place them at the creative core of the nation-state story as those who generated and performed nationalism's 'culture of politics'.[22]

Indeed, in almost every case where historians added new actors to the story of decolonization, the metanarrative was not just expanded, it began to transform in significant ways. When peasants or rural struggles came into sharp focus, the very discourse of nationalist mobilization—especially the meanings of independence—acquired a much longer and more contested history, one that was located as much in peripheral rural areas as in urban centres.[23] Elizabeth Schmidt's work on Sékou Touré's 'Non!' in 1958 powerfully demonstrated that nationalist scripts were written and often driven 'from below'.[24] Popular pressure from women, from peasants, from workers, and from veterans—rather than decisive leadership from above—led to the no-vote in that historic referendum. Similarly, Lonsdale's work on ethnicity and 'tribal nationalism' focused on the importance of 'moral ethnicity' in the development of political language—on the centrality of the local in shaping broader political debate.[25]

Some of the most significant challenges to the metanarrative of decolonization, however, have been launched by Frederick Cooper, whose initial work on the labour question in East Africa has been followed by a series of field-defining publications that explore the theoretical and epistemological underpinnings of nationalism and decolonization. Cooper's work persistently transcends the imperial history/nationalist history divide that has long separated the work of Africanists from that of historians of European empires and reveals the important insights that can be garnered from comparative research.[26] Perhaps most importantly, Cooper has opened up the realm of political imagination to rigorous historical scrutiny and reminded historians, time and again, that we should not read history backwards. In the era of decolonization, a range of social and political possibilities opened up and the nation-state was neither the only nor the inevitable outcome.[27] In the political imaginations of workers, of peasants, of urban women, we can trace motivations, goals, and struggles that do not always fit neatly within the nationalist rubric, nor should they be forced to. Even some of the most famous of nationalist leaders had visions, at least initially, that transcended the nation-state: Léopold Senghor wished to transform French Empire, not escape it, to build a federation in which free citizens shared equal rights and responsibilities. And Nkrumah's ultimate aim was not the independence of the colonial Gold Coast, but a United States of Africa.[28] In its call for non-linear histories of decolonization, in its posing of the national question in dynamic dialogue with other political questions, and in its search for the sovereign African state in a conjuncture of movements, Cooper's work has not only challenged the decolonization metanarrative, but has set the agenda for the next generation of historians.

WHOSE DREAMS AND WHICH DREAMS?

The next generation is as concerned with *which* dreams as it is with *whose* dreams narrated decolonization. Increasingly, decolonization is being freed from its moorings as either the triumphal 'end' of colonial history or the opening scene in an ongoing tale of 'what went wrong'. In part, this is a consequence of what has gone before—that is, debates within the historiography—but it also reflects new and very different political, economic, social, and academic realities. Globalization and the consolidation of a neo-liberal world order have foregrounded the seemingly endless reach of the multinational corporation, which at times seems to trump the nation-state as the most significant form through which power, might, wealth, and hegemony are organized and exercised. It is perhaps easier now than it was fifty years ago to imagine a nation-state that is neither natural nor inevitable. And as they begin to conceive of alternative forms of protest and power, historians today are also drawing from new kinds of theoretical models, such as postcolonial theory, cultural studies, and queer theory, and they are in dialogue, across the global South, with scholars of other parts of the vast postcolonial world. Of equal, if not more, significance for historians of decolonization today is the fact that, with the passing of fifty years since the Year of Africa, most, though certainly not all, of the documentation relevant to decolonization housed in various government archives is opening up. There are now, for the first time, fairly extensive archival records to consult about the era of decolonization, while some of the individuals who were witnesses to the events unfolding around struggles for sovereignty are still here to share their stories. New sources, new perspectives, new questions, in other words, mark the current juncture.

David Anderson's reconstruction of the Mau Mau rebellion and the end of empire in Kenya is a notable example of how new archival sources are transforming histories of resistance and decolonization. Historians have been grappling with the meanings of Mau Mau for decades. Was it a nationalist movement, a tribal rebellion, or a Kikuyu civil war? Did it contribute to decolonization or was it an obstacle? What, if any, were its connections to effective nationalist mobilization in Kenya? Anderson uncovered a vast repository of trial records pertaining to the over one thousand Mau Mau detainees who were sent to the gallows by the colonial government during one of the most brutal suppressions of African resistance in British imperial history. (At one point the colonial state had imprisoned 12 per cent of all male Kikuyus.) From the trial records and from a broad range of government documents housed both in Kenya and Britain, Anderson has crafted a complex story focused on the lives of ordinary men and women who were caught in the devastation that became known as 'Mau Mau' and provided unparalleled insight into its long-term consequences for Kenya's unfolding political landscape.[29]

New archival sources are, in part, also responsible for a burgeoning literature on political imagination, which builds from some of the scholarly work the 1980s and 1990s by locating the origins of political discourse outside the nationalist frame or at hybridized meeting places between the local and national. James Brennan's work on Tanzania, for example, takes aim at a historiography that has been primarily concerned with the structures of nationalist mobilization and has, for the most part, not taken seriously the intellectual content of Tanzanian nationalism. By tracing a shifting Kiswahili political vocabulary in Dar es Salaam, Brennan demonstrates that TANU had no monopoly on the generation of nationalist discourse.[30] Focusing on village politics in the Grassfields of Cameroon, Meredith Terretta undertakes a similar excavation of political imagination, demonstrating how the anti-colonialism of the UPC (Union des populations du Cameroun) and village concepts of sovereignty and nation coalesced to form a 'hybrid' political discourse of 'village nationalism'.[31]

It is not simply in excavating and analysing a range of political discourses that recent historians have complicated and at times subverted the metanarrative of decolonization. By exploring the varied ways in which political imagination was expressed, articulated, and performed, they have drawn insight from postcolonial and cultural studies scholarship and encouraged us to look beyond the print capitalism so central to Benedict Anderson's explanation of 'imagined communities'. Inspired by Geiger's work on the performance of nationalism by TANU women, for example, Marissa Moorman's *Intonations* turns to 'sonorous capitalism' (riffing on Anderson), specifically to popular music in Luanda and the vibrant dance clubs where it was played. 'Angolan musicians and audiences', Moorman argues, 'transformed autonomous spaces into an experience of sovereignty as they began to imagine an Angola in and on their own terms'.[32]

Pointing a wide-angle lens at political imagination and discourses of self-determination in the era of decolonization, historians have also brought into focus new political actors, who have seldom been taken very seriously. While 1980s and 1990s scholarship brought women, workers, and peasants into the frame of decolonization, some fascinating recent scholarship has looked at the particular role of youth in both imagining and contesting nation dreams. Most recently, Jay Straker's *Youth, Nationalism, and the Guinean Revolution* places Guinea's youth at centre stage in a story of mobilization and nation-building that defies the pessimism of earlier generations of scholars. In this account, Sékou Touré emerges not as an inevitable despot-in-the-making but as a 'beleaguered political artisan trying to come to terms with a youth-centered social dynamic'.[33] Straker follows the 'youth across the border of independence', right up to the death of Touré in 1984, in a narrative that is never overwhelmed by 'what went wrong', but rather foregrounds the complex nature of national citizenship and national imagining.

While much of the recent literature on decolonization is still generally situated within the confines of individual nation-states, there has been a growing scholarship that is comparative and transnational, and is blurring the boundaries between European imperial and African nationalist histories. Because of the assimilationist imperative of French decolonization, the literature on French West Africa has been the most expansive in this regard, but there are interesting developments in other areas as well.[34] Historians with very different repertoires of area expertise, for example, are bringing fresh insight to the study of decolonization. Kevin Gaines's *American Africans in Ghana*, for example, follows stories of freedom and nation through a cast of extraordinary women and men of African descent who converged on Ghana in the midst of the US civil rights movement, the Cold War, and the decolonization of the continent. Christopher Lee has looked to Bandung and the rise of Afro-Asian solidarity at the dawn of African independence and James Brennan, in a similar vein, has explored the impact of Radio Cairo on the East African freedom struggle—a context in which the global aspirations of Afro-Asian solidarity confronted the real political and economic disparities between Africans and Asians in East Africa.[35] In these recent transnational accounts, the Cold War figures far more prominently than it has in earlier scholarship and, indeed, grappling with the real impact of the Cold War on African decolonization is a critical area of investigation at the current juncture.[36]

Finally, historians are beginning to historicize their own discipline in the context of decolonization, and to examine questions of memory and public history as fiftieth-anniversary golden jubilees of independence are celebrated. This scholarship has taken a number of forms. Some of it is aimed at exploring knowledge production about Africa generally over the past fifty years.[37] Toyin Falola's recent work has grappled with nationalism, the academy, and the role of African intellectuals, while some of the early European scholars involved in the establishment of African history as a subject of professional academic inquiry have penned their memoirs.[38] In addition, historians have joined a range of scholars from other disciplines in probing sites of national memory and of public or popular culture in the context of decolonization.[39]

'LEAVE THE DEAD SOME ROOM TO DANCE'

The Year of Africa is now a half-century behind us; it is emerging out of the shadows, out of what Kelly and Kaplan term the 'twilight of history'.[40] But what does the future of this history hold? Certainly, historians of decolonization over the next decade must continue to heed Cooper's warning not to read history backwards, not to interpret every

word, action, or reaction as leading always and inevitably to the constitution of a single sovereign postcolonial nation-state. Historians of decolonization must, to borrow
the words of Nigerian playwright Wole Soyinka, 'leave the dead some room to dance'.[41]
We know from the scholarship of the past two decades that in 1960 women and men
were imagining new worlds of all kinds. We must continue to reconstruct these political
imaginaries, the dreams of winners and of losers. What was deemed possible in those
critical years? How and why did those possibilities, that promise, begin to narrow? In
answering these questions—of dreams deferred or, worse, disappeared—we cannot
just look to the 'failed' or 'compromised' nation-state or to its former colonial overlord.
African decolonization unfolded as a transnational, not just as an imperial, story, and we
must work to capture its multifaceted and multi-sited complexity, from Manchester to
Bandung and beyond.[42] And though we must look beyond nation-state borders in reconstructing histories of decolonization, we must also be cognizant of those ever-tightening
borders. How did they come to be marked or enacted, and engaged as lived experience?
How did they define or demarcate citizenship: who belonged and who did not?

Borders mattered, especially in the Cold War world in which African decolonization
unfolded. Indeed, one of the many challenges historians currently face is understanding
just how Cold War rivalries shaped, facilitated, constrained, or subverted not just
processes of decolonization, but how the postcolonial world could be imagined. For
example, it was in the context of the Cold War that international espionage came into
its own. Although it is unclear at this stage how much of the documentary record will
survive, we must more firmly take on global questions of Cold War politics in histories of African decolonization, including grappling with the new forms of intelligence
gathering that emerged after the Second World War. Who was collecting information,
from whom, and how, and to what end? How did those global practices refract locally,
within families, between generations? Equally important, given the critical role it would
assume in seizing and holding state power in so many countries, is the military. While
I suspect access to records will plague this area of research in the years to come, new
histories of decolonization must begin to interrogate far more carefully the legacy of
colonial militaries in the postcolonial era.

The challenges scholars face, as decolonization moves into the light of historical
inquiry, are not just about the big players on the big stage—US and USSR rivalries,
military power, or the CIA. One of the more exciting directions towards which current scholarship points is the gendered politics of decolonization. While we now have
a much better sense of the critical roles women played in mobilizing, performing, and
imagining nation in the years of nationalist struggle, we have much to learn about
the gendered dynamics of citizenship, politics, and governance in the immediate
postcolonial period.[43] What, for example, is the fate of women activists in the context of the centralization and consolidation of state power after independence? Does
decolonization inevitably result in a masculinization of the political sphere, no matter how central women were to independence struggles? Connected to questions of
gender, state power, and politics are issues of marriage, family, and sexuality. How

are these reinvented, articulated, and consolidated in the new 'modern' sovereign nation-states?

Fifty years on, the questions are many, but one thing is certain: the grand social science metanarrative of decolonization is under assault; it is being complicated, overturned, fractured into multiple micro-histories, and grafted onto transnational histories. It no longer fits neatly within borders of any kind. How, indeed, can we tell the story of any territorially bound nation-state as a singular story of triumph or tragedy when, for the very women and men who sought to build a new world in 1957, 1960, 1975, or 1994, it was not a singular, linear story? Certainly the archives for this project-in-the-making must be similarly nuanced and complex. Our research cannot be confined to the national archive of the postcolonial state or the former imperial power. Evidentiary fragments are strewn across the globe, from Cape Town to Cairo, from Beijing to Moscow to Washington, DC. They are in the intelligence archives of the CIA and the KGB, in the paintings of Tshibumba Kanda Matulu and Tom Feelings, in the prose of Chinua Achebe, Ngugi wa Thiong'o, and Maya Angelou, and in the memories and tin trunks of ordinary women and men. The challenges, of course, are immense and daunting: how to grapple with such an extraordinary, transnational range of sources and still 'discern the movements', as Fanon insisted, that gave decolonization 'its historical form and content'. Can we, in other words, recount this story so that it is neither a triumphal end nor a tragic beginning?

Notes

1. Frantz Fanon, *The Wretched of the Earth* (New York: Grove Press, 1963), 36.
2. 'Harold Macmillan: Winds of Change', in Jussi M. Hanhimäki and Odd Arne Westad, eds, *The Cold War: A History in Documents and Eyewitness Accounts* (Oxford: OUP, 2003), 357.
3. John D. Kelly and Martha Kaplan, *Presented Communities: Fiji and World Decolonization* (Chicago: University of Chicago Press, 2001), p. vii.
4. Frederick Cooper, 'Conflict and Connection: Rethinking Colonial African History', *American Historical Review*, 99/5 (1994), 1522.
5. Bill Freund, *The Making of Contemporary Africa: The Development of African Society since 1800* (Bloomington, Ind.: Indiana University Press, 1984), 8.
6. James S. Coleman, *Nigeria: Background to Nationalism* (Berkeley, Calif.: University of California Press, 1958); Dennis Austin, *Politics in Ghana, 1946–1960* (London: OUP, 1964); Robert I. Rotberg, *The Rise of Nationalism in Central Africa: The Making of Malawi and Zambia, 1873–1964* (Cambridge, Mass.: Harvard University Press, 1965); Ruth Schacter Morgenthau, *Political Parties in French-Speaking West Africa* (Oxford: Clarendon Press, 1964).
7. Thomas Hodgkin, *Nationalism in Colonial Africa* (London: Frederick Muller, 1956).
8. Austin, *Politics in Ghana*, see esp. 49–102.
9. See Morgenthau, *Political Parties in French-Speaking West Africa*.
10. Fanon, *Wretched of the Earth*; Amilcar Cabral, 'Is Colonialism Rationalized Imperialism?', in William Worger, Nancy Clark, and Edward Alpers, eds, *Africa and the West: A Documentary History, ii. From Colonialism to Independence* (New York: OUP, 2010), 181.

11. Kwame Nkrumah, *Class Struggle in Africa* (New York: International Publishers, 1970), 9.

12. Bob Fitch and Mary Oppenheimer, *Ghana: End of an Illusion* (New York: Monthly Review Press, 1966); Colin Leys, *Underdevelopment in Kenya: The Political Economy of Neo-Colonialism, 1964–1971* (Berkeley, Calif.: University of California Press, 1975).

13. Fanon, *Wretched of the Earth*, 35. See e.g. John S. Saul, *The State and Revolution in Eastern Africa: Essays* (New York: Monthly Review Press, 1979); Lionel Cliffe and John S. Saul, *Socialism in Tanzania: An Interdisciplinary Reader* (Dar es Salaam: East African Publishing House, 1972); John S. Saul, ed., *A Difficult Road: The Transition to Socialism in Mozambique* (New York: Monthly Review Press, 1985).

14. Freund, *Making of Contemporary Africa*, 288.

15. Michael Crowder, 'Whose Dream was it Anyway? Twenty-Five Years of African Independence', *African Affairs*, 86/342 (Jan., 1987).

16. Cooper, 'Conflict and Connection', 1522–3.

17. Frederick Cooper, 'Africa's Pasts and Africa's Historians', *Canadian Journal of African Studies*, 34/2 (2000), 304.

18. John Lonsdale, 'Africa's Pasts in Africa's Futures', *Canadian Journal of African Studies*, 23/1 (1989), 126–35.

19. Lonsdale, 'Africa's Pasts in Africa's Futures', 130.

20. An exception, perhaps, is the History Workshop, founded by radical white scholars at the University of the Witswatersrand in 1977.

21. Nina Mba's University of Ibadan Ph.D. dissertation, which was published as *Nigerian Women Mobilised: Women's Political Activity in Southern Nigeria, 1900–1965* (Berkeley, Calif.: University of California, 1982), laid important groundwork for what would follow in the 1980s.

22. Susan Geiger, *TANU Women: Gender and Culture in the Making of Tanganyikan Nationalism, 1955–1965* (Portsmouth, NH: Heinemann, 1997), 15. See also LaRay Denzer, 'Towards a Study of the History of West African Women's Participation in Nationalist Politics: The Early Phase, 1935–1950', *Africana Research Bulletin*, 6/4 (1976).

23. Steve Feierman's *Peasant Intellectuals: Anthropology and History in Tanzania* (Madison, Wis.: University of Wisconsin Press, 1990), laid important groundwork.

24. Elizabeth Schmidt, *Mobilizing the Masses: Gender, Ethnicity, and Class in the Nationalist Movement in Guinea, 1939–1958* (Portsmouth, NH: Heinemann, 2005).

25. John Lonsdale, 'The Moral Economy of Mau Mau: Wealth, Poverty and Civic Virtue in Kikuyu Political Thought', in Bruce Berman and John Lonsdale, *Unhappy Valley, ii. Violence and Ethnicity* (Athens, O.: Ohio University Press, 1990), 315–504. My own work on decolonization and the National Liberation Movement in Ghana sought to add to the metanarrative actors whose histories long predated the nation-state and whose visions of sovereignty differed markedly from Nkrumah's—grounded as they were in the long and contested past of Asante as a precolonial state: Jean Allman, *Quills of the Porcupine: Asante Nationalism in an Emergent Ghana* (Madison, Wis.: University of Wisconsin Press, 1993).

26. Cooper has also demonstrated the importance of engaging theoretical paradigms from outside African studies: see esp. his 'Conflict and Connection', and *Colonialism in Question: Theory, Knowledge, History* (Berkeley, Calif.: University of California Press, 2005).

27. Frederick Cooper, *Decolonization and African Society: The Labor Question in French and British Africa* (Cambridge: CUP, 1996), 1.

28. Frederick Cooper, 'Possibility and Constraint: African Independence in Historical Perspective', *Journal of African History*, 49/2 (2008), 174–5.

29. David Anderson, *Histories of the Hanged: The Dirty War in Kenya and the End of Empire* (New York: Norton, 2005). For an example of the importance of new sources for understanding decolonization in Francophone Africa, see Todd Shepard, *The Invention of Decolonization: The Algerian War and the Remaking of France* (Ithaca, NY: Cornell University Press, 2006), 5.

30. James R. Brennan, 'Blood Enemies: Exploitation and Urban Citizenship in the Nationalist Political Thought of Tanzania, 1958–1975', *Journal of African History*, 47/3 (2006), 391.

31. Meredith Terretta, ' "God of Independence, God of Peace": Village Politics and Nationalism in the Maquis of Cameroon, 1957–71', *Journal of African History*, 46/1 (2005), 75; see also David Anderson, ' "Yours in Struggle for Majimbo": Nationalism and the Party Politics of Decolonization in Kenya, 1955–64', *Journal of Contemporary History*, 40 (2005), and James R. Brennan, 'Lowering the Sultan's Flag: Sovereignty and Decolonization in Coastal Kenya', *Comparative Studies in Society and History*, 50/4 (2008).

32. Marissa J. Moorman, *Intonations: A Social History of Music and Nation in Luanda, Angola, from 1945 to Recent Times* (Athens, O.: Ohio University Press, 2008), 7.

33. Jay Straker, *Youth, Nationalism, and the Guinean Revolution* (Bloomington, Ind.: Indiana University Press, 2009), 10; see also James R. Brennan, 'Youth, the TANU Youth League and Managed Vigilantism in Dar es Salaam, Tanzania, 1925–1973', *Africa*, 7/6 (2006).

34. See e.g. Shepard, *Invention of Decolonization*, and Tony Chafer, *The End of Empire in French West Africa* (New York: Berg, 2002).

35. Kevin Gaines, *American Africans in Ghana: Black Expatriates and the Civil Rights Era* (Chapel Hill, NC: University of North Carolina Press, 2006); Christopher J. Lee, ed., *Making a World after Empire: The Bandung Moment and its Political Afterlives* (Athens, O.: Ohio University Press, 2010). In Lee's volume, see esp. James R. Brennan, 'Radio Cairo and the Decolonization of East Africa, 1953–1964'.

36. See Elizabeth Schmidt, 'Cold War in Guinea: The Rassemblement Démocratique Africain and the Struggle over Communism, 1950–1958', *Journal of African History*, 48/1 (2007), and *Cold War and Decolonization in Guinea, 1946–1958* (Athens, O.: Ohio University Press, 2007); Matthew Connelly, 'Rethinking the Cold War and Decolonization: The Grand Strategy of the Algerian War for Independence', *International Journal of Middle East Studies*, 33 (2001), 222; Ebere Nwaubani, *The United States and Decolonization in West Africa, 1950–1960* (Rochester, NY: University of Rochester Press, 2001).

37. Paul T. Zeleza, *The Study of Africa* (East Lansing, Mich.: Michigan State University Press, 1996 and 1997), i and ii.

38. Toyin Falola, *Nationalism and African Intellectuals* (Rochester, NY: University of Rochester Press, 2001); see also Toyin Falola and Saheed Aderinto, *Nigeria, Nationalism and Writing History* (Rochester, NY: University of Rochester Press, 2011). Two notable examples of these memoirs are Jan Vansina, *Living with Africa* (Madison, Wis.: University of Wisconsin Press, 1994), and Roland Oliver, *In the Realms of Gold: Pioneering in African History* (Madison, Wis.: University of Wisconsin Press, 1997).

39. See e.g. David E. Apter, 'Ghana's Independence: Triumph and Paradox', *Transition*, 98 (2008); also Cooper, 'Possibility and Constraint'; and Annie Coombes, *History After Apartheid: Visual Culture and Public Memory in a Democratic South Africa* (Durham, NC: Duke University Press, 2003).

40. Kelly and Kaplan, *Represented Communities*, 7.

41. Wole Soyinke, *A Dance of the Forests, from his Five Plays* (London: OUP, 1964), 39, cited in Lonsdale, 'Africa's Pasts in Africa's Futures', 126, 141.

42. Lee, *Making a World After Empire*.
43. Andrew Ivaska's recent *Cultured States: Youth, Gender and Modern Style in 1960s Dar es Salaam* (Durham: NC: Duke University Press, 2011) is an excellent example of where these new areas of inquiry might lead.

BIBLIOGRAPHY

Allman, Jean, *Quills of the Porcupine: Asante Nationalism in an Emergent Ghana* (Madison, Wis.: University of Wisconsin Press, 1993).

Anderson, David, *Histories of the Hanged: The Dirty War in Kenya and the End of Empire* (New York: Norton, 2005).

Austin, Dennis, *Politics in Ghana, 1946–1960* (London: OUP, 1964).

Coleman, James S., *Nigeria: Background to Nationalism* (Berkeley, Calif.: University of California Press, 1958).

Cooper, Frederick, *Decolonization and African Society: The Labor Question French and British Africa* (Cambridge: CUP, 1996).

——*Africa since 1940: The Past of the Present* (Cambridge: CUP, 2002).

Davidson, Basil, *Let Freedom Come: Africa in Modern History* (London: Little, Brown & Co., 1989).

Falola, Toyin, *Nationalism and African Intellectuals* (Rochester, NY: University of Rochester Press, 2001).

Fanon, Frantz, *The Wretched of the Earth* (New York: Grove Press, 1963),

Freund, Bill, *The Making of Contemporary Africa: The Development of African Society since 1800* (Bloomington, Ind.: Indiana University Press, 1984).

Geiger, Susan, *TANU Women: Gender and Culture in the Making of Tanganyikan Nationalism, 1955–1965* (Portsmouth, NH: Heinemann, 1997).

Hargreaves, John D., *Decolonization in Africa*, 2nd edn (New York: Longman, 1996).

Hodgkin, Thomas, *Nationalism in Colonial Africa* (New York: New York University Press, 1956).

Kelly, John D., and Martha Kaplan, *Presented Communities: Fiji and World Decolonization* (Chicago: University of Chicago Press, 2001).

Lee, Christopher J., ed., *Making a World After Empire: The Bandung Moment and its Political Afterlives* (Athens, O.: Ohio University Press, 2010).

Moorman, Marissa, *Intonations: A Social History of Music and Nation in Luanda, Angola, from 1943 to Recent Times* (Athens, O.: Ohio University Press, 2008).

Morgenthau, Ruth Schacter, *Political Parties in French-Speaking West Africa*. (Oxford: Clarendon Press, 1964).

Schmidt, Elizabeth, *Mobilizing the Masses: Gender, Ethnicity, and Class in the Nationalist Movement in Guinea, 1939–1958* (Portsmouth, NH: Heinemann, 2005).

Shepard, Todd, *The Invention of Decolonization: The Algerian War and the Remaking of France* (Ithaca, NY: Cornell University Press, 2006).

Straker, Jay, *Youth, Nationalism, and the Guinean Revolution* (Bloomington, Ind.: Indiana University Press, 2009).

PART III

RELIGION AND BELIEF

CHAPTER 13

··

ISLAM

··

MARIE MIRAN-GUYON AND JEAN-LOUIS TRIAUD

ISLAM has had a centuries-long presence in Africa, both north and south of the Sahara, before colonial encounters added a new layer to the continent's richly textured Muslim history. The extent to which nineteenth- and twentieth-century European domination brought about meaningful changes in Muslim lives and outlooks—and not simply within the religious domain—cannot be underestimated. Yet, at the same time, Muslim communities and Islamic thought continued to evolve in their own, enduring ways. Weaving together local, endogenous initiatives, on the one hand, and global, cosmopolitan influences from the *umma*, the world Muslim community in and out of Africa, on the other, Muslim actors went on making and remaking their own histories of religious renewal and crises, expansion and downturn. This goes beyond acknowledging the importance of the *longue durée* in comprehending Islam's colonial past or questioning the Eurocentric division of African history centred on the colonial moment. It underlines that Muslim Africa's colonial trajectories concurrently belonged to different, and partly overlapping, 'regimes of historicity'—Western imperial, Islamic, and African—and that these various trajectories cannot be reduced to a single aspect.[1]

As with conceptions of time, diversity characterized Muslim Africa's vast spaces, the southern frontiers of which were mapped anew on an unprecedented scale in the colonial period under the twin processes of migration and conversion. A major ecological fault line runs between countries north and south of the Sahara. Medieval Arab historiography portrayed the desert as an inner sea, imagining the Maghrib (the 'West' in Arabic, for North Africa was then Islam's westernmost lands) as an island, remote from the *bilad al-Sudan*, 'the land of the Blacks', stretching from modern Senegal to Ethiopia. The Maghrib itself was distanced from the heartlands of Islam by the interposition of Egypt—the gateway to the 'Orient' of olden days, today's Middle East—with the metropolis of Cairo as a high place of Islam in its own right. But the colonial interlude did reify this fault line to a certain extent, as British and French policies were bent on keeping Mediterranean and sub-Saharan Africa as separate as possible, even when their empires bridged both sides. This divide also translated into an academic split between specialists of both cultural areas, which never fully receded despite recent claims that the contrary would be more fruitful.

This binary vision, however, unduly downplays the far-reaching networks of scholarly and other contacts which have nurtured the intellectual and social life of sub-Saharan Muslim leaders, students, pilgrims, and traders over generations. Such networks paved the way for the integration of these societies into a broad moral community of African followers of Muhammad, in the Sunni branch of Islam and predominantly the Maliki school of law, even though Egypt, the Horn, and eastern Africa follow the Shafi'i *madh'hab*, as in parts of the Indian Ocean world. Under colonial pressure, some of these long-distance networks faltered. Yet many proved resilient, while others were transformed or moved in new directions.

Islam's foundational principle of unity of creed and *umma* does not negate the breathtaking diversity of Muslim Africa's vast spaces. Unity does not mean uniformity. Indeed, physical and cultural ecologies have always marked out porous territories where local societies ceaselessly endeavoured to domesticate Islam's universal message. It is clear that Muslim life in cosmopolitan urban centres such as Cairo or Zanzibar contrasted strongly with that in a Berber village in Morocco or in a settlement of new converts in coastal West Africa, to the extent that the value of the term 'Islam' itself as an analytical category has been questioned by both historians and social scientists. Alternate heuristic phrasings include 'discursive tradition' and 'Islamic religious culture', along with their plural forms.[2] Recent demographic statistics (in the absence of accurate ones for the colonial period) allude to the scale of Islamic pluralism: roughly half of Africa is Muslim and one in four Muslims worldwide is African.

All this points to the limits of our task of synthesis, at a time when grand narratives on Islam in Africa no longer feature in the research agenda. This chapter therefore privileges the Maghrib and West Africa, and British and French colonial situations. Within those zones it concentrates on Muslim religious elites and self-made entrepreneurs, almost exclusively male, although this does not mean that ordinary believers, in particular women, were any less Muslim. The focus on the *modi operandi* of colonial states and on Muslim experiences where the symbolic reference of Islam played a central role, moreover, is not to say that religion was the only factor defining Muslims' personal or collective engagements: many historical actors discussed throughout the chapters of this book happened to be Muslim, although they did not always act primarily *as* Muslims. The chapter begins with a review of past and current historiographical trends and methodological issues, before delving into major historical themes in order to sketch a composite picture of the interactions between Islam, imperial power, and religious change in the era of colonial encounter.

STUDIES IN AFRICAN ISLAM: CONSTRUCTION OF THE DISCIPLINE

Local Muslim societies never failed to produce their own internal knowledge in literate, oral, or material forms. But what we may call 'African Islamic studies' only began in earnest within the colonial sphere. It is important to discuss the historicity of this field of research, not only because the early period was foundational for the discipline in and of itself but because it had a direct impact on the unequal power relations that unfolded between the infidel colonizers and the Muslim colonized—especially, but not only, under French rule. It also matters because the colonial production of knowledge on African Islam has had a lasting legacy within the discipline well past the threshold of independence, to the point that recent research trends continue to situate themselves in contradistinction to it. Returning to early elaborations in the historiography of Islam in Africa is thus more than an erudite exercise: it speaks to the genesis of our current knowledge.

Egypt was the first focus of African Islamic studies and the ten-volume *Description de l'Egypte* (1809–28) its first major work. As the scholarly by-product of the 1798 Bonaparte expedition, it inaugurated a distinctive French tradition of exploration and encyclopedic output under the sacrosanct guise of 'science', soon to become the norm in newly conquered lands. In contrast, the writings of the leading British Arabicist scholar, Edward William Lane (1801–76), were far less imbued with imperial-minded Orientalism. His work included the anthropological bestseller *Manners and Customs of the Modern Egyptians* (1836) and the reputable *Arabic–English Lexicon* (1863–93).

After the 1830 conquest, Algeria became the French laboratory for Muslim policies and 'Islamological' theories, similar to the role played by India and later Sudan and Nigeria for the British. Algiers was a key site for the production of Islamological studies, geographical and historical works, and translations from medieval Maghribi scholars such as the famous Ibn Khaldūn (d. 1406). The French devoted particular attention to the translation of treatises in Islamic law, so essential to colonial jurisdiction. This project focused on the key *kutub* or authoritative Islamic 'books' used in the Maghrib (but authoritative in sub-Saharan Africa too) from as early as the eleventh century; so important were these books for local societies that they were—and often remain—essential readings in advanced Quranic education. Prominent among these *kutub* were the *Mukhtar* (published 1848–57), a concise handbook authored by Khalīl b. Ishāq (d. 1374), and the *Risāla* (1914), a treatise in Maliki Law by Ibn Abī Zayd al-Qayrawānī (d. 996). With the exception of Maliki-oriented Nigeria, the British drew more attention to the Shafi'i and Hanafi legal systems of their East African and Middle Eastern empires. This intense colonial literary production had a major impact throughout the twentieth century in that it induced a specifically text-based representation of African Islam, encompassing all of its history, geography, customs, and institutions.

This strong Orientalist trend to some extent continued south of the Sahara in the first three decades of the twentieth century. Sub-Saharan Africa became more of a research ground for ethnologists and linguists who put orality first and saw Islam as alien to what they imagined to be the pristine 'authenticity' of African society.[3] Only a few scholars looked to local manuscripts written in Arabic or in vernacular languages transcribed in the Arabic script (known as *ajami*). Nonetheless, these pioneers were noteworthy. Among them were the Maurice Delafosse, Octave Houdas, Henri Gaden, and Herbert Palmer; the well-known Orientalist Louis Massignon also worked for a while on Mauritania.

Primus inter pares was Delafosse (1870–1926), one of the founding fathers of African studies in France. Trained as a linguist, ethnologist, and historian, he served as the Director of Political Affairs for the government of French West Africa and worked together with his professor (and later father-in-law), the Arabicist Houdas, whose career had begun in Algiers. Between 1898 and 1901, either alone or with Delafosse, Houdas edited both in Arabic and in French translation the three famous historical chronicles written in the seventeenth and eighteenth centuries by Sudanese intellectuals from the Niger bend: the *Ta'rīkh al-Sūdān*, the *Ta'rīkh al-Fattash*, and the *Tadhkirat al-Nisiān*.[4] These works would play a central role in the writing of the history of the great 'Sudanese Empires' and, made available in print to a majority non-Arabophone African readership, in public memory and the self-fashioning of identities, in postcolonial Mali. This ongoing process is a reminder that colonial encounter served to intertwine African and European destinies in often unforeseen ways, linking the precolonial past to the postcolonial present.

Herbert Richmond Palmer (1877–1958) was Delafosse's distinguished British counterpart. A Cambridge graduate, he spent twenty-six years in Northern Nigeria, becoming its lieutenant-governor at the end of his stay. Colonial Northern Nigeria was unique in many ways. West Africa's most densely populated Muslim area, it bore the legacy of the 1804 jihad of 'Uthman dan Fodio that gave rise to the Sokoto Caliphate, sub-Saharan Africa's principal shari'a-minded Islamic state. Defeated by British forces in 1903, the caliphate was largely incorporated into the protectorate of Northern Nigeria under the governorship of Sir Frederick Lugard (1900–1906), later to become Nigeria's governor general (1914–19). Born in India, with service in Sudan and East Africa, Lugard is a central figure of British imperialism in Africa. He is best known as the architect of indirect rule, as expounded in his manifesto *The Dual Mandate in British Tropical Africa* (1922). Northern Nigeria witnessed the emergence of what Murray Last called the 'Colonial Caliphate': a hybrid arrangement in which Islamic institutions and leading ruling families were kept in place under discreet British control.[5] Northern Nigeria also houses one of Sudanic Africa's richest bodies of Arabic and *ajami* written sources, mostly about Sokoto. This was the peculiar political and intellectual context in which Palmer was able to write extensively on Muslim states and societies, making use of manuscripts collected throughout the region.[6] Notwithstanding later critiques, these documents too, most importantly the Kano Chronicle, became reference works for later generations of scholars and African actors alike.

French and British translation endeavours receded by the late 1920s, although they resumed on a smaller scale in the nationalist period at the initiative of Abdullahi Smith (1920–84), a British-Nigerian professor at the University of Zaria and a convert to Islam. Smith launched a systematic exploitation of Sokoto manuscripts, promoting at the same time a rich historical 'mine' and the caliphate's political position within the new and turbulent federation of Nigeria.[7] Albeit no longer a central endeavour, the concern to catalogue, preserve, and translate Muslim Africa's primary sources has not been relegated to the past, as demonstrated by the series of regional volumes edited by Rex O'Fahey and John Hunwick.[8]

Concomitantly to the textual approach based on scholarly translations, African Islamic studies further developed with the writings of colonial officials in charge of monitoring Muslim societies. Collectively, these writings were more 'discourses' on Islam, often ideological in nature in their articulation of the colonial perception of Islam (sometimes mere Eurocentric fantasies or paranoia) at the expense of local developments. Nonetheless, these writings played a major role both in colonial politics and in shaping the field's historiography on an enduring basis.

The French stand out in this respect. Two main themes emerge from this literature: the *confrérie* or 'brotherhood' theme (*tariqa* in Arabic) and the concept of *Islam noir* or 'Black Islam'. The former was born in Algeria. In the face of half a century of armed resistance to French conquest, specifically the lengthy struggle led by 'Abd al-Qādir, *shaykh* of the Qādiriyya brotherhood in western Algeria between 1832 and 1847, French army officers developed the influential theory of a 'brotherhood plot'. This fell within broader fears about the danger posed by Islam, as if brotherhoods were in a way coextensive with Islam itself. More than the British—even though they too fought Islamic leaders and organizations in Nigeria, the Sudan, and Somalia—the French were convinced that Islam was a dangerous transnational religion. This persuasion was in part built upon the anticlericalism of the Third Republic and civic officials' deep distrust of 'clerical' or 'feudal' Muslim hierarchies: Islamic brotherhoods were viewed as the Oriental equivalent of nineteenth-century European revolutionary secret societies.

In Algeria, the administration established a process of systematic data collection in an effort to distinguish friendly from hostile brotherhoods. The Tijāniyya, which had been 'Abd al-Qādir's foe and whose *shaykh*, a grandson of its founder Ahmad al-Tijani, married a French woman in 1870, progressively appeared as the model of the 'good' brotherhood, meaning one which could work with the French for the latter's interests. In Cyrenaica in western Libya, in contrast, the Sanūsiyya, whose founder was from Algeria and which was open to fleeing emigrants from Algeria, became the epitome of the 'bad' brotherhood, meaning one so drastically hostile to the French that it had to be suppressed.[9]

The brotherhood theme subsequently crossed the Sahara. Alfred Le Châtelier, a soldier and scholar who became a professor at the Collège de France, is a telling example of this process. Although Le Châtelier worked primarily on Morocco, he published the first survey of Islam in Senegal and the French Sudan (now Mali), *L'Islam dans l'Afrique occidentale* (1899). His preface explains how he travelled south of the Sahara in the 1880s in search of brotherhoods, but finding few traces of them concluded that the anxieties of the Algiers school were misplaced. Yet the French administration never ceased cataloguing and monitoring brotherhoods (as it also catalogued 'races', 'tribes', and 'ethnic groups'), despite the fact that mass brotherhood organizations which arose at the dawn of the twentieth century—in the Senegalese context at least—never actually threatened the colonial regime.

As situations and interests changed over time and space, so did the specific actors classified under the categories of 'good' or 'bad' Muslims. In French West Africa, the Tijāniyya was first deemed hostile because of its association with the nineteenth-century jihadist al-Ḥājj 'Umar, whose militarized state-building project had clashed with that of the French. By the early twentieth century, that perception was beginning to change, due in large part to the efforts of more 'accommodationist' Muslim cultural brokers. By the 1950s, young graduates returning to French West Africa from Arab universities, referred to as 'Wahhabi', became the new 'bad' Muslims, while 'traditionalist' Sufis were promoted to the rank of 'good' ones. But the Manichaean vision itself persisted, remaining in place well past decolonization under the new binary of 'moderate'/'tolerant' Muslims versus 'radical'/'extremist' Islamists.[10] The single most prominent theme in recent scholarship on African Islam is the attempt to deconstruct such brazenly ideological fabrications and to suggest more nuanced interpretations of complex realities.

It was Delafosse who in the 1910s can be credited with coining the concept of 'maraboutisme'; that is, the notion that *marabouts* (the French label for all types of Muslim clerics but especially the leaders of brotherhoods), were the pivotal figures behind the structuring of West African Muslim communities. The French colonial state went on to bestow such an inflated prominence upon this Muslim elite (provided, that is, that it was of the 'good' type) that it can be argued the figure of the *grand marabout* was in large part a colonial invention. This too proved to be an astoundingly enduring colonial legacy, with the *grands marabouts*—despite the recent challenge to their authority in some regions from more radical clerics—remaining influential leaders within many West African Muslim societies.

Although less prominent in British colonial discourse, the brotherhoods were not entirely ignored. C. Armine Willis, for instance, depicted Sudanese Islam through the sole prism of its brotherhoods, his dispassionate reportage standing in contrast to the conspiracy theories that characterized French accounts.[11] The concept of *Islam noir*, however, was the exclusive elaboration of French imperialism. It was meant to cut off sub-Saharan Islam from its supposedly subversive Arab connections, at a time when Arab nationalism was on the rise in the Middle East. According to French colonial theory, 'Black Islam' was heavily influenced by traditional animist practices and was therefore a milder, less radical version of the faith than that found elsewhere in the Islamic world. That this perception contradicted the brotherhood theory of bad *marabouts* did not seem to bother the colonial state, which even attempted, without great success, to induce religious syncretism in some areas. Yet the concept of *Islam noir* has also persisted, continuing to pervade not only French views of Africa and its own Muslim citizens but paternalistic Western public opinion at large.

The main propagator of the concept of *Islam noir* was the prolific Paul Marty. An official at the Bureau of Muslim Affairs in Dakar, Marty gathered intelligence reports about Muslims and Islam from the four corners of French West Africa. Over the course of eighteen years, he produced ten publications on Muslim societies in each of the federation's colonies, from *Les Mourides d'Amadou Bamba* (1913) to *L'Islam et les tribus dans la colonie du Niger* (1930–31), which were authoritative works of reference throughout the colonial period. Although Marty's interpretive framework has subsequently been critiqued, his corpus contains a great deal of material useful to the historian, when handled with caution. British overviews of African Islam came later, in the form of a series of works by John Spencer Trimingham (b. 1904). Trimingham's perspective was different: a member of the Church Missionary Society who worked successively in Sudan, Ethiopia, and West Africa, he gathered a large amount of field data and between 1949 and 1971 published seven books on Islam in different countries.[12] His method, like that of Marty, was later contested, but his books were the only available reference works of the kind in English before the 1970s, bestowing a scholarly status on the study of sub-Saharan Islam.

The era of decolonization in the 1960s opened up a new chapter for African Islamic studies, as it did for African history generally. Breaking free from the colonial stranglehold was the new ideological order of the day, carried along by nationalist sympathies and humanistic ideals. One way out of the colonial predicament was to focus anew on precolonial Islamic history by means of Arabic manuscripts, which located the now academic rather than administrative experts in Muslim matters in an erudite, philological enclave. Although the political focus of early nationalist historiography and the prediction by the modernization paradigm of the social irrelevance of religion served to confine Islam to the margins of the new Africanist project, pioneering historians such as Nehemia Levtzion excelled in the re-engagement with Arabic sources.[13] It would be the 1979 Iranian revolution, a defining moment in the recent history of Islam, which served to propel the faith and its followers to the centre of the scholarly stage.

In this early period, nonetheless, contributions from fields of inquiry as varied as anthropology, sociology, and geography have to be reckoned with. Most shared a concentration on Egypt, Morocco (and even more restrictively, on societies of the Atlas mountains), and Senegal. This narrow focus—to which we may add English-language literature on Northern Nigeria—lasted until recently, when dissonant voices began to argue that these areas do not encompass the whole spectrum of Muslim Africa and that, transnational phenomena notwithstanding, one should avoid the extrapolation of analyses from one region to another. One legacy of these geographical monopolies remains a deficit in studies on East African Islam. In line with E. E. Evans-Pritchard's functionalist and structuralist approach was Ernest Gellner's *Saints of the Atlas* (1969). Among the first anthropologists to put 'Islam' in a book title was Clifford Geertz: his seminal *Islam Observed* (1968) discussed the fertile tensions between Islamic texts and local contexts in a broad comparison between Moroccan maraboutism and Indonesian Sufism, at the polar ends of the Muslim world. South of the Sahara, Donal Cruise O'Brien's *The Mourides of Senegal* (1971) and Paul Pélissier's *Les Paysans du Sénégal* (1966) signalled an emerging 'mourido-centrism' (i.e. focus on the Muridiyya brotherhood) within studies of Senegalese Islam.

The dramatic arrival of 'political Islam' onto the international stage following the Iranian revolution has had a huge and complex impact on African Islamic studies. Never before has the field attracted so much intellectual interest. Scholarly output continues to grow by leaps and bounds, to the extent that it would be reductive to chart the achievements of individual scholarship, even when limiting oneself to works on the colonial period. If the field's multidisciplinary and international collaborative edge is more critical than ever, however, it is far from being univocal. Exemplary of this trend are the bilingual journals *Islam et sociétés au Sud du Sahara* launched in 1987 by Jean-Louis Triaud and the more recent *Sudanic* (now *Islamic*) *Africa*.[14] Likewise, Brill—the Netherlands-based publishing house which supervises the ongoing rewriting of the revered multi-volume *Encyclopaedia of Islam* (first edition 1922)—recently created a new space for the field's output in its new series 'Islam in Africa'.[15]

On the downside, the anxiety associated with the rise of political Islam in Iran and the Arab world and later in Muslim diasporas in the West has at times threatened to return the discipline to its early colonial concern with the monitoring of radicalizing external influences on the local, grassroots forms of the faith. This was especially true for the Maghrib and Egypt, where an avalanche of contemporary political science almost buried historical research on Islam in earlier periods. Sub-Saharan Africa was generally spared this fate, although studies of Islam there in the 1980s and 1990s did share a bias towards the faith's socio-political aspects. Recently, calls have been made to cease neglecting the intellectual, spiritual, material, and economic dimensions of the Muslim African experience. New studies addressing Muslim architecture, visual arts, music, or creative literature are among those starting to fill the gap—which may well in turn fuel a counter-critique of an all-out 'cultural turn'.[16]

In reality, the shift in the historiography of African Islam was more than the mere by-product of the faith's worldwide resurgence. It was part of the major intra- and trans-disciplinary 'turns' of the time: the postmodern, the postcolonial, the subaltern, and, especially, the debate generated by Edward Saïd's book *Orientalism* (1978). Full discussion of these intellectual currents lies beyond the scope of this survey, but it is crucial at least to note the ways in which they contributed to the renewal of the epistemology and methodology of African Islamic studies.

The most important advance is the injunction to avoid the reification or essentialization of Islamic experience across time and space. As already noted, the use of the concept 'Islam' itself is not unproblematic; Muslim actors continue to use and cherish it, of course, but in ways and for reasons that need carefully to be deconstructed *in situ*. New studies insist on Islam's dazzling diversity, with multiple interpretations coexisting in any given context. Though prone to dogmatic dispute or genuine conflict, hegemonic interpretations of Islam may exert reciprocal influences on one another and thus have overlapping and shifting boundaries. So, we need to reconsider our entrenched visions of a mystical Sufi version of Islam in contradistinction to a Wahhabi, Salafi, or reformist one. As Roman Loimeier argues with regard to the concept of the Sufi brotherhood or *tariqa* (but the same argument would hold true for 'Wahhabi' movements too), it may well be a mere 'essentialist abstraction, an idealization of realities, since a *tariqa* should more properly be viewed as a spectrum of potentially competing branches and networks loyal to prominent families of scholars or charismatic personalities (saints) who themselves embody a multitude of Sufi teachings'.[17] Even more broadly, Islam cannot be abstracted from the all-encompassing environment in which Muslim societies evolve. Muslim dynamics, moreover, have to be studied through their multifaceted interactions with both Christianity and indigenous African belief systems—and not simply in terms of conversion.[18]

Internal plurality extends to just about everything: from ritual practices and religious imaginaries to the micro-political strategies of agonistic Muslim actors. The impact of these strands of Islam on different social groups varies widely, yet all are worthy of academic inquiry: the learned and the powerful, but also ordinary Muslims and subalterns such as slaves, women, and even children. In fact, most studies on African Islam now take pains to include at least some discussion of women's roles (while the academic profession has become much more open to women). In tune with recent gender theory, a new focus on Muslim masculinities is also emerging, as in the milieu of the *tirailleurs sénégalais* or other colonial conscripts.[19] The question whether the latest cutting-edge research is commensurate with Muslims' own preoccupations or arises more from postmodern Western anxieties is open to debate. But the new celebration of Muslim complexity is welcome indeed.

Elaborating on the concept of 'agency' so central to subaltern studies, the new scholarship on African Islam's interface with colonialism further maintains that Muslims, both individually and collectively, remained to varying degrees masters of their own destinies rather than passive victims. It goes without saying that colonial oppression was no fiction. But colonialism was rarely powerful or coherent enough to prevent Muslims from manœuvring through its contradictions and shortcomings. Muslims were thus able to take initiatives for their own benefit—or to the disadvantage of local rivals. These goals were often pursued openly via a working understanding—and sometimes misunderstanding—with the colonial state, which has been labelled 'accommodation' by David Robinson and others.[20] More subtle, discreet, and subversive tactics were also employed, often unbeknownst to colonial rulers and therefore often more resistant to historical reconstruction. Accordingly, today's priority is to rewrite the colonial past from the indigenous perspective, as opposed to that of the colonial state. Recent studies tend to relegate the colonial apparatus to the background: a faint presence not quite meaningless but certainly not central to Muslims' daily lives.

To shed light on these daily lives and on semi-hidden initiatives, the injunction is to pay close attention to Muslim voices. This requires a new combing of colonial (and in some cases, Christian mission) records to decipher untapped echoes between the lines; the interpretation of neglected written sources in Arabic, *ajami,* and colonial languages such as devotional poetry, treatises, prayers, *fatawa* or legal opinions, narratives of pilgrimages and other journeys; and the construction of a corpus of oral accounts. A new ethics of writing further invites scholars, especially non-Muslims based in the West, to deploy polyphonic devices in order to accentuate the concert of variegated indigenous voices. It has been anthropologists of Islam who have taken the lead in reflecting on many of these methodological issues. Dale Eickelman, a specialist of Morocco and the Arab Middle East, dubbed this new approach a 'political economy of meaning'.[21] A notable recent shift has been the emergence of a respected Muslim African academic voice in African and in Western universities, especially among historians. This voice, combining scholarly rigour with internal knowledge and respect for religious sensibilities, is beginning to redefine the field in yet uncharted ways.

UNFOLDING HISTORIES: AFRICAN MUSLIMS
AND COLONIAL RULE

As with other colonized peoples, for most African Muslims the loss of sovereignty was a cruel condition. What was specific to Muslims was that they were defeated and subdued by Christian *kuffâr* (infidels): the conquest was therefore experienced as much as a spiritual as a political calamity. If this reality was plainly shared by all Muslims, reactions to it were more complex. As discussed above, however, contemporary interpretations were unsubtle: colonial administrations accounted for Muslim actors' varied strategies through the distorting prism of surveillance, often caricaturing both initial opposition and later forms of cooperation. Conversely, nationalist historiography from the 1960s tended to celebrate Muslim warrior chiefs as resistance heroes. Among them was the Senegal valley-born *shaykh* Al-Hājj 'Umar (d. 1864), the principal propagator of the Tijāniyya in West Africa.[22] 'Umar was an important and complex figure. He launched a jihad of the sword against 'pagan' populations between the Senegal and Niger rivers, but also against a rival Muslim power, the Qādiriyya-oriented Dina of Masina. Recalling his confrontation with expansionist French forces, postcolonial Senegal mainly celebrates the staunch resistance hero, whom the French typified as a dangerous *marabout*. Both historical interpretations tend to overlook a more complex reality: the fact that 'Umar, like 'Abd al-Qādir in Algeria, once also signed a truce with the French.

Further south was Samori Touré (d. 1900). Originating from Upper Guinea, Samori created an empire extending to northern Côte d'Ivoire. He proclaimed himself *almamy* (imam), but this did not stop him from destroying the town of Kong, a centre of Islamic scholarship, and his later policy of forced Islamization also met with strong opposition. If Samori has featured strongly in the resistance fighters' hall of fame (albeit more ambiguously on the Ivorian side than in Sékou Touré's Guinea), it is owing to his direct clashes with the expanding, rival imperialism of the French.[23] It can be noted that Samori's framed portrait can be seen today looking down from the wall of the Moroccan-style central mosque in Paris—a building of historic interest in itself, inaugurated in 1926 and funded in part by metropolitan taxpayers to thank Muslim conscripts who fought in defence of France in the First World War.

In Sudan, the British faced Muhammad Ahmad ibn Abd Allah, aka the Mahdī (d. 1885) and in Somalia, Muhammad 'Abdallah Hasan, aka the 'Mad Mullah' (d. 1920).[24] From 1911, when they set in motion the conquest of the Ottoman province of Libya, the Italians confronted the opposition of the Cyrenaica-based Sanūsiyya brotherhood. A peaceful missionary organization in origin, the Sanūsiyya effectively assumed control of much of eastern Libya following the collapse of Ottoman power. From the turn of the twentieth century, Sanūsī troops fought against the French, the Italians, and the British in Libya, Egypt, Algeria, and Niger. The final defeat came in 1931 with the execution of military commander 'Umar al-Mukhtār and the exile of the brotherhood's surviving leaders. A year after the United Nations voted for the creation of the Libyan state in 1949, the *shaykh* of the Sanūsī order became its new king. King Idris was deposed in 1969 by Muammar al-Qaddafi, a pan-Arab and pan-African leader with 'Islamic socialist' tendencies and a new spirit of non-compliance with Western imperialism.

On a smaller scale, messianic figures self-proclaimed as the *mahdī* or 'Promised Saviour' led local and sometimes bloody insurrections against colonial conquest. Muslim-led armed resistance against colonial encroachment, then, was real enough. But in no way was it peculiar to Muslim societies: in many regions, non-Muslim communities often offered much tougher resistance. Muslim responses, moreover, varied hugely. Facing the unprecedented situation of *kuffār* rule over the *dar al-Islam* (abode of Islam), Muslim clerics resorted to the vast resources of Islamic casuistry to devise canonical solutions: jihad; physical emigration (or mental withdrawal) on the model of the Prophet Muhammad's *hijra* or exile to Medina; and *taqiyya* or dissimulation in the face of repression.[25] Clerical families sometimes divided over the best course of action to adopt for safeguarding the same Islamic ideals. In the Senegal valley, for instance, the more conciliatory Sa'ad Būh was pitted against his *mujahid* brother Mā al-'Aynīn; meanwhile, Agibu, al-Hājj 'Umar's seventh son, stayed and cooperated with the French, while his cousin Hashimi led his followers eastwards towards Mecca. The Sanūsī and other Algerian families were similarly divided.[26] When armed jihad was finally defeated, compromise prevailed as an alternative option. Most *hijra* episodes were discreet and quiet, but some are well documented. Muhammad Bello Maiwurno, fifth son of Sultan Al-Tāhiru—Sokoto's eleventh sultan who was killed in action against the British in 1903—led a massive migration towards the Sudan (where he happened to be well received by the same British). Algeria was the scene of a similar exodus in 1911, when hundreds of Tlemcen Muslims fled military recruitment and other woes.

Ulamā also mobilized the concept of *taqiyya*—derived from a Quranic term meaning 'fear'—to legitimate strategies of accommodation. It refers to Muslims facing a major danger, in which case it becomes permissible to interact with an adversary 'with the tongue, not the heart'. Another legitimizing concept borrowed from Islamic law was *maslaha*, meaning the common good of the community. With these canonical references in mind, individual spiritual guides had to adjust their tactical choices, juggling their own convictions with the local balance of power. Based upon mutual—albeit unequal—advantage, these compromises offered valuable interlocutors to colonial powers as well as an opportunity for Islamic leaders to create or secure their own clienteles through protection and mediation. In this respect, 'accommodation' should be analysed as a long-term process of Muslim reappropriation and renewal of older forms of power, paving the way for postcolonial forms of empowerment.

Where and when colonial authorities endorsed such policies of mediation, it led to many different Muslim 'paths of accommodation' in French and British territories. This was also the case in Italian-ruled Eritrea (1890–1941) and Ethiopia (1935–41), where, unlike in Libya, the Italians favoured the development of Islam and protected its institutions as a counterbalance to the Amhara monarchy, local powers, and the Orthodox Church.[27] One major difference must nonetheless be noted between French and British colonial situations. In the French Empire, the potential agency of Islamic leaders was curbed by the requirement publicly to acknowledge subservience to the colonial state—at one and the same time a secular republic and a self-proclaimed 'Muslim power'. Some Muslim leaders only paid lip service to this requirement, while others agreed to it unabashedly as a means to other ends. A list of accommodationist *marabouts* from the four corners of French West Africa would include Sa'ad Būh (d. 1917), Sidiyya Shaykh Baba (d. 1924), Amadu Mokhtar Sakho, Boghé's *cadi* (d. 1934), Shaykh Fanta Madi Cherif of Kankan in Guinea (d. 1955), al-Hajj Malik Sy (d. 1980), and Seydu Nuru Tall (d. 1980). A grandson of Al-Hājj 'Umar, the latter may have appeared the most obsequious of them all. Yet the conviction of his modern-day peers that he rendered invaluable services to his transnational Tijani community now supersedes this perception.[28] Those who evaded the colonial pledge of allegiance faced repression, as in the best known cases of Amadu Bamba, founder of the Muridiyya, in his early preaching career, and Sheikh Hamallah, founder of the Hamawiyya, a peculiar branch of the Tijāniyya, who died in 1943 in exile in France. Yet neither 'resistance' nor 'collaboration'—oversimplified binary terms fraught with value judgements—were on the agenda of any of these Islamic actors as an end in itself. What mattered urgently for them was to safeguard Islamic social ties as best as possible given the uneasy circumstances, and preserve a future while waiting for *kuffâr* rule to come to an end.

In British colonies, Islamic elites could have greater autonomy and visibility. Unlike the French, the British did not abhor religious fiefdoms. Rather, they developed elective affinities with local aristocracies, in the political as much as the religious domain. The outstanding French exception was Hubert Lyautey, Morocco's résident general from 1912 to 1925, who conducted an experiment in indirect rule similar to that in Northern Nigeria by retaining and protecting established political and religious institutions.

In short, complexity now prevails in the treatment of Muslim–colonial encounter; nowhere and at no time was there an automatic and unique Islamic response, and trajectories must be contextualized carefully. The variety of Muslim adaptive responses to colonial conquest and rule provides a key theme for ongoing historical analysis.

HISTORY FROM WITHIN: ISLAMIC THOUGHT AND COMMUNITY DYNAMICS IN COLONIAL SITUATIONS

The conventional outlook long held that the 'colonial interlude', in Africa and elsewhere, had an overall negative impact on the inner workings of Islamic religious culture. The fact that young cohorts of reform-minded Muslim activists held discourses in the same vein seemed to corroborate this scholarly conclusion. At worst, the colonial era amounted to a dark age of disruption and crisis, when 'larger or smaller doses of western secular thought and "methodological atheism"' were perfidiously injected into Muslim 'intellectual horizons', relegating believers to social marginality in an all-encompassing imperial political economy.[29] Traditional Quranic education based on rote memoriz-ation of sacred texts in Arabic (a language few sub-Saharan pupils were taught to master) seemed doomed to irrelevance.[30] Everywhere, those trained in secular or Christian schools seemed to hold the upper hand.

Overtaken by events, gullible crowds of devout Muslims were characterized as easy prey for new entrepreneurial *marabouts* displaying their newfound material wealth as *baraka*, or blessing. Admittedly, nowhere did the colonial yoke break down deep-rooted feelings of belonging to Islam or the transmission of the faith. This was especially true in North Africa, where the Arabic language added to the shaping of the religious realm into a spiritual refuge. It was also the case south of the Sahara, where local communities kept living their daily lives clinging to their own rules. Yet the colonial environment was seen as unpropitious for Islamic development, to say the least.

Recent post-Orientalist literature, while not completely overthrowing this view, is more nuanced and positive in outlook. It shows that, in continuity with precolonial experience, Muslim leaders and societies never ceased to question the relevance of Islamic laws and values to the context of colonial modernity. This emerges from new studies that seek to understand Muslims on their own terms. Debates on Islamic dogma and orthodoxy, and on practice and ritual differences, proper guidance and leadership, and means to achieve social justice can be seen to have been as intense in the colonial period as before, producing new, fruitful responses. Colonial times were thus also a period of renewal (*tajdid*) and reform (*islah*).

Over the eighteenth and nineteenth centuries, the *tariqa* landscape had under-gone major transformation in many regions of the Muslim world, including Africa, as exemplified by the legacy of the Moroccan mystic and theologian Ahmad b. Idrīs. Idrīs inspired numerous followers throughout the continent and as far away as South-East Asia; some of his disciples founded new brotherhoods, including the Sanūsiyya and the Sudanese Khatmiyya.[31] Sufi thought and practice tended to restate the centrality of shari'a (the exoteric legal code) and *'ilm* (knowledge through Islamic books) as foun-dational steps towards *tasawwuf* (mysticism or spirituality) and *ma'arifa* (inner esoteric knowledge): a complex movement towards 'a less mystical mysticism, a more rigor-ous orthodoxy,... or a marrying of Wahhabism with a reformist form of Sufism'.[32] In an authoritative article, Rex O'Fahey and Bernd Radtke debunked the label 'neo-Sufism' coined to describe those transformations, arguing that they did not represent doctrinal innovation; rather, they were inscribed in the history of older Sufi renewals.[33] Yet both agreed that brotherhoods were significantly reshaped as they became more centrally institutionalized and moved from being exclusive elite circles confined to a few ascetics to become more like mass movements.

This landscape continued to evolve in the colonial period. Brotherhoods segmented according to their time-honoured fissiparous nature, with the emergence of new charis-matic *shaykh*s and devout communities of *talaba* (sing. *talib*, student), but also along new intra-Sufi lines of division. In Senegal, Amadu Bamba Mbacké (1853–1927) founded the Muridiyya, named after the collective term in Arabic for disciple or *murid*: the most important brotherhood founded in sub-Saharan Africa. Ascetic and erudite, Amadu Bamba preached the 'greater jihad' or *jihād al-nafs* in Quranic terminology (as opposed to the lesser jihad of the sword), stressing spiritual devotion, study, and disciplined work in a quest for personal piety and exemplary behaviour in this world, and salvation in the hereafter.[34] Central to the Muridiyya's socio-religious architecture was the *dara* or rural *zawiya* (Sufi lodge), where Murids working in the community's peanut fields received spiritual guidance as part of *khidma* or service in the name of the *shaykh* (and later of his *khalifa* or successor). When Murids began moving to towns after the Second World War and diversifying their occupations, they founded *dairas*, the urban equivalent of the *dara*, also tied by hierarchical networks of *marabouts* caring for their local religious clientele. Confronted by the polluted colonial environment, Murids endeavoured to Islamize their own sacred space. This included the growing settlement of Touba (today Senegal's second largest city), which after Bamba's death became the destination of a yearly pilgrimage known as the Great Maggal.

New branches of the Tijaniyya also developed in French West Africa. Shaykh Hamallah (1883–1943) founded a distinct path in Nioro (in what is now Mali) known as the 'eleven-beads' Hamawiyya, which the 'twelve-beads' Tijaniyya of the Al Hājj 'Umar line fiercely opposed from the outset.[35] In Senegal, the long understudied but highly influential Ibrahima Niasse of Kaolack (1900–75) launched his own Tijani community (though not a separate *tariqa*) variously known as Niassene, Ibrahimiyya, *Tarbiya* (Arabic for education), and *Fayda* (spiritual flood). At its centre was the peculiar *tarbiya* developed by Niasse: a new kind of spiritual training reserved for the initiated which accelerated the attainment of *ma'arifa* (ecstatic knowledge). Though Niasse himself insisted on strict rules in the transmission of his *tarbiya*, it soon fuelled controversy as an increasing number of believers joined the ranks of his community and claimed to have seen God. While the Muridiyya remained tied to its Wolof base in Senegal, the more cosmopolitan Fayda expanded throughout West Africa and especially in the Gold Coast and Nigeria, which Shaykh Niasse regularly visited from the early 1950s.[36] A few of the Fayda *muqaddam* (authorized transmitters of Niasse's path) were women.[37] Both Amadu Bamba and Ibrahima Niasse aimed at spiritual *tajdid* (renewal) through education and were prolific writers of religious texts in Arabic.

Straddling the precolonial and the colonial periods, the Salafiyya (from the Arabic *salaf* or 'pious forebears') inaugurated another major course of change within Islamic thought. Starting as an intellectual trend associated with Jamal al-Din al-Afghani (1838–97), Muhammad Abduh (1849–1905), and Rashid Rida (1865–1935), who called for the renewal and reform of Islam in order to resist Western cultural and scientific domination, its late nineteenth-century African bastion was Egypt. All three criticized *taqlid* (blind adherence to tradition) and some non-Islamic practices labelled *bid'a* (innovation), which they associated with Sufi excesses. Instead, they advocated *ijtihad*, the individual effort based on the Qur'an and Sunna, with a view to adapting Islamic law to modern problems.

Salafi teachings inspired the Muslim Brotherhood (*Al-Ikhwān*), which began as a socio-religious movement when it was founded in 1928 by the Egyptian primary schoolteacher Hasan al-Banna. By the 1940s, it claimed to have one million members and sympathizers, and had turned to political activism. After resorting to terrorism, it was severely repressed and Al-Banna was executed in 1948. Sayyid Qutb, who had joined the Brotherhood in 1953 and published influential writings condemning Nasser's and other Arab regimes as *jahili* (pre-Islamic idolators), was also put to death in 1966. The radical wing of the Salafiyya later inspired many so-called 'Islamist' groups in different parts of the Muslim world.[38] In Algeria, Salafi ideas influenced Shaykh Abdelhamid Ben Badis (1889–1940), who founded the Association of Muslim Algerian Ulama in 1931. Despite its impact remaining limited, the association was noteworthy for defending the Arabic language, establishing new Islamic schools, and coalescing religious, cultural, and nationalist sentiments. Its leader Tawfiq al-Madani authored the famous slogan 'Islam is my religion, Arabic is my language, Algeria is my fatherland'.[39]

The reformist wave gained some ground in the 1950s in West Africa, mostly in cities where a new generation of graduates from al-Azhar and other Arab universities, as well as pilgrims returning from Mecca, began questioning the competence and legitimacy of the old, often hereditary, religious guard. It swept through the Malinke/Jula world, bridging the present-day states of Mali, Burkina Faso, Côte d'Ivoire, and Guinea, leading to violent clashes for the control of mosques in cities such as Bamako, Bouaké, and Kankan. Shaykh Ture (1925–2005), who founded the Muslim Cultural Union in Dakar in 1953, was vigorous in his condemnation of the alleged collaboration with the colonial state of some *marabouts*, who were prompt to denounce in return the assumed Arab-fomented sedition of these young sub-Saharan Muslims misleadingly labelled 'Wahhabis'.[40] In East Africa, the main reform-oriented movement was led by the Zanzibari Shaykh al-Amîn b. 'Alî al-Mazrû'î (1890–1947) and 'Abdallâh Sâlih al-Farsy (1912–82).[41]

Although Salafis remained a minority, their concern to reform Islamic education had a broad, long-term impact on local Muslim societies. To borrow Louis Brenner's terminology, classical Quranic schools or *majlis* were part of an 'esoteric episteme' where the transmission of knowledge was hierarchical, restricted, and centred around a teacher whose legitimacy derived from his *silsila*, i.e. genealogical chain of previous masters.[42] Reformed Islamic schools or *madrasa*—with classrooms, timetables, and exercise books as in colonial and Christian schools—introduced an epistemic shift towards a 'rationalistic episteme' characterized by a democratization of knowledge though printed books in Arabic, now taught as a foreign language along with some secular topics. Generalizations about the '*madrasa* turn' have their limits, however, for it had hybrid roots and distinct developments according to local context. A case in point is the Ansar-Ud-Deen Society of Nigeria, the oldest and largest educational association of Yoruba Muslims, founded in Lagos in 1923, which brought together influences from the Indian Ahmadiyya, Protestant missions, and local Yoruba dynamics.[43]

In short, beyond the variety of sectarian differences, Muslim communities underwent broadly analogous changes over the colonial interlude. Such change typically involved the revisiting of old notions of religious truth and ignorance; finding relevant means to forbid the wrong and command the right; the redefinition of *irshad* or religious guidance; the rise of new religious entrepreneurs and communities of knowledge; the restructuring of community organization and new means of communication; a relative empowerment of Muslim youth and to a lesser extent of women; and the emergence of less local and more generic or standardized ways of 'being Muslim'. In the context of French West Africa, Robert Launay and Benjamin Soares advance the idea of the emergence of an 'Islamic sphere', autonomous from and evading the control of the colonial state, and where Muslims debated, disagreed, and, at times, divided on all these matters.[44] Whether all of these transformations meant a modernization of Islam or the making of a vernacular Islamic modernity will be the subject of ongoing academic debate.

Colonial Conversion: Sub-Saharan Africa's Expanding Islamic Frontiers

The eighteenth- and nineteenth-century jihads and the rise of mass Sufism resulted in a new wave of Islamization in those regions of Sudanic Africa where Muslims had hitherto formed a minority. In what has been described as one of the greatest albeit unintended and paradoxical consequences of European imperial conquest, this expansion continued on an even broader scale throughout the colonial period. Oddly, the issue of conversion to Islam remains poorly researched despite the debate on African conversion to world religions initiated by Robin Horton and Humphrey Fisher in the 1970s.[45] One reason for this is that historical data are not readily available. Conversion tended not to be publicly visible and was a gradual, sometimes lifelong, and often instable process which did not preclude reversion to the older or further change to another faith (this holds true for conversion to Christianity too). If the sometimes alarmist vision of Christian missions and colonial officials of the inexorable progress of Islam should not be taken at face value, the phenomenon was striking nonetheless. Despite the lack of reliable religious statistics, it can be estimated that the Muslim population from Senegal to Cameroon and from Sudan to Mozambique probably at least doubled in the era of colonial encounter.

In the late nineteenth-century *bilad al-Sudan*, Islam tended to be concentrated in distinct towns, territories, and ethnic groups, notably the Jula and Hausa tied by their long-distance trading networks. As the colonial economy developed new axes of communication through plantation agriculture, the monetization of exchange, and new urban centres in the forest belt and along the Gulf of Guinea, Muslim merchants and migrant workers sought to seize new opportunities. Clerical lineages benefited from the loss of power of established warrior clans after colonial conquest. Some followed in the paths forged by mobile merchants to serve a heterogeneous clientele of forced and voluntary labour migrants from all walks of life, many of whom left the 'microcosm' of their ancestral cults for Islam and the 'macrocosm' of the colonial world.[46] Mossi migrants became Muslim in southern Côte d'Ivoire and contributed via circular movement to Islamize their native regions in Upper Volta (present-day Burkina Faso). In eastern Africa, Islam made inroads in a reverse direction, from the Swahili coast into the hinterland. In need of social reconstruction after colonial conquest, the Yao of the Tanganyika, Nyasaland, and Mozambique frontier converted en masse to Islam. In both West and East Africa, many freed slaves became Muslim in a quest for a new identity and enhanced social status. Some iconoclastic Muslim preachers advocating a break with past practice burnt fetishes, as among the Baga in French Guinea.[47] In Accra in the 1930s, some members of the Methodist Church converted to Islam, many citing dreams as their inspiration. In a striking example of ongoing dialogue between the two world religions, these new Muslims interpreted certain passages in the Bible as foretelling the rise of Islam, launching Islamic Sunday schools in which they continued to use their Bibles to preach in the name of Muhammad.[48] Everywhere, peripatetic Muslim healers and proselytizing Sufi *shaykh*s contributed to expanding the African Muslim map space.

Independence, moreover, did not represent a watershed in the history of Islamic societies and religious cultures in Africa. As in their response to colonial intrusion, Muslims were neither united nor collectively mobilized in nationalist struggles. Postcolonial state power fell into secular hands and Islam generally kept evolving away from the public scene. As in the scholarly literature, a change of course would come later with the post-1979 international Islamic revival. Meanwhile, the diversity of Africa's Islamic movements—the Sufi brotherhoods, the Egyptian *Ikhwān*, the 'Wahhabis', and all the rest—continued to be reshaped by the dialectic between internal patterns of development and new global contexts.

NOTES

1. As defined by F. Hartog in his *Régimes d'historicité: Présentisme et expérience du temps* (Paris: Seuil, 2003).

2. See, respectively, T. Asad, 'The Idea of an Anthropology of Islam', *Occasional Papers* (Washington, DC: Center for Contemporary Arab Studies, 1986), and L. Brenner, 'Histories of Religion in Africa', *Journal of Religion in Africa*, 30/2 (2000).

3. R. Launay, 'An Invisible Religion? Anthropology's Avoidance of Islam in Africa', in M. Ntarangwi, D. Mills, and M. H. M. Babiker, eds, *African Anthropologies: History, Critique, and Practice* (London: Zed Books, 2006).

4. For an English translation of the first, see J. Hunwick, *Timbuktu and the Songhay Empire: al-Sa'di's Ta'rikh al-Sudan down to 1613 and other contemporary documents* (Leiden: Brill, 2003).

5. M. Last, 'The "Colonial Caliphate" of Northern Nigeria', in D. Robinson and J.-L. Triaud, eds, *Le Temps des marabouts* (Paris: Karthala, 1997).

6. H. R. Palmer, *Sudanese Memoirs*, 3 vols (Lagos: Government Printer, 1928).

7. See H. F. C. Smith, 'A Neglected Theme of West-African History: The Islamic Revolutions of the Nineteenth Century', *Journal of the Historical Society of Nigeria*, 2/1 (1961).

8. *Arabic Literature of Africa*, 4 vols (Leiden: Brill, 1994–2003).

9. See J.-L. Triaud, *La Légende noire de la Sanûsiyya* (Paris: Éditions de la MSH, 1995).

10. See O. Kane, 'Islamism: What is New, What is Not? Lessons from West Africa', *African Journal of International Affairs*, 11/2 (2008).

11. C. A. Willis, 'Religious Confraternities of the Sudan', *Sudan Notes and Records*, 4 (1921).

12. Trimingham's books include *Islam in the Sudan* (1949), *Islam in East Africa* (1964), *Islam in Ethiopia* (1965), and *The Influence of Islam on Africa* (1968).

13. See esp. N. Levtzion and J. F. P. Hopkins, eds, *Corpus of Early Arabic Sources for West African History* (Cambridge: CUP, 1981; repr. by Markus Wiener, 2000).

14. See http://islamicafricajournal.org.

15. See http://www.brill.nl/isaf.

16. See e.g. T. Insoll, *The Archaeology of Islam in Sub-Saharan Africa* (Cambridge: CUP, 2003); A. F. Roberts and M. N. Roberts, *A Saint in the City: Sufi Arts of Urban Senegal* (Los Angeles: UCLA Fowler Museum, 2003); K. Harrow, *Faces of Islam in African Literature* (Portsmouth, NH: Heinemann, 1991).

17. R. Loimeier, *Between Social Skills and Marketable Skills: The Politics of Islamic Education in 20th century Zanzibar* (Leiden: Brill, 2009), 61.

18. B. Soares, ed., *Muslim-Christian Encounters in Africa* (Leiden: Brill, 2006).

19. G. Mann, 'Old Soldiers, Young Men: Masculinity, Islam, and Military Veterans in Late 1950s Soudan Français (Mali)', in L. A. Lindsay and S. F. Miescher, eds, *Men and Masculinities in Modern Africa* (Portsmouth, NH: Heinemann, 2003).

20. D. Robinson, *Paths of Accommodation: Muslim Societies and French Colonial Authorities in Senegal and Mauritania, 1880–1920* (Athens, O.: Ohio University Press, 2000).

21. D. F. Eickelman, 'The Political Economy of Meaning', *American Ethnologist*, 6 (1979).

22. See D. Robinson, *The Holy War of Umar Tal: The Western Sudan in the Mid-Nineteenth Century* (Oxford: Clarendon Press, 1985).

23. Y. Person, *Samori: Une révolution dyula*, 3 vols (Dakar: IFAN, 1968–75).

24. See K. Searcy, *The Formation of the Sudanese Mahdist State: Ceremony and Symbols of Authority, 1882–1898* (Leiden: Brill, 2011); S. S. Samatar, *In the Shadow of Conquest: Islam in Colonial Northeast Africa* (Trenton, NJ: Red Sea Press, 1992).

25. See e.g. M. S. Umar, *Islam and Colonialism: Intellectual Responses of Muslims of Northern Nigeria* (Leiden: Brill, 2006).

26. See J. A. Clancy Smith, *Rebel and Saint: Muslim Notables, Populist Protest, Colonial Encounters. Algeria and Tunisia, 1800–1904* (Los Angeles: University of California Press, 1994).

27. J. Miran, 'A Historical Overview of Islam in Eritrea', *Die Welt des Islam*, 45/2 (2005).

28. Robinson and Triaud, *Le Temps des marabouts*.

29. J. Hunwick, 'Sub-Saharan Africa and the Wider World of Islam: Historical and Contemporary Perspectives', *Journal of Religion in Africa*, 26/3 (1996), 231.

30. See C. A. Kane's semi-autobiographical novel, *The Ambiguous Adventure* (Portsmouth, NH: Heinemann, 1972).

31. R. S. O'Fahey, *Enigmatic Saint: Ahmad Ibn Idris and the Idrisi Tradition* (Evanston, Ill.: Northwestern University Press, 1994).

32. R. S. O'Fahey, 'Islamic Hegemonies in the Sudan: Sufism, Mahdism, and Islamism', in L. Brenner, ed., *Muslim Identity and Social Change in Sub-Saharan Africa* (Bloomington, Ind.: Indiana University Press, 1993), 25.

33. R. S. O'Fahey and B. Radtke, 'Neo-Sufism Reconsidered', *Der Islam*, 70 (1993).

34. C. A. Babou, *Fighting the Greater Jihad: Amadu Bamba and the Founding of the Muridiyya of Senegal, 1853–1913* (Athens, O.: Ohio University Press, 2007).

35. Benjamin F. Soares, *Islam and the Prayer Economy: History and Authority in a Malian Town* (Edinburgh: EUP, 2005), 69–105.

36. R. Seesemann, *The Divine Flood: Ibrahim Niasse and the Roots of a Twentieth-Century Sufi Revival* (Oxford: OUP, 2011).
37. See A. S. Hutson, 'The Development of Women's Authority in the Kano Tijaniyya, 1894–1963', *Africa Today*, 46/3–4 (1999).
38. R. Mitchell, *The Society of the Muslim Brothers* (Oxford: OUP, 1969; 2nd edn, 1993); G. Kepel, *Muslim Extremism in Egypt*(Berkeley, Calif.: University of California Press, 1984).
39. A. Merad, *Le Réformisme musulman en Algérie de 1925 à 1940: Essai d'histoire religieuse et sociale* (Paris and The Hague: Mouton, 1967) ; Pessah Shinar, *Modern Islam in the Maghreb* (Jerusalem: Hebrew University of Jerusalem, 2004).
40. See L. Kaba, *The Wahhabiyya : Islamic Reform and Politics in French West Africa* (Evanston, Ill.: Northwestern University Press, 1974).
41. For their biographies, see R. Pouwels, 'Sh. al-Amin b. Ali Mazrui and Islamic Modernism in East Africa, 1875–1947', *International Journal of Middle Eastern Studies*, 13 (1981); and R. Loimeier, 'Patterns and Peculiarities of Islamic Reform in Africa', *Journal of Religion in Africa*, 33/3 (2003).
42. L. Brenner, *Controlling Knowledge: Religion, Power and Schooling in a West African Muslim Society* (London: Hurst, 2000).
43. S. Reichmuth, 'Education and the Growth of Religious Associations among Yoruba Muslims: The Ansar-Ud-Deen Society of Nigeria', *Journal of Religion in Africa*, 26/4 (1996).
44. R. Launay and B. Soares, 'The Formation of an Islamic Sphere in French Colonial West Africa', *Economy and Society*, 28/4 (1999); see also R. Seesemann and B. Soares, ' "Being as Good Muslims as Frenchmen": On Islam and Colonial Modernity in West Africa', *Journal of Religion in Africa*, 39 (2009).
45. For a comprehensive bibliography, see A. Mary, 'Retour sur la "conversion africaine": Horton, Peel et les autres', *Journal des africanistes*, 68/1–2 (1998); and for recent exceptions, see F. Becker, *Becoming Muslim in Mainland Tanzania, 1890–2000* (Oxford: OUP, 2008) and B. J. Peterson, *Islamization from Below: The Making of Muslim Communities in Rural French Sudan, 1880–1960* (New Haven, Conn.: Yale University Press, 2011). See also Nehemia Levtzion, ed., *Conversion to Islam* (New York: Holmes & Meier, 1979).
46. To use R. Horton's key concepts in 'African conversion', *Africa*, 41/2 (1971).
47. R. Sarro, *The Politics of Religious Change on the Upper Guinea Coast: Iconoclasm Done and Undone* (Edinburgh: EUP, 2008).
48. M. Miran, 'D'Abidjan à Porto Novo: Associations islamiques, culture religieuse réformiste et transnationalisme sur la côte de Guinée', in L. Fourchard, A. Mary, and R. Otayek, eds, *Entreprises religieuses transnationales en Afrique de l'Ouest* (Paris: Karthala, 2005).

Bibliography

Abun-Nasr, Jamil, *A History of the Maghrib in the Islamic Period* (Cambridge: CUP, 1987).

Anta Babou, Cheikh, *Fighting the Greater Jihad: Amadu Bamba and the Founding of the Muridiyya of Senegal, 1853–1913* (Athens, O.: Ohio University Press, 2007).

Brenner, Louis, *Controlling Knowledge: Religion, Power and Schooling in a West African Muslim Society* (London: Hurst, 2000).

Christelow, Allan, *Muslim Law Courts and the French Colonial State in Algeria* (Princeton: PUP, 1985).

Eickelman, Dale F., *Knowledge and Power in Morocco: The Education of a Twentieth-Century Notable* (Princeton: PUP, 1992).

Hanretta, Sean, *Islam and Social Change in French West Africa: History of an Emancipatory Community* (Cambridge: CUP, 2009).

Levtzion, Nehemia, and Randall Pouwels, eds, *The History of Islam in Africa* (Athens, O.: Ohio University Press, 2000).

Loimeier, Roman, *Islamic Reform and Political Change in Northern Nigeria* (Evanston, Ill.: Northwestern University Press, 1997).

Loimeier, Roman, and Rudiger Seesemann, eds, *The Global Worlds of the Swahili: Interfaces of Islam, Identity and Space in 19th- and 20th-Century East Africa* (Berlin: LIT Verlag, 2006).

Martin, B. G., *Muslim Brotherhoods in Nineteenth-Century Africa* (Cambridge: CUP, 1976; 2nd edn, 2003).

Miran, Marie, *Islam, histoire et modernité en Côte d'Ivoire* (Paris: Karthala, 2006).

Reese, Scott, *Renewers of the Age: Holy Men and Social Discourse in Colonial Benaadir* (Leiden: Brill, 2008).

Robinson, David, and Jean-Louis Triaud, eds, *Le Temps des marabouts: Itinéraires et stratégies islamiques en Afrique occidentale française, 1880–1960* (Paris: Karthala, 1997).

Robinson, David, *Paths of Accommodation: Muslim Societies and French Colonial Authorities in Senegal and Mauritania, 1880–1920* (Athens, O.: Ohio University Press, 2000).

Robinson, David, *Muslim Societies in African History* (Cambridge: CUP, 2004).

Sani Umar, Muhammad, *Islam and Colonialism: Intellectual Responses of Muslims of Northern Nigeria to British Colonial Rule* (Leiden: Brill, 2006).

Seesemann, Rüdiger, *The Divine Flood: Ibrahim Niasse and the Roots of a Twentieth-Century Sufi Revival* (Oxford: OUP, 2011).

Soares, Benjamin F., *Islam and the Prayer Economy: History and Authority in a Malian Town* (Edinburgh: EUP, 2005).

CHAPTER 14

···

CHRISTIANITY

···

DAVID MAXWELL

DURING the first century AD, Christianity evolved from an obscure sect of Galilean Jews into a religion of thousands centred upon the Mediterranean world. Christian adherence grew faster in Roman North Africa than in any western province of the empire and by the end of the third century it was one of probably three places in the world where Christians were the majority, the others being Armenia and modern Turkey. Chapter 8 of the Acts of the Apostles reveals that the first gentile to convert to Christianity was an 'Ethiopian' from 'Nubia', or black Africa, probably the northern part of modern Sudan. The origins of monasticism derive from the northern borders of this region. Moreover, 'in the first Christian centuries, northern Africa provided some of the keenest intellectuals and most influential apologists in Christendom'.[1] Tertullian (c.160–240), a citizen of Carthage, was the first cleric to write in Latin instead of Greek and the theologian who advanced the doctrine of the Trinity, while the premier theologian of Christian antiquity, St Augustine, was from 396 to 430 Bishop of Hippo (colonial Bône or today's Annaba in Algeria). As Islam made its way up the Nile and traversed the Red Sea in the seventh century, Nubia adopted the new religion and the Church in what is today Ethiopia became increasingly isolated from European Christianity. Nevertheless, the Ethiopian Church survived so that when the Portuguese arrived on the shores of the Red Sea in the early sixteenth century, they brought Roman Christianity into a region that had been connected to the Eastern Church through the Coptic patriarch of Alexandria for over a thousand years. This deep history of Christianity in North Africa serves the purpose of challenging the still widespread misconception that the Christian religion was diffused from an imperial European centre into a passive Africa.

Important lessons can also be drawn from the first European missionary encounter with Africa which began in 1483 in the kingdom of Kongo. This initiative emerged in the informal Portuguese mercantile empire where relations with African leaders were finely balanced and the triumph of the Church was by no means inevitable. Indeed, as Adrian Hastings observed, the 'religious sensibilities' of sixteenth-century Iberians were not dissimilar from those of their pagan African cousins. Both were 'absolutely pre-Enlightenment', sharing similar notions about the causality of misfortune and the omnipresence of good and evil forces in daily life.[2] The proselytizing endeavours of the Portuguese missionaries were undermined by disease, powerful chiefdoms, and the rise of the slave trade. Moreover, the missionaries' imperial masters were always more interested in Asian spices than in Christian converts. Thus, the initially successful establishment of a Kongo Christian court lay as much in the genuine religious enthusiasm of King Afonso, whose son was ordained bishop in 1521, as in the endeavours of missionaries. Kongo Christianity subsequently spread beyond the court elites, and the resulting popular faith was a sign of things to come. It endured, with little missionary oversight, as an intensely laicized and indigenized religion through the commitment of the *maestri*, or catechists. To consider Africa's Christianization in terms of how missionaries imposed their ideas and practices ascribes them too much agency and obscures how Africans have actively sought out the material, spiritual, and intellectual resources of Christianity and made them their own.

Africa's Christianization, however, began in earnest in the late nineteenth century, when the infrastructure and technologies of empire made it possible for missionaries to function in hitherto remote and inhospitable environments. Yet recent scholarship has disentangled the missionary enterprise from empire, and African Christianity from mission. Over the past three decades, African religious history has increasingly come to be written from the point of view of the congregation. Emphasis has shifted from the history of theological ideas and the mostly male-dominated missionary organizations that spread them across the continent, to a concern with indigenous Africans as religious consumers and as missionaries in their own right. This growing interest in popular religiosity, which Terence Ranger describes as 'grass roots adherence to religious ideas, symbols and rituals', has been marked by a broader intellectual shift that interprets religion as an intrinsic part of culture.[3] Historians of class, gender, and ethnicity have grasped the significance of Christian ideas and practices in the construction of these identities. The emergence of cultural history has generated an interest in what Christianity meant for ordinary adherents, including the mental transformations involved in conversion and the significance of pilgrimage, baptism, and death rites. This desire to reconstruct religious cultures has also led to a more grounded understanding of missions. Some of the best work, such as Patrick Harries's study of the Swiss Romande Mission in Mozambique, shows missionaries transforming as they were transformed. Harries demonstrates how Thonga ideas, images, and expertise informed the renowned missionary Henri-Alexandre Junod's research in a range of sciences from ethnography to botany and entomology.[4]

These new interests have been furthered by a greater sensitivity towards sources and consideration of new types of evidence.[5] A significant impetus came from the 'linguistic turn', a growing interest with texts and representation, and more recently, in the processes of their production. Scholars have studied the impact of Christian self-help manuals and other instructive literature on social and economic behaviour. Isabel Hofmeyr's study of the transnational reception of John Bunyan's Protestant classic *The Pilgrim's Progress* (1678), which was translated into eighty African languages, demonstrated how formative such texts were.[6] Other literary scholars such as Liz Gunner have examined how the spiritual autobiographies, canonical histories, and hagiographies produced by African Independent Churches can be 'read' as legitimating charters intended to establish the identity of emergent movements.[7] And scholars researching ethnicity and nationalism now recognize the formative contribution of religious ideas to these identities. Joel Cabrita, for example, has explored the processes by which Zulu Christian nationalism was imagined through scripture and sacred text.[8]

Missionaries, of course, excelled at producing texts, as did their converts who were usually the first literate Africans and Derek Peterson has demonstrated the importance of a range of literary productions including lists, record books, and memoirs in the shaping of political culture in Kenya.[9] Missions were also some of the first organizations to grasp the significance of photography as a means of propaganda and historian. Basel Mission archivist Paul Jenkins has played a pioneering role in demonstrating how these visual sources portray a more complex encounter between missionary and African than was represented in the simple oppositions found in evangelical reports to the guardians of orthodoxy at home.[10] The growing interest in visual cultures is part of a broader exploration of how new media such as books, images, and ritual objects transform relations between religious practitioners and change the relationship between worshippers and the divine. A pioneering study in this field was Matthew Engelke's *A Problem of Presence*, which examines materiality within a Zimbabwean independent Christian movement known as the Friday Apostles.[11] All of these developments have made the study of African Christianity one of the most innovative and lively areas of research in recent years.

MISSIONARIES AND CULTURAL ENCOUNTER

The notion of cultural encounter has become the key framework with which to think about Africa's Christianization. The extraordinary and unpredictable nature of contact, in which the actors found themselves in unfamiliar and challenging circumstances, presented situations where values were laid bare. The interaction of religions with contrasting codes of belief and practice has provided rich examples of how the construction of difference or 'otherness', foundational in the construction of African and European identities, has occurred. There has been a good deal of discussion about the vocabulary used to analyse the religious encounter. Scholars with a postcolonial outlook argue that the idea of conversion has a Western bias, suggesting a one-way process from non-Christian to Christian adherence. Such a totalizing concept obscures important processes of rejection or of selection and adaptation.[12] Such a term, however, is needed to describe the radical choices individuals and communities made in rejecting their old religion and embracing the new during the conversion movements that swept Africa in the first centuries of the twentieth century.

In their provocative study of the encounter between the London Missionary Society (LMS) and the Tswana of southern Africa, Jean and John Comaroff introduce the idea of the 'long conversation' between missionary and African. This notion of dialogue captures the changes that occurred on *both* sides of the encounter in the lives of missionaries and adherents.[13] The Comaroffs' work also raises the question of whether religion should be defined in terms of 'beliefs and doctrines, which must somehow be internalised or publically observable rituals and practices'.[14] They choose the latter, defining it broadly to argue that LMS missionaries had an unspoken symbolic relation to empire, whose civilization they performed through dress, architecture, biomedicine, time-keeping, literacy, and numeracy. Such practices inculcated cultural imbalances, which made colonialism possible. They suggest that the terms of the conversation were weighted heavily in favour of the missionaries in a 'dialectic of domination and resistance'.

Here, one must distinguish exactly what is being studied. The Comaroffs tell us a good deal about the social and cultural effects of one influential mission in southern Africa and provide us with a useful method for studying missionary practices. It is true that missionaries often had sympathy with the broader imperial project, sharing similar aims when it came to literacy, health, hygiene, and industrial development. In the Belgian Congo that relationship was explicit, whereby Belgian Catholics (but not Protestants) were part of a 'Holy Trinity' of Church, state, and big business that governed the colony. But the Comaroffs advance a model religious encounter, one which is overly dualistic, showing white Christians colonizing the minds of black pagans in territories being occupied by white colonists. They tell us little about Christian ideas that could rapidly escape missionary control and almost nothing about the indigenous agents who transmitted them. In the same southern African context, Elizabeth Elbourne has shown how crucial were the mediating effects of frontierspeople such as the Khoi in pushing Christianity well beyond missionary eyes. Many Khoi had been victims of brutal violence and enforced servitude, and had also been forced or chosen to participate in violence. To such groups the evangelical conversion narrative offered a language for the expiation of guilt and the rhetoric of rejuvenation.[15]

It is evident that the context of the encounter also profoundly influenced subsequent patterns of Christianization. This becomes clear in J. D. Y. Peel's major study of Christian encounter amongst the Yoruba of today's south-western Nigeria. By the nineteenth century, the complex coastal kingdoms and polities in this part of West Africa had a long tradition of trade and diplomacy with Europe. They also had a tradition of interaction with Islam. Thus, the Yoruba were not so much crushed or colonized by a monolith of Christian doctrine and practice which they were forced to accept wholesale, but able to select from it in order to enlarge and recast their existing worldview, responding in particular to its modernizing promises. Moreover, the Yoruba responded to Christianity and Islam in a similar manner, assessing both faiths for the material benefits they offered and for their ability to mediate between God and man. Because Islam had arrived before Christianity, Yoruba Christian leaders such as Samuel Crowther were able to adapt Muslim religious ideas for Christian use.[16]

As all of this suggests, there was never a single monolithic missionary movement. Missionaries were as diverse as their national origins, social background, and theologies.[17] They debated and disagreed on a range of topics within their own organizations and often acrimoniously with others. And they often changed their views as they encountered local ideas and new metropolitan theories. Although this chapter focuses on the African side of the encounter, it is worth sketching some of the broad shifts in missionary outlook during the late nineteenth and twentieth centuries, as these profoundly shaped the forms African Christianization could take.

By the mid-1910s, as colonial rule was shifting from processes of conquest and occupation to consolidation and governance, missionaries were beginning to change their theology and practice. They began to shed their ethnocentric self-confidence and the accompanying belief that African cultures were diabolical and in need of eradication before Christianization could occur. By the interwar period, African cultures had become the object of legitimate scientific study and some missionaries such as Edwin Smith began to see within them traces of an original monotheism.[18] Diedrich Westermann, a former lay-worker with the North German Missionary Society, warned of the dangers of destroying African beliefs and practices before understanding their purpose. An accomplished scholar of African languages and an early director of the International African Institute (founded in 1926), Westermann symbolized the age in which missionaries turned to ethnography with gusto. Missionary research contributed to a new functionalist anthropology, which assumed the existence of bounded tribal societies and sought to arrive at an explanation of how they worked in terms of their customs, institutions, and traditions. Missionaries often made their findings available to colonial officials in the process of constructing systems of indirect rule through the use of African traditional leaders. Thus, while many missionaries have been criticized for the radical cultural changes they required of their African converts, others may be taken to task for their political conservatism. When the leading African American historian and educationalist W. E. B. du Bois visited West African in 1923, he criticized the emphasis on the preservation of traditional culture as part of a white man's plot to maintain the African as a willing but useful servant of the imperial cause. After 1945, the pace of industrialization and urbanization quickened, bringing new social problems and the challenge of African nationalism. There was also a growing tide of Christian Independency, a movement of churches that were free from missionary control. Missionaries such as Bengt Sundkler, John V. Taylor, and Dorothea Lehmann researched these issues in the light of the future development of the Church, thus shaping the emerging disciplines of religious studies, African theology, and urban sociology.

These shifts in missiological thinking amongst the historic mission churches were complicated by denominational changes within Western Christianity. Following the calamity of the First World War, Britain declined as a recruiting ground and many of the former missionary agencies suffered a crisis of confidence. But new types of missionaries emerged, Evangelical, Pentecostal, and 'Faith Mission' in background and often North American in origin.[19] Meanwhile, the Catholic movement, fortified by recruits from rural and working-class backgrounds, became increasingly Ultramontane, ever more loyal to Rome, and focused on neo-scholastic theology and liturgical conformity. Convinced of their own orthodoxy, these ascendant wings of the missionary world remained intensely proselytizing. They also devoted a good deal of energy to fighting each other—as exasperated colonial officials across Africa found to their cost. Such conflicts were yet another spur to Christianization, as both Catholics and Protestants struggled to stake first claim to new territories by training local agents and erecting village churches.

Missionary encounter continued into the postcolonial era. The widely publicized call for a missionary moratorium made by leading African Christian thinkers in the early 1970s was ignored by many. The Protestant missionary impetus remained for the most part driven by North Americans, with Pentecostals and Charismatic Christians in the ascendant from the 1980s onwards. These missionaries placed great stress on conversion experience and the gifts of the spirit as marks of faith. Within Catholicism, traditional fields of recruitment such as Ireland, France, and the Netherlands declined, but more than a thousand new missionaries from Poland filled the gap. Catholics and the historic mission churches increasingly engaged with issues of development, the *raison d'être* of postcolonial states. They also did less welcome work on human rights advocacy, as good governance became a fundamental issue.[20]

AFRICAN MOVEMENTS OF MASS CONVERSION

Missionaries' most important contribution to African history in the nineteenth century was the translation, printing, and distribution of the Bible, while in the twentieth century, it was education. Convinced of the value of schooling as a tool of evangelization, missionaries managed to persuade colonial governments to support mission-sponsored education and refrain from establishing their own competing secular system. While the initial impetus for schooling came from Protestants, Catholics too came to grasp its significance. The idea of 'trusteeship', initiated in part by the mandate system under which Germany's confiscated colonies were distributed among the Allied powers, stimulated a greater sense of responsibility towards developing territories. In many regions this notion of development did not amount to much, but a series of commissions coordinated by the Phelps-Stokes Fund (1919 and 1924) and the British Colonial Office (1923) did examine the issue of African education and led to the creation of subsidies for education, for which mission organizations competed. For the majority, education was delivered at primary level through so-called bush schools staffed by African teachers-cum-evangelists and pastors. A small number of elites received a secondary education in high-quality secondary schools such as Mfantsipim in Ghana and Alliance in Kenya. These graduates became the first generation of Africans to govern newly independent states in the 1960s, helping to smooth the Church's transition to independence.

Despite all of this, Hastings has observed that there seems to have been 'almost no direct relationship between mass conversion and missionaries'.[21] Missionary pioneers were responsible for vast tracts of territory; few and far between, their priorities were first to explore and map the lands to which they had been sent. Much of their time was then occupied by translation work, the construction of a mission infrastructure, and schooling, while many struggled simply to survive disease and to learn local languages.

Christianization was therefore predominantly the work of African Christians themselves. The first wave of mass conversions coincided with the imposition of colonial rule, which provided their context. From the 1880s, the exploitative and rapid social change that accompanied mining, plantations, and white settlement created intense social, intellectual, and religious disturbance. Established systems of meaning often shattered in the face of new technologies and the enlargement of horizons that accompanied labour migration, trade, and eviction from ancestral lands. Africans sought a measure of conceptual control over these forces by turning to the revolutionary new ideas and tools offered by the world religions of Christianity or Islam. Their response to Christianity was as much ideological as material or instrumental: 'Confronted with new epidemic diseases, natural disasters and widespread political and economic destruction in wake of colonial conquest, Africans sought new religious concepts to regain moral control over their lives.'[22]

The broad parameters of these movements of mass conversion have been described by Adrian Hastings in his classic study *The Church in Africa*. The first major example happened in the kingdom of Buganda in the closing fifteen years of the nineteenth century. The conversion of a group of pages at the royal court in the early 1880s, followed by their martyrdom and ensuing civil conflict, led to the full-scale Christianization of the kingdom by 1900. From Buganda the movement spread into surrounding states. Some of its impetus flowed from Ganda imperialism but it was also marked by a sincere African missionary commitment to the propagation of Anglican and Catholic traditions. Inspired by a local revival in 1893–4, Ganda Protestants volunteered to proselytize in places as distant as Nkore, Toro, Bunyoro, Busoga, Acholi, Teso, and Sukuma.[23] In 1896, the Ganda evangelist Apolo Kivebulaya arrived on the Semeliki escarpment in the north-eastern Congo Free State, devoting the next thirty-seven years of his life to the extension of the Anglicanism of the Church Missionary Society which he had encountered in Uganda.[24] Not to be upstaged, Ganda Catholics launched their own initiatives, animated by the likes of Yohana Kitigana who founded popular Catholicism in the Bunyarunguru region of Uganda twenty years before the White Fathers arrived there.

Along the West African coast, a series of conversion movements began around 1910. The most prolific of these occurred in Côte d'Ivoire and was led by the dynamic Liberian Grebo, the Prophet William Wadé Harris, who travelled with a cross, calabash, and Bible, baptizing tens of thousands. Harris had no intention of setting up his own church and channelled his converts into Catholicism and Methodism; only where mission Christianity was not present did the distinctive Harris Church appear. A number of his acolytes became significant Christian prophets in their own right. One such was John Swatson, who gathered a considerable number of followers on the western Gold Coast (modern Ghana) before shepherding them into the Anglican fold, where they were formally accepted by the Diocese of Accra in 1915.[25]

The trauma of the First World War was another impetus to mass conversion. The forced recruitment of porters and workers, the requisitioning of crops, the influenza pandemic of 1918–20, and postwar price rises and shortages further destabilized traditional structures of meaning. In the Belgian Congo the most famous example occurred in the 1920s amongst the Bakongo, in which the prophet and former Baptist catechist, Simon Kimbangu, was the most prominent of a number of actors.[26] But there was a significant movement amongst the Luba and Lunda peoples as well. These movements and many others like them represented a seismic shift in adherence to Christianity. Conversion was marked by stronger recognition of the unity and sovereignty of God, some personal attachment to Christ, and a belief in the value of baptism as a sign of these changes. Vigorous hymn singing (often strongly Christo-centric in content) and the public reading and discussion of the scriptures were the most prominent public features of this new mass Christianity. It was also marked by the keeping of a Sabbath and new moral strictures such as the prohibition of human sacrifice, the murder of twins, and trial by poison ordeal—practices which had been outlawed by colonial authorities but in some regions continued in locations far from state surveillance. Such movements were self-consciously modernizing, aggressively rejecting traditional religious objects that were often burnt in public bonfires and displaying a strong desire for bush schools and literacy. Nevertheless, the resulting network of village Christianities that now traversed much of sub-Saharan Africa retained a good deal of former cosmological beliefs, especially those relating to the family and kinship which were so central to personal security.

Mission Christianity was severely tested in the successive crises of the Great Depression and the Second World War between 1929 and 1945. The pace of development slowed, agricultural production diminished, and colonialism became increasingly conservative, blocking the advance of educated elites and consolidating its alliance with traditional leaders. Because the colonial state was in good part a religious construct, legitimated by both the ideologies of modernizing mission Christianity and customary law, it was logical that much resistance was expressed in religious terms.[27] In southern Africa, prophetic leaders emerged from the traditions of Pentecostalism and revivalism, their Zionist or Apostolic label an indication of their Western antecedents. Isaiah Shembe's Nazaretha Church and the *Vapostori* (i.e. Apostles) of the Shona Prophets, Johanna Maranke and Johanna Masowe, were prime examples, but a host of smaller movements also established themselves in this period. Because these movements were deeply critical of worldly missionaries and 'pagan' customary rulers, two key pillars of the colonial order, it is hardly surprising that they so unsettled imperial officials. These movements were not explicitly proto-nationalist; rather, they saw themselves as providing personal security through prayer, healing, and exorcism.[28] A similar collection of churches, known as the Aladura movement, arose amongst the Yoruba of Nigeria. Mission Christianity did not wither away, however, but was saved by the revivalist activities of women and youth. Revival was most vigorous in East Africa, where the movement spread from its first manifestation in Rwanda in 1939 into surrounding territories, affecting numerous Protestant churches. It became popularly and universally known as the *Balokole* movement—the 'saved people' in the Luganda language. Drawing on the biblical language of renewal, revivalists preached against the institutionalization of mission and called for the public confession of personal sin.

While we know the names of the leaders of the larger movements of Christianization, many other unknown Africans were involved. Christianization was low-key, spontaneous, and haphazard, often moving rapidly ahead of missionaries who struggled to control it. The first groups of local agents of Christianity were former slaves. More than 70,000 slaves were freed by the Royal Navy in Sierra Leone following the British abolition of the slave trade in 1807. Dispersed into Christian villages around Freetown, many adopted Christianity and subsequently returned home along the West African coast with their new-found faith. The most prominent example was Samuel Crowther, a Yoruba former slave who became an Anglican bishop in 1864. A similar movement occurred in the far south of the continent in Cape Town, where over 10,000 slaves were released between 1808 and 1885. Members of this Christianized immigrant community, known as Mozbiekers, subsequently led Anglican missionaries back into Central Africa. Most notable was Bernard Mizeki, who played a leading role in founding of Anglican Christianity in Southern Rhodesia, for which he was later martyred. In the twentieth century, Luba and Lunda slaves freed by Portuguese decree in Angola in 1910 returned to Belgian Congo as missionaries to their own people. In southern and Central Africa, migrant labour became an important carrier of Christianity, as Africans travelled south in search of work, converted along the way, and then returned home to spread the faith to their kin and neighbours. Labour migration was an important factor in the Christianization of Nyasaland (now Malawi), a colony that exported a high proportion of its inhabitants. Missionary organizations such as the American Methodists located themselves in the mining towns of Katanga in the Belgian Congo to proselytize these workers. Traders were another group of informal proselytizers. R. A. Coker, the Yoruba Anglican cleric who witnessed the Ijebu conversion movement, recorded in 1897 that 'We often have pleasant surprises of adherents in many places we little dreamed of. Again as the converts are all traders, they go as preachers of the word taking with them their Bibles and Prayer books.'[29]

CONVERSION AND RELIGIOUS CHANGE

Religious conversion is a complex and often extended process, occurring at both individual and group level. Initially changes might appear quite shallow, based upon the hope of material gain, healing, or in response to a challenging event. Yet once transformation has begun it can take on a momentum of its own, drawing converts into a new, often unforeseen world where moral, aesthetic, cognitive, and organizational patterns are considerably different. A spectrum of change is possible: radical and immediate conversion, or a slower process of gradual transformation over a lifetime or even several generations. The former often occurs with evangelical Protestantism, the latter with Catholicism. Yet the process is often far from linear: individuals can backslide, unable to live up to the cultural changes demanded by Christianity. As cohorts 'age', moreover, some grow weary of the ceaseless battle of faith against the ancestors, witches, and evil spirits, once again acquiring magical substances to supplement the protection offered by the Holy Spirit. A sudden crisis of illness, infertility, drought, or witchcraft might prompt an individual or community to change denomination, to convert *from* Christianity to Islam, or to return to a pre-Christian state.

It is possible, nonetheless, to identify broad processes involved in the initial adoption and evolution of Christianity. Missionaries generally made few conversions prior to colonial occupation. African leaders sought them out for knowledge of how to manage the growing number of whites entering their territories or for help in procuring arms and trade in order to get ahead of their enemies, but were often unwilling to accept the changes in lifestyle and government that missionaries demanded. For the first five years following the founding of F. S. Arnot's Brethren mission to Bunkeya in the south-eastern Congo Free State in 1886, it made little headway. Despite the pleas of missionaries, the Yeke warlord Msiri who ruled this Central African trade emporium had no intention of ending the brutal treatment of his subjects or his participation in the slave trade. It was only after his death in 1891 that conversions occurred at Luanza, the successor mission to Bunkeya. Its founder, Dan Crawford, became Konga Bantu, the 'gatherer of people', a white Christian chief, whose station provided security for those fleeing the break-up of Msiri's polity.[30] Other pioneer missionaries found themselves in a similar role, protecting those without kin or as patrons in the vacuum of political authority that accompanied colonial conquest.

Colonialism created new prospects for different social groups and shaped patterns of Christianization across Africa. The process has been explained most effectively by J. D. Y. Peel, whose model of 'opportunity costs' used to account for conversion amongst the Yoruba has an explanatory value for many other instances of mass conversion. Initial converts were often those on the social periphery such as outsiders and ex-slaves, who were more religiously biddable than those of higher status. They had lost the spiritual support of home communities and, in the absence of relatives, were more at liberty to make revolutionary religious choices. The first major social category to adopt Christianity was often young men, who bore the brunt of gerontocratic power in many societies and were least locked into existing religious institutions prior to their first marriage. In their hands it often became a mass movement. As well as an exit strategy, Christianity offered in its ideology of individualism 'a ready legitimation to the new cultural choices which now beckoned to the young'.[31] Young men were often the zealous foot soldiers of conversion movements who burnt 'fetishes', destroyed sacred sites, and challenged traditional hierarchies. Sensing the future belonged to them, many became catechists and evangelists, later on introducing Christianized notions of patriarchy into the rural society as they became elders themselves.

It is also possible to discern patterns of reception amongst women. They formed a high proportion of those who fled to mission stations during the early colonial period as they sought refuge from domestic slavery, unhappy or unwanted marriages, or widowhood.[32] Whether or not women subsequently converted in larger numbers hinged upon the extent to which they held status and power in precolonial society. In the history of southern Africa it is often taken as axiomatic that Christianity was 'a woman's movement' in the early twentieth century.[33] Among the Shona of Zimbabwe, most women lacked any religious or political authority. Christianity directly undermined elder male notions of patriarchy by demonizing the male ancestor spirits which legitimated it. Moreover, the prayer band and the fellowship meeting offered a vital source of solidarity for women otherwise divided by exogamy, polygamy, and fear of witchcraft accusation.[34] Among the Yoruba, women's reproductive capacities made their status more complementary to that of men, rather than subordinate to it. Hence they were anxious to pursue any spiritual power which might aid their chances to bear children, and in the early days this locked them more firmly into local *orisa* cults than men. Furthermore, missionary strictures about Christian marriage seemed to limit their options to bear and successfully rear children.[35] However, this same desire to maximize the chances of biological reproduction drew many women to Christianity once they grasped the benefits of missionary medicine and midwifery. Indeed, as women organized into Anglican Mothers Unions, Wesleyan fellowships, East African Revival sororities, and the rest, they became a profound influence in African churches as fundraisers and evangelists. It was female groups such as these that did much to save mission Christianity in the 1930s by instituting revival.

The emergence of groups of African woman characterized by white starched uniforms, zealous in their hymn singing, proselytizing, and domesticity reminds us that Christianity could dramatically advance the position of previously marginal social categories, profoundly reshaping notions of gender and class. Mission stations provided the material basis for a new class of white-collar workers: clerks, teachers, translators, printers, and evangelists. In the 1920s, missions took up state subsidies for education to expand this class of what were pejoratively called 'trousered blacks' for service in the wider colonial economy. Elite Christians embraced their new identity, adopting new patterns of dress and consumption to enhance their status. Christian ideas and practices also shaped African class formation, providing new sets of manners and mores. These new codes, best described as 'respectability', stressed temperance, orderliness, cleanliness, fidelity in sexual relations, and economic independence. In the African press, which they often controlled, the respectable contrasted themselves with those who frequented beer halls and indulged in new urban cultures of gambling, prostitution, and drunkenness.[36]

Women were integral to this new middle-class identity. In South Africa, a spectrum of missions—Anglican, Methodist, American Board—chose to educate small numbers of women in order to make respectable wives for their elite male workers. Some were destined for nursing or teaching, but most were intended for domestic service. Missionaries emphasized 'motherhood' as the basis of a settled family life, their lessons focusing on the virtues of diet and hygiene, and the arts of washing, ironing, and needlework. While African women did not necessarily share the objectives of missionary social engineering, they did adopt aspects of Christian domesticity as part of their self-definition.[37] More generally, women's status itself became a key marker of the respectable class in which female virtue symbolized all that needed protection from threatening under-classes. Respectable Christians defined themselves against others: the feckless, the backward, the uncivilized, and the superstitious, zealously adopting missionary prejudices. In this many desired recognition from whites, and it was wounded pride caused by missionary slights to their newfound respectability, combined with the colour bar, that prompted the first generation of mission elites to found their own churches. A pioneering figure in this movement was the South African Mangena M. Mokone. Splitting from the Wesleyan Church in 1892 and drawing inspiration from the ancient traditions of Christian Ethiopia, Mokone founded his own 'Ethiopian Church'—from which this new Ethiopian Movement of Christian Independency took its name.

There has been a good deal of debate concerning the extent to which conversion can be explained in terms of continuity with African culture or as a radical break with it.[38] In practice, continuity and rupture combine to shape conversion. There has to be some degree of continuity between the new and the old because the former can only be grasped in terms of what has already been understood and practised. Indeed, missionaries made great attempts to establish verbal continuities with the names of God, to build Christian messages upon African proverbial wisdom, and to replace charms with Catholic medals or crucifixes. Recognizing that the landscape had sacred meaning, its mountains, caves, and pools associated with the ancestors or local spirits, missionaries and Africans sought to resacralize it in Christian fashion. Catholics built grottos, places of pilgrimage to the saints or Mary, while Anglicans created new holy ground by constructing cemeteries.[39] Christianity also brought new and compelling ideas about heaven and hell, sin and judgement.[40] Psychologically, the element of discontinuity, a faith worth persecution, dominated in the early stages. If converts were to give up a system of belief and practice that shaped their worldview and public conventions and adopt another religion, they often did so with great rigour. Subsequently, the dimension of continuity could reappear. Once the convert was established in the new faith they grasped the congruity of much that went before. This was truer for the second generation of Christianized children who never experienced the rupture of conversion nor the old life as a social and spiritual entity. They often sought a self-conscious rapprochement with their parents' former culture. This act of 'reprise' is seen in contemporary Botswana, where Apostolics in Gaborone's independent churches have reintroduced in Christian form the practices of divination and witchcraft eradication rejected by their parents. Similarly, in Pentecostal services, drums and xylophones initially banned due to their association with ancestor veneration have been reintroduced as a harmless aspect of heritage.

Missionaries often looked for continuities in response to pressure from African Christians. Missionaries from the Berlin Missionary Society working amongst the Ndebele in South Africa re-oralized the Bible, becoming raconteurs of the great Old Testament narratives such as 'Jonah and the Swallowing Fish', ensuring that their message resonated with local story-telling traditions.[41] The idea of dialogue also captures the manner in which ancestor cults and oral traditions could be transformed through encounter. In Zimbabwe, spirit mediums responsible for recounting the genealogies of the ancestors have embellished them with the names of Hebrew patriarchs such as Noah and Abraham to give them greater legitimacy.[42] Where missionaries and their agents failed to be culturally sensitive, African church prophets often arrived at more satisfying syntheses of old and new. Their movements evolved continuities with food taboos, models of leadership, and, most importantly, with healing traditions. In an attempt to meet Africans' enduring concerns for health and personal security, the prophets Kimbangu and Shembe chose to elevate Christ's healing ministry over his sacrifice, founding centres of healing and prayer in their headquarters-cum-holy cities.

THE CHRISTIANIZATION OF THE POPULAR MIND

A common missionary complaint was that Africans embraced them not so much for their religious message but for access to the tools and knowledge of modernity. While it is true that initial encounter may have taken place for instrumental reasons, we have seen how conversion could develop its own momentum and lead in unexpected directions. Moreover, the simple dichotomy between sacred and secular made by pioneer missionaries bore little relation to African realities in the nineteenth and early twentieth centuries. Peel argues that 'the search for power, individual or collective, was the dominant orientation of the Yoruba towards all religions...There were both social and technical aspects to this power, but the former—power in and over material things, power as practical knowledge—was primary, an end in itself, as well as a means to the latter.'[43] His notion that Christianity was yet another, albeit significant, route to power can be generalized across many African cases. Given the integral relationship between religion and culture, this meant that initially 'Christianity for Africans was inseparable from European customs and the power and effectiveness of the Christian God was part and parcel of the power and effectiveness of European technology, economy and ideas.'[44]

The search for power in Christian religion was forcefully illustrated by African responses to literacy. Writing was viewed as a manifestation of a greater force, the ability to communicate data over time and space without having to learn it. African Christian movements were usually animated by a grassroots adoption of literacy, in which schooling and church were synonymous in representing progress. Once again the African catechist or evangelist, who was often also the village schoolteacher, was an important conduit of this new technology. His new faith, together with his adoption of reading, new types of cultivation, new notions of cleanliness, and his connections with white missionaries made him the local embodiment of modernizing Christianity. His sons (and sometimes daughters) might well advance to secondary schooling at the mission station and a white-collar job. Unsurprisingly, a frequent label given to Yoruba Christians was *Onibuku*, 'the people of the book'; for the Kikuyu of Kenya, it was *athomi*, 'readers'.

The translation into African languages of the scriptures, hymn books, and catechisms turned literacy into a tool of popular Christianization that stretched well beyond the control of missionaries. The impact of vernacular religious texts was enhanced because

Africans themselves were intimately involved in the translation process. Missionary linguists quickly realized that African expertise was necessary to ensure that the vernacular properly conveyed new Christian concepts in local terms. Indigenous intermediaries thus had the opportunity to put their own ideas and images into the final texts. Amongst the Kikuyu, the young men who participated in the translation process shaped the scriptures to legitimate their struggle against their elders. 'By writing themselves and their elders into Jesus' critique of the Pharisee's hypocrisy, readers contrasted new forms of knowledge with old ... Bible translation made it possible for readers to argue that they were the leaders in changing times.'[45]

The impact of the vernacular scriptures, or just a single gospel or language primer, could be electrifying.[46] Once the Bible was in the hands of Africans, they quickly seized control of its message, finding all manner of things that missionaries had omitted to tell them about and that resonated with local cultures: healing miracles, visions, exorcisms, angels and demons, food taboos, and polygamy.[47] It was no accident that the great independent prophetic churches emerged soon after the appearance of vernacular scriptures. In Kenya, the publication of the Gikuyu New Testament in 1926 spurred revival and later inspired a new Christianity, embodied in the 'praying' or *akurinu* church. Likewise, the imagery of power, place, and prophecy that animated the laws, hymns, meditations, and canonical history of Isaiah Shembe's Nazaretha Church drew heavily from the Zulu scriptures. Where the Bible remained in English or French, or in the hands of authoritarian Catholic priests, the chances of independency were far more limited.

Beyond its religious impact, the Bible also shaped ethnicity. Among the eastern Shona of Zimbabwe, a combination of Anglican, Jesuit, and American Methodist missionaries chose to elevate the Manyika dialect over its neighbours. Through processes of language classification and codification, the production of vernacular scriptures, and their diffusion via church and mission school networks a new Manyika identity was created in the 1920s. Closely shaped by progressive Christians, it was embraced by other eastern Shona who saw it as a means of enhancing their chances in the migrant labour economy.[48] In Kenya, scripture had a significant ideological input into the discursive arena of 'moral ethnicity', by which Kikuyu sought to understand and define themselves. They had read the Bible as 'an allegory of their own history—a story of servitude and salvation, exile and return'.[49] In the early stages of their struggle to forge an ethnic nationalist consciousness, on the eve of the Mau Mau emergency, they embraced the Exodus story, comparing themselves to the Children of Israel and the British to Pharaoh's Egyptians. The force of such a comparison was based upon the Gikuyu Old Testament, published in 1951.

Adrian Hastings has similarly argued that Christianity contributed to the development of African nationalism. While the examples he provided, such as Buganda, were old kingdoms or newer ethno-linguistic entities rather than what became Africa's new states, he convincingly argued that the Bible provided the original model of the nation, sanctifying it as the God-given unit of political action.[50] It is certainly true that by 1950, 'everyone claimed...the sanction of religion in some form' and that this profoundly shaped the decolonization process.[51] In Northern Rhodesia in March 1953,

Harry Nkumbula, an ex-mission teacher, publicly burnt the government's White Paper outlining plans for federation in the presence of a number of chiefs and a large crowd after singing 'O God our Help in Ages Past'.[52] Six years later, in neighbouring Nyasaland, nationalist leader Hastings Banda told jubilant crowds 'To Hell with federation' and 'Let us fill their prisons with our thousands shouting Hallelujah'.[53]

Many missionaries did not rate the prospects of mission-derived churches particularly highly during the era of decolonization. They feared that a successful nationalism would promote either a revived paganism or communism, or both. If Africa had a Christian future, it seemed to lie with the so-called African Independent Churches. However, although empire had assisted the spread of Christianity, the faith outlasted its framework of transmission. Between 1900 and 1950, Christian adherence increased from 4 million to 34 million, reflecting a significant shift in the balance of power between black and white Christians.[54] As African Christians came to control the religious initiative and the message, so any formal connection between Christianity and empire diminished. Given that Christianity was now deeply indigenized, there was no contradiction between a sharp increase in Christian adherence and the growth of anti-colonialism. Christianity's African future turned out to be far from bleak. Indeed, the remarkable growth in Christian adherence continued to accelerate in the postcolonial period: from approximately 75 million in 1965 to 351 million in 2000, with much of the growth happening in the former mission churches. These trajectories of growth and indigenization marked a fundamental shift in the centre of gravity of world Christianity to the global South.

Notes

1. Elizabeth Isichei, *A History of Christianity in Africa: From Antiquity to the Present* (London: SPCK, 1995), 1.
2. Adrian Hastings, *The Church in Africa, 1450–1950* (Oxford: Clarendon, 1994), 74–5.
3. Terence Ranger, 'Religious Movements and Politics in Sub-Saharan Africa', *African Studies Review*, 29/2 (1986), 1.
4. Patrick Harries, *Butterflies and Barbarians: Swiss Missionaries and Systems of Knowledge in South East Africa* (Oxford: James Currey, 2007).
5. David Maxwell, 'Writing the History of African Christianity: Reflections of an Editor', *Journal of Religion in Africa*, 36/3–4 (2006).
6. Isabel Hofmeyr, *The Portable Bunyan: A Transnational History of* The Pilgrim's Progress (Princeton: PUP, 2003).
7. Elizabeth Gunner, *Man of Heaven and the Beautiful Ones of God: Writings from Ibandla lama Nazaretha, a South African Church* (Leiden: E. J. Brill, 2002).
8. Joel Cabrita, *Texts and Authority in the South African Nazaretha Church* (Cambridge: CUP, 2012).
9. Derek Peterson, *Creative Writing: Translation, Bookkeeping and the Work of Imagination in Colonial Kenya* (Portsmouth, NH: Heinemann, 2004).
10. Paul Jenkins, 'On Using Historical Missionary Photographs in Modern Discussion', *Le Fait Missionnaire*, 10 (Jan. 2001), 73.

11. Matthew Engelke, *A Problem of Presence: Beyond Scripture in an African Church* (Berkeley, Calif.: University of California Press, 2007).

12. David Lindenfield, 'Indigenous Encounters with Christian Missions in China and West Africa, 1800–1920', *Journal of World History*, 16/3 (2005).

13. Jean Comaroff and John Comaroff, *Of Revelation and Revolution: Christianity, Colonialism and Consciousness in South Africa* (Chicago: University of Chicago, 1991).

14. Lindenfeld, 'Indigenous Encounters', 334.

15. Elizabeth Elbourne, *Blood Ground: Colonialism, Missions, and the Contest for Christianity in the Cape Colony and Britain, 1799–1853* (Montreal: McGill-Queen's University Press, 2002).

16. J. D. Y. Peel, *Religious Encounter and the Making of the Yoruba* (Bloomington, Ind.: Indiana University Press, 2000).

17. Andrew Porter, *Religion Versus Empire : British Protestant Missionaries and Overseas Expansion, 1700–1914* (Manchester: MUP, 2004).

18. Patrick Harries, 'Missions and Anthropology', in Norman Etherington, ed., *The Oxford History of the British Empire Companion Series: Missions and Empire* (Oxford: OUP, 2005); Olivier Servais and Gérard van't Spijker, eds, *Anthropologie et missiologie XIXe–XXe siècles: Entre connivance et rivalité* (Paris: Karthala, 2004).

19. Brian Stanley, 'Introduction', in Brian Stanley, ed., *Missions, Nationalism and the End of Empire* (Grand Rapids, Mich.: Eerdmans, 2003).

20. David Maxwell, 'Post-Colonial Christianity in Africa', in Hugh McLeod, ed., *The Cambridge History of Christianity, ix. World Christianities, c.1914–c.2000* (Cambridge: CUP, 2006).

21. Hastings, *Church in Africa*, 463.

22. Thomas Spear, 'Toward the History of African Christianity', in Thomas Spear and Isaria Kimambo, eds, *East African Expressions of Christianity* (Oxford: James Currey, 1999), 3.

23. Spear, 'Toward the History of African Christianity', 12.

24. Emma Wild-Wood, *Migration and Christian Identity in Congo (DRC)* (Leiden: Brill, 2008).

25. Bengt Sundkler and Christopher Steed, *A History of the Church in Africa* (Cambridge: CUP, 2000), 219.

26. Jean-Luc Vellut, *Simon Kimbangu, 1921: De la prédication à la déportation. Les Sources, i. Fonds missionnaires protestants* (Brussels: ARSOM, 2005).

27. John Iliffe, *A Modern History of Tanganyika* (Cambridge: CUP, 1979), 342–79.

28. Ranger, 'Religious Movements', 54–8.

29. Hastings, *Church in Africa*, 440.

30. R. I. Rotberg, 'Plymouth Brethren and the Occupation of Katanga, 1886–1907', *Journal of African History*, 5/2 (1964).

31. Peel, *Religious Encounter*, 238.

32. Marcia Wright, *Strategies of Slaves and Women: Life Stories from East/Central Africa* (London: James Currey, 1993).

33. Bengt Sundkler, 'African Church History in a New Key', in Kirsten Holst-Peterson, ed., *Religion, Development and African Identity* (Uppsala: Scandinavian Institute of African Studies, 1987), 83.

34. David Maxwell, *Christians and Chiefs in Zimbabwe: A Social History of the Hwesa People, c.1870s–1990s* (Edinburgh: EUP, 1999), 103–8.

35. Peel, *Religious Encounter*, 234–40.

36. David Maxwell, *African Gifts of the Spirit: Pentecostalism and the Rise of a Zimbabwean Transnational Religious Movement* (Oxford: James Currey, 2006), 60–108.

37. Deborah Gaitskell, 'Housewives, Maids or Mothers: Some Contradictions of Domesticity for Christian Women in Johannesburg 1903–39', *Journal of African History*, 24/2 (1983).

38. Joel Robbins, 'Continuity Thinking and the Problem of Christian Culture', *Current Anthropology*, 48/1 (2007).

39. Terence Ranger, 'Taking Hold of the Land: Holy Places and Pilgrimages in Twentieth-Century Zimbabwe', *Past and Present*, 117 (1987).

40. Richard Gray, *Black Christians and White Missionaries* (New Haven, Conn.: Yale University Press, 1990).

41. Isabel Hofmeyr, *'We Spend our Years as a Tale that is Told': Oral Historical Narrative in a South African Chiefdom* (Portsmouth, NH: Heinemann, 1993), 41–58.

42. Michael Bourdillon, 'Gleaning: Shona Selections from Biblical Myth', in Wendy James and Douglas Johnson, eds, *Vernacular Christianity: Essays in the Social Anthropology of Religion* (Oxford: JASO, 1988).

43. Peel, *Religious Encounter*, 217.

44. Lindenfeld, 'Indigenous Encounters', 356.

45. Peterson, *Creative Writing*, 85.

46. Harries, *Butterflies and Barbarians*,182–205.

47. Lamin Saneh, *Translating the Message: The Missionary Impact on Culture* (New York: Orbis Books, 1989).

48. Terence Ranger, 'Missionaries, Migrants and the Manyika: The Invention of Ethnicity in Zimbabwe', in Leroy Vail, ed., *The Creation of Tribalism in Southern Africa* (London: James Currey, 1989).

49. John Lonsdale, 'Kikuyu Christianities: A History of Intimate Diversity', in David Maxwell, ed., with Ingrid Lawrie, *Christianity and the African Imagination: Essays in Honour of Adrian Hastings* (Leiden: Brill, 2002), 158.

50. Adrian Hastings, *The Construction of Nationhood: Ethnicity, Religion and Nationalism* (Cambridge: CUP, 1997), 4.

51. Adrian Hastings, *A History of African Christianity* (Cambridge: CUP, 1979), 17.

52. Henry Swanzy, 'Quarterly Notes', *African Affairs*, 52 (1953), 232–3, cited in Hastings, *A History of African Christianity*, 89.

53. Quoted in R. Rotberg, *The Rise of Nationalism in Central Africa* (Cambridge, Mass.: Harvard University Press, 1967), 293.

54. Sundkler and Steed, *History of the Church*, 906.

BIBLIOGRAPHY

Comaroff, Jean, and John Comaroff, *Of Revelation and Revolution: Christianity, Colonialism and Consciousness in South Africa* (Chicago: University of Chicago, 1991).

Elbourne, Elizabeth, *Blood Ground: Colonialism, Missions and the Contest for Christianity in the Cape Colony and Britain, 1799–1853* (Montreal: McGill-Queens University Press, 2002).

Etherington, Norman, ed., *Oxford History of the British Empire Companion Series: Missions and Empire* (Oxford: OUP, 2005).

Hastings, Adrian, *The Church in Africa, 1450–1950* (Oxford: Clarendon Press, 1994).

Isichei, Elizabeth, *A History of Christianity in Africa: From Antiquity to the Present* (London: SPCK, 1995).

Maxwell, David, ed., with Ingrid Lawrie, *Christianity and the African Imagination: Essays in Honour of Adrian Hastings* (Leiden: Brill, 2002).

Peel, J. D. Y., *Religious Encounter and the Making of the Yoruba* (Bloomington, Ind.: Indiana University Press, 2000).

Ranger, Terence, 'Religious Movements and Politics in Sub-Saharan Africa', *African Studies Review,* 29/2 (1986).

Spear, Thomas, and Isariah Kimambo, eds, *East African Expressions of Christianity* (Oxford: James Currey, 1999).

Sundkler, Bengt, and Christopher Steed, *A History of the Church in Africa* (Cambridge: CUP, 2000).

CHAPTER 15

....

INDIGENOUS AFRICAN
RELIGIONS

....

ROBERT M. BAUM

THIS chapter focuses on religions which were created by African communities and which have relied primarily on the inspiration of African prophets, mediums, and elders, rather than on sacred texts that originated outside the continent. These religious systems developed in ways that have played an important role in fostering a distinct sense of cultural and ethnic identity within particular African communities. While open to borrowing ideas and practices from other religious traditions, innovations were assimilated in such a way that they did not directly challenge ideas of ethnic identity. Indigenous African religions are highly instrumental in emphasis, seeking to enhance the physical, economic, and cultural well-being of their adherents in this world rather than in a world to come. Followers of indigenous religions do not usually proselytize; rather, they tend to assume that people born into or living in their community will practise its religious tradition, an obligation to their society's civil religion. Following from that, they are less concerned about the use of Christian or Muslim ritual practices as long as people fulfil their obligations to their religious community.

There are over one thousand African religions, with significant differences within and between ethnic groups, and between regional and/or linguistic groupings. Religious concepts and practices are often taught through the performance of oral traditions and intensive instruction during periods of initiation or rites of passage. Individual young people may also seek out and 'sit at the feet' of elders who share their knowledge based on the younger individuals' ability to handle responsibly the power associated with the acquisition of knowledge. Although there are considerable debates about the relative importance of the supreme being in African religions, there is convincing evidence that most African religions do have a central deity who begins the process of creation and is involved in the ongoing process of creating life and passing judgement on life after death. African religions stress the importance of lesser gods, spirits, and ancestors who address different types of religious concerns and appeal to different forms of social groupings.

Indigenous African religions were first studied exclusively by anthropologists, colonial administrators, and missionaries who became intrigued by the religious practices and ideas with which they came into contact. Neither historians nor scholars of religions concerned themselves with African religions prior to the growth of Christianity and Islam in particular regions of the continent. Western scholars often shared the view of Hegel that Africa was a place on the mere threshold of history, a region without religion or morality, where only sorcery and superstition reigned.[1] When historians turned their attention to African religions, they focused on the growth of Christianity and Islam, utilizing indigenous African religions as an 'ethnographic base line' from which to chart their sustained interaction and gradual loss of influence to the incoming Abrahamic faiths.

As African religion and belief became part of religious studies or theology programmes within African universities, Western missionaries and African theologians began to publish on the subject. However, they had internalized this view of a relatively static indigenous tradition which was acted upon by historical 'world religions', notably Christianity and Islam. Thus, John Mbiti, the author of the most influential textbook of African religions in the English-speaking world, wrote: 'In the traditional set-up where the African concept of time is mainly two dimensional, human life is relatively stable and almost static. A rhythm of life is the norm, and any radical change is either unknown, resented, or so slow that it is hardly noticed.' For Mbiti, major religious change began in 'the second half of the nineteenth century and swiftly gaining momentum towards the middle of the twentieth century' during the colonial era.[2] Indigenous religions, according to Mbiti, changed very little until they encountered Islam and Christianity and the disruptive influences of colonialism.

As pioneering scholars of African religions in the first half of the twentieth century struggled to account for the extraordinary diversity of indigenous religious practice and belief on the continent, they tended to embrace evolutionary models of religious change, to emphasize the role of outside agents in the transformation of African religions, or to acknowledge change while suggesting that there were insufficient reliable sources to reconstruct a history of these religious traditions. Evolutionists were strongly influenced by social science research directed at discovering the origins of religion itself and entertained the strong possibility that Africa could well be the site of such a genesis. Edward Tylor, James Frazer, and other evolutionists assumed that the West embodied the highest stages of religious life, either a form of monotheism or the decline of organized religion altogether, and that Africa was a living laboratory for the understanding of the origins of religion.[3] One finds this type of work articulated in the works of anthropologists such as Jean Girard, who thought that Diola religion in the Senegambia region was somewhere on the evolutionary scale between fetishism and polytheism.[4] One finds it resurfacing in some cognitive studies of religion that suggest that humans evolve into higher forms of religious consciousness that closely parallel developments in the Western world.

A second form of historical explanation, the so-called Hamitic Hypothesis, originated with the British explorer John Hanning Speke in the 1860s. It suggested that African religions and African civilizations in general were the product of small groups of 'Hamites' (occasionally Semites—hence the idea of King Solomon's mines being located at Great Zimbabwe or the Yorubas as the Canaanite descendants of Nimrod) who wandered south of the Sahara, intermarried with local rulers' daughters and became the leaders of many sub-Saharan African states. Some went so far as to suggest that African ruling classes had lighter pigmentation than ordinary African people. This belief, however, denied African agency in the construction of basic cultural and political institutions, relying instead on various groups of Caucasians as a kind of *deus ex machina* of cultural innovation.[5] This theory would have tragic consequences in Rwanda and Burundi where the upper class Tutsi became associated with Hamitic wanderers who were given all sorts of special privileges by their German and Belgian colonizers.[6] In both Rwanda and Burundi, Europeans felt a special kinship with the Tutsi 'Hamites' and consistently favoured them in school admissions and for positions in government service. Such favouritism was deeply resented by the Hutu majority who mobilized against both foreign occupation and the local aristocracy, culminating in massacres of Tutsis in both countries after independence and the Rwandan genocide of 1994.

SOURCES AND METHODS

Pioneering scholars claimed that there was insufficient evidence to uncover the history of African religions, reinforcing the resistance to historical research on African religions. This claim, first articulated by Geoffrey Parrinder, was developed further by Jack Goody and Jan Vansina.[7] It focused on two sets of claims: first, the paucity of written documents before Christianity and Islam became important influences; and second, the nature and richness of oral traditions concerning these religious traditions. The first is subject to little debate: ancient Egyptian, Geʾez, Greek, Latin, and medieval Arabic texts do not provide sufficient detail to reconstruct the deep history of indigenous religions. European documents prior to the nineteenth century were similarly sparse and largely confined to the coastal regions or to what became South Africa. Nineteenth- and twentieth-century accounts produced by missionaries, colonial administrators, travellers, and the first academic researchers provided far more detail, but were restricted by where outsiders travelled and what they were allowed to see.[8]

Given the paucity of written sources, the debate about the history of indigenous African religions has focused on the reliability of oral traditions. Since the 1950s, African historians have utilized oral traditions collected through field research to gain insights into the history of African societies before the colonial conquest. Some of those pioneers, however, have suggested that religious history is a far more difficult area of research, both because oral traditions concerning political and economic history overshadow religious history and because of a tendency for oral traditions to edit out or lose memories of dissident traditions which might highlight significant changes in African religious traditions. Furthermore, African religious traditions rely primarily on direct forms of instruction about ritual knowledge, to which access is accorded only to those who have achieved a particular status or demonstrated their individual acumen in handling responsibly the power that accompanies any transmission of knowledge. This makes field research-based studies particularly difficult, because of the lack of both time and linguistic skills necessary to establish the type of rapport crucial to gaining access to such esoteric knowledge.[9]

Goody and Vansina have gone beyond the issue of the difficulties in obtaining access to oral traditions about religious topics to consider the question of whether such materials exist or are reliable. Goody has written extensively on the contrast between literate and oral cultures and argued that the absence of written texts causes people in oral cultures to think 'mythically' about the past (a view shared by Joseph Miller) and that a 'true' historical consciousness does not emerge until the development of literacy. He sees oral cultures as relatively homogeneous, governed by a need to eliminate incongruities between the needs of the present and prior practices. He suggests that oral cultures have a marked tendency 'towards cultural homeostasis: those innumerable mutations of culture that emerge in the ordinary course of verbal interaction are either adopted by the interacting group or they get eliminated in the process of transmission from one generation to the next'.[10] Vansina makes a similar argument about the difficulty of gathering oral traditions about the history of African religions:

> Religious practice was so tied up with other institutions that it lacked sufficient autonomy and visibility to develop systematic traditions of its own. It is diffused throughout society. Furthermore, change in the representations and in the practice of ritual was so slow as often to be unconscious and hence could not be remembered.
>
> Where change was not slow, the need to adhere to the new consensus effectively prevented development of traditions that would indicate what previous representations of ultimate reality might have been. Oral traditions are therefore, sources that are not promising for intellectual history in general and religious history in particular...[11]

A growing number of African historians, anthropologists, and scholars of religion, however, contend that sustained research using oral traditions in combination with a range of linguistic, archaeological, and written sources can provide insight into the history of indigenous religions. Furthermore, once they moved away from elite performative traditions, such as those associated with the West African griots, they were able to obtain oral traditions from various social groupings, representing different classes, ethnic minorities, and women. Even in 'acephalous' societies that were relatively egalitarian, different perspectives may be collected and compared in an effort to ascertain the broad outlines of a history of an African religion. Such research has served significantly to reduce the picture of homoeostasis suggested by Goody and Vansina. Furthermore, these oral traditions often include quite pragmatic explanations of why a particular spirit cult or ritual practice was abandoned or a new one introduced. Indeed, historians of African religions have found that local oral historians often reflect critically on reasons for religious change and the significance of such changes.

The historical richness of oral testimony has become evident in research on African religions conducted since the end of the First World War. One of the earliest examples was the now-classic anthropological work by E. E. Evans-Pritchard on the religion of the Nuer peoples of present-day South Sudan, conducted in the 1930s and published in the 1950s. Despite the relatively ahistorical training he had received in his own discipline, Evans-Pritchard found significant amounts of evidence that Nuer religion had sustained substantial changes in the nineteenth century. He focused his attention on an expanding category of lesser spirits that he called 'Spirits of the Above', which had been fairly unimportant to the Nuer before the nineteenth century. During the turbulent era of the Sudanese slave trade, they became a major force in religious life. These spirits included Deng, a spirit of Dinka origin who was seen as a son of Kwoth Nhial, the supreme being, and who revealed itself to a significant number of people whom Evans-Pritchard labelled as prophets. The most famous of these prophets was Ngundeng Bong, who led success- ful military campaigns against the Dinka and northern Sudanese slave traders and who sought to gather up all the life-destructive forces afflicting his land and bury them inside an earthen pyramid. Ngundeng Bong died leading a revolt against the British, who also levelled his pyramid, which they misunderstood to be a symbol of anti-colonial resist- ance. Other Spirits of the Above created during this time included Mahdi and Issa (Arabic for Jesus), who inspired resistance to the northern Sudanese Mahdist state in the waning years of the nineteenth century. The irony of spirits with the names of the final reformer of the Islamic world and of Jesus leading Nuer resistance to an Islamic state is also eloquent testimony to the innovative capacities of 'traditional' religion in a time of crisis.[12]

Since Evans-Pritchard's pioneering work, historians such as Douglas Johnson have written monographs on these Nuer prophets, looking at the ways that religious leaders successfully enabled Nuer communities to meet the challenges of a century of social turmoil following the opening of navigation on the Upper Nile. Sharon Hutchinson's work on the Nuer of the late twentieth century demonstrated the innovative quality of this prophetic tradition as it adapted to a newly hegemonic Christianity on the eve of the second Sudanese civil war in the 1980s.[13]

Similarly, Matthew Schoffeleers's work on the Mbona cult in Malawi and Iris Berger's work on spirit mediums in the interlacustrine region of East Africa demonstrated the existence of important religious movements based on revelatory experience in the pre- colonial era.[14] Other historians using both oral and documentary sources have demon- strated the importance of clan migrations, trade, and the expansion of African states in fostering religious innovations.[15] Oral traditions concerning droughts, famines, and epi- demics demonstrated the close connection between environmental and religious change. Studies of precolonial African religions were conducted through the collection of oral tra- ditions, ethnographic field research (including participant observation), archaeological evidence, and the analysis of the relatively few written sources relevant to these studies.

African Religions and the Atlantic Slave Trade

Beginning with important work by K. O. Dike, David Northrup, and Bernard Belasco, there has been increasing attention to the connections between the Atlantic slave trade and the history of African religions. Their work on Aro-Chukwu in present-day south-eastern Nigeria and its entanglement with the Atlantic slave trade, as well as the involvement of lesser spirit cults among the Yoruba and Igbo peoples, demonstrates the complexity of religious changes directly linked to the enslavement of people in the region. The participation of the Aro-Chukwu oracle itself and the priesthood of other cults profoundly changed the role of the oracles and their priesthoods.[16] John Janzen's work on the history of the Lemba cult in Equatorial Africa and its spread across the Atlantic was one of the first to look at the impact of the slave trade in the development of new spirit cults. It is also one of the first studies of the emergence of a shrine of affliction in its historical context.[17] Judy Rosenthal has studied the ongoing influence of slaves from northern Togo as a special kind of ancestor for the coastal peoples of the south who sold them into the Atlantic slave trade and who then venerated them at various ritual sites.[18]

My own study of precolonial Diola religion in the Casamance region of southern Senegal traces the way in which religious authorities and their spirit shrines regulated participation in the Atlantic slave trade, how they shaped Diola involvement in accordance with their system of thought and religious and political practice, and how, in the process of doing so, they were profoundly changed. The introduction of new shrines was specifically related to the organization of the slave trade and in response to the growing economic inequality of a previously egalitarian society. Spirit shrines of the family cult, of male initiation, of male elders, and of the town council all had their specific rules for the nomination of priests radically changed, thereby transforming the nature of the priesthood itself. Some shrines were replaced by new cults that emphasized wealth as a means to ritual office and charismatic experience was downplayed as a means of access to ritual authority.[19]

More recently, Rosalind Shaw has demonstrated the enduring legacies of memories of the Atlantic slave trade among the Temne of Sierra Leone. Shaw traced attitudes towards witchcraft, divination, the spirit world, and the postcolonial realm of politics back to the terror of centuries of slave raiding and random violence generated by this commerce in human beings.[20]

Religion, Resistance, and Colonization

Since the 1970s, a growing number of historians have turned to the history of indigenous African religions during the era of European colonial rule. At the start of that decade, Terence Ranger and Isaria Kimambo, both associated with the Dar es Salaam historical school, edited an important collection of essays focusing mainly on East and Central Africa, including work on the history of the Mbona cult of Malawi, the Maji Maji rebellion in Tanganyika, and Shona resistance in Southern Rhodesia.[21] Much of Ranger's initial interest concerned the role of indigenous religions in inspiring and organizing what he labelled as 'primary' forms of resistance; that is, rebellions against the initial attempts by colonial powers to establish their authority, levy taxes, demand forced labour, impose cash crops, and mediate disputes between African communities. He noted that a central part of many of these resistance movements was an attempt to forge a multi-ethnic or regional religious identity capable of overcoming long-standing political or ethnic boundaries. This primary resistance, Ranger argued, would be supplanted by more modern, secular, forms of political resistance which would eventually lead to the establishment of independent African states.[22]

Ranger's pioneering work on the role of priests and other ritual officials of the Mwari cult in the Shona revolt of 1896 in Southern Rhodesia inspired a growing interest in the religious element in resistance against colonization, from the 1905–1907 Maji Maji rebellion against the Germans in Tanganyika, to Nongqawuse's revelations of prophecies that led to the so-called Xhosa Cattle Killing of 1856, and the prophetic movement of a Diola woman named Alinesitoué Diatta in southern Senegal during the Second World War.[23] In the case of Maji Maji, the religious leader Kinjikitile went on a shamanic journey to the abode of the regional deity Bokero and returned with knowledge of a special medicine that would protect warriors who used it in their armed revolt against the Germans, inspiring a movement that united many of the peoples of south-eastern Tanganyika. The revolt was suppressed and its prophet was executed, but it served as an inspiration to other forms of nationalist struggle and became a symbol of the new nation of Tanzania.[24] Although the authors of these studies admired the tenacity of resistance inspired by indigenous African religions, there lingered, perhaps from Ranger's own model of political evolution, a sense that this was all a form of 'false consciousness', self-destructive and ultimately futile. Secondary and tertiary forms of political organization, more secular and Westernized, would be necessary in order to free African states from their colonial masters. Yet the central role of spirit mediums (*mhondoro*) in the liberation struggle in Zimbabwe in the 1970s and of warrior rituals in the war for independence in Guinea-Bissau raise serious questions about the separation of these three phases of resistance.[25]

WITCHCRAFT AND HISTORY

In recent decades, the rise of witch-finding movements and understanding African forms of witchcraft have become increasingly important concerns for historians of African religions. African concepts were initially understood in terms of Western ideas of witchcraft, something more analogous to what Evans-Pritchard meant by sorcery or others might determine as the anti-social practice of medicines, oaths, and healing rituals.[26] Within most African belief systems, witchcraft is associated with the nocturnal activities of spiritually powerful individuals, whose souls travel in the night and consume the spiritual essence or parts of other people, their crops, their livestock, or their children. Such activities are crimes for which there is no material evidence, only the evidence of dreams, visions, and divination. Still, local administrators and missionaries were astounded by the proliferation of anti-witchcraft movements at the time of the colonial conquest. Works by Peter Geschiere and Rosalind Shaw have demonstrated how effectively ideas about witchcraft have been useful in explaining many of the more destructive forces and phenomena of the eras of the Atlantic slave trade and the colonial and the postcolonial social world that the peoples of Africa encountered.[27]

Nongqawuse's religious movement linked European expansion in southern Africa directly to the prevalence of witchcraft among the Xhosa people, which contaminated their land, crops, and cattle. In the early 1850s, Xhosa cattle were dying and, as Jeff Peires has shown, the lung sickness which killed them strongly resembled symptoms associated with the attack of witches against humans: a consumption of one's inner vitality and energy ultimately leading to death.[28] In order to rid the Xhosa territories of the pollution associated with witchcraft, Nongqawuse claimed that the ancestors insisted they destroy their cattle and grain, thereby purifying themselves and demonstrating the faith necessary to usher in a new age of peace and prosperity. When the sacrifices were completed the ancestors would return from the dead, leading vast herds of cattle and transporting vast quantities of grain, and the Europeans would disappear from southern Africa. To Nongqawuse, witchcraft was the cause of conquest. Europeans were a scourge in the hands of an angry supreme being and ancestors, and the way to end this threat was through a reaffirmation of one's commitment to a Xhosa community and the abandonment of all the wealth acquired through witchcraft. Only then would a time of peace and harmony ensue. The failure of her prophecies played a major role in the defeat of the Xhosa chiefdoms and the conversion of many Xhosa to Christianity.

In other parts of Africa, witch-finding movements were also central to the response to European conquest. The conquest itself was often seen as clear evidence that there must be active witches in many African communities. Among the Balanta, Diola, Papel, and Manjaco of southern Senegal and Portuguese Guinea, an epidemic of poison ordeals to determine which people in the community were witches and which people were innocent led to the deaths of thousands of people in rural communities throughout the region.[29] The desire to cleanse the community of witches whose activities were linked to the conquest was also true of the interlacustrine region of East Africa and played a role in the Maji Maji rebellion in Tanganyika.

Because most Western Europeans in the early twentieth century did not share African views of the importance of witches, colonial administrations often made it a criminal offence to accuse someone of witchcraft. Many did believe, however, that some Africans practised cannibalism as part of clandestine rituals. I have studied a series of such accusations against members of an alleged cannibal society known as the Kussanga, among the Diola of Senegal. By translating trial transcripts written in French back into the original testimony given in the vernacular, a persistent misunderstanding of two Diola idioms, 'to see in the night' and 'to eat in the night' is apparent. The former term refers to the special ability to see in dreams and to observe events in the dream world; the latter refers to the type of eating done by witches, who consume the spiritual essence of people, their body parts, grain, or other items, as they travel in their dreams. French administrative officials did not understand this meaning of 'eating in the night' or that testimony about people eating other people in the night referred to witches rather than cannibals. The series of trials in the late 1920s, conducted by local French administrators, illustrates the problems of conducting legal procedures when there was no agreement on what was real, as well as the role of interpreters and other local officials in choosing when to alert French officials to the cultural ambiguities generated by very different systems of thought.[30]

Recent work on witchcraft has focused on its ability to explain disruptive powers associated with growing social inequality, the failures of independent governments and development schemes, and the devastating consequences of epidemics such as AIDS in postcolonial societies. Andrew Apter's analysis of the Atinga cult among the Yoruba has shown how unequal economic development among cocoa farmers in colonial Nigeria exacerbated witchcraft accusations within extended families concerned about differential rates of economic success.[31] Birgit Meyer's work on the Ewe people of eastern Ghana demonstrates the importance of witchcraft in explaining illness and misfortune for both Christian and non-Christian communities.[32] James Howard Smith has studied the use of witchcraft as a critique of political corruption and the limitations of economic development in postcolonial Kenya.[33] Adam Ashcroft has demonstrated the continued importance of witchcraft in explaining the persistence of disease and economic equality in post-Apartheid South Africa.[34] All of these studies provide clear evidence of the continuing ability of ideas of witchcraft to explain the challenges confronting African societies in the twentieth and twenty-first centuries.

Gender and Indigenous Religions

The prominence of female deities, priests, and spirit mediums has also generated historical work on changes in gender relations and the position of women in African religious systems. Iris Berger conducted some of the earliest historical work on female spirit mediums in the Abacwezi cults in the interlacustrine region of East Africa. Ifi Amadiume has examined the role of the female deity of wealth, Idemili, among the Igbo of south-eastern Nigeria. She focused on the role of the deity in the support of local commerce and the celebration of female wealth associated with the cult, examining the types of gender fluidity permitted in the cult of Idemili and in Igbo religious systems in general. Finally, she examined the role of British colonialism and Christian missions in suppressing both women's leadership roles and much of the flexibility of an Igbo system of gender relations.[35]

In my own work, I have been studying the history of a prophetic tradition of direct revelation from the Diola supreme being, Emitai, that during the precolonial era was entirely male, but since the colonial conquest has included over forty women prophets.[36] The most famous of these prophets, Alinesitoué Diatta, only taught for two years before being arrested, convicted of the crime of obstructing government initiatives in southern Senegal, and exiled until she died a year later at age 23. During that short time, Diatta introduced a new ritual, *Kasila*, which focused on the sacrifice of a black bull to end droughts and emphasized the importance of community solidarity against the forces of the colonial economy, migrant labour, and growing divisions of the Diola community into Christian, Muslim, and indigenous factions. She also turned her attention to French agricultural policies, arguing that the introduction of new forms of Asian rice (*Oryza sativa*) which offered higher yields but were more susceptible to drought should not lead to the abandoning of those varieties of African rice (*Oryza glaberrima*) which the supreme being had provided and were required for ritual sacrifice and meals. Finally, she prohibited the cultivation of the dominant Senegalese cash crop, groundnuts, which required the cutting down of substantial forest land, diverted men from their important roles in ploughing the rice paddies and maintaining the irrigation systems, and weakened the status of women who were excluded from the benefits of the new crop while being burdened with all responsibilities for cultivating the staple rice. All of these teachings were based on what Diatta claimed were revelations from the supreme being. She has inspired other women to come forward and claim similar powers—women prophets who remain central to the continued vitality of Diola religion.

Conversion to Islam and Christianity

The dramatic growth of Christianity and Islam throughout Africa in the twentieth century and the apparent decline of indigenous religions inspired another area of an emerging religious history focused on the issue of conversion. Guided by evolutionary models of religious change and the sheer numbers of Africans embracing these new world religions, many scholars assumed that indigenous belief systems would cease to exist as independent forces in most of the continent, maintaining only subtle or peripheral influences in most societies. Louis Vincent Thomas, one of France's leading anthropologists of African religions in the twentieth century, predicted in the 1960s that the indigenous religion of the Diola of Senegambia would wither away and that he was witnessing the last generation of circumcision rituals, as Christianity and Islam became virtually universal in the region.[37] Yet these male circumcision rituals continue to be performed today and Diola religion retains a visible and autonomous role in Diola society. Scholars of African Christianity and African Islam saw indigenous African religions as fundamentally rigid and brittle, incapable of adapting to the challenges of colonialism, modernization, and decolonization.

In 1971, however, Robin Horton, a British sociologist based at Port Harcourt in Nigeria, challenged this orthodoxy. Building from his earlier work comparing African traditional thought and Western science, Horton argued that most African religions had a two-tiered structure, a supreme being and lesser spirits. The supreme being was dominant in the 'macrocosm', associated with large-scale phenomena, while the lesser spirits dominated the 'microcosm', focusing on daily life and issues of morality. Horton argued that colonialism shattered the microcosm that dominated most of Africa, forcing Africans into a twentieth-century world dominated by macrocosmic experience. This, in turn, generated a need for a religious tradition more focused on the supreme being and a moral order related to this new realm of social interaction. He suggested that the destabilization of African microcosms was largely responsible for conversion to Christianity and Islam, although he argued that indigenous religions too were capable of making the shift to a macrocosm focused on morality and on a supreme being.[38] This is where he antagonized some critics, such as Humphrey Fisher, who suggested that the idea that African religions could develop a stronger idea of a supreme being by themselves was naive and was a kind of romantic sentimentalism.[39] Horton's other work on south-eastern Nigeria, however, provides clear evidence of waxing and waning influences of particular religious cults and organizations both in relationship to their perceived efficacy and the particular religious needs of the society at large.[40] Despite his emphasis on African religious innovation, however, he accepts the idea that a macrocosmic world demands a macrocosmic supreme being or, put in another way, he conveys a sense that a belief in many deities or lesser spirits has little place in an increasingly global society.

Although it is clear that the colonial occupation of Africa greatly accelerated the spread of Christianity and Islam on the continent, some scholars have focused less on the shattering of the microcosm and its implicit assumption that lesser spirits are marginal to a macrocosmic society and more on the ways in which the dramatic loss of autonomy raised questions about the ability of African religious systems to interpret or explain the significance of the conquest for indigenous adherents.[41] The idea that African societies were far less local and homogeneous than Horton assumed would suggest that they responded to their growing integration into a world economic system and colonial empire in a variety of ways. New cults focused on lesser spirits with special powers emerged to address anxieties generated by colonial conquest, such as growing inequalities of wealth, rising incidence of disease, and the perception of an increase in witchcraft. Population mobility and the development of new African diasporas in the rapidly growing urban centres of colonial empires did not necessarily entail either conversion to an Abrahamic tradition nor an expanding role for a supreme being.

Indeed, African religions have proven quite adept at integrating themselves into the urban context. Monica Hunter (Wilson) and Philip Mayer have studied the spread of Xhosa religion to the townships of South Africa since the Great Depression.[42] Similar studies have documented the thriving role of indigenous religions in the urban centres of southern Ghana and Nigeria.[43] More recent studies have examined the rise of the West African cult of Mami Wata, whose devotees address the complex interplay of the quest for wealth, power, and sexual expression over the last century of colonial and post-colonial developments, often in urban contexts.[44]

RELIGION, LIBERATION, AND THE
POSTCOLONIAL ERA

Although indigenous religious leaders played an important role in the nationalist movements that led to the liberation of African states, no African ruler since independence has identified him or herself publically as a practitioner of an indigenous African religion. In the liberation of Zimbabwe, *mhondoro* spirit mediums, associated with the land, played an important role in disciplining the guerrilla army and reaffirming its sense of purpose.[45] Since independence, Zimbabwe has celebrated their role by naming two major roads after these spirit mediums, but otherwise made little space for indigenous belief in the official religious life of the nation. Indigenous African oathing rituals, binding people to the cause for which they struggled, played an important role in the Mau Mau rebellion in Kenya and in other nationalist movements. In Portuguese Guinea, independence forces sought the blessings of local territorial priests to protect the rebels in the lengthy war against the Portuguese.[46] More than any other African states, Togo and Benin celebrate their traditions of Vaudou as a national heritage and even, to some extent, as an object of tourism. The continuing links between Vaudou and the Yoruba traditions of *orisa* worship on the one hand and their diaspora counterparts in Brazil, Cuba, and more recently in the United States on the other, are celebrated on both sides of the Atlantic.[47] In South Africa and Nigeria, associations of traditional healers have been established in an effort to professionalize this instrumental aspect of African religions. In Senegal, a research institute on Serer divination and healing traditions attracts considerable attention from local government officials and scholars.

Despite their active roles in liberation movements, adherents of African religions have felt marginalized by postcolonial states, as the doors of government offices seemed to be reserved for Christians or Muslims who had attended government or religious schools. In their recent *Worlds of Power*, Gerrie Ter Haar and Stephen Ellis argue that many African leaders, most notably President Mobutu of Zaire, have consulted diviners and healers and practised forms of sorcery, but they do not mention other indigenous religious influences. Ter Haar and Ellis tend to reduce African religions to such negatively regarded practices, ignoring ethical teachings that informed ideas of African Socialism in Tanzania, African Humanism in Zambia, *négritude* in Francophone Africa, and Muntu in South Africa. Furthermore, they rely primarily on the gossip of 'radio trottoir' for evidence of these nefarious practices.[48] In predominantly Muslim or Catholic countries where traditions of naming children reflect their religious adherence, traditionalists feel discriminated against in employment because of their non-Christian or non-Muslim names. In Guinea, Sekou Touré led a campaign of 'demystification' against indigenous practitioners in the coastal areas in the late 1950s and early 1960s, seeking to root out the secret societies known as Poro (for men) and Sande (for women). In South Africa, the Xhosa religious healer (*sangoma*), Nokuzola Mndende, left both the comforts of a university teaching position at the University of Cape Town and the ruling African National Congress because of its insistence that African culture was best represented in post-Apartheid South Africa by African-Initiated Churches that regularly denounced her as a witch.[49]

Similar problems affect indigenous religions in terms of economic assistance in the postcolonial era. Non-governmental organizations affiliated with non-African Christian churches and Islamic foundations funnel aid through local religious organiz-ations for projects ranging from building houses of worship to improving chicken varieties and helping the handicapped acquire wheelchairs. This is compounded by the tendency of many government agencies, both national and foreign, to chan-nel assistance through the same organizations which already have an infrastructure for distribution of local aid. This approach reinforces Christian and Muslim claims to represent modernity and for African religions to be relegated to the past. I remember a bishop in Senegal who likened Christianity to a nice car (Senegalese Catholic priests are encouraged to drive their cars to church even when it is only a short distance away). If you had a car, he argued, it would be foolish to travel by bicycle or on foot (though I remembered some of the treacherous roads and thought foot or bicycle were better for some destinations).

The lesson learnt by local leaders and activists in many areas is that it is easier to mobilize one's followers along religious lines than in regional, ethnic, or racial group-ings; that there is a group waiting to help you mobilize politically or build new devel-opment projects as long as it is associated with international religious organizations. One example was the shift in emphasis from race and ethnicity to religion as the ration-ale for the persecution cited in southern Sudanese information pamphlets during the Second Sudanese Civil War and their far greater success in enlisting the aid of the West in support of their fellow Christians against persecution by a Muslim northern Sudan. Reliance on foreign assistance from Christian and Muslim groups became even more important as the International Monetary Fund imposed structural adjustment pro-grammes on many countries in the 1980s and as the end of the Cold War curtailed the volume of foreign aid to Africa. The Mungiki and other neo-traditionalist movements can be seen, in part, as efforts of people to reassert the importance of indigenous African religions in the life of the nation and of their own ethnic group.[50]

Conclusion

This chapter demonstrates that oral traditions and oral testimonies, along with the consultation of government, missionary, and other written records provide rich materials for the history of indigenous African religions, especially since the nineteenth century. African historians have found rich sources on precolonial religious responses to political, economic, and environmental changes as well as the destabilizing effects of the Atlantic slave trade. The colonial conquest also served as an important catalyst for religious change, not just in terms of conversion to Christianity or Islam, but in generating various types of religious movements of resistance. These included movements which prepared warriors for armed resistance and movements which looked to the corrupting power of witchcraft as an explanation for the European occupation. This history also reveals shifts in gender relations within the leadership of these religious traditions, prophetic movements that challenged the efficacy and morality of colonial and postcolonial agricultural schemes, and the difficult challenges to indigenous religions that persist into the postcolonial era. Finally, environmental shifts, including severe and persistent drought, have been major forces for change in indigenous religions. The history of indigenous religious belief and practice remains an underdeveloped field within African history, but one which may provide profound insights into the history of the peoples of the continent.

Notes

1. G. W. F. Hegel, *Philosophy of History* (New York: Dover, 1958), 91–9. For a broader discussion of the history of representations of Africa, see Valentin Mudimbe, *The Invention of Africa: Gnosis, Philosophy, and the Order of Knowledge* (Bloomington, Ind.: Indiana University Press, 1988).

2. John Mbiti, *African Religions and Philosophy* (Oxford: Heinemann, 1990), 4, 211.

3. See E. E. Evans-Pritchard, *Theories of Primitive Religion* (Oxford: Clarendon Press, 1965), 6–15, 20–1, and *passim*.

4. Jean Girard, *Genèse du pouvoir charismatique en Basse Casamance (Sénégal)* (Dakar: IFAN, 1969).

5. Benjamin Ray, *African Religions: Symbols, Ritual and Community* (Englewood Cliffs, NJ: Prentice Hall, 1976), 11; Edith Sanders, 'The Hamitic Hypothesis: Its Origins and Functions in Time Perspective', *Journal of African History*, 10/4 (1969); Reverend Samuel Johnson, *The History of the Yorubas* (Lagos: CMS Bookshops, 1960 [1921]), 6–7.

6. Timothy Longman, *Christianity and Genocide in Rwanda* (Cambridge: CUP, 2010).

7. Geoffrey Parrinder, *West African Religion* (New York: Barnes & Noble, 1970), 8; Jack Goody, *The Domestication of the Savage Mind* (Cambridge: CUP, 1977); Jan Vansina, *The Children of Woot: A History of the Kuba Peoples* (Madison, Wis.: University of Wisconsin Press, 1978).

8. For a discussion of the limitations of documentary research, see Robert M. Baum, *Shrines of the Slave Trade: Diola Religion and Society in Precolonial Senegambia* (New York: OUP, 1999), 13–17.

9. Baum, *Shrines*, 18–23.

10. Goody, *Domestication*, 12; see too Joseph Miller, 'The Dynamics of Oral Tradition in Africa', in B. Bernardi, C. Poni, and A. Triulzi, eds, *Fonti Orali—Oral Sources—Sources Orales: Anthropologia e Storia—Anthropology and History—Anthropologie et Histoire* (Milan: F. Angeli, 1978), 89–90.

11. Vansina, *Children of Woot*, 197; see too Jan Vansina, 'History of God among the Kuba', *Africa*, 28 (1983), 17.

12. E. E. Evans-Pritchard, *Nuer Religion* (Oxford: OUP, 1956); see too Douglas Johnson, *Nuer Prophets: A History of Prophecy from the Upper Nile in the Nineteenth and Twentieth Centuries* (Oxford: Clarendon Press, 1994).

13. Sharon Hutchinson, *Nuer Dilemmas: Coping with Money, War, and the State* (Berkeley, Calif.: University of California Press, 1996).

14. Matthew Schoffeleers, *River of Blood: The Genesis of a Martyr Cult in Southern Malawi, c. 1600* (Madison, Wis.: University of Wisconsin Press, 1992); Iris Berger, *Religion and Resistance: East African Kingdoms in the Precolonial Period* (Tervuren: Musée Royal de l'Afrique Centrale, 1981); see too David Anderson and Douglas Johnson, eds, *Revealing Prophets: Prophecy in Eastern African History* (London: James Currey, 1995).

15. M. L. Daneel, *The God of the Matopo Hills: An Essay on the Mwari Cult in Rhodesia* (Leiden: Mouton, 1970), 22–35; Jean Allman and John Parker, *Tongnaab: The History of a West African God* (Bloomington, Ind.: Indiana University Press, 2005), 1–71; D. J. E. Maier, *Priests and Power: The Case of the Dente Shrine in Nineteenth Century Ghana* (Bloomington, Ind.: Indiana University Press, 1983).

16. K. Onwuka Dike, *Trade and Politics in the Niger Delta, 1830–1885* (Oxford: Clarendon, 1956); David Northrup, *Trade without Rulers: Pre-Colonial Economic Development in Southeastern Nigeria* (Oxford: Clarendon Press, 1976); Bernard Belasco, *The Entrepreneur as Culture Hero: Preadaptations in Nigerian Economic Development* (New York: J. P. Begin, 1980).

17. A shrine of affliction is a spirit cult whose priests are chosen by virtue of their successful recovery from a particular illness. John Janzen, *Lemba (1650–1930): A Drum of Affliction in Africa and the New World* (New York: Garland, 1982).

18. Judy Rosenthal, *Possession, Ecstasy, and Law in Ewe Voodoo* (Charlottesville, Va.: University Press of Virginia, 1998).

19. Baum, *Shrines,* 108–29.

20. Rosalind Shaw, *Memories of the Slave Trade: Ritual and the Historical Imagination in Sierra Leone* (Chicago: University of Chicago Press, 2002).

21. Terence Ranger and I. Kimambo, eds, *The Historical Study of African Religion* (Berkeley, Calif.: University of California Press, 1972).

22. Terence Ranger, 'Connexions Between "Primary Resistance" Movements and Modern Mass Nationalism in East and Central Africa', *Journal of African History*, 9 (1968).

23. Terence Ranger, *Revolt in Southern Rhodesia, 1896–1897: A Study in African Resistance* (Evanston, Ill.: Northwestern University Press, 1967); J. B. Peires, *The Dead will Arise: Nongqawuse and the Great Xhosa Cattle Killing Movement of 1856–1857* (Bloomington, Ind.: Indiana University Press, 1989); Robert M. Baum, 'Alinesitoué: A West African Woman Prophet', in Nancy Falk and Rita Gross, eds, *Unspoken Worlds: Women's Religious Lives* (Belmont, Calif.: Wadsworth, 2001).

24. James Giblin and Jamie Monson, eds, *Maji Maji: Living the Fog of War* (Leiden: Brill, 2010).

25. David Lan, *Guns and Rain: Guerillas and Spirit Mediums in Zimbabwe* (Berkeley, Calif.: University of California Press, 1985); Eve Crowley, 'Contracts with the Spirits: Religion, Asylum, and Ethnic Identity in the Cacheu Region of Guinea-Bissau', Ph.D. Thesis (Yale University, 1990), 179–80.

26. E. E. Evans-Pritchard, *Witchcraft, Oracles, and Magic among the Azande* (Oxford: Clarendon Press, 1937).

27. Shaw, *Memories*; Peter Geschiere, *The Modernity of Witchcraft: Politics and the Occult in Post-Colonial Africa* (Charlottesville, Va.: University Press of Virginia, 1997).

28. Peires, *The Dead will Arise.*

29. Robert M. Baum, 'Crimes of the Dream World: French Trials of Diola Witches in Colonial Senegal', *International Journal of African Historical Studies*, 37 (2004);

C. Maclaud, 'La Basse Casamance et ses habitants', *Bulletin de la Société de Géographie Commerciale de Paris* (1907).

30. Baum, 'Crimes'.

31. Andrew Apter, 'Atinga Revisited: Witchcraft and the Cocoa Economy, 1950–1951', in Jean Comaroff and John Comaroff, eds, *Modernity and its Malcontents: Ritual and Power in Postcolonial Africa* (Chicago: University of Chicago Press, 1993).

32. Birgit Meyer, *Translating the Devil: Religion and Modernity among the Ewe of Ghana* (Edinburgh: EUP, 1992),188–204.

33. James Howard Smith, *Bewitching Development: Witchcraft and the Reinvention of Development in Neoliberal Kenya* (Chicago: University of Chicago Press, 2008).

34. Adam Ashcroft, *Witchcraft, Violence, and Democracy in South Africa* (Chicago: University of Chicago Press, 2005).

35. Berger, *Religion and Resistance*; Ifi Amadiume, *Male Daughters, Female Husbands: Gender and Sex in an African Society* (London: Zed Books, 1987).

36. Baum, 'Alinesitoué'.

37. Louis Vincent Thomas, *Les Diola: Essai d'analyse fonctionelle sur une population de Basse Casamance* (Dakar: IFAN, 1959).

38. Robin Horton, 'African Conversion', *Africa*, 41 (1971) and 'On the Rationality of Conversion', *Africa*, 45 (1975).

39. Humphrey Fisher, 'Conversion Reconsidered: Some Historical Aspects of Religious Conversion in Black Africa', *Africa*, 43 (1973).

40. Robin Horton, 'A Hundred Years of Change in Kalabari Religion', in John Middleton, ed., *Black Africa: Its Peoples and their Cultures Today* (New York: Macmillan, 1970).

41. Robert M. Baum, 'The Emergence of a Diola Christianity', *Africa*, 60 (1990).

42. Philip Mayer, 'Religion and Social Control in a South African Township', in Heribert Adam, ed., *South Africa: Sociological Perspectives* (London: OUP, 1971); Monica Hunter (Wilson), *Reaction to Conquest* (London: OUP, 1961 [1936]).

43. Meyer, *Translating the Devil*, 175–212.

44. Meyer, *Translating the Devil*, 202–4.

45. Lan, *Guns and Rain*.

46. Donald I. Barnett and Karari Njama, *Mau Mau from within* (New York: Monthly Review Press, 1966).

47. J. Lorand Matory, *Black Atlantic Religion: Tradition, Transnationalism and Matriarchy in the Afro-Brazilian Candomblé* (Princeton: PUP, 2003); Joseph Murphy, *Working the Spirit: Ceremonies of the African Diaspora* (Boston: Beacon, 1994); Emmanuelle Kadya Tall, 'Stratégies locales et relations internationales des chefs de culte au Sud-Bénin', in Laurent Fourchard, André Mary, and René Otayek, eds, *Entreprises religieuses transnationales en Afrique de l'Ouest* (Paris: Karthala, 2005).

48. Stephen Ellis and Gerrie Ter Haar, *Worlds of Power: Religious Thought and Political Practice in Africa* (New York: OUP, 2004).

49. Nokuzola Mndende, *The Pride of Izizikazi: Some Aspects of African Indigenous Religion* (Cape Town: Icamagu Institute, 2000); personal communication, Aug. 2000.

50. Smith, *Bewitching*, 39.

Bibliography

Amadiume, Ifi, *Male Daughters, Female Husbands: Gender and Sex in an African Society* (London: Zed Books, 1987).

Anderson, David, and Douglas Johnson, eds, *Revealing Prophets: Prophecy in Eastern African History* (London: James Currey, 1995).

Baum, Robert M., *Shrines of the Slave Trade: Diola Religion and Society in Precolonial Senegambia* (New York: OUP, 1999).

Berger, Iris, *Religion and Resistance: East African Kingdoms in the Precolonial Period* (Tervuren: Musée Royal de l'Afrique Centrale, 1981).

Evans-Pritchard, E. E., *Nuer Religion* (Oxford: OUP, 1956).

Geschiere, Peter, *The Modernity of Witchcraft: Politics and the Occult in Post-Colonial Africa* (Charlottesville, Va.: University Press of Virginia, 1997).

Goody, Jack, *The Domestication of the Savage Mind* (Cambridge: CUP, 1977).

Horton, Robin, 'On the Rationality of Conversion', *Africa*, 45 (1975).

Janzen, John, *Lemba, 1650–1930: A Drum of Affliction in Africa and the New World* (New York: Garland, 1982).

Johnson, Douglas, *Nuer Prophets: A History of Prophecy from the Upper Nile in the Nineteenth and Twentieth Centuries* (Oxford: Clarendon Press, 1994).

Lan, David, *Guns and Rain: Guerillas and Spirit Mediums in Zimbabwe* (Berkeley, Calif.: University of California Press, 1985).

Meyer, Birgit, *Translating the Devil: Religion and Modernity among the Ewe of Ghana* (Edinburgh: EUP, 1999).

Peires, J. B., *The Dead will Arise: Nongqawuse and the Great Xhosa Cattle Killing Movement of 1856–1857* (Bloomington, Ind.: Indiana University Press, 1989).

Ranger, Terence, and I. Kimambo, eds, *The Historical Study of African Religion* (Berkeley, Calif.: University of California Press, 1972).

Rosenthal, Judy, *Possession, Ecstasy, and Law in Ewe Voodoo* (Charlottesville, Va.: University Press of Virginia, 1998).

Schoffeleers, Matthew, *River of Blood: The Genesis of a Martyr Cult in Southern Malawi, c.1600* (Madison, Wis.: University of Wisconsin Press, 1992).

Shaw, Rosalind, *Memories of the Slave Trade: Ritual and the Historical Imagination in Sierra Leone* (Chicago: University of Chicago Press, 2002).

Smith, James Howard, *Bewitching Development: Witchcraft and the Reinvention of Development in Neoliberal Kenya* (Chicago: University of Chicago Press, 2008).

Vansina, Jan, *The Children of Woot: A History of the Kuba Peoples* (Madison, Wis.: University of Wisconsin Press, 1978).

CHAPTER 16

NEW RELIGIOUS MOVEMENTS

SEAN HANRETTA

The Triumph of 'Religion'

In 1970, Ugandan poet and scholar Okot P'Bitek asserted that Africans were fundamentally 'atheistic in their outlook'.[1] With this polemical claim he meant to draw attention to the way European conceptions of religion failed to describe or translate highly varied African beliefs and practices. P'Bitek believed that African cultures had been deformed by channelling them into the monotheistic and metaphysical strictures of the 'world religions' and he championed a vision of renewal and modernization that rejected the relevance of both Christianity and Islam, calling instead for both policy and art to be founded on the sociological excavation of 'authentic' pre-existing practices.

P'Bitek would likely be disappointed by how both his analysis and his hopes have fared as of the early twenty-first century. 'Religion' seems to be everywhere in contemporary Africa. The category itself provokes little anxiety for those describing or living in an Africa where it has become commonplace to see virtually every facet of life as informed by 'religiosity'. As for the two faiths that so troubled P'Bitek, Christianity and Islam not only dominate public life but indeed underpin normative and creative ways of 'being-in-public' to a degree probably unprecedented in human history.[2]

P'Bitek's radical cultural nationalism was never a majority position, but other analysts of his time might have been equally surprised by the trajectory of contemporary religiosity in Africa. It is a cliché, if largely a justified one, that modernization theorists—which included colonial planners and nationalist leaders as much as academics—imagined that the social relevance of religion would fade with industrialization, scientific education, and either liberal or socialist rationalism. But a different position—one that sees Africans as inherently religious—had long been the shadow assumption of such models. When, for instance, in 1969, H. W. Turner presented as paradoxical the thesis that religion was playing a major role in modernization, he did so with some caution. Hoping that 'the benefits of secularization [could] be secured at the same time as the profoundly religious nature of African life [was] protected against the inroads of a materialistic secularism and reformed within a modern historical world-view', he saw the persistence of 'magical' practices as evidence that the 'task of modernization' had far to go and worried that the failure of modernization might prompt 'escapism into "spiritual" religion'.[3]

Indeed, while official religious neutrality has been the norm for most sub-Saharan African states, it has long been difficult to find proponents of the radical secularization of African societies outside the occasional revolutionary junta or military barracks.[4] However secular they might have been in policy, colonial regimes generally perceived both Christianity and Islam as potentially modern ways of being—in sharp contrast to their treatment of 'traditional' practices—and the structures of rule they set up reflected this. Certainly P'Bitek had good reason to suspect that the category of religion and the apparent conformity of Islam and Christianity to its practical definition served colonial interests. David Chidester, Jean and John Comaroff, and others have shown the deep connections between colonial rule and not just religion but the very idea of religion. J. P. Daughton has shown how even in France's colonies—where it might have been expected that the metropole's political anti-clericalism and the formal separation of church and state would have restricted religious activity—missionaries played a crucial role in practical administration and social transformation.[5] For their part, early independence leaders were typically sanguine (at least in public) about the utility of religion and many openly welcomed religious institutions into the project of governing.[6] Thus, while it has only recently become commonplace to speak of 'religious modernities', it has long been implicit in rhetoric and policy that development in Africa would involve religion; partisans and observers merely argued over the implications for modernization of particular Christian or Muslim orientations or of those beliefs that they called 'traditional', 'historical', or 'local'.

Nonetheless, few predicted the specific changes in spiritual practices and attitudes towards spirituality that have swept across Africa (and beyond) during the last fifty years. These include a great increase in those identified as Christian or Muslim; the loss of control by many of the dominant Muslim and Christian institutions of the early colonial period over religious activity; the creativity with which Africans have transformed and refigured the quotidian practices of inherited or adopted systems; and the centrality of those practices to public debates over nearly every aspect of social life, from legal reforms, to health policies, to geopolitics, and to finance.

Africa's most significant contribution to the ongoing global transformations in faith would seem to rest with the connection between these new religious movements and the quest for modernization. In the nineteenth and twentieth centuries, religiosity had great salience in the US and Europe as a critique or 'great negation' of the modernist projects that seemed to dominate the landscape. By contrast, the near-universal sense—within the continent and without—that to be African is to be perpetually in need of modernity has placed intense pressure on religious institutions to demonstrate their modern-ness. This has meant that both audaciously radical and profoundly reactionary uses of faith have had little leverage.[7] Religious life rather seems to have moved largely in sympathy with most other social dynamics and its recent history thus becomes a kind of displaced commentary on other processes.

It is, to a limited extent, possible to trace some of the developments that produced this situation. Colonial administrators and then independent states were eager to deploy universal categories for analysing and acting on myriad practices, resulting in a tableau of religiosity that was superficially diverse but homogeneous underneath. The decades between the Second World War and the 1970s were what Jonathan Reynolds has called (translating a Hausa expression) a 'time of politics', when the struggles for self-rule, first against imperialism and then to establish independent nations and give them real meaning, saturated most aspects of public life. Subsequent decades saw ideological and political struggles fade out in much the way modernization theorists had predicted that religion would. Religion was thus brought forcefully into public life in the 1950s and 1960s only to have the very idea of a public quickly hollowed out in the 1970s and 1980s. Since then, the rise of the development industry and what James Ferguson has called its 'anti-politics machine', accompanied by the de-ideologizing effects of the end of the Cold War, have made technocratic, instrumental, and idiosyncratic ways of imagining change dominant.[8]

Such forces have, of course, aided and drawn on transnational movements of people, ideas, and capital that have seen Africans play major roles in transforming global cultures even as they adapt and reconfigure those cultures for their own uses. A crucial part of the global economy in the seventeenth and eighteenth centuries, sub-Saharan Africa became in the twentieth century more institutionally connected to the rest of the world; but that mode of integration has remained fundamentally extractive. In this context, Africans persistently made complex and morally charged claims about their membership (or lack thereof) in a global 'imagined community', claims that often explicitly mobilized religious language. In doing so, Africans engaged on a practical and intellectual level with the term 'religion' and its transnational meanings. As the ideology of neoliberalism came to dominate, analysts and actors alike discovered that 'religion' could be treated sociologically and economically as a set of cultural resources, ideological commitments, and identity markers. The conceptual supremacy of 'religion' configured in this way seems secure, at least for the near future.

In the end, however, while it is possible to use this construct to produce meaningful narratives and chronologies for individual 'religious' movements or communities, the weakness of the analytic category becomes clear as soon as one turns to aggregation or generalization. Studies of the newer forms of religiosity on a regional, continental, or global basis—particularly within Christianity—are remarkable for their paucity of dates, meaningful turning points, or multi-directional processes. Studies of Islamic movements have been more likely to posit key points of inflection, such as the 1967 Six-Day War, the Saudi oil boom of the mid-1970s, or the 1979 Iranian Revolution; but viewed from sufficient distance—or proximity—any such periodization is hard to sustain.[9] Furthermore, the gulf between the vocabularies typically used from 1945 until the 1970s to discuss religious changes and those used in the following decades is so vast that few specific continuities in practical evolution can be discerned. Instead one is left with the impression simply of ever-growing, ever-diversifying, and ever-intensifying communities of the faithful, a narrative whose simplicity does little to alleviate suspicions that apparent changes may have as much to do with the terms of analysis as with the phenomena themselves.

THE 'TIME OF POLITICS': NATIONALISM AND POSTCOLONIALITY

Religious movements had been a visible feature of the early twentieth century and they had often produced anxiety among those who held the reins of power (including African elites) for reasons amounting to the opacity of their motivations and their challenge to the rationality of the colonial apparatus. As early as the 1980s, scholars such as Terence Ranger had abandoned earlier efforts to identify such movements as proto-nationalist. Yet the repression that movements such as the Hamawiyya or the Harrists in French West Africa, the Kimbanguists in the Belgian Congo, or the frequent anti-witchcraft movements of the Gold Coast all faced at the hands of the colonial state did give them a retrospective political significance. The fact that unpredictability or inscrutability were not synonymous with anti-colonial resistance was understood by many administrators (perhaps better than by subsequent historians), but for a system in which indiscipline posed an inherent threat, official responses were generally highly repressive. David Robinson's research into the accommodation between officials and African elites has revealed how effective their strategies were in squelching insurgent movements, turning those that survived into conduits for patronage and governance.[10] The colonial era thus saw the processes of religious change and adaptation—long an important dynamic in Africa as elsewhere—become entangled with interests widely perceived as alien, with serious consequences for the popular legitimacy of powerful religious institutions.[11]

Following the Second World War, early nationalist leaders found the mobilizing capacities of insurgent religious movements attractive, while nationalism provided religious leaders with the opportunity to ally themselves with figures or groups that could offer both extrinsic meaning and crucial political protection. Insofar as they presented themselves as vehicles for regaining control of history, self-governance campaigns and nationalist movements were useful both to existing religious elites as a way of shaking the stigma of accommodation and to new actors optimistic that a wide range of social questions might at last be broached.

In the long run, however, independent states proved less effective at containing religious mobilization than had their predecessors and were able to make good on few of their promises of renovation and liberation. However much Africa's many single-party states would have liked to have heavily influenced religious organizations, the overall trend was in the opposite direction. The reasons for this are largely exogenous. Many states lacked serious capacity from the moment of independence while others saw external pressures grow with Cold War politicking. Economic crises in the 1970s and the era of structural adjustment that followed further limited the ability of states to shape popular institutions. It was the 1980s—perhaps the worst decade of the century for many Africans—that saw the most rapid growth of both Pentecostalism and the kind of Islamic reform often called 'Salafism' for its focus on a return to the Islam of the ancestors (the *salaf*). Both movements challenged what they perceived as the routinization of spiritual guidance as well as the legitimacy of older elites' control of institutions and their monopoly on access to religious knowledge and authority.

It is tempting to read much into the timing of these successes. Many scholars have interpreted the apparently new direction in African religiosity as an active response to state dysfunction and hollowness. Beginning in the 1990s, analysts started looking to 'civil society' as the locus of African agency in social change and turned to models of the 'public sphere' derived from the sociologist Jürgen Habermas and to postmodernist theories about new types of communities to explain religious change. Such efforts implicitly or explicitly argue that religious creativity is essentially compensatory or even a progressive alternative to modern forms of sovereignty. Indeed, the shifts in state power that dominated the late 1980s and early 1990s—and which occasioned much of the interest in civil society—saw religious institutions and spokespeople play key roles in pushing for democratization, including Christian leaders in Benin, Gabon, Togo, Zaire (now Democratic Republic of Congo), Kenya, Uganda, Malawi, Madagascar, Zambia, and South Africa, and Muslim ones in Senegal, South Africa, Nigeria, Niger, Mali, and across Anglophone East Africa.[12]

But some caution here is warranted. Most of these developments revealed more about the weakness of state institutions and the paucity of other forms of opposition than they did about the liberating potential of religion. It has been the dysfunctions of many states—their spectacles of power, accumulation, and global connectivity; their corruption; their unpredictability; their personalism and high-stakes competition—rather than the rhetoric or mechanisms of democratically competing civil interest groups that have contributed to the imagery and vocabularies of contemporary religiosity. The 'public sphere' has thus often meant more in the negative, as a way of labelling ineffective governance, than in the positive as a site of any specific new political ethics. Indeed, some cases suggest almost the opposite trajectory. In South Africa, for instance, where the state has had much greater capacity than virtually anywhere else in the continent, Pentecostal and Muslim reformist movements emerged to criticize or even struggle against the state rather than to fill a political vacuum with an alternative structure of authority. Nigeria, which has been the home to much of Africa's religious creativity, is also illustrative. In the 1960s, the first generation of independent political elites found their efforts to build a new nation end in disastrous civil war. But more successful efforts to create Nigerian unity followed in the 1970s and it was at the height of the country's wealth and optimism—which was also the height of hyper-materialism and political spectacle—that most of the now-dominant religious forms began to expand. Nigeria's boom soon foundered on the contradictions of a petro-economy, but the ensuing disillusion (there and elsewhere) proved equally compatible with the new movements.

Ghana's story is nearly Nigeria's in reverse as its recent relative affluence, stability, and 'good governance' have only furthered the successes of religious movements born of earlier austerity.[13]

Thus, insofar as the direct political consequences of new religious movements are concerned, patterns are elusive. Even straightforward efforts to link mainline churches to elites and Pentecostalism or charismatics to subalterns—or vice versa—have not held up to broad empirical scrutiny.[14] The most that can probably be said, then, about the long-term trend in relations between religious and political institutions is that those states that had seen the most effective institutionalization (and bureaucratization) of religious authority in the late colonial and early independence era—such as Senegal and its Sufi orders or the Catholic Church in Rwanda—subsequently saw innovation take place largely within the organization and staffing of these networks. In those states, 'mainline' religious elites have been relatively effective at resisting the institutional forms—if not the devotional content—of both Pentecostalism and 'Salafi' Islam. When for instance the close alignment in Senegal between Muslim *shaykh*s and government ministers weakened during the 1990s, it made a resurgence after 2000, although with more competition among religious leaders for positions of power. In Ethiopia, by contrast, the jarring back-and-forth between a co-opting Italian occupational force and a negligent Ethiopian Orthodox state left the networks by which Muslim elites could interact with state power highly personalized and fragmented. As a result, insurgent 'Salafi' preachers have experienced unchecked success in certain communities. Elsewhere, interactions between spiritual figures and the state have often been powerful, but also typically fluid, fragile, and highly personal, exemplified by such phenomena as Gambian president Yahya Jammeh's claim to cure AIDS and asthma via Qur'an-inspired remedies or the brokers of *sorcellerie* and *fétichisme* in Central Africa. The most distinctive discontinuities during the last half of the twentieth century were thus in the content, experience, and discourse of religiosity rather than in its political influence.[15] One recent exception has been the radical Islamic movements that have directly confronted (or replaced) governmental authorities in Somalia, Nigeria, Mali, and elsewhere. Sometimes continuous with older conflicts over reform, more often simply borrowing some of their vocabularies, such groups have mobilized around (and drawn material sustenance from) geopolitical struggles and the perceived or actual failings of neoliberal states. The role of Libya—and particularly of the collapse of the Qaddafi regime—in some of these events remains an intriguing open question.

SOCIAL CHANGE AND PERSONAL FAITH

The content of much contemporary religious language and experience draws attention to its own professed newness. As the insightful work of J. D. Y. Peel has revealed, missionary conceptions of conversion had widespread influence on narratives of religious change, shaping them in self-consciously ahistorical terms and deliberately positing a rupture with both past social norms and older expressions of Christianity or Islam.[16] At the same time, converts engaged critically with what they thought of as traditional African cultures in ways that ranged from cautious reappropriation to outright condemnation. The evangelical or holiness Protestantism of missionaries of the late nineteenth and early twentieth centuries had emphasized a short, explosive experience of conversion as the central objective of Christian life and made this the vehicle by which the experience of the divine was linked to projects of social transformation. More recently, enthusiasm for religious discontinuity has become entangled with the aspiration for radical social transformation embedded in the rhetoric of Africa's perpetual underdevelopment and deferred modernity.

African theology in all religious traditions has come to centre on the same questions of poverty, moral weakness, and the relationship between cultural heritage and ethical behaviour as have haunted the technocrats of the developmentalist state. Pioneering work by Birgit Meyer on changing conceptions of evil has revealed much about this theological shift. The rise of affluence or prosperity churches from the 1980s onwards built directly on older ideas about radical rupture, but shifted the target of transformation more towards personal suffering and the individual experience of evil. In this respect, Pentecostalism has been the most ambitious. Its major breaks with evangelicalism over 'dispensations' (the temporality of god's relations with humans, particularly the issue of whether miracles still occur or are confined to the distant past) and over faith healing and worldly affluence (themselves largely the result of the different attitude towards dispensation) have served to liberalize access to Christianity's perceived transformative spiritual power and to pluralize the paths to personal breaks with the present. New Christian and Islamic movements share with both the socialist and, especially, neo-liberal projects a rhetorical commitment to total social reinvention. But by crafting personal techniques for attacking the 'evil' of what are perceived as traditional beliefs and practices, and by linking these traditions to underdevelopment, new movements have seized the mantle of modernization and economic rationality.[17]

The insistence by these movements on discontinuity—through the process of being 'born again' or of returning to a true Islam stripped of innovations—as the critical prerequisite for spiritual actualization has also influenced growing debates about the nature of secularism. Such debates are especially pronounced in Francophone countries where the official commitment to laïcité on the part of newly independent states made secularism one of the stakes of postcolonial ambitions. The failures of those states and their simultaneous commitment to social management—whether in the language of nationalism, heritage, or revolution—turned secularism into one of the social evils that religions strove to overcome. This position in turn has been compatible with the rhetoric in which African societies are depicted as being in permanent crisis, beset by corruption, and in need of redemption.[18]

In all this, the instrument of social transformation has clearly remained the spiritualized self, a focus of contemplation and engagement that is often difficult to distinguish from a broader technology of self-mastery and self-discipline. Post-Second World War socio-economic transformations accelerated and deepened this tendency as the self-in-society (sometimes expressed as a distinctive religious 'worldview') became a dominant figure of debate, inspection, and the exercise of power. As Achille Mbembe has pointed out, this has provided the moralistic mirror image of the amoral technocracies of nation-building, structural adjustment, and neo-liberal development.[19]

Muslims have been more resistant—but not immune—to the prosperity trope, and have generally exhibited greater confidence in the state as an effective tool for enabling pious behaviour, whether through shari`a courts in Nigeria, institutionalizing Muslim family law in Mali and Niger, or struggling over public heritage in South Africa.[20] Rather than reflecting hoary Orientalist models of Islam's inherent propensity to fuse religion and state, these dynamics seem to suggest relatively less atomization and personalization of the goals of spiritual fulfilment than among Christians. But, as a new type of anthropology of Islam exemplified by the work of Benjamin F. Soares has shown, Muslim piety has itself seen the emergence of new ways of imagining the search for ethical self-improvement and new consociational institutions to facilitate those quests.[21]

Studies of Islam in Africa and elsewhere have often grappled with the apparent rise of 'militancy' or 'Islamism', but such labels often confuse a variety of reform efforts and a diversity of political and social movements. Popular understandings of African Islam as a 'tolerant', 'Sufi' form of Islam counterpoised to Salafism as a Middle Eastern, 'fundamentalist' form bolstered by globalization and oil revenue misapprehend highly complex long-term processes and the intricate interplay of local and transnational forces. In the 1970s and 1980s, expanding resources for Islamic education and training outside of sub-Saharan Africa combined with local crises in reproducing institutions of religious authority to produce a series of conflicts over practice and doctrine. Many of these drew on very old debates but with new, regionally specific institutional implications. By the late 1990s most of these conflicts had dwindled considerably in the face of several developments: generational and ethnic disputes over institutions were resolved; states moved to exercise greater control over 'national' religious organizations; democratization channelled reform efforts into campaigns for new legislation; and popular fatigue with conflicts forced community leaders into rapprochement.

What had made these conflicts meaningful was an underlying shift in the way religion and daily life intersect and this has left its marks. Older Sufi orders have seen the emergence of more individual, free-floating ties between disciple and master, capturing some of the independence of personal judgement enabled by the expansion of Arabic literacy and the weakening of ascriptive ties to religious communities. Most dramatically, religious modernizers have themselves shifted their attention to development work. Individual *shaykh*s often sponsor the building of schools and clinics and the digging of wells, while more organized *da`wa* missions—outreach groups whose preaching aims to inform and reform—have structures and goals very similar to those of development NGOs. *Da`wa* movements have been a major feature of the social landscape ever since the increase in intra-Islamic competition that began after the 1979 Iranian Revolution.[22]

The idea that religion is about bringing techniques of control and transformation to bear upon the self as a way to become modern and free of various kinds of evil has had a substantial impact on religious education. Following the ground-breaking work of Louis Brenner, scholars such as Roman Loimeier have shown how Islamic schools began, after 1945, to internalize both the rationalistic pedagogies of European schools and their education-for-development goals, resulting in massive changes in the practical meaning of 'being Muslim' for most people and providing a compelling alternative to state schools for many. Among Christians, missionary education had been such a hallmark of the colonial era that one of the main ways that independent states sought to demonstrate their capacity and legitimacy was through the secularization and nationalization of schools. Yet here too independent schools quickly took advantage of unmet demand, while the limited restrictions that postcolonial governments were able to impose on faith-based schools in the 1990s and 2000s (such as 'teaching without preaching') actually furthered the image of evangelical Christianity and reformist Islam as legitimate alternative forms of developmentalist modernity. Even in Côte d'Ivoire, where de-missionization was highly limited, state-church corporatism has given way to increasing privatization and entrepreneurialism.[23]

The numerous formal syntheses of religious and secular education that have emerged since 1945 highlight one important gap: the difficulty practitioners of so-called traditional religions have faced in asserting their commitment to modernity. The classic theory, according to which indigenous religions declined in response to objective material and social changes—as a result, for instance, of the transition from a society based on personal relationships and personalized power to one based on institutions and bureaucratic rationalism—is unconvincing once we recognize how trans-local, complex, and mediated the institutions were that supported many African religions.[24] A more likely cause of the reduced public visibility of such religions is the relatively lower access their practitioners have to the symbols and circuits of modernizing institutions. But while some practices have actually declined, others have merely been channelled in directions that have tended to obscure their importance, while others still have grown and diversified. Since 1945, for instance, anthropologists have reported the growth and spread of several forms of spirit possession, practices that had been socially marginal in the colonial period but which have been moving to the centre of many communities' systems for conflict resolution and are being taken up by individuals seeking to improve their lives. Part of a transnational growth in the belief in active spirits, this process seems even to be taking place in some Muslim communities, such as in Kano in northern Nigeria where techniques of possession and exorcism previously restricted to stigmatized *bori* practitioners have made their way into the toolkits of *bori*'s powerful reformist enemies.[25]

Some areas where religion had been tightly integrated into powerful precolonial states—Yoruba city-states and Asante—saw 'traditional' religion become highly fused with the rituals and claims to authority of colonial intermediaries, particularly in zones of British indirect rule. This may have allowed institutionalized alternatives to Islam and Christianity to persist as socially respectable ways of being in public. Adherents of these religions often simultaneously commit themselves to a world religion, but more important is the fact that 'traditional' practices and world religions have all taken part in the same turn to instrumentalism, personalization of power, and spiritualization. In areas where spiritual authority had been less centralized, as in much of Central Africa, or more fully overrun by Christianity, such as in Buganda, it has circulated and blended into the vague categories of 'witchcraft' or 'sorcery', operating either as an antisocial technique for advancement or its antithesis in anti-witchcraft movements. In these areas there has thus been more room for entrepreneurialism and eclectic borrowing from the global diffusion of spiritual techniques, although as the Nigerian exorcism case suggests, this is not unknown even in areas with very hierarchical, powerful, and conservative religious institutions.

Often it is impossible to separate out such movements from innovations within Islamic or, particularly, Christian practice. The Brotherhood of the Cross and Star in Nigeria illustrates this complexity. Emerging in the 1950s, the movement drew on terminology and symbolism from both Protestantism and a wide variety of local and transnational spiritualities, while explicitly attacking 'traditional' forms of social authority including polygyny and cultural preservation groups. More extreme is the case of Alice Lakwena, whose anti-witchcraft healing movement in Uganda was driven by a global array of spirits including an Italian officer, various Acholi *jok* spirits, and the Holy Spirit; linking personal suffering directly to national politics, Lakwena's movement quickly evolved into an armed insurrection, setting the stage for Joseph Kony's Lord's Resistance Army.[26]

Lakwena's case highlights the major linkage between changing gender and age norms and religious change during the twentieth century. Born Alice Auma, this young female medium channelled male and female spiritual entities—something with strong precedents in Acholi possession techniques—while also tapping into the freedom from clan affiliations that non-local *jok* spirits provided. Nonetheless, gender ambiguity and spiritual inventiveness quickly collapsed under the pressures of military mobilization; young men took over roles previously played by elders, even as women's conspicuous place among the causalities of war was glossed as a reflection of 'modernity'.[27] Movements among Christians and Muslims alike have seen women play important leadership roles during early insurgent phases only to find their options narrow as institutionalization proceeds. But key changes have also taken place within established or newly majoritarian denominations. Membership in Pentecostal, Charismatic, and Independent churches skews heavily towards young women and women increasingly play important leadership roles within them—though usually not at the very top levels. Women's influence in these churches and in Islamic reformist circles range from drawing attention to the use of spiritual power to remedy infertility or resolve marital disputes, to harnessing religious authority to reform social and legal institutions, to challenging deep assumptions about women's bodies and ritual purity.[28] The centrality of the body to many spiritual traditions has made religion equally useful for those hostile to broader social changes in gender norms; but the key lines of debate are typically over what constitutes proper, ethical modern gender relations rather than the wholesale rejection of transformation. Far more complex than simply a matter of measuring the effects of a particular set of theological positions on women or men's identities, dialogue between the gender norms dramatized in religious texts and those prevalent in the communities using those texts has in some areas resulted in considerable diversifications of publicly and privately defensible roles grounded in local terms.[29] Even for those who find themselves beyond the limits of their coreligionists' tolerance—such as the `yan daudu, 'feminine men', in northern Nigeria where the personalization of religious morality and its perceived significance for social well-being have diminished acceptance of 'alternative' gender identities or sexualities—religious vocabularies and logics remain personally compelling and useful.[30]

Rapid social change in other domains has had an equally ambiguous relationship with religious change. Many movements that cannot easily be labelled as either religious or social have mobilized Islamic or Christian ideas and practices to offer more-or-less liberal critiques of racial inequality, slavery, colonialism, and so on. But it is with regard to those issues where liberalization has been least successful that the patterns are most revealing. The failures of malaria eradication efforts in the 1970s, the explosion of the HIV/AIDS crisis in the 1980s, intensifying struggles over the environment (both its destruction and conservation), and the violence of late decolonization in southern Africa, and of the civil and regional wars that became pandemic after 1989 have all given a very literal edge to the long-noted healing orientation of African religions.[31] Religious pluralism has been seen by many as a deep structural property of many African societies, reflecting pragmatic accommodation to the decentralization of legitimate authority in communities and the role of extended kin groups in managing therapies. Studies of religious healing over the *longue durée*, such as those by Steven Feierman, Jan Janzen, and Neil Kodesh, have highlighted the rapid transformations that took place during times of extreme social stress, such as with the onset of colonial rule. The depths of the crises of the last four decades, their suddenness, and their defiance of the rhetoric of modernization and development have brought an extreme kind of eclecticism. Phenomena such as President Jammeh's Quranic healing, the rise of fertility and healing churches in the urban areas of the Democratic Republic of Congo, the transformations wrought on spirit mediumship by Zimbabwean guerrillas, or the flocking of AIDS pilgrims to the prophet Chisupe in Malawi reflect instead an unfettered experimentalism that, while perhaps facilitated by pluralism, expresses the breakdown of social units rather than their synthesis.[32] While one can hear in this cacophony the uniting theme of a shared, cosmopolitan spiritual malevolence—a translated devil, portable and polyvalent and serving as a kind of universal currency—part of the important work performed by the apparently metaphysical 'Satan' (as opposed to the merely fickle spirit) derives from its ability to circulate between various different scales.[33] But which scales are these, exactly?

AFRICA AND THE WORLD

African religious practices have been part of global and 'cosmopolitan fields of migration, commerce, and communication' for centuries,[34] but the period since 1945 has seen profound shifts in these global connections. Communication technologies have helped detach contemporary religious transnationalism from large-scale popu-lation movements and the legacies of political imperialism. To be sure, the post-Second World War era has seen a renewed flow of African labour out of the continent and this has in many cases contributed to new forms of interaction. These have been as diverse as the growing influence of the Senegalese Muridiyya Sufi order in North America, the accumulation of social and spiritual capital by Muslim scholars who train in the Middle East and then return home, and the struggles of African Initiated Churches in Israel.[35] Migration into Africa, largely from South and East Asia, as well as international Africa–Asia cooperation efforts, have themselves promoted the growth of visible—if still tiny—urban followings for Baha'ism, Shi`ism, Buddhism, and Krishna Consciousness among Africans, alongside the religions of immigrant enclaves.

But whereas the patterns of religious globalization from the 1600s until the mid-1900s piggy-backed on and were circumscribed by such population diasporas and imperial connections, even when driven by individual cultural entrepreneurs or cosmopolitan practitioners, more recent currents tend to take the form of semiotic and discursive movements rather than social ones and are thus even more eclec-tic. It is perhaps Rastafarianism—born of Jamaican images of Ethiopia and then embraced and refashioned from Dakar to Cape Town—that best sums up the free-floating, polysemic nature of Africa's place in a field of sharing and comparison in which race and place articulate in complex ways.[36] Migration to and from South Asia may not, for example, have resulted in the rapid growth of Hinduism in Africa, but the carrier wave of Bollywood has touched many corners, such as with the controversial incorporation of Indian film music into Hausa-language devotional songs in Kano.[37]

The most famous way African religion has entered the global stage has been through the 'southerning' of Christianity, an overall shift in the centre of gravity of this world religion away from Europe and North America. In 1900, Africa, Asia, and Latin America accounted for around 17 per cent of census-identified Christians worldwide. In 1970, that portion had leapt to 42 per cent and by 2010 the estimate was around 60 per cent. In 1945, Africa alone accounted for about 8 per cent of the world's Christian population; in 2010 that figure was around 20 per cent.[38] As a result, forms of Christian piety and institutional politics developed or fostered in Africa have come to have pro-found—though hardly uncontested—consequences for practitioners and institutions outside Africa. Sudden worldwide significance has given Africa-oriented theologians great confidence and an ambitious agenda. Islam has not seen such a decisive shift—the demographic centres of the faith remain, as they have for centuries, in South and South-East Asia, while the authority of the Hijaz centres of Mecca and Medina has been bolstered by the increasing number of pilgrims to Saudi Arabia. The efforts of African Muslims have, however, given greater visibility to issues such as racism and poverty within the global *umma*.

Beyond sheer numbers, the rhetorical and interpretive repertoires of many religious actors have become deterritorialized. Globe-trotting evangelists such as Reinhard Bonnke, a massive international trade in pamphlets, and newer media such as Warner Bros./Campus Crusade's *Jesus* film (1979)—with its textualism, historical positivism, and narrative unity—helped forge fundamentalist Protestant scriptural techniques into a template for wider spiritual and cultural discourses.[39] Among Muslims, Ahmed Deedat's itinerant polemics and the techniques of the Wahubiri wa Kislamu of Kenya and Tanzania have adapted styles of textual criticism and argumentation from sources as wide-ranging as evangelical apologists and the India-born Ahmadiyya movement.[40] In the US, where the influence of Muslims in the early-modern diaspora had been stronger than in other parts of the new world,[41] organizations such as the Sankore' and Zaytuna Institutes have in recent years turned explicitly to West and East Africa for models of pedagogy, legal interpretation, ritual practice, and proselytism, mostly among African American Muslims. In doing so they have provided an alternative to both immigrant-dominated Middle Eastern or South Asian practices and idiosyncratic forms such as the Nation of Islam. While 'globalization' might be thought to favour the so-called world religions, the long-standing transoceanic development of religions linked to the Kongo, Fon, and Yoruba areas that contributed heavily to diaspora cultures has continued apace.[42] Meanwhile, subsidized air travel has enabled Hausa women to bring 'non-Islamic' healing goods and services (long popular in North Africa) right to Mecca.[43]

The international development industry has long been intertwined with religious proselytizing. Saudi Arabia, Libya, and Iran have all directed funding towards mosques, educational institutions, public health centres, basic infrastructure, and development-oriented NGOs as part of a multi-pronged project of social and spiritual transformation that has both required and enabled them to act as privileged voices in defining Islamic practice. Christian missionaries have benefited equally from the shift from national and international aid organizations to NGOs.[44]

But the socio-economic effects of global neo-liberalism provide more than context for these new movements. If the failures of development discourses have facilitated the rise of new modes of religiosity, it is primarily because such failures have paradoxically increased the purchase on people's daily lives of developmental thinking and the technocratic, rationalist epistemologies that underwrite it. The more thoroughly developmentalism intertwines with religiosity the more self-consciously global and globalizing religion becomes as the comparison with the 'developed world' becomes a constitutive spiritual fact. Religion is thus more and more explicitly *about* global modernity. Among Muslims, for instance, transnational ties—whether through charitable giving, the Organization of the Islamic Conference, or the use of book, media, and internet networks for circulating 'Islamic' norms—have become crucial markers of modernity. As they actively appropriate free-floating technologies and techniques, many African practitioners stage commentaries on what it means to be part of a global community of competing, communicating world religions. This sense of global membership can intensify polarization when participants generate 'radically different readings of global politics',[45] resulting in many fraught local rivalries with bidirectional links to national and geopolitical struggles.

Yet this type of politics does not match up easily with conventional ideological orientation. Novel or non-conforming Christian lines may have the comparative advantage of being unsullied by visible links to imperialism but this has not usually resulted in the development of active anti-imperialist movements. Muslim reformists may have greater claim to anti-imperial credibility, but their readings of the global order typically present that imperialism as something other than classical political control over territory. Their focus is rather on forms of oppression and on threats to the freedom of Muslims to practise their religion fully, freely, and as an empowered community. Similarly, religious identity can provide a form of grounding that allows labour migrants to move through complex transnational spaces while actively rejecting cosmopolitan values. Nor does technological mediation necessarily erode parochialism, such as with West Africa's own home-grown industry of 'Jesus films' that are less interested in meta-commentary on global proselytization than in simply rendering existing belief visible.[46]

In light of this, the more prosaic links between globalization and new religious movements cry out for more research. It would be useful to know, for instance, whether the retreat from capital controls after 1971 greatly facilitated the emergence of transnational Pentecostalism and Islamic reform in purely institutional ways; whether spasms of media diversification and consolidation had shaping effects on the technological mediation of spirituality; and to what extent labour struggles, as opposed to labour flows, have affected these processes. It is striking, for instance, that despite some rhetoric about Islamic syndicalism (*niqâbiyya islâmiyya*), connections between Islam and concrete labour movements are elusive. Even in the movements of the so-called Arab Spring in, say, Egypt and Tunisia, the relation has been more one of cautious alliance than fusion. Genuine Islamic social movements are thus largely restricted to the highly abstract sphere of Islamic finance or the very local domain of Muslim Brotherhood-style social welfare and small business development.[47]

Such research would supplement the great insights that have come from investigation into meanings and styles and help generate more complex chronologies and a clearer sense of the tensions within the convergence of neo-liberalism and religious expression. Current approaches tend towards a methodological individualism that emphasizes African agency at the expense of tracing the implications of accumulated decisions or real structural constraints on activity. In the end, face-to-face social dynamics such as generational struggle and household organization, alongside changing literacy rates, nationalist sentiments, patterns of state formation and governance, and responses to changing macroeconomic conditions, provide much of the context within which Africans have understood and used global networks and spaces, even as those social dynamics themselves reflect processes on the world scale. The case of the Ahmadiyya in Ghana can stand as a final example. South Asians created the movement in the 1890s and established its beachheads in West Africa in the 1920s. But whatever kinds of cosmopolitanism its transnationalism is generating or may generate in the future, its local purchase was provided by community competition over the authority to define

Muslim-ness and by the techniques of British indirect rule.[48] The legacy of the early and mid-twentieth century thus remains powerful even in the face of over thirty years of assault on states and societies alike.

NOTES

1. Okot P'Bitek, *African Religions in Western Scholarship* (Kampala: East African Literature Bureau, 1971), 100.
2. Stephen Ellis and Gerrie ter Haar, *Worlds of Power: Religious Thought and Political Practice in Africa* (London: Hurst, 2004); Terence O. Ranger, 'Scotland Yard in the Bush: Medicine Murders, Child Witches and the Construction of the Occult', *Africa*, 77/2 (2007).
3. James Beckford, 'The Restoration of "Power" to the Sociology of Religion', *Sociological Analysis*, 44 (1983); H. W. Turner, 'The Place of Independent Religious Movements in the Modernization of Africa', *Journal of Religion in Africa*, 2/1 (1969), 61–2. Cf. William J. Samarin, 'Religion and Modernization in Africa', *Anthropological Quarterly*, 39/4 (1966).
4. Key exceptions include Ethiopia from 1974 to 1978, while in Mozambique from 1975 to 1982 something like P'Bitek's project was put into action, though even the FRELIMO government eventually came to rely on the churches.
5. David Chidester, *Savage Systems: Colonialism and Comparative Religion in Southern Africa* (Charlottesville, Va.: University Press of Virginia, 1996); Tomoko Masuzawa, *The Invention of World Religions* (Chicago: University Press of Chicago, 2005); Jean Comaroff and John L. Comaroff, *Of Revelation and Revolution*, 2 vols (Chicago: University of Chicago Press, 1991 and 1997); J. P. Daughton, *An Empire Divided: Religion, Republicanism, and the Making of French Colonialism, 1880–1914* (Oxford: OUP, 2006).
6. David Westerlund, 'Christianity and Socialism in Tanzania, 1967–1977', *Journal of Religion in Africa*, 11/1 (1980); John S. Pobee, *Kwame Nkrumah and the Church in Ghana, 1949–1966* (Accra: Asempa, 1988); Marie Miran, 'The Political Economy of Civil Islam in Côte d'Ivoire', in H. Weiss and M. Bröening, eds, *Politischer Islam in Westafrika: Eine Bestandsaufnahme* (Berlin: Lit, 2006).
7. James Ferguson, *Expectations of Modernity: Myths and Meanings of Urban Life on the Zambian Copperbelt* (Berkeley, Calif.: University of California Press, 1999); Marie Miran, *Islam, histoire et modernité en Côte d'Ivoire* (Paris: Karthala, 2006).
8. Jonathan T. Reynolds, *The Time of Politics (Zamanin Siyasa): Islam and the Politics of Legitimacy in Northern Nigeria, 1950–1966* (San Francisco: International Scholars Publications, 1999); James Ferguson, *The Anti-Politics Machine: 'Development', Depoliticization, and Bureaucratic Power in Lesotho* (Cambridge: CUP, 1990).
9. See, for instance, the long perspectives provided by Nehemia Levtzion and John O. Voll, eds, *Eighteenth-Century Renewal and Reform in Islam* (Syracuse, NY: Syracuse University Press, 1987); Roman Loimeier, 'Patterns and Peculiarities of Islamic Reform in Africa', *Journal of Religion in Africa*, 33/3 (2003).
10. Terence O. Ranger, 'Religious Movements and Politics in Sub-Saharan Africa', *African Studies Review*, 29/2 (1986); Sean Hanretta, *Islam and Social Change in French West Africa: History of An Emancipatory Community* (Cambridge: CUP, 2009); René Bureau, *Le Prophète de la lagune: Les Harristes de Côte d'Ivoire* (Paris: Karthala, 1996). Compare the argument made about indiscipline by Achille Mbembe, 'Domaines de la Nuit et Autorité Onirique dans les Maquis du Sud-Cameroun (1955–1958)', *Journal of African History*, 32/1 (1991), with that on accommodation in David Robinson, *Paths of Accommodation: Muslim*

Societies and French Colonial Authorities in Senegal and Mauritania, 1880–1920 (Athens, O.: Ohio University Press, 2000).

11. See, for e.g. Cynthia Hoehler-Fatton, *Women of Fire and Spirit: History, Faith, and Gender in Roho Religion in Western Kenya* (Oxford: OUP, 1996); Louis Brenner, *Controlling Knowledge: Religion, Power and Schooling in a West African Muslim Society* (Bloomington, Ind.: Indiana University Press, 2001); Norman Etherington, 'Recent Trends in the Historiography of Christianity in Southern Africa', *Journal of Southern African Studies*, 22 (1996).

12. On these, see Leonardo Villalón and Ousmane Kane, 'Senegal: The Crisis of Democracy and the Emergence of an Islamic Opposition', in Villalón and Phillip Huxtable, eds, *The African State at a Critical Juncture: Between Disintegration and Reconfiguration* (Boulder, Colo.: Lynn Rienner, 1998); Holger Bernt Hansen and Michael Twaddle, eds, *Religion and Politics in East Africa: The Period Since Independence* (London: James Currey, 1995); Paul Gifford, *The Christian Churches and the Democratization of Africa* (Leiden: Brill, 1995); Terence O. Ranger, ed., *Evangelical Christianity and Democracy in Africa* (Oxford: OUP, 2008).

13. Daniel Magaziner, *The Law and the Prophets: Black Consciousness in South Africa, 1968–1977* (Athens, O.: Ohio University Press, 2010); Andrew Apter, *The Pan-African Nation: Oil and the Spectacle of Culture in Nigeria* (Chicago: University of Chicago Press, 2005); Ruth Marshall, *Political Spiritualities: The Pentecostal Revolution in Nigeria* (Chicago: University of Chicago Press, 2009).

14. Paul Gifford, *African Christianity: Its Public Role* (Bloomington, Ind.: Indiana University Press, 1998), 47–8.

15. Rebecca Cassidy and Melissa Leach, 'Science, Politics, and the Presidential Aids "Cure"', *African Affairs*, 108/433 (2009); Filip De Boeck 'Le "Deuxième monde" et les "enfants-sorciers" en République Démocratique du Congo', *Politique africaine*, 80 (2000); Florence Bernault, 'De la modernité comme impuissance: Fétichisme et crise du politique en Afrique équatoriale et ailleurs', *Cahiers d'études africaines*, 49/3/195 (2009); Leonardo Villalón, 'Sufi Modernities in Contemporary Senegal: Religious Dynamics between the Local and the Global', in Martin van Bruinessen and Julia Day Howell, eds, *Sufism and the 'Modern' in Islam* (London: I. B. Tauris, 2007); Terje Østebø, *Localising Salafism: Religious Change among Oromo Muslims in Bale, Ethiopia* (Leiden: Brill, 2011).

16. J. D. Y. Peel, 'For Who Hath Despised the Day of Small Things? Missionary Narratives and Historical Anthropology', *Comparative Studies in Society and History*, 37/3 (1995).

17. Birgit Meyer, *Translating the Devil: Religion and Modernity among the Ewe in Ghana* (Edinburgh: EUP, 1999); Marshall, *Political Spiritualities*; David Maxwell, *African Gifts of the Spirit: Pentecostalism and the Rise of a Zimbabwean Transnational Religious Movement* (Oxford: James Currey, 2006); Benjamin F. Soares, 'Islam in Mali in the Neoliberal Era', *African Affairs*, 105 (2006). On theology, see Kofi Appiah-Kubi and Sergio Torres, eds, *African Theology en Route: Papers from the Pan-African Conference of Third-World Theologians, December 17–23, 1977, Accra, Ghana* (Maryknoll: Orbis Books, 1979); V. Y. Mudimbe, *Tales of Faith: Religion As Political Performance in Central Africa* (London: Athlone Press, 1997).

18. Marshall, *Political Spiritualities*; Hervé Maupeu, 'Mungiki et les elections: Les Mutations politiques d'un prophétisme kikuyu (Kenya)', *Politique africaine*, 87 (2002).

19. Gayatri Spivak and Achille Mbembe, 'Religion, Politics, Theology', *boundary* 2, 34/2 (2007), 154.

20. See, for e.g. Abdulkader Tayob, 'Muslim Public Claiming Heritage in Post-Apartheid Cape Town', *Journal for Islamic Studies* (Cape Town), 24/25 (2005).

21. Benjamin F. Soares, *Islam and the Prayer Economy: History and Authority in a Malian Town* (Edinburgh: EUP, 2005).

22. For the previous two paragraphs, see Soares, *Islam and the Prayer Economy*; Benjamin F. Soares, 'Saint and Sufi in Contemporary Mali', in van Bruinessen and Howell, *Sufism*; Dorothea Schulz, 'Piety's Manifold Embodiments: Muslim Women's Quest for Moral Renewal in Urban Mali', *Journal for Islamic Studies* (Cape Town), 28 (2008); Miran, *Islam en Côte d'Ivoire*.

23. Brenner, *Controlling Knowledge*; Roman Loimeier, *Between Social Skills and Marketable Skills: The Politics of Islamic Education in 20th Century Zanzibar* (Leiden: Brill, 2009); Amy Stambach, *Faith in Schools: Religion, Education, and American Evangelicals in East Africa* (Stanford, Calif.: Stanford University Press, 2010); Eric Lanoue, '"Le Temps des missionnaires n'est plus!": Le devenir postcolonial de l'enseignement catholique en Côte-d'Ivoire (1958–2000)', *Cahiers d'études africaines*, 43/ 169/170 (2003).

24. Jean Allman and John Parker, *Tongnaab: The History of a West African God* (Bloomington, Ind.: Indiana University Press, 2005); J. Lorand Matory, *Sex and the Empire that is No More* (Minneapolis: University of Minnesota Press, 1994).

25. Susan M. O'Brien, 'Gender, Islam, and Hierarchies of Treatment in Postcolonial Northern Nigeria', in Steven Pierce and Anupama Rao, eds, *Discipline and the Other Body: Correction, Corporeality, Colonialism* (Durham, NC: Duke University Press, 2006).

26. Friday M. Mbon, *The Brotherhood of the Cross and Star: A New Religious Movement in Nigeria* (Frankfurt: Peter Lang, 1992); Heike Behrend, *Alice Lakwena and the Holy Spirits: War in Northern Uganda, 1985–97* (Oxford: James Currey, 1999).

27. Sverker Finnström, 'Wars of the Past and War in the Present: The Lord's Resistance Movement/Army in Uganda', *Africa*, 76/2 (2006); compare Alcinda Honwana, 'Undying Past: Spirit Possession and Modernity in Mozambique', in Birgit Meyer and Peter Pels, eds, *Magic and Modernity: Interfaces of Revelation and Concealment* (Stanford, Calif.: Stanford University Press, 2003).

28. Deidre Helen Crumbley, 'Patriarchies, Prophets, and Procreation: Sources of Gender Practices in Three African Churches', *Africa*, 73/4 (2003); Birgit Meyer, 'Christianity in Africa: From African Independence to Pentecostal-Charismatic Churches', *Annual Review of Anthropology*, 33 (2004); Joel Robbins, 'The Globalization of Pentecostal and Charismatic Christianity', *Annual Review of Anthropology*, 33 (2004); Ousseina Alidou, *Engaging Modernity: Muslim Women and the Politics of Agency in Postcolonial Niger* (Madison, Wis.: University of Wisconsin Press, 2005); Adeline Masquelier, *Fashioning Islam: Women and Islamic Revival in a West African Town* (Bloomington, Ind.: Indiana University Press, 2009); Dorothea Schulz, *Muslims and New Media in Africa: Pathways to God* (Bloomington, Ind.: Indiana University Press, 2011).

29. Stephan Miescher, 'The Challenges of Presbyterian Masculinity in Colonial Ghana', *Transactions of the Historical Society of Ghana*, NS 9 (2005).

30. Rudolph Pell Gaudio, *Allah Made Us: Sexual Outlaws in an Islamic African City* (Oxford: Wiley-Blackwell, 2009).

31. See, for e.g. Terence Ranger, *Voices from the Rocks: Nature, Culture, and History in the Matopos Hills of Zimbabwe* (Oxford: James Currey, 1999); Niels Kastfelt, ed., *Religion and African Civil Wars* (London: Hurst, 2005).

32. Steven Feierman and John M. Janzen, eds, *The Social Basis of Health and Healing in Africa* (Berkeley, Calif.: University of California Press, 1992); Neil Kodesh, *Beyond the Royal*

Gaze: Clanship and Public Healing in Buganda (Charlottesville, Va.: University Press of Virginia, 2010); David Lan, *Guns and Rain: Guerillas and Spirit Mediums in Zimbabwe* (London: James Currey, 1985); René Devisch, 'La Violence à Kinshasa, ou l'institution en négatif', *Cahiers d'études africaines*, 38/150–2 (1998); J. M. Schoffeleers, 'The AIDS Pandemic, the Prophet Billy Chisupe, and the Democratisation Process in Malawi', *Journal of Religion in Africa*, 29/4 (1999).

33. Meyer, *Translating the Devil*; Clifton Crais, *The Politics of Evil: Magic, State Power and the Political Imagination in South Africa* (Cambridge: CUP, 2002).

34. J. Lorand Matory, *Black Atlantic Religion: Tradition, Transnationalism, and Matriarchy in the Afro-Brazilian Candomblé* (Princeton: PUP, 2005); Roman Loimeier and Rüdiger Seesemann, eds, *The Global Worlds of the Swahili* (Berlin: Lit, 2006); Edward Simpson and Kai Kresse, *Struggling with History: Islam and Cosmopolitanism in the Western Indian Ocean* (New York: Columbia University Press, 2008).

35. Cheikh Anta Babou, 'Brotherhood Solidarity, Education and Migration: The Role of the Dahiras among the Murid Muslim Community of New York', *African Affairs*, 101/403 (2002); Galia Sabar, 'African Christianity in the Jewish State: Adaptation, Accommodation and Legitimization of Migrant Workers' Churches, 1990–2003', *Journal of Religion in Africa*, 34/4 (2004).

36. Neil Savishinsky, 'Transnational Popular Culture and the Global Spread of the Jamaican Rastafarian Movement', *New West Indian Guide*, 68/3–4 (1994); Louis Chude-Sokei, 'Post-Nationalist Geographies: Rasta, Ragga, and Reinventing Africa', *African Arts*, 27/4 (1994).

37. Brian Larkin, 'Bandiri Music, Globalization, and Urban Experience in Nigeria', *Social Text*, 22/4 (2004).

38. Compiled from Todd M. Johnson and Brian J. Grim, eds, *World Religion Database*. http://www.worldreligiondatabase.org.

39. Freeda Bakker, 'The Image of Jesus Christ in the Jesus Films Used in Missionary Work', *Exchange*, 33/4 (2004).

40. David Westerlund, 'Ahmed Deedat's Theology of Religion: Apologetics through Polemics', *Journal of Religion in Africa*, 33/3 (2003); Brian Larkin, 'Ahmed Deedat and the Form of Islamic Evangelism', *Social Text*, 26/3 (2008); Chanfi Ahmed, 'The Wahubiri wa Kislamu (Preachers of Islam) in East Africa', *Africa Today*, 54/4 (2008).

41. Michael Gomez, *Black Crescent: The Experience and Legacy of African Muslims in the Americas* (Cambridge: CUP, 2005).

42. Robert Farris Thompson, *Flash of the Spirit: African and Afro-American Art and Philosophy* (New York: Vintage Books, 1983); Suzanne Preston Blier, *African Vodun: Art, Psychology and Power* (Chicago: University of Chicago Press, 1996); Harry G. Lefever, 'Leaving the United States: The Black Nationalist Themes of Orisha-Vodu', *Journal of Black Studies*, 31/2 (2000).

43. Susan M. O'Brien, 'Pilgrimage, Power, and Identity: The Role of the Hajj in the Lives of Nigerian Hausa Bori Adepts', *Africa Today*, 46/3–4 (1999).

44. See, for e.g. Julie Hearn, 'The "Invisible" NGO: US Evangelical Missions in Kenya', *Journal of Religion in Africa*, 32/1 (2002).

45. Barbara Cooper, *Evangelical Christians in the Muslim Sahel* (Bloomington, Ind.: Indiana University Press, 2006), 25; compare Harri Englund, 'Christian Independency and Global Membership: Pentecostal Extraversions in Malawi', *Journal of Religion in Africa*, 33/1 (2003).

46. Olivier Roy, *L'Islam mondialisé* (Paris: Seuil, 2002); Bruno Riccio, ' "Transmigrants" mais pas "nomads": Transnationalisme mouride en Italie', *Cahiers d'études africaines*, 46/1/181

(2006); Birgit Meyer, 'Religious Remediations: Pentecostal Views in Ghanaian Video-Movies', *Postscripts*, 1/2–3 (2005).

47. Holger Weiss, ed., *Social Welfare in Muslim Societies in Africa* (Uppsala: Nordic Africa Institute, 2002); Goolam Vahed and Shahid Vawda, 'The Viability of Islamic Banking and Finance in a Capitalist Economy: A South African Case Study', *Journal of Muslim Minority Affairs*, 28/3 (2008); Benjamin F. Soares 'An Islamic Social Movement in Contemporary West Africa: NASFAT of Nigeria', in Stephen Ellis and Ineke van Kessel, eds, *Movers and Shakers: Social Movements in Africa* (Leiden: Brill, 2009), 178–96.

48. Humphrey J. Fisher, *Ahmadiyyah: A Study in Contemporary Islam on the West African Coast* (London: Nigerian Institute of Social and Economic Research, 1963); on the local contexts of its cosmopolitanisms, John H. Hanson, 'Jihad and the Ahmadiyya Muslim Community: Nonviolent Efforts to Promote Islam in the Contemporary World', *Nova Religio*, 11/2 (2007).

Bibliography

Brenner, Louis, *Controlling Knowledge: Religion, Power and Schooling in a West African Muslim Society* (Bloomington, Ind.: Indiana University Press, 2001).

Cooper, Barbara, *Evangelical Christians in the Muslim Sahel* (Bloomington, Ind.: Indiana University Press, 2006).

Gifford, Paul, *African Christianity: Its Public Role* (Bloomington, Ind.: Indiana University Press, 1998).

Hoehler-Fatton, Cynthia, *Women of Fire and Spirit: History, Faith, and Gender in Roho Religion in Western Kenya* (Oxford: OUP, 1996).

Larkin, Brian, 'Ahmed Deedat and the Form of Islamic Evangelism', *Social Text*, 26/3 (2008).

Loimeier, Roman, *Between Social Skills and Marketable Skills: The Politics of Islamic Education in 20th Century Zanzibar* (Leiden: Brill, 2009).

Magaziner, Daniel, *The Law and the Prophets: Black Consciousness in South Africa, 1968–1977* (Athens, O.: Ohio University Press, 2010).

Marshall, Ruth, *Political Spiritualities: The Pentecostal Revolution in Nigeria* (Chicago: University of Chicago Press, 2009).

Meyer, Birgit, *Translating the Devil: Religion and Modernity among the Ewe in Ghana* (Edinburgh: EUP, 1999).

Miran, Marie, *Islam, histoire et modernité en Côte d'Ivoire* (Paris: Karthala, 2006).

Schulz, Dorothea, *Muslims and New Media in Africa: Pathways to God* (Bloomington, Ind.: Indiana University Press, 2011).

Soares, Benjamin F., 'Islam in Mali in the Neoliberal Era', *African Affairs*, 105 (2006).

Spivak, Gyatri, and Achille Mbembe, 'Religion, Politics, Theology', *boundary 2*, 34/2 (2007).

Tayob, Abdulkader, 'Muslim Public Claiming Heritage in Post-Apartheid Cape Town', *Journal for Islamic Studies* (Cape Town), 24/25 (2005).

Van Bruinessen, Martin, and Julia Day Howell, eds, *Sufism and the 'Modern' in Islam* (London: I. B. Tauris, 2007).

PART IV

SOCIETY AND
ECONOMY

....

CHAPTER 17

EDUCATION AND LITERACY

....

CAROL SUMMERS

IN 1935, the educationist C. T. Loram summarized the aims of education and literacy in colonial Africa by asserting that 'education is the process by which a human being is changed from what he is to something that those in authority wish him to be'. Loram argued that 'the objective of education in Africa is to produce the good African—the Native who is proud to be an African, appreciative of the finer elements in his culture, willing and anxious to accept European culture in so far as it is complementary and supplementary to his own, quite unwilling to be an imitative or unoriginal White man'.[1]

Loram's definition of education as planned by the powerful for the social construction of useful and 'good' Africans, along with his implicit concerns about bad or disruptive literate individuals, represented the views of many educationists during the colonial era. Such views, moreover, survived the end of colonial rule, re-emerging at the centre of shifting debates over how educational institutions and pedagogies should either persist or be challenged. Social utility defined education, not its specific content in reading, arithmetic, religious faith, business, or gardening. Struggles over educational planning were less over whether it was a form of social control than over what sort of future should be planned: either one in which educated elites led Africans towards a European-style model of civilization, or one rooted in an adapted form of education that emphasized established African identity and sought gradually to develop the masses in locally appropriate ways with an emphasis on community cohesion and social peace. Yet these alternative pathways only very partially capture the lived experiences of schoolchildren and teachers, parents and administrators, graduates and dropouts, in formal and informal schools across Africa in the nineteenth and twentieth centuries.

Recent histories of education and literacy in modern Africa have drawn less on the elaborate plans of experts and more on the experiences of individuals who acquired and deployed the technologies of literacy for their own purposes and who struggled to access, escape from, or transform schools. These newer histories pay attention not simply to official intentions and institutional structures but to people such as the Tanzanian speaker who told secondary school graduates in 1992 that 'Any parent who loves a child...will do everything possible, if it is to sell their banana grove, if it is to sell a cow, if it is to sell a shirt...so that the parent can pass on education to the child...we do not have any valuable inheritance that we can give our children that is more valuable than education.'[2] For the speaker, it was education itself, rather than a more abstract civilizational goal, that was important enough to demand parental sacrifices that upended social orders based on land, cattle, and patriarchal authority. New histories which place students and parents at their centre in many ways echo colonial warnings of how schooling and literacy might unleash unintended and unsettling social change. Yet they routinely celebrate the resulting transformations as evidence of creativity and possibility in a volatile and changing world.

COLONIAL LEARNING

The beginnings of literate education in much of Africa in the nineteenth century represents a key development in the continent's modern history. The libraries of Timbuktu containing manuscripts in Arabic and *ajami* (i.e. vernacular languages written in Arabic script) and those of the Ethiopian Orthodox Church containing works in Ge'ez are important symbols of precolonial African literary culture. They lack direct continuity, however, with modern writing, books, schools, and literate communities that emerged on the continent in the context of the encounter with European missionaries, traders, and colonial states. Knowledge transfer, intellectual activity, and most other valued aspects of life are, of course, possible without literacy. Intellectuals both within Africa and beyond, though, have seen distinctively *modern* selves, communities, and politics as fundamentally connected to a world of printed books, documents, and news, usually accessed through some sort of formal schooling. From at least the nineteenth century, as in some earlier cases, African intellectuals sought mastery of literacy in both European and vernacular languages and saw education as a way to make the continent modern and strong, transforming it from a source of human captives to a centre of new ideas and renewed civilization. The Sierra Leonean doctor James Africanus Horton, for example, exhorted the youth of Africa in 1868 to 'study...to obtain the combined attractive influence of knowledge and wisdom...book-learning and virtue, so that they may...bring their happy influences to bear on the regeneration of their country'. Pioneering pan-Africanist thinker Edward W. Blyden went even further in his inaugural address as president of Liberia College in 1881, delineating a curriculum organized around educating young men as the future leaders to take forward his idea that 'the African must advance by methods of his own'.[3] Even within West Africa's nineteenth-century jihadist states such as the Sokoto Caliphate, recent scholarship has emphasized that literate education and propaganda was as key as military power in transforming territories seized into properly Muslim parts of new Islamic realms.[4]

By the beginning of the twentieth century, literacy and education in Africa were more firmly connected to Christian missions and European imperial ideas of civilization and progress than to concepts of continent-wide regeneration or Islamic purification. Mission adherents across the continent were popularly referred to as 'book people' or 'readers', as Protestant missions routinely required basic literacy for baptism and even Catholics sought converts through education.[5] Mission schools taught the elements of literacy and colonial practice, catechizing the young and their elders throughout the week and then holding Sunday services that were often mandatory for school-goers. Successful graduates reaped real rewards in colonial systems as they mobilized new skills to become not simply evangelists and teachers, but also government-appointed interpreters, clerks, and chiefs. Historical anthropologists Jean and John Comaroff, impressed by the meticulous records kept by both missionaries and Tswana converts in nineteenth-century southern Africa, have seen this as the core of a hegemonic colonial project. Literacy—a basic ability to read vernacular translations of the Bible and other religious and moral literature—was a key element of conversion and aim of the mission educational project. But even in the earliest years, literacy and schooling were linked to secular employment, social mobility, class formation, and cultural transformation. Curricula thus explicitly incorporated timetables that would introduce students to colonizers' ideas of time. Teachers championed new sorts of clothing and consumption patterns that included suits, soap, and square houses, educating bright youth to be useful as servants and workers in colonial enterprises. And successful students internalized the messages of transformation, routinely emerging from these schools with ideas of themselves as progressive leaders of their people.[6]

By the late nineteenth century, in elite schools from Sierra Leone's Fourah Bay College to South Africa's Lovedale College, young men left schools with explicitly modern identities. These individuals wrote in English and other languages, including Yoruba, Luganda, Sotho, Xhosa, and Zulu, grappling with the politics of language, community, and identity and in some cases becoming the pioneers of an indigenous print culture. The missions that saw literacy as basic to Christian identity actively translated scriptures and liturgies, and sponsored local printing presses that also produced books, pamphlets, and newspapers. Colonial and Christian influences began to impact upon the reformulation of local identities and visions of the past and the future, inscribed in publications that became iconic for subsequent generations, such as Samuel Johnson's *History of the Yorubas* (1921, but completed 1897), Apolo Kaggwa's *Basekabaka be Buganda* (*The Kings of Buganda*, 1901), and Tiyo Soga's journalism and Xhosa translations.

The strong association between Christian missions and schools could cause problems for Muslims. Quranic schools during the colonial era generally lacked the social prestige or usefulness of Christian or secular schools, a distinction which reshaped the class basis of mixed societies like Uganda, where Muslims without government-recognized schooling were pushed out of government posts and grew to dominate trade. In regions dominated by Muslims, such as much of French West Africa, which often had few if any Christian missions, Western education was therefore sparse. Government schools, often begun as elite institutions for the 'sons of chiefs', provided an amalgam of Western and Islamic education that often satisfied no one.[7]

Schools in colonial Africa, whether affiliated with missions or not, were at the centre of hopes and fears of social change and disruption for missionaries, officials, students, parents, and others. Conventional typologies of colonial schooling in Africa emphasize conquering states' distinct ideologies of education and development: British colonies emphasizing vernaculars in the service of indirect rule, French colonies assimilating students through French curricula and culture, and the Belgian Congo paternalistically developing an emphasis on primary education coupled with a rejection of secondary and higher education.[8] Detailed studies across the continent, however, show more nuanced, often overlapping patterns of educational policy and provision, as all colonial governments and educators struggled with limited material and human resources and widespread fears of unrest. Loram and others might see schools as basic to colonial development, but colonial states routinely left them underfunded. Colonized Africans, however, increasingly sought schooling for their children and sometimes themselves, often supporting schools when colonial state funds proved inadequate. At times, this moved school practices far from the intentions of colonial planners. In Uganda, notables taxed themselves and their clients and provided money and land for schools, from a flagship college built on Buganda's coronation grounds to simple rural classrooms sponsored by local chiefs. Even in tightly regulated Southern Rhodesia (now Zimbabwe), students rejected government limits on their education, pushing for—and achieving—post-primary education. By the middle decades of the colonial rule, parents and patrons often valued schooling. Children's work experiences, apprenticeships, and initiation might continue to provide important knowledge, but school mattered enough to justify forfeiting children's work to provide time for education, paying fees and buying supplies, or donating labour and resources.

Even as students, parents, and community leaders demanded school places, capacity remained limited even for basic primary schooling, let alone secondary education. Many students worked as servants or taught lower level pupils as part of their training, with limited time for their own lessons. Teachers' qualifications varied dramatically and pedagogy could be basic, with students subject to corporal punishment. Parents usually contributed tuition fees, but expense did not, sadly, guarantee educational quality: government inspectors in Southern Rhodesia in 1923 reported community-supported schools that spent most of their two-hour days on attendance taking and Bible stories, had less than one slate for every ten attending students, lacked classrooms, and taught students to memorize wall syllable charts rather than actually learning to read them—producing 'deadening monotony' and 'parrot-like repetition'.[9] Seniors at elite schools such as King's College, Budo, in Uganda and Domboshawa in Southern Rhodesia often also initiated new students with buying rituals or 'hazing'.

By the interwar years, early mission endeavours had become increasingly secularized and two models of colonial education emerged among experts who agreed on the need for African transformation, but differed over how best to plan education to manage change. Planners categorized educational plans as emphasizing either quality or quantity: elite, often assimilationist colonial-language education versus mass, 'adapted', vocational, and usually vernacular training. In French West Africa, and to a lesser extent in those parts of British colonies such as Uganda, Sierra Leone, and the Gold Coast that possessed strong local pressures capable of influencing colonial policy, education policies approximated those of the metropole in the provision of elite schools that taught in the metropolitan language and trained small numbers of carefully chosen students. In French- or in Portuguese-ruled Africa, education offered a tiny number of the most successful youth the possibility of legal assimilation.[10] In British Africa, graduates of elite Anglophone 'public' schools such as King's College (Budo) in Uganda, the Prince of Wales' College (Achimota) in the Gold Coast, and Gordon College, Khartoum, in the Sudan viewed simple assimilation as below them: instead of seeking equality with Britons, they planned to lead the country.[11] For advocates of elite schooling, any mass expansion of education would come only *after* a corps of highly qualified Africans had been trained. French administrators believed, according to Louis Brenner, that 'if future generations of African leaders...were imbued with the values of French culture, and facility in the French language, the...colonial project would be assured'.[12]

In a speech to a 1938 conference discussing the establishment of Makerere University College, Uganda's governor Sir Philip Mitchell echoed such calls for elites to be taught as colonial aristocrats:

> No civilization in the world has arisen...upon any other foundation than...an aristocracy of culture...The widespread education of the masses...may be a consequence of that, but cannot precede it, indeed I should regard with horror as a crime against the people of these countries the partial education of great numbers...unless at the same time we were making every effort to provide for them, in their own environment, a means whereby there may be produced the leaders and guides of their own race...Our task, indeed, if we have any faith in our civilization and in ourselves, is boldly to lead the African peoples forward along the road we are ourselves following, confident that if we do that we shall have discharged our duty.[13]

Combining faith in the superiority of his own civilization with an equally strong sense that Africans were somehow different, Mitchell did *not* suggest that Britain should create some sort of inferior or second-class education system, but that it should teach what it knew best, even if such teaching could reach only small numbers.

Yet Mitchell's perspective was a minority one in British colonial circles and controversial even amidst the more 'progressive' missions. Such elitist goals represented one model of education, but the other drew heavily on ideas developed in the United States by African American educationist Booker T. Washington and advocated by the Phelps-Stokes Foundation, which produced influential surveys of educational practice in Africa.[14] Phelps-Stokes intellectuals criticized the pretensions of elite Africans and instead emphasized mass vocational education. Rather than educating a tiny elite to European standards, such planners called for community education and development. Education, it was asserted:

> should be adapted to the mentality, aptitudes, occupations and traditions of the various peoples...Its aim should be to render the individual more efficient in his

or her condition of life...and to promote the advancement of the community as a whole...The first task of education is to raise the standard alike of character and efficiency of the bulk of the people.[15]

The most concrete policy initiatives of this sort emphasized agricultural and industrial education or other forms of community development, such as those in Togo associated with Booker T. Washington's Tuskegee Institute or those sponsored in Kenya, Southern Rhodesia, and elsewhere by the Anna T. Jeanes Foundation. Community-centred development education sought to go beyond slates and sums and use demonstration techniques to model new economic initiatives. Schools would become centres for community debate and the dissemination of new ideas not just about curricula and pedagogy, but everything from how to wean a baby to the management of scouting troops.[16] While voicing an ideal of progressive methods and gradual community adaptations for orderly development, such initiatives sometimes provoked serious clashes as they mobilized factions who struggled over authority, land, and propriety.

Official British policy from the 1920s explicitly privileged mass over elite education, despite difficulties in applying this policy choice. Planners criticized 'aristocratic' systems that might produce over-ambitious individuals able to demand equality of opportunity with metropolitan officials or professionals. Phelps-Stokes models of an apolitical development-centred educational policy, however, proved utopian. Such programmes were unsettling and expensive, government efforts to build technical schools costing more than the distribution of modest grants-in-aid to established mission schools. Policies promoting a mass applied education via community development proved unpopular and unworkable.

Looking back at policy-makers' arguments over elite education versus locally adapted mass education, it is easy to see both the merits, and the problems, of each approach. Elite education was, accurately, associated with the development of a new class of Africans with expensive needs and wants, new aspirations, and sometimes only limited and tense connections to their home communities. Joyce Cary's novel *Mister Johnson* (1939) captured the essence of this colonial critique by portraying the array of awkward problems raised by an intelligent, articulate, ambitious, and even loyal educated Nigerian who had learnt to refer to England as home. The figure of Mister Johnson might be an exaggerated creation, but his educated and alienated colleagues have been staples of African creative writers from Camara Laye to Tsitsi Dangarembga. For many observers (including those who experienced it), elite colonial education produced loss as well as opportunity: it involved leaving home and family but in a context where membership in a race-blind community was not viable. For the educated individual, results could be tragic.[17]

Despite such dangers, both colonial planners and ambitious Africans understood that the alternative—adaptive, mass education—sought to limit students' individual ambitions and the emergence of an elite class of upwardly mobile Africans. In the Belgian Congo, official rhetoric might emphasize social welfare, but actual policies aimed to divert political challenges into ideals of community welfare, domesticity, and public health, without offering students access to secondary and tertiary education.[18] In South Africa, such policies were even blunter and more explicitly racist. They culminated in the Apartheid regime's efforts to develop a system of 'Bantu Education' that brought unprecedented numbers of African children into schools but restricted their access to English, facilitating economic growth but preserving the racial order.[19] Education for girls and women was often a part of adapted models of education, as teaching girls offered administrators a way of acting to provide potentially volatile educated men with wives, and preventing them from challenging white political or domestic power.[20] Adaptive education for both genders taught basic literacy and faith along with messages about health, work, and obedience, but students, parents, and teachers generally wanted more than training as, in the often repeated phrase of the colonial era, 'hewers of wood and drawers of water'. Student activism, ranging from routine strikes in interwar Southern Rhodesia to the establishment of independent schools in the Kikuyu region of Kenya and the dramatic clashes of the Soweto uprising of 1976, testified to students' rejection of education as a non-political route towards development without revolution.[21] Across the continent, students and their parents repeatedly blocked educational planners' efforts to use schools as centres of social control and guided development.

National Development

The idea of using education to define and plan the future persisted into the era of anti-colonial nationalism and the emergence of new independent African states in the 1950s and 1960s. Education was one of the most popular demands to emerge from the grass-roots of nationalist movements, and educated individuals from a variety of backgrounds were prominent as political leaders and as the inheritors of new nations. These individuals, belonged, as Brenner notes with regard to Mali, to a social class 'invented during the colonial period primarily through the process of Western schooling'.[22] The efforts on the part of nationalist leaderships to develop new ideas of education often reiterated colonial debates about elite and adapted community education, and they were subject to many of the same political and economic pressures that had shaped the choices of colonial planners.

International rhetoric increasingly rejected the racism that once sought to justify European leadership and a second-class status for Africans. Elite students took up opportunities to study not simply in Africa, where from the late 1940s new universities began to be established in some colonies, but in increasing numbers in France, Britain, and the United States. Such newly educated men and women, though, tended to move into administrative and technical posts or into private enterprise and generally failed to transform the very basic schools where increasing numbers of ordinary students experienced standards of education that were similar to, or even a deterioration from, the standards set in colonial-era mission schools. Despite the establishment of teachers' unions and calls for professional respect, elementary schoolteaching remained a relatively underpaid job with little prestige, serving the upwardly mobile as a way-station towards better things and the less ambitious as a fallback.[23] New nationalist regimes, like their colonial predecessors, routinely saw education as expensive, potentially destabilizing, and capable of creating a dangerously demanding citizenry. Departments of education, faced with vigorous demands for schools from both parents and children, often operated overcrowded schools that resembled those of the colonial era: they taught discipline, demanded physical labour, and emphasized (not always successfully) deference to the country's leadership.

Ironically, men and women who had been successful students demonstrated the socializing power of colonial education as they became nationalist leaders and teachers. Like their predecessors, they believed in schools as possibly transformative institutions that could be centrally planned and directed to achieve a new social and cultural world. Elite education—of almost any sort—provided a qualification for leadership in this brave new world as teachers, lawyers, doctors, and others sought power. These elites eagerly seized international scholarships and opportunities offered by competing Cold War powers during the 1960s and 1970s, Nigerian, Ghanaian, and other students being sent off to higher education in the United States, Britain, the Soviet Union, and elsewhere. They also imported international faculty and expanded the new universities established in the late colonial years. The new elite was increasingly transnational, able to move between Africa, Europe, America, and sometimes even Asia. As in the colonial era, though, the price of this global status was high—and not simply in economic terms, as individuals sought resources to support the soaring levels of personal consumption that they considered basic to their newfound prestige. Most also retained connections to their families and broader home communities. As the hopes of their communities, demands on them for patronage, payback, and salvation produced complicated and contradictory pressures that fundamentally undermined ideals of impersonal meritocracy.

Ideas of adapted community education also survived the transition from colonial to national departments of education. After the Second World War, during the period referred to as the 'second colonial occupation' underwritten in British colonies by the Colonial Development and Welfare Act, all European powers had sought to expand investment in schools as loci of 'community development'. Grants-in-aid were increased to support growing numbers of mission schools with more highly qualified teachers and improved infrastructure. In Nigeria, for example, official spending on schools doubled from 1941 to 1942, doubled again by 1947–8, and again by 1950–1.[24] Universal education, however, was considered unaffordable.[25] Ironically, the globalized educated elite emerged in newly independent African states in parallel with a vision of adapted education as a resource for cheap nation-building. Nationalist propaganda could be as blunt as that of colonial powers in using school materials to convey political messages. Some of the crudest uses of such educational propaganda came from armed revolutionary movements. The Zimbabwe African National Union (ZANU), for example, produced reading primers with cover illustrations of young guerrillas toting guns and English grammar lessons that consisted of such useful phrases as 'we have guns', 'the settlers are few', and 'grandmother is fighting for Zimbabwe'.[26] Outside a context of warfare, the assertively progressive government of Kwame Nkrumah in Ghana sought to use state-sponsored schools and curriculum, supplemented by new youth organizations such as the Young Pioneers, to produce a new national culture in Ghana that would block ethnic or local loyalties otherwise likely to challenge the central state and party.[27]

Julius Nyerere, Tanzania's teacher-president, offered in 1967 what was perhaps one of the most thoughtful analyses of postcolonial education. While acknowledging that schools were one of the principal demands of people in Tanzania, Nyerere argued that:

> It is now time that we looked again at the justification for a poor society like ours spending almost 20 per cent of its Government revenues on providing education...and began to consider what that education should be doing...it is impossible to devote Shs. 147,330,000 every year to education for some of our children...unless its result has a proportionate relevance to the society we are trying to create.[28]

Training teachers, engineers, and administrators for membership of an educated elite did not, according to Nyerere, fit national policy. Instead, he emphasized that education should:

> foster the social goals of living together...inculcate a sense of commitment to the total community, and help the pupils to accept the values appropriate to our kind of future...[It] must emphasize cooperative endeavour, not individual advancement; it must stress concepts of equality and the responsibility to give service...And, in particular, our education must counteract the temptation to intellectual arrogance.

An educational system inherited from the colonial era, he continued, was designed 'for the few who are intellectually stronger than their fellows; it induces among those who succeed a feeling of superiority and leaves the majority of the others hankering after something they will never obtain...It induces the growth of a class structure in our country'. Nyerere called instead for self-supporting schools engaged in production and emphasized that students must work as well as learn. His roadmap towards affordable education in socialist Tanzania substantially retraced colonial experts' calls for community development and schools as collective effort rather than individualism.

Neither Nkrumah's efforts to cultivate unity through progressive schooling in a national culture nor Nyerere's plans to teach harmony and productivity through work and community orientation proved especially effective in producing communal cohesion. Instead, people routinely sent children to school and hoped education would be what they imagined it as in the colonial era—an almost magical way of gaining access to success (usually measured in money) in the modern world. Reformist ideas failed to transform the culture of schools characterized by rigid hierarchies, rote learning, and competitive examinations. From the 1980s, with the rise of World Bank-IMF structural adjustment programmes, austerity, and neo-liberalism, most governments and international overseers across Africa had abandoned radical ideas of education as an inexpensive way to catalyse political change and community development. Instead, like colonial critics, they calculated the cost of schooling populations with accelerating proportions of children and youth. Education might be important but it was a budgetary elephant: huge, powerful, and potentially damaging or destabilizing.

LIBERAL LITERACY AND LEARNING

In 1997, President Museveni of Uganda publically pushed the World Bank to spend money in Uganda on feeder roads, not on schools. If people wanted education, he argued, the best way to get it was to foster economic growth and prosperity that would allow people to afford the sorts of education they found useful.[29] Museveni's energetic neo-liberalism sat awkwardly with international donors' perspectives on educational investment and he soon gave way and put forward a programme for universal primary education.[30] But his government maintained pressure on institutions to act entrepreneurially, particularly at university level, where not just trade schools but the nation's flagship, Makerere University, admitted private fee-paying students, paid staff on a piecework basis, and left departments to generate their own funds from students and donors by developing practical degree programmes in subjects such as 'Organizational Studies' or Tourism.[31]

Museveni's reluctance to see centrally planned and funded schools as basic for social development and cultural control reflects the actual (as opposed to theoretical) significance of literacy, learning, and education in modern Africa. New historical research, which is now looking beyond mission, imperial, or government initiatives to the lives and struggles of ordinary people, has begun to offer a vision of the development of education in modern Africa centred not on institutions and ideologies but on the new sorts of selfhood forged by literacy and the ways these self-identified educated men (and a few women) built connections and networks through new forms of knowledge, writing, literature, histories, and values.

This emerging approach starts with the people who were necessary but dangerous to planners' visions of education for social control: those who successfully learnt for themselves both in schools and beyond. These literate individuals, far from being unformed children remade by schooling, could more accurately be characterized as entrepreneurs of a new sort of consciousness. They experimented with new resources of literacy and print culture, both for themselves as individuals and for the communities they belonged to and, in many cases, actively built.[32] As we have seen, these sorts of new men and women were emerging from new outposts of literacy at early as the nineteenth century. In West Africa, literate networks of traders, brokers, and interpreters spread inland from the coastal towns of Sierra Leone, the Gold Coast, and Nigeria, becoming the educated notables and clerks of newly formalized colonies.[33] On the other side of the continent, Malagasy-reading and writing individuals cultivated an Indian Ocean community that linked regions as disparate as Mauritius, Magadascar, and Cape Town.[34] Inland in Buganda, ambitious youth in the royal court learnt to read and write, mobilizing their status as readers and converts in the 1880s to build political factions to the point that a threatened King Mwanga had dozens tortured and burnt to death.[35] Literacy, as a technology of communication and recordkeeping, as a way to access, understand, and disseminate new ideas and resources, could be transformational and revolutionary.

Recent scholarship has therefore emphasized that education and literacy, rather than being simply imposed by colonial planners, could be a freely chosen and potentially liberating path, especially for those who lacked other options. In the Igbo region of south-eastern Nigeria, for example, schooling was notoriously associated with *osu*, low-status individuals often of slave background, who lacked the resources and support of more elite members of society. Similarly, the young men who vied with each other to improve their translation and writing skills in Kenya were often those lacking cattle and land, so needed an alternative route to livelihood and self-fulfilment. And far from being colonial pawns, readers in the Gold Coast 'produced distinctive cultural meanings for themselves' through their literacy in ways that served local aesthetics rather than imported or imposed structures.[36]

The records of literary societies and debating clubs from South Africa to the Gold Coast show us the creativity of African readers, as they imported Western literature either in translation or in English and sought to make it meaningful to local cultural contexts. Southern African intellectuals saw imported materials as valuable resources for individuals and groups confronting rapid social change. Tiyo Soga, for example, published his Xhosa translation of Bunyan's evangelical allegory *The Pilgrim's Progress* in 1868, complete with an introduction that offered advice on how to read and a contextualization of the work's production that made it directly relevant to many of the controversies in contemporary South African politics. As Isabel Hofmeyr shows in her fine study, Soga, rather than perceiving the work as alien, translated it in a way that allowed subsequent generations of South African students in both formal classes and less formal literary societies to negotiate their place in the world.[37]

Stephanie Newell, writing about the Gold Coast, demonstrates how central books and reading became to the construction of elite male identity and sociability from the late nineteenth century. Formal schooling in the Gold Coast was far from widespread: even in 1920, only 42,339 students were enrolled in recognized primary and secondary institutions, a number that only rose to 91,047 by 1940. But books in English had been sold from at least the 1850s and in vernacular languages from the 1860s to an expanding class of literate men with money. Protestant missionaries established book depots and presses for the local market, and by 1892, the Wesleyan Methodist Mission's depot alone reported annual sales of a thousand pounds. These initiatives sought to meet local demand for 'good Christian literature' and provide an alternative to 'books not suitable', according to the first manager of the Basel Mission's Accra book depot.[38] Depots and presses became bookstores and publishers, readers established book clubs and private libraries, and sociability around reading expanded. Products included Christian devotional materials and self-help manuals but also increasing ranges of both locally produced and international publications, from local primers to British detective thrillers. Newell documents nearly eighty literary societies or clubs in the Gold Coast from 1831 to the 1950s. One member, Henry Ofori, recalled clubs being what one did when posted to rural locations: the need 'to relieve the tedium of that rural place, where you would be coming home to nothing at the end of the day'.[39]

Mr Ofori's account provides hints of how books and reading culture moved beyond the reworking of a religious canon described in Hofmeyr's study of *The Pilgrim's Progress* to the making of a literate class who rewrote themselves and their world through their textual activities. Whether using English or vernacular languages, these individuals distinguished themselves from the 'tedium' of less literate, ordinary places, privileging clubs and words over more material or traditional versions of home. Beyond reading, they also wrote. Leading Gold Coast intellectuals in the early twentieth century such as J. E. Casely Hayford and Kobina Sekyi produced both fiction and non-fiction that expressed new sorts of class values and new cultures. The readers who bought, circulated, discussed, interpreted, and in some cases eventually wrote the books were part of a minority but vibrant culture rooted in literacy and self-directed learning. Both readers and clubs often had links to elite Gold Coast schools such as Achimota and Mfantsipim. But their members brought to their intellectual lives habits of apprenticeship, initiation, and ongoing adult learning.[40]

Newell's work documents the growth of this new class on the Gold Coast, but similar patterns characterized other regions as well. In both Southern and Northern Rhodesia, successful middlemen understood learning as central to both personal and professional identities, pursuing it at high cost and investing in it for their families.[41] In Uganda, young men who graduated from the country's top schools and went to work throughout the country organized Old Boys' Associations that brought together religious, professional, civic, literary, and cultural aims. The vernacular newspapers they supported became so popular that by the 1950s observers joked that subscribing to them and reading them publically to both literate and non-literate audiences was one of the new duties of chiefship.[42] In Natal, South Africa, Zulu intellectuals paralleled Gold Coast men in their intense constructions of identity through writing.[43] Historical accounts of such groups remain rare, outnumbered by histories of schools and nationalist politics. Such associations appear, however, to have been an elite or bourgeois alternative to modern identities grounded in straightforwardly religious, economic, or political associations such as churches, trade unions, or networks such as southern Africa's Industrial and Commercial Workers' Union (ICU) or Uganda's Bataka Union.

Those men and women able to buy books, as well as those who aspired to do, also wrote letters and kept journals. Caches of letters, diaries, and other ephemera— so-called 'tin trunk' writings—remain rare and require careful interpretation and contextualization. But as anthropologists and historians have increasingly looked beyond official archives to unofficial and personal papers, materials that might once have been seen as too difficult to interpret now support new ways of thinking about self-development and networking among correspondents.[44] It is now apparent that, in South Africa, letter writing was crucial not only to the formation of elite Christian identity, but spread beyond to migrant labourers, medical workers, and religious entrepreneurs. Parallel patterns of letter writing, greeting card exchange, and journal-keeping have been reported for the Gold Coast: one A. K. Boakye Yiadom collected seventy years of journal-keeping and correspondence in a special glass-fronted bookcase—a 'shrine to literacy' for a man who was otherwise an undistinguished clerk of the high colonial era.[45] Nor were such literary selves and relationships solely the constructions of men. Lynn Thomas and Kenda Mutongi have documented how romance could define the modernity of young women, both through love letters and those written to *Drum* magazine's 'Dear Dolly' column.[46]

The elites of newly literate societies fashioned one sort of new selfhood, complete with the ability to refer to the classics and the great works of English literature; ordinary women and men, meanwhile, employed writing and print cultures for their own ends. But these were not the only identities constructed from written words by entrepreneurial readers in the colonial era. Another major genre built by writing was that of 'tradition'. From the 1980s, a wave of historical work on the invention of tradition has challenged older assumptions about ethnicity and cultural identities as primordial and organic. [47] Instead, historians now look at how literate Africans, sometimes in conjunction with colonial rulers, missionaries, ethnographers, and others, imagined and wrote such identities into reality.

An early and well-documented example of such cultural construction was Yoruba identity. J. D. Y. Peel's work offers a careful history of the process of making identity through text and words. Peel shows that the ethnonym 'Yoruba' began to take on its modern meaning when the Reverend Samuel Crowther used it in his 1843 publication *Grammar and Vocabulary of the Yoruba Language* and the Church Missionary Society and other missions accepted it as a name for the language and people they sought to convert. Peel is careful to note that this was only part of what made Yoruba identity. But words, and especially publications ranging from Samuel Johnson's landmark *History of the Yorubas* to more recent works such as those of playwright Wole Soyinka, have been essential to pulling together the pasts of diverse city-states and peoples, varied religious beliefs and practices, and energetically competitive social groups, into a recognizable, self-conscious whole.[48] Indeed, Soyinka's memoirs of his father's intensely bookish family intimately portray how this process felt.[49]

Peel portrays literate Yoruba Christians as writing an identity as an alternative to the more violent methods of the war-torn regional city-states or the encroaching British Empire. On the other side of the continent in Buganda, the literacy of early converts similarly allowed key individuals to negotiate with British agents to determine the shape of the protectorate. The literacy of the country's discontents, with their own version of history, also allowed Ganda to transcribe a vivid history and litigate over lands and rights throughout the colonial period and beyond. In Shambai in Tanganyika, too, education and schooling provided a basis for educated peasants to challenge the king and chiefs, seeking literally to overwrite one version of tradition with a new one that linked previous traditions of protest to new ideas of modernity. Recent analyses of the work of early literate entrepreneurs in such disparate regions have begun to offer insights into their work of reimagining the past and codifying 'custom'.[50]

Derek Peterson explores similar themes in the history of the Kikuyu people of Kenya. Peterson portrays a process in which landless, subordinate young men used literacy and language entrepreneurially to achieve personal social status and then went further to build identity (and fight for it) through orthography, spelling, and discussions of loan words and grammar, as well as more usual clan histories and traditions.[51] For both Peel and Peterson, as well as other scholars who have looked at work by 'organic intellectuals', writing, translation, grammars, vocabulary books, and canonical histories remade Africans' worlds under colonialism in ways that have persisted since. All this was connected to the formal institutions of schools and missions, but it spread out catalytically, beyond the wishes or the control of imperial authorities. Readers and writers, with their words and institutions, built new selves, new associations, new consumption patterns, new faiths and values, and even new histories and identities. The new historiography demonstrating the power of literacy seeks to document all of these complex processes. Even where transformations were limited to narrow literate elites, those classes shaped aspirations, actions, and access to resources not just during the years of colonialism, but after.

Neo-Liberalism and its Limits

Much recent historical and anthropological scholarship on education and literacy fits surprisingly well with today's dominant political and economic narratives of neo-liberalism. Recent works acknowledge state rhetoric, interests, and power, but show the lives of individuals and groups who bent school resources to meet their own goals. Kristen Cheney, for example, explains Ugandan teachers' insistence that students pay fees in defiance of the government's Universal Free Primary Education policy not simply because schools need the money, but also from a strong sense that education should come from individual and familial sacrifice. Catie Coe describes how school practices—from teachers' refusal to teach the government cultural curriculum to Christian messages in state schools' drama competitions—subverted the nationalist plan that understood schools as sites for forging Ghanaian identity. And Amy Stambach has noted that 'education for self-reliance' in Tanzania has in practice generated discussions amongst women about forms of self-reliance not envisaged by its official proponents, such as leaving patriarchal or marital homes to establish their own households, thereby subverting the emphasis on socially conservative ideas of tradition and domesticity.[52]

Such work emphasizes the gap between the ambitions of planners and the realities on the ground, offering analysis of where and why grandiose visions of the potential of education can go astray. It emphasizes—often with vivid anthropological detail—the creativity of individuals and networks of people who sought schooling, acquired literacy, and used it as capital to pursue their own goals rather than those of the state. As in discussions of literacy in colonial Africa, recent depictions of educational practice have found much to celebrate in individual triumphs over inadequate resources and competitive, conservative school structures. These postcolonial case studies not only point to the failure of planning to shape intended results, but also provide evidence of the intense conservatism and parochialism of an educational system that is driven by efforts to belong to a privileged elite and to maintain the distinction between the privileged few and the rest.

Recent studies such as those of Cheney, Coe, and Stambach, especially when combined with novels by Chimamanda Adichie, Adaobi Tricia Nwaubani, and Helon Habila, serve to delineate the ongoing centrality of literacy and education to modern Africa.[53] Poverty, debt, corruption, illness, infrastructure problems, and sheer lack of access to opportunities have been and remain real problems that education and the literate may propose solutions for, but often lack resources to solve. Today, education in Africa succeeds neither by the standards of its official planners, who wanted it to change people from what they were to what those in power wish them to be, nor those of the parents, sponsors, and entrepreneurs willing to sacrifice security and wealth, banana gardens and cattle, to provide their children with the basis of success. At once a crucial resource and a source of frustration and disappointment, it remains a central arena for those who struggle to reshape identity and opportunity anew in each generation.

NOTES

1. C. T. Loram, 'Fundamental Principles of African Education', in *Report of Interterritorial 'Jeanes' Conference held in Salisbury, Southern Rhodesia on 27 May to 6 June 1935* (Lovedale, South Africa: Lovedale Press, 1936), 7–14.

2. Quoted in Amy Stambach, *Lessons from Mount Kilimanjaro: Schooling, Community and Gender in East Africa* (New York: Routledge, 2000), 30.

3. Quoted in W. H. Worger, N. L. Clark, and E. A. Alpers, eds, *Africa and the West: A Documentary History from the Slave Trade to Independence* (Phoenix, Ariz.: Oryx Press, 2001), 168–72, 189–94.

4. See Beverly Mack and Jean Boyd, *One Woman's Jihad: Nana Asma'u, Scholar and Scribe* (Bloomington, Ind.: Indiana University Press, 2000), 76–91.

5. See J. D. Y. Peel, *Religious Encounter and the Making of the Yoruba* (Bloomington, Ind.: Indiana University Press, 2000), 130.

6. Jean Comaroff and John Comaroff, *Of Revelation and Revolution: Christianity, Colonialism and Consciousness in South Africa* (Chicago: University of Chicago Press, 1991), esp. 231–6; also Michael West, *The Rise of an African Middle Class: Colonial Zimbabwe, 1898–1965* (Bloomington, Ind.: Indiana University Press, 2002), esp. 36–67.

7. On Uganda, see A. B. K. Kasozi, *The Life of Prince Badru Kakungulu Wasajja* (Kampala: Progressive Publishing House, 1996), 46–60, 82–4; on French West Africa, Louis Brenner, *Controlling Knowledge: Religion, Power and Schooling in a West African Muslim Society* (London: Hurst, 2000).

8. See e.g. Bob White, 'Talk about School: Education and the Colonial Project in French and British Africa (1860–1960)', *Comparative Education*, 32/1 (1996), 9–26.

9. Quoted in Carol Summers, *Colonial Lessons: Africans' Education in Southern Rhodesia, 1918–1934* (Portsmouth, NH: Heinemann, 2002), 6.

10. See Jeanne Penvenne, '"We are all Portuguese!" Challenging the Political Economy of Assimilation: Lourenço Marques, 1870–1933', in Leroy Vail, ed., *The Creation of Tribalism in Southern Africa* (Berkeley, Calif.: University of California Press, 1989).

11. Gordon McGregor, *King's College Budo: A Centenary History 1906–2006* (Kampala: Fountain Publishers, 2006); Heather Sharkey, *Living with Colonialism: Nationalism and Culture in the Anglo-Egyptian Sudan* (Berkeley, Calif.: University of California Press, 2003).

12. Brenner, *Controlling Knowledge*, 39; see also Alice Conklin, *A Mission to Civilize: The Republican Idea of Empire in France and West Africa, 1895–1930* (Stanford, Calif.: Stanford University Press, 1997).

13. *Proceedings of the Inter-territorial Conference Held at Makerere, Uganda, 21–24 May, 1938, to Examine the Practical Steps Necessary to Implement the Recommendations of the Commission on Higher Education in East Africa for the Establishment of a Higher College* (Entebbe: Government Printer, 1938).

14. Thomas Jesse Jones, *Education in Africa: A Study of West, South, and Equatorial Africa* (New York: Phelps-Stokes Fund, 1922) and *Education in East Africa: A Study of East, Central and South Africa* (New York: Phelps-Stokes Fund, 1925).

15. Advisory Committee on Native Education in the British Tropical African Dependencies, *Memorandum on Educational Policy in British Tropical Africa*, Cmd 2374 (London: HMSO, 1925).

16. See Andrew Zimmerman, *Alabama in Africa: Booker T. Washington, the German Empire and the Globalization of the New South* (Princeton: PUP, 2010); Summers, *Colonial Lessons*, 117–43; Derek Peterson, *Creative Writing: Translation, Bookkeeping, and the Work of Imagination in Colonial Kenya* (Portsmouth, NH: Heinemann, 2004), 99–103.

17. For depictions of the alienation induced by education, see Camara Laye, *The Dark Child*, tr. J. Kirkup and E. Jones (New York: Farrar, Straus & Giroux, 1971 [orig. 1954]) and Tsitsi Dangarembga, *Nervous Conditions* (London: Women's Press, 1988).

18. Nancy Rose Hunt, 'Domesticity and Colonialism in Belgian Africa: Usumbura's Foyer Social, 1946–60', *Signs*, 15/3 (1990); Crawford Young and Thomas Turner, *The Rise and Decline of the Zairian State* (Madison, Wis.: University of Wisconsin Press, 1985), 38–9.

19. Jonathan Hyslop, *The Classroom Struggle: Policy and Resistance in South Africa 1940–1990* (Pietermaritzberg: University of Natal Press, 1999).

20. See Summers, *Colonial Lessons*, 176–96, and Carol Summers, '"If You Can Educate the Native Woman...": Debates over the Schooling and Education of Girls and Women in Southern Rhodesia, 1900–1934', *History of Education Quarterly*, 36/4 (1996).

21. See Summers, *Colonial Lessons*; Peterson, *Creative Writing*, 139–62; Hyslop, *Classroom Struggle*; Baruch Hirson, *Year of Fire, Year of Ash* (London: Zed Press, 1979).

22. Brenner, *Controlling Knowledge*, 13.

23. See Summers, *Colonial Lessons*, 87–116, 197–202.

24. David Abernethy, *The Political Dilemma of Popular Education: An African Case* (Stanford, Calif.: Stanford University Press, 1969), 95. Later figures become more difficult to track with the rise of provincial education depts.

25. See Joanna Lewis, *Empire State-Building: War and Welfare in Kenya 1925–52* (Athens, O.: Ohio University Press, 2000), 326–32, which shows that policy moved from 'mass

education' to a model of 'community development' that officials hoped would depoliticize education and be less expensive.

26. Julie Frederikse, *None But Ourselves: Masses vs Media in the Making of Zimbabwe* (Harare: Anvil Press, 1982), 14–15. Compare these with the colonial era Luganda grammar for British administrators, which in lesson one offers the following for translation: 'I strike', 'I rebel', 'you distribute', 'we guard', and 'they rule': J. D. Chesswas, *Essentials of Luganda Grammar* (London: OUP, 3rd edn, 1963), 3.

27. Cati Coe, *Dilemmas of Culture in African Schools: Youth, Nationalism, and the Transformation of Knowledge* (Chicago: Chicago University Press, 2005), esp. 60–70.

28. Julius Nyerere, 'Education for Self-Reliance' (1967) in *Ujamaa: Essays on Socialism* (London: OUP, 1968).

29. *World Bank: The Great Experiment*, part 1 (dir. Peter Chappell, 1997).

30. See Kristen E. Cheney, *Pillars of the Nation: Child Citizens and Ugandan National Development* (Chicago: University of Chicago Press, 2007), 75–100.

31. For a vivid depiction of this process, see Mahmood Mamdani, *Scholars in the Marketplace* (Kampala: Fountain Publishers, 2007), 57; for a general history of Makerere, see Carol Sicherman, *Becoming an African University: Makerere, 1922–2000* (Trenton, NJ: Africa World Press, 2005).

32. The term 'entrepreneur' is that of Derek Peterson in *Creative Writing*.

33. For examples, see Peel, *Religious Encounter*, 123–51.

34. Pier M. Larson, *Ocean of Letters: Language and Creolization in an Indian Ocean Diaspora* (Cambridge: CUP, 2009).

35. J. C. Ssekamwa, *History and Development of Education in Uganda* (Kampala: Fountain Publishers, 1997), 25–45, offers a basic textbook history of the episode. The martyrs were later canonized by the Catholic Church and Mwanga's surviving Protestant enemies, notably Apolo Kaggwa, went on to dominate Buganda's politics and intellectual life in the early colonial era.

36. Misty Bastian, 'Young Converts: Christian Missions, Gender and Youth in Onitsha, Nigeria, 1880–1929', *Anthropological Quarterly*, 73 (2000); Peterson, *Creative Writing*; Stephanie Newell, *Literary Culture in Colonial Ghana: 'How to Play the Game of Life'* (Bloomington, Ind.: Indiana University Press, 2002), 7.

37. Isabel Hofmeyr, *The Portable Bunyan: A Transnational History of* The Pilgrim's Progress (Princeton: PUP, 2004), 113–36.

38. Newell, *Literary Culture*, 9.

39. Mr Henry Ofori, founding member of New Tafo Club, quoted in Newell, *Literary Culture*, 35.

40. See Stephen Miescher, *Making Men in Ghana* (Bloomington, Ind.: Indiana University Press, 2005) on how apprenticeships, working as servants, and learning on the job were as important as official schooling for many men.

41. Terence Ranger, *'Are We Not Also Men?': The Samkange Family and African Politics in Zimbabwe, 1920–64* (Portsmouth, NH: Heinemann, 1995); Summers, *Colonial Lessons*; Anthony Simpson, *Half London in Zambia: Contested Identities in a Catholic Mission School* (Edinburgh: EUP, 2003).

42. Carol Summers, 'Catholic Action and Ugandan Radicalism: Political Activism in Buganda, 1930–1950', *Journal of Religion in Africa*, 39 (2009) and 'Radical Rudeness: Ugandan Social Critiques during the 1940s', *Journal of Social History*, 39 (2006).

43. Paul la Hausse de Lalouvier, *Restless Identities: Signatures of Nationalism, Zulu Ethnicity and History in the Lives of Petros Lamula and Lyman Maling* (Pietermaritzburg: University of Natal Press, 2001).

44. See the essays in Karin Barber, ed., *Africa's Hidden Histories: Everyday Literacy and Making the Self* (Bloomington, Ind.: Indiana University Press, 2006).

45. Stephen Miescher, '"My Own Life": A. K. Boakye Yiadom's Autobiography', in Barber, *Africa's Hidden Histories*.

46. Lynn Thomas, 'Schoolgirl Pregnancies, Letter-Writing and "Modern" Persons in Late Colonial East Africa', in Barber, *Africa's Hidden Histories*; Kenda Mutongi, 'Dear Dolly's Advice', in Jennifer Cole and Lynn M. Thomas, eds, *Love in Africa* (Chicago: University of Chicago Press, 2009).

47. See the chapter by Richard Waller in this volume.

48. Peel, *Religious Encounter*, 284, 304–13.

49. Soyinka even refers to his father as 'Essay': Wole Soyinka, *Isara: A Voyage around Essay* (New York: Random House, 1989).

50. Holly Hanson, *Landed Obligation: The Practice of Power in Buganda* (Portsmouth, NH: Heinemann, 2003); Carol Summers, 'Grandfathers, Grandsons, Morality and Radical Politics in Late Colonial Buganda', *International Journal of African Historical Studies*, 38 (2005); Stephen Feierman, *Peasant Intellectuals: Anthropology and History in Tanzania* (Madison, Wis.: University of Wisconsin Press, 1990), 138–45.

51. Peterson, *Creative Writing*, 80–5, 97–134; for other examples of writing and ethnogenesis, see also Derek Peterson and Giacomo Macola, eds, *Recasting the Past: History Writing and Political Work in Modern Africa* (Athens, O.: Ohio University Press, 2009).

52. Cheney, *Pillars of the Nation*, 88–97; Coe, *Dilemmas of Culture*; Stambach, *Lessons from Mount Kilimanjaro*, 49.

53. Chimamanda Adichie, *Purple Hibiscus* (2003); Adaobi Tricia Nwaubani, *I Do Not Come to You by Chance* (2009); Helon Habila, *Measuring Time* (2007).

BIBLIOGRAPHY

Barber, Karin, ed., *Africa's Hidden Histories: Everyday Literacy and Making the Self* (Bloomington, Ind.: Indiana University Press, 2006).

Brenner, Louis, *Controlling Knowledge: Religion, Power, and Schooling in a West African Muslim Society* (Bloomington, Ind.: Indiana University Press, 2001).

Cheney, Kristen E., *Pillars of the Nation: Child Citizens and Ugandan National Development* (Chicago: University of Chicago Press, 2007).

Coe, Cati, *Dilemmas of Culture in African Schools: Youth, Nationalism, and the Transformation of Knowledge* (Chicago: Chicago University Press, 2005).

Comaroff, Jean, and John Comaroff, *Of Revelation and Revolution*, 2 vols (Chicago: University of Chicago Press, 1991 and 1997).

Dangarembga, Tsitsi, *Nervous Conditions* (London: Women's Press, 1988).

Jones, Thomas Jesse, *Education in Africa: A Study of West, South, and Equatorial Africa* (New York: Phelps-Stokes Fund, 1922).

—— *Education in East Africa: A Study of East, Central, and South Africa* (New York: Phelps-Stokes Fund, 1925).

Larson, Pier M., *Ocean of Letters: Language and Creolization in an Indian Ocean Diaspora* (Cambridge: CUP, 2009).

Newell, Stephanie, *Literary Culture in Colonial Ghana: 'How to Play the Game of Life'* (Bloomington, Ind.: Indiana University Press, 2002).

Peel, J. D. Y., *Religious Encounter and the Making of the Yoruba* (Bloomington, Ind.: Indiana University Press, 2000).

Peterson, Derek, *Creative Writing: Translation, Bookkeeping, and the Work of Imagination in Colonial Kenya* (Portsmouth, NH: Heinemann, 2004).

Soyinka, Wole, *Ake: The Years of Childhood* (New York: Vintage, 1981).

Stambach, Amy, *Lessons from Mount Kilimanjaro: Schooling, Community and Gender in East Africa* (New York: Routledge, 2000).

Summers, Carol, *Colonial Lessons: Africans' Education in Southern Rhodesia 1918–1935* (Portsmouth, NH: Heinemann, 2002).

White, Bob W., 'Talk about School: Education and the Colonial Project in French and British Africa (1860–1960)', *Comparative Education*, 32/1 (1996), 9–26.

CHAPTER 18

WOMEN AND GENDER

BARBARA M. COOPER

ONE of the strengths of African history from the 1970s has been its attentiveness to women. Nancy Hafkin and Edna Bay's 1976 classic *Women in Africa: Studies in Social and Economic Change* offered studies of women's centrality to trade, protest movements, agricultural change, and political structures.[1] Historians since the 1990s have tended to explore the history of how both men and women, masculinity and femininity, have been understood and constructed over time: an important work marking this turn in the context of Africa was the 1997 collection *Gendered Colonialisms in African History*.[2] The shift in the focus to gender has revealed a continent in which the division of labour by sex is striking, while gender itself can be extremely fluid. In *Male Daughters, Female Husbands*, Ifi Amadiume argued that Western scholars had misunderstood the flexible gender system among the Igbo peoples of south-eastern Nigeria, failing to see that women could occupy the position of 'husband' and in so doing pursue the same kinds of strategies as men. She also argued that to read such relations as homosexual was a Western projection: the expansion of class difference, patriarchal inheritance linked to the body, and Christianity's male god and male priesthood had intruded to disrupt this more egalitarian pattern.[3]

It is true that one of the few major texts to undertake a synthesis of the history of women on the continent, Catherine Coquery-Vidrovitch's *African Women: A Modern History*, suffers somewhat from a tendency to treat women as passive victims of male patriarchy rather than as active social agents shaping the meanings of marriage, family, and gender.[4] Yet the counter-claims of those who reject the notion that African women had historically been subjugated by their own societies rather than by colonialism frequently rest on observations drawn from the unique circumstances of West Africa's coastal zone.[5] Examples of highly patriarchal societies in Africa have tended towards southern African cases such as the Shona, Zulu, and Tswana, where, again, historical circumstances are ill suited to continent-wide generalization.[6] Narratives of female power and of female subordination in Africa both disguise tremendous variation in time and space and occlude the history of turbulence and change in the nineteenth and twentieth centuries. It is in exploring the changeable nature of gender constructions that we gain purchase on the ongoing agency of African men and women.

The meanings of male and female bodies are bound up with constructions of seniority that engage understandings of age, sexuality, reproductive capacity, spiritual aptitude, physical strength, and wealth. The history of modern Africa is marked by significant redefinitions of these elements of seniority as a result of the expansion of Islam and Christianity, new modes of education, and new global economic flows. As the ways in which gender is constructed shift, avenues of discursive possibility are closed down, leaving less room to renegotiate the implications of inhabiting a body marked as male or female. Yet the complex flows of ideas, peoples, cultures, and material goods over the past two centuries have also introduced novel constructions of gender that have in turn been adapted and transformed in the African context, generating new avenues of manœuvre. No single credible narrative of either ascension or decline can be told about women's experiences in the history of modern Africa because what it has meant to be a woman has been constantly renegotiated. Male bodies and masculinity have shifted in meaning and potential as well.

MAJOR THEMES IN EARLY AFRICA

In an influential 1995 article, Jane Guyer and Samuel Belinga argued that political formations in Africa prior to the nineteenth century tended towards the absorption and accretion of multiple modes of power.[7] Rather than eliminate alternative nodes of power, African states and societies have had a marked tendency to integrate and co-opt them. This assemblage of different sources of power can contribute to 'heterarchy', enabling diverse interest groups to pool different modes of production, knowledge, and spirituality. In the middle Niger region, this meant the cooperation of fisherfolk, herders, agriculturalists, blacksmiths, hunters, and so on.[8] Early occupants might be recognized as having particular kinds of power over resident spiritual forces, while incomers had gifts in cultivation, ironworking, or pastoralism. This pattern of accretion might tend, as in the case of the eventual rise of the Mali Empire, towards the absorption of different nodes of power into one centralized state structure. Centralizing states could incorporate different clans, lineages, ethnicities, or occupational groups, yet such groups often preserved a considerable degree of autonomy.

In such contexts, the particular contributions of women might be recognized and valued. Heidi Nast has shown for the Hausa-speaking Kano region how the accumulation of concubines from neighbouring regions could be critical to state power; concubines served as important links to and sources of information about a centralizing state's hinterland.[9] In *East African Kingdoms*, Iris Berger found that women's particular aptitude for mediation with spirits could provide them with entrée into structures conferring status.[10] In urbanizing societies, women's significance in trade could lead to powerful women's market associations, a typical pattern in the coastal towns of West Africa. The symbolic representation of women as 'mothers' gave rise to titled positions for influential women, particularly in the Sudanic zone.[11] Multiple nodes of authority, then, could serve women's interests. Authority did not extend to all women, but rather depended upon lineage, age, productive activity, and spiritual function. Women were not understood to have a single collective interest.

Seniority could be established in a variety of ways, one of which was temporal precedence, an insight articulated by Oyeronke Oyewumi in *The Invention of Women*. Oyewumi insists that gender did not exist in precolonial Yoruba culture, only a sense of temporal precedence.[12] So, a woman is subordinate to the man whose house she enters not because she is a woman, but in the same way that the first people to settle an area had certain rights over the settlement of subsequent strangers. Wherever virilocal marriage entailed the movement of a woman to her husband's home, a woman was always subordinate to him. Any women who entered the household after her, whether as co-wives, daughters-in-law, or captives, would be under her authority, with generational distinctions forming the same logic of precedence and priority. In a cogent rebuttal of Oyewumi, however, John Peel argues that 'where a norm of virilocal marriage goes with the rule that relative seniority within the compound is determined not by actual age but by the length of one's attachment to it, women are subject to a form of seniority-discrimination from which men are immune: if Yoruba life is set on a status gradient based on seniority, then women are forced back to square one when they marry'.[13] Oyewumi's emphasis on temporal precedence does not convincingly undermine the logic of gender hierarchy.

Cognatic ties could have salience not erased by conjugal ties; that is, women often retained status and authority in their birth families. In the Great Lakes region, as David Schoenbrun points out, the power of an aunt over her brothers' children included authority over marriage arrangements. Women's importance in arranging funerals and in identifying male heirs could also give them a great deal of leverage.[14] Seniority could also be a function of success in reproduction. A woman successful in providing children for her father's or husband's lineage could have authority over women who had proven infertile. As African societies have tended to be gerontocratic, temporal precedence and successful reproduction could often coincide with greater age. Some societies marked the importance of generation through age grades with associated rituals that emphasized hierarchies through tattoos, hairstyles, or genital cutting. Rather than understood as 'natural', socially appropriate manhood and womanhood were therefore created through ritual. A girl who fell behind her peers in ritual accomplishment would become junior to them, a highly humiliating occurrence.

Despite variation across the continent, agriculture has to a significant degree been marked as appropriately female; in contrast, pastoralism, hunting, and fishing have tended to be appropriately male. By extension, labour-intensive tasks generally have been understood to be appropriately female. Both men and women, therefore, historically have worked to maximize access to female labour and junior male labour, whether by attracting clients, acquiring captives, claiming the labour of wives and sons-in-law, or by producing able-bodied children. Men and women have often pursued parallel strategies for gaining wealth and authority; patriarchy in Africa has entailed attempts by *both* to control the labour of juniors, while resisting the attempts of others to control their own labour, production, and offspring. Where women had an important role in agricultural production, their contributions could be recognized through their control of land, labour, particular crops, or a portion of the household's surplus production. In regions where women left agriculture with the advance of Islam, as Jerome Barkow was to observe in Hausa communities, non-Muslim women who farmed might have greater status than Muslim women in seclusion.[15] With access to and control of their own productive wealth, women in both agricultural and pastoral societies could have influence and autonomy.

Women often directed the labour of their own offspring and of their children's spouses. Women in a position to capitalize upon their authority as heads of matrifocal units could therefore become quite powerful. This could be particularly significant in pastoral societies, despite the tendency for cattle to be associated with men.[16] A woman's success in reproduction could be as important to her personally as it could be to her husband's or father's lineage. Even matrilineal societies therefore could demonstrate the patriarchal tendencies through which control over female productive and reproductive labour is established, and those tendencies could privilege some women's access to labour and authority over other women's. The division of labour by sex has meant that women have had a particularly pressing need to secure the labour of other women as a means of displacing demands upon their own. The strong demand for female slaves over male slaves that typified the African slave market reflects both the heavy burden of domestic, productive, and reproductive labour on women and the efforts of senior women to acquire female labour to free up their own.[17]

In some societies, women could act as 'husband' to other women in order to gain control over their productive and reproductive labour. In other words, what makes an individual a 'husband' or 'son' has not always entailed inhabiting a male body, but rather performing the social functions associated with the position of a head of household or a genitor for a lineage. It is not clear that such strategies were widely available to women, or that other components in struggles to gain authority did not have greater importance. Even where women have occupied a masculine gender position, both by acquiring wives and disposing of wives to attract male clients, the goal has been to reproduce the mechanisms through which patriarchy operates, namely to control the productive and reproductive labour of women and to lay claim to children.

Men in roles gendered as female could have unusual latitude in their affective behaviour, their access to feminine homosocial settings, their capacity to enter into spiritual practices marked as feminine, and their ability to enjoy same-sex sexual relationships.[18] In some societies, particularly in Sudanic Africa, castration could in effect generate a gender position that did not threaten the reproductive supremacy of powerful men. Eunuchs could be extremely powerful in both public and domestic domains of governance. They also enabled women to sustain activities normally reserved for males through a proxy while providing senior male figures with surveillance of exclusively feminine spaces. Because in Africa eunuchs were generated through forcible surgery upon young male slaves, they disrupted the normal hierarchy of slave and free. As Sean

Stillwell illustrates in the context of the Sokoto Caliphate in the nineteenth century, access to the kinds of power available only to royal slaves meant that abstract 'freedom' was not necessarily desirable for those well situated within relations of patronage.[19] While in principle such slave officials could not reproduce, in practice it was not unusual for such offices eventually to belong to particular slave lineages that had been built up through the familiar reproductive strategies available to men in matrilineal societies and women in patrilineal societies: acquiring women, claiming their offspring as legitimate children, and attracting male clients by providing them with wives.

Claude Meillassoux's observation that control of female labour and of marriage has often served as a means to cement ties to junior men (whether soldiers, clients, or sons-in-law) continues to have salience.[20] In the context of recognized marriages, such ties were generally marked by a gift transaction from the husband and his lineage to that of the bride. Control over the goods and wealth necessary to transact such a marriage, then, has also proven to be a significant element of processes through which wives have been acquired, male labour secured, and authority established. Where marriage transactions entailed an exchange of cattle, as was common in much of eastern and southern Africa prior to the twentieth century, masculine control of pastoral wealth permitted men to secure and transfer rights in female productive and reproductive labour. Schoenbrun argues that the emergence of cattle keeping as a peculiarly masculine activity was an important moment in the history of gender in the Great Lakes region.

Seniority generated through wealth in people was thus a function of access to goods and increasingly to engagement with trade circuits. European traders arriving on the shores of Africa from the fifteenth century found that, in facilitating the transit trade in captives from one location to another, they could begin to acquire the trade goods they desired—principally gold. Technologies that could facilitate the acquisition of labour in the form of captives or brides were particularly coveted in African markets. Those with privileged access to the means of warfare preyed on other groups, or struggled to retain or gain control of trade routes. In the context of the coastal trade, African societies were often willing to trade male war captives, prisoners, or 'criminals' for the prestigious technologies of war. George Brooks has shown that women often served critical functions as brokers between Europeans and indigenous trade networks. Such women, known on the Upper Guinea coast as *signares*, could combine the qualities of business partner, caretaker, 'landlord', and wife to European merchants, contributing to the emergence of small but influential enclaves of Euro-African populations in coastal ports.[21]

The expansion of Islam in Sudanic West Africa had contradictory implications for women. In regions of militarized state-building and of jihadist reform movements, women from 'pagan' societies were often highly vulnerable to capture, enslavement, pawning, and sale. However, elite women educated in Islamic literary traditions could have important roles in the shaping of Muslim societies and could benefit from legal protections. The case of Nana Asma'u, daughter of the founder of the Sokoto Caliphate, 'Uthman dan Fodio, reveals that contests over the definition of orthodoxy could hinge in part on the question of whether women could indeed be full members of Islamic societies. 'Uthman dan Fodio insisted that free women have access to Islamic education and Asma'u was charged with socializing defeated populations into the Islam of the jihadists, a task she took on with vigour. Her movement, claiming Islamic orthodoxy, was built upon the adaptation of modes of female representation borrowed from an earlier mode of governance. Taking on the authority and male dress of the Inna ('Mother', the title of the female aristocrat overseeing spirit possession in the court of Gobir), Asma'u attempted to spread the jihadists' brand of orthodoxy through an inventive combination of vernacular poetry, the co-optation of indigenous modes of feminine authority, and the institution of women's study and pilgrimage groups.[22]

THE NINETEENTH CENTURY

By the nineteenth century, the heterarchy of an earlier era was under threat from increasingly centralized states engaged in a cycle of acquisition of trade goods suited to enhancing power and prestige in exchange for less desirable captives, predominantly male, seized through raids and warfare. Healthy female captives were typically retained to provide wives for soldiers (who were often themselves male captives absorbed into local military structures), to shore up the agricultural base, and to contribute to the demographic growth of centralizing states. Societies were increasingly hierarchical, with implicit and explicit distinctions of class, ranked lineage, and political power. For women at the top of the hierarchy, positions of extraordinary wealth and power were possible: in states such as Asante we have particularly rich records of elite women because of their significance in diplomatic and military struggles as the Atlantic trade increasingly tended towards direct contest with European powers.[23] However, for those highly vulnerable women who were the object of slave raiding and warfare, the expansion of powerful states and the increasing importance of high value imported goods was often the source of great instability and oppression.

Decentralized societies found themselves having to devise ever more innovative ways to evade attack. Relations of clientage and pawnship that had in the past facilitated survival in periods of ecological stress tended increasingly to blur into captivity and slavery. The heterarchal cooperation previously common between nomadic and agricultural societies gave way increasingly to competition and struggles to fix relations of power in hierarchical terms. In such contexts, women taken into households as concubines and captives were more likely to be sold into chattel slavery than had been the case in the past. Differences between slave and free were accentuated in ways that the previously absorptive and non-hierarchical tendencies of African societies had tended to de-emphasize. In short, free or captive status became as important as gender or age in the determination of authority and the capacity to control labour, while the definition of 'free' increasingly overlapped with specific dominant ethnic, economic, or religious groups.

The growth of the abolition movement in the nineteenth century had contradictory implications for women and gender on the continent. On the one hand, women stood to benefit disproportionately from the elimination of slavery. On the other hand, because slave women served to protect free women from the demands of productive and reproductive labour, more privileged women stood to lose ground. The paternalist abolitionist movement justified European intervention into African societies and markets in the name of protecting vulnerable women. Defining women as weak, vulnerable, subordinate, and in need of protection significantly altered the terms on which women participated in society at large.

Furthermore, the gradual and contradictory manner in which abolition occurred over two centuries generated tremendous instability. Marcia Wright's work on slave narratives in East and Central Africa shows how women could slip from the status of wife to slave and back again. The protection of a powerful figure, whether husband or master, was critical to women's security.[24] As the abolitionist movement gained strength in Europe and the United States, 'legitimate' trade goods increasingly replaced captives in export markets. Where legitimate goods were produced in large-scale agricultural enterprises, captives were redirected to local production rather than export and the enslavement continued; indeed, at times it increased. Cash crops such as cloves, coffee, and palm oil often displaced food crops and entailed significant retooling of productive arrangements. In the process, women often lost access to land and agro-pastoral products, rendering them less autonomous and less able to parlay their access to surplus into control of junior labour.

The end of slavery in Africa occurred slowly, in part because colonial rulers declined to see captive females as distinct from wives for fear of disrupting productive systems and alienating key male allies.[25] If in the long term the decline of the slave trade certainly benefited women vulnerable to enslavement, in the shorter term the demand for labour meant that pawning and polygyny became mechanisms for controlling labour on an unprecedented scale.[26] Struggles to redefine marriage became commonplace, as seniors attempted to co-opt junior female labour and as women sought protection in marriage that could distinguish brides from mere captives or concubines.

In areas better patrolled by abolitionist powers, contraband captives seized from slave ships were deposited in cities along the West African coast, notably Freetown, Monrovia, and Libreville. These dislocated Africans often attracted the particular solicitude of European missionaries, becoming privileged mediators between coastal societies and increasingly intrusive external forces. In the cosmopolitan coastal towns of West Africa, educated elites began to emerge as a significant intermediate class, exhibiting domestic arrangements that resembled typical monogamous European companionate marriage. Among such 'creole' populations, women could become quite wealthy through trade.[27]

THE COLONIAL PERIOD

Since the 1970s, the historiography of Africa has focused increasingly on the period of colonial rule. I have here set out at some length the significance of earlier patterns in order to highlight the depth of the transformations in gender examined in recent work on the twentieth century. Such work has tended to focus upon how colonial structures, capitalist relations, and increasing integration into global circuits of production and trade transformed gender relations. Feminist theory of the 1970s struggled to gain analytical acuity through the concept of patriarchy without losing all local specificity; such work, as Amadiume and others have noted, suffered at times from a lack of historical and cultural depth. By the 1980s, the challenge for feminist historians of Africa was to accommodate the theoretical fixity of patriarchy to the necessarily historical requirements of Marxist theory.

A significant body of work on women and gender in colonial Africa was shaped by debates within Marxism and feminism about how best to understand the implications of shifts in labour mobilization, in the reproduction of the labour force, and in how value might be generated. These debates culminated in Sharon Stichter and Jane Parpart's largely sociological volume *Patriarchy and Class: African Women in the Home and the Workforce*, published in 1988. Claire Robertson's study of Ga women in Accra offers a particularly interesting approach to the marriage of Marxist and feminist analysis. In the precolonial period, Robertson argued, the dominant mode of production, while insisting ideologically upon male superiority, in practice provided for a relatively cooperative sexual division of labour. The colonial period enabled Ga market women to increase their economic and spatial autonomy as markets expanded and male hierarchies were undermined. By the post-independence period, however, the capitalist mode of production had driven women out of production, as they lost access to the means of production in the domain of fishing. The result was that gender hierarchies in Accra were increasingly coterminous with class relations; that is, women had effectively become an underclass.[28]

With the global political transformations of the 1990s, Marxist analysis has lost considerable traction, so that the language of 'articulation' and 'modes of production' has fallen largely by the wayside. Nevertheless, it is worth retaining a few key insights from that historiographic moment: the problem of women's ability to sustain access to the means of production (whether labour, land, or capital) has continued to have tremendous importance; the question of how decisions are made regarding fertility and reproduction is one of the most pressing on the continent; and the capacity of women to monetize their domestic services remains stubbornly relevant. The implications of agency on the part of actors in a range of registers have often been 'contradictory' in the Marxian sense, in that they have generated productive tensions that have contributed to change. While the vocabulary preferred by a later cohort of scholars has tended to be less inflected by Marxist theory, many of the key problems explored in the 1980s were carried forward in the 1990s, although less schematically and with less rigid demarcations in chronology.

In many ways, the colonial period marked the amplification of trends that began with the decline of the slave trade and the shift to legitimate commerce. Pamela Scully charts these dynamics in a fine study of South Africa's western Cape: the increasing concentration of political power in the hands of men; the growing exclusion of women from control of land, labour, and productive surplus; and the rise of struggles over the definition of marriage and 'tradition' in the service of enhanced control over female and junior male labour.[29] Missionaries, soldiers, traders, and administrators mistook the turbulent conditions of the early nineteenth century as typical of the vulnerable condition of women and of the abusive relations between African men and women. Casting themselves as the saviours of African women in the face of slave-owners or brutal African men, colonial agents set themselves the task of reforming what they took to be backwards African understandings of womanhood, masculinity, family, and marriage.

Across the continent, colonial interventions purported to protect women from the abuses of early marriage, summary divorce, polygamy, and other perceived injustices. One of the most striking means deployed by colonial states to alter the status of women was to intervene in the legal domain, legislating against a variety of practices that were deemed repugnant to civilized values. Thus, the early colonial period presented unprecedented opportunities for young women in particular to escape arranged marriages, lay claim to monogamous relations, and insist upon support from their spouses as dependants.[30] In some regions, women seized upon the presence of missions to escape from unwelcome marriages and the servitude they sometimes entailed as *de jure* slavery fell into decline.

These novel openings set off an outcry on the part of senior figures, both male and female, European and African, to rein in 'wayward' women. In the absence of control over young women, it was difficult for seniors to provide brides for young men, ensure labour supplies, and provide the production necessary to meet colonial tax demands. Furthermore, the very construction of seniority was predicated upon the ability of some to mobilize the labour of others. Jean Allman's study of the detention of Asante 'spinsters' in the interwar years captures the dynamics of this pivotal moment, as local chiefs, initially supported by colonial officials, intervened into the negotiation of marriage in an effort to continue male exploitation of the labour of wives in the blossoming cocoa economy.[31] In order to shore up the authority figures so necessary to sustain the ideologies of indirect rule in British Africa and of 'association' in French Africa, it was important to restore the ability of seniors to mobilize female productive and reproductive capacity as brides and workers. Independent women were recast as 'wicked'—often as prostitutes or witches, whose debased or detribalized mores threatened both indigenous morality and the colonial order.[32] Increasingly, colonial administrations favoured patriarchal controls over unruly women. By bolstering male and ignoring female authority, colonial powers narrowed women's political and economic options.[33] By the interwar years, avenues of action closed down and an increasingly rigid construction of gender relations and the division of labour by sex emerged. In his landmark study of law in colonial Malawi and Zambia, Martin Chanock argued that 'customary law' was a product of capitalism that served as a means for elders to gain control of the labour and income of young male migrants and for husbands to secure the labour of wives.

Another way in which the 'unruly' woman was contained was the elimination of the mechanisms through which female interests could be expressed. Previously recognized offices for women were vacated of meaning or transferred to male occupants, female spiritual offices were derided as pagan and backwards, and flexible gender constructs such as female husbands were treated as aberrant signs of African licentiousness. Actors differently situated within the economic and political landscape vehemently disputed the implications of purportedly 'traditional' rights and duties with regard to land, labour, and productive wealth in an effort to secure advantage in an uncertain environment.

One of the most significant shifts was in the kinds of transactions through which legitimately recognized indigenous marriages were marked. In most regions of Africa, marriage entailed a long sequence of gifts and counter-gifts between the groom's family and that of the bride. Gifts of livestock and labour service from the former to the latter ('bride-wealth' or 'bride-price') were essential to establishing a relationship and to securing the groom's rights to any offspring. Gifts from a woman's family to the new couple as a kind of dowry could be very important in securing a new bride's position in a household and in marking her as having powerful and supportive female kin. As colonial era economies increasingly emphasized cash over the livestock and goods produced in established agro-pastoral economies, older women's ability to contribute to these gift exchanges and thereby establish their daughters' worth and their own seniority was imperilled.[34]

Young men sought access to brides through wages earned outside family production, prompting elders to attempt to gain access to those wages by extracting ever higher bride-wealth. Senior women might benefit from their ability to extract wealth from junior males, but younger women who sought to leave unwelcome or unsuccessful marriages often found that, unless they could return the extensive marriage payments, they could not secure a divorce. Bride-wealth, often given to the senior members of a bride's family, might have in turn been used to secure a bride for a woman's brother. The increasing commoditization of marriage transactions contributed to a tendency for male and female relations to be marked and experienced through the medium of gifts of cash and goods associated with the globalizing market economy. Both men and women found themselves in an ever more desperate search for money through which to secure the most basic of social relations for themselves and their children: sexual intimacy and marriage. With characteristic obtuseness, colonial administrators and missionaries tended to read the increasing commoditization of gift transactions as proof that African marriage was tantamount to the sale of women.

Not surprisingly, the confusion, moral panic, and fading opportunities of the interwar period prompted a variety of protest actions, often articulated in the idioms of 'heterarchy' that women had invoked in the past. Such idioms famously emerged in the case of the 1929 Women's War in south-eastern Nigeria, which drew upon an Igbo institution known as 'sitting on a man'. Whether these were anti-colonial protests, 'female' protests, or, more accurately, the protests of wives, mothers, daughters, market women, or taxpayers, is subject to debate.[35] What is clear is that women in south-eastern Nigeria and elsewhere were far from passive in the face of threats to their autonomy and livelihoods posed by colonial rule, whether the creation of new modes of authority such as the Igbo 'warrant chiefs', the imposition of new categories of subjecthood such as 'femmes libres' when single women struggled to tap urban male incomes, and newly defined 'crimes' such as 'conjugal abandonment' in French Soudan.[36]

In French West African territories in particular, Islam increasingly provided a useful discourse through which various parties could articulate legal claims to land, labour, and moral authority. For women this had complex and contradictory implications, for the social heterarchy of the precolonial period had often recognized feminine spiritual authority, women's productive importance, and the right of wives to seek the support of kin in marital disputes. Prior to the nineteenth century, many Muslim societies had combined established modes of female authority with elements of Islam in ways that did not undermine local conventions regarding land and labour. In the context of reform movements of the nineteenth century and of colonial rule in the twentieth, some elements of more legalistic Islamic practice could be appealing to young men and women. Islamic legal principles guaranteed individual sons and daughters the right to inherit parental property in freehold, a practice very much at odds with the communal land tenure arrangements of an earlier era. Dependent status in a Muslim marriage could, in principal at least, provide a woman with support and some respite from the arduous work typical of productive arrangements in non-Muslim marriages in an era of heavy labour extraction. While Islam inscribed husbands' rights to multiple wives into law, that right was limited to four, which in some contexts would have represented a significant limitation on powerful men's prerogatives to take multiple wives in order to maximize their access to labour.

In exchange, however, wives often lost their usufruct rights to land as part of their productive contribution to the household. Stricter readings of Islam also posed a challenge to recognized female authority, such as that associated with *bori* spirit mediumship in the Hausa-speaking region of northern Nigeria and Niger. In areas of expanding cash-crop production and rising population density, such as the Hausa region, the fragmentation of landholdings with divisible inheritance meant that wives tended to lose direct access to farmland and to the products of their own farm labour.[37] Women have scrambled to maintain incomes in a context in which their means of earning cash have often narrowed over time. If in principle Islam upholds the right of women to education, the reality has been that in some regions women's education was seen as less urgent than the need to marry girls off young.

Across colonial Africa, education (whether Islamic, Christian, or secular) was understood to be more relevant to men as breadwinners and potential colonial interlocutors than to women. Consequently, women's capacity to manœuvre in colonial and then postcolonial economies was often constrained. Education for women tended to be limited to matters deemed appropriate to generating a bourgeois household and an appropriately domestic helpmeet for both Christian and Muslim men. With the recent cultural turn in the historiography, scholars have begun to examine how domesticity was constructed through education and consumption, how social and cultural practices were modified through mission interventions, and how resistance might be embodied and Christianity transformed. The effort to transform cultural forms in ways that sustained structures of dominance was an important part of colonial rule, particularly in the encounter between Africans and missionaries. Both Christian and Muslim women often managed to parlay their training into means to earn income, whether by selling cooked foods or needlework or by offering domestic services such as laundering, sewing, ironing, or childcare for cash.[38] A number of forward-looking women, such as the midwife Aoua Keita in Mali and journalist Mabel Dove in the Gold Coast, succeeded in putting their educations to significant political uses in the lead up to independence.[39]

The construction of femininity entailed a parallel transformation in masculinity. In a reversal of the precolonial pattern, work in the colonial era—whether on agricultural schemes, mines, railways, or in government bureaucracies—overwhelmingly favoured male labour over female labour. As Elizabeth Schmidt documents for Southern Rhodesia, even domestic servants were often men, in part because senior African men and women did not relish placing junior women in positions of sexual vulnerability, and in part because European women feared sexual competition from African women. Colonial rule redefined masculinity in ways that were racialized, increasingly rigid and hierarchal, and, above all, contradictory. To be fully masculine was to be a breadwinner, in control of the female members of one's household, and the sole intermediary with the state. At its limit in white settler colonies, to be truly masculine was to be a white man. Yet colonial labour relations consistently infantilized black male labourers as 'boys'.[40] Because white women could have more authority than black men, race regularly destabilized gender hierarchies, creating anxiety and moral panic in the face of potential miscegenation. African women sometimes earned impressive sums of money through trade in beer, cooked foods, and services such as hair dressing in urban settings, unsettling the ideal of the male as the primary income earner. As Luise White demonstrated, prostitutes in colonial Nairobi could earn independence and capital by providing all the 'comforts of home' to men far from their wives or too poor to marry.[41]

Although the constructions of femininity and masculinity emerging in the colonial era were profoundly marked by Western conceptions of domesticity and race, it would be inaccurate to suppose that Africans played little role in reshaping gender norms. As Kristin Mann has shown for early colonial Lagos, African women could have strong preferences for Westernized modes of marriage that they perceived as advantageous to them, while men, as Lisa Lindsay demonstrates for Nigerian railway workers, could find attractions in the 'modernity' of new labour and household arrangements.[42] The ideal masculinity of the colonial system was in reality very difficult to sustain, for wages were rarely adequate for a man to support all his wives and children without feminine support. In practice women continued to have economic significance and unrecognized moral authority. As Margaret Jean Hay argued for the Luo in Kenya, women's agricultural labour often subsidized male wages and sustained land claims that might otherwise be weakened if land were left dormant.[43] Low and unreliable male wages often meant that urban women's earnings through informal trade and marketing made up a significant part of household income. The dissonance between the ideal of male control of the household and the reality of women's independent sources of income continues to generate, as Richard Schroeder documented convincingly in the context of the Gambia, considerable friction.[44] The redefinition of household and marital relations, often termed 'Victorian' in the literature, was the combined product of missionary understandings of womanly Christian submission, bourgeois conceptions of modern domestic arrangements and marriage, and Islamic preferences for the segregation of the sexes and heightened sexual restraint. This proved to be a radical departure from the complementarities, heterarchy, and fluid gender formations so typical prior to the nineteenth century.

CONTEMPORARY CONCERNS:
THE TURN TO SEXUALITY

The rigidification of conceptions of masculinity and femininity served to inscribe African gender relations in an increasingly hetero-normative paradigm. Once fluid gender constructions rapidly closed down amid claims to the moral superiority and 'authenticity' of patriarchal heterosexual relations. Marc Epprecht has argued that the homophobia so common in Africa today is a relatively recent phenomenon, generated to a significant degree by European mission ideologies.[45] The history of sexuality in Africa remains relatively unexplored, in part because of the ways in which purportedly deviant African sexuality was deployed by outsiders to justify conquest and cultural imperialism. The supposed hypersexuality of Africans, institutionalized in polygamy, secret societies, and genital cutting (to name a few of the fixations of Western observers) served to legitimate the racist and paternalist intrusions of colonialism. As colonialism progressed, the growing unease over women's mobility and autonomy generated a great deal of attention to 'prostitution', the catch-all term for the sexual practices of independent single women. Regulating unruly African women's sexuality simultaneously served to reinforce notions of white moral superiority and to undergird claims of the need for patriarchal control.

One effect of the homophobia on the continent today is that it is difficult to interpret sexual practices in the past without triggering polemical responses. The distaste of some female African scholars for the suggestion that practices such as female husbands had recognized social dimensions does make it hard to even broach the subject of lesbian sociability in Africa. While there have been a number of efforts to study homosexual and bisexual practices in Africa historically, on the whole the topic has not yet received the attention it deserves. The surge in attention to the purported deviance of African sexual habits in the wake of the AIDS epidemic has not made broaching an already sensitive topic any easier. The recent politicization of homosexuality in Uganda, linked to evangelical circles in the United States, suggests that the subject cannot be evaded much longer.

One of the most compelling issues in the history of modern Africa is how women's fertility and sexuality has been understood and controlled. The perception fuelling the recent surge in homophobia in Uganda, that homosexuality is somehow linked to a genocidal imperialist conspiracy to prevent Africans from reproducing, may gain its resonance from the historical importance of fertility in so many African societies. In the colonial period, the regulation of African sexuality was often limited to containing prostitution and casting men as 'boys'. Only in some settler colonies did regimes try to contain or reduce the fertility of African populations seen to compete with white settler prerogatives. Such efforts at population control contributed to an enduring mistrust on the part of some African nationalists, who suspected that birth control was a mechanism of colonial subjugation.[46]

Elsewhere, colonial administrations and missionaries actively intervened in an attempt to increase African fertility. This was particularly the case where African practices—from genital cutting to polygyny—were perceived to be 'unnatural', unhealthy, and acting to reduce the available labour force.[47] Lynn Thomas has examined the contradictory and politically explosive intrusions of the British colonial administration as it attempted to control female circumcision in Kenya, in an effort to alter marriage patterns, reduce abortion, and prompt population growth. Attempts to modify African birthing practices were often highly contradictory, embroiling administrators in intimate bodily issues and prompting unexpected responses from local populations. As Nancy Rose Hunt has shown in the context of the Congo, such intrusions often entailed the mediation of African figures—often male nurses—to translate Western biomedical practices into local idioms. Given the centrality of claims about population growth to debates about issues as wide-ranging as the impact of slavery, the emancipation of women, and prospects for development, understanding how local populations have understood their own fertility and attempts to regulate it is likely to be an important area of future study.

If gender relations in twentieth-century Africa continued to be bound up with issues of production and reproduction, they nevertheless also had a significant, if elusive, affective dimension. A history of gender should undoubtedly include reflections on how the shifting meanings of bodies and sexualities affected the emotional lives of Africans and an attention to the ways in which political economy and emotional life are intertwined. Recent research on the concept of love promises to provide an avenue through which to explore this important aspect of lived experience. The colonial era ushered in an unprecedented and often unruly flow of media in the form of print culture, film, and music. Many Africans gained tantalizing glimpses of life in America through Westerns, while others reimagined romance and family life through Hindi films and debated appropriate courtship through magazine advice columns. The growing salience of notions of 'love' and companionate marriage coincided with increasing monetization, so emotional relations could be bound up with gifts and cash in ways that defied the Western ideal that love transcends money. They were also linked to conceptions of what constituted modernity in rather contradictory ways: was it modern to enter into affective relations in a companionate marriage, or did modernity entail the independence of the single girl clothed in recognizably cosmopolitan garb? Love did not necessarily imply greater female power in a relationship; indeed, monogamous companionate marriage could imperil women's ability to draw upon kin support in disputes and could imply female subservience to their beloved, something Kristin Mann noted long ago for colonial Lagos. Not surprisingly, some young 'modern' women skirted both 'traditional' and 'romantic' marriage in pursuit of greater autonomy, giving rise to predictable accusations of moral laxity.[48]

Love takes on particular complexity and poignancy in the era of AIDS. Making sense of the AIDS epidemic in Africa requires a longer history of the geography of intimacy, including the implications of Apartheid, circulatory migration, women's autonomy, and the materiality of everyday life.[49] Because of the link between colonial racism and attention to African fertility, discussion of the history of sexuality in Africa can be sensitive and polemical. This is unfortunate, because reducing the history of gender and power in Africa to discussions of production and reproduction or of 'transactional sex' evacuates sexual relations of their intimacy and human complexity. It also leaves major issues such as AIDS to be debated by specialists in other fields, who may have little gift for interpreting the nuances of African sexualities and therefore may impose solutions that at best have little traction and at worst reinscribe denigrating paradigms of African hypersexuality. In thoughtful studies, historian John Iliffe and medical practitioner Helen Epstein have in different ways worked hard to render the AIDS epidemic in Africa legible, human, and solvable.[50]

WOMEN AND POLITICS

The stresses of colonialism in Africa were felt as acutely by women as by men, prompting the former to enter into anti-colonial movements with more vigour than was recognized in established nationalist narratives of the 1960s. Armed resistance movements beginning in the 1950s in Algeria and Kenya and continuing into the 1970s in much of southern African gave tantalizing promise of greater recognition of women's contributions to African society. Women had important roles in mobilizing popular sentiment, carrying information, provisioning guerrillas, and articulating grievances through a variety of forms of protest.[51] Socialist movements, in particular, seemed to promise a future of gender equality. However, women faced with multiple modes of subordination often failed to win the equality in postcolonial regimes that liberation struggles had so often promised to deliver.

In the postcolonial period, the egalitarian promise of nationalism often gave way to class, ethnic, religious, and gender competition that continues to the present. Major positions of visible power have, with only a few notable exceptions, gone to men in male-dominated states that had, in the end, always been ambivalent at best about gender equity.[52] Despite some gains for women in education and health in the early postcolonial period, subsequent economic decline has left many women even more vulnerable than their grandmothers had been.[53] Where women have made gains through micro-enterprise, the push back from men has often proven strong, as Schroeder illustrates in the contests over women's market gardens in Gambia.[54]

South Africa in the post-Apartheid era may prove to be a shining example in a turn for the better: the new constitution enshrines gender and sexual equity in ways that are unparalleled in most other democracies and women have found major positions in government. The history of popular protest in South Africa may have generated a strong enough civil society that women's claims will continue to be voiced. Whether they will be heard is, of course, another matter. As women move into bureaucratic positions there is some danger that the women's movement will lose some of the strong leaders it once had; the prospect of feminist issues being dismissed as Western-imposed distractions from the 'real' business of reversing the heritage of racism continues to be real.[55] Yet the dynamism of the adaptive strategies of the deep past continues to have salience: in rejecting the unproductive identity politics that feeds divisiveness, women have often generated styles of political engagement that draw upon established nodes of authority while seizing upon the opportunities offered by a shifting political economy.[56]

Other recent bright spots on the continent suggest that women's persistence in insisting upon their importance in resolving the problems of contemporary Africa is paying off. Women are increasingly present in African parliaments as a variety of quota bills have required greater efforts on the part of male-dominated parties to provide genuine female representation. In the far more open media context of Africa since the 1990s, women activists have been increasingly vocal, sometimes successfully shaping the legislative agenda in light of their own experiences and their perceptions of women's and society's needs. Women have engaged the new media in ways that at times bring together religious debate and political concerns.[57] Effectively drawing upon women's information networks, they have also mobilized in contexts not always immediately identified as female concerns. Kenyan biologist Wangari Maathai was awarded the Nobel Peace Prize in 2004 for her environmental work, while in 2005 Ellen Johnson Sirleaf became the first woman to be elected head of state in Africa when she became president of Liberia. In 2011, Johnson Sirleaf was herself a recipient of the Nobel Peace Prize, along with fellow Liberian activist Leymah Gbowee and the Yemeni journalist Tawakoll Karman. As in the past, women have drawn upon the seniority conferred by motherhood and age, but have not hesitated to use new institutions to ensure that their interests are met. The visibility of African women in continental and international political movements today is very much in keeping with the centrality and malleability of gender in the history of Africa.

Notes

1. Nancy Hafkin and Edna Bay, eds, *Women in Africa: Studies in Social and Economic Change* (Stanford, Calif.: Stanford University Press, 1976); for other excellent historical overviews, see Iris Berger and E. Frances White, *Women in Sub-Saharan Africa: Restoring Women to History* (Bloomington, Ind.: Indiana University Press, 1999); Jean Allman, Susan Geiger, and Nakanyike Musisi, eds, *Women in African Colonial Histories* (Bloomington, Ind.: Indiana University Press, 2002).

2. Nancy Rose Hunt, Tessie P. Liu, and Jean Quataert, eds, *Gendered Colonialisms in African History* (Oxford: Blackwell, 1997). Andrea Cornwall's *Readings in Gender in Africa* (Bloomington, Ind.: Indiana University Press, 2005) provides a sample of central readings and a cogent introduction to major debates.

3. Ifi Amadiume, *Male Daughters, Female Husbands: Gender and Sex in an African Society* (London: Zed Books, 1987). Amadiume's *Reinventing Africa: Matriarchy, Religion, and Culture* (London: Zed Books 1997) was considerably less compelling in its blurry definition of gender. For a recent recasting of the Igbo family emphasizing the importance of consanguinity over conjugality, see Nkiru Nzegwu, *Family Matters: Feminist Concepts in African Philosophy of Culture* (Albany, NY: State University of New York Press, 2006).

4. Catherine Coquery-Vidrovitch, *African Women: A Modern History* (Boulder, Colo.: Westview, 1997).

5. See e.g. Bolanle Awe, 'The Iyalode in the Traditional Yoruba Political System', in Alice Schlegel, ed., *Sexual Stratification: A Cross-Cultural View* (New York: Columbia University Press, 1977); Kamene Okonjo, 'The Dual Sex Political System in Operation: Igbo Women and Community Politics in Midwestern Nigeria', in Hafkin and Bay, *Women in Africa*; Ama Ata Aidoo, 'Asante Queen Mothers in Government and Politics in the 19th Century', in Filomena Chioma Steady, ed., *The Black Woman Cross-Culturally* (Rochester, VT: Schenkman, 1981).

6. On gender constructions among the Zulu, see Sean Hanretta, 'Women, Marginality and the Zulu State: Women's Institutions and Power in the Early Nineteenth Century', *Journal of African History*, 39 (1998); for the Tswana, see Margaret Kinsman, '"Beasts of Burden": The Subordination of Southern Tswana Women, ca. 1800–1840', *Journal of Southern African Studies*, 10 (1983).

7. Jane Guyer and Samuel M. Eno Belinga, 'Wealth in People as Wealth in Knowledge: Accumulation and Composition in Equatorial Africa', *Journal of African History*, 36 (1995).

8. Roderick McIntosh, *The Peoples of the Middle Niger: The Island of Gold* (Oxford: Blackwell, 1998).

9. Heidi Nast, *Concubines and Power: Five Hundred Years in a Northern Nigerian Palace* (Minneapolis: University of Minnesota Press, 2005).

10. Iris Berger, *Religion and Resistance: East African Kingdoms in the Precolonial Period* (Tervuren: Musée Royal de l'Afrique Central, 1981).

11. Barbara M. Cooper, *Marriage in Maradi: Gender and Culture in a Hausa Society in Niger* (Portsmouth, NH: Heinemann, 1997).

12. Oyeronke Oyewumi, *The Invention of Women: Making an African Sense of Western Gender Discourses* (Minneapolis: University of Minnesota Press, 1997). For an alternative analysis, see J. Lorand Matory, *Sex and the Empire that is No More: Gender and the Politics of Metaphor in Oyo Yoruba Religion* (New York: Berghahn, 2nd edn, 2005).

13. J. D. Y. Peel, 'Gender in Yorùbá Religious Change', *Journal of Religion in Africa*, 32 (2002), 139; see too J. Lorand Matory, 'Is there Gender in Yorùbá Culture?', in Jacob K. Olupona and Terry Ray, eds, *Òrìsà Devotion as World Religion: The Globalization of Yorùbá Religious Culture* (Madison, Wis.: University of Wisconsin Press, 2008).

14. David Schoenbrun, *A Green Place, A Good Place: Agrarian Change and Social Identity in the Great Lakes Region to the 15th Century* (Portsmouth, NH: Heinemann, 1998).

15. Jerome H. Barkow, 'Muslims and Maguzawa in North Central State, Nigeria: An Ethnographic Comparison', *Canadian Journal of African Studies*, 7 (1973).

16. Dorothy L. Hodgson, ed., *Rethinking Pastoralism in Africa: Gender, Culture, and the Myth of the Patriarchal Pastoralist* (Oxford: James Currey, 2000).

17. Claire Robertson and Martin Klein, eds, *Women and Slavery in Africa* (Madison, Wis.: University of Wisconsin Press, 1983).

18. Stephen Murray and Will Roscoe, eds, *Boy Wives and Female Husbands: Studies of African Homosexualities* (London: Macmillan, 1988); Marc Epprecht, *Hungochani: The History of a Dissident Sexuality in Southern Africa* (Montreal: McGill-Queens University Press, 2004).

19. Sean Stilwell, *Paradoxes of Power: The Kano 'Mamluks' and Male Royal Slavery in the Sokoto Caliphate, 1804-1903* (Portsmouth, NH: Heinemann, 2004); Emily Ruete, *Memoirs of an Arabian Princess from Zanzibar* (Princeton: Markus Weiner, 2000).

20. Claude Meillassoux, *Maidens, Meal and Money: capitalism and the domestic community* (Cambridge: CUP, 1981).

21. George E. Brooks, *Eurafricans in Western Africa: Commerce, Social Status, Gender and Religious Observance* (Athens, O.: Ohio University Press 2003).

22. Beverly Mack and Jean Boyd, *One Woman's Jihad: Nana Asma'u, Scholar and Scribe* (Bloomington, Ind.: Indiana University Press, 2000).

23. Ivor Wilks, 'She Who Blazed a Trail: Akyaawa Yikwan of Asante', in Patricia Romero, ed., *Life Histories of African Women* (London: Ashfield Press, 1988).

24. Marcia Wright, *Strategies of Slaves and Women* (New York: Lillian Barber Press, 1993).

25. Paul E. Lovejoy and Jan S. Hogendorn, *Slow Death for Slavery: The Course of Abolition in Northern Nigeria, 1897-1936* (Cambridge: CUP, 1993); Suzanne Miers and Richard Roberts, eds, *The End of Slavery in Africa* (Madison, Wis.: University of Wisconsin Press, 1988).

26. Jane Guyer, *Family and Farm in Southern Cameroon* (Boston: Boston University, 1984); Barbara M. Cooper, 'Reflections on Slavery, Seclusion and Female Labor in the Maradi Region of Niger in the Nineteenth and Twentieth Centuries', *Journal of African History*, 35 (1994).

27. Mary H. Moran, 'Woman and "Civilization": The Intersection of Gender and Prestige in Southeastern Liberia', *Canadian Journal of African Studies*, 22 (1988); E. Frances White, 'Creole Women Traders in the Nineteenth Century', *International Journal of African Historical Studies*, 14 (1981).

28. Claire Robertson, *Sharing the Same Bowl: A Socioeconomic History of Women and Class in Accra, Ghana* (Bloomington, Ind.: Indiana University Press, 1984).

29. Pamela Scully, *Liberating the Family? Gender and British Slave Emancipation in the Rural Western Cape, South Africa, 1823-1853* (Portsmouth, NH: Heinemann, 1997).

30. For an exceptional study, see Richard Roberts, *Litigants and Households: African Disputes and Colonial Courts in the French Soudan, 1895-1912* (Portsmouth, NH: Heinemann, 2005); see too Margaret Jean Hay and Marcia Wright, *African Women and the Law: Historical Perspectives* (Boston: Boston University Papers on Africa, 1982), and Martin Chanock, *Law, Custom and Social Order: The Colonial Experience in Malawi and Zambia* (Cambridge: CUP).

31. Jean Allman, 'Rounding up Spinsters: Gender Chaos and Unmarried Women in Colonial Asante', *Journal of African History*, 37 (1996).

32. Dorothy Hodgson and Sheryl A. McCurdy, eds, *'Wicked' Women and the Reconfiguration of Gender in Africa* (Portsmouth, NH: Heinemann, 2001).

33. Elizabeth Schmidt, *Peasants, Traders and Wives: Shona Women in the History of Zimbabwe, 1870-1939* (Portsmouth, NH: Heinemann, 1992).

34. See Barbara M. Cooper, 'Women's Worth and Wedding Gift Exchange in Maradi Niger, 1907-89', *Journal of African History*, 36 (1995).

35. The literature on the Igbo Women's War is particularly rich: see Judith Van Allen, '"Sitting on a Man" and "Aba Riots" or "Igbo Women's War": Ideology, Stratification and the Invisibility of Women', in Hafkin and Bay, *Women in Africa*; Nina Mba, *Nigerian Women Mobilized: Women's Political Activity in Southern Nigeria, 1900-1965* (Berkeley, Calif.: University of California, 1982); Susan Kingsley Kent, Misty L. Bastian,

and Marc Matera, *The Women's War of 1929: Gender and Violence in Colonial Nigeria* (Basingstoke: Palgrave, 2011); Toyin Falola and Adam Paddock, *The Women's War of 1929: A History of Anti-Colonial Resistance in Eastern Nigeria* (Durham, NC: Carolina Academic Press, 2011).

36. See e.g. Marie Rodet, 'Le Délit d'abandon de domicile conjugal ou l'invasion du pénal colonial dans les jugements des tribunaux indigènes au Soudan français, 1900–1947', *French Colonial History*, 10 (2009); Nancy Rose Hunt, 'Noise over Camouflaged Polygamy, Colonial Morality Taxation and a Woman-Naming Crisis in Belgian Africa', *Journal of African History*, 32 (1991).

37. Cooper, *Marriage in Maradi*.

38. Karen Tranberg Hansen, ed., *African Encounters with Domesticity* (New Brunswick, NJ: Rutgers University Press, 1992).

39. LaRay Denzer, 'Gender and Decolonization: A Study of Three Women in West African Public Life', in J. F. Ade Ajayi and J. D. Y. Peel, eds, *People and Empires in African History: Essays in Memory of Michael Crowder* (Harlow: Longman, 1992).

40. A groundbreaking collection is Lisa A. Lindsay and Stephan F. Miescher, eds, *Men and Masculinities in Modern Africa* (Portsmouth, NH: Heinemann, 2003).

41. Luise White, *The Comforts of Home: Prostitution in Colonial Nairobi* (Chicago: University of Chicago Press, 1990).

42. Kristin Mann, *Marrying Well: Marriage, Status and Social Change among the Educated Elite in Colonial Lagos* (Cambridge: CUP, 1985); Lisa A. Lindsay, *Working with Gender: Wage Labor and Social Change in Southwestern Nigeria* (Portsmouth, NH: Heinemann, 2003).

43. Margaret Jean Hay, 'Luo Women and Economic Change during the Colonial Period', in Hafkin and Bay, *Women in Africa*.

44. Richard A. Schroeder, *Shady Practices: Agroforestry and Gender Politics in the Gambia* (Berkeley, Calif.: University of California Press, 1999).

45. Marc Epprecht, *Heterosexual Africa? The History of an Idea from the Age of Exploration to the Age of AIDS* (Athens, O.: Ohio University Press, 2008); for an excellent overview, see his 'Sexuality, Africa, History', *American Historical Review*, 114/5 (2009).

46. Amy Kaler, *Running After Pills: Politics, Gender, and Contraception in Colonial Zimbabwe* (Portsmouth, NH: Heinemann, 2003); Susanne M. Klausen, *Race, Maternity, and the Politics of Birth Control in South Africa, 1910–39* (New York: Palgrave, 2004).

47. Lynn Thomas, *Politics of the Womb: Women, Reproduction, and the State in Kenya* (Berkeley, Calif.: University of California Press, 2003); see too Nancy Rose Hunt, *A Colonial Lexicon: Of Birth Ritual, Medicalization, and Mobility in the Congo* (Durham, NC: Duke University Press, 2000).

48. Jennifer Cole and Lynn M. Thomas, eds, *Love in Africa* (Chicago: University of Chicago Press, 2009).

49. See Mark Hunter, *Love in the Time of AIDS: Inequality, Gender, and Rights in South Africa* (Bloomington, Ind.: Indiana University Press, 2010).

50. John Iliffe, *The African AIDS Epidemic: A History* (Athens, O.: Ohio University Press, 2006); Helen Epstein, *The Invisible Cure: Why we are Losing the Fight Against AIDS in Africa* (Picador: 2008).

51. See e.g. Susan Geiger, *TANU Women: Gender and Culture in the Making of Tanganyikan Nationalism, 1955–1965* (Portsmouth, NH: Heinemann, 1998); Stephanie Urdang, *And Still they Dance: Women, War and the Struggle for Change in Mozambique* (New York: Monthly Review Press, 1989); Cora Ann Presley, 'The Mau Mau Rebellion,

Kikuyu Women, and Social Change', *Canadian Journal of African Studies*, 22 (1988); Wambui Waiyaki Otieno, *Mau Mau's Daughter: A Life History* (Boulder, Colo.: Lynne Reiner, 1998).

52. Sita Ranchod-Nilsson, 'Gender Politics and the Pendulum of Political and Social Transformation in Zimbabwe', *Journal of Southern African Studies*, 32 (2006).

53. Meredeth Turshen and Clotilde Twagiramariya, *What Women Do in Wartime: Gender and Conflict in Africa* (London: Zed, 1998); Christina Gladwin, *Structural Adjustment and African Women Farmers* (Gainesville, Fla.: University Press of Florida, 1991); Jane L. Parpart and Kathleen A. Staudt, eds, *Women and the State in Africa* (Boulder, Colo.: Lynne Rienner, 1989); Meredeth Turshen, *Privatizing Health Services in Africa* (New Brunswick, NJ: Rutgers University Press, 1999).

54. Schroeder, *Shady Practices*.

55. Gisela Geisler, '"Parliament is Another Terrain of Struggle": Women, Men and Politics in South Africa', *Journal of Modern African Studies*, 38 (2000).

56. See e.g. Leslie Bank, 'Beyond Red and School: Gender, Tradition and Identity in the Rural Eastern Cape', *Journal of Southern African Studies*, 28 (2002).

57. Ousseina Alidou, *Engaging Modernity: Muslim Women and the Politics of Agency in Postcolonial Niger* (Madison, Wis.: University of Wisconsin Press, 2005).

BIBLIOGRAPHY

Allman, Jean, Susan Geiger, and Nakanyike Musisi, eds, *Women in African Colonial Histories* (Bloomington, Ind.: Indiana University Press, 2002).

Amadiume, Ifi, *Male Daughters, Female Husbands: Gender and Sex in an African Society* (London: Zed Books, 1987).

Boyd, Jean, *The Caliph's Sister, Nana Asma'u, 1793–1865: Teacher, Poet and Islamic Leader* (London: Frank Cass, 1989).

Cole, Jennifer, and Lynn M. Thomas, eds, *Love in Africa* (Chicago: University of Chicago Press, 2009).

Cooper, Barbara M., *Marriage in Maradi: Gender and Culture in a Hausa Society in Niger* (Portsmouth, NH: Heinemann, 1997).

Cornwall, Andrea, *Readings in Gender in Africa* (Bloomington, Ind.: Indiana University Press, 2005).

Epprecht, Marc, *Heterosexual Africa? The History of an Idea from the Age of Exploration to the Age of AIDS* (Athens, O.: Ohio University Press, 2008).

Geiger, Susan, *TANU Women: Gender and Culture in the Making of Tanganyikan Nationalism, 1955–1965* (Portsmouth, NH: Heinemann, 1998).

Hafkin, Nancy, and Edna Bay, eds, *Women in Africa: Studies in Social and Economic Change* (Stanford, Calif.: Stanford University Press, 1976).

Hansen, Karen Tranberg, ed., *African Encounters with Domesticity* (New Brunswick, NJ: Rutgers University Press, 1992).

Hodgson, Dorothy, and Sheryl A. McCurdy, eds, *'Wicked' Women and the Reconfiguration of Gender in Africa* (Portsmouth, NH: Heinemann, 2001).

Hunt, Nancy Rose, *A Colonial Lexicon: Of Birth Ritual, Medicalization, and Mobility in the Congo* (Durham, NC: Duke University Press, 2000).

Hunt, Nancy Rose, Tessie P. Liu, and Jean Quataert, eds, *Gendered Colonialisms in African History* (Oxford: Blackwell, 1997).

Lindsay, Lisa, and Stephan F. Miescher, eds, *Men and Masculinities in Modern Africa* (Portsmouth, NH: Heinemann, 2003).

Robertson, Claire, and Martin Klein, eds, *Women and Slavery in Africa* (Madison, Wis.: Wisconsin University Press, 1983).

Schroeder, Richard A., *Shady Practices: Agroforestry and Gender Politics in the Gambia* (Berkeley, Calif.: University of California Press, 1999).

Thomas, Lynn, *Politics of the Womb: Women, Reproduction, and the State in Kenya* (Berkeley, Calif.: University of California Press, 2003).

CHAPTER 19

URBANIZATION AND URBAN CULTURES

JOHN PARKER

UTOPIA/DYSTOPIA

IN the year 2008, according to United Nations figures, the proportion of the world's population living in towns and cities reached 50 per cent. The urban revolution of the past two centuries had, statistically at least, arrived at a watershed: in that moment, humanity made the transition from being a predominantly rural to a predominantly urban species. This historic shift in the nature of human habitation has in recent decades been fuelled largely from Africa and Asia. Although in neither of these continents has the proportion of urban dwellers yet matched that of Europe or the Americas, both have experienced explosive rates of urbanization over the past fifty years. And this explosion is set to continue: in the next twenty-five years, it is estimated that Africa and Asia's combined urban population will double, adding a further 1.6 billion people to already overcrowded cities. Africa, at present, remains the world's least urbanized continent. Only eleven of its more than fifty nations contain a majority of urban dwellers and it boasts just two 'megacities', Cairo and Lagos, with populations of over 10 million, compared to some fifteen in Asia. Yet as recently as 1960, more than four out of five Africans lived in the countryside, and by 2020—i.e. in the space of one lifetime—it too will contain an absolute majority of city dwellers. Urbanization and the creation of new urban cultures are amongst the most dramatic social transformations in Africa's modern history.

The sheer speed and magnitude of these processes tell us something about the historiography of African cities and city life. It is, in short, widely considered to be in a state of underdevelopment. The editors of a landmark volume on the continent's urban past published in 2000 noted that 'urban history as a recognizable sub-field has not made a significant impact upon African historiography'.[1] Two years later, the editor of another important collection focusing on eastern Africa concurred: 'these are early days', he wrote, 'in the emergence of an African urban historiography'.[2] The belated engagement of historians with African urbanism, a tendency to write about things that happened to unfold in cities rather than about cities themselves, uncertainties about just how distinctively 'urban' the continent's precolonial towns really were, or how 'African' the colonial cities of the twentieth century: all of these factors are seen to have hindered the emergence of a literature able fully to get to grips with the complexities of urban social histories or to develop clear lines of theoretical debate.

Considerable advances have been made in the decade or so since the publication of the two volumes quoted here. While few would claim that the literature has reached the level of sophistication of that on other regions—more has probably still been written on the history of Paris, London, or New York than on all of Africa's cities combined—a more nuanced understanding of the continent's urban past is now emerging.[3] Dramatic urbanization in contemporary Africa has underlined the imperative to engage with the deeper history of individual cities and of regional urban networks—even if that history extends in many parts of the continent only to the era of colonial rule. It has also contributed to the setting aside of nagging issues concerning the definition, the attributes, and the typology of the African city. If at the beginning of the twentieth century, towns throughout much of the continent were an exception, by the 1940s urban society was a widespread reality and within a few decades was beginning to dominate that of the countryside. Far from being exceptional, urban settlement patterns in Africa have begun to follow the same broad historical trajectory as that of other continents.

The issue of historical exceptionalism is an important one, for another impact of unrestrained urban growth in postwar Africa and elsewhere in the global South has been a tendency to view the contemporary third world metropolis as a dystopia—either a calamitous aberration or a portent of a universalized future of alienation, inequality, physical decay, and social breakdown.[4] If Africa's two megacities, Cairo and Lagos, plus Kinshasa (also fast approaching the 10 million mark, and projected to be the continent's largest city by 2025) are most frequently cited as exemplars of this dystopian nightmare, then it is a vision that extends to contemporary African urbanism generally.[5] It is a vision, moreover, that is only partially offset by a contrary image of the African city as a site of human resilience and resourcefulness, where 'apparent constraints can point to unforeseen possibilities in livelihood and in the elaboration of vibrant urban cultures'.[6] Even the most celebratory accounts of against-the-odds inventiveness are often forced to concede that the outlook for the vast majority of Africa's city dwellers is bleak: 'for all its imaginative and creative exuberance', the editors of the tellingly named volume *Under Siege* admit, 'the contemporary African city is today in crisis'.[7] Thus, the dystopian megalopolis emerges as the monstrous inversion of the orderly, integrated city, such as that envisaged for French-ruled North Africa by Le Corbusier in his modernist manifesto, *The City of Tomorrow and its Planning* (1929). Meanwhile, the iconic modernist figure of the Baudelairean *flâneur* is supplanted by the wily street hustler and grifting survivor—the *lambwaza* of the decaying towns of the Zambian Copperbelt or the *sauveteur* of Douala's New Bell slums.[8] The Afro-pessimism of the 1970s and 1980s can be seen to be taking on a distinctively urban hue, as the historical struggle for the city is being supplanted by a struggle *with* the city itself.

It may be a mistake, however, to view the modern African city as essentially dysfunctional and aberrant. Here a comparative understanding of the urban past is crucial. Africa's individual cities have their own particular histories—political, economic, social, cultural, and intellectual—and the first task of their historians must be to reconstruct that history in all its complexity. The challenge then is to integrate our understanding of the continent's diverse urban past with that of other world regions; as that task proceeds, the less divergent the contemporary urban crisis may well seem. It is important to remember that modern European capitals too expanded by way of great bursts of rural migration: descriptions of early twentieth-century Moscow as 'a big village, a one- and two-storey bastion of patriarchal provincialism' within which most people grew much of their own food; of the 'vast shanty-towns' that ringed interwar Paris, where as recently as 1968 some 45 per cent of dwellings lacked a flush toilet; or of postwar Rome's 'sprawling, chaotic penumbra' of rural migrants, would all sound familiar to any student of the contemporary African city.[9]

With regard to perceptions of the urban, too, it can be seen that giant cities have long been regarded in many cultures with a profound ambivalence—as concentrations of dread and delight, at once sublime and grotesque, the best and the worst of human existence. Africa's teeming primate cities are far from the first to be viewed with apocalyptic foreboding: in the course of the nineteenth century, the inexorable rise of Europe's great industrial capitals spawned a profound strain of anti-urbanism in Western thought. If Walter Benjamin's famous *Arcades Project* was a celebration of the enchantment of nineteenth-century Paris, then for others that enchantment had a darker, more threatening face, deeply subversive of established social, political, and sexual norms.[10] By the end of the century, fears of an inevitable progress from metropolis to megalopolis and on to necropolis—the dead city—gave rise to the modern science of town planning and the garden city movement.[11] Emerging at the moment that Africa fell to European conquest, these radical new conceptions of urbanism would have a significant impact on the development of the twentieth-century colonial city. That the colonial city and its inhabitants would confound both the worst fears of urban pessimists and the visionary schemes of modernist planners was in no way peculiar to the African continent. As architectural historian Joseph Rykwert notes, 'literate critics of the city have been clamorous. Nevertheless, people have always crowded into cities, and their praises have also been sung.'[12]

AFRICAN URBAN STUDIES

It was from such divergent perceptions of city life that research into urban Africa took shape. North Africa's great cities had, of course, long attracted the attention of both indigenous and foreign chroniclers. Mamluk Cairo possessed a recognizable and extensive urban history in the form of Ahmad al-Maqrizi's *Khitat* as early as 1400; half a millennium later, René Lespès's *Alger* (1930) was a detailed account of a century of French interventions into the built environment and social fabric of the Algerian capital.[13] In sub-Saharan Africa, however, scholarly concern with towns emerged only in the terminal phase of European colonial rule. With the exception of early planning initiatives, its roots lay in the era of accelerating social change spanning the Depression and the Second World War, when rapid urbanization threatened to disrupt control over migrant labour and to erode the stereotype of traditional, rural African society on which the edifice of colonial rule was precariously constructed. As colonial officials struggled to assert control over worryingly 'detribalized' urban migrants, social scientists began to turn their attention to the new forms of town life. In British-ruled Africa, urban social science was pioneered by the anthropologists of the Rhodes-Livingstone Institute in Northern Rhodesia, who from the 1940s began to explore the variety of innovative social relations and cultural institutions created by migrant workers in the mining towns of the Copperbelt and elsewhere. In French Africa, the key figure was Georges Balandier, whose *Sociologie des Brazzavilles noires* (1955) drew a picture of restless, rapidly changing indigenous life in the Equatorial African capital at odds with the orderly visions of colonial planners.[14] Similar findings in other cities soon followed, with the publication the following year of the proceedings of a UNESCO conference held in Abidjan on the 'Social Impact of Industrialization and Urban Conditions in Africa'. As many colonies moved rapidly towards independence, the scope of research also widened from an early focus on the social 'adaptations' of migrants to the dynamics of urban politics; landmark works by Michael Banton on Freetown and Abner Cohen on Ibadan portrayed the complex connections between the two.[15] The new field of 'African urban studies' pointed to the ways in which the continent's cities encapsulated both the modernizing aspirations and the social challenges of the era of nationalism and decolonization.

The first generation of Africanist historians made only a limited contribution to this emerging interdisciplinary endeavour. In an era when the imperative was to reconstruct the precolonial past and when twentieth-century archives were only partially accessible, the urban revolution of the colonial period did not attract immediate attention. Despite the occasional celebratory nod in the direction of Africa's deeper urban past, the recent advent of cities in much of the continent meant that a self-consciously urban history began to be decoupled from labour history only in the 1970s. Since then, the recognition that African urbanism *was* often ephemeral and in a state of flux, and that towns *were* unrepresentative of wider society—odd, protean places full of minorities, strangers, and diasporic settler communities, often hailing from beyond Africa's shores—has begun to facilitate a more robust engagement with precolonial urban history. The transformations of Africa's tumultuous nineteenth century, in particular, provide fertile ground to explore continuity and change in urban forms from the precolonial to the colonial eras.

NINETEENTH-CENTURY COSMOPOLITANISMS

It may be overstating the case to say that Africa's modern urban revolution had clear roots in the nineteenth century, yet recent research has demonstrated that internal dynamics in combination with the expansion of global trade served to reconfigure established urban networks and to create new forms of city life in many parts of the continent. Two regions of long-established West African urbanism in particular underwent significant transformation: Hausaland, where the forging of the Sokoto Caliphate strengthened the role of Islam as the glue that bound together city culture, and neighbouring Yorubaland to the south, where decades of internecine warfare and internal migration reshaped the network of city-states and gave rise to a great new city of warriors and refugees, Ibadan. Escalating violence and indigenous imperial ambitions also resulted in the rise of new urban centres in north-eastern, eastern, and central Africa: Khartoum, established in the 1820s as the headquarters of the Egyptian conquest state in the Sudan—joined sixty years later by Omdurman, its Mahdist rival on the opposite bank on the Nile; Kampala, the expansive capital of the kingdom of Buganda; Addis Ababa, founded in 1886 and emerging as the new, permanent capital of Menelik's Shewan-centred Ethiopian Empire; as well as numerous examples of what Giacomo Macola, writing of Lunda royal capitals, refers to as the 'militarised and defensive urbanism' of the nineteenth century.[16] Like the so-called 'agro-towns' of southern African peoples such as the Tswana, just how urban the latter were remains an open question. Reflecting on the stockaded settlements of the eastern African interior, John Lonsdale writes that 'none of them were towns in the sense that they were governed by institutions distinct from those which ordered rural life'; yet Macola's analysis of Kazembe's *musumba*, with its distinctive quarters and hierarchies of power, does suggest a degree of divergence from established rural norms.[17]

Much of the best recent writing on the nineteenth century, however, has explored the social histories of those coastal towns and cities most open to the transformative impact of global flows of commodities, peoples, and ideas. Earlier scholarship often characterized such entrepôt ports as peculiarly 'hybrid', yet the more it becomes apparent that that is exactly, by definition, what all modern cities are, the less useful the term becomes. Over the course of the century, two cities arose at the northern and southern extremities of the continent that exemplified Africa's incorporation into expanding global networks: Alexandria and Cape Town. The great metropolis of the classical eastern Mediterranean, Alexandria had declined to a small village when in the 1820s it was refounded by Muhammad Ali as the gateway to modernizing Egypt and his planned Nile Valley empire beyond. The Egyptian ruler signalled his intent by building himself a residence on the Ras el Tin headland; an 1839 daguerreotype of the new palace is the first known photograph taken in Africa.[18] The construction of the Mahmoudiya Canal, a new harbour, and the Stock Exchange brought the city back to life, attracting a cosmopolitan mix of Greek, Italian, Jewish, Levantine, and indigenous Egyptian migrants. By

1871, its population was some 200,000 (compared to Cairo's 300,000) and by the First World War, half a million. Alexandria was a self-consciously modern boom town, a town on the make. Yet a fundamental social and cultural divide opened up between the cosmopolitan city—centred on the fashionable shops, restaurants, and theatres of Rue Chérif Pasha—and the teeming lower-class quarters populated by indigenous labourers and artisans. Much is known of the former, but less of the latter. Yet it is clear that the gulf between the two encapsulates the contradictions of Egypt's 'semi-colonial' economy, as it slid in the second half of the nineteenth century towards decadence, bankruptcy, and foreign intervention.

In contrast with Alexandria, Cape Town was an unambiguously colonial outpost from its foundation in 1652. Yet by the time the city passed from the control of the Dutch East India Company to the British at the start of the nineteenth century, it had developed a variety of contrasting urban cultures, from respectable Dutch burghers to free labourers and on to the large population of Coloured slaves. Like all port towns, Cape Town could be a rough and tumble place. Its famous *taphuisen*, taverns, served as a focus for the social life of the working classes, and criminal gangs were identified as a social problem as early as 1826. But religion, both Christianity and Islam, was also a key factor in town life. As slavery ended in the 1830s, the latter attracted many Coloured converts and by mid-century Cape Town's 6,000 Muslims or 'Malays' worshipped at six mosques. Afrikaans served as the language of instruction in the city's *madrasas*; indeed, the earliest known examples of written Afrikaans are the textbooks of Muslim students, using the Arabic script.[19]

On Africa's west coast, port towns that had developed as entrepôts in the era of the Atlantic slave trade were also reshaped by the gradual transition to legitimate commerce and colonial rule. From St Louis at the mouth of the Senegal River, to Cape Coast and Accra on the Gold Coast, Ouidah and Lagos on the Slave Coast, and south to Luanda in Angola, such coastal ports often grew up around European trading forts but soon took on local African characteristics. So too, to varying degrees, did the newly founded settlements of liberated slaves and African American returnees, Freetown and Monrovia. These towns remained too small in the nineteenth century to dominate their surrounding hinterlands: like Cape Town, as well as inland imperial capitals such as Kumasi and Abomey, they typically ranged from 15,000 to 20,000 in population. Within towns such as Accra and Ouidah, moreover, urban values and institutions were often strongly contested between competing hierarchies of local rulers, imperial overlords, religious specialists, mixed-race Euro-Africans, migrant communities, and the officials of European forts.[20] Yet in these coastal outposts of cosmopolitanism arose innovative new lifestyles, forms of consumption, technologies, and media of communication. Key here was literacy, including by mid-century a vigorous English-language press—which not only reflected the special character of West Africa's nineteenth-century coastal urban network but, crucially, has served to facilitate its reconstruction by historians. Recent research has begun to flesh out the precolonial social history of some of these eclectic port towns, as well as to articulate their internal dynamics with changes in the regional urban networks of which they were part. Robin Law's book on Ouidah together with that by Kristin Mann on Lagos demonstrate how the shift in focus of the slave trade in the Bight of Benin from the former to the latter in the first half of the nineteenth century impacted upon both. This suggests the way forward for a more connected urban history of regions such as Senegambia and the Gold Coast.[21]

Similar patterns are also emerging in research on Africa's east coast in the pre-colonial period, particularly with regard to the maritime Swahili civilization of present-day Tanzania and Kenya. Characterized by vibrant urban cultures and blessed with rich sources, including archaeological and written records, the Swahili towns occupy an important place on the cutting edge of African urban history. Much attention has been focused on Mombasa and, especially, on Zanzibar, which grew dramatically following the development of slave-worked clove plantations and the relocation of the capital of the Omani trading empire to the island in the 1830s. By the 1870s, Zanzibar was East Africa's largest city, its population of some 50,000 comprising indigenous Swahili, Arab settlers, 3,000 Indian traders, and a large number of mainland Africans subject to varying degrees of servitude. While the wealthier inhabitants were concentrated in the so-called Stone Town or Mji Mkongwe (literally 'Old Town'), poorer families were from mid-century spreading across the lagoon to Ng'ambo, or the 'Other Side'. Historians of Zanzibar are divided on the dynamics of this spatial dichotomy and the degree to which it is reflective of older patterns of Swahili urbanism, although the debate exhibits a mobilization of architectural evidence that offers rich possibilities for the history of established urban centres elsewhere on the continent.[22]

So too does Jeremy Prestholdt's *Domesticating the World*, on the consumption of material goods in the nineteenth-century Swahili towns. Consumerism has long been a key theme in the social history of European and American cities, most emblematically in Benjamin's exploration of Paris's glittering shopping passages in the *Arcades Project*. Yet despite the recognized role played by luxury imports in generating the Atlantic slave trade, consumerism—and its more specific associated activities, retailing and shopping—are only beginning to register as a feature of African urbanism. Drawing on sources that include the Swahili verse of the Mombasa poet Muyaka bin Haji and Krapf's Swahili–English dictionary—the 'most extensive reflections of social life in any East African city before the 1860s'—Prestholdt detects a restless cosmopolitanism in the avid consumption of goods in Mombasa, Zanzibar, and Mutsamudu town in the present-day Comoros Islands.[23] The role of the city in 'domesticating' global commodities and technologies is nowhere more evocative than in Sultan Barghash's development of Zanzibar's waterfront in the 1880s, which included the construction of the Beit al Ajaib, the 'House of Wonders', a three-storey palace displaying an eclectic range of exotic manufactures, scientific instruments, and photographs, a public water cistern in the shape of a ship's hull, and a striking clocktower-cum-lighthouse. Dominating the city's skyline and installed with four large clocks, Barghash's tower might be seen as a portent of the imposition of Western notions of temporal order, were it not for the fact that the clocks were set not to European but to Zanzibari time, with daybreak as one o'clock. Such customized cosmopolitanism is also apparent in late nineteenth-century Massawa, on the coast of present-day Eritrea. The 'Zanzibar of the Red Sea', Massawa too emerged as a dynamic port city under a local imperial tutelage, that of Egypt, from the 1860s.[24] Like its Indian Ocean counterpart, its diverse population originating from both land and sea was held together by ties of economic interest and by a distinctively Islamic urban culture.

Colonial Cities

It was from these port cities clinging to Africa's Mediterranean, Atlantic, and Indian Ocean littorals that at the end of the nineteenth century the European conquest of the continent's interior was launched. As indigenous imperial projects, states, and trading operations subsided in the face of better equipped and more ruthless European rivals, diverse coastal cosmopolitanisms gave way to a more ideologically structured version of urbanism: the 'colonial city'. Colonial capitals in particular were intended as projections of European power, although they originated in a variety of ways and subsequently took a variety of forms. Some, such as Lagos, Accra, and Kampala, were planted upon older African towns; others, like Dakar, Luanda, and Cape Town, grew from existing colonial outposts; whereas a third type, often sprouting from military encampments or at strategic points of communication, were entirely new creations. Examples of the latter include Conakry, Nairobi, and Salisbury (present-day Harare), as well as Brazzaville and Léopoldville (Kinshasa)—the twinned capitals of the French and Belgian imperial domains in Equatorial Africa, eying each other warily across the Congo River—plus, it should be added, Addis Ababa, Menelik's new Ethiopian imperial capital. In only a few cases did either existing or new urban centres challenge the dominance of colonial capitals within individual territories: notable examples are Ibadan, after Cairo the continent's largest city in 1900 and still almost twice the size of Lagos at Nigerian independence in 1960; Alexandria, Cairo's reinvigorated rival; Johannesburg, which outstripped Cape Town within a few years of its foundation in the mid-1880s and has remained South Africa's largest city since; and Casablanca, which retained its status as Morocco's largest city despite the French decision to locate their headquarters up the coast at Rabat. Elsewhere, colonial capitals tended to emerge as undisputed primate cities, especially where, as around the West African coast, they doubled as a colony's main entrepôt port.

The transformation of older cities and the foundation of new ones point to two fundamental issues in the history of the global urban revolution: the changing form of cities, and the reconfiguration of wider urban networks. The creation of built environments and the regulation of urban space in colonial Africa has received considerable attention and has made a notable contribution to the comparative study of the twentieth-century city. In contrast, the dynamics of regional urban networks, predicated as they are on an understanding of individual African cities, is only now beginning to emerge. Together, they form the necessary context for three other great themes of modern urban history: social and economic life; urban politics and governance; and the creation of urban cultures, including artistic production. Let us examine the current state of knowledge with regard to Africa of each of these themes in turn, with the aim of identifying emergent research agendas.

BUILT ENVIRONMENTS AND
URBAN NETWORKS

Insofar as European planners began to consider the spatial organization of new and existing cities from the very outset of colonial rule, it was the form of towns that represented the first sustained engagement with the idea of urbanism in twentieth-century Africa, predating the rise of urban social science in the 1940s. A number of recent works examine the history of town planning and architecture, with an important line of debate emerging on the degree to which such ventures were mechanisms of imperial order and control. While some scholars see the built environment as symbolically reinforcing colonial domination, others question its ability to do so—or at least detect limits to its hegemonic designs.[25] Much of the best research concerns the French Empire, particularly in North Africa, where proconsuls such as Marshal Lyautey in Morocco envisaged civic design as a tool to curb local resistance as well as to win support for colonialism in the metropole. As early as 1914, just two years after the declaration of the French protectorate, Lyautey appointed Henri Prost as head of his new Architecture and Urbanism Department, which the following year produced the first large-scale redevelopment scheme for Casablanca. Prost's vision of drawing both indigenous Moroccans and European settlers into 'a public life of leisure, consumerism, and civic pride' combined paternalistic social engineering with a healthy dose of imperial authoritarianism.[26] Like other North African cities, Casablanca was regarded as a *champ d'expérience*, an 'experimental terrain', where new ideas in urbanism might be applied unhindered by democratic accountability. This planning culture culminated in the International Congress on Urbanism in the Colonies held as part of the 1931 Colonial Exposition in Paris. Over the following decade, Le Corbusier, inspired by a grandiose vision of a corridor of modernism spanning the Mediterranean, drew up a sequence of plans for the redevelopment of Algiers.[27] Yet none was ever implemented, as a combination of economic depression, war, social change, and indigenous political aspirations widened the gulf between colonial vision and local reality. Despite a final burst of postwar planning in Casablanca by Le Corbusier's disciple Michel Écochard, the transformative power of modernist design was beginning to look as flimsy as the papier mâché simulacra of iconic African buildings in Paris's Parc de Vincennes in 1931.

A failure to assert control over the demographic and spatial expansion of established cities such as Casablanca and Algiers points to real limitations in the ability of colonial power to impose itself in African urban space, even in colonies with significant white settler communities. Lyautey and Prost's dream of turning Casablanca into a modern French city accommodating Europeans and an assimilated indigenous middle class soon began to evaporate as increasing numbers of dispossessed rural migrants poured into town. By the early 1920s, the spontaneous settlements springing up on the outskirts of the city had acquired a local name: Bidonville, the 'tin can' or 'oil drum' town—a term which in the following decade was being used generically for shanty-towns across the French Empire. Rather than the city projecting a model of orderly, assimilationist colonial culture into the countryside, the disorderly native countryside came to the city: by 1931, Casablanca's population of 160,000 was half Muslim (plus 20,000 Moroccan Jews); two decades later, on the eve on independence, its 473,000 Muslims comprised 69 per cent of the population (and the number of Jews had risen to 75,000).[28] Nor should the incorporation of vernacular motifs into a hybrid imperial architecture be seen as a simple appropriation of local culture in the service of colonial rule. As Cohen and Eleb point out, 'while the French were susceptible to the charms of Moroccan exoticism, some Muslims and Moroccan Jews were just as eager to embrace the exotic nature of the West, keen to possess Western clothes, housing, furniture and other objects'.[29] In common with Sultan Barghash's development of the Zanzibar water-front in the 1880s, colonial-era appropriations of modernity did not necessarily imply hegemonic cultural subjugation.

A similar conclusion may be offered with regard to the region south of the Sahara, although here the historiography of the built environment, with some partial exceptions such as Zanzibar, Asmara, and the older West African coastal towns, is less advanced than that for North Africa.[30] Like that for North Africa, moreover, it is still only par-tially integrated into the social history of urban life. Reflecting on the ideological intent of 'neo-Sudanic' architecture or dissecting colonial planning schemes—both those that got beyond the drawing board and the greater number that did not—provide insights into one set of perceptions of urban space and its future, but more attention needs to be given to how diverse urban populations, indigenous and settler, envisaged their chang-ing environment in the 'double cities' of the colonial era. Marissa Moorman's recent book on music in twentieth-century Luanda is instructive in this respect. Although concerned with the social history of Angolan pop music, Moorman situates its emer-gence in the culture of the *musseques*, Luanda's sandy shantytowns, that from the 1950s came increasingly to be defined in opposition to the *baixa*, the 'official' asphalted city.[31] As Lonsdale argues with regard to colonial Kenya, 'municipal social engineers did not so much initiate new social history as try to control the ways in which Africans were already exploiting new opportunity'.[32]

These attempts at control have attracted sustained interest from historians of the African colonial city. Much is now known about the role of racial segregation, sanitation and housing regulations, labour laws, and policing in the ordering of urban space, as well as of the jaundiced view that indigenous rural patriarchs sometimes held of the activities of women in towns. Yet just as access to new opportunity differed greatly according to gender and other social variables, so too was it shaped by the reconfiguration of regional urban networks. While new colonial capitals and a handful of dynamic industrial centres such as Johannesburg in South Africa and Elizabethville in the Belgian Congo (present-day Lubumbashi) experienced burgeoning growth by at least the interwar period, older towns often entered into long periods of decline. Such was the case when emergent primate cities greedily dominated economic and demographic expansion at the expense of established rivals, some of which had served for a time as early colonial headquarters before decaying into sleepy backwaters: witness the ascendancy of Dakar, Abidjan, Accra, Brazzaville, Léopoldville, and Dar es Salaam relative to St Louis, Bingerville, Cape Coast, Libreville, Boma, and Bagamoyo, respectively. Meanwhile, centres of indigenous political power were often bypassed, sometimes deliberately, by colonial communication links. The impact of such policy decisions is nowhere more apparent than in the contrasting twentieth-century history of the royal seats of the two most powerful precolonial states in the West African forest: the Asante capital, Kumasi, and that of Dahomey, Abomey. Whereas the railway from the Gold Coast arrived in the heart of Kumasi in 1903, acting as a catalyst for its regeneration as the colony's second city and a rival to upstart Accra, the French rulers of Dahomey chose to terminate their railway not in royal Abomey but nearby Bohicon. Kumasi today is a heaving metropolis; in stark contrast, Abomey retains a distinct precolonial air, its crumbling royal palaces rising from verdant undergrowth and connected still by red dirt roads.

These examples remind us that modern urban histories, far from being processes only of unrelenting growth, must also include narratives of decline and decay. The ghost towns left behind by the boom-and-bust cycles on the white settler frontiers of North America and Australasia, as well as the more recent hollowing out of rustbelt cities such as Detroit, point to this factor elsewhere. While we are now developing a clearer picture of how first- and second-generation African townspeople forged new livelihoods, lifestyles, and cultures in rapidly expanding migrant quarters, much less is known of changing community life for older commercial elites who found themselves marooned in quaint backwaters or in crumbling 'historic' inner-city quarters. From the casbahs of the Maghrib and the historic centre of Cairo to the ramshackle clapboard downtowns of Accra, Lagos, and Cape Town, established urban communities struggled to come to terms with the influx of rough country migrants who threatened their monopoly on urbanity and respectability. By mid-century, many such communities had become minorities in their own towns, their loss of control over the terms of settlement shaping escalating tensions in the era of decolonization between 'hosts' and 'strangers'.

Social and Economic Life

This brings us to the social and economic life of cities, including new forms of sociability as well as social struggle. As we have seen, it was these facets that, in turn, attracted the attention of the first two generations of scholars of African urbanism: the social scientists of the 1940s–1960s, followed by historians of labour from the 1970s. While research into social change continues apace, however, that on urban economies—along with economic history generally—has fallen from fashion, or has at best been subsumed into the former. Indeed, the full panoply of urban institutions that from mid-century seemed to define the restless 'social situation' of the colonial city continue to fascinate: ethnic associations, youth groups, burial societies, religious movements, literary and sports clubs, and new forms of sociability, of leisure, of consumption, and of language. Such innovations were often documented in colonial-era social surveys and ethnographic accounts, which are now assiduously being mined for data and relocated in historical context. In contrast, the economic concerns so prominent in the first wave of specifically historical writing on African cities—the creation of urban workforces and subsequent labour struggles, the control of urban land, economic linkages between town and countryside and 'urban bias'—have receded. This must be a concern, as not only is a deeper understanding of the changing nature of work needed for many towns and cities, economic transitions remain crucial to the periodization of any urban history. In terms of consumption, moreover, the voracious appetites of great cities—first and foremost for food—lie at the heart of the creation of national integrated economies and the wider projection of urban culture.[33]

Yet significant strides have been made in reconstructing the dynamics in many twentieth-century African cities of families, of neighbourhoods, and of communities—the three fundamental structures of urban social life.[34] Twenty years ago, with the scholarly emphasis still on labour and its control, little was known about the history of pastimes and leisure, while as recently as 2005 John Iliffe could note that, outside of South Africa, the study of urban youth had been neglected.[35] Both topics—and, crucially, the links between them—are now firmly established in the literature. From the beer bars, football clubs, and dance societies of Brazzaville, to the *taarab* musical salons and cutting-edge ladies' fashions of post-slavery Zanzibar, the ways in which both established urban communities and newly arriving migrants struggled to create new forms of individual identity and of sociability are beginning to be pieced together.[36] As in burgeoning cities everywhere, these processes were shaped by gender as well as by generation. While a start has certainly been made in the task of excavating the lived experience of women in what was often overwhelmingly male urban space, much remains to be done in thinking about the many ways in which Africa's townswomen—at all levels of society—created the 'comforts of home'.[37]

Important individual cities, too, have begun to emerge from the historiographical shadows. A case in point is Dar es Salaam, which might be used to illustrate broader trends in research. Founded in the 1860s as an outpost of Zanzibari mercantile power on the Mrima coast before becoming the headquarters of German East Africa, of British Tanganyika, and, briefly, of independent Tanzania, Dar es Salaam formed part of the backdrop for some key pioneering works of African history, from Terence Ranger's *Dance and Society in Eastern Africa* (1975) to John Iliffe's *Modern History of Tanganyika* (1979). Yet the city itself remained in the background, lacking the distinctive character of its regional rivals Nairobi and Kampala or the cultural swagger of a Lagos or a Kinshasa. In 1974, the Nyerere regime moved the national capital to the interior town of Dodoma, a 'big village' regarded as more conducive to the building of rural-based African socialism than the 'capitalist' coastal metropolis. In subsequent decades, however, 'Dar' has emerged onto the continental—and, increasingly, global—stage. With a population of some 3 million, it is now East Africa's largest city and the subject of varied lines of historical inquiry into the evolution of its built environment, diverse communities, youth culture, musical and dance genres—from *beni ngoma* to *dansi* to *bongo flava*—and, crucially, its role in the forging of contested national cultures.[38]

URBAN POLITICS

That urban space was the principal arena of mass nationalist politics in the postwar period has long been recognized. It was with Dar es Salaam in mind that John Iliffe wrote that it 'was in the towns that Europeans first lost control of Africa'.[39] Colonial cities may have been envisaged by their rulers and planners as showcases of modernity and sound imperial governance, to which the mass of rural Africans would be exposed, if at all, under close supervision. As early as the 1930s, however, the socio-economic transformations and rising expectations generated by urban life were beginning to undermine the very order that cities were meant to exemplify. By the end of the Second World War, rapidly swelling urban populations were frustrated by shortages of housing, consumer goods, and services, and workers began to flex their collective muscle in concerted waves of industrial action. Then in 1948 came two events that can be seen to have encapsulated the growing contradictions of colonial urbanism: in the Gold Coast, Britain's 'model' African colony, mounting frustration exploded into rioting in the capital Accra and other towns; and in South Africa the white electorate, itself frustrated and frightened by the spectre of being overwhelmed by rural black Africa, narrowly voted the National Party into power, marking the beginning of the Apartheid era. Pioneering urban ethnographers across the continent would soon have to factor a further element into their analyses of the fluid 'social situation': political action in the form of determined anti-colonial nationalism.

As archives open up and historians turn their attention to Africa's era of decolonization, established narratives of national liberation begin to be contested and complicated. Urban politics were not simply nationalist politics. Neither did they emerge only in the 1950s: political struggles for the city and contested visions of its future extend back into the deeper past, as well as forwards into contemporary times. One neglected arena for such struggles was municipal government: experiments with modern town councils on the coast of West Africa date to the late nineteenth century, while the creation of a municipality in 1890 established Alexandria as the 'first self-governing city in the Middle East'.[40] Another was the more 'traditional' structure of town quarters and religious congregations presided over by hierarchies of secular and sacred office holders, such as those in the Yoruba towns of Nigeria. A third space of contest was the popular neighbourhood, often unregulated, rowdy shantytowns such as Cairo's *awhash*, or Luanda's *musseques*, whose everyday cultural practice, Moorman argues, must be relocated from the margins to 'the centre of national history'.[41] Far from being subsumed into a monolithic vision of anti-colonial liberation, many such communities and institutions survived to challenge the authority of new indigenous ruling elites to imprint unitary national cultures on urban space.

That said, the importance of tracing continuities across the colonial divide should not obscure the fact that, in some African cities, established ways of life and civic values were overthrown by the rise of the nation-state. In common with the end of multi-ethnic imperial cities in central and south-eastern Europe in the aftermath of the First World War, the cosmopolitan character of North Africa's great cities declined rapidly in the 1950s. This was particularly the case in Alexandria and Cairo, where, in a process of ethnic homogenization already witnessed in Mediterranean centres such as Salonica and Smyrna, diverse 'Levantine' cities were transformed into Egyptian cities. In a telling reflection of the decline of imperial merchant capital in the face of a new vision of autochthonous statehood, Colonel Nasser announced the nationalization of the Suez Canal in 1956 from the balcony of Alexandria's famous Bourse, which began life as the mansion of Michael Tossizza, the leading businessman in Muhammad Ali's new city, before becoming the world's second largest cotton exchange. In a further sign of the times—and of the ongoing importance of urban space as site of popular protest—the building would be destroyed in the 1977 food riots that swept Egyptian cities.[42]

Nationalism also brought an end to urban orders better described as hierarchical and racially exclusive than cosmopolitan and inclusive, as Europeans vacated the cities of white settler colonies from Algiers and Asmara to Luanda and Lourenço Marques and Zanzibar's Arab aristocracy was overthrown in the bloody 1964 revolution. Then, in processes that are only just beginning to be understood by historians, it was the turn of indigenous ruling elites to attempt to imprint their newly won power on the urban fabric.[43] Somewhat ironically, postcolonial design strategies tended to reject art deco neo-traditionalism in favour of modernist European functionalism, which was put to use in the reshaping of established cities as well as the construction of new ones. The Senegalese government, for example, set about demolishing swathes of Dakar's colonial-era Médina and replacing it with concrete *cités* that aimed to 'socialize' rural migrants; later, in the 1980s, socialist-orientated military regimes in Ghana and Burkina Faso would raze the central markets in their respective capitals in order to root out supposed opposition from 'profiteering' women traders. Anti-urban bias—or, at least, a bias against autonomous or 'neo-colonialist' vested interests in established capital cities—can also be detected in the construction of new capitals: Dodoma in Tanzania, and two 1980s Brasilia-like planned cities (minus Brasilia's heady optimism and visionary architecture, that is), Abuja in Nigeria and Yamoussoukro in Côte d'Ivoire. The latter, with the dome of its great Catholic basilica rising from the forest of what had been the late President Houphouët-Boigny's natal village, stands as a potent symbol of the over-inflated hegemonic pretensions of the era of personalized autocracy.

ARTS AND IMAGINARIES

It is primarily in the context of the postcolonial era that we turn to our final theme: the creation of urban cultures, in particular the production of visual, written, and performing arts generated by and reflecting on the city. This is not to say that new forms of culture and the arts were unimportant in earlier periods. As elsewhere in the world, their emergence was fundamental in distinguishing city life from that of the traditional countryside. In the realm of visual arts, one medium stands out as capturing the restless modernity of the city: photography, which by the late nineteenth century was being widely practised in both African- and expatriate-owned studios in the continent's coastal towns.[44] In the performing arts, the definitive medium in twentieth-century urban Africa has been popular music. Like photography, its evolution was energized by technological change and commercialization, as advances in recording in the 1920s facilitated stylistic interaction and innovation around the broader Atlantic and Indian Ocean worlds. From 'highlife' on the Gold Coast to *marabi* in South Africa and *taarab* on the Swahili coast, by the interwar period new hybrid, syncopated styles reflected the pace, energy, and bricolage of urban life.

Yet it was the explosive urbanization of the later twentieth century that led to the multiplication and amplification of these and other forms of cultural production. Whereas such innovations once set towns apart as strange new worlds—alluring to some and disturbing to others, but relatively self-contained as concentrations of modernity—recent decades have witnessed their diffusion into an increasingly urbanized countryside. The rising dominance of big cities has given much pause to observers of contemporary African urbanism, who turn to culture as the repository of what are often called urban 'imaginaries'; that is, in the words of Mamadou Diouf, 'beliefs, practices, histories, fears, phantasms, and readings of the world'.[45] The excavation of such imaginaries has a venerable tradition in the scholarship of the modern city beyond Africa, from Benjamin's reading of the urban fabric of Paris as a 'memory machine', to urban philosopher Henri Lefebvre's 'rhythmanalysis', the *dérive* or 'drift' of the Situationists, 'psychogeography', and on to a recent extrapolation of Baudelairean rag-picking: 'rubbish theory'.[46] Arising from a feeling that conventional sources, methods, and vocabularies are simply not adequate fully to capture the protean and ambivalent meanings of the modern metropolis, the cultural turn to 'imaginaries' has much to offer beyond the fleetingly fashionable (consider how the extension of a city's archive to its detritus might benefit an understanding of, say, Lagos)—if, that is, the 'history' part of Diouf's description is taken seriously.

Certainly, some of the most interesting recent work on African urbanism has been on the role of the arts in the visible social fabric of the city and in the evocation of the imagined or 'invisible' city.[47] The liberation promised by towns as well as the moral threat they pose has long been reflected in forms as diverse as the novel, popular music, and the painted scenes of rural idyll that decorate bars and clubs across the continent.

Here, we return to where we began: to the central paradox of the city as both utopia and dystopia, delightful and dreadful in equal measure. For, as in cities elsewhere, it is art that provides an obvious entry into the tensions between these multiple identities. If the advent of expressionism and atonal music can be seen as symptoms both of urban alienation and of urban inventiveness in early twentieth-century Europe, so too can the work of Congolese painter Chéri Samba, whose canvasses confront the atrophy, quotidian hardships, aggressive consumption, and sexualization, and, to use Achille Mbembe's term, 'vulgarity' of contemporary Kinshasa.[48] Again, the danger here is the temptation to fixate on the contemporary and invisible at the expense of the historical and visible city. Yet as Africa and its exploding population of city-dwellers enter the post-Cold War era of escalating global inequality and urban hypertrophy, such imaginaries will only continue to resonate.

Notes

1. David M. Anderson and Richard Rathbone, eds, *Africa's Urban Past* (Oxford: James Currey, 2000), 9.
2. Andrew Burton, ed., *The Urban Experience in Eastern Africa c.1750–2000* (Nairobi: British Institute in Eastern Africa, 2002), 1.
3. The recent appearance of an excellent textbook signals a maturing historiography: Bill Freund, *The African City: A History* (New York: CUP, 2007); see too Catherine Coquery-Vidrovitch, *The History of African Cities South of the Sahara: From the Origins to Colonization* (Princeton: Markus Wiener, 2005), and Laurent Fourchard, 'Between World History and State Formation: New Perspectives on Africa's Cities', *Journal of African History*, 52 (2011).
4. See Mike Davis, *Planet of Slums* (London: Verso, 2006).
5. Projected populations for Africa's largest cities in 2025 are: Kinshasa 16.8 million; Lagos 15.8 million; Cairo 15.6 million; Luanda 8.2 million, 'Wealth Gap Creating a Social Time Bomb', *Guardian*, 23 Oct. 2008; 'Mega-Slums Danger Warning for Africa as Population Passes 1bn', *Guardian*, 24 Nov. 2010.
6. AbdouMaliq Simone and Abdelghani Abouhani, eds, *Urban Africa: Changing Contours of Survival in the City* (Dakar: CODESRIA Books, 2005), 1; see too AbdouMaliq Simone, *For the City Yet to Come: Changing African Life in Four Cities* (Durham, NC: Duke University Press, 2004).
7. Okwui Enwezor et al., eds, *Under Siege: Four African Cities. Freetown, Johannesburg, Kinshasa, Lagos* (Kassel: Hatje Cantz, 2002), 14.
8. See James Ferguson, *Expectations of Modernity: Myths and Meanings of Urban Life on the Zambian Copperbelt* (Berkeley, Calif.: University of California Press, 1999); and Basile Ndijo, 'Douala: Inventing Life in an African Necropolis', in Martin J. Murray and Garth A. Myers, eds, *Cities in Contemporary Africa* (New York: Palgrave Macmillan, 2006).
9. The quotations are from Anthony Sutcliffe, ed., *Metropolis, 1890–1940* (London: Mansell, 1984), 22, 28; and Peter Clark, *European Cities and Towns, 400–2000* (Oxford: OUP, 2009), 239.
10. Walter Benjamin, *The Arcades Project* (Cambridge, Mass.: Belknap, 1999).
11. Theo Baker and Anthony Sutcliffe, eds, *Megalopolis: The Giant City in History* (London: Macmillan, 1993).

12. Joseph Rykwert, *The Seduction of Place: The City in the Twenty-First Century* (New York: Pantheon Books, 2000), 5; see too Edward Glaeser, *Triumph of the City: How Urban Spaces Make us Human* (London: Macmillan, 2011).

13. André Raymond, *Cairo: City of History* (Cairo: American University in Cairo Press, 2001), 149; Patricia M. E. Lorcin, 'Historiographies of Algiers: Critical Reflections', in Zeynep Çelik, Julia Clancy-Smith, and Frances Terpak, eds, *Walls of Algiers: Narratives of the City through Text and Image* (Los Angeles: Getty Research Institute, 2009), 234.

14. On Balandier, see Frederick Cooper, *Colonialism in Question: Theory, Knowledge, History* (Berkeley, Calif.: University of California Press, 2005), 33–55.

15. Michael Banton, *West African City: A Study of Tribal Life in Freetown* (London: OUP, 1957); Abner Cohen, *Custom and Politics in Urban Africa: A Study of Hausa Migrants in Yoruba Towns* (Berkeley, Calif.: University of California Press, 1969).

16. Giacomo Macola, 'The History of the Eastern Lunda Royal Capitals to 1900', in Burton, *Urban Experience*, 44.

17. John Lonsdale, 'Town Life in Colonial Kenya', in Burton, *Urban Experience*, 209.

18. Michael Haag, *Vintage Alexandria: Photographs of the City, 1860–1960* (Cairo: American University in Cairo Press, 2008).

19. Nigel Worden, Elizabeth van Heyningen, and Vivian Bickford-Smith, *Cape Town: The Making of a City* (Claremont: David Philip, 1998), 76–9, 124–7.

20. John Parker, *Making the Town: Ga State and Society in Early Colonial Accra* (Portsmouth, NH: Heinemann, 2000); Robin Law, *Ouidah: The Social History of a West African Slaving 'Port', 1727–1892* (Oxford: James Currey, 2004).

21. Law, *Ouidah*; Kristin Mann, *Slavery and the Birth of an African City: Lagos, 1760–1900* (Bloomington, Ind.: Indiana University Press, 2007).

22. Abdul Sheriff, 'The Spatial Dichotomy of Swahili Towns: The Case of Zanzibar in the Nineteenth Century', in Burton, *Urban Experience*.

23. Jeremy Prestholdt, *Domesticating the World: African Consumerism and the Genealogies of Globalization* (Berkeley, Calif.: University of California Press, 2008), 37.

24. Jonathan Miran, *Red Sea Citizens: Cosmopolitan Society and Cultural Change in Massawa* (Bloomington, Ind.: Indiana University Press, 2009).

25. For examples of the former, see Thomas M. Shaw, *Irony and Illusion in the Architecture of Imperial Dakar* (Lewiston, NY: Edwin Mellen Press, 2006); Garth Myers, *Verandahs of Power: Colonialism and Space in Urban Africa* (Syracuse, NY: Syracuse University Press, 2003); and the latter, Gwendolyn Wright, *The Politics of Design in French Colonial Urbanism* (Chicago: University of Chicago Press, 1991); Jean-Louis Cohen and Monique Eleb, *Casablanca: Colonial Myths and Architectural Ventures* (New York: Monacelli Press, 2002); William Cunningham Bissell, *Urban Design, Chaos, and Colonial Power in Zanzibar* (Bloomington, Ind.: Indiana University Press, 2011).

26. Wright, *Politics of Design*, 106.

27. Zeynep Çelik, *Urban Forms and Colonial Confrontations: Algiers under French Rule* (Berkeley, Calif.: University of California Press), 40–2.

28. Cohen and Eleb, *Casablanca*, 169–70, 286.

29. Cohen and Eleb, *Casablanca*, 441.

30. Jacques Soulillou, ed., *Rives Coloniales: Architectures, de Saint-Louis à Douala* (Marseilles: Éditions Parenthèses, 1993); Edward Denison, Guang Yu Ren, and Naigxy Gebremedhin, *Asmara: Africa's Secret Modernist Town* (London: Merrell, 2003).

31. Marissa J. Moorman, *Intonations: A Social History of Music and Nation in Luanda, Angola, from 1945 to Recent Times* (Athens, O.: Ohio University Press, 2008).

32. Lonsdale, 'Town Life in Colonial Kenya', in Burton, *Urban Experience*, 221.
33. On food in Libreville, see Jeremy Rich, *A Workman is Worthy of his Meat: Food and Colonialism in the Gabon Estuary* (Lincoln, Neb.: University of Nebraska Press, 2007).
34. See Clark, *European Cities*, 303.
35. John Iliffe, *Honour in African History* (Cambridge: CUP, 2005), 368.
36. Phyllis Martin, *Leisure and Society in Colonial Brazzaville* (Cambridge: CUP, 1995); Laura Fair, *Pastimes and Politics: Culture, Community, and Identity in Post-Abolition Urban Zanzibar, 1890–1945* (Athens, O.: Ohio University Press, 2001).
37. Luise White, *The Comforts of Home: Prostitution in Colonial Nairobi* (Chicago: University of Chicago Press, 1990).
38. An excellent survey of recent developments is James R. Brennan, Andrew Burton, and Yusuf Lawi, eds, *Dar es Salaam: Histories from an Emerging African Metropolis* (Dar es Salaam: Mkuki na Nyota, 2007); see too James R. Brennan, *Taifa: Making Nation and Race in Urban Tanzania* (Athens, O.: Ohio University Press, 2012).
39. John Iliffe, *A Modern History of Tanganyika* (Cambridge: CUP), 381.
40. Michael Haag, *Alexandria: City of Memory* (New Haven, Conn.: Yale University Press), 16.
41. Moorman, *Intonations*, 53.
42. For two elegiac accounts of the twilight of Levantine cosmopolitanism, see Haag, *Alexandria*, and Philip Mansel, *Levant: Splendour and Catastrophe on the Mediterranean* (London: John Murray, 2010).
43. See Okwui Enwezor, ed., *The Short Century: Independence and Liberation Movements in Africa, 1945–1994* (Munich: Prestel, 2001), esp. Gwendolyn Wright, 'The Ambiguous Modernisms of African Cities', 225–33, and Nnamdi Elleh, 'Architecture and Nationalism in Africa, 1945–1994', 234–45.
44. From a rapidly growing literature, see Erin Haney, *Photography and Africa* (London: Reaktion, 2010).
45. Allen F. Roberts and Mary Nooter Roberts, *A Saint in the City: Sufi Arts of Urban Senegal* (Los Angeles: UCLA Fowler Museum, 2003), preface by Mamadou Diouf, 12.
46. A useful survey is Matthew Beaumont and Gregory Dart, eds, *Restless Cities* (London: Verso, 2010); see too Tom McDougal, ed., *The Situationists and the City* (London: Verso, 2009).
47. See e.g. Filip de Boeck and Marie-Francoise Plissart, *Kinshasa: Tales of the Invisible City* (Brussels: Ludion, 2005); Roberts and Roberts, *Saint in the City*; and on creative literature as an inspiration for social history, Terence Ranger, *Bulawayo Burning: The Social History of a Southern African City, 1893–1960* (Oxford: James Currey, 2010).
48. Achille Mbembe, *On the Postcolony* (Berkeley, Calif.: University of California Press, 2001).

BIBLIOGRAPHY

Anderson, David M., and Richard Rathbone, eds, *Africa's Urban Past* (Oxford: James Currey, 2000).
Brennan, James R., Andrew Burton, and Yusuf Lawi, eds, *Dar es Salaam: Histories from an Emerging African Metropolis* (Dar es Salaam: Mkuki na Nyota, 2007).
Burton, Andrew, ed., *The Urban Experience in Eastern Africa c.1750–2000* (Nairobi: British Institute in Eastern Africa, 2002).

Çelik, Zeynip, Julia Clancy-Smith, and Frances Terpek, eds, *Walls of Algiers: Narratives of the City through Text and Image* (Los Angeles: Getty Research Institute, 2009).

Cohen, Jean-Louis, and Monique Eleb, *Casablanca: Colonial Myths and Architectural Ventures* (New York: Monacelli Press, 2002).

Fair, Laura, *Pastimes and Politics: Culture, Community, and Identity in Post-Abolition Urban Zanzibar, 1890–1945* (Athens, O.: Ohio University Press, 2001).

Freund, Bill, *The African City: A History* (New York: CUP, 2007).

Martin, Phyllis, *Leisure and Society in Colonial Brazzaville* (Cambridge: CUP, 1995).

Moorman, Marissa J., *Intonations: A Social History of Music and Nation in Luanda, Angola, from 1945 to Recent Times* (Athens, O.: Ohio University Press, 2008).

Raymond, André, *Cairo: City of History* (Cairo: American University in Cairo Press, 2001).

Roberts, Allen F., and Mary Nooter Roberts, *A Saint in the City: Sufi Arts of Urban Senegal* (Los Angeles: UCLA Fowler Museum, 2003).

Van Onselen, Charles, *Studies in the Social and Economic History of the Witwatersrand, 1886–1914,* i. *New Babylon;* ii. *New Nineveh* (Harlow: Longman, 1982).

Worden, Nigel, Elizabeth van Heyningen, and Vivian Bickford-Smith, *Cape Town: The Making of a City* (Claremont: David Philip, 1998).

——— and —— *Cape Town in the Twentieth Century* (Claremont: David Philip, 1999).

Wright, Gwendolyn, *The Politics of Design in French Colonial Urbanism* (Chicago: University of Chicago Press, 1991).

CHAPTER 20

HEALTH AND HEALING

NANCY ROSE HUNT

WHAT do historians of Africa mean by 'health and healing'? The field emerged under this name only in the late 1970s, when Steven Feierman and John Janzen began steering the continent's history of medicine away from a focus on disease towards vernacular healing practice and the politics of health.[1] The appearance of two special issues in the journal *Social Science and Medicine* in 1979 and 1981 signalled the shift. While containing contributions from established historians of medicine in Africa, these collections expanded disciplinary and thematic frontiers, and included work of a new generation of scholars, including anthropologists of the body, religious practice, and healing.[2]

COLONIAL RESEARCHERS AT WORK

Feierman and Janzen were not the first scholars to take notice of healing and illness in Africa. Vernacular notions of affliction, the emergence and suppression of healing movements, and the meaning of therapeutic ritual all became subjects of serious anthropological study in colonial Africa, especially from the interwar period. E. E. Evans-Pritchard led the way with his foundational 1937 study of witchcraft, magic, and sorcery among the Azande of southern Sudan. Diet and nutrition became a vital topic with the appearance, two years later, of Audrey Richards's superb ethnography of food and hunger among the Bemba of Northern Rhodesia. In South Africa, the psychoanalyst Wulf Sachs invited a Rhodesian healer, John Chavafambira, onto his therapeutic couch in Johannesburg where he shared his life story. The result was a fascinating primary source, which reads more like ethnography and autobiography than a clinical account (and is now available in an edition with two splendid commentaries by Saul Dubow and Jacqueline Rose). First published in 1937, *Black Hamlet* revealed much, not only about Chavafambira's relationship with his father, his migration to the big city, and his healing practice, but also about the contradictions of a colonial therapeutic situation.[3] Also important are the enduring contributions of the French surrealist, Michel Leiris, a member of Marcel Griaule's Dakar–Djibouti expedition of 1931–3. Leiris's consideration of the healing role of spirit possession movements such as Zar in northern Ethiopia in his critique of French colonialism, *L'Afrique fantôme* (1934) influenced much subsequent anthropological work on spirit possession as well as most work in the French language on healing in Africa.[4]

This pioneering work expanded in scope in the 1950s, with a series of important ethnographies of the Ndembu of Northern Rhodesia by Victor Turner. Turner introduced the term 'drums of affliction' to speak to the widespread practice of healing through dance and drumming within an *ngoma* (literally, 'drum') association. The colonial anthropologist, Margaret Field, viewed the anti-witchcraft practices of the Akan and their neighbours in the Gold Coast as a form of psychic therapy; her ethnography is another fascinating primary source. Anne Retel-Laurentin, a French medical doctor and ethnologist, combined a biological lens with an ethnography of sorcery accusations to understand the extent of infertility and its social implications among the Nzakara in French Equatorial Africa (today's Central African Republic). Finally, J. Clyde Mitchell's famous analysis of *kalela*, a new dance form in the industrial towns of the Northern Rhodesian Copperbelt, appeared in 1956. *Kalela* was clearly about urban innovation and leisure, yet its theatrical routines included nurses and stethoscopes. More recently, Lyn Schumaker has demonstrated that *kalela* remains a kind of recreational *ngoma*; with its nurses still singing and dancing in their white uniforms, it has long valorized the crisp, clean style and class prestige of modern hygiene and nursing.[5]

POLITICS AND THE SOCIAL

These colonial ethnographies influenced the new engagement with health and healing pioneered by Feierman and Janzen in the late 1970s. Feierman, who has degrees in both history and anthropology, has shown how speech about 'healing and harming the land' operated as a key form of political discourse about good (or bad) leadership in the history of the Shambaa kingdom in today's Tanzania. His research on everyday therapeutic choices among a range of alternatives in the Shambaa region in the 1970s and 1980s, moreover, revealed that the same language of healing and harming resonated in how people understood prosperity, fertility, and belonging.[6] In a series of essays, Feierman has also explored questions of social efficacy, the work of healers, the social distribution of illness and vulnerability, and communities of care.[7]

Feierman also introduced the important concept of 'public healing'. It urges historians to rethink Africa's history of 'religious movements' as therapeutic movements with political and remedial dimensions. Dissent and healing combine in response to concerns about social reproduction, health, and survival.[8] From Nyabingi spirit mediums in the Great Lakes region, to the Maji Maji rebellion in German East Africa, to many other anti-sorcery and prophetic movements of colonial and postcolonial Africa, these forms of healing are not simply manifestations of religious syncretism or political 'resistance', but therapeutic forms of social criticism. 'Public healing' is one of the concepts that Africa's precolonial historians, notably David Schoenbrun and Neil Kodesh, have embraced to reinterpret the continent's deeper pasts.[9] Neither did 'public healing' end with the close of colonial rule. Africa's postcolonial conflict zones, from West Africa to Congo, the Great Lakes region, and southern Africa, are bound to push historians to see the conjoined healing and harming dynamics to making war, while more attention to the manufacture, use, and destruction of war medicines as healing and harming devices is needed.[10]

The historical anthropologist John Janzen was another innovator from the 1970s. Like Feierman, Janzen sought to link the historical with the contemporary. He moved between documentary evidence for an early 'drum of affliction', Lemba, which dates back to at least the seventeenth century, and the complex therapeutic itineraries of the Bakongo people in the 1970s. His path-breaking *Quest for Therapy* became a staple of medical anthropology classes in North America; it demonstrates that African patients in the lower Congo region rarely operated as individual decision-makers but rather became part of kin-based therapy management groups.[11] Such groups are critical in diagnosing the causes of illness—social or human-caused versus 'natural' or 'God'-caused—and in steering the movement of a patient between diverse healers, diviners, and therapeutic associations or modern, clinical settings. *Quest for Therapy* also discusses colonial practice, touching on the kinds of ambivalence and attachment this new kind of medical presence produced.[12] The significance of Lemba became more evident when Janzen published *Ngoma,* in which he shows how key concepts undergirding instances of *ngoma* have been present since ancient times in Bantu-speaking Africa and are still alive in eastern, central, and southern Africa today.[13]

Another concept in Feierman and Janzen's early work was therapeutic pluralism. Although not their intention, the notion of pluralism had dichotomizing and analogizing effects, with many scholars opposing and comparing two distinct medical 'systems': colonial-introduced biomedicine and public health versus 'traditional healing'. Murray Last spurned the language of therapeutic pluralism from the beginning. Long a maverick figure in the history and anthropology of Africa, Last, in a single powerful article, introduced the notion of 'not knowing' as a way of broaching more clandestine aspects to patterns of therapeutic resort. His point was that there are many worlds in which the ill and their kin combine from a spectrum of possibilities, but often with reticence, secrecy, and shame.[14] Last was questioning the notion of any 'system' in health and healing work. A scholar of the Hausa in northern Nigeria, Last was also one of the first to consider healing in a Muslim zone in Africa. He described a situation in which biomedical care and Muslim healing coexisted, but where most Muslims ostensibly rejected 'pagan' spirit possession practices as wrong and backward; the disapproval produced a silencing effect, with persons 'not knowing' (or not acknowledging) what remained a still thriving pattern of resort. Last's insights proved so important that they led to a whole collection on 'not knowing' in 2007, including two important postscripts added to his original essay. Last also joined Gordon Chavunduka in assembling a collection on healers in early postcolonial Africa, with rich material on their post-independence revalorization, their professionalization into associations, and the certification programmes of several postcolonial states.[15]

A landmark piece from this early generation of work is Feierman's 1985 review essay in *African Studies Review*. It offers a compelling historical narrative of health conditions, argues the importance of beginning analysis with patients rather than practitioners, and develops the notion of the 'social costs of production'. Feierman uses this concept as a model for analysing the threats posed by a particular political economy—such as the capitalist migrant labour system of southern Africa—to everyday household health, nutrition, and social reproduction. Many of these ideas reappeared in the introduction to the important anthology Feierman coedited with Janzen in 1992, *The Social Basis of Health and Healing in Africa*.[16]

In many ways, historians of health in South Africa had already arrived at this important line of thinking. As was true of many kinds of African history in the 1970s and 1980s, medical historians of southern Africa were more attuned to class and race, and tended to write with a sharper political economy edge. Shula Marks, another key figure who shaped Africa's historiography of medicine, began by analysing Apartheid, health, disease, and epidemics in twentieth-century South Africa in a series of publications, many of them coauthored and coedited with Neil Andersson. About the same time, Marks began working on women's health; this theme took her to the history of nursing, and then to mental illness and asylums. She also produced vital work on South Africa's early experiment with social medicine, while insisting that there should be a politics to all historical work on colonial medicine.[17] Thus, her work assured that a political economy approach to Africa's health history became salient, as did Randall Packard's powerful book on the history of tuberculosis, mining, and labour reserves.[18] Increasingly, scholars speak not of the 'social costs of production' but of 'structural violence', as this phrase grapples more capaciously with challenges to health and well-being in postindustrial Africa. Indeed, the effects of neo-liberalism, privatization, AIDS, and war since 1989 are producing new challenges for scholars of health, healing, and suffering in Africa.

THE CRITIQUE OF COLONIAL MEDICINE AND HEALTH WORKERS

Frantz Fanon's essay, entitled 'Medicine and Colonialism', first published in English translation in 1965, was a searing indictment of colonial medicine, violence, and torture in the context of the Algerian war of independence (1954–62). Few of the pioneering generation of scholars of health and healing, however, followed Fanon's lead in thinking about subaltern ambivalence in the face of colonial medicine.[19] With the publication of Megan Vaughan's *Curing their Ills* in 1991, a robust critical gaze met the workings and representations of colonial medicine. Through a discursive reading of medical texts, Vaughan pointed to the colonizing force and symbolic violence of pathologization. *Curing their Ills* shows how colonial medical power worked through texts, words, and practices. While drawing inspiration from Michel Foucault's discursive analyses of medicine, sexuality, and psychiatry, she argued that in Africa colonial medicine shaped less individual African subjects than the reified 'tribes' produced as part of indirect rule. Enthusiastically received for signalling that a linguistic turn had arrived in African historical writing, *Curing their Ills* also encouraged historians to reconsider the history of colonial health institutions and opened several domains to more serious historical study: madness, sexuality, reproduction, and maternal and infant health care.[20]

In its wake has come scholarship drawing on texts authored by African doctors, nurses, midwives, and patients demonstrating that colonial medicine *did* sometimes shape individuated selves. The history of health 'workers' in Africa includes not only nurses, midwives, and doctors, but also orderlies, pharmacists, pill-sellers, home-based providers of care, healers of all stripes, and mothers. In many ways, this spectrum is one of the richest and most concrete ways to bring alive themes of care and multiplicity; it may also reveal aspects of violence in the context of health care.

In many ways Adell Patton, Jr. introduced the theme of health workers with his study of the first generation of professional West African doctors, trained and practising from the middle of the nineteenth century. The theme has been elaborated many times since: in Paul Landau's essay about an evangelical doctor pulling teeth; in John Iliffe's book on East African doctors and tribal dressers since the 1880s; in Shula Marks's history of nursing; and in Julie Livingston's work on home-based and NGO-connected care in Botswana and more recently on cancer nurses and oncologists.[21] Sustained studies of African healers since Wulf Sach's *Black Hamlet* of the 1930s, however, remain rare. Important exceptions include Pamela Reynolds's study of healers and their work with children during and after the independence war in Zimbabwe, which includes an extraordinary set of primary source appendixes, and Catherine Burns's study of the South African healer, Louisa Mvemve.[22]

ETHNOGRAPHIC HISTORY AND GENDER MOVES

As research on colonial medicine and health work has developed, Africa's historians of medicine have also done much to forge a new and often microhistorical genre: ethnographic history. My own *A Colonial Lexicon* is one example, focusing on missionary medicine, nursing labour, reproductive process, childbearing, and mobility.[23] It is also about a primary health care network established jointly by the Belgian colonial state, plantation companies, and a Protestant evangelical medical mission. Rejecting the framing device of a colonial encounter between two opposed categories—colonizer and colonized, white and black—it instead uses the notion of 'middle figures' as a way to think about material objects, mixtures, mobility, and the kinds of translation that nurses and midwives do. *A Colonial Lexicon* also introduced the idea of approaching post-colonial situations as spaces of 'debris', of material remains, and complex memory work.

Several historical ethnographies of health, healing, and medicine have appeared since. Most also combine the colonial and postcolonial, archival evidence and memory work. Many deal with colonizing processes, ambivalence, or border work within state, missionary, and company institutions, hospitals, NGOs, and everyday life. Some have taken up innovative new themes: Livingston on debility, care, and chronicity in Botswana; Nguyen on AIDS and 'therapeutic citizenship' in Abidjan; Geissler and Prince on AIDS, infant illness, and touch in Kenya; and Langwick on the materiality of vernacular healing, malaria, medical science, and AIDS in Tanzania.[24] Much new work bridges the past and present, while demonstrating how healing, regardless of its form (whether razor-blade vaccination, spirit possession, prophetic healing, missionary health clinics, or traumatic story-telling), goes with crossing literal and metaphorical borders.[25]

Much of this work has also been strongly gendered in nature. Indeed, it has been in gendered histories of medicine that many compelling insights have emerged. Lynn Thomas was one of the first historians of Africa to demonstrate the usefulness of bio-politics for thinking about colonial campaigns directed at female bodies in her history of female circumcision in colonial Kenya. Other research has focused on reproductive health, childbearing, infertility, abortion, breast-feeding, birth spacing, and spirit possession.[26] One of the most creative fusions of history and anthropology is Janice Boddy's history of the unusual midwifery and maternity care programme in colonial Sudan, which was aimed at modifying rather than abolishing genital cutting practices. By using speech from women possessed in interstitial chapters, Boddy reminds readers that this other register of meaning-making was always at play as history unfolded.[27]

THE PSYCHIATRIC

While Shula Marks was one of the first to work on women's health, her most innovative work on healing may be *Not Either an Experimental Doll*. An interpretation of a rare collection of letters, the poetic title comes directly from the words of the most anguished letter writer, the Xhosa schoolgirl Lily Moya, writing to a British Fabian socialist with whom she had forged a relationship of deeply ambivalent patronage.[28] Moya's mental unravelling, perhaps triggered by having been raped at school, is evident in her letters to her distant, stern white patron. Thanks to Marks's careful research, the book contains material on Moya's time in a South African insane asylum as well as on her family's efforts to seek help for her from traditional healers. The result reveals an individual psyche, shaped by forms of colonial paternalism, kin interventions, and psychiatric treatment. *Not Either an Experimental Doll* is a history of adolescence, schooling, violence, and gender—the latter also emerging as a central theme in Marks's subsequent work on nursing in South Africa.[29]

With *Not Either an Experimental Doll,* Marks joined Megan Vaughan in reopening the theme of mental illness, a subject first broached in the colonial era by Wulf Sachs, Margaret Field, and Frantz Fanon. That Fanon's theoretical writings came out of his psychiatric work during the Algeria war of liberation has long invited re-engagement with the question of the degree of psychic damage wrought by the violence of colonialism and its overthrow.[30] Megan Vaughan shaped the field with an essay on Malawi's asylum, then a chapter in *Curing their Ills,* and more recently her introduction to *Psychiatry and Empire.* Jonathan Sadowsky was the first to find patient files in his work on psychiatry in colonial and postcolonial Nigeria, and he uses them in arresting ways, including to consider the persecutory effects of living under colonialism.[31]

The contrast of French approaches to matters psychiatric is stark. Very little research has been done on psychiatry in French-rule Africa—but then again, there is next to nothing on the subject for Italian, Portuguese, or Belgian Africa either.[32] The contrast with Anglophone Africa includes the unabashed search for Oedipus in Africa, the use of Freudian and Lacanian theory, the founding in the 1960s of an ethno-psychiatric institute that incorporated some African healing methods, and the ongoing journal with the audacious title *Psychopathologie Africaine.* That French scholars would have read Leiris's *L'Afrique Phantome* and his subsequent studies of *zar* spirit possession surely made them more open to African therapeutics, and far removed from the kinds of 'frontal lobe function' reasoning pervasive in late colonial Kenya.

Objects, Sorcery, and the Harming Register

Feierman has long pointed out that healing gets paired with harming in African political discourse. In therapeutic rituals called *libeli* and *lilwa* long practised in the Kisangani region of the Belgian Congo, these initiation practices were not only meant to reproduce a next generation, but also to eliminate enemies. Janzen and Wyatt MacGaffey point to the 'ambivalence' of medicinal charms and power objects in the lower Congo, with the same assembled *nkisi* item able to heal or harm. *Nkisi* objects, now ubiquitous in African art galleries around the world, include fearsome *nkondi* nail sculptures with each nail hammered into the figure's body suggesting a diagnostic encounter and therapeutic effect.[33] Art historians and visually minded anthropologists show how historians of many periods may use therapeutic objects as evidence. MacGaffey dug deep into Swedish missionary archives and unearthed the role of Congolese catechists in documenting the healing powers of *nkisi* figures. The journal *African Arts* is an important resource on village cleansing rituals, masquerades, and healing traditions. David Doris's *Vigilant Things* considers home-made theft prevention devices as aesthetic objects, which the Yoruba use to prevent misfortune and protect fields and property from burglary. [34] A visit to the closest museum with African art holdings to see masks, flywhisks, and other medicinal objects is a powerful way to teach students about 'vigilant' medicinal objects that can heal or harm. The same session may cover the commodification, ambivalence, and iconoclasm that resulted in such items ending up on display as 'art' in museums in North America and Europe.

In a historiographical essay published in 1994, however, Megan Vaughan posed critical questions about the field of African health and healing.[35] She suggested that scholars were perhaps romanticizing vernacular therapeutic practice by aligning it with the helpful and the beneficent, and that they were partially doing so through the word 'healing'. One effect, she argued, was to distort biomedical practice in Africa as singular and secular, as part of a universal science. This effect meant failing to see that a major share of medical practice since the 1850s had been the work of evangelical missionaries, focused on religious healing and conversion, even while using biomedical technologies—surgery, tooth-pulling, bandages, soap, injections, and pills—to do so. Vaughan was cautioning that the interpretation of healing, whether in shrines, households, marketplaces, or associations, in positive terms risked overlooking negative, violent dimensions. She was also suggesting, unwittingly perhaps, that the gloss of 'healing' enabled a kind of scholarly *unknowing* (to borrow from Murray Last) about the harming sometimes involved in therapeutic practice and care.

Vaughan was writing in 1994, a time when historians of Africa came to realize that romanticizing the past was no longer tenable. The Cold War had ended and neo-liberalism had arrived. So had AIDS, expanding war zones, widespread suffering and poverty, and, most significantly for everyday lives, 'cash and carry' payments for health care. Once state-of-the-art tertiary hospitals of the 1960s had become near morgues (as *Donka* by Belgian documentary film-maker Thierry Michel shows well).[36] Structural adjustment programmes (SAPs) and privatization were also working to produce a generation of newly wealthy African doctors with their own private clinics. Vaughan's intervention also came as AIDS was producing a boom in new health research in Africa. AIDS indeed had many questioning the singularity of biomedicine and the universality of biology; as a new kind of biomedical multiplicity was coming into view, so was the notion of local biologies.

This post-1989 era also witnessed an explosion of new research into connections between modernity and witchcraft, resulting in an immense body of work on sorcery idioms, witchcraft anxieties, 'spiritual insecurity' (to quote Adam Ashforth), and the use of medicines and cursing to harm. Most who have written on the 'modernity of witchcraft' or 'occult ecomomies' would not call themselves scholars of health and healing, and few are historians. Nor has their work been fully embraced into the medical history fold.[37] An important exception is Luise White's work on rumour and fear of the vampire-like technologies of modern medicine in colonial East and Central Africa, which serves to underline the importance of integrating sorcery idioms as a core strand to the continent's medical history.[38] Yet anthropologists of postcolonial witchcraft have given one of the oldest anthropological themes new life amid the disquiet of neo-liberal Africa. Their work has also highlighted the negative register of therapeutic practice; that is, the use of 'medicines', broadly defined, to hurt and harm, frighten, reproduce power, and eliminate enemies in high politics and in everyday life. The patterns of resort that go with such postcolonial afflictions, though studied on an intimate scale in Ashforth's study of one tormented man in Soweto, are still awaiting serious attention by scholars firmly engaged with the 'health and healing' field.

Why have sorcery-related dimensions been largely excluded, or set aside as separate, from healing matters? Feierman has pointed out that colonial regimes, in the wake of healing movements like Maji Maji, tried to abolish witchcraft legally. The attempt at suppression produced layers of acceptable and unacceptable healing. Work with *materia medica* by household and village-based practitioners and more mobile healer-entrepreneurs usually remained as benign and licit healing, while an underground realm of illegal anti-sorcery practice surfaced before the colonial gaze more rarely. Since it was dangerous for healers who specialized in diagnosing and treating human malice openly to practise, sorcery-related healing became a realm of relative unknowing in colonial Africa, glimpsed as a juridical or policing matter and separated from more visible forms of work with medicinal herbs and charms. Some historians have recuperated anti-sorcery practices into their histories of 'religious movements' under colonial rule, though these have rarely been conceptualized through a lens of heath and illness. Consider Karen Fields's history of Watchtower in Northern Rhodesia. Still the finest political analysis of a colonial religious movement available, there is little therapeutic about it; nor does it aim for parallel histories of illness or biomedical spaces. A book that comes closer to such a spectrum is Robert Edgar and Hilary Sapire's gripping history of a woman prophetess who ended up incarcerated in a South African mental asylum; her biography, therefore, produced a parallel history about colonial psychiatry. Precolonial historians have also glimpsed the healing aspects of a prophetic religious imagination, at least those working in the Lower Congo region, as can be seen in Thornton's retelling of Kimpa Vita's emergence in seventeenth-century Kongo.[39]

That the scholarship on witchcraft and sorcery still remains largely disconnected from the key thrusts of historical work on health, healing, and medicine is intriguing. It is not that historians are not making subtle interjections of sorcery idioms into ethnographic histories. But it will be interesting to track how historians stitch a more negative register about harming and violence (*as* therapeutics) into future work. My guess is that the history of war, particularly the use of killing and maiming to heal, will lead the way. Since the theme of health and war has been little considered by historians of Africa, such new work may not only probe recent pasts. Healing, health, and war might instead serve well as a theme to stem the most problematic epidemic in African historical writing today, the presentism and shallow time depths that dominate our field.

A TIME OF ACRONYMS: SAPS, AIDS, AND STS

If vernacular therapeutics has always had positive and negative registers, the same is true of biomedicine as practised in Africa and other postcolonial locations today. The effects of neo-liberalism and globalization mean expertise and monies from the North, and increasingly from China and India as well, are parachuted into zones of 'innovation', 'experimentality', and needy 'bare life' in Africa. The result is enclaves of humanitarianism, clinical trials, orphan adoption, and NGOs sitting alongside and within zones of instability, displacement, and warfare. Recent work forces reckoning with the new present, a time of 'global health' amid widespread infirmity, immiseration, and structural violence.[40]

Clearly, the academy—from history and anthropology departments to tropical research institutes—values fresh work about the history of health care and research in Africa. Recent decades have also witnessed rising numbers of medicine and health students from North America and Europe who seek global health training in Africa. These educational opportunities blur travel and internships with sentiments of rescue. Claire Wendland, who authored a splendid ethnography of a medical school in Malawi, calls this phenomenon 'clinical tourism'.[41] The sensibility has a long history, of course: dreams of redemption oriented to the poor and suffering in Africa are at least as old as those that inspired David Livingstone and other nineteenth-century medical missionaries. It might make a difference if the new, twenty-first-century generation of 'global health' humanitarians were taught something of the history of African ambivalence towards biomedical care; at least they might be more aware of their own salvationist aspirations, as well as the resentments and contradictions embedded in global health projects.

Central to the scholarly shift from the late 1970s away from disease and towards vernacular therapeutics was the idea that the history of medicine should *not* be broached first and foremost through biology, pathology, or epidemics. Rather, considering health and illness as social in the broadest political sense of the term was the first priority, though the approach turned more discursive, semiotic, and biomedical over time. By the 1990s, the impact of the AIDS pandemic coincided with neo-liberalism, a confluence that served as a catalyst for a further shift in the field. At the same, the new field of 'science and technology studies' (STS) emerged, in part from work on how French colonial medicine took shape within Pasteurian networks.[42] Since the 2000s, this new theoretical toolbox began to shake up the history and the anthropology of medicine in Africa.

Social histories of particular disease categories have been an important way of writing Africa's medical history since Philip Curtin, Maryinez Lyons, and Randall Packard did their pioneering work.[43] Some, like Eric Silla, Vinh-Kim Nguyen, and Elisha Renne, have used their strong ethnographic and political imaginations to understand the formation of disease-based patient communities (as 'therapeutic citizenship' in the case of Nguyen) and their treatment anxieties.[44] Today, a new wave of work on disease and science is available, with much of it focusing on the history of hospitals, biomedical campaigns, public health, scientific practice, laboratories, and clinical trials. Some scholars have sought to link a disease, such as leprosy, sleeping sickness, polio, and AIDS, not only to scientific interpretations and networks, but also to vernacular ones. When disability emerged as an important new focus of research and NGO funding, Julie Livingston broadened the term to 'debility' and produced a historical ethnography that periodizes impairment in Botswana, from workers who came home from the mines after accidents to home-based care for AIDS patients, thus combining political economy with intimate household relations, ageing, and the risks of 'toxic' relationships for kin-based networks of care.[45]

There is much to be welcomed in this new turn. Not until the 2000s did medical historians and anthropologists begin to speak of networks, boundaries, technopolitics, and experimentality,[46] or of pharmaceuticals as global objects.[47] Scholars have begun to write a different kind of history of medicine, using—and perhaps at times overusing—vocabulary from STS. This new body of work takes account of the changing ways Africa is positioned in the world, the impact of neo-liberalism on everyday lives, new medical marketplaces, and the use of Africa as a site for 'global health' endeavours, from clinical trials to medical education. But the new STS orientation does not simply mean a return to matters biomedical. Ethnographic history is still in play as methodology and as genre. Greater attention is being paid to multiple scales, while the best work is *not* moving away from the vernacular or the 'traditional'. Indeed, as Stacy Langwick's work on Tanzania shows, the STS approach may mean combining a global scale with a sharper focus on the vernacular within an intimate scale set in an African world.[48]

DEEPER PASTS AND NEW METHODS

This chapter has argued that historians of health and healing in Africa would do well to pay more attention to war, and in some ways this has already begun. I also predict a new era of creativity and rigour in the identification and use of evidence for all historical periods. Recent memory work has involved scholars raising important questions about the kinds of debris left over from past scientific and public healing schemes. The visual and the medical have hardly intersected so far in our histories, however, and surely they soon will. Moreover, the digital humanists among us are bound to sit down soon with archivists, librarians, and museum curators. Not only is there an urgency about source acquisition and preservation, but the promise of being able to scale up research through keyword searching is simply too intriguing to ignore. We also need to deepen the time scales of our histories of health and healing. One useful exercise might begin with a critical review of the literature on precolonial African history for evidence on healing, diviners, and spirit mediums, as well as the use of medicinal objects in war, state-building, and everyday life. Surely much evidence—little of it probably dubbed specifically as therapeutic—would be found. It also may be time to persuade our colleagues in archaeology to collaborate in the task of identifying material debris associated with health and healing in the deep past.[49]

That we do not yet have regional histories of healing for periods prior to the 1880s, with the exception of the Great Lakes and lower Congo regions, is significant. Karen Flint's *Healing Traditions* stretches back to the 1820s in a significant investigation of royal healing in the Zulu kingdom.[50] With the exception of Schoenbrun and Kodesh, however, few have followed Janzen's lead in thinking about the deep time to African healing. It is also significant that Janzen mined the therapeutic lexicon embedded in early Bantu languages. That West Africa has generally been underrepresented in the historiography is not unrelated to its exclusion from the Bantu proto-lexicon that has been the foundation for this field. The study of slavery in West Africa, 1500–1800, might well be reinvigorated through questions refracted through a health and healing prism.

Many historians use Janzen's *Lemba* to teach the history of African therapeutics in the era of the Atlantic slave trade. This healing association or 'drum of affliction' took on the functions of a polity, including control of trade routes and markets. Its members were often rich merchants who could afford Lemba's fees; they were also perhaps ailing from the contradictions of benefiting from the commoditization of human beings. Yet it has been historians of the Africa's Atlantic diaspora rather than those of the continent alone who have followed Janzen's lead, writing histories not only of African surgeons on slave ships and medical coercion on American plantations, but also of how African slaves kept alive therapeutic traditions both before and after emancipation. As these historians increasingly do African history as well, they are producing extraordinary accounts of healers, such as James Sweet's history of Domingos Álvares, an African healer who moved around the Atlantic world from Dahomey to Brazil to Portugal.[51]

It may also be time for a hermeneutic turn that enables a reconsideration of health and healing in those neglected centuries that might be labelled Africa's 'early modern' period. William Pietz is a maverick scholar who has helped a new generation of historians rethink African material objects, including therapeutic ones, through the mixed etymology for the word 'fetish', while simultaneously using European travel accounts about exchange on the African coast between the sixteenth and eighteenth centuries to new effect.[52] Historians of Africa would do well to rewrite West and West Central African history through attending to these and other kinds of European-produced texts with the kind of early modern hermeneutic sensibilities that historians have used for Europe and other parts of the world. This will mean rethinking not only encounters and objects, but also medicine, illness, and healing across these three centuries.

CONCLUSION

This chapter has sketched an interpretation of historical writing on health and healing in Africa since the articulation of the theme in the late 1970s. It identified three key turning points in the field. The first cut across all of African history in the 1990s, as Foucauldian questions about biopower, subject formation, and technologies of the self came to the fore. A second came with the development of ethnographic history and a greater attention to African textualities and materialities; in medical history, this new genre enabled more intimate understandings of medical routines, health work, and vernacular objects, words, interpretations, and action. A third was the arrival of STS-inspired questions about technological practice and experimentality within scientific and vernacular locations. Attention to phenomenological matters like memory, affect, and care have grown deeper across these three transitions, while the methods of ethnographic history and the urgencies of the present have meant that historians have been working with increasingly shallow time scales as they do important work in contemporary history. It is worth asking: are these the kinds of histories of health, healing, and medicine that are needed for Africa's present and future? The increasing presentism of recent work should not be shunned, since the value of these highly innovative histories of the present is immense. They grapple, after all, with an urgent topic: health. Still, there is a vast challenge facing the next generation of historians of health, healing, medicine, and the body, and it lies in finding ways to apply this same subtlety and resourcefulness to earlier time periods.

NOTES

1. For the older approach, see K. David Patterson, 'Disease and Medicine in African History: A Bibliographical Essay', *History in Africa*, 1 (1974); Gerald W. Hartwig and K. David Patterson, eds, *Disease in African History: An Introductory Survey and Case Studies* (Durham, NC: Duke University Press, 1978); Philip Curtin, 'Medical Knowledge and Urban Planning in Tropical Africa', *American Historical Review*, 90/3 (1985); Philip Curtin, *Disease and Empire: The Health of European Troops in the Conquest of Africa* (Cambridge: CUP, 1998).

2. John Janzen and Steven Feierman, eds, 'Special Issue on the Social History of Disease and Medicine in Africa', *Social Science and Medicine*, 13B/4 (1979); John Janzen and Gwyn Prins, eds, 'Special Issue on Causality and Classification in African Medicine and Health', *Social Science and Medicine*, 15B/3 (1981).

3. E. E. Evans-Pritchard, *Witchcraft, Oracles and Magic among the Azande* (Oxford: OUP, 1937); Audrey Richards, *Land, Labour, and Diet in Northern Rhodesia: An Economic Study of the Bemba Tribe* (Oxford: OUP, 1939); Wulf Sachs, *Black Hamlet: The Mind of an African Negro Revealed by Psychoanalysis* (Baltimore, Md.: Johns Hopkins University Press, 2nd edn, 1996).

4. Michel Leiris, *L'Afrique fantôme* (Paris: Gallimard, 1934); see too his collected essays in *Miroir de l'Afrique* (Paris: Gallimard, 1996). For some of the best recent work on spirit possession, see Janice Boddy, *Wombs and Alien Spirits: Women, Men, and the Zar Cult in Northern Sudan* (Madison, Wis.: University of Wisconsin Press, 1989); Adeline Masquelier, *'Prayer has Spoiled Everything': Possession, Power, and Identity in an Islamic Town of Niger* (Durham, NC: Duke University Press, 2001).

5. Victor Turner, *Chihamba, the White Spirit* (Manchester: MUP, 1962); Victor Turner, *The Drums of Affliction: A Study of Religious Processes among the Ndembu of Zambia* (Oxford: Clarendon Press, 1968); M. J. Field, *Search for Security: An Ethno-Psychiatric Study of Rural Ghana* (London: Faber & Faber, 1960); Anne Retel-Laurentin, *Oracles et ordalies chez les Nzakara* (Paris: Mouton, 1969); J. Clyde Mitchell, *The Kalela Dance: Aspects of Social Relationships among Urban Africans in Northern Rhodesia* (Manchester: MUP, 1956); Lyn Schumaker, 'The Dancing Nurse: Kalela Drums and the History of Hygiene in Africa', in Penelope Gouk, ed., *Musical Healing in Cultural Contexts* (Aldershot: Ashgate, 2000).

6. Steven Feierman, *The Shambaa Kingdom: A History* (Madison, Wis.: University of Wisconsin Press, 1974) and *Peasant Intellectuals: Anthropology and History in Tanzania* (Madison, Wis.: University of Wisconsin Press, 1990).

7. See notably Steven Feierman, 'Explanation and Uncertainty in the Medical World of Ghaambo', *Bulletin for the History of Medicine*, 74/2 (2000).

8. Steven Feierman, 'Healing as Social Criticism in the Time of Colonial Conquest', *African Studies Review*, 54/1 (1995).

9. David Schoenbrun, 'Conjuring the Modern in Africa: Durability and Rupture in Histories of Public Healing between the Great Lakes of East Africa', *American Historical Review*, 111/5 (2006); Neil Kodesh, *Beyond the Royal Gaze: Clanship and Public Healing in Buganda* (Charlottesville, Va.: University Press of Virginia, 2010).

10. For works gesturing towards the religious, medicinal, and healing dimensions of war and conflict, see Stephen Ellis, *The Mask of Anarchy: The Destruction of Liberia and the Religious Dimension of an African Civil War* (London: Hurst, 1999); John Janzen and Reinhild Kauenhoven Janzen, *Do I Still have a Life? Voices from the Aftermath of War in Rwanda and Burundi* (Lawrence, Kan.: University of Kansas Press, 2000); and Danny Hoffman, *War Machines: Young Men and Violence in Sierra Leone and Liberia* (Durham, NC: Duke University Press, 2011).

11. John Janzen, *The Quest for Therapy: Medical Pluralism in Lower Zaire* (Berkeley, Calif.: University of California Press, 1982).

12. John Janzen, *Lemba, 1650–1930: A Drum of Affliction in Africa and the New World* (New York: Garland, 1982).

13. John Janzen, *Ngoma: Discourses of Healing in Central and Southern Africa* (Berkeley, Calif.: University of California Press, 1992).

14. Murray Last, 'The Importance of Knowing about Not Knowing', in Roland Little, ed., *On Knowing and Not Knowing in the Anthropology of Medicine* (Walnut Creek, Calif.: Left Coast Press, 2007).

15. Murray Last and Gordon Chavunduka, eds, *The Professionalisation of African Medicine* (Manchester: MUP, 1986); see too Ismail Abdalla, *Islam, Medicine, and Practitioners in Northen Nigeria* (Lewiston, NY: E. Mellen Press, 1997).

16. Steven Feierman, 'Struggles for Control: The Social Roots of Health and Healing in Modern Africa', *African Studies Review*, 28/2–3 (1985); Steven Feierman and John Janzen, eds, *The Social Basis of Health and Healing in Africa* (Berkeley, Calif.: University of California Press, 1992).

17. See e.g. S. Marks and N. Andersson, eds, *Journal of Southern African Studies*, 13/2 (1987), Special Issue on the Political Economy of Health in Southern Africa; S. Marks, N. Andersson, and A. Zwi, eds, *Social Science and Medicine*, 27/7 (1988), Special Issue on Health, Apartheid and Frontline States; Shula Marks, 'What is Colonial about Colonial Medicine?', *Social History of Medicine*, 10 (1997); S. Marks and N. Andersson, 'The Epidemiology and Culture of Violence', in C. Manganyi and A. du Toit, eds, *Political Violence and the Struggle in South Africa* (London: Macmillan, 1990); Shula Marks, 'George Gale, Social Medicine and the State in South Africa', in S. Dubow, ed., *Science and Society in Southern Africa* (Manchester: MUP, 2000).

18. Randall Packard, *White Plague, Black Labor: Tuberculosis and the Political Economy of Health and Disease in South Africa* (Berkeley, Calif.: University of California Press, 1989). Packard's recent work has become more global: see his *The Making of a Tropical Disease: A Short History of Malaria* (Baltimore: Johns Hopkins University Press, 2007).

19. Frantz Fanon, 'Medicine and Colonialism', in *A Dying Colonialism*, tr. Haakon Chevalier (New York: Grove Press, 1965).

20. Megan Vaughan, *Curing their Ills: Colonial Power and African Illness* (Stanford, Calif.: Stanford University Press, 1991).

21. Adell Patton, Jr., *Physicians, Colonial Racism, and Diaspora in West Africa* (Gainesville, Fla.: University Press of Florida, 1996); Paul Landau, 'Explaining Surgical Evangelism in

Colonial Southern Africa: Teeth, Pain and Faith', *Journal of African History*, 37 (1996); John Iliffe, *East African Doctors: A History of the Modern Profession* (Cambridge: CUP, 1998); Shula Marks, *Class, Race, and Gender in South Africa: The Nursing Profession and the Making of Apartheid* (New York: St Martin's Press, 1994).

22. Pamela Reynolds, *Traditional Healers and Childhood in Zimbabwe* (Athens, O.: Ohio University Press, 1996); Catherine Burns, 'The Letters of Louisa Mvembe', in Karin Barber, ed., *Africa's Hidden Histories: Everyday Literacy and Making the Self* (Bloomington, Ind.: Indiana University Press, 2006).

23. Nancy Rose Hunt, *A Colonial Lexicon: Of Birth Ritual, Medicalization, and Mobility in the Congo* (Durham, NC: Duke University Press, 1999).

24. Julie Livingston, *Debility and Moral Imagination in Botswana: Disability, Chronic Illness, and Aging* (Bloomington, Ind.: Indiana University Press, 2005); P. Wenzel Geissler and Ruth J. Prince, *'The Land is Dying': Contingency, Creativity and Conflict in Western Kenya* (Oxford: Berghahn, 2010); Vinh-Kim Nguyen, *The Republic of Therapy: Triage and Sovereignty in West Africa's Time of AIDS* (Durham, NC: Duke University Press, 2010); Stacey Langwick, *Bodies, Politics, and African Healing: The Matter of Maladies in Tanzania* (Bloomington, Ind.: Indiana University Press, 2011).

25. The subject of a superb anthology: Tracey Luedke and Harry West, eds, *Borders and Healers: Brokering Therapeutic Resources in Southeast Africa* (Bloomington, Ind.: Indiana University Press, 2006); see too Hansjörg Dilger, Abdoulaye Kane, and Stacey Langwick, eds, *Medicine, Mobility, and Power in Global Africa: Transnational Health and Healing* (Bloomington, Ind.: Indiana University Press, 2012).

26. Lynn Thomas, *Politics of the Womb: Women, Reproduction, and the State in Kenya* (Berkeley, Calif.: University of California Press, 2003); Pamela Feldman-Salvesburg, *Plundered Kitchens, Empty Wombs: Threatened Reproduction and Identity in the Cameroon Grassfields* (Ann Arbor, Mich.: University of Michigan Press, 1999); Elisha Renne, *Population and Progress in a Yoruba Town* (Ann Arbor, Mich.: University of Michigan Press, 2003); and Nancy Rose Hunt, 'Between Fiction and History: Modes of Writing Abortion in Africa', *Cahiers d'études africaines*, 47/186 (2007).

27. Janice Boddy, *Civilizing Women: British Crusades in Colonial Sudan* (Princeton: PUP, 2007).

28. Shula Marks, *Not Either an Experimental Doll: The Separate Worlds of Three South African Women* (Bloomington, Ind.: Indiana University Press, 1988).

29. Marks, *Class, Race, and Gender*; Shula Marks, 'Every Facility that Modern Science and Enlightened Humanity have Devised: Race and Progress in a Colonial Hospital, Valkenberg Mental Asylum, Cape Colony, 1894–1910', in Joseph Melling and Bill Forsythe, eds, *Insanity, Institutions and Society, 1800–1914: A Social History of Madness in Comparative Perspective* (New York: Routledge, 1999); Shula Marks, 'The Microphysics of Power: Mental Nursing in South Africa in the First Half of the Twentieth Century', in Sloan Mahone and Megan Vaughan, eds, *Psychiatry and Empire* (Basingstoke: Palgrave Macmillan, 2007).

30. On Fanon and Algeria, see Richard Keller, *Colonial Madness: Psychiatry in French North Africa* (Chicago: University of Chicago Press, 2007).

31. Jonathan Sadowsky, *Imperial Bedlam: Institutions of Madness in Colonial Southwest Nigeria* (Berkeley, Calif.: University of California Press, 1999); see too Lynette Jackson, *Surfacing Up: Psychiatry and Social Order in Colonial Zimbabwe, 1908–1968* (Ithaca, NY: Cornell University Press, 2005); Julie Parle, *States of Mind: Searching for Mental Health in Natal and Zululand, 1868–1918* (Scottsville: University of KwaZulu-Natal Press, 2007).

32. For an exception, see Alice Bullard, 'L'Œdipe Africain: A Retrospective', *Transcultural Psychiatry*, 42 (2005), and 'Imperial Networks and Postcolonial Independence: The Transition from Colonial to Transcultural Psychiatry', in Mahone and Vaughan, *Psychiatry and Empire*.

33. John M. Janzen and Wyatt MacGaffey, *An Anthology of Kongo Religion: Primary Texts From Lower Zaire* (Lawrence, Kan.: University of Kansas, 1974); Wyatt MacGaffey, *Art and Healing of the Bakongo, Commented by Themselves: Minkisi from the Laman Collection* (Bloomington, Ind.: Indiana University Press, 1991); Wyatt MacGaffey, *Kongo Political Culture: The Conceptual Challenge of the Particular* (Bloomington, Ind.: Indiana University Press, 2000).

34. Zoë Strother, *Inventing Masks: Agency and History in the Art of the Central Pende* (Chicago: University of Chicago Press, 1998); David Doris, *Vigilant Things: On Thieves, Yoruba Anti-Aesthetics, and the Strange Fates of Ordinary Objects in Nigeria* (Seattle: University of Washington Press, 2011).

35. Megan Vaughan, 'Healing and Curing: Issues in the Social History and Anthropology of Medicine in Africa', *Social History of Medicine*, 7 (1994). For another useful and earlier historiographical survey, see Gwyn Prins, 'But What was the Disease? The Present State of Health and Healing in African Studies', *Past and Present*, 124 (1989), and the more recent *Crossing Colonial Historiographies: Histories of Colonial and Indigenous Medicines in Transnational Perspective* (Newcastle: Cambridge Scholars, 2010).

36. Thierry Michel, dir., *Donka: X-ray of an African Hospital* (1996). See too Adeline Masquelier, 'Behind the Dispensary's Prosperous Facade: Imagining the State in Rural Niger', *Public Culture*, 13/2 (2001).

37. See e.g. Jean Comaroff and John Comaroff, eds, *Modernity and its Malcontents: Ritual and Power in Postcolonial Africa* (Chicago: University of Chicago Press, 1993); Peter Geschiere, *The Modernity of Witchcraft: Politics and the Occult in Postcolonial Africa* (Charlottesville, Va.: University Press of Virginia, 1997); Adam Ashforth, *Madumo: A Man Bewitched* (Chicago: University of Chicago Press, 2000); and Jean Comaroff and John L. Comaroff, 'Occult Economies and the Violence of Abstraction: Notes from the South African Postcolony', *American Ethnologist*, 26 (1999).

38. Luise White, *Speaking with Vampires: Rumor and History in Colonial Africa* (Berkeley, Calif.: University of California Press, 2000).

39. Karen E. Fields, *Revival and Rebellion in Colonial Central Africa* (Princeton: PUP, 1985); Robert Edgar and Hilary Sapire, *African Apocalypse: The Story of Nontetha Nkwenkwe, a Twentieth-century South African Prophet* (Athens, O.: Ohio University Press, 2000); John Thornton, *The Kongolese Saint Anthony: Dona Beatriz Kimpa Vita and the Antonian Movement, 1684–1706* (Cambridge: CUP, 1998).

40. For an overview of the issues, see Craig R. Janes and Kitty K. Corbett, 'Anthropology and Global Health', *Annual Review of Anthropology*, 38 (2009), and for a superb historical ethnography of the issues involved, Julie Livingston, *Improvising Medicine: An African Oncology Ward in an Emerging Cancer Epidemic* (Durham, NC: Duke University Press, 2012).

41. Claire Wendland, 'Moral Maps and Medical Imaginaries: Clinical Tourism at Malawi's College of Medicine', *American Anthropologist*, 114 (2012), and *A Heart for the Work: Journeys through an African Medical School* (Chicago: University of Chicago Press, 2010).

42. Bruno Latour, *The Pasteurization of France* (Cambridge, Mass.: Harvard University Press, 1988); Guillaume Lachenal, 'Franco-African Familiarities: A History of the

Pasteur Institute of Cameroun, 1945–2000', in Mark Harrison and Belinda White, eds, *Hospitals beyond the West: From Western Medicine to Global Medicine* (New Delhi: Orient-Longman, 2009).

43. Curtin, 'Medical Knowledge', and *Disease and Empire*; Packard, *White Plague*; Maryinez Lyons, *The Colonial Disease: A Social History of Sleeping Sickness in Northern Zaire, 1900–1940* (Cambridge: CUP, 2002).

44. Eric Silla, *People are Not the Same: Leprosy and Identity in Twentieth-Century Mali* (Portsmouth, NH: Heineman, 1998); Nguyen, *Republic of Therapy*; Elisha Renne, *The Politics of Polio in Northern Nigeria* (Bloomington, Ind.: Indiana University Press, 2010). See too Melissa Leach and James Fairhead, *Vaccine Anxieties: Global Science, Child Health and Society* (London: Earthscan, 2007); Felicitas Becker and Wenzel Geissler, eds, *AIDS and Religious Practice in Africa* (Leiden: Brill, 2009).

45. Livingston, *Debility*.

46. Vinh-Kim Nguyen, 'Government-by-Exception: Enrolment and Experimentality in Mass HIV Treatment Programmes in Africa', *Social Theory and Health*, 7 (2009); Richard Rottenburg, 'Social and Public Experiments and New Figurations of Science and Politics in Postcolonial Africa', *Postcolonial Studies*, 12 (2009); Christian Bonah, ' "You Should Not Use our Senegalese Infantrymen as Guinea Pigs": Human Vaccination Experiments in the French Army', in Wolfgang Eckart, ed., *Man, Medicine and the State: The Human Body as an Object of Government Sponsored Medical Research in the 20th Century* (Stuttgart: Franz Steiner Verlag, 2006); Wolfgang Eckart, 'Medical Experiments at the Colonial Periphery: The Fight against Sleeping Sickness in German East Africa and Togo', in Volker Roelcke and Giovanni Maio, eds, *Twentieth Century Ethics of Human Subjects Research* (Stuttgart: Franz Steiner Verlag, 2004); Gabrielle Hecht, 'Hopes for the Radiated Body: Uranium Miners and Transnational Technopolitics in Namibia', *Journal of African History*, 51 (2010).

47. Susan Reynolds Whyte, Sjaak van der Geest, and Anita Hardon, *Social Lives of Medicines* (Cambridge: CUP, 2003); Dider Fassin, 'Illicit Sale of Pharmaceuticals in Africa: Sellers and Clients in the Suburbs of Dakar', *Tropical and Geographical Medicine*, 40/2 (1998); Kristin Peterson, 'AIDS Policies for Markets and Warriors: Dispossession, Capital, and Pharmaceuticals in Nigeria', in Kaushik Sunder Rajan, ed., *Lively Capital: Biotechnologies, Ethics, and Governance in Global Markets* (Durham, NC: Duke University Press, 2012).

48. Langwick, *Bodies*; see too Peter Redfield, 'Sacrifice, Triage, and Global Humanitarianism', in Michael Barnett and Thomas G. Weiss, eds, *Humanitarianism in Question: Politics, Power, Ethics* (Ithaca, NY: Cornell University Press, 2008); Didier Fassin and Richard Rechtman, *The Empire of Trauma: An Inquiry into the Condition of Victimhood* (Princeton: PUP, 2009); P. Wenzel Geissler and Catherine Molyneux, eds, *Evidence, Ethos and Experiment: The Anthropology and History of Medical Research in Africa* (New York: Berghahn, 2011).

49. See e.g. *Anthropology and Medicine*, 18/2 (2011), Special Issue: Shrines, Substances and Medicine in Sub-Saharan Africa: Archaeological, Anthropological and Historical Perspectives, ed. Timothy Insoll.

50. Karen Flint, *Healing Traditions: African Medicine, Cultural Exchange, and Competition in South Africa, 1820–1948* (Athens, O.: Ohio University Press, 2008); see too Gloria Waite, *A History of Traditional Medicine and Health Care in Pre-Colonial East-Central Africa* (Lewiston, NY: E. Mellen Press, 1992).

51. Sharla Fett, *Working Cures: Healing, Health, and Power on Southern Slave Plantations* (Chapel Hill, NC: University of North Carolina Press, 2002); Karol Weaver, *Medical*

Revolutionaries: The Enslaved Healers of Eighteenth-Century Saint Domingue (Urbana, Ill.: University of Illinois Press, 2006); James H. Sweet, *Domingos Álvares, African Healing, and the Intellectual History of the Atlantic World* (Chapel Hill, NC: University of North Carolina Press, 2011); Maarit Forde and Diana Paton, eds, *Obeah and other Powers: The Politics of Caribbean Religion and Healing* (Durham, NC: Duke University Press, 2012).

52. William Pietz, 'The Problem of the Fetish I', *Res*, 9 (1985), 'The Problem of the Fetish II', *Res*, 13 (1987), and 'The Problem of the Fetish IIIa', *Res*, 16 (1988).

BIBLIOGRAPHY

Boddy, Janice, *Civilizing Women: British Crusades in Colonial Sudan* (Princeton: PUP, 2007).

Curtin, Philip, *Disease and Empire: The Health of European Troops in the Conquest of Africa* (Cambridge: CUP, 1998).

Feierman, Steven, and John Janzen, eds, *The Social Basis of Health and Healing in Africa* (Berkeley, Calif.: University of California Press, 1992).

Geissler, P. Wenzel, and Catherine Molyneux, eds, *Evidence, Ethos and Experiment: The Anthropology and History of Medical Research in Africa* (New York: Berghahn, 2011).

Hunt, Nancy Rose, *A Colonial Lexicon: Of Birth Ritual, Medicalization, and Mobility in the Congo* (Durham, NC: Duke University Press, 1999).

Janzen, John, *Lemba, 1650–1930: A Drum of Affliction in Africa and the New World* (New York: Garland, 1982).

Kodesh, Neil, *Beyond the Royal Gaze: Clanship and Public Healing in Buganda* (Charlottesville, Va.: University Press of Virginia, 2010).

Langwick, Stacey, *Bodies, Politics, and African Healing: The Matter of Maladies in Tanzania* (Bloomington, Ind.: Indiana University Press, 2011).

Last, Murray, and Gordon Chavunduka, eds, *The Professionalisation of African Medicine* (Manchester: MUP, 1986).

Livingston, Julie, *Debility and Moral Imagination in Botswana: Disability, Chronic Illness, and Aging* (Bloomington, Ind.: Indiana University Press, 2005).

Luedke, Tracey, and Harry West, eds, *Borders and Healers: Brokering Therapeutic Resources in Southeast Africa* (Bloomington, Ind.: Indiana University Press, 2006).

Mahone, Sloan, and Megan Vaughan, eds, *Psychiatry and Empire* (Basingstoke: Palgrave Macmillan, 2007).

Marks, Shula, *Not Either an Experimental Doll: The Separate Worlds of Three South African Women* (Bloomington, Ind.: Indiana University Press, 1988).

Nguyen, Vinh-Kim, *The Republic of Therapy: Triage and Sovereignty in West Africa's Time of AIDS* (Durham, NC: Duke University Press, 2010).

Packard, Randall, *White Plague, Black Labor: Tuberculosis and the Political Economy of Health and Disease in South Africa* (Berkeley, Calif.: University of California Press, 1989)

Reynolds, Pamela, *Traditional Healers and Childhood in Zimbabwe* (Athens, O.: Ohio University Press, 1996).

Sachs, Wulf, *Black Hamlet: The Mind of an African Negro Revealed by Psychoanalysis* (Baltimore, Md.: Johns Hopkins University Press, 2nd edn, 1996).

Vaughan, Megan, *Curing their Ills: Colonial Power and African Illness* (Stanford, Calif.: Stanford University Press, 1991).

CHAPTER 21

....

YOUTH

....

NICOLAS ARGENTI AND DEBORAH DURHAM

SUB-SAHARAN Africa is the most youthful region of the world, with some 44 per cent of the population under the age of 15 in 2006 and persistent high birth rates in many countries.[1] While African governments may publicly celebrate their country's youth as the 'promise of the future', they also often fear them as a primary source of twenty-first-century instability, as boys and unemployed young men are associated with a propensity for civil unrest and girls and young women with a propensity for wayward sexuality. The sheer numbers of young people in contemporary Africa, together with a growing sense of their political and social importance, has in recent decades attracted considerable scholarly attention to the continent's youth.

WHO YOUTH ARE

....

Population figures may tell us roughly how many young people there are in Africa, but they do not accurately reflect the number of 'youth'. While 'young people' may be identified simply by biological age, 'youth' is a socially constructed—and often contested—category that may accommodate people of a wide range of biological ages. Who youth are has been subject to many struggles and debates in the context of rapid social change in twentieth-century Africa. While age structures utilized by various international agencies to analyse societies and devise interventions are often used by African governments, local cultural and social practices may recognize people in their forties as youths while considering those younger than their early twenties as 'only children'. In other places someone who has married, including girls of 13, or boys with steady jobs at 16, may be treated as adults. Such understandings are important: when a 25 year old considers herself only a child, she places her actions and situation in a particular moral frame of expectations; when a government considers a 16 year old to be a 'youth', it produces discourses about him or her that include not only verbal rhetoric, but also structured social opportunities, institutions to 'discipline' his or her behaviour, and constraints on rights and responsibilities. Being youth in Africa is shaped by structural, relational, situational, and increasingly intense global processes. Because there are so many frames within which to understand who youth are and what youth means, there is scope for considerable argument and negotiation, as well as creativity made possible through being youth, and some anxiety about being caught in an unending state of youth. In fact, youth includes a wide range of people involved in a wide range of experiences. As Deborah Durham argues, the process of identifying and describing them or of understanding one's own experience as youth (or not) necessarily involves 'discourses about power and authority, responsibility and the grounds of legitimate governance, sources of autonomy and of interdependence, and the obligations and exploitations that make up membership in such social groups as family and nation-state...critical issues of power, agency, and the moral configurations of society'.[2]

Classic anthropological studies of Africa from the colonial period, which typically examined rural societies, described well-defined life stages marked by ritual transitions from one to the next. Often these rituals marked a stage of youth—a period between childhood and full adulthood for which many African languages possess a specific term—although some societies did promote people from childhood directly to adulthood. Sometimes the period of youth was well-marked at its outset with elaborate initiation rituals, but the transition to the next life-stage was less clearly defined, and only elderhood marked a secure and respectable end to youth. East African pastoralists, who organized young men into age cohorts which progressed through life together, provided a model of a clearly demarcated life cycle often referred to by students of Africa. Among Maasai, for example, young males underwent an initiation ceremony after which they were designated *murran* and lived in camps in the bush, away from settlements dominated by older men. Now warriors, they hunted wild animals and sometimes their seniors' cattle, engaged in love affairs with the married women of the villages, and were attended to by a cohort of junior girls. The *murran* returned from their period in the bush in an elaborate ceremony to become adult men who would marry and develop households. Throughout their lives they would remain juniors to elder cohorts and seniors to junior ones, but their progression from youth to adult men to elders was clear and signalled by the foods they ate, their relationship to women, their household status, and their relationship to the cohorts above and below them. Their status as youth or elders was also reinforced through the ways in which colonial governments, and later postcolonial ones, recognized political power and property rights, and sustained selected characterizations of 'unruly' youth.[3]

In such societies where age status was organized through cohorts and was marked by rituals and formalized relationships to other organized cohorts, the members may have been of roughly the same chronological age—or they may not have been. The age sets organized by East African pastoralists, or the rather unusual 'age villages' set up for new cohorts of young people by the Nyakyusa in precolonial Tanzania, were composed of people in roughly the same age range, who remained cohorts as they progressed through the life course.[4] However, in other places where age transitions were marked by rituals that affected the status of cohorts, initiates to youth or to young adulthood may in fact have been of widely varying biological ages. Marc Schloss, in his study of Ehing of the

Casamance in Senegal, described an initiation ceremony, *Kombutsu*, that was staged only every twenty-five years or so. At the ceremony he witnessed in 1979, initiates ranged in age from eighteen months old to their later twenties: prior to initiation they were youth-children and after they became elders, *abiya*.[5] After the ritual, the two-year-old elders had several social privileges, including the ability to see a corpse, eat adult foods, and know sexual secrets and, in theory, to be procreative. Men in their twenties who missed the rite remained youths, at least technically and in public interactions, ignorant of sex and unable to manage death, until the next cycle. Age villages and two-year-old elders are, of course, somewhat extreme and unusual examples of how biological age intersects with organized age statuses. Yet they alert us to the wide ranges of practices and possibilities, provide some background for examining the new forms of assembling cohorts and recognizing statuses, and alert us to contradictory forms of cohort organization in postcolonial Africa.

But not all societies organized people into age cohorts, and even in many of those that did, other forms of reckoning and experiencing age status existed. Indeed, mid-twentieth-century anthropology often treated the age cohorts as an institution that cross-cut more fundamental sources of political order and social reproduction, that is, lineages or territorially based identities. In his classic study of the Nuer of present-day South Sudan. E. E. Evans-Pritchard wrote of the age-set system that it 'segments the male population of a tribe into stratified groups which stand in a definite relationship to one-another and it cuts across territorial divisions, giving identity of status where there is political disparity and differentiating status where there is political identity'.[6] Within lineages or lineage-based villages, generational relations which situated people as junior and senior, or as youth or elder, with respect to a variety of rights and privileges including leadership, property, and religious status, typically operated with little regard to age. As Meyer Fortes pointed out, a father's father's brother's son's son may be genealogically senior and have a wide array of rights and privileges, even though he is ten years old and his genealogical junior is in his seventies.[7]

Young people might therefore be elders at certain ceremonies or in certain legal contexts, but in other contexts, when participating with other people in an initiatory or chronological age cohort, might be youths. Fortes's paper reminds us that youth is not only a relative position, concerned with relations between people within a structure, but is also situational. Situations involving property or title inheritance, marriage discussion, public deference, or other genealogically inflected issues may invoke certain ways of recognizing youth or age; community celebrations may ask for chronologically young people to participate as youth or categorize those doing certain things—fetching, for example, or singing and dancing—as youth, no matter what their age; workplaces and forms of organizing labour may situate people quite differently, with older men remaining 'boys' to better educated or wealthier 'men' in their twenties. Life-course studies, which have traditionally seen people as moving from one stage of life to the next, have also begun to look at the ways in which people negotiate the life course in a non-linear fashion, taking on the role of adult, for example, upon marriage and having a child, but then returning to youth or childhood after a divorce or giving the child to a parent to raise.[8]

Anthropological studies conducted during the colonial period interpreted African institutions, including practices of and around youth, in functionalist terms: they saw them as contributing to the maintenance or reproduction over time of stable social and cultural systems. Even youthful rebellion, articulated especially in ritual, served to highlight the power of the elders to contain, or tap into it to strengthen or re-energize the existing social structures.[9] Since the 1990s, however, youth have more often been seen by anthropologists as sources of social change, who, as they seek ways of achieving adulthood, masculinity or femininity, or power and authority, themselves initiate important changes. In the last decade, historians of Africa have begun to join anthropologists in a new focus on youth as both participants in and engines of social change.[10]

While Evans-Pritchard suggests that the cross-cutting effect of age groups was a source of social stability, tying together groups that are otherwise only weakly connected, the situational nature of age statuses have probably always been a source of local dynamism, if not conflict. This more dynamic sense of age and life cycle is certainly prevalent in scholarship today, as we explore how multiple ways of being 'youth' intersect, including schooling, government policies, nationalist political discourses, and global media. Among the Herero in Botswana, for example, during the week of visiting prior to funerals, men in their twenties and forties often try to sit in the circle of older men known as the *kota*. They may even carry a walking stick, don a hat and coat typical of older men, and sit in one of the chairs around the fire. There the older men may tease them, make space for them, or drive them away; the same younger men will be called upon on the morning of the funeral to act as youths and dig the grave. But some of the older men, secure in membership around the funeral *kota*, may make themselves over into youth at a community civil ceremony, participating in events as members of a choir, whose role is 'just playing', instead of as respected seniors sitting in the shade near the chief. Meanwhile, their sons take charge of navigating government bureaucracy, organizing vaccinations or cattle sales, or making decisions concerning government (Western) medical care, while their uncles, fathers, or mothers deal with ancestors and 'traditional' medical consultations and invoke agricultural knowledge based on experience.[11] Focusing on the situational nature of youth—how people enter into being and not being youth in their daily lives—can supplement approaches that look at youth as inherently rebellious or inventive by drawing our attention to the dynamic nature of society and to the complex labour and affective exchanges that underlie generational relations. Understanding youth to emerge contextually in situated interactions draws our attention, too, to the ways in which subjectivities are engaged in social process; subjectivities which include a sense of playfulness and fun, of aspiration to respect and authority, of resentment and rebelliousness, and a sense of subjective interdependence that is part of traditional and modern African life.

Youth and Labour

A recurrent theme in recent studies of African youth concerns the inability of those categorized as young to achieve maturity or to reach adulthood. Many young people have been seen as 'stuck in the compound' or living a kind of 'social death', unable to find the employment or patronage that will lead to a mature independence.[12] Such studies probably overestimate the extent to which transitions to adulthood were smoothly and regularly achieved in earlier periods, even as they recognize the new challenges to achieving adulthood in changing economic and political contexts. Nonetheless, they do raise the complicated relationship of youth and labour. Although more contemporary accounts stress the lack of access to formal work as almost a synonym for youth, both in the past and in the present, being youth historically has been aligned closely with providing labour.

The studies of age-grade systems of East Africa, as well as accounts of initiation ceremonies in southern Africa such as those by Victor Turner and Jean Comaroff, seemed to describe the effectiveness of symbolic processes in transforming children into adults in 'traditional' social milieux in the colonial period.[13] Studies of West and Central African societies more often found a systematic failure by many polities to manage the transition of young men and women into social maturity. One explanation offered by G. I. Jones in an article on age-grades among the Igbo of south-eastern Nigeria was that in many West African societies young people underwent a long period of transition marked by sporadic and relatively minor rites and transactions, but had no clear-cut rite of passage.[14] Another explanation, however, refers to slavery and the impact of the trans-Atlantic slave trade.[15] Instead of highlighting the functional integration of youth into society through symbolic practices, these explanations refer to tensions surrounding power and conflicts over its exercise. Focusing in particular on youth as sources of labour and as people in whom others have rights, they describe resistance, struggle, and historical transformations. While Claude Meillassoux and Achille Mbembe have emphasized the apparently inescapable and totalizing oppression of youth under gerontocratic and colonial regimes, later studies have focused on more dynamic and unpredictable tensions and agonism between age grades.[16] These studies include children as well as youth and emphasize not the continuous reintegration of marginalized age groups into society, but rather the production of youth as a result of the often intractable nature of marginalization in unequal political formations, whether precolonial, colonial, or postcolonial.[17]

The concepts of rights and power in much of West and Central Africa included rights in persons, such that elders had rights over children and youth in their lineages or other political arrangements and could dispose of them for the interests of the lineage or group as a whole. This could include allocating them not only in marriage, but also allocating the right to arrange marriages (as among the Tiv) or, more commonly, pawning or selling them. As the trans-Atlantic slave trade intensified and had an increasing impact on local practices, those transacted for one reason or another became coded as youth. That is to say, whereas originally people were transacted because they were youth or children over whom elders had rights, under the Atlantic system those who were transacted came to be characterized as youth, even when they were not very young. Such categorizations are familiar from other parts of Africa under the impact of colonial labour systems, where older men came to be called 'boys' by white employers.[18] Indeed, in much of Africa, the poor, the marginalized, bachelors without dependants, and the childless can all find themselves classified as life-long youths despite their biological age.

Meillassoux suggested that the distinction between youth and elders was fundamentally a class division, organized around access to the means of production and reproduction. This perspective is analytically useful in its focus on conflict and attention to historical change, and yet limiting. In this approach, youth—a group not strictly demarcated by age—were forced into dependence on their elders, who monopolized the rights to allocate lineage resources, including land, livestock, and the right to make marriages—which in turn produced labour in the form of children and wives. Youth were kept in dependence as long as possible and were compelled to surrender their labour to their elders, who accumulated it and used it to maximize their own positions. Meillassoux's approach depends on a Marxist reading of local economies. Other approaches have analysed ideas about youth labour not as a form of expropriation, but as a means through which agency is exercised and forms of intersubjectivity are negotiated and sustained.[19] Young people's labour was not always as easy to control as Meillassoux suggested, as it was often allocated or called upon in diverse ways by different parts of society, affording room for agency, negotiation, and, sometimes, outright rebelliousness.[20] Even within family and villages, cohorts of the young might work or not work at field-clearing, public works, or other projects, and could offer their labour elsewhere. Labour, like forms of play or the 'laziness' displayed by Maasai *murran*, established bonds of interdependence and reciprocating selfhoods between youth, and between them and others, that were critical to establishing social personalities. Only through the exchanges of caring, manifest in work for others, can someone in Botswana develop recognized emotional maturity, manifest in the ability to shape others' emotional states through one's own actions and feelings in ways that extends one's social being. This is less a process of alienation of individual worth through the expropriation of labour than one of the shaping of certain kinds of interdependent selfhoods in a place where independent selfhood is a condition of childhood, and interdependence one of maturity.[21]

Transformations in the economic and political relations between age groups have undoubtedly marked all periods of African history, but they have been most extensively studied in the colonial and postcolonial eras. Colonial labour markets, whether for public works, private enterprises, new forms of domestic labour, or positions in government bureaucracies, afforded younger people new resources and new horizons. These transformations should not be characterized as setting a lineage-based economy with juniors dependent on elders against one in which young people suddenly had new opportunities for independence and resources for challenging elders' power. Specific historical narratives were more complicated, because the opportunities and labour of the young were always directed in various ways. The Zulu kingdom, for one well-studied example, was built up in the early nineteenth century through the control of social maturity by organizing youth into military regiments (and young women into marriage regiments); in doing so, the king extended his authority into household and lineage structures and weakened local patriarchies. Subsequent colonial policies, however, supported and bolstered the gerontocracies of local lineages and households (sometimes even inventing them where they had not previously existed), making household and village elders responsible for hut taxes as well as maintaining a 'traditional' social order.

Benedict Carton has described the tensions between local elders attempting to maintain authority and control over their juniors (and women) and the increasing opportunities for young men and women in the colonial economy as one where the young were caught between competing patriarchal powers, which ironically were mutually constituting each other even as they competed over youth.[22]

Colonial labour markets entered into the construction of youth in many ways. Julie Livingston has described the ways in which the demand for and screening of 'able-bodied' workers by recruitment agencies in southern Africa reshaped the entire life course.[23] Being able-bodied drew a line between childhood and a new workforce-oriented maturity, as well as consigning the disabled to a status where they often grew old without becoming elders. Contracts and wages, too, contributed to new ways in which labour itself was configured and labour relationships negotiated. While labour within family and small communities often built long-term relationships in ways that enabled life-course transformations and developed intersubjective personhood, waged work allowed for more independence. The impact on rural areas was, in some places, profound: while colonial authorities in West Africa claimed to be emancipating youth from traditions and rural indentures, the various calls on able-bodied labour emptied some areas of the able-bodied, including youth and younger adults. One such area was the Cameroonian Grassfields, where colonial labour policies led to levels of depopulation more drastic than that caused by four hundred years of slave raiding.[24] There, as in much of southern Africa, rural areas were left populated by the very young, women, and the elderly or disabled. This often led to a tightening control of women by male elders: in Cameroon it exacerbated polygamy and allowed some chiefs to command thousands of wives. In Botswana, however, the same factors enabled women to gain new powers and independence in running farms and households.

Migrant labourers often cast their experiences as heroic ventures that increased their own charismatic powers both at home and abroad.[25] In compounds that grew around mines and in the cities where they sought employment, young people joined together for amusement, self-help, and, increasingly from the 1940s, labour action and political mobilization. The resulting social, cultural, and political innovations would dramatically reshape both rural and urban life.[26] Young people in cities banded together in groups that forged new leisure activities and also in forms labelled 'gangs'. As young people became the front-line in the fight against Apartheid in South Africa in the 1970s–1980s, historians' attention turned to the older phenomena of Ma-Rashea ('the Russians') and other urban gangs.[27] Distinctive urban lifestyles took shape, characterized by cash, clothing, and more transient relationships of all kinds. Yet youth rarely lived entirely within one sphere, but moved back and forth from rural 'homes' to urban ones for education, work, food, and other social resources. Using case studies from Ghana, Esther Goody studied the adoption of children into urban families, arguing that it increased their social networks and their social skills in equal measure. Whether such practices represented an unmitigated opportunity for children and adolescents has, however, since been questioned.[28]

GENDER

Early anthropology often focused more on male than on female youth. Indeed, there were few female informants in much mid-twentieth-century anthropology in Africa. In some places, female life stages were either not the subject of elaborate public rituals or were not marked by ritual at all. In places that did mark female life stages, the important transition was from child to wife, leading some people to suggest that girls did not have a culturally recognized period of youth. In yet other places, girls entered a culturally celebrated period of maidenhood which might be treated as an institutionalized period of youth. In all cases, to focus on girls and women in Africa presses us to think about what we mean by youth and what youth might mean in very different social settings. Youth is often understood in the West as a phase intermediate between a childhood focused on the household and independent adulthood in a new household, so it is understood to take place 'outside' the home in many ways. But the lived experience of many young African women, which is primarily associated with households, may not fit that mould. A Western model accepts too easily the idea that marriage ends youth and that young married people are treated as mature adults—an idea that caused conflicts for young women being trained up as Igbo preachers' wives in colonial Nigeria.[29]

Young girls and women were not entirely invisible in classic anthropological accounts, however, appearing most often as problematic brides in new households. Audrey Richards shifted the standard focus on male rites of passage with her 1956 study of the *chisungu* initiation ceremony among the Bemba of Northern Rhodesia (now Zambia). Her account focused on the agency of the elders from what could be considered a male point of view and the many elaborate practices of the twenty-three days of ritual were presented as convincing girls that a 'girl's proper conduct is expressed in the phrase "be submissive, or make yourself soft and pliant before your elders"'.[30] Victor Turner's analyses of ritual among the neighbouring Ndembu took a more social perspective than Richards's psychoanalytic one. Following his earlier studies of boys' initiation rituals, Turner turned to those of girls, making use, like Richards, of the tripartite structure of separation–liminality–reincorporation originally set out by Arnold van Gennep.[31] Turner saw these rituals as a means of resolving the structural contradictions in Ndembu society, which was matrilineal but nevertheless practised virilocal marriage. For Turner, the rites dramatically enacted the conflicts between men and women, and between girls and women, overcoming them with assertions of the overarching 'solidarity of the widest effective social group, of the whole Ndembu people'.[32]

More recent studies of girls and women as youth now tend to focus on their lives outside the home. A notable exception is Minou Fuglesang's study of young Muslim women in Zanzibar as they consume global popular culture inside their homes and the homes of friends.[33] Many young women, however, have pursued a life outside family households and by doing so are producing new ways of being female youth. Churches have offered many young women a variety of opportunities, including ways of separating themselves from families, as well as new ways of living with parents or spouses. Girls' experiences in school can have intriguing parallels with ritual initiation such as that studied by Richards, but with an array of contradictory new symbols and values that offer a less clear sense of resolution than that suggested by Turner.[34] One important insight of such studies is the extent to which people move in and out of life-stage categorizations, accepting more adult roles as they leave school, get married, have children, or become head of a household, but then return to school, relinquish the primary parenting role to another woman, or move into a household as a junior member.

Studies of young women, whether in school or not, often focus on their sexuality, a topic that has generated more concern in the context of HIV/AIDS. In spite of the problems surrounding AIDS, recent literature often finds that girls' and women's sexuality seems to give them new power and agency when liberated from patriarchal controls. One might note that, while studies of young males' struggles with masculinity reach into a number of practices and domains, those on girls' femininity tend to focus on sexuality. While some studies depict young women as victims of male sexual dominance and aggression, suffering the consequences of pregnancies and sexually transmitted diseases and being set up as *deuxièmes bureaux* or 'outside wives' without the benefits of marriage, more attention is now being paid to how young women use their sexuality to promote their own interests. 'Transactional sex' has become a popular term in analysing young women's sexual activities, referring to how they exchange sex for various social and material rewards. As Jennifer Cole has pointed out in studies of Madagascar, however, transactional sex, while raising alarms among local and outside observers, has continuities with past sexual practices, and is driven by a variety of emotional as well as economic incentives.[35]

New Discources: Education and Youth Movements

Although colonial governments have been faulted for providing only very limited educational opportunities for their African subjects, those schools that were developed initiated a long transformation in the way in which youth came to be understood. Schools emerged as sites of new youth-centred movements, which in turn fed into broader political movements. As elsewhere in the world, schooling in Africa introduced novel ways of dividing up the life course, serving to focus the notion of youth more tightly on chronological age and on the removal of individuals from the labour economy. Today, for example, most national youth policies in Africa consider people of school age (typically up to age 16, but sometimes to 21) who are not in school to be 'a problem', and consider as youth people up to the age of 29 or 34 (the ages vary) who are not 'employed'. In some countries, such as Botswana, where people in their teens tend to be considered 'children', secondary school students have made active claims to the category of youth, arguing that literacy and other new forms of knowledge clearly distinguish them from children.

The possibilities of new forms of education opened early in the colonial period, as the literacy offered by mission schools allowed some young people to enter into the lower echelons of colonial administrations needing clerks, secretaries, and other indigenous intermediaries. Young men might no longer need to wait half a lifetime to attain adult status: they could take a shortcut through salaried government employment and wield considerable authority over traditional elders. When African countries achieved independence from the 1950s, many educated young men moved into positions of bureaucratic power, taking the jobs of departing colonial administrators and accelerating the shift in domestic power relations. As Jean-Francois Bayart put it, 'the era of the Whites became the era of insolence, when "children," "their mouths on fire," came out of their silence'.[36] With reference to children, Filip de Boeck has suggested that the recent child-witch panic in Kinshasa may have been a result of the social inversion wrought by illiterate elders coming to depend upon educated children for the household income.[37] Although Western education has provided an arena in which youth have claimed new forms of power and posed challenges to their elders, it should also be noted that at every historical juncture we find records of complaints about youths' lack of respect, misbehaviour, and political challenge.

In the era of late colonialism and independence, the emphasis in rapidly expanding secondary schools on producing a technocratic and political elite served to introduce new aspirational horizons for young people. More recently, however, a combination of factors has produced what can be seen to be a contraction of opportunities. In the 1980s, structural adjustment policies imposed by the World Bank and the IMF shrank government bureaucracies and opened borders to foreign capital. The government employment that supported the development of a middle class shrank, both in numbers and in the salaries paid to teachers, police, and others, while foreign capital sought mostly cheap labour and forged alliances with a small and very wealthy elite. Donal Cruise O'Brien wrote in the 1990s of the 'high order of built-in frustration' among Africa's 'lost generation'; frustration resulting from an educational system that prepared people for jobs that did not exist. Mbembe has similarly spoken of the African university as providing only a 'disapprenticeship of life'.[38] Such frustration has only grown in the twenty-first century. The educational system generally contributes to a rural–urban imbalance, a large segment of educated unemployed, and a brain drain as higher education channels students to advanced degrees and eventual employment abroad. The high level of education of a small minority, while contributing to the development of a new elite, has not led to the devolution of opportunities for participation to the majority of the young.

Although only a minority gain access to higher levels of education, schools are places where new kinds of cohorts are formed, based on age instead of common submission to local authorities or work practices. This is especially true of upper secondary schools and universities, which typically are filled with students from a wide region, sometimes the whole country. In Nigeria, the development of campus 'cults' among university students has recently drawn attention.[39] University associations were important in early political movements and nationalist movements had a natural home in universities, which reciprocally contributed to the imprimatur of youth on those who were mobilized in nationalist causes. Most African political leaders who fought for independence during colonial times were young rather than old men, their political parties often striving to identify themselves as 'youth' movements. The youth label can long outlast any other obvious markers of youth, and the original politicians or their successors have sometimes held onto the banner of youth for decades in the context of national politics.

In some states, however, postcolonial regimes have appropriated the symbolic structure of traditional hierarchies into national politics in the form of authenticity campaigns. Some heads of state have identified themselves as traditional elders and cast the nation's youth as wayward children in need of strong paternal leadership, who owe allegiance, obedience, and gratitude to their 'father'. Opportunities for political representation of young people, even in the multiparty political systems that have emerged since the 1990s, are thus often limited to the youth wing of the party in power, a youth wing itself sometimes dominated by people decades past university age. University students seeking to participate in national debates by organizing in groups that do not come under the aegis of the party youth wing are often harassed and sometimes subjected to arbitrary acts of violence and incarceration without charge. Universities may be occupied by security forces or closed, becoming key sites of confrontation between the state and a politically mobilized youth. Some scholars have considered the extent to which these confrontations represent struggles for free speech and education or are merely attempts of a new generation to form a new elite and appropriate their own slice of the 'national cake'.[40]

The ambiguity surrounding some of these student uprisings led to disillusionment and fostered the adoption of increasingly Machiavellian worldviews by some members of the student body. According to Bayart, since their experience of the state is typically of a place in which democratic ideals are of no value except as a rhetorical device, students cease to pursue these ideals themselves and instead become pragmatists who simply seek advancement within the status quo, adopting the 'politics of the belly' of the ruling class. This 'miseducation' has been said to produce at best a class of passive and silenced academics and government functionaries, and at worst a faction of pragmatists who reproduce the conditions of their own de-skilling. Students seeing that higher education does not lead to formal employment in either the private or public sector may resort to uprisings, protests, and insurrections that assume varying degrees of violence. Tactics of pacification and an ideal of cynical self-preservation apparent in state responses, often create further protests—leading to the assertion that the state bears the fruits of its persecution of students in the consequent disenchantment and outright criminalization of the young. In spite of this, it must be noted that the democratization movements that swept much of sub-Saharan Africa in the 1990s, as well as the more recent 'Arab Spring' in North Africa in 2011, witnessed a greater role for student and youth movements in genuine political change. In some ways, student movements in contemporary Africa recall the role of students in the emergent anti-colonial struggles of the 1930s to 1950s, and should not always be interpreted cynically.

CRITICAL YOUTH AND YOUTH CRISIS

Not all youth movements in Africa have taken shape in schools. Work sites, military conflict, religious practice, and leisure activities have all provided rich terrains for the organization and orientation of youth activity from precolonial to postcolonial times. Even as youth participation in the political sphere has been circumscribed by repressive authoritarian regimes with their regimented youth wings, scholars have looked at youth's other activities as expressly political interventions. The language of crisis, challenges to power, and trenchant social critique characterizes much writing on contemporary youth activities, from obvious sites such as civil unrest and militarization, vigilantism and violence, to leisure practices in dress, music, and open sexuality.

Youth have long been intimately involved in warfare in Africa. Richard Reid has argued for East Africa that young men were frequently both the victims of nineteenth-century violence and among its leading perpetrators, as they sought to establish their manhood, either within a social order that pressed young men to military accomplishment or against established power.[41] Just as much nineteenth-century violence had a generational aspect, so have the images of the child soldier draped in bandoliers and brandishing weaponry and of the girls raped or kidnapped to be domestic slaves to marauding fighters become icons of contemporary African conflict. Such images perpetuate the contradictory ideas of African children and adolescents as alternately or ambivalently vandals and victims, makers and breakers.[42] This is not to suggest direct continuity between past sources of conflict in Africa and current ones, only to note that the best analyses both recognize the contingent nature of conflicts and the symbolic and social structures within which young people's actions are motivated and through which they are experienced. Paul Richards's account of Sierra Leonean child soldiers notes their motivations within family structures, through encounters with popular media such as Rambo films, the political and economic framework of failed states, a Cold War influx of weaponry, and world demand for diamonds.[43] Many other accounts also go beyond restating a sense of outrage at child victims, in order to make sense of things such as young warriors donning women's wigs and dresses, new leadership opportunities for women in guerrilla operations, and the struggles ex-combatants and displaced youth face to re-establish moral compasses and livelihoods in fractured post-conflict economies.[44]

Dance, music, and dress have long been part of explicitly youthful activities across Africa, from the young men dancing around their campsites celebrating their oxen in Evans-Pritchard's ethnographies, to the hip-hop artists urging renunciation of drinking, and women in the embrace of Quranic principles in Tanzania. J. Clyde Mitchell's account of *kalela* dancers in the mining towns of Northern Rhodesia in the 1950s is one of the first studies to examine how young people mobilized new dress and performance styles in creative ways.[45] Mitchell's work notes how the movement took up the dance motifs that *ngoma* dancing from East Africa had borrowed from military marching bands and integrated those into existing inter-village dance competitions in the early twentieth century. In *kalela*, young men dressed in neat white shirts and pressed trousers on free weekend afternoons, gathering to sing songs celebrating their own sophistication and belittling groups of other 'tribal' origins. Like many other groups, the *kalela* teams also served as self-help societies, maintaining contact with rural homes while also catering to new urban needs. Mitchell argued that these practices created both a new 'traditional' social geography of tribes and rural–urban difference, promoting a modernity associated with colonial figures. In doing so, youth joined headmen and government-nominated elders in creating a new kind of traditional social world, one associated with cities.

Terence Ranger's critical response to Mitchell's work delved further back into the history of *kalela* and its origins in Beni *ngoma* dancing, which Ranger attributed not to mere imitation or pantomime of European forms of symbolic authority, but to an embodied memory of the trauma of slavery and colonial occupation.[46] Later authors examining leisure in mining compounds and urban areas in southern Africa noted how the organization of space and the sponsorship of certain activities enmeshed competitive dancers and football teams in inter-ethnic rivalries that facilitated capitalist interests. As with *ngoma*, young men carried the music, dance, and dress from their labour sites back to villages, where they became intertwined with wedding and other dance and music, re-emerging from both to join with African American music and become part of a dynamic music business.[47] Whether youth performance genres represent a form of autonomy and resistance for youth or their appropriation to the interest of powerful elders and business and political elites is a question that is again brought up by the Ode Lay dances of Freetown, Sierra Leone. Describing the militarization of a traditional dance style in Freetown, John Nunley evokes the ambiguity of a performative genre promoted by elite political patrons in which the line between the adulation of elite elders and the institutions they represent on the one hand and their satirization on the other is never clearly resolved.[48]

One of the most remarked upon sartorial phenomena concerns the SAPE, the self-styled 'Société des Ambianceurs et des Personnes Elégantes', of Brazzaville.[49] So-called *sapeurs* would travel to Paris where they would take on demeaning and gruelling work, living in the most penurious conditions, to save the money with which to buy high-end designer clothing. They would return to Brazzaville with their new *gamme* and engage in competitive partying, hoping to become, however briefly, the best dressed men in town. The political and economic elites of Congo, whose profligate display of wealth the *sapeurs* mimicked, referred to these competitive dressers as delinquents. Scholars have praised them for offering a social critique of the obscene display of illegitimate wealth by African elites, even as the *sapeurs* also reveal the alienating effects of postcolonial proletarianization. Interestingly, early *sapeurs* of the 1960s were typically married men: their double marginalization in Africa and in the global economy, along with their creative appropriation of high fashion, has meant that they are analysed as youth and the SAPE as a youth movement, in spite of being heads of households with access to the low rungs of the global labour market. More recent studies of hip-hop have also focused on the double-edged critique and embrace of wealth and power in a transnational cultural economy.[50] Some simply celebrate illegitimately obtained wealth and its fleeting benefits of women and friends; other hip-hop artists have linked these motifs with new religious movements, both Muslim and Christian.

Churches and new religious movements too have long been important for Africa's youth. Young people gravitated towards Christian missions for a variety of reasons: sent experimentally by their elders, as well as taking their own initiative to seek out new opportunities for knowledge, literacy, and social advancement. Spiritual healing churches in southern Africa provided new homes and caring parenting by charismatic leaders for young people who felt rejected or neglected by their own families, and have been important sources of care for young people dying of AIDS or orphaned by it.[51] Pentecostal churches and Muslim brotherhoods, among others, have offered many opportunities for meaningful participation in civil society that are often denied young people in politics, more established churches, and traditional religious practice focusing on elderhood and ancestorhood. Rijk van Dijk's analysis of the Born-Agains, a Pentecostal movement that emerged in Malawi in the 1970s, highlights the youth of its participants. The preachers ranged in age from 9 to 30 and emphasized to their followers the need to make a break with the traditions of their elders. While the Banda regime of the day was reinventing a traditional Chewa past to facilitate rule over all Malawians, young Pentecostal preachers promoted a church with a power and authority 'beyond the clutches of tradition and its gerontocracy'.[52] In Ghana, Pentecostal demands to make a 'complete break with the past' are set against state projects to celebrate national cultural heritage and build allegiance to the nation and its state.[53] While Pentecostals regularly appeal to the global character of their religious practice and to its modernity, they also embrace a very literal belief in satanic agents, whom they identity as the spirits of traditional religions.

In the first decade of the twenty-first century, Africa has become more and more open to global flows through the rapid spread of cell phones, the internet, and increased traffic of people, capital, and consumer goods. In the context of the rise of the neo-liberal world order, this traffic is increasingly involving China, and what this means for Africa's youth is yet to be discovered. At present, through the prosperity so profligately displayed by the very small minority of wealthy elites, many young people in Africa come to recognize their youth as constituted through marginality and deprivation. West Africans, in particular, often describe their youth as a yearning for escape, both from their locality and from the state of youth with which it is intertwined and by which it is constituted. While youth in other parts of the continent are not all described with such desperation—and certainly there are young people who are successfully navigating jobs and entrepreneurial enterprises—much recent scholarship has come to identify African youth with marginalization and the marginalized as youth. In this sense, to describe Africa as a continent of youth refers not only to the age statistics cited at the beginning of the chapter, but also to the sense that the continent is increasingly marginalized in the global economy. Whereas in nineteenth-century abolitionist literature, Africa was portrayed as a continent robbed by the slave trade of its youth, a realm of abandoned mothers, children, and the infirm, in today's literature it is often represented as a continent robbed of its adulthood, a continent of youth.

Notes

1. Lori S. Ashford, *Africa's Youthful Population: Risk or Opportunity?* (Washington, DC: Population Reference Bureau, 2007), www.prb.org/pdf07/africayouth.pdf.

2. Deborah Durham, 'Disappearing Youth: Youth as a Social Shifter in Botswana', *American Ethnologist*, 31/4 (2004), 590; see also Deborah Durham, 'Youth and the Social Imagination in Africa', *Anthropological Quarterly*, 73/3 (2000).

3. P. T. W. Baxter and Uri Almagor, eds, *Age, Generation and Time: Some Features of East African Age Organizations* (New York: St Martin's Press, 1978); Thomas Spear and Richard Waller, eds, *Being Maasai* (London: James Currey, 1993); Richard Waller, 'Bad Boys in the Bush? Disciplining Murran in Colonial Maasailand', in Andrew Burton and Hélène Charton-Bigot, eds, *Generations Past: Youth in East African Prehistory* (Athens, O.: Ohio University Press, 2010).

4. Monica Wilson, *Good Company: A Study of Nyakyusa Age-Villages* (London: OUP, 1951).

5. Marc Schloss, *The Hatchet's Blood: Separation, Power, and Gender in Ehing Social Life* (Tucson, Ariz.: University of Arizona Press, 1988).

6. E. E. Evans-Pritchard, *The Nuer* (Oxford: OUP, 1940), 260.

7. Meyer Fortes, 'Age, Generation, and Social Structure', in David I. Kertzer and Jennie Keith, eds, *Age and Anthropological Theory* (Ithaca, NY: Cornell University Press, 1984).

8. Jennifer Johnson-Hanks, 'On the Limits of Life Stages in Ethnography: Towards a Theory of Vital Conjunctures', *American Ethnologist*, 104/3 (2002).

9. See Max Gluckman, 'Rituals of Rebellion in South-East Africa', in his *Order and Rebellion in Tribal Africa* (London: Cohen & West, 1963).

10. Anthropological works include Nicolas Argenti, *The Intestines of the State: Youth, Violence and Belated Histories in the Cameroon Grassfields* (Chicago: University of Chicago Press, 2007); Nicolas Argenti, 'Youth in Africa: A Major Resource for Change', in Nicolas Argenti and Alex de Waal, eds, *Young Africa: Realising the Rights of Children and Youth* (Trenton, NJ: Africa World Press, 2002); Catrine Christiansen, Mats Utas, and Henrik Vigh, eds, *Navigating Youth, Generating Adulthood: Social Becoming in an African Context* (Uppsala: Nordiska Afrikainstitutet, 2006); Alcinda Honwana and Filip de Boeck, eds, *Makers and Breakers: Children and Youth in Postcolonial Africa* (Oxford: James Currey, 2005). For recent work from historians, see the useful survey by Richard Waller, 'Rebellious Youth in Colonial Africa', *Journal of African History*, 47 (2006); and Burton and Charton-Bigot, *Generations Past*. Note Deborah Durham's critique of assumptions about youth agency and social change: 'Apathy and Agency: The Romance of Youth and Agency in Botswana', in Jennifer Cole and Deborah Durham, eds, *Figuring the Future: Globalization and the Temporalities of Children and Youth* (Santa Fe: SAR Press, 2008).

11. Deborah Durham, 'Just Playing: Choirs, Bureaucracy, and the Work of Youth in Botswana', in Honwana and de Boeck, *Makers and Breakers*, and Durham, 'Love and Jealousy in the Space of Death', *Ethnos*, 67/2 (2002).

12. Karen Tranberg Hansen, 'Getting Stuck in the Compound: Some Odds Against Social Adulthood in Lusaka, Zambia', *Africa Today*, 51/4 (2005); Donal Cruise O'Brien, 'A Lost Generation? Youth Identity and State Decay in West Africa', in Richard Werbner and Terence Ranger, eds, *Postcolonial Identities in Africa* (London: Zed Books, 1996); Henrik Vigh, 'Social Death and Violent Life Chances', in Christiansen et al., *Navigating Youth*.

13. Victor Turner, '*Mukanda*, the Rite of Circumcision', in his *The Forest of Symbols: Aspects of Ndembu Ritual* (Ithaca, NY: Cornell University Press, 1967); Jean Comaroff, *Body of Power, Spirit of Resistance: The Culture and Power of a South African People* (Chicago: University of Chicago Press, 1985).

14. G. I. Jones, 'Ibo Age Organization, with Special Reference to the Cross River and North-Eastern Ibo', *Journal of the Royal Anthropological Institute*, 92/2 (1962).

15. Claude Meillassoux, *Maidens, Meal and Money: Capitalism and the Domestic Community* (Cambridge: CUP, 1981).

16. Achille Mbembe, *Les Jeunes et l'ordre politique en Afrique noire* (Paris: L'Harmattan, 1985).

17. Jean-Francois Bayart, *The State in Africa: The Politics of the Belly* (London: Longman, 1993); Argenti, *Intestines of the State*; Nicolas Argenti, 'Things that Don't Come by the Road: Folktales, Fosterage, and Memories of Slavery in the Cameroon Grassfields', *Comparative Studies in Society and History*, 52/2 (2010).

18. Karen Tranberg Hansen, ed., *African Encounters with Domesticity* (New Brunswick, NJ: Rutgers University Press, 1982).

19. e.g. Bayart, *The State in Africa*.

20. Richard Reid, 'Arms and Adolescence: Male Youth, Warfare, and Statehood in Nineteenth-Century East Africa', in Burton and Charton-Bigot, *Generations Past*.

21. Deborah Durham, 'Making Youth Citizens: Empowerment Programs and Youth Agency in Botswana', in Jennifer Cole and Deborah Durham, eds, *Generations and Globalization: Children, Youth, and Age in the New World Economy* (Bloomington, Ind.: Indiana University Press, 2007).

22. Benedict Carton, *Blood from your Children: The Colonial Origins of Generational Conflict in South Africa* (Charlottesville, Va.: University Press of Virginia, 2000).

23. Julie Livingston, *Debility and the Moral Imagination in Botswana* (Bloomington, Ind.: Indiana University Press, 2005).

24. Argenti, *Intestines of the State*.

25. David Coplan, *In the Time of Cannibals: The Word Music of South Africa's Basotho Migrants* (Chicago: University of Chicago Press, 1994); see too the ethnographic films by Jean Rouch, *Jaguar* (1955) and *Les Maîtres Fous* (1955).

26. See the classic study by Terence Ranger, *Dance and Society in Eastern Africa 1890–1970: The Beni Ngoma* (London: Heinemann, 1975).

27. See Gary Kynoch, 'Marashea on the Mines: Economic, Social and Criminal Networks on the South African Goldfields, 1947–1999', *Journal of Southern African History*, 26/1 (2000); Clive Glaser, *Bo-Tsotsi: The Youth Gangs of Soweto, 1935–1976* (Portsmouth, NH: Heinemann, 2000). For elsewhere in Africa, see Andrew Burton, 'Urchins, Loafers and the Cult of the Cowboy: Urbanization and Delinquency in Dar es Salaam, 1919–61', *Journal of African History*, 42/2 (2001); Laurent Fourchard, 'Lagos and the Invention of Juvenile Delinquency in Nigeria, 1920–60', *Journal of African History*, 47/1 (2006).

28. Esther Goody, *Parenthood and Social Reproduction: Fostering and Occupational Roles in West Africa* (Cambridge: CUP, 1982); and compare Erdmute Alber, 'Grandparents as Foster Parents: Transformations in Foster Relations between Grandparents and

Grandchildren in Northern Benin', *Africa*, 74/1 (2004); Argenti, 'Things that Don't Come by the Road'; Suzanne Lallemand, *Adoption et mariage: Les Kotokoli du centre du Togo* (Paris: L'Harmattan, 1994).

29. Misty Bastian, 'Young Converts: Christian Missions, Gender, and Youth in Onitsha, Nigeria 1880–1929', *Anthropological Quarterly*, 73/3 (2000).

30. Audrey Richards, *Chisungu: A Girl's Initiation Ceremony among the Bemba of Zambia* (London: Tavistock, 1956), 149.

31. Arnold van Gennep, *The Rites of Passage* (Chicago: University of Chicago Press, 1960 [1909]).

32. Victor Turner, *The Drums of Affliction: A Study of Religious Processes among the Ndembu of Zambia* (Oxford: Clarendon Press, 1968), 268.

33. Minou Fuglesang, *Veils and Videos: Female Youth Culture on the Kenyan Coast* (Stockholm: Stockholm University Press, 1994).

34. Amy Stambach, *Lessons from Mount Kilimanjaro: Schooling, Community, and Gender in East Africa* (New York: Routledge, 2000); Lynn Thomas, 'Schoolgirl Pregnancies, Letter-Writing, and "Modern" Persons in Late Colonial East Africa', in Karen Barber, ed., *Africa's Hidden Histories: Everyday Literacy and Making the Self* (Bloomington, Ind.: Indiana University Press, 2006).

35. Jennifer Cole, *Sex and Salvation: Imagining the Future in Madagascar* (Chicago: University of Chicago Press, 2011).

36. Bayart, *The State in Africa*, 151.

37. Filip de Boeck, 'The Divine Seed: Children, Gift and Witchcraft in the Democratic Republic of Congo', in Honwana and de Boeck, *Makers and Breakers*.

38. O'Brien, 'A Lost Generation?'; Mbembe, *Les Jeunes*.

39. Misty Bastian, 'Vulture Men, Campus Cultists, and Teenage Witches: Modern Magics in the Nigerian Popular Press', in Henrietta Moore and Todd Sanders, eds, *Magical Interpretations, Material Realities: Modernity, Witchcraft and the Occult in Postcolonial Africa* (London: Routledge, 2001); Daniel Jordan Smith, *A Culture of Corruption: Everyday Deception and Popular Discontent in Nigeria* (Princeton: PUP, 2007).

40. Bayart, *The State in Africa*; O'Brien, 'A Lost Generation?'; Jeremy Seekings, *Heroes or Villains? Youth Politics in the 1980s* (Johannesburg: Raven Press, 1993).

41. Reid, 'Arms and Adolescence'.

42. Jon Abbink and Ineke van Kessel, eds, *Vanguards or Vandals: Youth, Politics, and Conflict in Africa* (Leiden: Brill, 2005); Honwana and de Boeck, *Makers and Breakers*.

43. Paul Richards, *Fighting for the Rainforest: War, Youth and Resources in Sierra Leone* (Oxford: James Currey, 1996).

44. Mary Moran, *Civilized Women: Gender and Prestige in Southeastern Liberia* (Ithaca, NY: Cornell University Press, 1990); Chris Coulter, *Bush Wives and Girl Soldiers: Women's Lives through War and Peace in Sierra Leone* (Ithaca, NY: Cornell University Press, 2009); Harry West, 'Girls with Guns: Narrating the Experience of War of Frelimo's "Female Detachment"', *Anthropological Quarterly*, 73/4 (2000); Rosalind Shaw, 'Displacing Violence: Making Pentecostal Memory in Postwar Sierra Leone', *Cultural Anthropology*, 22/1 (2007).

45. J. Clyde Mitchell, *The Kalela Dance* (Rhodes-Livingston Papers, 27; Manchester: MUP, 1956).

46. Ranger, *Dance and Society*.

47. Veit Erlmann, *African Stars: Studies in Black South African Performance* (Chicago: University of Chicago Press, 1991).

48. John Nunley, *Moving with the Face of the Devil: Art and Politics in Urban West Africa* (Urbana, Ill.: University of Illinois Press, 1987).

49. Justin-Daniel Gandoulou, *Dandies à Bacongo: Le Culte de l'élégance dans la société Congolaise contemporaine* (Paris: L'Harmattan, 1989); Justin-Daniel Gandoulou, *Au Cœur de la Sape: Mœurs et aventures de Congolais à Paris* (Paris: L'Harmattan, 1989); C. D. Gondola, 'Dream and Drama: The Search for Elegance among Congolese Youth', *African Studies Review*, 42/1 (1999).

50. Brad Weiss, 'Chronic Mobb Asks a Blessing: Apocalyptic Hip-Hop and the Global Crisis', in Cole and Durham, *Figuring the Future*.

51. Fred Klaits, *Death in a Church of Life: Moral Passion during Botswana's Time of AIDS* (Berkeley, Calif.: University of California Press, 2010).

52. Rijk van Dijk, 'Pentecostalism, Cultural Memory, and the State: Contested Representation of Time in Postcolonial Malawi', in Richard Werbner, ed., *Memory and the Postcolony: African Anthropology and the Critique of Power* (London: Zed Books, 1998), 166.

53. Birgit Meyer, 'Make a Complete Break with the Past: Memory and Postcolonial Modernity in Ghanaian Pentecostal Discourse', in Werbner, *Memory and the Postcolony*.

BIBLIOGRAPHY

Abbink, Jon, and Ineke van Kessel, *Vanguards or Vandals: Youth, Politics, and Conflict in Africa* (Leiden: Brill, 2005).

Argenti, Nicolas, *The Intestines of the State: Youth, Violence and Belated Histories in the Cameroon Grassfields* (Chicago: University of Chicago Press, 2007).

Bayart, Jean-Francois, *The State in Africa: The Politics of the Belly* (London: Longman, 1993).

Burton, Andrew, and Hélène Charton-Bigot, eds, *Generations Past: Youth in East African History* (Athens, O.: Ohio University Press, 2010).

Carton, Benedict, *Blood from your Children: The Colonial Origins of Generational Conflict in South Africa* (Charlottesville, Va.: University Press of Virginia, 2000).

Christiansen, Catrine, Mats Utas, and Henrik Vigh, eds, *Navigating Youth, Generating Adulthood: Social Becoming in an African Context* (Uppsala: Nordiska Afriainstitutet, 2006).

Cole, Jennifer, *Sex and Salvation: Imagining the Future in Madagascar* (Chicago: University of Chicago Press, 2011).

Cole, Jennifer, and Deborah Durham, eds, *Figuring the Future: Globalization and the Temporalities of Children and Youth* (Santa Fe: SAR Press, 2008).

Durham, Deborah, 'Youth and the Social Imagination in Africa', *Anthropological Quarterly*, 73/3 (2000).

Honwana, Alcinda, and Filip de Boeck, eds, *Makers and Breakers: Children and Youth in Postcolonial Africa* (Oxford: James Currey, 2005).

Mbembe, Achille, *Les Jeunes et l'ordre politique en Afrique noire* (Paris: L'Harmattan, 1985).

Richards, Audrey, *Chisungu: A Girl's Initiation Ceremony among the Bemba of Zambia* (London: Tavistock, 1956).

Richards, Paul, *Fighting for the Rainforest: War, Youth and Resources in Sierra Leone* (Oxford: James Currey, 1996).

Waller, Richard, 'Rebellious Youth in Colonial Africa', *Journal of African History*, 47 (2006).

CHAPTER 22

ECONOMIC GROWTH

MORTEN JERVEN

'*AVANTI*, economic historians!' sounded the call from Patrick Manning to African economic historians in 1987.[1] But instead of surging ahead, the discipline in the following decade arguably went into relative decline.[2] In the past ten years, however, there has been a resurgence of scholarship on the long-term economic performance of Africa. Whereas earlier scholarship was dominated by economic historians, the recent impetus has mainly come from economists seeking to explain the historical roots of African development.[3] This chapter seeks to reconnect the work of economists with that of economic historians. First, it considers what kind of challenge lies in the recent declaration of a 'new African economic history', and attempts to bridge the somewhat unfortunate divide between 'old' and 'new' directions in the discipline. It then reviews some of the main drivers of macroeconomic change over the past two hundred years, revisiting fundamental debates about the impact of the decline of the Atlantic slave trade, the commercial transition to 'legitimate' commerce and subsequent cash-crop revolutions, and on whether colonial regimes acted as brakes on growth or were conducive to economic development. In light of these questions on long-term patterns of development, I analyse the different trajectories of growth and stagnation in postcolonial Africa. Finally, the chapter maps some of the potential paths that current and future scholars of the history of economic development in Africa may take.

BEYOND OLD AND NEW IN AFRICAN ECONOMIC HISTORY

The economic dimension of the African past was a central theme in the development of African history as a discipline, from the appearance of K. Onwuka Dike's seminal *Trade and Politics in the Niger Delta* in 1956 through to the heyday of African economic history in the

1970s.[4] Although the field subsequently went into relative decline, important contributions continued to be made in the 1980s and 1990s, particularly with regard to the history of slavery and the slave trade.[5] Important publications in later years include landmark works of synthesis by Ralph Austen, Frederick Cooper, and Paul Zeleza, as well as John Iliffe's demographic interpretation of Africa's long-term history and his history of poverty.[6]

The first wave of African economic history was concerned with applying concepts of classical and neo-classical economics to the continent's past, specifically in order to analyse prices, supply and demand responses, and the allocation of productive resources in the precolonial and colonial eras. In short, much pioneering research was focused on the functioning of markets, seeking to reject the approach of the 'substantivist' school that held that resource allocation was determined by cultural rather than economic factors.[7] The market approach was crowned with the appearance of A. G. Hopkins's major work on the economic history of West Africa.[8] Other early scholarship emphasized African agency in explaining economic change, with the work by Polly Hill on the Ghanaian cocoa farmers being of particular importance in this regard.[9]

While pioneering work on African economic history was dominated by an emphasis on demonstrating the rationality and agency of African actors, a second generation of scholars pointed to the use of coercion and the role of conflict in the development process. This set the stage for a more radical, Marxist revisionism.[10] Perhaps the most important target for criticism was the use of dual sector models, such as that developed by the American economist W. A. Lewis and applied to the study of settler economies, where the European-dominated or 'modern' sector was viewed as intrinsically dynamic as opposed to the stagnant, 'traditional' African sector.[11] This view was rejected, research showing that African farmers in settler colonies did responded positively to the emergence of markets for food crops. Furthermore, it was demonstrated that colonial administrations in these territories intervened with taxes and land alienation in order to drive African farmers out of the produce markets and into the market for labour on European-owned farms and mines.[12]

An influential development since the 1980s has been the application of the so-called new institutional economics to African history. A leading innovator in this respect was the political scientist Robert Bates, who sought to apply the principle of rational choice to economic and political decision-making in postcolonial Africa. Bates argued that postcolonial states were dominated by the interests of urban elites and were therefore stuck in a low growth equilibrium where urban interests were catered for at the expense of over-taxed rural producers.[13] This interpretation became an important justification for the drastic scaling back of state intervention in IMF and World Bank-sponsored structural adjustment reforms in the 1980s and 1990s.

More recently, the principles of the 'new institutional economics' have been applied to the continent's long-term macroeconomic history.[14] These have served to extend the debates on the effects of colonization, notably in two important articles by Acemoglu, Robinson, and Johnson in which they set out two controversial theses on the 'reversal of fortune' and the 'colonial origins of comparative development'.[15] The former argues that five hundred years ago, the poorest non-European areas of the world are now among the richest and that conversely, the formerly richest areas now are among the poorest. This apparent reversal of fortune, they argue, can be explained by the fact that Europeans settled in great numbers in poorer areas and invested in the creation of costly but economically 'good' institutions. The latter thesis builds on the first, explaining the current comparative development levels in the non-European world using an instrumental variable approach. It is argued that mortality levels of European settlers determined the numbers of settlers that colonies attracted, which in turn determined the quality of the institutions that were established. Specifically, the argument distinguishes between colonies where 'extractive' institutions were introduced, on the one hand, and those where 'productive' institutions were established, on the other—the latter being the richest ex-colonies today.

During the past decade, a field that since the 1980s was in danger of being marginalized by the dominance of social and cultural history has begun to be reinvigorated by these and other innovative studies of long-term development. Indeed, A. G. Hopkins identified a 'new African economic history' in a recent review article which sought to introduce non-specialists to some of this new work by economists on the continent's long-term development problems.[16] Hopkins highlighted the 'reversal of fortune' thesis as an explanation for current income differentials, and the use of 'ethno-linguistic fractionalization' measures to capture weak, perverse, or dysfunctional institutions in sub-Saharan Africa. These were, he argued, arguments and findings with which Africa's economic historians—and historians more generally—should and could engage.

In response to Hopkins's declaration of a new African economic history, James Fenske produced another review of the literature with a somewhat different emphasis.[17] Fenske associated 'new' not with the arguments, but with the methods used to investigate the cause and effects of historical economic change, arguing that scholarly contributions to the discipline will be judged by their methods and not by the ideas they put forward.[18] In a contribution to this debate, I have argued for a middle ground, one that will accommodate the differing methodological imperatives of history and economics.[19] A common research agenda must appreciate interdisciplinary methods. This means that there are equally valuable yet different ways of 'coming to know' something about African economic change. The most robust way of asserting knowledge regarding economic phenomena is not always related to the sophistication of the method applied, but must be judged carefully with regard to the quality of the underlying data that are used to generate the results and the nature of the question at hand. Some issues call for generating large cross-country databases; others for specific micro-studies. Others again are better approached through careful archival work, source criticism, and the subjective judgement and interpretation of the researcher.

It is clear that the recent study of African economic development over the long term has been invigorated by the adoption of a broader approach in the search for, and mobilization of, quantitative evidence. These big ideas have by and large been put forward by economists using econometric techniques. Even so, the lack of reliable and consistent data over time is the most fundamental challenge for the practice of African economic history. The paucity of reliable time series data complicates the evaluation of the importance of key historical events, such as the slave trades and the development of colonial economies, as compared to 'initial conditions' of geography and resource endowment. In the search for root causes of underdevelopment, there has been a tendency to overlook considerable divergence in economic performance across the continent. Institutional change over time has also been downplayed, resulting in what Austin has called a 'compression of history'.[20]

Approaching Long-Term Growth in Africa

It is with this background in mind that I proceed to sketch out a history of macro-economic growth in modern Africa. The emphasis here is on considering how some of the key themes in the 'old' literature cohere with, contradict, or otherwise shed light on the main issues raised in the 'new' literature. In doing so, I have chosen to focus quite narrowly—and often in very generalized terms—on one particular aspect of Africa's modern economic history: economic growth at the aggregate level. There are other issues of great importance to the study of Africa's economic history which will be largely ignored here: infrastructural development, labour migration, urbanization, demographic change, and, perhaps most importantly, poverty. Moreover, the emphasis is on the external sector, which at times comes at the expense of analysing the dynamics of domestic economies. The justification for this is that most recent contributions to African economic history have focused on the aggregate and on explaining persistent divergence in Gross Domestic Product (GDP) per capita. There remains much more to explain in terms of spatial and temporal variation in GDP per capita over the past two centuries, including institutional change and causation between institutions and economic performance over the long term. Taking inspiration from the concept of recurring growth, I investigate periods of per capita income increases in precolonial, colonial, and postcolonial times.[21]

The study of economic growth is supported and aided by the availability of a reliable dataset of GDP per capita estimates. Yet in most African states these have only been published regularly by national statistical offices in the period since the Second World War. For most other regions of the world, economic historians have access to national accounts, but for the majority of African economies such estimates are not available before about 1950.[22] The Angus Maddison dataset only provides a few single-year estimates of GDP per capita for Africa before 1950, which are provided in Table 22.1. These estimates indicate slow but steady progress, at a rate of 0.3 per cent per annum between 1820 and 1870, 0.6 per cent between 1870 and 1900, and 0.4 per cent between 1900 and 1913, before accelerating to 0.9 per cent between 1913 and 1950.

These data give a misleadingly generalized picture of slow and steady growth, particularly because aggregating statistics from the entire continent obscures large regional diversity. Rising per capita figures were driven mostly by the higher per capita

Table 22.1 African GDP per capita, 1820–1950

Year	1820	1870	1900	1913	1940	1950
GDP per capita ($)	420	500	601	637	813	890

Source: Angus Maddison, *The World Economy* (Paris: Development Centre of the OECD, 1990).

incomes in North Africa and in South Africa. Furthermore, the sluggish growth rates seem inconsistent with what is known of economic and political change taking place during this period. The average data may well be within the reasonable range of guesses one could make, but it is of greater interest to see what happened to particular states, societies, and regions. Finally, it is important to emphasize that African economic data are limited both in availability and quality. These growth 'data' are only partially based on firm historical evidence and rely first and foremost on assumptions and projections. Consequently, the study of growth, particularly during the precolonial era but also during the colonial, and to some extent the postcolonial era, must make use of much circumstantial evidence and interpret visible trends in trade, population, and taxation to make conjectures on rates and direction of economic change.

To begin with, it is useful to distinguish between intensive and extensive economic growth. Extensive growth is a simple expansion of production by adding more factors of production, which is essentially observed by historians as more people using more land. It is this process that John Iliffe stresses in his demographic interpretation of Africa's long-term history.[23] The study of growth in the modern period, in contrast, focuses on intensive growth. This refers to the process of getting more for the same, and thus is the type of economic growth associated with technological change and 'development'. Such changes also increase living standards, which, if properly recorded and measured, could be summarized as increases in GDP per capita.[24]

The most important source of intensive growth in the pre-modern period was the introduction of new cultigens from Asia and the Americas. Exotic food crops such as cassava, banana, and maize had a considerable impact on productivity throughout much of the continent. Similarly, crops primarily grown for export, such as cocoa and tobacco, could be interpreted as growth arising from the introduction of new technologies and investment. Another important stimulant of economic growth is market integration. When markets integrate, specialization takes place, opportunities for expansion arise, and growth occurs as economies of scale make production more efficient. Moreover, an expanded market may serve to release underutilized factors of production, such as land and labour, generating new production for the market. Growth arising from production for the market goes back many centuries. It should be stressed that not all production in the pre-modern era was orientated towards subsistence: internal markets for agricultural goods, handicrafts, textiles, metals, and currencies were all widespread and important. Moreover, the interaction of markets preceded the slave trade and went beyond Atlantic commerce. Northern and sub-Saharan Africa were linked by the trans-Saharan trade and in the Horn, and in eastern and southern Africa, Indian Ocean trade was vibrant. However, until the twentieth century only a small part of the territorial gross product entered external trade.[25]

These positive gains from engagement with external markets have to be weighed against the negative effects. Some were indirect, such as the spread of diseases, while others were direct, most obviously the removal of millions of productive people during the era of slave trades. The spread of cheaper imports, such as textiles and iron, often replaced existing domestic production. The role and effect of coercion in inducing Africans to produce for the world market (instead of producing food for their own use) are equally contested. It will be argued here that increases in production for the market in the late nineteenth and early twentieth centuries were by and large a net benefit for African producers.

The growth perspective adapted here largely ignores and only marginally touches upon concurrent developments in patterns of poverty. Following Iliffe, poverty is best approached by understanding it as having two distinct causes. Conjunctural poverty is the hardship resulting from episodic crises such as war and insecurity, drought, famine, and other disasters. Structural poverty is a long-term phenomenon that derives from social or political factors. According to Iliffe, with the exception of North Africa and Ethiopia, the continent historically has a much lower incidence of structural poverty than elsewhere. Structural poverty resulting from lack of access to land, however, became prevalent in some parts of the continent during the colonial period. This was in part due to trends in population growth, but in colonies of white settlement discriminatory access to land was more important.[26] With industrialization and urbanization, a distinctly urban poverty also appeared. Urbanization was held back in many regions during much of the colonial period, but from the mid-twentieth century African cities received more migrants than the labour market could accommodate, resulting in high urban unemployment and an increase in the incidence of deprivation caused by conjunctural poverty.[27]

A focus on episodes of growth represents an important reorientation from the previous emphasis on explaining the lack of growth, relative underdevelopment, and persistence of poverty in Africa. Earlier approaches have tended to underestimate institutional change and the role of local agency in the process of specialization. Specialization in the slave trade testifies to the power of African elites and states. From the perspective of those who controlled them, the slave trades were a means of securing returns through exports in lieu of a land tax. During and after the closing of the trans-Atlantic slave market, growth in 'legitimate commerce' did, in some places, occur—often in spite of rather than because of the actions of both precolonial and colonial states. Peasant farmers were the leading agents of change in this period. By the mid-twentieth century, marketing boards, an institutional innovation of late colonialism, provided the basis for the state to reassert itself. When these revenues were undermined by external markets and internal rent-seeking in the 1980s, so-called structural adjustment was implemented and state intervention in markets was limited. The most recent growth episodes since the 1990s have been based predominantly on exports of minerals and other raw materials. The internal revenue base of the state has remained limited and taxation through marketing boards has been curtailed. But as long as external market demand has remained buoyant, economic growth has been sustained.

These recurring episodes of economic growth in Africa between 1800 and the present were rooted in trade and the world economy. Yet growth was only possible due to a reorganization of factors of production, an increase in investment, and technological growth, all of which had significant consequences for political economy. In these episodes of growth, factors of production could be relocated relatively smoothly and producers were able to change patterns of specialization with temporary social costs. However, patterns of boom and bust crucially affected state revenue and thus necessitated the reorientation of the state, a process that was often slow, costly, and associated with conflict.

From Slave Trade to Legitimate Commerce

One of the key questions in African economic history concerns the impact of the slave trade on the continent's social, political, and economic structures. It is quite obvious that the slave trades had a negative impact on demographic growth in many regions, particularly in the short and medium term, and this may have been on the whole detrimental for polities that were already characterized by a shortage of labour.[28] Exactly how it affected the total population and the evolution of domestic markets has been the subject of much debate.[29] It is generally agreed that African participants, whether states or networks of merchants, were motivated to engage in the external slave trade because they were able to realize economic gains from these transactions. In West Africa, for example, polities such as Asante, Dahomey, and Oyo grew from small kingdoms to extensive imperial systems, owing in large parts to their participation in the slave trade.

In 1807, Britain made it illegal for its own subjects to trade in slaves, and other nations followed suit by the middle of the century. The ban was actually followed by an intensification of trade in slaves from some parts of Atlantic and eastern Africa to the middle of the nineteenth century, while domestic slavery persisted in many regions into the twentieth century. Whether the closing of the trans-Atlantic slave trade led to a 'crisis of adaptation' as the external trade shifted to 'legitimate commerce' in the middle of the nineteenth century is a highly contested question.[30] The basic reasoning underlying this claim is that the end of profitable slave exports undermined the fiscal capabilities of centralized states, and that the income terms of trade (i.e. the price of exports over that of imports) deteriorated as the slave trade ended. The general consensus is that this crisis has been overstated.[31] While the transition to legitimate trade in general constituted an evolutionary, rather than revolutionary, process, there were important regional transformations in political, economic, and social structures. In the Sokoto Caliphate, slavery for domestic production increased after the abolition of the trans-Atlantic slave trade, thus minimizing any 'crisis of adaptation'; in contrast, coastal kingdoms such as Dahomey did see their financial basis undermined.

In West Africa more generally, the ongoing coercion of labour contributed to the process by which the cash-crop economies developed as the region made the transition to legitimate commerce. For example, it has been estimated that over 30 per cent of the population of French West Africa were slaves at the turn of the twentieth century. For slave-owning elites, at least, this system of production made economic sense. With abundant land in the region in the nineteenth century, free wage rates would have been too high and thus coercion was an important mechanism of mobilizing labour. Slaves contributed to the labour force in important zones of nineteenth-century legitimate commerce such as groundnut production in Senegambia and palm oil production in south-eastern Nigeria, while the use of pawned labour was important in the early twentieth-century expansion of cocoa production in the Akan forest kingdoms of the Gold Coast and the Yoruba region of south-western Nigeria.[32]

At the beginning of the twentieth century, however, the institution of slavery was also made illegal by European colonial powers, and slaves in large numbers were freed or escaped their masters. This created a short-term downward dip in production of cash crops for the market. Growth did return as production adapted to the use of free labour. Overall, the main trend in the organization of production was towards the use of free family labour, which was true for both forest and savanna zones, so there was definitely a long-term evolutionary shift towards the use of free labour after the ending of the slave trade in West Africa. However, the crisis of adaptation thesis is probably overstated, mainly because the early literature overlooked the importance of coerced labour within the region during the early phases of the cash-crop revolution.

In eastern Africa, the slave trade continued to be important for commercial exchange until the end of the nineteenth century. Here, a similar dynamic can be observed to that in West Africa, with some communities suffering greatly from slave raiding while others benefited as suppliers or operators of slave caravans from the interior to the ports of the Indian Ocean coastline. Those who benefited did so by trading textiles and beads in return for supplying slaves directly or producing food for the caravans. These exchanges allowed for new commodities to circulate in the local economies. On the white settler frontier of southern Africa, commercial farming was implemented by settlers whose labour force was sometimes comprised of slaves, but more often of African workers who had had their own production displaced by the confiscation of their cattle and/or land. This latter pattern would continue and expand with the creation of new colonies of white settlement following the European partition of the continent by the early twentieth century.

COLONIALISM AND ECONOMIC GROWTH

Beginning in the nineteenth century and continuing into the period of colonial rule, there was an expansion in the production of primary products for export in many parts of Africa. This could be considered rural capitalism, not necessarily because of its reliance on wage labour—although that also featured in some regions—but because it entailed the investment of borrowed or saved capital for expansion in production for the market. New land was colonized and cleared, and investments were made in perennial crops. The archetypal peasant-led cash-crop revolution was that of cocoa in the forest zone of the Gold Coast (present-day Ghana) and subsequently other West African colonies. But it also occurred in other crops, such as coffee, cotton, tobacco, palm oil and kernels, kola nuts, rubber, and groundnuts, and in other parts of the continent.

A key question in the literature on the cash-crop revolution in general has been how to interpret the visible aggregate export data. Increases in export quantities or income terms of trade should not be equated directly with economic growth. The rapid expansion of exports may facilitate growth in the domestic economy, yet it may also displace other production for the domestic market. We have the external trade statistics, but less is known regarding the impact of this trade on local economies.[33] There is consensus, however, that there must have been some economic growth. A lot of this growth was extensive, generated by the application of more factors of production, but there was also intensive growth. There was growth both through specialization and though the entrepreneurial adaptation of new technologies and capital investment in the form of planting of tree crops. However, it has been argued that the economic growth arising from international trade was probably limited because exports were confined to staples while imports were dominated by consumer goods. Furthermore, because the total export proceeds were too small to support the formation of a wide range of enterprises on the continent and because income inequality was high, the growth in traded goods did not allow the formation of mass consumer markets. Other scholars, however, not only take issue with the assumptions of abundance or scarcity, but point to the importance of the political economy of growth. Dependency scholars would argue that growth in exports was fundamentally driven by power and redistribution of returns. Specifically, the colonial state was interested in increasing taxable activities and increasing labour supply, and thus had an incentive to undermine food production and promote export production. It did so by introducing taxes or by alienating land to various degrees across the continent.

The basic methodological tool used to analyse this process is the vent-for-surplus model from classical economics. It assumes that there was a surplus of factors of production, particularly labour and land, and that the world market provided a vent for these factors. Thus, when we see increased export volumes, the opportunity cost is zero. Scholarship has in different ways contested these assumptions and by extension the validity of the model.[34] It has been pointed out that labour was only seasonally abundant and was very scarce in certain periods—particularly in areas outside the West African forest belt.[35] Furthermore, the production of exports involved both innovation and capital; that is, investment in new technologies, and expansion in production was made possible through labour migration.[36] Most importantly, the opportunity costs of engaging in production for exports were not necessarily zero, as they could have an impact on food quality and security, the division of labour, and on local manufacturing.[37] These, and other empirical contributions, remind us that when we see aggregate modern sector growth it is not equivalent to observing aggregate economic growth.[38]

The observed growth in exports was impressive in some colonies, whereas in other areas colonial efforts to spur production were futile. The rapid expansion of cocoa production in the Gold Coast from the 1890s was fundamentally an entrepreneurial response by African peasants, and this pattern spread to other areas of West Africa's forest zone. The success of the cocoa economy in the Gold Coast appears to have occurred in spite of, rather than because of, the British colonial administration, which, for instance, was reluctant to formalize private land rights. In neighbouring Côte d'Ivoire, cocoa production did not take off until after the terminal phase of colonial rule in the 1950s. This is probably because French settler farmers demanded *corvée* labour from African peasants during colonial rule. Thus, there was not enough wage labour available for land clearing and planting until this labour regime was abolished after the Second World War. The role of the British and French colonial administrations in the cocoa economies of the Gold Coast and Côte d'Ivoire can therefore be seen to have been crucial only with regard to their respective policies governing coercion in labour markets.[39]

In some cases, coercion contributed directly to export production. Most infamously, the boom in rubber exports from the Congo Free State in the 1890s–1900s was built on brute force and was sustained with disastrous consequences for the local population. However, evidence suggests that coercion tended to be both weak and futile, and that the crude violence of the concessionary company regimes of Belgian- and French-ruled equatorial Central Africa in the opening decades of colonial rule were the exceptions to this rule. In savanna regions, both British and French colonial administrations found it very hard to urge smallholders to increase their production of cotton. In Egypt, producers and the state took full advantage of the increased demand for cotton in the mid-nineteenth century, and colonial powers envisaged the same kind of supply from their sub-Saharan possessions. Their efforts to increase production, however, were largely unsuccessful. One contributing factor was competition from local demand for cotton for spinning, but another was the unwillingness of smallholders to increase their food security risk. The planting season of cotton corresponds with the food planting cycle, and thus producers were unwilling to specialize in cotton production.[40]

The distinction between colonies dominated by peasant production on the one hand and those dominated by production by white settlers on the other is important when it comes to interpreting visible export growth in the colonial era. South Africa, the Rhodesias, and Kenya provide the most pronounced examples of settler colonies. Here, settlers faced two basic constraints: first, as food producers and cattle rearers, they faced competition from local producers, and secondly, the competing peasants were unwilling to engage fully in wage labour. This was most acutely felt in relation to mining in South Africa and on the Copperbelt in Central Africa. But the same problem arose in those settler colonies where white farmers found it difficult to attract wage labour for employment on commercial farms. In both cases the problem was to attract labour while preventing it from becoming prohibitively expensive.

In effect this means that observed growth production quantities in these areas came at a cost. The basic logic here is contained in the Lewis model of 'economic development with unlimited supplies of labour'.[41] In this classical dual economy model, land was assumed to be scarce and so the marginal productivity of labour in the rural sector was zero. Therefore the opportunity cost of modern sector growth, defined as labour moving to the modern industrial sector, was also zero. This sets the wage rate at very close to subsistence. In the settler colonies, however, land was abundant and peasants found no compelling reason to leave their land for wages that were lower than their marginal output on their own farms. Unable to find solutions to this labour problem, colonial administrations sometimes resorted to coercion. In both peasant and settler colonies, some of this problem was relieved by instituting a head tax. In order to obtain cash to pay taxes, Africans had to engage in wage labour. However, this did not secure a regular supply of labour, as peasants would, if allowed to do so, often be better off earning cash to satisfy the tax demands by their own production. The solution in settler colonies was found in alienating African farmers from their land and reserving land for settlers. In Kenya, growing coffee was legal only for white farmers, while in Nyasaland production of tobacco was also reserved for settlers. Such restrictions made labour available for both capitalist farming and mining. In effect this may have resulted in slower growth equilibrium in the economies where the growth in the export sector came at a high opportunity cost. Furthermore, it artificially put the wage rate at a lower level in these colonies, with the observable effect of higher poverty and lower real wages in settler colonies compared to peasant colonies.[42]

Another key question is whether colonial rule acted as a brake on industrial development in sub-Saharan Africa. African colonies were integrated in the world economy as producers of primary products prior to colonization, a pattern which continued and was strengthened during colonial rule. There was some industrialization, which took place mainly to satisfy the domestic market. There was also some industrial growth directly associated with mineral extraction and railways to transport goods for the market. The main settler colonies (South Africa, Algeria, Kenya, Southern Rhodesia, and the Belgian Congo) had a larger consumer market for such goods, and therefore industry was more developed in these places. Furthermore, the presence of white settlers provided an articulated political will to industrialize. Settlers had an economic interest in securing a market for their own output that was not subject to the volatility of the world market, together with a political interest in increasing the autonomy of their respective colonies.

Thus, in colonies with a very marginal settler presence, industrialization may have been relatively delayed. However, manufacturing was less profitable than primary extraction activities. Protection of local industries from foreign competition proved costly for colonial administrations and expansion placed an additional demand on a limited labour force. And as Peter Kilby's calculations show, it was only in the 1950s that the domestic market in Nigeria could have supported basic light manufacturing industries across the board. There were, however, some exceptions. The size of the Nigerian domestic economy would have justified a start-up of cement and textile production as early as the 1920s and the 1890s respectively, but these sectors were not in fact started until 1957.[43]

Indeed, most of Africa's progress in manufacturing occurred only after the Second World War. Arriving on the heels of the Great Depression of the 1930s, the war gave impetus to local industry because the colonies had to be self-sufficient in consumer goods. As the period of decolonization approached, however, African economies by and large remained dependent on imports of manufactured goods financed by exports of unprocessed primary products. The potential for industrialization was therefore seen as a promising opportunity when African countries became independent. As a result, it was anticipated that, as independent states developed, rapid advances in industry would follow and that these would not only be associated with established mining sectors but also extended to basic manufacturing.

On the eve of African independence, then, there was a large variation in incomes based on different growth patterns during the colonial period. Some economies, such as Sierra Leone and Zambia, were rich from mineral extraction; others such as Belgian Congo had developed a wider industrial base. The Gold Coast (from 1957, Ghana) had a fully specialized agricultural economy, whereas opportunities for expansion were still available and untapped in Côte d'Ivoire. Some territories, such as those of Sahelian region of French West and Equatorial Africa from Mali to Chad and down to the Central African Republic, did not have much in the way of either mineral deposits or fertile agricultural land, whereas other poor economies, such as Kenya and Malawi, had their agricultural sector geared towards the needs of a privileged white settler minority. This rich variation of economic and political outcomes made for distinct paths of economic development in the postcolonial period.

AFRICAN ECONOMIES SINCE INDEPENDENCE

In the 1980s, most African economies were characterized by stagnation and economic crisis. This period was followed by a convergence in policy orientation in the 1990s, as almost all economies adopted very similar policies contained in IMF- and World Bank-sponsored structural adjustment reforms. Economic growth performance between the late 1970s and the early 1990s was, with very few exceptions, dismal throughout sub-Saharan Africa. Neither OECD countries nor the world economy as a whole were booming during this period, but African economies still performed much worse than most other economies. In response, scholars turned their attention to what was called a chronic failure of growth in Africa, seeking to disentangle the historical character flaws that inhibited economic advance.[44] This ahistorical approach to economic growth in Africa ignores periods of growth, not only in the postcolonial period, but, as has been demonstrated here, also in precolonial and colonial Africa.[45] Furthermore, the diversity of country experiences in the postcolonial period has tended to be overlooked in the search for characteristics that can explain the failure of growth across the board.

What general observations can be made about African economic performance between the 1950s and the present day? To obtain an answer I have used the Maddison dataset that contains GDP per capita data for all African economies from 1950 until 2009 in order to search for patterns in periods of sustained growth.[46] Different methods can, and have, been used to identify and define periods of sustained growth or shorter-term accelerations. In this exercise growth is classified as 'sustained' if the nine-year moving averages of GDP per capita growth are 3 per cent or higher.[47] Comparatively, this is quite a strict criterion. The average annual GDP per capita growth in the world according to the same dataset over the same period was 2 per cent.[48] Sustained growth failure is defined as occurring when the nine-year moving average of real GDP per capita growth is less than 0 percent, which represents an overall and lasting deterioration in income per capita. Those economies which were neither growing nor failing were classified as preserving. Figure 22.1 provides the summary information.

The interpretation of Figure 22.1 is straightforward: many African colonies were experiencing high growth towards the end of the colonial period. As territories gained their independence, the prevalence of sustained growth increased further. By 1967–8, half of Africa's economies were in the middle of a decade of sustained rapid growth. This trend of more countries joining a path of growth was reversed by the beginning of the 1970s. Following the second oil shock of 1979–81, only a handful of countries achieved sustained growth in the 1980s—most notably Mauritius and Botswana, which are widely recognized as African growth 'miracles'. Less recognized in the literature are Cape Verde, Equatorial Guinea, Lesotho, and the Seychelles, but given their past growth and current relative position in terms of GDP per capita, they do deserve the same kind of attention given to Mauritius and Botswana.[49] Liberia and Chad also experienced a

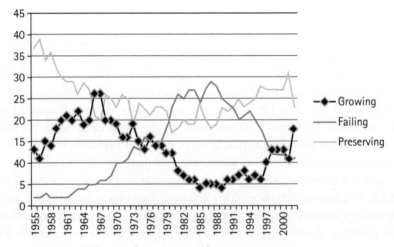

FIGURE 22.1. Growing, failing, and preserving African economies, 1950–2006.

four-year period of sustained growth in the late 1980s. By 1998, a quarter of African economies were again experiencing sustained growth.

It is of course the phenomenon of failed growth that has received far more attention in economic literature on African development. Figure 22.1 also tracks the occurrence of growth failure in Africa each year between 1955 and 2002. Until the 1980s, sustained growth failure was the exception: between 1950 and 1960 only Benin, Tanzania, and Morocco experienced sustained periods of stagnation and negative growth. In the 1960s, Chad and the Central African Republic were also stagnating. This group of ill-performers (Tanzania and Morocco subsequently improved on their performance) was joined by Senegal, Niger, and Somalia in the late 1960s and the early 1970s. A sudden spike in the list of ill-performers then occurred in the late 1970s. By the 1980s, the failure of growth became the rule rather than the exception. While some economies were failing, however, a number of economies such as Botswana were growing in a modest fashion: adding these economies gives the full picture of the distribution of economic growth in independent Africa. Yet it is evident that the recent African growth episode has been less widely shared than the boom in the earlier period.

Underlying this growth was a notable change in development strategies. In all colonies, agricultural marketing boards were instituted in the interwar and immediate postwar years. In common with similar marketing boards instituted in North America and elsewhere in the aftermath of the Depression, these institutions were originally devised to provide seeds and other inputs and to secure stable prices for agricultural goods. Yet they soon became a mechanism by which the late colonial state and its post-colonial successors extracted revenue from peasant farmers and redirected it towards attempts at import-substitution industrialization. In tune with the postwar development agenda that emphasized state planning and 'modernization' through rapid industrialization, infant industries were protected from external competition and foreign exchange policy sought to secure cheap imports of capital goods and other inputs in industrial production. Some countries, such as Tanzania and Ghana, favoured a more interventionist approach, with the state directly involved in industrial activities. In one manner or another, all of the newly independent countries attempted to facilitate rapid manufacturing growth through some kind of state intervention. The distinction between self-styled 'capitalist' and 'socialist' economies in Africa masked a consensus on industrial development strategy. Even determinedly capitalist Kenya had five-year plans and tariff protection from imports.

This active role of the state represented a discontinuity from the colonial period. The change in policy meant that increased capital was available in a more conducive environment for manufacturing development. As a result, steps towards self-sufficiency in consumer goods continued. To remove bottlenecks in the existing infrastructure, large-scale improvements in energy provision and transport were undertaken. In some countries, particularly Kenya, Nigeria, Côte d'Ivoire, and South Africa, there was expansion in the production of capital goods. The growth in manufacturing was mainly geared towards domestic demand, and only some countries exported a small share of their manufactured output. The early rapid growth soon turned to stagnation, and it is generally conceded that the industrialization project in sub-Saharan Africa was a failure. The quality of data on manufacturing in Africa is notoriously poor, and aggregation hides important facets of the development story. However, the broad picture that emerges from the aggregate statistics is unambiguous.[50] Rapid growth in industrial output took place in the 1960s, and although it slowed somewhat, growth continued into the 1970s. The 1980s and 1990s is most aptly described as a period of stagnation in industrial production. Many countries experienced sustained deindustrialization in these two decades.

Since the mid-1990s, growth has returned to many African economies. Growth is largely stimulated by external demand for exports, and African economies have become more liberalized and open than ever before during the past five decades. Some commentators have thought that African economies have now reached a turning point, and that years of policy reform are finally paying off.[51] As has been shown in this survey of economic growth in Africa over the past two centuries, growth has been recurring. There is ample evidence from both the immediate present and the past that shows African economies are capable of economic growth. Rather than being stuck in low growth equilibrium, African economies are able both to profit from and to be vulnerable to changing fortunes in external markets. The most recent growth period, however, is distinguished from earlier periods in that it is even more dependent on exports and external demand. This suggests some cause for concern regarding future prospects for growth and development.

Conclusion

The slave trades from Africa enabled economic growth to be captured by some states and elites at the expense of the economic development of the continent as a whole. Slave-trading states and elites were able to internalize revenues that they otherwise would not have been able to capture, with the costs borne by surrounding communities. In the long term, the slave trade was not sustainable and increased existing problems of labour scarcity. Yet in the short term, it helped some states to accumulate wealth and to expand. It also provided incentives for market growth, as slave-trading caravans carried other commodities for exchange and allowed for imports of currencies that facilitated domestic economic exchange.

While the decline and termination of the slave trade was temporarily detrimental to many of those states and merchant elites which had hitherto benefited from it, in the long run there was a transition to cash-crop exports based on family and wage labour. Although there was a problem of adaptation in some regions, the aggregate trends in economic growth were less impaired. In the mean time, slave labour was increasingly used in domestic economies, serving as the foundation for the cash-crop revolution at the end of the nineteenth century. In the twentieth century, this explosive growth in agricultural production of goods for export was made possible by a free labour market. Colonial rule appears to have had only a limited impact on those territories dominated by indigenous peasant agriculture, where the lack of state intervention tended to favour economic growth. In settler colonies, growth was less widely shared as states intervened to the benefit of white producers. The lesson from the transition to cash crops is that growth was rapid and sustained over a long period. Although production was largely taking place in spite of, not because of, the state, it enabled the colonial state and its post-colonial successor to expand its revenue base. According to most indicators, the increase in financial and other resources caused widespread development, also spurring positive institutional change such as the development of markets in land, labour, and credit.

The growth of export crop production in the nineteenth and early twentieth centuries led to considerable improvements in GDP per capita, which were enjoyed, sometimes directly, by the peasant population. Recent research indicates that in both Kenya and Ghana, living standards were increasing during this period, and that in British Africa as a whole real wages also increased in the colonial period.[52] The opportunity to capture rents from this growth in exports was eventually seized by the colonial state through the formation of marketing boards. These revenues facilitated the emergence of what has been called the 'developmental state' in the late colonial period, which continued to expand in the postcolonial era until structural adjustment policies were undertaken in the 1980s. In many cases, such as in Ghana in the 1960s and 1970s, states engaged in predatory rent-seeking, setting the producer price for commodities at a small fraction of the world market price. Inflation and overvalued currencies contributed strongly to this trend. In neighbouring Côte d'Ivoire, in contrast, ruling elites did not favour heavy tax-ation of export crops. Nevertheless, both of these fiscal models ultimately failed, as both were forced to undergo structural adjustment in the 1980s. After some two decades of general stagnation, growth has returned to most African economies since the end of the 1990s. This recent and ongoing upturn indicates that the imperative for those interested in the economic history of modern Africa is now to explain growth, analyse its causes, and understand its political distribution, rather than, as in the past, explain its absence.

The marked decline in the study of African economic history in the 1980s and 1990s corresponded with a pessimism about the prospects for growth in the continent. As a generation of historians focused their attention on other aspects of the continent's past, the responsibility for the study of long-term development in Africa was taken up by economists, motivated mainly by the pressing task of explaining how Africa fell behind relative to other world regions. The past decade has witnessed a renewed interest in African economic history, coinciding with a newly found optimism stemming from the recent upturn in growth in the region. This provides the opportunity to reconnect and revisit themes of economic and political change in Africa.

This chapter has faced a limitation that all similar efforts must face: a severe paucity of data on the period before 1960. We lack basic data on population, commodity yields, and prices, both for consumers and for those supplying factor markets. Without such data, we cannot estimate total factor productivity and thereby secure reliable measures of growth. However, a mix of qualitative accounts and careful use of the data that are available may give substance to the analysis of growth episodes. Thus the datasets are biased in two respects: we know much less about economic change before 1960 than after 1960, and we know much more about exports than about actual production.

The use of quantitative approaches means that we may understate the importance of economic change in the precolonial and colonial periods, while emphasizing external linkages at the expense of internal dynamics over the whole period.

Despite these periods of growth, however, African economies continue to make up the majority of the poorest economies in the world. The emphasis on variation and fluctuation in growth rates is not merely making a point about getting the history right, but, as has been argued here, these changes have had a fundamental impact on institutional, social, and political change in the region. The emphasis in the 'new African economic history' has been on the importance of historical legacies for present-day development and institutions. Thus, these historical episodes, revolutions, and evolutions are fundamental to understanding and disentangling the conditions under which African economic performance improved and deteriorated over the past centuries.

Notes

1. Patrick Manning, 'The Prospects for African Economic History: Is Today Included in the Long Run?', *African Studies Review*, 30/2 (1987).
2. A. G. Hopkins, 'The New Economic History of Africa', *Journal of African History*, 50/2 (2009).
3. Morten Jerven, 'A Clash of Disciplines?: Economists and Historians Approaching the African Past', *Economic History of Developing Regions*, 26/2 (2011).
4. K. Onwuka Dike, *Trade and Politics in the Niger Delta, 1830–1885: An Introduction to the Economic and Political History of Nigeria* (Oxford: OUP, 1956; 2nd edn, with a foreword by Gareth Austin, Ibadan: Bookcraft, 2011).
5. See e.g. Paul E. Lovejoy, *Transformations in Slavery: A History of Slavery in Africa* (Cambridge: CUP, 1983; 3rd edn, 2011); Joseph C. Miller, *Way of Death: Merchant Capitalism and the Angolan Slave Trade, 1730–1830* (Madison, Wis.: University of Wisconsin Press, 1988); and more recently, Paul. E. Lovejoy, *Slavery, Commerce and Production in the Sokoto Caliphate of West Africa* (Trenton, NJ: Africa World Press, 2006).
6. Ralph Austen, *African Economic History: International Development and External Dependency* (Oxford: James Currey, 1987); Frederick Cooper, 'Africa and the World Economy', *African Studies Review*, 24/2–3 (1981); Paul T. Zeleza, *A Modern Economic History of Africa* (Dakar: CODESRIA, 1993); John Iliffe, *Africans: The History of a Continent* (Cambridge: CUP, 2nd edn, 2007); John Iliffe, *The African Poor: A History* (Cambridge: CUP, 1987).
7. See Robin Law, 'Posthumous Questions for Karl Polanyi: Price Inflation in Pre-Colonial Dahomey', *Journal of African History*, 33 (1992).
8. A. G. Hopkins, *An Economic History of West Africa* (Harlow: Longman, 1973).
9. Polly Hill, *The Migrant Cocoa-Farmers of Southern Ghana: A Study in Rural Capitalism* (Cambridge: CUP, 1963; 2nd edn, with preface by Gareth Austin, Hamburg: LIT, 1997).
10. See e.g. Walter Rodney, *How Europe Underdeveloped Africa* (Washington, DC: Howard University Press, 1972); and P. Gutkind and I. Wallerstein, eds, *The Political Economy of Contemporary Africa* (Beverly Hills, Calif.: Sage, 1976).
11. W. A. Lewis, 'Economic Development with Unlimited Supplies of Labour', *Manchester School of Economic and Social Studies*, 20 (1954); W. J. Barber, *The Economy of*

British Central Africa: A Case-Study of Economic Development in a Dualistic Society (London: OUP, 1961). Lewis did not claim that his model of unlimited supply of labour applied to Africa, as he was quite aware that sub-Saharan Africa was short of labour.

12. Giovanni Arrighi, 'Labour Supplies in Historical Perspective: A Study of the Proletarianization of the African Peasantry in Rhodesia', *Journal of Development Studies,* 3 (1970); Colin Bundy, *The Rise and Fall of the South African Peasantry* (Cape Town: David Philip, 1988).

13. Robert H. Bates, *Markets and States in Tropical Africa* (Berkeley, Calif.: University of California Press, 1981), and *Essays on the Political Economy of Rural Africa* (Cambridge: CUP, 1983).

14. Gareth Austin provides a full-length historical test case of the rational choice theory of induced institutional innovation focused on the Akan forest region of present-day Ghana in his *Labour, Land and Capital in Ghana: From Slavery to Free Labour in Asante,1807–1956* (Rochester, NY: Rochester University Press, 2005).

15. Daron Acemoglu, Simon Johnson, and James A. Robinson, 'The Colonial Origins of Comparative Development: An Empirical Investigation', *American Economic Review,* 91 (2001); Daron Acemoglu, Simon Johnson; and James A. Robinson, 'Reversal of Fortune: Geography and Institutions in the Making of the Modern World Income Distribution', *Quarterly Journal of Economics,* 118 (2002).

16. Hopkins, 'The New Economic History of Africa.

17. James Fenske, 'The Causal History of Africa: A Response to Hopkins', *Economic History of Developing Regions,* 25/2 (2010).

18. James Fenske, 'The Causal History of Africa: Replies to Jerven and Hopkins', *Economic History of Developing Regions,* 26/2 (2011).

19. Morten Jerven, 'A Clash of Disciplines? Economists and Historians Approaching the African Past', *Economic History of Developing Regions,* 26/2 (2011).

20. Gareth Austin, 'The "Reversal of Fortune" Thesis and the Compression of History: Perspectives from African and Comparative Economic History', *Journal of International Development,* 20 (2008).

21. Morten Jerven, 'African Growth Recurring: An Economic History Perspective on African Growth Episodes, 1690–2010', *Economic History of Developing Regions,* 25/2 (2010).

22. Morten Jerven, 'An Unlevel Playing Field: National Income Estimates and Reciprocal Comparison in Global Economic History', *Journal of Global History,* 7/1 (2012).

23. Iliffe, *Africans.*

24. E. L. Jones, *Growth Recurring: Economic Change in World History* (Oxford: Clarendon Press, 1988).

25. Philip D. Curtin, *Economic Change in Precolonial Africa: Senegambia in the Era of the Slave Trade* (Madison, Wis.: University of Wisconsin Press, 1975).

26. Paul Mosley, *The Settler Economies: Kenya and Southern Rhodesia, 1900–1963* (Cambridge: CUP, 1983).

27. Iliffe, *The African Poor.*

28. Gareth Austin, 'Resources, Techniques, and Strategies South of the Sahara', *Economic History Review,* 61 (2008).

29. J. I. Inikori, 'Africa and the Globalization Process: Western Africa, 1450–1850', *Journal of Global History,* 2 (2007).

30. Hopkins, *An Economic History of West Africa.*

31. Robin Law, ed., *From Slave Trade to 'Legitimate' Commerce: The Commercial Transition in Nineteenth-Century West Africa* (Cambridge: CUP, 1995).

32. Gareth Austin, 'Cash Crops and Freedom: Export Agriculture and the Decline of Slavery in Colonial West Africa', *International Review of Social History*, 54 (2009).

33. Frederick Cooper, 'Africa and the World Economy', in Frederick Cooper, Allen F. Isaacman, Florencia E. Mallon, William Rosebury, and Steve J. Stern, eds, *Confronting Historical Paradigms: Peasants, Labor and the Capitalist World System in Africa and Latin America* (Madison, Wis.: University of Wisconsin Press, 1993).

34. For a review of this literature and a reformulation of factor endowment perspective for sub-Saharan Africa, see Austin, 'Resources, Techniques, and Strategies'.

35. John Tosh, 'The Cash-Crop Revolution in Tropical Agriculture: An Agricultural Reappraisal', *African Affairs*, 79 (1980).

36. Sara Berry, *No Condition is Permanent: The Social Dynamics of Agrarian Change in Sub-Saharan Africa* (Madison, Wis.: University of Wisconsin Press, 1993).

37. S. Smith, 'An Extension of the Vent-for-Surplus Model in Relation to Long-Run Structural Change in Nigeria', *Oxford Economic Papers*, 28/3 (1976).

38. Although in some periods and places the assumptions of the vent-for-surplus model largely hold: see e.g. Susan M. Martin, *Palm Oil and Protest : An Economic History of the Ngwa Region, South-Eastern Nigeria, 1800–1980* (Cambridge: CUP, 1988).

39. Gareth Austin, 'African Economic Development and Colonial Legacies', *International Development Policy Series*, 1 (2010).

40. Richard Roberts, *Two Worlds of Cotton: Colonialism and the Regional Economy in the French Sudan, 1800–1946* (Stanford, Calif.: Stanford University Press, 1996).

41. W. A. Lewis, 'Economic Development with Unlimited Supplies of Labour', *Manchester School of Economic and Social Studies*, 22 (1954).

42. Sue Bowden, Blessing Chiripanhura, and Paul Mosley, 'Measuring and Explaining Poverty in Six African Countries: A Long-Period Approach', *Journal of International Development*, 20 (2008).

43. Peter Kilby, 'Manufacturing in Colonial Africa', in Peter Duignan and L. H. Gann, eds, *Colonialism in Africa, 1870–1960, iv. The Economics of Colonialism* (Cambridge: CUP, 1975).

44. See Morten Jerven, 'The Quest for the African Dummy: Explaining African Post-Colonial Economic Performance Revisited', *Journal of International Development*, 23/2 (2011), and 'A Clash of Disciplines?'.

45. Austin, 'The "Reversal of Fortune" Thesis'.

46. For some issues with regard to the use of this data set, see Morten Jerven, 'Random Growth in Africa? A Report on the Quality of the Growth Evidence in East–Central Africa, 1965–1995', *Journal of Development Studies*, 46/2 (2010).

47. The nine-year moving average is calculated by taking the average of nine annual observations from the middle year observation and the four years on each side.

48. For a full list of countries and the observations of sustained growth by country, see Jerven, 'African Growth Recurring'. Of course, when nine-year moving averages are calculated, the dataset only covers 1955 to 2002.

49. Morten Jerven, 'The Relativity of Poverty and Income: How Reliable are African Economic Statistics?', *African Affairs*, 109 (2009).

50. Roger C. Riddel, *Manufacturing Africa: Performance and Prospects of Seven Countries in sub-Saharan Africa* (London: James Currey, 1990).

51. Edward Miguel, *Africa's Turn* (Cambridge, Mass.: MIT Press, 2009).

52. Alexander Moradi, 'Confronting Colonial Legacies: Lessons from Human Development in Ghana and Kenya', *Journal of International Development*, 20 (2008); Ewout Frankema and

Marlous van den Wajenburg, 'Structural Impediments to African Growth? New Evidence from Real Wages in British Africa, 1880–1965' (*Working Papers, 24*; Utrecht University, Centre for Global Economic History, 2011).

BIBLIOGRAPHY

Austen, Ralph, *African Economic History: International Development and External Dependency* (Oxford: James Currey, 1987).

Austin, Gareth, *Labour, Land and Capital in Ghana: From Slavery to Free Labour in Asante,1807–1956* (Rochester, NY: University of Rochester Press, 2005).

——'Resources, Techniques and Strategies South of the Sahara: Revising the Factor Endowments Perspective on African Economic Development, 1500–2000', *Economic History Review*, 61/3 (2008).

Cooper, Frederick, 'Africa and the World Economy', *African Studies Review*, 24/2–3 (1981).

Hill, Polly, *The Migrant Cocoa-Farmers of Southern Ghana: a study in rural capitalism*, 2nd edn, with preface by Gareth Austin (Hamburg: LIT, 1997).

Hopkins, A. G., *An Economic History of West Africa* (London: Longman, 1973).

—— 'The New Economic History of Africa', *Journal of African History*, 50 (2009).

Iliffe, John, *The Emergence of African Capitalism* (London: Macmillan, 1983).

—— *The African Poor : A History* (Cambridge: CUP, 1987).

Inikori, Joseph, 'Africa and the Globalization Process: Western Africa, 1450–1850', *Journal of Global History*, 2/1 (2007).

Jerven, Morten, 'African Growth Recurring: An Economic History Perspective on African Growth Episodes, 1690–2010', *Economic History of Developing Regions*, 25/2 (2010).

PART V

ARTS AND
THE MEDIA

CHAPTER 23

··

VISUAL CULTURES

··

SIDNEY LITTLEFIELD KASFIR

IN the history of art and artefacts there are periods of 'fast and slow happening'.[1] From the late nineteenth to the mid-twentieth centuries in Africa, 'fast happening' was certainly the prevalent mode as the European colonial presence foreclosed upon or reconfigured established genres and practices of art, performance, and material culture, at the same time encouraging new ones. This chapter begins with European exploration and the colonial encounter as a framework for understanding how African art and visual culture has changed and been changed by the Western practices of collecting and connoisseurship. After this I trace the development of three major aesthetic expressions: masquerades, urban painting, and photography, in order to give a broad sense of how African art is simultaneously rooted in practices which are centuries old and an important constituent in the thrust of modernity. Reasons of length preclude the discussion of myriad expressive forms such as architecture, fashion, and precolonial art genres other than masquerade, although each of these is worthy of an essay of its own.

I will use Nigeria as the main focus for the discussion of masking history because it is there that scholars have done the most work on reconstructing its deep past. Research on Sierra Leone, Liberia, and the Casamance region of Senegal will also be used to illustrate recent shifts in scholarly approaches to masking. Since modern African art is primarily urban, the discussion of painting and photography will be more wide-ranging geographically, from Kinshasa to Dakar and Johannesburg to Bamako. At the same time, I will describe the changing methodologies and research agendas which have accompanied the study of African art as an academic discipline born out of both European art history and anthropology, two fields which had their own beginnings in the late nineteenth century.

COLONIZATION AND COLLECTING

··

The study of African art based on field observation and collection began with the exploration accounts of the great nineteenth- and early twentieth-century travellers to

West and Central Africa such as Georg Schweinfurth, Emin Pasha, Emil Torday, Leo Frobenius, and Alfred Mansfeld.[2] The earlier of these journeys coincided with and were in some cases constitutive of the first significant contact with Europeans (and in the case of the Upper Nile region, with Arab ivory and slave traders as well). Herein lies a problem: these collectors were looking for 'pure' cultural products unsullied by external influence, but contact brings change by its very presence. With the collections made by these travellers, moreover, came the realization by African rulers and ritual specialists that material objects which previously had only local or regional value as inalienable possessions or 'enclaved commodities' were now valued in faraway Europe as well.[3] Such items were purchased from their owners or caretakers (or given as part of gift exchanges) as specimens for newly formed natural history collections; later, after 1900, they became valued as art objects and sought by influential modern art dealers such as Henri Kahnweiler and Paul Guillaume in Paris and written about by critics such as Vladimir Markov and Carl Einstein.[4]

A revealing example of how this new trajectory in the life of aesthetic objects also marked a change in their form can be seen in what happened to the Kuba royal *ndop* or king figures after 1913. In that year, King Kwete Peshanga Kena gave a statue of himself to Commandant V. Knauer, a Danish mercenary who had done him a service. It differed in several respects from the *ndop* previously owned exclusively by Kuba kings and set a new prototype for effigies which thereafter were made for expatriates as well.[5] Even the earliest ethnographic collections usually bear the evidence of such change. In today's intellectual climate with its greater acceptance, even celebration, of hybridity, such objects have been reconsidered as part of a more complex view of the European–African encounter. But in the era of high modernism born out of the work of Picasso and Braque and the writings of Einstein, the pure expression of African sculpture was thought to be inevitably compromised, even destroyed, through its alienation from its original context. This set in motion a search for what was deemed an authentic, precontact art, creating a collector's value scale in which old ('used') was good and new ('unused') was suspect.

Ironically then, what was potent about African art in the eyes of European artists such as Picasso was derived from a past antithetical to the modernity newly prized in their own work. He described this power, at some times, as *raisonnable*, obeying its own formal logic, but at others as a form of magic, standing between ourselves and a hostile universe.[6] The notion of African magic, popularized as the concept of 'fetish' in the writings of early travellers and missionaries, held a fascination for Europeans, the remnants of which can still be seen in their dramatic mode of installation in the new Musée du Quai Branly in Paris, the successor to the old Palais Trocadero and then the Musée de l'Homme.[7] The French poet Apollinaire, African art collector and friend of Picasso and other early modernists, wrote of these power figures as 'lesser Christs of obscure hopes' ('*Christ inférieurs des obscures espérances*').[8] What this tells us is that the study, collection, publication, and display of African art has been intimately connected to the colonial enterprise through the channels this commerce created for its export. If Paris became the centre for what was called *Art Nègre*, London, Berlin, and Lisbon competed briskly as well. Both French Cubism and German Expressionism bore witness to this influx of African masks and shrine sculpture which had begun in the last quarter of the nineteenth century.

Not a small proportion of these objects came as the direct result of conquest: the British conquest of the West African forest kingdom of Asante in 1896 and, a year later, the punitive expedition against the kingdom of Benin in what would become Nigeria. Many objects from Asante in British collections date from this period, though some, such as the royal axe, were acquired earlier in the nineteenth century through negotiations over trade. The Benin conquest resulted in hundreds of exquisitely wrought symbols of royal power, from commemorative cast brass heads and low-relief plaques to ivory tusks and sculpture, being carried away as booty and then placed on the auction block in order to recoup the costs of the expedition. The result was the scattering of these objects across museums in England, Germany, and Austria. In conquering the kingdom of Dahomey and looting the Fon's palace in the capital Abomey in 1893, the French came away with the famous figure of Gu, the god of iron, wielding his double-edged sword, which now graces the African and Oceanic gallery at the Louvre.

It is possible to read whole histories of colonialism in European and sometimes American museum collections. While the massive shipments of art from the Congo found their way through various expeditions to the Congo Museum in Tervuren (now the Musée Royal de l'Afrique Centrale), the British Museum, and the American Museum of Natural History, other major collections were made by German military officers and colonial administrators in Cameroon prior to the First World War. These were dispersed to Frankfurt, Berlin, and Stuttgart as well as various other Museums für Volkerkunde. In the competition among colonial regimes, these collections were both premise and proof of the need to pacify despotic rulers who nonetheless held out the possibility of developing sophisticated relations with the colonial metropole, proven by their ability to produce fine artefacts. These treasures of course also added lustre to the image of the colonizing cultures that now owned them.

Stimulated in part by the attempts by anthropologists Alfred Kroeber, Franz Boas, and Clark Wissler to map trait complexes among Native American populations, European scholars used the vast collections now in Europe to develop theories on the diffusion of object types. Such work gave rise to the new discipline of museum ethnology, collection-based and not requiring travel to Africa. In Britain the schema of comparative evolutionary theory made possible the didactic installations in the Pitt Rivers Museum at Oxford, which worked well enough with spears and baskets but unfortunately also meant displaying visually and culturally disjunctive African shrine sculpture next to Japanese Buddha figures in the same vitrines. Although by the 1930s fieldwork became the *sine qua non* for studying culture among British and American anthropologists, in France and elsewhere on the continent it was still possible, even in the 1950s and 1960s, for a museum ethnologist to spend a respected career studying, say, the massive collections housed in the Musée de l'Homme acquired by Marcel Griaule and others in the course of the 1931–3 Dakar-Djibouti expedition and subsequent seasons in Dogon country.

MASQUERADES: A BRIEF HISTORY
AND TYPOLOGY

Masquerades represent the pre-eminent expressive form linking aesthetic practices with ritual and social life across broad swathes of sub-Saharan Africa: the West African forests and savannas from the Senegambian region and Mali east to Cameroon; and Central Africa from the equatorial forests of the Congo basin south to Angola and Mozambique and as far east as Tanzania. Shrine sculpture, another important aesthetic practice, is found over an even wider region, including among peoples such as the Akan of Ghana where masquerades are absent. It is important to note that many kinds of African masks from these regions never found their way into Western art collections, which are primarily limited to objects sculpted or constructed in wood. Despite their local importance, masks—or those parts of masks and their accompanying costumes and ritual accoutrements—fabricated from materials such as bark, leaves, raffia fibre, and cloth, were often left behind by collectors as they did not match accepted Western notions of fine art. Masks of natural materials, such as the 'Mumbo Jumbo' fashioned from the bark of the *fara* tree which Francis Moore saw near the Gambia River in 1738, are likely to predate both textile and sculptural masquerades.[9] The only older mask form than this is the acoustic or 'invisible' mask spirit found all over the continent, even in places such as the Ituri Forest in the eastern Congo where no other forms of masking exist. They are recognized by their special sound effects, and usually are heard at dusk or after dark (hence their frequent name, 'night mask').

Textile masquerades, the most elaborate of which are found around the Benue and Lower Niger Rivers in what is today Nigeria, developed sometime after the tenth century following the importation of the double-heddle loom along the trans-Saharan trade routes into West Africa. Moore's account, perhaps the first by a 'literate alien' of an African mask, coincides roughly with the dating from oral accounts of the origins of Egungun among the Oyo Yoruba, said to have been adopted from Nupe across the Niger. Egungun are incarnated ancestors and although the Yoruba version had the specific political function of intimidating rival factions with its display of supernatural power, there are good reasons to believe that its prototype originated further east in the Middle Benue region in a cluster of small states known in the Kano and Bornu Chronicles as Kwararafa and to themselves as Apá. Both linguistic and morphological evidence points to two of these states, Doma (which is early enough to appear on a map of Leo Africanus) and Jukun, as the likely origins. In both, the Ashama lineages owned a textile masquerade wrapped in a burial shroud of white *opa* cloth and indigo-dyed *odu mele*, the first an important trade item along the Benue and the second traded from Doma and Wukari eastwards into the Cameroon Grassfields, where it is known as *ndop*.[10]

From the fifteenth century onwards, non-Muslim Hausa known in the Benue region as Abakwariga or Abakpa filtered southwards as they resisted Islam. These were elephant hunters, traders, artisans, and ritual specialists, who together played an important role in the transmission of the cloth ancestral masquerade westwards from Apá along the Benue and towards its confluence with the Niger. There are important versions of it in Idoma, Igala, Ebira, and among the Onitsha Igbo. This elongated masquerade, considered numinous because it contains relics of the deceased ancestor, reached Nupe, where it is a spectacular shape-changing cloth tube called Ndako Gboya, and later Yorubaland, where it appears as Egungun.[11]

Sculpted wooden masks have a very different genealogy and character in this same region. The pioneering German ethnographer and collector Leo Frobenius had theorized that masks had developed from skull cults.[12] He was wrong about this as a grand theory, but one type of mask, associated with warriorhood between the Cross River and the Benue in Nigeria and Cameroon, did develop from earlier dances with human crania. After a victory, the headwinners publicly displayed their trophies and later danced with them atop their heads. Soon after the first British military patrols into the interior around 1910, both headhunting and dances with skulls were outlawed by the colonial administration. Warriorhood under the *pax britannica* became a metaphorical performance of masculinity in the form of a masquerade, in which local sculptors made versions of enemy crania from wood.[13] Many of these, especially in the Cross River region, were starkly realistic, covered tightly with antelope skin and with the addition of local scarification patterns burnt into the surface.

Most of these mask forms still exist and continue to be performed at least occasionally, though the social and religious structures which support their use have undergone radical change in the course of the twentieth century due to the effects of Islamic and Christian proselytizing, especially by evangelical churches since the 1980s. In rural Nigerian communities they are still a major form of spectacle, which has meant the continual emergence of new masquerades. This same level of twentieth-century creativity in individual mask invention and performance has been described for communities as disparate as the Dogon peoples of Mali and the Pende of the Democratic Republic of Congo.[14] They are also irreplaceable in certain ritual contexts, such as bush initiation schools in various parts of Africa. In Casamance in southern Senegal, Ferdinand de Jong has documented the continuing relevance of these initiation schools held in sacred bush, which now draw migrant workers from Dakar and even Paris back to their home villages to participate.[15]

As mask-using communities have migrated to towns, so masks have followed. One result has been the commoditization of what had been ritual culture, one consequence of performing before strangers. In the Casamance, for example, de Jong shows how small boys allowed to watch the Kankurang mask dress in someone's house subsequently learn to perform their own 'Kankurang' for coins. Another is the role of masks in urban violence: there have been street confrontations among Kankurang supporters and non-supporters in the same towns, resulting in deaths and court cases. This theme of mask violence has been reported in Sierra Leone, Liberia, and Nigeria, where youth gangs, sometimes in the guise of political party youth wings, use masks as a form of intimidation.[16] As if in illustration of Gregory Bateson's famous essay on play and fantasy, at some point 'nip turns to bite' and what began as a piece of theatre turns into real violence.[17]

In south-east Nigeria, this is the modern iteration of a good deal of traditional mask behaviour, stemming back to the warrior dances with trophy heads a century ago. From the 1920s, Idoma masquerades such as Oglinye, drawing upon their nineteenth-century association with young warriors and headwinners, became law enforcers and vigilantes, recruited by councils of elders to punish those who broke the community's laws, but often stealing and intimidating with impunity.[18] In today's idioms for the testing of masculinity in a neighbouring region, David Pratten found similarly transgressive behaviour by Annang youth enacting Agaba masquerade performances to demonstrate their toughness, amidst community disapproval.[19] To mask is to 'play' in West African pidgin; playing, however, is usually serious business.

MASQUERADES: LOCAL AND TEXTUAL INTERPRETATIONS

It is not easy to disentangle masking as a performative act from its study and its description by scholars, since material objects are never entirely separable from the discourse which forms around them. From as early as Moore's 1738 description of the 'Mumbo Jumbo', the idea of the mask as an instrument of social control has been the most durable explanation for its existence. For the outsider to African cultures this appeared the only rational explanation for what seemed an otherwise mysterious and arbitrary exercise of power. It was noted by Moore that, while men used and controlled masks, women were barred from close contact with them and were subject to harsh penalties if these rules were broken. The interpretation of this observed social asymmetry has undergone changes by successive generations of writers from a functionalist to structuralist to feminist reading, in keeping with the reigning social theories of the day.

There is also no shortage of local explanations for these asymmetries. In some regions, masquerading by men is seen by community members as the social and ritual counterpart to spirit possession by women (although possession also exists where masking does not, such as in Ethiopia, Somalia, and Morocco). Alternatively, masking is understood as parallel to and a bulwark against witchcraft, as among the Ebira of the Niger–Benue Confluence in Nigeria who asserted that 'God made all things double: masquerading for men and witchcraft for women'.[20] What is cogent about these observations is that, like witchcraft and possession by spirits, masquerading is socially powerful and potentially dangerous in the hands of those who control it, not only for subordinating women and strangers but even, among the Idoma and Yoruba and various Cameroonian cultures in the precolonial period, for trying and executing criminals as well as leading warriors into battle.[21]

The most important exception to the dominance of men in the ownership of masks is the Sande society of Sierra Leone and Liberia. Scholarship on Sande and its parallel male society, Poro, is exemplary of the changing theoretical approaches to masking in the twentieth century. Indeed, the missionary George Harley, who collected Poro masks for the Peabody Museum at Harvard, wrote the first widely read essay on African masks as agents of exerting patriarchal social control over women and uninitiated males. Harley was followed by the anthropologist Warren d'Azevedo, a student of Melville Herskovits committed to a functionalist approach, who carried out extensive fieldwork among the Gola of Liberia, especially among artists, from the late 1950s. D'Azevedo viewed the Sande and Poro societies and their respective masquerades as existing in a state of complementary opposition to one another, each alternating control of the ritual life of the community for a fixed period while the society was in session.[22] The only point at which the symmetry of power relations broke down was in the creation of the Sande masks themselves, which were commissioned by women but carved by men. For the Gola and their neighbours, mask-making is the line in the sand which women may not cross.

By the 1970s, the functionalist approach to masking had been replaced by a structuralist analysis which contrasted the 'culture' of the village with the 'nature' of the forest or bush, exemplified for M. C. Jedrej by the disappearance of Sande initiates from the village to a forest training camp and their re-emergence and reincorporation led by the *sowei* masquerade.[23] At the same time, feminist anthropologists such as Carol MacCormack and Edwin Ardener factored male and female into the bush/village, nature/culture syllogism by arguing that women were said to be seen by men as 'closer to nature' due to the dominance, both socially and ritually, of their reproductive roles.[24] Such clear-cut categorization now seems simplistic and suspect. Masking, like other social phenomena, is seen more as a hybrid mix of changing religious and social values, attitudes towards gender, and opportunistic political deployment. Most recently, the practice of sacred forest initiation and its accompanying use of masks by Jola migrant workers in southern Senegal has been interpreted by de Jong as an attempt to produce a locally grounded social identity as a counter-narrative to the effects of globalization.[25]

Although anthropologists have dominated the theoretical discourse on masking, by the end of the 1960s Africanist art historians had also established intellectual beachheads of their own which reacted against the old museological model of the mask as static object encased in a vitrine. In a series of influential articles in 1969 about art as process, Herbert Cole stepped back from the finished artefact to consider how, when, and why it was brought forth. Another major redefinition occurred when Robert Farris Thompson curated the ground-breaking exhibition *African Art in Motion*, which argued that a mask's enactment was the focal point of its meaning. In most of Africa, a mask stored in a shrine house lacked ritual efficacy until it was actually performed publicly before an audience.[26] Throughout these repositionings, anthropologists have tended to concentrate on the ritual and social context in which masking is embedded, while art historians typically begin with the aesthetic object and the affect derived from the sheer power of the image itself. With the rise of Foucauldian theory, this affect is now said to be propagated as much by speech acts surrounding the mask performance as by its physical attributes.[27]

Comparing anthropological and art historical approaches to objects allows several problems to surface: the first is that of artistic geography, and the second is history itself. Geographies of art establish boundaries and centres of production and use, but also vectors of movement. The earliest models developed out of the *Kulturkreslehre* diffusion studies of German and Austrian scholars, but it was Melville Herskovits in the United States and Eckart von Sydow in Germany, both writing in 1930, who established the approach to cultural and artistic geographies in Africa as broadly defined 'culture areas', a classificatory system which still exists in many museum installations of African art today.[28] Von Sydow's *Handbuch der Africanischen Plastik* further subdivided works of art into distinct styles produced by geographically bounded 'tribal' units. This was followed in 1935–8 by Carl Kjersmeier's four-volume *Centres de style de la sculpture Nègre africaine*, which identified 'style centres' of African sculpture (a form assumed to be synonymous with African art in general) in conformity with supposed tribal boundaries.[29] By the middle decades of the twentieth century, then, when the canon of African art was being formed by curators, critics, dealers, and private collectors, artistic geography was assumed to be a simple matter of tribal boundaries. The model was derived from the prevailing notion of timeless, traditional society, which supposedly began to change only after 1900 and was then inexorably destroyed by colonial contact and modernity. Leading scholars such as William Fagg, Keeper of African Ethnography at the British Museum and by the 1950s the leading authority on Nigerian art, was convinced of what he called this essential 'tribality'. In a series of influential exhibitions and publications beginning with *Tribes and Forms in African Art* in 1965, Fagg sought to demonstrate the one-tribe–one-style model of African art.[30]

The first challenge to this paradigm came in a 1973 exhibition curated by René Bravmann, who argued that, contrary to Fagg's view, tribal life has always been one of 'open frontiers'. This allowed artistic geographies to be rethought in a more complex way, but the lack of a historical dimension remained.[31] Although there have been dozens of richly detailed accounts of masking and shrine sculpture since the 1970s, almost all have been couched in a shallow time depth focusing on a real or fictive present seen against, at best, one or two previous generations. Often, in accounts by anthropologists, the diachronic dimension is limited to the life histories of the principal African collaborators or informants. While there are dozens of important studies of Yoruba art, there has not yet been a detailed treatment of its history.

To use another example from Nigeria's rich artistic tradition, the canon formed in the 1950s and 1960s for sculpture in the Middle Belt by William and Bernard Fagg, Roy Sieber, and others took no cognizance of the nineteenth-century jihad waged by 'Uthman dan Fodio and his successors, which by mid-century had caused the scattering of populations on the north bank of the Benue. Peoples fled with their most valued possessions, such as the contents of their shrines, forming refugee enclaves on the south side of the river. Yet shrine sculptures in the region were assumed to come from the places where they were collected by British administrators in the early twentieth century. This ahistorical treatment has been responsible for a series of misattributions which, once published by a reputable scholar, curator, or even auction house, are very difficult to dislodge. Major reassessments taking history into account are finally being written for central Nigeria, but other parts of the continent may remain frozen in their old classificatory schemes in major museums for many years to come.[32]

URBAN FORMS OF POPULAR CULTURE

If masks were and often remain the currency of popular culture in many rural areas of sub-Saharan Africa, the processes of urbanization which accompanied colonialism produced new genres such as studio painting, photography, popular musical styles, and a taste for modern fashion and sports. Underlying these innovations were literacy and the allure of imported media and technology. Bogumil Jewsiewicki has argued that literacy in Congolese cities such as Kinshasa and Lubumbashi conferred a form of power associated initially with colonial and missionary authority.[33] The growth of African cities created a distinctive urban class of consumers whose tastes and aspirations diverged from those in rural areas, though such clear-cut distinctions today are becoming obsolete as global consumption patterns spread outwards from cities. When Western ideas and goods were appropriated they were creolized and reinvented in this new African setting: for example, in popular painting intended for local audiences, images were often heavily embedded with explanatory text creating a parallel narrative. These cities, because they consisted of multiple streams of migrants, were also mosaics of cultural borrowings among many indigenous subcultures. Taken together, this heady mix of imported and reinvented forms signalled a distinctive or 'alternative' modernity, different from that which had reshaped the Western world from the nineteenth century.

Unlike in the West, where naturalistic painting preceded photography by centuries, studio-based painting and photography emerged in parallel as new forms of African visual culture in the late nineteenth century. Easel painting arrived in sub-Saharan Africa as academic-style portraiture, usually credited first to Aina Onabolu (1882–1963) in Nigeria at the turn of the twentieth century. Portrait photography had emerged in Lagos some years earlier and the patrons for both, as in other cosmopolitan coastal cities, were the new urban elites. By the late nineteenth century, there were thriving studios run by expatriate and local photographers in cities from Alexandria to Algiers, on to Dakar, Freetown, Accra, and Lagos, down to Cape Town and Durban, and up to Zanzibar. Portraiture rapidly became a key mode of self-fashioning for the rising commercial elites and the emergent professional class of African doctors and lawyers. In Lagos and elsewhere, another important clientele was the traditional elite of powerful title-holders; a third source of patronage was European colonial administrators, who hired these same photographers as personal portraitists and to document official gatherings. Photography, like painting, was tied to both colonial and anti-colonial ideologies in its initial development. Unfortunately, until now, much more has been known about these portrait subjects than about the individuals who wielded the cameras.[34]

Researching these photographers is now an emerging field: one who has received recent attention is Jonathan Adagogo Green, whose iconic portrait of Oba Ovanranwen of Benin on board the SS *Ivy* as he was being sent into exile by the British following the 1897 punitive expedition was published in the *Illustrated London News* that year and widely thereafter.[35] This archival function of the photograph is emblematic of its dual nature as both art and documentary evidence, and has made photography the medium of choice in the study of visual culture by a number of social historians. By contrast, art historians have focused upon analyses of style or of modern subjectivity, published in exhibition catalogues of African photography such as *In/sight* (1996), *Snap Judgments* (2006), and *Darkroom* (2009).[36]

The first post-1950 black African photographer to gain international recognition was Seydou Keita, whose work appeared anonymously as 'Unknown Photographer, Bamako, Mali' in the New York exhibition *Africa Explores* in 1991. The French curator Andre Magnin saw the show and was determined to find the photographer, so travelled to Bamako where another photographer, Malick Sibidé, led him to the older Keita. After agreeing to print his negatives in Paris and for his work to be exhibited there, Keita described his studio method from the early 1950s, when he hung a printed textile backdrop and invited his customers to use props that he provided as symbols of modernity: Western men's clothing, a large portable radio, a motorbike, eyeglasses, cigarettes. Women more often preferred to be photographed in their own 'traditional' clothes and jewellery, an interesting gender disjuncture still seen today at formal occasions, especially in West African countries. Looked at now, Keita's black-and-white studio portraits have a classic detachment, posed carefully in a timeless yet modern style, itself a reflection of the late colonial city. Sibidé, his younger Bamako counterpart, took his 1960s and 1970s subjects out of the studio into nightclubs and onto the beaches along the Niger river, where they cavort in swimsuits, dance the Twist, and pose with prized Western pop records, placing them in an effervescent early postcolonial moment when all things seemed possible. Sibidé's subjects have the uneven exposure and ephemeral quality of news photos.

The connection of Sibidé's kind of photography to that found in newspapers and magazines collapses the old categories of high ('fine') art and low ('popular') art into a single phenomenon which fits the more capacious definition of visual culture better than those of conventional art history. Nothing demonstrates this better than the fact that photojournalists' work has appeared in major exhibitions such as *Short Century*, *In/sight*, and *Darkroom*.[37] A legendary vehicle for this work was the popular culture and entertainment magazine *Drum*, which began publication in 1951 in South Africa and also had East, Central, and West African editions. Photographers such as Peter Magubane captured images of everyday life ranging from cafés and weddings to glimpses of the underworld in Johannesburg townships and (very carefully, given the possibility of being shut down by the Apartheid regime) political protest. More than anything else, *Drum* documented the irresistible reach of modernity in African cities from Johannesburg to Nairobi, Lagos, and Accra in the 1950s and 1960s.

At about the same time that modern photojournalism got its start, the British education establishment began a fine art programme at the Nigerian College of Arts, Science, and Technology, Zaria, later part of Ahmadu Bello University. The outbreak of the Nigerian civil war in 1967 forced some of the Zaria art students to leave the north and return to the secessionist Eastern Region where, after the end of the war in 1970, the University of Nigeria at Nsukka became fertile ground for a new kind of modernism. Uche Okeke had christened this style 'Natural Synthesis', drawing upon both Western modernist media and indigenous design such as *uli* body and shrine decoration practised by Igbo women and *nsibidi* script used by the Cross River Ngbe or Leopard Society. The Zaria to Nsukka story reads at first like a narrative of progress, overcoming the strictures of narrow-minded colonialism to create a new art form combining elements of tradition and modernity. The closer one gets to the contemporary, the more difficult it is to react critically towards such narratives, especially since the careers of some of these artists are still active. A more reflective account of Nsukka is just in the process of being written.[38]

The complex twists and turns in the development of fine art (by which I mean art based in academic training and intended for an elite market) have varied widely. While formally trained artists, who are often university educated, are different in terms of their subject matter and their intended audience from the minimally trained 'popular' street painters working for a clientele of urban workers, there has long been a middle ground: the informal workshop. During the late colonial and early independence periods these were usually set up by outsiders acting as cultural brokers, but in recent years have typically been initiated by local artists themselves, looking to expand their business by training apprentices. A fundamental condition of African cities is the scarcity of formal employment, which means that nearly everyone works in the informal sector, where there is a high degree of competition for patronage. Within this social and economic space, apprenticeship to a successful painter is the hoped-for path to recognition. What is passed on to the apprentice may be either a specific technique or a style of representation. Both master and apprentice are considered and consider themselves craftsmen (whose gender is nearly always male).[39] In this they differ from the academically trained artist, who, in passing through a Western-style formal curriculum in a university or an *école des beaux arts*, has learnt to regard art as a form of self-actualization, in which critical recognition matters less than monetary reward. Yet, formally trained artists in Africa must survive in the same economic and political climate as street and workshop artists, so although their patrons are drawn from the elite sectors of society and their work is shown in galleries, museums, or cultural centres, there are not usually enough of these in African cities. In that sense they are more vulnerable than the street painter who treats his work as merchandise which can be sold anywhere.

Under these circumstances, a generous patron can perform the roles of cultural broker and underwriter to the artist's success. Such a situation occurred during the presidency of Léopold Senghor in Senegal from 1960 to 1980. As a young man, Senghor had spent years in Paris with other Francophone artists and intellectuals, some such as Léon-Gontran Damas and Aimé Césaire active in the *négritude* literary movement, others such as Picasso a part of the artistic avant-garde. He would later draw on this experience in fashioning a policy for the visual arts in Senegal, a predominantly Muslim country without the strong image-making traditions of Nigeria, Cameroon, or the Congo. To fill this gap, Senghor proposed a national art curriculum which would address both the conventional training found in French academies and research in the plastic arts based on his own interest in *négritude*, which he described as 'an aesthetics of feeling'. He saw Picasso as an exemplar, an artist who was at the forefront of modernism but able to retain his Andalusian roots. In what later became the École National des Beaux-Arts du Sénégal, this dual agenda was realized in a Department of Fine Arts and a separate Workshop for Research in Black Visual Arts. In 1965, an offshoot of the latter became a separate tapestry workshop in Thiès. Senghor argued that tapestry had its origins in ancient Egypt so possessed an African pedigree. It was this art form which established contemporary Senegalese art, in the form of large-scale public commissions.

There were limitations to Senghor's patronage: in order to enjoy it fully, artists had to subscribe to the ideology of *négritude* and work within its parameters. Eventually this hardened into its own form of academicism, with artists reacting against its strictures by forming their own counter-movement in a converted army barracks known as the Village des Arts, which included theatre, film, and jazz workshops as well as art studios. In the 1980s, experimental collectives such as Laboratoire AGIT-Art dedicated to performance art were also formed by artists such as El Hadji Sy, Issa Samb, and Amadou Sow.[40]

In 1990, Dakar staged its first international art biennale.[41] In the two decades since, the international art market has become increasingly globalized, extending beyond Europe and North America to Africa, Asia, and Latin America and giving rise to bien-nales in cities as diverse as Havana, Johannesburg, and Cairo. Dak'Art, as Dakar's bien-nale is called, has survived for twenty years despite shaky finances and organizational problems. While participation is heaviest from Francophone West African countries and others with relatively developed art worlds such as Nigeria, Egypt, and South Africa, its aim is to have a continent-wide reach. In contrast, the Cairo biennale is aimed at the Islamic world, while the Johannesburg biennale did not last beyond 1995 and 1997. Meanwhile, Angola's Trienal de Luanda has been conceived as a primarily digital site, and a new biennale has also started in Tanzania's increasingly vibrant capital, Dar es Salaam. These shows have not been without their critics. Dak'Art, drawing many of its visitors from beyond Africa, has been criticized for being both too international and too parochial. In the former case, 'biennale art' is seen by some as catering to new media, such as video, which attempt to be internationally current rather than rooted in Africa.[42]

A very different strand of painting developed as a part of popular, rather than elite, culture, most famously in Congolese cities in the 1970s. Emerging from a burgeoning, newly literate urban culture exposed to print media and later to films and television, Congolese popular painting also looked to Christianity and the Bible to provide par-ables, proverbs, and illustrations of sin and redemption. In cities such as Kinshasa and Lubumbashi, paintings on flour sacking were sold on the street to ordinary workers seek-ing to improve the appearance of their rented rooms.[43] In Kinshasa, the most renowned painters were Moke and Cheri Samba, both astute social critics and moralists. Samba, with his images of proud owners of television sets, electric fans, and refrigerators as well as portrayals of his own moral temptation, acquired two distinct levels of patronage: his original Kinshasa clientele; and, after exhibiting at the *Magiciens de la Terre* exhibition in Paris in 1989, international collectors willing and able to pay much more for his work. For Samba, this created a dilemma over which direction to follow.

In the 1970s and 1980s, such moral temptations were personified in images of La Sirene or Mamba Muntu (Snake Woman) in Central Africa, and as Mami Wata in the towns of coastal West Africa. Some interpretations, such as that of Johannes Fabian, have seen these temptresses as the alluring yet exploitative spirit of international capitalism, while evangelical Christian readings depict them as Jezebels attempting to snare the unwary Christian.[44] A different genre of painting also developed in the mining city of Lubumbashi, where street painters such as Tchibumba Kanda Matulu created a series of templates repeated over and over, such as the history paintings called 'Colonie Belge' which recalled the violence of Belgian colonialism.[45] Nowadays a combination of poverty and the dominance of photography has brought local patronage for these paintings to a halt.[46]

Indeed, by the closing decades of the twentieth century, it was photography that was cementing itself as the pre-eminent medium of visual culture across much of Africa. From the documentary work of South Africa's David Goldblatt, Santu Mofokeng, and Zwelethu Mthethwa, to the subversive and interrogative self-portraits of the Central African Republic-based Cameroonian, Samuel Fosso, photographers were in many ways best placed to capture the continent's ambiguous embrace of modernity. While the work of Goldblatt and Mthethwa, like that of Keita and Sidibé, is framed as fine art by critics and audiences, Ghanaian studio photographer Philip Kwame Apagya's work is constructed as disarmingly entertaining fantasy instead of realism, unabashedly aimed at a popular audience. Apagya's portraits are intimately tied to the consumption desires of his clients, who pose in front of painted backdrops of modern homes with gleaming bathroom fittings, appliances, and well-stocked refrigerators, or at a computer, or boarding a plane.[47] Finally, it is worth noting that virtually every African town, however small, has a local photographer. In that sense, it is the most egalitarian of visual media, and the primary one through which African modernism is felt and propagated.

THE DISCOURSE ON AFRICAN MODERNISM

As African art and material culture were transformed over the twentieth century in response to colonialism, urbanization, and the expansion of Christianity and Islam, so also did the methods of studying it. By the 1970s, a wave of young art historians and anthropologists on both sides of the Atlantic travelled to Africa in order to conduct ethnically based case studies of the art and expressive culture of 'the X people'. There was a sense of scholarly urgency surrounding this enterprise, often referred to as 'salvage anthropology', in order to record what were thought of as rapidly disappearing cultures and customs. At the same time that young Africanist historians were expected to carry out tape-recorded oral interviews, their art-history counterparts were documenting their research with 35 mm or super-8 film cameras. But to the detriment of both history and art history as disciplines, there was little cross-over in these fieldwork techniques. A 1984 survey of African art history by Jan Vansina exposed some of these methodological shortcomings, but it was not until historians accepted the validity of 'visual culture' as a field of inquiry in the 1990s that visual documentation became routine for historians.[48]

A more radical shift occurred from the late 1980s, when the serious study of the new urban genres of art began to gain ground. By the turn of the twenty-first century it had largely overtaken the established study of village- and court-based art forms. From outside the discipline, this appears as a fundamental split between the study of precolonial art forms and those which developed in response to the colonial and postcolonial experience. But whereas the split began as a tiny fraction of scholars pursuing the study of modern genres, the younger generation of scholars are now focused overwhelmingly on art emerging from the postcolonial African city. This is accompanied by a distaste for the old salvage anthropology paradigm, which to many younger scholars seems rooted in colonial-era perceptions of tribal styles or in the romantic notion of disappearing cultures. Yet it is clear that, while cultures may not actually disappear, many are being transformed in ways which would have seemed unimaginable two generations ago.

The new scholarship raises fundamental questions concerning the concepts of the postcolonial and the contemporary. Exemplified by the paradigm-shifting exhibitions of photography noted earlier, much of this scholarship has emerged not primarily in Africanist journals and monographs but in exhibition catalogues and journals of contemporary criticism. There are advantages but also limitations to the presentation of large ideas in short, profusely illustrated essays in exhibition catalogues. The exhibition format has the power of immediacy and emphatic visuality, but there is less space for sustained and nuanced argument. What substitutes for deep observation is often the apt turn of phrase, picked up and passed into public discussion. Not only are the vehicles of the debates different, but so are the interlocutors: while the academic study of precolonial art is still mainly the prerogative of a shrinking older generation of European, American, and African scholars trained in the 1970s, intellectual leadership in the study of the contemporary comes from younger scholars, including a number of Nigerians teaching in American universities, curating major exhibitions, and writing criticism.

Three terms are in current use by this cohort to describe the art which emerged around the mid-twentieth century: 'modern', 'contemporary', and 'postcolonial'. While often treated in catalogues and textbooks as if they are roughly interchangeable, each reflects a different theoretical approach to the art of the past half-century. To call African art 'modern' is to use the most capacious of these concepts: in art history, modernism is a disposition or aesthetic choice made possible by the condition of modernity. In Western art, the emergence of modernism is usually associated with a handful of late nineteenth-century Post-Impressionist painters in Paris; in other words, in a very specific time and place. Modernism introduced the notion of an avant-garde, connected to the bourgeoisie, in Clement Greenberg's famous phrase, by 'an umbilical cord of gold'.

Many African and Latin American cultural critics, however, argue that there have been many modernisms in different places and times, and that there is no defensible reason to regard these 'alternative modernisms' as necessarily derivative from the European one. The most overtly political argument, advanced by Okwui Enwezor in his exhibition *The Short Century* (2001), is that African modernity arose primarily from liberation struggles, emerging 'out of the ruins of colonialism' through the new cultural self-awareness which came with political autonomy.

One difficulty with this position is that it collapses modernism in the arts with the much broader condition of modernity. Another is the absence of strong exemplars: the theme of cultural resistance to colonialism is quite explicit in African literature of the 1950s and 1960s, but more submerged in the visual arts. There is no straightforward visual equivalent to the clash-of-two-worlds theme in Achebe's *Things Fall Apart* (1958) or *Arrow of God* (1967). Indeed, the 'Natural Synthesis' genre pioneered by artists from Achebe's own Igbo culture did not require traumatic rupture.[49] In a contrasting example, the emergence of a theorized and historically situated 'Resistance Art' in Apartheid South Africa emerged following the 1976 Soweto Uprising, but a fully formed South African modernism emerged as early as the 1950s in informal workshops such as Polly Street in Johannesburg, at the same time that art students of the Zaria school were attempting to actualize their notion of an appropriate modernism. The South African case demonstrates that modernism need not arrive on the wings of revolution but in fact can creep in well before the revolution begins.

The alternative argument to modernism developing with anti-colonial resistance and political autonomy is that it made its inroads with the incursion of colonialism itself. Africa is a large and complex continent: both arguments have had immediacy at different times and places. The politically driven explanation is about modernity, not modernism: what artists then did with this new condition is a different issue. Some responded to modernity by looking to export markets and the emergence of global tourism in order to keep on producing the genres they already knew.[50] Others began to create new forms. In the end, we can conclude that modernism as an aesthetic developed in places (primarily cities) where traditional art genres no longer had their former currency but also where there were artists who were looking, with a newly formed self-awareness, for means of expression which would reflect the world they now lived in.

'Postcolonial', like 'modern', suggests both a time frame and a state of being. At its simplest, it is a historical marker meaning 'after the end of colonial rule', but in expressive culture it is usually taken to mean a principled opposition to the ideological imprint of colonialism and its lingering after-effects. In this second sense, it is the successor to anti-colonial struggle. The condition of postcoloniality was embodied in the work of the African novelists who came of age in the late 1950s and 1960s, as well as in the philosophical writings of Frantz Fanon from the same period; it was then given theoretical nuance by a generation of Indian intellectuals such as Homi Bhabha and Gayatri Spivak. But its *métier* was the written or spoken word: it was not incorporated into African visual art discourse until the 1990s. For a decade prior to this, the British art journal *Third Text* had couched the analysis of Black art in a First World/Third World template.

Part of the reason for the neglect of the postcolonial in the art world was the parallel discourse of postmodernism which preoccupied the critical establishment.[51] Now that postmodernism is 'over', not as a condition but as a specific movement in the visual arts, postcoloniality may also be approaching the end of its usefulness as a descriptor.

One reason for this is that postcolonial consciousness is nowadays beginning to blur in Africa itself, losing its intellectual underpinnings as colonial memory, now fifty years old or more in the majority of countries, fades. Though a number of African cultural critics continue to use the postcolonial paradigm, most are too young to have experienced colonialism personally, so that it is expressed instead as a considered intellectual position from a certain temporal distance. Its most important staging was the mega-exhibition Documenta 11, in Kassell, Germany, in 2002, which for the first time in its postwar existence appointed an African artistic director, Okwui Enwezor, who in turn included African contemporary art in the exhibition. In response to this expansion of African art into the global art narrative, 'postcolonial' has become a useful, if uncritically deployed, place-marker in Western writing on contemporary art, giving recognition to art that was previously invisible on the international stage, while alluding to its different historical narrative.[52] At the same time, what has been labelled a postcolonial subjectivity is morphing into the transnational and diasporic as more African artists move into the stream of globalization.

This brings us to the fraught issue of the 'contemporary', also a term of periodization and a normative category, but with a moving time frame, since it is always assumed to imply 'recent'. In Western art history it has usually meant the post-Second World War period, though this too is moving forwards as the war recedes in memory; in African art history its parallel beginning was formerly the late colonial period, or frequently, after about 1950. Younger scholars are beginning to amend these dates by positioning African art from the 1950s, 1960s, and 1970s within the larger 'modern' time frame and revising the 'contemporary' to encompass only the past generation, from about 1980 to the present.[53] It should be noted that all contemporary art need not be modern in genre, since non-elite artists continue to produce such expressive forms as masks, a kind of contemporary art couched within a traditional genre.

What has also been subject to debate has been the rapidly expanding cultural geography of contemporary African art. By its most capacious measure it includes artists who have lived in the West since childhood but who have a family and emotional connection to Africa. Conversely, many artists who practise in Africa and the West resist the 'African artist' label. Because of their greater international visibility, it is this small cadre of diaspora artists who have come to represent the cutting edge of contemporary African art in Western public forums. This has occurred not only because of increasing migration but also because of a series of changes in the global art world from the 1980s, most importantly the ascendance of the independent curator and the expansion of the biennale system. A major consequence has been the rising interest of younger scholars in artists of African descent who practise in the West, further guaranteeing their greater visibility.

While all African countries have contemporary art, those with their own critics or curators (such as Nigeria, Senegal, and South Africa) have greater impact because they accrue written histories and a more global audience. Moreover, the established critical focus on the plastic art of sub-Saharan Africa has been replaced by a more inclusive artistic geography which includes Islamic North Africa. Since elite art from these countries is usually secular, it can be integrated seamlessly into pan-African exhibitions. So despite uneven coverage, current knowledge about African art is much broader than in the past, and Egyptian, Tunisian, and Sudanese artists figure prominently.

Finally, the study of contemporary African art is beginning to interact with that of Western contemporary art, an inevitable result of the latter's encroachment into the African diaspora. The response of art history departments in the United States has been increasingly to replace former non-Western specializations such as African or Asian art with one in 'world art', a trend reflected also in the renaming of European ethnology museums as museums of 'world culture'. The pessimistic view of all this is that African art and its study are in danger of disappearing beneath a globalizing steam-roller which flattens out distinctions among different visual cultures. But as the study of globalization has progressed it has become clear that with each homogenizing thrust, there is a corresponding increase in the number of ways to reconfigure the new local contexts it creates. This constant remaking of both idea and practice is as true for art as it is for politics and would seem to assure a future for the study of African visuality.

NOTES

1. George Kubler, *The Shape of Time: Remarks on the History of Things* (New Haven, Conn.: Yale University Press, 1962), 83.
2. See Enid Schildkrout and Curtis A. Keim, eds, *The Scramble for Art in Central Africa* (Cambridge: CUP, 1998).
3. Arjun Appadurai, *The Social Life of Things* (Cambridge: CUP, 1986).
4. See Vladimir Markov, 'Negro Art (*Iskusstvo negrov*, 1913)', and Carl Einstein, 'African Sculpture (*Negerplastik*, 1915)', in Jack Flam and Miriam Deutsch, eds, *Primitivism and Twentieth-Century Art* (Berkeley, Calif.: University of California Press, 2003).
5. Albert Maesen, letter cited in 'A Fine Kuba Figure of a King, *ndop*', Christie's sale catalogue, New York, 19 May 1992, 85.
6. William Rubin, 'Modernist Primitivism', in William Rubin, ed., '*Primitivism*' *in 20th Century Art*, i (New York: Museum of Modern Art, 1984), 18.
7. Sally Price, *Paris Primitive: Jacques Chirac's Museum on the Quai Branly* (Chicago: University of Chicago Press, 2007).
8. Michel Leiris and Jacqueline Delange, *Afrique noire: La Création plastique* (Paris: Gallimard, 1967), 14.
9. Francis Moore, *Travel into the Inland Parts of Africa* (London: Edward Cave, 1738), 40.
10. Sidney Kasfir, 'The Ancestral Masquerade: A Paradigm of Benue Valley Art History', in Marla C. Berns, Richard Fardon, and Sidney Littlefield Kasfir, eds, *Central Nigeria Unmasked: Arts of the Benue River Valley* (Los Angeles: UCLA Fowler Museum, 2011).

11. See Constanze Weise, 'Ndako Gboya Masquerades of the Nupe', and John Willis, 'Power and Gender in the History of Egungun', in Berns et al., *Central Nigeria Unmasked*, 123–9, 129–33.

12. Leo Frobenius, *Masken und Geheimbünde Afrikas* (Leipzig, 1898).

13. Sidney Littlefield Kasfir, *African Art and the Colonial Encounter* (Bloomington, Ind.: Indiana University Press, 2007), 120.

14. Walter Van Beek, 'Enter the Bush: A Dogon Mask Festival', in Susan Vogel, ed., *Africa Explores: 20th Century African Art* (New York: Center for African Art, 1991); Zoë Strother, *Inventing Masks: Agency and History in the Art of the Central Pende* (Chicago: University of Chicago Press, 1998).

15. Ferdinand de Jong, *Masquerades of Modernity: Power and Secrecy in Casamance, Senegal* (Bloomington, Ind.: Indiana University Press, 2007).

16. See John Nunley, *Moving with the Face of the Devil: Art and Politics in Urban West Africa* (Urbana, Ill.: University of Illinois Press, 1987).

17. Gregory Bateson, 'A Theory of Play and Fantasy', *Steps to an Ecology of Mind* (San Francisco: Chandler, 1972).

18. Kasfir, *African Art*, 121.

19. David Pratten, 'Masking Youth: Transformation and Transgression in Annang Performance', *African Arts*, 41/4 (2011), 44–59.

20. John Picton, 'Some Ebira Reflections on the Energies of Women', *African Languages and Cultures*, 1/1 (1988), 61–76.

21. Kasfir, *African Art*, 59, 84–5.

22. George Harley, 'Masks as Agents of Social Control in Northeast Liberia', *Papers of the Peabody Museum, Harvard University*, 32/2 (1950); Warren D'Azevedo, 'Gola Poro and Sande: Primal Tasks of Social Custodianship', *Ethnologische Zeitschrift Zurich*, 1 (1980).

23. M. C. Jedrej, 'Structural Aspects of a West African Secret Society', *Ethnologische Zeitschrift Zurich*, 1 (1980).

24. Carol MacCormack, 'Sande: The Public Face of a Secret Society', in Bennetta Jules-Rosette, ed., *The New Religions of Africa* (Norwood, NJ: Ablex, 1979), and 'Nature, Culture and Gender: A Critique', in Carol MacCormack and Marilyn Strathern, eds, *Nature, Culture and Gender* (Cambridge: CUP, 1980); Edwin Ardener, 'Belief and the Problem of Women', and 'The Problem of Women Revisited', in Shirley Ardener, ed., *Perceiving Women* (London: J. M. Dent, 1975).

25. De Jong, *Masquerades of Modernity*; Arjun Appadurai, *Modernity at Large: Cultural Dimensions of Globalization* (Minneapolis: University of Minnesota Press, 1996), 178–99.

26. Herbert Cole, 'Mbari is Life', *African Arts*, 2/3 (1969); 'Mbari is a Dance', *African Arts*, 2/4 (1969); and 'Art as a Verb in Igboland', *African Arts*, 3/1 (1969); Robert Farris Thompson, *African Art in Motion: Icon and Act* (Los Angeles: University of California, Los Angeles, 1974).

27. Kasfir, *African Art*, 184–5; Christopher Tilley, 'Michel Foucault: Toward an Archaeology of Archaeology', in Christopher Tilley, ed., *Reading Material Culture: Structuralism, Hermeneutics and Post-Structuralism* (Oxford: Basil Blackwell, 1990).

28. Bernard Ankermann, 'Kulturkreise und Kulturschichten in Afrika', *Zeitschrift für Ethnologie*, 37 (1905), 54–90; Melville Herskovits, 'The Culture Areas of Africa', *Africa*, 3 (1930); Eckart von Sydow, *Handbuch der Afrikanischen Plastik* (Berlin: Dietrich Reimer, 1930).

29. Carl Kjersmeier, *Centres de style de la sculpture Nègre africaine*, 4 vols (New York: Hacker, 1930).

30. William Fagg, *Tribes and Forms in African Art* (New York: Tudor, 1965), and *African Sculpture* (Washington, DC: International Exhibitions Foundation, 1970).

31. René Bravmann, *Open Frontiers: The Mobility of Art in Black Africa* (Seattle: University of Washington Press, 1973); Sidney Kasfir, 'One Tribe, One Style? Paradigms in the Historiography of African Art', *History in Africa*, 11 (1984).

32. Berns et al., *Central Nigeria Unmasked*; for similar reappraisals for Central Africa, see Strother, *Inventing Masks*; Allen F. Roberts and Mary Nooter Roberts, eds, *Memory: Luba Art and the Making of History* (New York: Museum for African Art, 1996).

33. Bogumil Jewsiewicki, 'Painting in Zaire: From the Invention of the West to the Representation of Social Self', in Vogel, *Africa Explores*, 130–51, and *A Congo Chronicle: Patrice Lumumba in Urban Art* (New York: Museum for African Art, 1999), 13–27.

34. For an excellent recent survey, see Erin Haney, *Photography and Africa* (London: Reaktion, 2010).

35. Martha G. Anderson and Lisa L. Aronson, 'Jonathan A. Green: An African Photographer Hiding in Plain Sight', *African Arts*, 44/3 (2011), 38–9.

36. Clare Bell et al., eds, *In/Sight: African Photographers, 1940 to the Present* (New York: Guggenheim Museum, 1996); Okwui Enwezor, ed., *Snap Judgments: New Positions in Contemporary African Photography* (Göttingen: Steidl, 2006); Tosha Grantham, ed., *Darkroom: Photography and New Media in South Africa since 1950* (Richmond, Va.: Virginia Museum of Fine Arts, 2009).

37. Okwui Enwezor, ed., *The Short Century: Independence and Liberation Movements in Africa, 1945–1994* (Munich: Prestel, 2001).

38. Chika Okeke, 'The Quest: From Zaria to Nsukka', in Clémentine Deliss, ed., *Seven Stories about Modern Art in Africa* (Paris: Flammarion, 1995); Chika Okeke-Agulu, *Postcolonial Modernism: Art and Decolonization in 20th-Century Nigeria* (Durham, NC: Duke University Press, forthcoming).

39. Till Förster, 'Work and Workshop: The Iteration of Style and Genre in Two Workshop Settings', in Sidney Littlefield Kasfir and Till Förster, eds, *African Art and Agency in the Workshop* (Bloomington, Ind.: Indiana University Press, 2012).

40. Ima Ebong, 'Négritude: Between Mask and Flag. Senegalese Cultural Ideology and the "École de Dakar"', in Vogel, *Africa Explores*, 198–209; Elizabeth Harney, *In Senghor's Shadow: Art, Politics and the Avant-Garde in Senegal, 1960–95* (Durham, NC: Duke University Press, 2004).

41. Yacouba Konaté, 'The Invention of the Dakar Biennial', in Elena Filipovic, Mieke Van Hal, and Soveig Øvstebø, eds, *The Biennial Reader*, i (Bergen: Kunsthall, 2010), 104–21.

42. See Namubiru Rose Kirumira and Sidney L. Kasfir, 'An Artist's Notes on the Triangle Workshops', in Kasfir and Förster, *African Art and Agency*.

43. Jewsiewicki, 'Painting in Zaire'.

44. Johannes Fabian, 'Popular Culture in Africa: Findings and Conjectures', *Africa*, 48/4 (1978); Rosalind Hackett, 'Mermaids and End-Time Jezebels: New Tales from Old Calabar', in Henry John Drewal, ed., *Sacred Waters: Arts for Mami Wata and Other Divinities in Africa and the Diaspora* (Bloomington, Ind.: Indiana University Press, 2008), 405–12.

45. Johannes Fabian, *Remembering the Present: Painting and Popular History in Zaire* (Berkeley, Calif.: University of California Press, 1996).

46. Bogumil Jewsiewicki, 'Building Social Selves: Contemporary Post-Scriptural Creativity in Congo', in Danielle de Lame and Ciraj Rassool, eds, *Popular Snapshots and Tracks to the Past: Cape Town, Nairobi, Lubumbashi* (Tervuren: Royal Museum for Central Africa, 2010), 53.
47. Tobias Wendl and Philip Kwame Apagya, 'Photography as a Window to the World', in *Flash Afrique!* (Göttingen: Steidl, 2001).
48. Jan Vansina, *Art History in Africa: An Introduction to Method* (London: Longman, 1984).
49. Uche Okeke, 'Natural Synthesis' and 'Growth of an Idea', in Deliss, *Seven Stories about Modern Art*, 208–11.
50. Christopher Steiner, *African Art in Transit* (Cambridge: CUP, 1994).
51. Kwame Anthony Appiah, 'Is the Post- in Postmodernism the Post- in Postcolonial?', *Critical Inquiry*, 17/2 (1991).
52. Terry Smith, *What is Contemporary Art?* (Chicago: University of Chicago Press, 2009).
53. Okwui Enwezor and Chika Okeke-Agulu, *Contemporary African Art since 1980* (Bologna: Damiani, 2010).

BIBLIOGRAPHY

Appadurai, Arjun, *Modernity at Large: Cultural Dimensions of Globalization* (Minneapolis: University of Minnesota Press, 1996).
Bell, Clare, Okwui Enwezor, Olu Oguibe, and Octavio Zaya, eds, *In/Sight: African Photographers, 1940 to the Present* (New York: Guggenheim Museum, 1996).
Berns, Marla C., Richard Fardon, and Sidney Littlefield Kasfir, eds, *Central Nigeria Unmasked: Arts of the Benue River Valley* (Los Angeles: UCLA Fowler Museum, 2011).
D'Azevedo, Warren, 'Gola Poro and Sande: Primal Tasks of Social Custodianship', *Ethnologische Zeitschrift Zurich*, 1 (1980).
De Jong, Ferdinand, *Masquerades of Modernity: Power and Secrecy in Casamance, Senegal* (Bloomington, Ind.: Indiana University Press, 2007).
Deliss, Clémentine, ed., *Seven Stories about Modern Art in Africa* (Paris: Flammarion, 1995).
Enwezor, Okwui, ed., *The Short Century: Independence and Liberation Movements in Africa, 1945–1994* (Munich: Prestel, 2001).
Frobenius, Leo, *The Voice of Africa: Being an Account of the Travels of the German Inner Africa Exploration Expedition in the Years 1910–1912* (New York: B. Blom, 1968).
Kasfir, Sidney Littlefield, *African Art and the Colonial Encounter* (Bloomington, Ind.: Indiana University Press, 2007).
——and Till Förster, eds, *African Art and Agency in the Workshop* (Bloomington, Ind.: Indiana University Press, 2012).
Markov, Vladimir, 'Negro Art (*Iskusstvo negrov*)', in Jack Flam and Miriam Deutsch, eds, *Primitivism and Twentieth-Century Art* (Berkeley, Calif.: University of California Press, 2003).
Moore, Francis, *Travel into the Inland Parts of Africa* (London: Edward Cave, 1738).
Strother, Zoë, *Inventing Masks: Agency and History in the Art of the Central Pende* (Chicago: University of Chicago Press, 1998).
Tilley, Christopher, ed., *Reading Material Culture: Structuralism, Hermeneutics and Post-Structuralism* (Oxford: Basil Blackwell, 1990).
Vansina, Jan, *Art History in Africa: an introduction to method* (London: Longman, 1984).
Vogel, Susan, ed., *Africa Explores: 20th Century African Art* (New York: Center for African Art and Prestel, 1991).

CHAPTER 24

MUSIC IN MODERN AFRICAN HISTORY

VEIT ERLMANN

Fluid Genres, Blurred Boundaries: The 'Modern' in African Music

THE emergence of African history as an object of serious scholarly inquiry in the 1950s and 1960s was accompanied by the rapid growth of the study of African music among anthropologists, ethnomusicologists, and historians. Pioneered by scholars such as Alan P. Merriam (1923–80), Gerhard Kubik (b. 1934), John Blacking (1928–90), Hugh Tracey (1903–77), and, most significantly, African ethnomusicologists such as Kwabena Nketia (b. 1921), much of this scholarship was driven by the desire to map the extraordinary wealth and antiquity of the continent's musical practices. 'Tradition' was the core concept around which this scholarship developed.

But 'tradition' was also the antithesis to many of the performance practices that were gaining prominence during the colonial era and that pioneering researchers pejoratively associated with the growth of urban centres, mass media, and the introduction of 'foreign', usually meaning Western, styles. With few exceptions, precolonial 'tradition' was perceived to persist in various stages of adaptation or 'acculturation' to these new developments. And while such emerging 'syncretic' styles were said to preserve many elements of precolonial tradition, the forces driving these processes were perceived to be located elsewhere, outside Africa. In the history of modern African music, then, the 'modern' was something that was initially seen not as African and in the definition of which Africans themselves had only a minor stake.

From the 1980s, several factors led to a major shift in this traditional–modern dichotomy. Foremost among these is the failure of the postcolonial African state to shore up legitimacy and to suppress political, ethnic, religious, or cultural divisions through the 'nationalization' of precolonial tradition and the concurrent ossification of such 'traditions' in carefully calibrated ethnic and stylistic categories. Second, the publication in 1983 of Eric Hobsbawm and Terence Ranger's ground-breaking collection *The Invention of Tradition* set the scholarly agenda for the interrogation and historicization of the notion of tradition, particularly with regard to twentieth-century ethnic identities in Africa.[1] Rather than being seen as primordial, timeless categories, now ethnic identities or 'tribes' were seen to have been reformulated or even invented by the agency of colonial rulers and indigenous brokers. The third factor that led to a rethinking of the traditional–modern dichotomy and the parallel temporal divisions between precolonial, colonial, and postcolonial Africa was the emergence in the 1980s of what is variously called 'world music' or 'worldbeat'. A self-consciously global style, 'worldbeat' involved musicians exploring and expanding upon on the historical connections between Africa, Europe, and the Americas, such as in the *al-andalus* musical tradition of southern Spain and North Africa, or creating entirely new hybrid forms without any historical precedent. Worldbeat recognized African performing arts as a major presence on the global stage at a time when many observers had written off Africa as the 'lost' continent and as peripheral to the global economy. The new global visibility of African music in turn inspired a major reassessment, most prominently in Paul Gilroy's *The Black Atlantic*, of the historical significance of these practices and of the continent as a vital cultural link between the Americas, Europe, and Asia.[2]

The net effect of these shifts is twofold. First, the history of African music in the twentieth century must be based on a vastly more differentiated set of concepts. Thus, 'the modern' functions not as a static category defined in opposition to tradition; rather, it is a category in a dynamic field that is characterized by fluid genres and blurred boundaries, whether between musical styles, national and ethnic markers of such styles, historical periods, between 'art' music and 'popular' music, or between rural and urban performance practices. Second, the history of modern African music is one of displaced correlation in which the relationship between historical sequence, social structure, cultural practice, and expressive forms cannot be subsumed under an overarching logic. While larger geo-political processes such as colonization and decolonization did shape the broader development of musical genres and the meanings audiences invested in them, such impact did not follow a straight line of influence everywhere. A host of factors, including geographic location, economic structure, and continuities of language or religious practice, complicate the larger picture of shared traits and developments, lending the history of modern African music a certain degree of autonomy.

THE COLONIAL LEGACY

The colonial impact on African music has been less profound and in many ways less direct than in other world regions such as Latin America. Nevertheless, colonial power did shape the musical terms through which the colonized were to make sense of the larger social, economic, and cultural configuration being grafted upon precolonial life-worlds during the first half of the twentieth century. A key role in this process was played by Christian missions, which were often hostile to indigenous forms of musical practice. More often than not this impact led to the decline if not complete disappearance of numerous performance genres, particularly those embedded in ritual practice and which involved instruments the missionaries deemed to be offensive, such as drums.

Only a small number of early Christian communities were able to maintain the complete range of precolonial musical traditions. But those that did, such as the Church of Nazareth in South Africa, founded in 1900 by Isaiah Shembe, created a unique blend of the ancestral Zulu heritage and Western elements. But the missions also introduced new forms of music making, such as four-part choral singing, and new instruments, especially keyboards such as the harmonium and the piano. Some denominations, such as the Salvation Army, even sponsored brass bands as part of the congregation's social activities. In several regions, particularly in eastern and southern Africa, the new forms of four-part choral performance (commonly referred to as *kwaya*, 'choir') have become the mainstay of community-based organizations from churches to schools to football clubs.[3] While these mission-inspired musical forms set out to imbue African converts with Western concepts of civilization, performers and audiences often reinterpreted them as assertions of the desire for equality with whites or, in mission-sponsored choral contests, used them as a mould within which to reaffirm the vitality of precolonial forms of social organization and group identity in the face of colonial power.

Less prominent than the missionary impact has been the role of the military. Military brass bands were an important part of the urban colonial soundscape, especially in colonies with a large numbers of European settlers such as South Africa, Kenya, or Southern Rhodesia. In addition to offering training in key Western musical skills such as sight reading, the sound (and sight) of marching bands also provided modernizing Africans with a symbol of discipline and power. In some instances, these symbols were appropriated and reinterpreted to support counter-images of modern African statehood; in others, such as the East African *beni* dance, they served to reinforce established models of social order. Unlike guitars, brass instruments were beyond the economic means of most Africans, so musicians in some regions designed their own kazoo-like instruments to emulate the sound of brass, such as in the *malipenga* music of Malawi.

Finally, vestiges of colonial culture were also felt for decades after independence in institutionalized musical education, especially in countries formerly under British rule. Several institutions of higher education in colonial Nigeria, the Gold Coast (now Ghana), Southern Rhodesia (Zimbabwe), and South Africa boasted music departments, many of which admitted African students. While the overall emphasis in these institutions was (and in some cases still is) on Western music, attempts to 'Africanize' the curriculum date back to the 1920s and 1930s, when Ephraim Amu (1899–1995) in the Gold Coast and Reuben T. Caluza in South Africa began introducing indigenous instruments.

THE GROWTH OF CITIES

Cities have always played a crucial role in the history of African music, both north and south of the Sahara.[4] During the precolonial era, much of this history was shaped by the role of urban centres as nodes of political power and long-distance trade, particularly in North, West, and East Africa, where seaports and endpoints of caravan routes served as gateways to regional and often international exchange. North African cities such as Cairo, Tunis, Algiers, Oran, and Casablanca all gave rise to vibrant musical cultures, while in East Africa port cities such as Mombasa and Lamu in Kenya later became centres of such Arab-influenced popular genres as *taarab*, a blend of vocals sung in Swahili accompanied by Egyptian-style light classical music played by an ensemble with strings and hand-held percussion. In Timbuktu in present-day Mali, North African Arab musical practices blended with West African traditions, while black slaves introduced musical instruments such as the *gimbri*, a three-stringed skin-covered bass plucked lute, and metal castanet-like instruments to Morocco. Such instruments and accompanying musical forms often featured in rituals of spirit possession, such as *stambeli* in Tunisia.[5]

During the early phases of European colonization, administrative centres such as Luanda, Angola, and Cape Town, South Africa (founded 1575 and 1652, respectively) provided fertile ground for the emergence of some of the first modern hybrid musics that blended African, European, Indian, Arab, Malay, and Portuguese elements. While in Cape Town this mix is at the heart of the culture of the 'Cape Coloured' community, Luanda's *musseques* (popular neighbourhoods) became home to an important Luso-African culture.[6] Similar cultural nodes emerged in the nineteenth century along the West African coast in cities such as Freetown in Sierra Leone, Accra on the Gold Coast, and Lagos in Nigeria. Here, Christian choral singing, military brass bands, piano-based 'parlour' music, guitar bands, accordions, and indigenous traditions were by the 1920s blending into innovative styles such as the Gold Coast's 'highlife', which remained influential into the era of independence (often transcending ethnic and class boundaries and providing an expressive medium for anti-colonial politics). Towards the end of the twentieth century, however, as Africa's cities experienced accelerating levels of migration from the rural hinterland, many of these older hybrid Euro-Asian-African cultures have become restricted to the middle classes and, in some cases, are on the verge of extinction. Thus, the golden era of Ghanaian guitar-band highlife was all but over by the 1970s, while *rebita* accordion music in Luanda by the 1970s had become little more than a tourist attraction.[7] Increasingly, musical creativity is shifting to the huge slum districts that surround Africa's major metropolitan areas such as Johannesburg, Kinshasa, and Nairobi. In addition to being hotbeds of poverty, crime, and disease, these informal settlements constitute an important sector of the informal economy, as centres of consumption (including pirated music) and of vibrant, youth-centred cultural production.

Other important musical centres were the mining regions of southern Africa. Although not generally located within cities, the mines of the Katanga province of the

Belgian Congo, the Northern Rhodesian Copperbelt, and of South Africa emerged as powerhouses of musical innovation in the colonial period. Prominent in this regard are the 'finger-style' acoustic guitar pioneered by Mwenda wa Bayeke (1930–90) from Katanga and the *kalela* dance performed by migrants during the 1940s and 1950s.[8] While the music played by these performers drew on traditional techniques, *kalela* in particular was an important vehicle of urban adaptation, prompting anthropologist Max Gluckman to proclaim, perhaps somewhat prematurely, that 'an African towns-man is a townsman'.[9] Meanwhile, migrants from Lesotho working in the South African mines developed a poetic genre known as *lifela* that addresses their experience of dislocation, alienation, and poverty as members of one of the largest industrial work-forces on the continent.[10]

THE IMPACT OF NATIONALISM

The rise of nationalism as a broad-based anti-colonial ideology in the middle decades of the twentieth century represented a key point in Africa's modern history. Its effects were felt in all spheres of life, from political organization and economic development to edu-cation and health services. The agendas of many nationalist movements also included a significant cultural component that was fuelled by widespread anti-colonial sentiment and the persistence of vibrant local traditions. Culture constituted a vital element in the emergence of nationalist ideology, often drawing on earlier forms of production and of so-called 'primary' resistance. In Zimbabwe, for example, in what became known as the First Chimurenga of 1896–7, Ndebele and Shona peoples joined forces to con-front the British South Africa Company. Led by charismatic spiritual leaders, the insur-gents found sustenance and guidance in *bira* spirit possession rituals and the associated music of the lamellaphone *mbira dza vadzimu*. Although it subsequently fell into near oblivion, *mbira* music experienced a major revival during the Second Chimurenga, the guerrilla war against white minority rule of 1966–79, when it became the basis of a new electric guitar style called *chimurenga*.[11]

However, nationalist movements did not always mobilize the symbols and musical practices of the precolonial past. In many cases, nationalist ideology entailed a mod-ernizing cultural agenda based on the idea that a new nation should theoretically be forged from a synthesis of the best local practices and the best of modern, Western cul-ture. This was the case in countries with a sizeable minority of European settlers such as Zimbabwe and Kenya, but also in Tanzania.[12] In actual practice, however, a genu-ine synthesis of such divergent cultural elements under the banner of nationalist ide-ology was rarely achieved, primarily because many early nationalist leaders and culture brokers had attended mission schools where they were exposed to Western, middle-class notions of aesthetic value. Hence, in determining value, early nationalists often privileged the adaptation of Western standards—part of the process of 'development'—over authenticity, thus getting caught in a dilemma. On the one hand, music was said to be the true and, hence, immutable expression of the national 'spirit'. On the other hand, this notion clashed with modern ideas of history as steadily unfolding progress.

In South Africa, the incorporation of the 'best of the West' was a highly contested project, as the ruling white minority regarded the appropriation of Western culture by the country's disenfranchised African majority as a Trojan horse: once admitted into the realm of 'modern' culture, demands by the majority for a just share in the economic and political benefits of that culture would follow. It is for this reason that the work of early nationalist composers such as Reuben T. Caluza (1895–1969)—and in some cases *all* Western music made by black South Africans—was denigrated as imitative and intrinsically inferior.[13]

After independence, expressions of nationalist sentiment became increasingly enmeshed with the public display of autocratic power. Typically, such displays occurred under the guise of celebrating national unity and were often accompanied by token gestures of largesse on the part of the leader or ruling party. Another method of 'staging the nation' involved performances by ensembles supposedly representing the ethnic make-up of the country as a harmonious whole, displays that often served to paper over social tensions and the lack of democratic representation. A classic example of the latter type of nationalism is *authenticité*, the official state ideology of the Mobutu regime in Zaïre (now Democratic Republic of Congo) during the 1970s. A key component of *authenticité* was *animation politique*, a system of state-sponsored events featuring singing and dancing based on a careful selection of local symbols of authority.[14] 'Mobutism' had many parallels, as autocrats such as Hastings Banda in Malawi and Sékou Touré in Guinea, along with more 'liberal' figures such as Léopold Senghor in Senegal, Julius Nyerere in Tanzania, and Jomo Kenyatta in Kenya sought to appropriate traditional and nationalist symbols to boost their image as benevolent fathers of the nation and to obscure the sharpening divisions of class, age, ethnicity, and gender.

The sound of African nationalism, by and large, has been a male sound: male singers and instrumentalists shaped the image of a continent proudly rising up against foreign domination. However, in many countries women also occupied central roles on the musical stage, linking the notion of cultural continuity with deeply entrenched ideals such as motherhood and nurturing. The Zanzibar-born *taarab* singer Siti bint Saad (1880–1950) belongs to this category, as does South African icon Miriam Makeba (1932–2008), often dubbed 'Mama Afrika'. From the 1990s, however, growing numbers of prominent female musicians questioned the subordination of women to an agenda that is national only in name. While some, such as the Malian *wassulu* vocalist Oumou Sangaré (b. 1968) and Benin-born singer Angélique Kidjo (b. 1960), address politically charged issues such as polygamy, others, such as South African bubblegum performer Brenda Fassie (1964–2004), Cameroon's supposedly 'pornographic' *bikutsi* singer K-tino, and a growing number of female hip-hop artists, intervene in postcolonial gender politics by providing models for the construction of fluid forms of female desire and identity.

THE ROLE OF THE STATE

Throughout the nineteenth and twentieth centuries, the emergence of various (and for the most part Western) forms of statehood has had a profound impact on African music. But it was only with the emergence of sovereign African nation-states from the late 1950s that various forms of government intervention in the arts became more systematic and, at least until the late 1980s, sustained. Performance, in the postcolonial order, constitutes a major stage for the state to represent itself to its subjects, just as it provides the latter with a resource with which 'to protect themselves from or to gain a purchase on the intervention of the state'.[15] Accordingly, the uses of music by the state range from attempts by the ruling elite to legitimize its rule by depicting itself as being in continuity with the tradition of chiefly power to the construction of networks of patron–client relationships between musicians and politicians, the use of mass media to regulate the flow of nationally and internationally produced music, to the harassment, incarceration, and even killing of musicians perceived to be a threat to state power. Meanwhile, musicians and other artists have sought to forge spheres of popular culture shielded from or directly challenging state power.

Among the first cultural projects pursued by newly independent states were the formation of national dance troupes. Lavishly funded and carefully assembled from each country's most talented performers, these troupes toured the world in an attempt to portray decolonization and the modernization of African societies as simultaneously developing and being compatible with traditional cultures. Pioneers of this trend were the *Ballets Africains* of Guinea and the National Ballet of Senegal.[16] Although few countries have been in a position to maintain ballets of this size for extended periods, the pageantry of 'tribal' customs sharing the stage in a display of national unity provided the format for festivals such as FESTAC in 1977, when oil-rich Nigeria hosted the Second World Festival of Black Arts and Culture.[17] National ballets also served as training grounds for a great number of musicians who gained international prominence during the 'worldbeat' boom of the 1980s and 1990s.

Another form of state intervention is the complex system of patronage that Jean-François Bayart has called the 'politics of the belly'. Many ruling elites have sought to use popular music either as the soundtrack for populist rhetoric or as a distraction from the dreary reality of daily life—or both.[18] The giant of Congolese rumba music, François Luambo Makiadi, aka Franco (1938–89) for the better part of his career enjoyed the patronage of Zaïrean dictator Mobutu, even if he occasionally clashed with the regime and was even incarcerated. In the Mande-speaking region of West Africa, where for centuries the *jeli*, or *griots*, have forged alliances with the rich and powerful, autocratic regimes such as that of Sékou Touré in Guinea have employed a mixture of patronage and coercion in enlisting the support and the praise of these musicians.[19]

A different approach was that of 'progressive' military regimes such as that of Seyni Kountché in Niger. In the 1980s, Kountché sought to repress the widespread practice of patrons hiring semi-professional musicians to sing their praises. Such practices, he claimed, were 'unproductive' and at odds with the modernization and development of Niger. In reality, however, the musicians were an important part of the country's informal sector who, in trying to generate additional income to complement their meagre earnings as farmers plagued by drought, economic mismanagement, and market fluctuations, contributed to a 'moral economy' based on solidarity and mutuality.[20]

State intervention in South Africa between the 1950s and 1980s, often aimed at suppressing musicians' opposition to Apartheid, had a crippling effect on the country's vibrant jazz and popular music scene as the segregation of performance venues and audiences along racial lines deprived many black musicians of their livelihood. A number of the most talented performers such as Miriam Makeba, jazz trumpeter Hugh Masekela (b. 1939), and jazz pianist Abdullah Ibrahim (b. 1934) left their country of birth for the uncertainty of exile, while continuing to denounce the Apartheid regime and creating some of the most poignantly nostalgic music.[21]

Another area in which the impact of the state on musical practice is manifest is censorship, especially in areas that are most vulnerable to government scrutiny, the media. From the immediate post-independence period of the 1960s to the era of neoliberal deregulation of 1990s, control of broadcasting tended to be centralized in the hands of the single-party or military regime. Usually legitimized as being essential to nation-building, these state-run media deployed a broad range of censorship techniques, from the outright banning of oppositional content to the refusal of airplay on grounds of obscenity, to the marginalization or silencing of ethnic minorities or religious communities and their expressive forms.[22] 'Obscenity' is frequently cited by government censors. One example was the banning in 1990 of Remmy Ongala's song 'Mambo kwa Soksi' (Things with Socks), a song advocating the use of condoms in HIV/AIDS-stricken Tanzania; another was Franco's brief imprisonment in 1979 after having recorded a song about a prostitute who feeds one of her customers excrement in a bowl of soup. Critics of the court's ruling claimed that the obscenity clause in the country's penal code was a mere pretext for Mobutu to humiliate the singer in retaliation for his thinly veiled criticism of the dictator and his cronies. In recent times, a type of Congolese rumba called *ndombolo* became the subject of fierce controversy, prompting governments in Cameroon, Kenya, and the Democratic Republic of Congo to ban performances of the fast, hip-swaying dance music from the airwaves.

In recent years, African governments have taken a more nuanced approach to freedom of expression and censorship, the most high-profile examples being two cases of hate speech in music in which censorship and even the criminal prosecution of the artist were legitimized by invoking human rights and constitutional law. The first example concerned Simon Bikindi, a Rwandan singer who in the genocide of 1994 composed and broadcast on the radio station Radio-Télévision Libre des Mille Collines several songs in which he called on Hutu militias (of which he was himself a member) to kill the Tutsi 'cockroaches'. In the wake of the mass slaughter (in which hundreds of thousands perished) the UN's International Criminal Tribunal for Rwanda charged the singer on six counts of genocide-related crimes and sentenced him to fifteen years prison in 2008. A slightly different approach was taken by the South African government in the case of Mbongeni Ngema and his song 'AmaNdiya' (The Indians). In the song, Ngema, a renowned playwright ('Sarafina') and anti-Apartheid activist, lashed out against Indian South Africans and their alleged exploitation of Africans in the KwaZulu-Natal region. Although the South African constitution guarantees freedom of artistic creativity, the Broadcasting Complaints Commission, the regulatory body overseeing broadcasting, ruled that Ngema's song amounted to hate speech, that the song should be banned from broadcast, and that a warning sticker should be attached to CDs sold in retail stores.[23]

Not all African musicians gave in to such state pressures. Many openly confronted autocratic regimes, most famously Nigerian Afrobeat star Fela Anikulapo Kuti (1938–97), who was frequently jailed and whose legendary 'Kalakuta Republic' centred on his Lagos club was often raided by police for alleged drug consumption and currency smuggling.[24] Several Zimbabwean musicians rose to prominence because of the stance they took against the white minority regime of Ian Smith, the best known being Thomas Mapfumo (b. 1945), who after playing rock and soul for many years turned to the *mbira* to create the revolutionary genre of *chimurenga*. In some cases, musicians suffered severe physical abuse, received death threats, or were even murdered. In 2001, for instance, Malawian reggae star and outspoken critic Evison Matafale died in police custody, allegedly of torture, and in 2008, Cameroonian musician Lapiro de Mbanga was sentenced to three years in prison for allegedly taking part in anti-government riots.

PUBLICS AND COUNTER-PUBLICS: FROM THE GRAMOPHONE TO COMMUNITY RADIO

The history of the recording industry in Africa dates to the dawn of the twentieth century. The Gramophone Company of London (with its famous 'His Master's Voice' label) first recorded in Cairo in 1903, followed by the German company Odeon and the Baidaphon label from Beirut, and within a few years the Egyptian capital had emerged as a important centre for the recording and sale of phonograph records. At the other end of the continent in South Africa, records were on sale by 1907. Over the following decades and up to the Second World War, this market grew significantly and was dominated by the major foreign labels such as HMV, Odeon, Columbia, Zonophone, and Pathé. Precise figures are scarce, but the fact that by 1939 HMV/Zonophone had sold over 200,000 records in East Africa alone (of which 80,000 were in vernacular languages) gives an indication of the scope of this development. Until about 1930, most recording occurred in the colonial metropolises, with African performers travelling to London, Paris, and elsewhere; some East African pioneers, such as *taarab* singer Siti bint Saad, first recorded in Bombay. From the late 1920s, mobile recording units from the big companies were travelling to North and West Africa and, from the mid-1930s, to South Africa. After the Second World War, smaller independent record labels began to be set up. One thriving musical centre was the capital of the Belgian Congo, Léopoldville, where in the late 1940s three local labels, Ngoma, Opika, and Loningisa—all established by immigrant Greek businessmen—would capture and disseminate the emerging sound of rumba. Across the continent, 78 RPM gramophone records were a major vehicle in the formation of new transnational styles such as South African jive and Congolese rumba—the latter strongly influenced by recordings of Cuban music. The possession of records and gramophones were seen as signs of achievement, upward mobility, and modernity.

Mirroring the profound technological shifts in the distribution of music elsewhere in the world, the emergence of cheap and easily bootlegged audio cassettes in the 1970s marked the beginning of the end of the African music industry. By the late 1990s, Africa's share in the global music industry had plummeted to an all-time low. According to the International Record Industry Association, the retail value of soundcarrier sales in Africa in 1999 represented a mere 0.5 per cent of the global value of sales, and of that figure 95 per cent had been realized in South Africa alone.

The history of African radio began in the 1920s, coinciding with the introduction of broadcasting in the West. The first radio station was established in South Africa in 1924, followed by Algeria in 1926, and Kenya in 1927. But most African countries only introduced radio as late as the 1960s and even at the end of the twentieth century distribution remained low, with only 20 per cent of the population owning a receiver.[25] Cinema also played an important role in shaping Africans' consumption of music, mostly by familiarizing audiences with an array of foreign musical styles such as Bollywood *filmi* music in parts of West and East Africa. In southern Africa, films produced in Great Britain and the United States played an essential part in conveying images of urban sophistication, including the music of the swing era. From the 1990s, the impact of cinema was superseded by the massive spread of video parlours, the availability of cheaply produced VCD, and since 2005, MTV's first African television channel, MTV Base, a pan-African network accessible to some 50 million viewers across the continent.

The future of African music in the information age is uncertain. The deregulation of the media that began in the 1990s, the growing concentration of media ownership, and the ensuing decline of the public sector model of national media have greatly diminished the ability of local artists and art forms to challenge the hegemony of the global music industry. At the same time, the past decade has seen a significant increase in the number of locally operated, independent electronic media. These include commercial FM stations that target urban youth as well as rural and community-based stations. Usually supported by NGOs and religious organizations, the latter in particular have become important agents in strengthening grassroots participation and artistic expression.

MAKING DO: MUSIC IN TIMES OF CRISIS

Musicians throughout the African continent have historically held an ambiguous social position, frequently revered and reviled at the same time. Often sought out by those in power as counsellors and spokespersons and given special privileges, they are also kept separate from the rest of society as members of a distinct occupational caste. Yet while the ambivalent status of ancient musical castes such as the *griots* of Mande-speaking West Africa has generated much scholarly research, the precarious position of musicians in the twentieth century has much less frequently been noted.[26] The West's image of African musicians has largely been shaped by two extremes: the spectacular and glamorous aspects derived from the Western star system, with its emphasis on the uniquely gifted and inspired individual, and the idea of the musician as a member of his or her 'traditional' community. Yet between these two poles, the vast majority of African musicians occupy liminal and shifting positions in a rapidly changing social, economic, and cultural environment that offers fewer and fewer opportunities for upward social mobility. As elsewhere, popular music (along with sports) has become one of the arenas in which dreams of fame and wealth have served to propel some career trajectories—while destroying many others.

In Kinshasa, the capital of the Democratic Republic of Congo, the structure and micro-politics of popular bands offer ordinary musicians a variety of strategies for making do in uncertain times. These strategies are designed to counterbalance often exploitative work conditions and to render more supple the rigid power relationships between the band leader and subordinate band members. At the same time these strategies enable musicians to explore alternative sources of revenue and symbolic capital through what scholars have called a logic of 'splintering'. Whether or not such strategies reproduce broader Congolese patterns of 'big man' politics, or enable the redistribution of wealth and increase access to networks, 'splintering' from a band to set up a band of one's own has empowered Kinois musicians and endowed them with an extraordinary sense of resilience.[27]

Performers of South African *isicathamiya* choral music after the Second World War devised a different strategy for coping with the fluctuations of the labour market and the insecurity of life at the margins of society. Instead of building ever larger networks of reciprocity as in Kinshasa, these musicians withdraw into replicas of a social universe shattered by the migrant labour system. Although these choral groups often celebrate the city and its promise, however elusive, of upward mobility, in their organization and in the structure of their songs, *isicathamiya* choirs re-enact the social relationships of the labour reserve, complete with the symbols of chiefly power, inter-clan antagonism, and the subordination of women.[28]

A different set of circumstances hampering the growth of thriving communities of musicians and their audiences is the implosion over several decades of a legitimate African music industry, on the one hand, and the growing leverage of the global music industry in shaping concepts of ownership and cultural authority, on the other hand. Copyright protection is fundamental in this regard. Although most African countries have signed the TRIPS (Trade-Related Aspects of Intellectual Property Rights) agreement, a multilateral instrument administered by the World Trade Organization that governs the globalization of intellectual property laws, many lack the resources or political will to enforce existing national copyright laws other than those benefiting US or European software or pharmaceutical companies. In addition, African countries have made little headway in extending legal protection to musical creations not covered by intellectual property law such as 'traditional' music or folklore, still a significant part of everyday musical production throughout the continent. One exception is Ghana, where legislation was introduced in 1985 that vests works of anonymous folklore in the state for perpetuity and prohibits their use without permission from the Ghana Folklore Board of Trustees. South Africa also has a robust system of licensing bodies and since its transition to democracy has moved aggressively towards protecting authors' rights, most famously in 2006 when the heirs of Solomon Linda (1909–62), the composer of the song 'Mbube', aka 'The Lion Sleeps Tonight', won a lawsuit against Walt Disney, Inc., which had infringed on Linda's rights by using the song in the movie and Broadway show *The Lion King*.

Paris Africain: African 'Worldbeat' in Europe

African music, it might be argued, has always been 'global'. The trans-Atlantic slave trade served to transplant African music to the Americas, from where it subsequently returned in a variety of new forms to reshape musical practice to this day. But the twentieth century also witnessed the emergence of distinctly 'modern' forms of African performance in locations outside the African continent. The most emblematic of these new transnational spaces is Paris. Other imperial capitals such as London saw a steady presence of performers from the colonies during the first half of the twentieth century, but it was Paris that acquired a distinctly African hue during the 1970s and 1980s, as the city absorbed, at times reluctantly, an ever-growing number of immigrants from both North and sub-Saharan Africa.[29]

Musicians were in many ways the most visible of these immigrants, contributing in large part to the French capital's reputation as the world centre of African 'world-beat': *Paris Africain*. The first musicians began to arrive in the late 1970s, spearheaded by two Cameroonian artists, Francis Bebey and Manu Dibango. They were soon joined by a larger contingent from West Africa such as Lamine Konté, Mory Kanté, and Touré Kunda. Others, such as Ray Lema, came from Congo (then still called Zaïre). By the mid-1980s, African music had become a fixture on the Parisian cultural scene, a process aided by the inclusionist policies of socialist president François Mitterand and his minister of culture Jack Lang. These policies met with an enthusiastic response from some of the capital's newly deregulated radio stations such as Radio Nova, print media such as *Libération*, and independent record labels specializing in 'worldbeat' such as Celluloïd and Syllaphone, the latter founded by Senegalese producer Ibrahim Sylla.

This scene flourished into the early 1990s, even as attempts to curb immigration reduced Africans' ability to gain a permanent foothold in French cultural life. The international success of performers such as Salif Keïta and Mory Kanté (the latter's

1987 'Yéké Yéké' became one of worldbeat's biggest hits) was also helped by the backing of prominent rock musicians such as Peter Gabriel, the founder of the WOMAD (World of Music, Arts and Dance) festival held annually in Britain since 1982 and now in over twenty countries.

The later 1990s, however, saw the fortunes of African performers in France decline. Aggressive anti-immigration policies, the rise of anti-Muslim sentiment among the French public, and the absorption of independent labels by major music corporations such as Time-Warner, Sony, and BMG all led to shrinking opportunities in the 'worldbeat' industry. While some musicians continued to operate illegally as so-called *sans papiers* (undocumented immigrants), others returned to Africa, including stars such as Salif Keïta. Here they collaborated with foreign and local musicians in trying to revitalize what was left of an African-based recording industry. Foremost in this regard was Ali Farka Touré (1940–2006), the Malian guitarist whose signature blend of blues and local *griot* styles, coupled with down-to-earth production, struck a chord with both African and international audiences. A similar development is the re-emergence of seemingly long-forgotten instruments such as the *ngoni*, a skin-covered lute-like instrument of West African origin, or the popularity of what one might call scrapyard music by the Congolese band Konono No. 1, that combines outdated audio-technology with *likembe* lamellaphone sounds.

Global Africa: From Minstrelsy to Hip-Hop

Africa has been at the centre of some of the modern world's most creative and influential cultural developments, with musical forms passing back and forth across what Gilroy called the Black Atlantic. While African slaves and their descendants made a huge contribution to the popular music of the Americas, some of the continent's most vibrant twentieth-century styles emerged as a result of African performers' familiarity and experimentation in turn with American, European, and Asian musical traditions. During the colonial period, African audiences experienced an unprecedented influx of new sounds, performance styles, and aesthetic concepts. As we have seen, brass bands had a major impact on the development of urban popular culture in East Africa, as populations formed associations engaged in competitive dancing known as *beni ngoma*.[30] In southern Nigeria, the interaction between Saro ('Sierra Leonean') Christians, Muslims, and repatriated slaves from Brazil during the early decades of the twentieth century led to the emergence of *juju*, a syncretic blend of styles popular among urban Yoruba in and around Lagos.[31] Likewise, highlife, a guitar-based style that emerged in the early 1900s on the Gold Coast and subsequently spread to Liberia and Nigeria, is primarily an amalgamation of local 'palm wine' guitar music and a particular two-fingered style of guitar playing reputedly spread by Kru sailors from Liberia.

Even more influential was the music of African Americans. Orpheus McAdoo and the Virginia Jubilee Singers toured South Africa during the 1890s, familiarizing middle-class black audiences with the politics of post-reconstruction America as well as images of black American educational progress and, above all, musical traditions such as the 'spiritual'.[32] But McAdoo also brought blackface minstrelsy, a tradition popular among South African urban whites from as far back as the 1840s, to the attention of black audiences. In Ghana, minstrelsy constituted the core of a genre of performance called Concert Party. Popular since the 1920s, these were variety shows that combined material appropriated from 'highlife', the music of precolonial *asafo* military associations, and African American spirituals.[33] Despite their racist connotations, minstrel shows were appreciated by local audiences because of the subtle ways in which they enacted, and thereby enabled audiences to make sense of increasingly complex urban landscapes and the growing distinctions of class, gender, and ethnicity operating within them.

In Cape Town, African, Dutch, South-East Asian, and British traditions blended to form a range of distinct musical styles such as the moppies or *gommaliedjes* of the local Minstrel Carnival (traditionally known as 'Coon Carnival') and, later, with American input, Cape jazz.[34] Far from merely being derivative of American jazz, however, Cape jazz also drew on Christian hymnody, indigenous Xhosa styles, and those of 'Cape Malay', descendants of Javanese slaves brought to the Cape by the Dutch East India Company.

By far the most pervasive 'global' style prior to the 1960s was the wave of Afro-Cuban music that swept the Belgian Congo from the 1940s. Popularized by musicians such as Joseph Kabasele Tshamala (Le Grand Kalle) and his orchestra African Jazz (later OK Jazz), 'Congo rumba' was sung in the *lingua franca* of Léopoldville's up-country migrants, Lingala. But rumba's interethnic, interregional appeal was also bolstered by the city's record labels and a record-buying public which by 1955 is reported to have purchased some 600,000 records a year.[35]

After independence, *soukous* or *kwasa kwasa* as Congolese rumba became known, spread to eastern and southern Africa, becoming the first truly transnational African style. Its success was rivalled only by the growing influence of rock'n'roll. Initially decried as 'immoral' and 'un-African' and banned from some state-controlled media, various fusions of rock and local traditions eventually gained tremendous popularity among the growing number of disenfranchised African youth in the larger cities. Prominent examples within this genre are Fela Kuti's 'afro-beat' in Nigeria and *mbalax*, pioneered by Senegalese Youssou N'Dour (b. 1959). In South Africa, where rock's rise met with particular circumspection from the Apartheid regime, African American music none-theless filtered into *jive*, a potent blend of funk, soul, and Zulu guitar styles, that subsequently became known as *mbaqanga* and was popularized by performers such as the female vocal quartet the Mahotella Queens. It should be noted, however, that such pan-African appropriations, apart from celebrating the connections between the Civil Rights movement and the anti-Apartheid struggle, often also fed into the resurgence of ethnic particularism that was increasingly colouring black oppositional politics.[36] Parallel with the explosion of rock, reggae also became an important part of the African soundscape, particularly following Bob Marley's seminal performance at the Zimbabwean inde-pendence festivities in Harare in 1980.

These developments have been dwarfed, however, by what is undoubtedly the most popular 'international' musical style to have gained a foothold on the African conti-nent: hip-hop.[37] Scholars have tended to consider African hip-hop as largely derivative of African American hip-hop, minus some of the more violent and misogynist content of gangsta rap. Local practitioners, however, frequently contest this narrative, insisting that the structural and technical similarities between hip-hop (such as the use of 'beats') and vernacular forms obscure the fact that local audiences consider the latter as sites of making history and much less so as opportunities for asserting authentic 'Africanness'.

Another debate surrounding the emergence and growing hegemony of hip-hop in many African countries concerns the position from which African artists engage with issues of globalization, poverty, and disempowerment. South African *kwaito*, for instance, after an early phase in the 1990s in which artists of the 'post-struggle' gener-ation such as Boom Shaka were seen as uncritically accepting global, free-market stand-ards of consumption and personal identity, seems to have diversified into a complex mix of styles and stances. In espousing causes such as the fight against HIV/AIDS while at the same time retreating from narrow definitions of the political in terms of 'national reconciliation', a younger generation of performers such as Chicco and Zola, Brassis Vanni Kaap, and even white crews such as Die Antwoord are playing a major, 'noisy' role in shaping public culture.[38] Elsewhere, vernacular forms such as *bongo flava* in Tanzania and *genge* in Kenya (sung in the slum lingo Sheng) afford unemployed youths a plat-form from which to challenge Western cultural hegemony while carving out niches of self-empowerment between officially mandated patriotism, global stardom, and social responsibility.[39]

African music at the end of the first decade of the twenty-first century is shot through with ambiguity, conflict, and lost opportunities. Despite the gains made in many coun-tries in opening up the public sphere to the creative engagement of artists and com-munities through locally and democratically controlled media, disillusionment and cynicism are widespread. Under such turbulent conditions, much of contemporary African music making is now articulated with a rediscovered, revitalized, and even reinvented religious sphere as a site where the fissures of war-torn societies are healed and supposedly more 'real' and meaningful forms of living are nurtured. The rise of gospel music is an example. Distinct from *kwaya*, gospel in many countries is a major component of the public soundscape, second only to hip-hop as the top-selling musi-cal category. Another is the increasingly contested role of music in Islam. The rise of political Islam, in particular the introduction of shari'a law in northern Nigeria, has turned various syncretic musical styles such as *bandiri* music into sites of contestation.[40] An Islamic chant accompanied by frame-drums, *bandiri* has been popular among Qādiriyya sufis in Kano since the 1950s, its contemporary popularity also stemming from its catchy melodies borrowed from Hausa popular song and Bollywood film music. Yet *bandiri* has drawn the ire of the Wahhabi-influenced clergy, primarily on account of Bollywood's alleged licentiousness.[41]

Far from merely reflecting history, African music during the twentieth century has been a major site of social, cultural, and political contestation and transformation. Musical forms and practices have been important vehicles in fostering resistance to colonial rule, in shaping new patterns of identity, in providing powerful narratives of justice, freedom, development, and belonging, and in forging notions of indigenous or cosmopolitan modernity. Not all of these forms and practices are 'modern' or of predominantly Western provenance: many long-standing African musical traditions have also proven remarkably resilient, often by articulating differences of class, race, ethnicity, and religion, especially among the marginalized and the disempowered whose aspirations and visions of social and cultural order are ignored by the elites and the forces of the global market economy.

NOTES

1. Eric Hobsbawm and Terence Ranger, eds, *The Invention of Tradition* (Cambridge: CUP, 1983).
2. Paul Gilroy, *The Black Atlantic: Modernity and Double-Consciousness* (Cambridge, Mass.: Harvard University Press, 1992).
3. Gregory Barz, *Performing Religion: Negotiating Past and Present in Kwaya Music of Tanzania* (Amsterdam: Rodopi, 2003).
4. David Coplan, 'The Urbanisation of African Music: Some Theoretical Observations', *Popular Music*, 2 (1982).
5. Richard C. Jankowsky, *Stambeli: Music, Trance, and Alterity in Tunisia* (Chicago: University of Chicago Press, 2010).
6. Marissa J. Moorman, *Intonations: A Social History of Music and Nation in Luanda, Angola, from 1945 to Recent Times* (Athens, O.: Ohio University Press, 2009).
7. John Collins, *West African Pop Roots* (Philadelphia: Temple University Press, 1992).
8. J. Clyde Mitchell, *The Kalela Dance* (Manchester: MUP, 1956).
9. Max Gluckman, 'Anthropological Problems Arising from the African Industrial Revolution', in A. Southall, ed., *Social Change in Modern Africa* (Oxford: OUP, 1961), 69.
10. David Coplan, *In the Time of Cannibals: The Word Music of South Africa's Basotho Migrants* (Chicago: University of Chicago Press, 1994).
11. Thomas Turino, *Nationalists, Cosmopolitans, and Popular Music in Zimbabwe* (Chicago: University of Chicago Press, 2000).
12. Kelly Askew, *Performing the Nation: Swahili Music and Cultural Politics in Tanzania* (Chicago: University of Chicago Press, 2002).
13. Veit Erlmann, *African Stars: Studies in Black South African Performance* (Chicago: University of Chicago Press, 1991).
14. Bob White, *Rumba Rules: The Politics of Dance Music in Mobutu's Zaire* (Durham, NC: Duke University Press, 2008).
15. John Lonsdale, 'States and Social Processes in Africa: A Historiographical Survey', *African Studies Review*, 24 (1981), 161.
16. Francesca Castaldi, The Pan-African Nation: *Choreographies of African Identities: Négritude, Dance, and the National Ballet of Senegal* (Urbana, Ill.: University of Illinois Press, 2006).
17. Andrew Apter, *The Pan-African Nation: Oil and the Spectacle of Culture in Nigeria* (Chicago: University of Chicago Press, 2005).

18. Jean-François Bayart, *The State in Africa: The Politics of the Belly* (London: Longman, 1993).

19. Jay Straker, *Youth, Nationalism, and the Guinean Revolution* (Bloomington, Ind.: Indiana University Press, 2009).

20. Veit Erlmann, 'Data on the Sociology of Hausa Musicians in the Valley of Maradi (Niger)', *Paideuma*, 27 (1981).

21. David Coplan, *In Township Tonight! South Africa's Black City Music and Theatre* (Chicago: University of Chicago Press, 2nd edn, 2008).

22. Michael Drewett and Martin Cloonan, eds, *Popular Music Censorship in Africa* (Aldershot: Ashgate, 2006).

23. Further information on censorship is available on the website of Freemuse, a watchdog organization advocating freedom of expression for musicians and composers worldwide (www.freemuse.org).

24. Michael Veal, *Fela: The Life and Times of an African Musical Icon* (Philadelphia: Temple University Press, 2000).

25. Krister Malm and Roger Wallis, *Big Sounds from Small Peoples: The Music Industry in Small Countries* (New York: Pendragon Press, 1984); Dina Ligaga, Dumisani Moyo, and Liz Gunner, eds, *Radio in Africa: Publics, Cultures, Communities* (Johannesburg: Witswatersrand University Press, 2012).

26. Thomas Hale, *Griots and Griottes: Masters of Words and Music* (Bloomington, Ind.: Indiana University Press, 1999).

27. White, *Rumba Rules*.

28. Veit Erlmann, *Nightsong: Performance, Power, and Practice in South Africa* (Chicago: University of Chicago Press, 1996).

29. James A. Winders, *Paris Africain: Rhythms of the African Diaspora* (New York: Palgrave Macmillan, 2006).

30. Terence Ranger, *Dance and Society in Eastern Africa, 1890–1970: The Beni Ngoma* (Berkeley, Calif.: University of California Press, 1975).

31. Christopher Waterman, *Juju: A Social History and Ethnography of an African Popular Music* (Chicago: University of Chicago Press, 1990).

32. Erlmann, *African Stars*, 21–53.

33. Catherine Cole, *Ghana's Concert Party Theatre* (Bloomington, Ind.: Indiana University Press, 2001).

34. Denis Constant-Martin, *Coon Carnival: New Year in Cape Town, Past to Present* (Cape Town: David Philip, 1999).

35. Gary Stewart, *Rumba on the River: A History of the Popular Music of the Two Congos* (London: Verso, 2004).

36. Louise Meintjes, *Sound of Africa! Making Music Zulu in a South African Studio* (Durham, NC: Duke University Press, 2003).

37. P. Khalil Saucier, *Native Tongues: An African Hip-hop Reader* (Trenton, NJ: Africa World Press, 2011).

38. Gavin Steingo, ed., *Kwaito* (Berlin: VWB, 2008).

39. Mwenda Ntarangwi, *East African Hip Hop: Youth Culture and Globalization* (Bloomington, Ind.: Indiana University Press, 2009).

40. Adeline Masquelier, *'Prayer has Spoiled Everything': Possession, Power, and Identity in an Islamic Town of Niger* (Durham, NC: Duke University Press, 2001).

41. Brian Larkin, 'Bandiri Music, Globalization and Urban Experience in Nigeria', *Cahiers d'études africaines*, 168 (2002).

BIBLIOGRAPHY

Askew, Kelly, *Performing the Nation: Swahili Music and Cultural Politics in Tanzania* (Chicago: University of Chicago Press, 2002).

Castaldi, Francesca, *Choreographies of African Identities: Négritude, Dance, and the National Ballet of Senegal* (Urbana, Ill.: University of Illinois Press, 2006).

Coplan, David, *In the Time of Cannibals: The Word Music of South Africa's Basotho Migrants* (Chicago: University of Chicago Press, 1994).

Erlmann, Veit, *African Stars: Studies in Black South African Performance* (Chicago: University of Chicago Press, 1991).

Erlmann, Veit, *Nightsong: Performance, Power, and Practice in South Africa* (Chicago: University of Chicago Press, 1996).

Meintjes, Louise, *Sound of Africa! Making Music Zulu in a South African Studio* (Durham, NC: Duke University Press, 2003).

Moorman, Marissa J., *Intonations: A Social History of Music and Nation in Luanda, Angola, from 1945 to Recent Times* (Athens, O.: Ohio University Press, 2009).

Ntarangwi, Mwenda, *East African Hip Hop: Youth Culture and Globalization* (Bloomington, Ind.: Indiana University Press, 2009).

Stewart, Gary, *Rumba on the River: A History of the Popular Music of the Two Congos* (London: Verso, 2004).

Turino, Thomas, *Nationalists, Cosmopolitans, and Popular Music in Zimbabwe* (Chicago: University of Chicago Press, 2000).

Veal, Michael, *Fela: The Life and Times of an African Musical Icon* (Philadelphia: Temple University Press, 2000).

Waterman, Christopher, *Juju: A Social History and Ethnography of an African Popular Music* (Chicago: University of Chicago Press, 1990).

White, Bob, *Rumba Rules: The Politics of Dance Music in Mobutu's Zaire* (Durham, NC: Duke University Press, 2008).

Winders, James A., *Paris Africain: Rhythms of the African Diaspora* (New York: Palgrave Macmillan, 2006).

CHAPTER 25

....

AFRICAN LITERARY HISTORIES AND HISTORY IN AFRICAN LITERATURES

....

STEPHANIE NEWELL

A consideration of history in African literatures involves far more than the study of narratives about the past. While literary material is often attuned to historical specificities, it is never simply a mirror reflecting sociological realities. Alive with voices, opinions, and interpretations of the past and present in specific locales, African literatures offer a particularly rich but complex resource for historians. What sort of vector for modern African history is a work of the creative imagination? Packed with opinion and character, African literatures are useful to historians for the manner in which they foreground individual subjectivity, but how should we approach the vexed historical status of the fictional subjects we encounter? This chapter will offer a series of approaches to and questions about the different types of historical engagement to be found in African literatures.

The Nigerian philosopher Emmanuel Eze asks of the continent's writers, 'What does the thought of history in fiction tell us about suspended histories of peoples, traditions, societies, and cultures in modern Africa, including Africa's experiences of its own past?'[1] In what follows, I will suggest that historians should approach African literatures for biased and intimate and thus ideologically significant visions of local cultures at particular moments in time. Whether or not a text is self-consciously 'historical'—in the manner of Chinua Achebe's canonical novel about the coming of colonialism, *Things Fall Apart* (1958), Chimamanda Ngozi Adiche's best-selling Biafran war novel, *Half of a Yellow Sun* (2007), or M. K. Vassanji's revisionary novel about the Mau Mau in Kenya, *The In-Between World of Vikram Lall* (2003)—African creative writing often furnishes us with carefully fleshed-out subjects who exist in particular times and settings. In reading this material as cultural historians, we can adopt a three-tiered methodology in which we consider, first, the time and place of literary production; second, the ways in which works of literature engage with the concepts of time, memory, and historical consciousness; and third, the temporal and geographical distances separating literary works from their current audiences.

CONSIDERATION OF THE TIME AND PLACE OF LITERARY PRODUCTION

Attention to the social and political currents within which an author is situated can furnish us with vital clues about a writer's choice of themes and settings. What political factors, for example, led Ken Saro-Wiwa to publish his Biafran war novel, *Sozaboy: A Novel in Rotten English* (1985), with its searing critique of corruption among the country's ruling elites from a disempowered 'small' man's point of view, and with its refusal to grant moral authority to either side in the conflict? From this perspective, *Sozaboy* must be regarded as a novel about the breakdown of civil society in postcolonial Nigeria as much as it is an apocalyptic anti-war novel about the Biafran conflict of 1967–70. Similarly, we need to ask what political considerations subsequently led the British publisher, Longman, to include *Sozaboy* in its African Writers Series in 1994, nearly a decade after the book's first publication in Nigeria. By this time, the author was in prison for treason on a charge that caused international condemnation of the regime that went on to execute him the following year. Often ignored in favour of content analysis, an examination of the times and places of literary production can thus reveal the ways in which texts and authors actively become a part of history.

For another example of the historical agency and cultural clout of literatures, we can turn to the earliest printed materials to circulate in Africa. As many scholars have pointed out, the history of books on the continent is closely connected to the rise of missionary presses in the nineteenth century and the expansion of the colonial education system in the early twentieth.[2] Christianity and colonialism formed two substantial vested interests in the field of early African literary production. Often anxious about the circulation of politically 'incendiary texts' among newly literate (and thus supposedly naïve and morally corruptible) 'natives', colonial authorities designed an array of techniques to regulate and reform people's literary interests.[3] Alongside punitive measures such as anti-sedition legislation and press registration laws, one method of monitoring African literacy was the prize essay and story competition, common throughout the continent in the colonial period. In the Gold Coast (today Ghana) from 1914 onwards, for example, Governor Hugh Clifford's wife, Lady Clifford (famous in her own right as the novelist Mrs H. de la Pasture), held regular prize essay and story competitions for newly literate Africans in an effort to harness people's literacy to morally worthy ends. In May 1914, she announced the first competition, calling for essays by women on the theme 'House-Keeping on the Gold Coast'.[4] A silver tea service was the first prize, a silver coffee pot was second prize, and third was a silver salver. Clearly, this was an effort to graft European, upper middle-class modes of consumption and feminine behaviour onto African women through the medium of their literacy.

Lady Clifford's second competition, launched in June 1918, provides further insights into the ways in which writing for public consumption, or public writing, was gendered and monitored in colonial settings in an effort to lay the foundations for African literary expression. Alongside the main competition—600 words on 'A Day of My Life', open to anybody—Lady Clifford created two further competitions: the first was aimed specifically at African schoolgirls, inviting them to write letters on the topic, 'Why educated girls ought to be able to keep house, clean and cook, better than uneducated girls'; meanwhile, in a separate competition, she invited boys to write letters on, 'What work do I wish to do in the world when I am a man, and why'.[5] Such an obvious gendering of literacy demonstrates the ideological biases with which literacy was imbued in colonial Africa.

The form, content, and style of texts cannot therefore be regarded as historically neutral. In the colonial period, most African readers would have been taught to read in mission schools, supplied with 'good' Christian literature from local bookshops. If mission Christianity contributed to the formation of African literary values, Christianity continues to dominate local print cultures. Evangelical and Pentecostal titles such as *The Challenge of Marriage, Sex, Friendship and Marriage,* and *Delivered from the Powers of Darkness* circulate widely throughout the continent, with numerous local variations in response to debates in particular regions.[6] In East Africa, for example, large numbers of Christian novels and self-help pamphlets circulate on the topic of the causes and spread of HIV/AIDS;[7] meanwhile, in West Africa, debates about lesbianism and homosexuality, particularly in schools and college campuses, find expression in popular novels.[8]

Published on urban printing presses, the most popular pamphlets are reprinted regularly and may remain on sale for several decades: David A. Dartey's *Hints for a Happy Marriage* (1981), which contains practical advice on maintaining a strong relationship, has undergone numerous revisions and reprints since the early 1980s, and can still be found in Christian bookshops in Ghana's capital, Accra. Copies of North American evangelical self-help books, including titles by the American founders of the Family Life Mission, Walter and Ingrid Trobisch, can also be found on the shelves of urban African bookshops and on sale at open-air bookstalls. The circulation of such morally 'good' material, and the debates provoked by these texts, help to consolidate postcolonial African reading cultures in which books are widely expected to furnish what might be labelled the 'three Es': education, ethical guidance, and entertainment. These 'three Es' and the interpretative conventions they generate are not simply a product of Christian missionary history, however: as shown in more detail below, African readers are often trained from birth to extrapolate socially relevant meanings from the figurative folktales and dilemma tales narrated by *griots* and senior family members.

With these historical biases in view, several literary scholars have pointed out that the novel as a genre in Africa is inextricable from the print cultures generated by colonialism.[9] Some critics go so far as to label the novel an 'alien' import to the continent.[10] Of all the literary genres to circulate around Africa today, the novel has the clearest European ancestry and, as a consequence, remains ideologically the most problematic for scholars. In Simon Gikandi's words, African 'novelists could not fall back on precolonial forms of writing; novelists in search of an epistemological or formal breakthrough had nowhere to turn except to the European novel itself'.[11]

Imported to Africa in the late nineteenth century—a time when representations of the continent were often filled with racist stereotypes and colonial prejudice—the novel does not exist in an aesthetic realm divorced from the exercise of power. As Achebe wrote in his famous essay on racism in Joseph Conrad's *Heart of Darkness* (1902), 'white racism against Africa is such a normal way of thinking that its manifestations go completely unremarked' by literary scholars.[12] The Kenyan author, Ngugi wa Thiong'o, agrees: commenting on the literate African's sense of 'colonial alienation', he describes how 'Europe was always the centre of the universe' in the literature, geography, and history taught in colonial African classrooms.[13] In choosing to write fiction above other literary genres, African novelists such as Achebe and Ngugi therefore enter into tense, potentially fraught, relationships with colonial history.

According to some literary scholars, the novel did not find a generically recognizable, stable form in Africa until the 1950s and 1960s when it came of age in anti-colonial and nationalist modes: these modes, however, did not give rise to 'radical breakthroughs' or an abandonment of colonial literary paradigms.[14] This coming of age is evidenced by novels such as Ayi Kwei Armah's *The Beautyful Ones are Not Yet Born* (1968), Yambo Ouologuem's *Bound to Violence* (1968), and, from a later period, Dambudzo Marechera's short-story cycle *House of Hunger* (1978), all of which share a common concern for urban poverty, slum life, sexuality, political violence, and corruption in the postcolonial city. An aesthetic of excess can be found in these texts, which show a preoccupation with dirt, odours, vermin, disease, and bodily excretions. Taken together, these diverse urban novels illustrate the disengagement of African fiction from the European missionary and colonial encounter.

In a recent manifestation of this current, in South Africa since the early 1990s novels focusing on whiteness have challenged the authority of Afrikaner history with images of incest, bodily disintegration, rape, and dirt in white households. In a similar manner to Armah's and Marechera's work, Afrikaans-language novels such as Marlene van Niekerk's *Triomf* (1994; translated into English in 1999) and Mark Behr's *Die Reuk van Appels* (1993; published the same year in English as *The Smell of Apples*) use sexual and scatological material to expose the hypocrisy of a regime whose self-justification revolved around a racist insistence on white people's physical and moral superiority to blacks. These path-breaking novels bring incest to the fore of debates about whiteness in post-Apartheid South Africa, exposing the concept of ethnic purity as an idea that stems from abusive and violent relations.

These examples demonstrate that one cannot simply dismiss colonial genres such as the novel as alien imports to Africa. To do so ignores the diversity of vernacular and regional literary cultures on the continent, and fails to include the circulation of Arabic texts in North Africa and Amharic texts in Ethiopia. Textual objects always articulate with social contexts. As Roger Chartier insists in his work on the history of reading in

Europe, neither meaning nor value is inherent in a printed object; rather, 'the same texts can be differently apprehended, manipulated, and comprehended' by readers situated in different material and historical contexts.[15] Similarly, African novelists and readers rework and transform the genres they encounter, whether these genres appear to be 'traditional' and local, or new and 'foreign'. Genres might contain elements that supposedly originated in Europe and America—such as literary realism—but they are not necessarily transmitted in European languages or even via the printed page.

In an essay on cultural translation, Gikandi insists that 'we need...to question the assumption that the colonial situation simply manufactured colonial subjects, and to consider, instead, how colonial subjects also manufactured their own identities, processes, and versions of the colonial process'.[16] While largely persuasive, the 'coming-of-age' story about the African novel is therefore too teleological in that it ignores the polymorphous narrative genres which preceded the emergence of the novels identified as mature by critics, and it neglects the ways in which colonial subjects 'manufactured their own identities'. From the outset, if African creative writers made use of genres inherited from Europe, they also extended those genres far beyond their established limits, working within and also beyond colonial cultural histories. In a literary work published in, say, the 1880s or the 1920s, the 'present' that is portrayed—and the representation of the past—contributes to our understanding of the social and cultural currents with which authors engage, and from which they emerge. Whether fictional or non-fictional, African literatures carry their moment of publication on their sleeves, as it were.

Alongside a discussion of the content of literatures, in examining evidence such as missionary and colonial uses of print, or a writer's choice of publisher, we can find out about the ways in which African authors participate in and produce political discourses about their present moment. From this perspective, African literatures can be regarded as a powerful 'sign of the times', giving us an entry point to debates, categories, ideas, and reactions from periods that have informed but are no longer necessarily relevant to contemporary themes in historiography and literary study. Sensitivity towards a book's material and cultural contexts can therefore reveal a great deal about the history of ideas and the development of debates within the texts under scrutiny.

CONSIDERATION OF CONTENT AND THEMES

A second mode of historical appreciation is to study how works of literature engage with time through the production of characters with historical consciousness and through the thematization of the past. Ben Okri's *The Famished Road* (1991) and Chenjerai Hove's *Bones* (1988) exemplify the latter process, focusing, respectively, upon the countdown to Nigeria's independence and the role of women in Zimbabwe's liberation struggle. From an earlier period, Thomas Mofolo's Sotho-language novel, *Chaka* (1925) and Sol Plaatje's English-language *Mhudi* (1930) bring to life pivotal moments in South

Africa's history and, in the process, establish a tradition of South African historical war fiction inherited by novelists such as Zakes Mda (*Heart of Redness*, 2000).

Always anachronistic and always revisionary because of their inescapable immersion in the author's own world, these works nevertheless convey detailed, intimate, and carefully researched accounts of the past. Crucially, these historical narratives ask how the present might have been different if history had been otherwise. Wole Soyinka's best-known play, *Death and the King's Horseman* (1960), exemplifies this genre, as does the work of his fellow Yoruba playwrights Ola Rotimi (*Kurunmi: An Historical Tragedy*, 1971) and Femi Osofisan (*The Chattering and the Song*, 1977). Similarly, many Francophone African novelists write about the Islamic faith and postcolonial quests for Islamic identity, asking how the present might have been otherwise. Chiekh Hamidou Kane's seminal novel about the quest for Islamic identity, *L'Aventure ambiguë* (1961; translated as *Ambiguous Adventure*,1963) is caught up in the histories of French colonialism in West Africa and Quranic education: unlike anti-colonial novels such as *Things Fall Apart*, the protagonist's identity and future direction are rendered 'ambiguous' by both cultural histories.

The emphasis on alternative historical pathways is particularly common in African feminist creative writing, as well as in literary projects which seek to recreate or to 'retrieve' voices that have been lost or silenced in the official archives.[17] The prominence of black South African authors as historical novelists is hardly surprising in this context, given the ways in which Apartheid misrepresented and demeaned 'tribal' cultures and histories. The authors of historical stories deliberately ignore the time of literary production and reimagine history as lived through the individual experiences of their protagonists. Carrying the weight of what happened next, 'what ifs' are inserted into familiar accounts of the past; in the process, the provisional status of the present is highlighted and the tense used for historical narration is destabilized.

The 'production of historical consciousness' is rather more difficult to identify than the thematization of history in African literatures, for it includes both texts which are not overtly historical in subject matter and those that experiment with literary realism. Historical consciousness here refers to the ways in which authors problematize the representation of time and memory in their narratives, as well as a fictional character's reflexive sense of being in time. In Ngugi's *The River Between* (1965), for example, the author juxtaposes a chronological model of narration (the realist 'what happened next' format) with an epic, cyclical model of time in which ancient prophecy and destiny fulfilment take precedence over linearity. The protagonist Waiyaki finds himself caught up in and finally caught out by these two contrasting modes of thinking about time: is he the 'black messiah' prophesied by the ancestors and eagerly awaited by Christian converts, or is he an ordinary man in the here-and-now, with a duty to lead his community out of their cycle of mutual distrust? In depicting Waiyaki's failure of leadership and passive overinvestment in the myth of the messiah, Ngugi politicizes linearity itself and asks us to think about the 'truths' and temporalities carried by particular narrative forms. Loyal to his own version of Marxist principles, he insists on the necessity for people to step into history as decisive agents of their own destinies and not to wait passively to be rescued by divinely sanctioned leaders, the source of whose authority is without time or place.

Other African Marxists also express scepticism towards mythological and cyclical ways of representing time in literature. In this respect, the Nobel prize-winning author Wole Soyinka has been the target of especially virulent criticism by Marxist scholars who feel that his life-long promotion of African traditional values does not avoid the pitfalls of nativism. To his critics, Soyinka's writing produces a static, essentialist vision of African cultures, sapping history of the human agency which, for Marxists, moulds future possibilities from the status quo.[18] Put bluntly by one of his most outspoken critics, Chidi Amuta: 'The religious practices and beliefs which have been used [by Soyinka] to characterize the African world view belong to an advanced neolithic phase in the development of human societies', and those who promote such a vision manifest a 'non-rational' and 'pre-scientific' mentality.[19] Judged from this troublesome (and itself essentialist) evolutionary perspective, if Soyinka hopes to criticize neo-colonialism through his representation of non-colonized African traditions in his work, the model he produces serves only to give African audiences an escapist, mystical view of life which denies their human agency and lacks historical dynamism.[20]

Soyinka has a commitment to the rejuvenation and modernization of Yoruba mythologies, rituals, deities, and ways of thinking about time, especially in poems such as 'Idanre' (1967) and plays such as *Death and the King's Horseman* and *A Dance of the Forests* (1963). He is a writer, intellectual, and political activist who rejects 'imported' discourses, temporalities, and narrative forms—including Marxism—in favour of indigenous African models for the interpretation of African cultures.[21] 'Does the African critic', Soyinka asks in an attack on his detractors, 'take the trouble to find out the sensibility of the Kilimanjaro goatherd towards his mountains, or does he simply ingest these claims into the language of his own class myths?'[22]

The desire of intellectuals such as Soyinka to accommodate 'precolonial' beliefs and timescales has generated some distinctive literary forms since the 1940s. In Senegal in the 1950s and 1960s, the poet-president Léopold Senghor produced a theory of 'African socialism' which combined key features of his philosophy and poetry of *négritude* with the promotion of 'Western technology' and 'universal civilization'.[23] Much of this was conveyed through poetry, both Senghor's own and that of his fellow *négritude* poets Aimé Césaire, Léon Damas, and Birago Diop. As president of Senegal from 1960 to 1980, Senghor's investment in the notion of a shared African identity allowed him to think beyond the limits of the postcolonial nation-state and to promote his political and cultural model for the entire continent.

Other African writers draw attention to the production of historical consciousness in literature by deploying 'oral' narrators as framing devices, or by staging the difficulties of representing the past without bias. Several stories in Bessie Head's *The Collector of Treasures, and Other Botswana Village Tales* (1977) highlight the social effects of the masculine ownership of oral historical genres. In the opening tale, 'The Deep River: A Story of Ancient Tribal Migration', Head explores the ways in which male oral historians in her village trivialize companionate romantic love in their interpretations of the past, preferring instead to blame the politically disruptive power of women for the break-up of the clan.[24] In a less partisan vein, Ama Ata Aidoo (*No Sweetness Here,* 1970) and Kofi Anyidoho (*A Harvest of Dreams,* 1985, and *Ancestral Logic and Caribbean Blues,* 1993) make use of oral genres and narrators in their work in order to draw attention to the socially positioned nature of narration, both on and off the printed page.

One of the richest literary sites for the production of historical consciousness can be found in contemporary South African fiction. The recent upsurge in experimental and non-realist writing presents us with narratives which confront—often in the form of trauma—the country's history of institutionalized racial violence. This trajectory of South African literature probes the problem of how to represent the past in language. In the wake of Apartheid, numerous authors, from Zoe Wicomb to Achmat Dangor and Antjie Krog, have employed experimental, fragmented narrative forms to convey the impossibility of simply recounting their country's history in plain language and linear fashion through coherent, self-aware subjects.[25] How can creative writers fully represent the traumatic effects of South African history on individual lives, they ask, in fragmented, polygeneric texts which, at a structural level, repeatedly perform the shattering of identity and the failure of coherence.

With several major exceptions, literature under Apartheid represented the cultural wing of the political struggle, 'bearing witness' to atrocities, speaking out against racial hatred, making visible the necessity for armed resistance, and imagining racial emancipation. (Some popular literature disengaged from the political sphere in favour of spectacle and entertainment, including Gibson Kente's township melodramas and the steamy romances produced by Afrikaans-language authors for white female readerships.) From Peter Abrahams's *Mine Boy* (1946) to Athol Fugard's *Sizwe Bansi is Dead* (1974) and the 'theatre for development' projects of the 1980s, South African literature under Apartheid summoned readers into urgent and immediate political relationships, insisting on the power of present audiences to shape future society.[26] With the exception of magazines such as *Drum* in the 1950s and *Staffrider* in the 1970s and 1980s, however, the imprisonment or banishment of politically oppositional writers combined with rigid state control of the media to inhibit the emergence of local South African literatures. Large numbers of the country's writers made their calls to arms from exile, for unlike the dynamic world of literary production in other parts of Africa, the censorious regime prevented the emergence of indigenous publishers and printing presses.

In stark contrast to the literatures of protest and self-assertion from preceding decades, post-Apartheid authors such as Wicomb, Dangor, and Krog dwell upon the inexpressible and unrepresentable aspects of history. They replace empirical (or 'representable') history with one of trauma, traced through images of people screaming, of nervous breakdown, of tortured, raped, silenced, and abject bodies. (Bessie Head's 1973 novel *A Question of Power* can be regarded as a precursor to this non-realist mode of writing about South Africa.) In this way, the genres through which history is articulated, as well as the ideals of truth and reconciliation which accompany the open airing of stories in post-Apartheid South Africa, are interrogated and problematized by contemporary authors. As with Ngugi's juxtaposition of temporalities in *The River Between,* these authors' refusal to adhere to linear or realist narrative forms draws attention to the implications and effects of different styles of narrating the past. In the process, readers are forced to become self-conscious about the form, as well as the content, of historical narration.

CONSIDERATION OF READERSHIPS

If the times and places of literary production significantly affect a text's overall meaning, then a historically sensitive approach to African literatures must also include a consideration of the gaps—historical and geographical—which separate literary works from their audiences. No matter how permanent a printed text appears to be as a material object, literary themes and debates are mobile because readers have histories and cultural contexts which influence the ways they interpret works of literature. The critical reception of canonical texts, such as Plaatje's *Mhudi,* Achebe's *Things Fall Apart,* or Ngugi's *Petals of Blood* (1977), changes considerably over time and in different locations.

A dramatic example of this mobility in readers' responses is Amos Tutuola's novel, *The Palm-Wine Drinkard* (1956), published in London by Faber & Faber. The novel was received with some embarrassment by Nigerian critics in the 1950s and 1960s for its seemingly incorrect use of English, yet it was simultaneously celebrated by British and American critics for the African 'authenticity' of its language.[27] *The Palm-Wine Drinkard* underwent a renaissance in the late twentieth century as scholars started to trace alternative African literary histories through Tutuola's work: indeed, recent critics see in it the beginnings of an avant-garde trajectory of African writing that is unconcerned with the grand narratives of nationalism, colonialism, and cultural identity that have dominated realist African writing since the publication of *Things Fall Apart.*[28] The example of *The Palm-Wine Drinkard* reveals the manner in which reader responses echo transformations in debates about African cultures and postcolonial literatures, shifting with the times to reflect contemporary preoccupations.

Literature cannot be separated from current social debates in many parts of Africa. Locally situated readers often interpret literary material by connecting it with immediate concerns, using familiar texts in order to discuss moral dilemmas or social problems.[29] Such a mode of reading has its ancestry in oral narratives (as well as in the missionary modes of reading discussed above), where storytellers are often expected to embellish familiar texts and apply socially relevant morals at the end. Aware of these expectations, the Swahili writer Shaaban Robert has published many collections of poetry which derive directly from didactic folktale currents.[30]

Often, the mark of a good storyteller in Africa is his or her ability to update and improvise material, to take well-known tales and characters and add new details, to engage listeners and encourage them to identify, situate, and apply the lessons and dilemmas contained within the story. These interpretative processes are not confined to locally produced and oral literatures. Since the colonial period, readers have shown an aptitude for 'resettling' European literatures in African contexts. In the Gold Coast in the early twentieth century, Charles Dickens was a particular favourite because his novels furnished local readers with a vibrant cast-list of larger-than-life characters who could be unfastened from the surrounding narrative and used to develop interpretations of colonial society. So popular was Dickens in colonial Accra that the pseudonymous author (actually, multiple authors) of the 'Women's Corner' column in the *Times of West Africa*, Marjorie Mensah, declared his writing to be 'unsurpassed in the history of English literature'.[31]

Part of the reason that Dickens permeated African literary cultures so rapidly and successfully is that his novels were regularly rewritten by colonial educators, published as abridged versions to suit different grades at school. Thus students in Standard Two would first encounter Dickens through a simplified version of *A Tale of Two Cities*, *The Pickwick Papers*, or *Oliver Twist*. The same story would appear again in Standards Four and Six, extending and stretching the earlier encountered version with more ambitious vocabularies while remaining condensed in comparison with the original text. Given that Dickens originally wrote his novels for serialization in journals, it is possible that his work was peculiarly open to this process of adaptation and condensation into shorter texts for circulation outside the world of the book. Just as Dickens produced episodic scenes for each instalment, so his novels, in turn, were 'unravelled' by colonial educationists and resettled by African readers.[32]

Throughout Africa, local readers continue to import their own interpretative styles and creative protocols into international and local literatures.[33] In discussing African literatures, it is therefore vital to consider the 'currency' of literary reception alongside the ways in which African authors engage with the present and the past inside the pages of their publications.

THE HISTORICITY OF ORAL LITERATURES IN RELATION TO PRINTED TEXTS

Literary activity in Africa encompasses an enormous array of genres, styles, and languages, including vernacular praise songs, funeral dirges, oral epics, folktales, abuse songs, religious pamphlets, popular novels, printed autobiographies, hymns and testimonials, political protest poems written to be performed, self-help booklets, novels in international languages, poetry, and plays. Each genre carries its own entanglement with the past and the present alongside distinct conceptions of authorship and audience. As indicated by genres such as abuse songs or testimonials, many forms of African literature are inextricable from politics and society. 'Art for art's sake' is not an aesthetic that is commonly adhered to, either by African authors or by their audiences, a point which is forcibly made by the Kenyan author and intellectual, Ali

Mazrui, in his novel about the role of art in the Biafran war, *The Trial of Christopher Okigbo* (1971).

In extreme circumstances, some literary practitioners have found themselves firmly and fatally harnessed to political bandwagons. In the latter parts of their presidencies, for example, both Kwame Nkrumah in Ghana and Ahmed Sékou Touré in Guinea made use of literary genres in order to produce visions of 'authentic' and 'traditional' precolonial Africa which justified their increasingly authoritarian regimes. In the view of Gikandi, their 'political leadership cult was performed through the invocation of a mythical past, which was, at the same time, the African mask for Eurocentric ideas'.[34]

What is intriguing about both leaders' self-representation is the manner in which they employed oral praise poets, or *griots*, in the manner of wealthy chiefs and patrons of old, cleverly gaining public recognition through their adoption of established figures and formulae. Using song, the two men's public poets declared the leaders' authority to crowds and viewers, masking the leaders' excesses, soothing their neuroses, and explaining away their violence towards political opponents.[35] Indeed, one of the smears on the political record-card of Frantz Fanon is his praise for Sekou Touré. By 1969, the Guinean president had grown so paranoid about the words (not deeds) of his official praise-poet, Keita Fodeba, that he had Fodeba executed, an action that has generated a forceful critical debate about the degree of Fanon's—and Marxism's—complicity with this West African dictatorship.[36] These and other leaders' uses of oral narrators at public occasions demonstrates the vitality and public importance of oral literary genres in Africa and the ongoing importance of oral history in establishing (or destroying) the names of 'big men' in Africa.[37]

If these examples imply a rigid division between objective or fixed printed literatures and subjective or biased oral literatures, however, it must be remembered that paper archives are no more politically neutral or historically objective than orally transmitted narratives. Oral forms may lack fixity for the manner in which they combine formulae with the performer's interpretive bias, but printed texts are also flexible and temporal, pulsing with historicity in a similar manner to oral genres. As Aileen Julien argues in her ground-breaking study, *African Novels and the Question of Orality* (1992)—and as suggested above in relation to shifts in the critical reception of texts—books and manuscripts do not remain static as the years pass by, in spite of the visual permanence of print on a page.

Furthermore, oral texts are not uncontrollably 'open' to transformations or modifications by individual narrators such as the *jeli,* or *griots*, of the Mande peoples of West Africa. Just as printed literatures follow generic rules and conventions, oral texts also have formulae and rules for transmission. Oral African literatures follow nuanced, sometimes strict, aesthetic codes. The narrators of the *Sunjata* epic, recorded and transcribed by Gordon Innes in the late 1960s and early 1970s, travelled widely through Mandinka-speaking territories, embellishing their versions of the historical epic about thirteenth-century Mali with details and verbal flourishes learnt from other *griots*.[38] Innes locates at least three separate levels of discourse in performances of the epic: first, the 'speech mode', where words are freely chosen and delivered in an ordinary voice;

secondly, the 'recitation mode', in which praises or observations are delivered using fixed phrases and formulae passed down through the generations; and thirdly, the 'song mode', in which fixed sets of songs are performed.[39] The 'recitation mode' is illustrated by the fact that narrators of the *Sunjata* epic include terms and historical references which are too archaic even for themselves to comprehend or translate. In this way, an ancient archive is preserved within a form that allows for embellishment and creativity.

Many hundreds of miles away from these Mande *griots*, in Yoruba areas of Nigeria, the *babalawo*—priests and diviners trained in specialist oral genres—also oscillate between formulaic phrases and innovative discourses of their own creation. As with printed texts, then, fixed words and formulae often have an important place alongside individualistic creative embellishment by the oral historian or performer; and, in all of these cases, authorship and audience should be regarded as collaborative and socially engaged, rather than as singular and solitary.[40]

Throughout the continent, oral genres are mobilized within printed texts, reworked by authors for political, aesthetic, or moral ends. The Tunisian feminist author, Fatima Mernissi, frequently makes use of North African folktales to demonstrate the cleverness and subversive audacity of women.[41] Similarly, in his Gikuyu-language novel, *Devil on the Cross* (1982), Ngugi makes use of the *marimu* (ogre) from local folktales in order to cast negative judgements on postcolonial Kenyan politicians and businessmen. Other authors, including Tutuola and his Booker Prize-winning protégé, Ben Okri, play with popular folktales, utilizing familiar folk characters in ways that work against the moral framework of the tales from which they are borrowed. Tutuola in particular unravels the morals of his borrowed tales by refusing to engage with or apply closure at the end.[42]

Alongside this insertion of local oral sources into printed materials, several African authors have experimented with the 'transliteration' of African languages into European-language texts, transplanting local grammars and genres into European languages, producing inventive results that often challenge the 'host' languages and cause critical controversy. A prize-winning example of this vernacularization of European languages is *En attendant le vote des bêtes sauvages* (1998; translated in 2003 as *Waiting for the Wild Beasts to Vote*) by Ivorian author Ahmadou Kourouma. As with his earlier novels, Kourouma fills this narrative with the voices of local interpreters and storytellers who comment, often comically, on the vulgarity and corruption of barely fictionalized postcolonial despots. Nigerian author Gabriel Okara's *The Voice* (1964) achieves a similar, often intensely comic effect, in its transliteration from Ijaw syntax into English.

In regions where 'oral literatures' circulate widely with their own complex histories of transmission and reception, literary genres remain a great deal more dynamic than in book-dominated cultures. Efua Sutherland's play *The Marriage of Anansewa* (1967) is a particularly successful example of a writer's experimentation with oral genres. Filled with song and dance, written to be performed, the play revels in the outrageous behaviour and cunning of the Akan folktale hero, Mr Kwaku Ananse, as he manipulates four wealthy chiefs who wish to marry his daughter, exposing the faults in the marriage payment system at the same time as comically enriching himself. Alongside its folktale content and themes, and its gentle social criticism of Ghanaian marriage practices,

The Marriage of Anansewa involves a full range of performance modes drawn from Akan traditional theatre, from mime to music and dance.[43]

Sutherland insists upon audience participation in the play by scripting in an active, visible narrator who addresses the audience and the cast. 'Ananse is lying', the Storyteller announces to the audience in Act 4, adding, 'You were here, weren't you, when Ananse started drilling his daughter, Anansewa, in pretending dead?'[44] At other points in the play, the Storyteller and the Property Man re-enact Ananse's actions in order to remind the audience—from a critical distance—of what has gone before. As Sutherland writes in the introduction to her play, the Akan storyteller has 'a conventional right to know everything' and 'a right to be personally involved in the action'.[45] In this way, the suspension of disbelief, so common to European theatre, is prevented, especially when the Property Man distributes objects to the cast on-stage, drawing attention to their status as actors.

Examples such as this reveal the dynamic status of anonymously authored folktales and their power to be updated in ways that absorb contemporary moods, opinions, and representations. Printed African literatures are characterized by a similar versatility, often combining oral and published materials, fictional and factual narratives, local and transnational influences, and conventional and experimental styles.[46] For this reason, African literatures cannot simply be classified according to the genres commonly used in European literary criticism, where poetry, drama, prose fiction, and non-fiction have widely recognizable styles, subgenres, and historical trajectories, and where printed materials are central to the identification and study of literary histories.

Conclusion

Three key points arise from the issues examined in this chapter. First, African literatures adopt many shapes and styles, but books and pamphlets have a history rooted in missionary and colonial encounters, and are bound up with postcolonial debates about politics, urbanization, gender, migration, and cultural difference. Printed African literatures are part of and products of a history of conflicted cultural encounters. Second, literatures give us access to intimate encounters with historically situated subjects. Whether produced in the 1880s, the 1930s, the 1960s, or the present, creative writing offers snapshots of contemporary life, including people's hopes and dreams for the future. Each instance of African literature is also part of an *emergent history*. It thus represents a uniquely biased—because uniquely engaged and intimate—type of historical discourse.

Third, unlike the archives and other official sources of information for historians, African creative writing frequently offers us full and integral worlds which are filled with unrealized social ideals and alternatives to the status quo. As historians, what we find in African literatures is the imagination *in* history and the imagination *as* history. History, in African literatures, is not therefore a term that applies simply to narratives which engage with the past. Never simply a historical 'source', these texts supply us with interpretations of and perspectives on the continent's colonial and postcolonial history. In particular, African literatures personalize history, inserting characters, voices, and opinions into specific times and places. As articulations of time, as much as articulations about the past, the continent's diverse literatures possess a unique historicity, fleshing out the subjective realm—that is, the very space that tends to be lost to scholars in the archives.

Notes

1. Emmanuel Eze, *On Reason: Rationality in a World of Cultural Conflict and Racism* (Durham, NC: Duke University Press, 1998), 195.

2. Tim White, 'The Lovedale Press during the Directorship of R. H. W. Shepherd, 1930–1955', *English in Africa*, 19/2 (1992); Gareth Griffiths, *African Literatures in English: East and West* (Harlow: Longman, 2000); Isabel Hofmeyr, *The Portable Bunyan: A Transnational History of* The Pilgrim's Progress (Princeton: PUP, 2004); Stephanie Newell, *Literary Culture in Colonial Ghana* (Manchester: MUP, 2002).

3. See Robert Darnton, 'Literary Surveillance in the British Raj: The Contradictions of British Imperialism', *Book History*, 4 (2001).

4. Lady Clifford, 'Prize Essay Competition', *Gold Coast Nation*, 21–28 May 1914, 607–8.

5. Lady Clifford, 'Prize Essay Competition', *Gold Coast Nation*, 8 June 1918, 4–5.

6. Uchi Nwani, *The Challenge of Marriage* (Agbor, Bendel State: Central Books, 1988); Joshua Adjabeng, *Sex, Friendship and Marriage* (Accra: Olive Publications and Pentecost Press, 1991); Emmanuel Eni, *Delivered from the Powers of Darkness* (Ibadan: Scripture Union, 1987).

7. See Evan Mwangi, 'AIDS/HIV', in Simon Gikandi and Evan Mwangi, *The Columbia Guide to East African Writing in English since 1945* (New York: Columbia University Press, 2007), 23–5; see also Agnes Muriungi, ' "Chira" and HIV/AIDS: The (Re)Construction of Sexual Moralities in Popular Fiction', in James Ogude and Joyce Nyairo, eds, *Urban Legends, Colonial Myths: Popular Culture and Literature in East Africa* (Trenton, NJ: Africa World Press, 2007).

8. See Esther de Bruijn, ' "What's Love" in an Interconnected World? Ghanaian Market Literature for Youth Responds 1', *Journal of Commonwealth Literature*, 43 (2008).

9. Simon Gikandi, 'Novel', in Simon Gikandi, ed., *Encyclopedia of African Literature* (London: Routledge, 2003).

10. J. Roger Kurtz, *Urban Obsessions, Urban Fears: The Postcolonial Kenyan Novel* (Trenton, NJ: Africa World Press, 1998), 13–14; see also Emmanuel Obiechina, *Culture, Tradition and Society in the West African Novel* (Cambridge: CUP, 1975); Adrian Roscoe, *Mother is Gold* (Cambridge: CUP, 1971).

11. Gikandi, 'Novel', 390.

12. Chinua Achebe, 'An Image of Africa: Racism in Conrad's Heart of Darkness', in *Hopes and Impediments: Selected Essays, 1965–1987* (London: Heinemann, 1988), 8.

13. Ngugi wa Thiong'o, *Decolonising the Mind: The Politics of Language in African Literature* (London: James Currey, 1981), 17.

14. Gikandi, 'Novel', 389–90.

15. Roger Chartier, *The Order of Books* (Stanford, Calif.: Stanford University Press, 1994), 8.

16. Simon Gikandi, 'Cultural Translation and the African Self: A (Post)Colonial Case Study', *Interventions*, 3/3 (2001), 358.

17. See Lauretta Ngcobo, *And They Didn't Die* (New York: Feminist Press at CUNY, 1999); Yvonne Vera, *Butterfly Burning* (Harare: Baobab, 1998); Buchi Emecheta, *The Joys of Motherhood* (London: Heinemann, 1979).

18. Geoffrey Hunt, 'Two African Aesthetics: Soyinka vs. Cabral', in Georg M. Gugelberger, ed., *Marxism and African Literature* (London: James Currey, 1985).

19. Chidi Amuta, *The Theory of African Literature* (London: Zed, 1989), 39–41.

20. Amuta, *Theory of African Literature*, 39–41; Hunt, 'Two African Aesthetics'.

21. Wole Soyinka, *Myth, Ritual and the African World* (Cambridge: CUP, 1976; 2nd edn, 1992), 48; see also Jane Wilkinson, 'Conversations with Wole Soyinka', in Jane Wilkinson, ed., *Talking with African Writers* (London: James Currey, 1992).

22. Wole Soyinka, *Art, Dialogue and Outrage: Essays on Literature and Culture* (New York: Pantheon, 1982; 2nd edn, 1993), 109.

23. Léopold Sédar Senghor, *Négritude et humanisme (Negritude and Humanism)* (Paris: Éditions du Seuil, 1964).

24. Bessie Head, *The Collector of Treasures and other Botswana Village Tales* (Oxford: Heinemann, 1977).

25. Zoe Wicomb, *David's Story* (New York: Feminist Press at CUNY, 2001); Achmat Dangor, *Bitter Fruit* (Cape Town: Kwela Books, 2001); Antjie Krog, *Country of my Skull* (London: Vintage, 1998).

26. Zakes Mda, *When People Play People* (London: Zed, 1993); see also Wally Serote, Sipho Sepamla, and the other black consciousness poets who emerged in the 1970s; for autobiographical writing, see Es'kia Mphahlele, *Down Second Avenue* (London: Faber, 1959) and Bloke Modisane, *Blame Me on History* (London: Thames & Hudson, 1963).

27. See Bernth Lindfors, ed., *Critical Perspectives on Amos Tutuola* (Washington, DC: Three Continents Press, 1975).

28. Achille Mbembe, 'Life, Sovereignty, and Terror in the Fiction of Amos Tutuola', *Research in African Literatures*, 34/4 (Winter 2003); Sarah Nuttall, 'Reading, Recognition and the Postcolonial', *Interventions*, 3/3 (Nov. 2001).

29. See Stephanie Newell, *Ghanaian Popular Fiction: 'Thrilling Discoveries in Conjugal Life'* (Oxford: James Currey, 2000).

30. Shaaban Robert, *Utenzi wa Vita Vya Uhuru (The Epic of the Struggle for Independence)* (Arusha: Eastern African Publications, 1978 [1961]); *Pambo ya Lugha (A Question of Language; or The Adornment of Language)* (Nairobi: OUP, 1966).

31. Marjorie Mensah, 'Women's Corner', *Times of West Africa*, 19 Feb. 1932, 2.

32. See Newell, *Ghanaian Popular Fiction*.

33. James Ogude and Joyce Nyairo, eds, *Urban Legends, Colonial Myths: Popular Culture and Literature in East Africa* (Trenton, NJ: Africa World Press, 2007).

34. Simon Gikandi, 'Theory, Literature and Moral Considerations', *Research in African Literatures*, 32/4 (2001), 8.

35. Kwesi Yankah, 'Creativity and Traditional Rhetoric: Nkrumah's Personal Poet and his Son', in Ernest Emenyonu, ed., *Literature and National Consciousness* (Ibadan: Heinemann Educational Books, 1989), 78–88; Gikandi, 'Theory, Literature, and Moral Considerations'.

36. Christopher Miller, *Theories of Africans: Francophone Literature and Anthropology in Africa* (Chicago: Chicago University Press, 1990), 50–64; Gikandi, 'Theory, Literature, and Moral Considerations'.

37. See Achille Mbembe, *On the Postcolony* (Berkeley, Calif.: California University Press, 2001); Leroy Vail and Landeg White, *Power and the Praise Poem: Southern African Voices in History* (Charlottesville, Va.: University Press of Virginia, 1991).

38. Gordon Innes, *Sunjata: Three Mandinka Versions* (London: School of Oriental and African Studies, 1974), republ. as Bamba Suso and Banna Kanute, *Sunjata* (London: Penguin, 1999).

39. Suso and Kanute, *Sunjata*, 15–16; see too Ralph A. Austen, ed., *In Search of Sunjata: The Mande Oral Epic as History, Literature and Performance* (Bloomington, Ind.: Indiana University Press, 1999); Alain Ricard, *The Languages and Literatures of Africa* (Oxford: James Currey, 2004).

40. Karin Barber, *I Could Speak Until Tomorrow: Oriki, Women and the Past in a Yoruba Town* (Edinburgh: EUP, 1991); Ricard, *Languages and Literatures of Africa*.

41. See e.g. Fatima Mernissi, 'Who's Cleverer, Man or Woman', in Margot Badran and Miriam Cooke, eds, *Opening the Gates: An Anthology of Arab Feminist Writing* (Bloomington, Ind.: Indiana University Press, 2004), 317–21.

42. See Ato Quayson, *Strategic Transformations in Nigerian Writing* (Oxford: James Currey, 1997); Brenda Cooper, *Magical Realism in West African Fiction* (London: Routledge, 1994).

43. Pietro Deandrea, *Fertile Crossings: Metamorphoses of Genre in Anglophone West African Literature* (Amsterdam: Rodopi, 2002), 186–94.

44. Efua Sutherland, *The Marriage of Anansewa and Other Plays* (Harlow: Longman, 1989 [1976]), 68.

45. Sutherland, *Marriage of Anansewa*, 4.

46. See Camara Laye, *The Guardian of the Word* (London: Vintage, 1978).

Bibliography

Andrzejewski, B. W., S. Pilaszewicz, and W. Tyloch, eds, *Literatures in African Languages: Theoretical Issues and Sample Surveys* (Cambridge: CUP, 2010).

Bertoncini-Zubkova, Elema, M. D. Gromov, and S. A. M. Khamis, *Outline of Swahili Literature: Prose, Fiction and Drama* (Leiden: Brill, 2008).

Gikandi, Simon, ed., *Encyclopedia of African Literature* (London: Routledge, 2003).

Julien, Aileen, *African Novels and the Question of Orality* (Bloomington, Ind.: Indiana University Press, 1992).

Korang, Kweku Larbi, *Writing Ghana, Imagining Africa: Nation and African Modernity* (New York: Rochester University Press, 2004).

Mehrez, Samia, *Egyptian Writers between History and Fiction: Essays on Naguib Mahfouz, Sonallah Ibrahim, and Gamal Al-Ghitani* (Cairo: American University in Cairo Press, 2nd edn, 2005).

Miller, Christopher, *Nationalists and Nomads: Essays on Francophone African Literature and Culture* (Chicago: University of Chicago Press, 2nd edn, 1999).

Mirmotahari, Emad, *Islam in the Eastern African Novel (Literatures and Cultures of the Islamic World)* (Basingstoke: Palgrave Macmillan, 2011).

Newell, Stephanie, *Ghanaian Popular Fiction: 'Thrilling Discoveries in Conjugal Life and Other Tales'* (Oxford: James Currey, 2000).

Ogude, James, and Joyce Nyairo, eds, *Urban Legends, Colonial Myths: Popular Culture and Literature in East Africa* (Trenton, NJ: Africa World Press, 2007).

Peek, Philip M., and Kwesi Yankah, *African Folklore: An Encyclopedia* (New York: Routledge, 2004).

Ricard, Alain, *The Languages and Literatures of Africa* (Oxford: James Currey, 2004).

Thomas, Dominic, *Nation-Building, Propaganda and Literature in Francophone Africa* (Bloomington, Ind.: Indiana University Press, 2002).

CHAPTER 26

··

COMMUNICATIONS AND MEDIA IN AFRICAN HISTORY

··

JAMES R. BRENNAN

THE media present a paradoxical topic for historians of Africa. Unlike the mechanisms of state power or resource allocation, the media seem initially transparent, fixed in speech, text, or image. Yet the media's surrounding systems of production and transmission are deviously complicated amalgams of individual agency of writers and artists, profit-minded firms, and control-minded authorities, all of which work across multiple levels of local, regional, and international information and technology. Moreover, changes in Africa's media accelerate with dizzying speed as one approaches the present. The developments of the printing press, telegraph, film, radio, television, and internet demonstrate that Africa's media landscape is, at least in one sense, just one of several sites in which global technologies have accelerated the transmission of information, creating new communities while challenging the authority of older ones. Yet African cultures and historical experiences have also shaped the form and content of the continent's media. The persistence of oral forms of communication and the African appropriation of global information and technologies have been foci of the best literature on African media. This chapter surveys this historiographical focus, while also demonstrating that a fuller view of the media's multiple political economies remains a central task for future historical research in the field of African media.

The chapter is organized around the chronological progression of global media technologies. The most arresting feature of communications in the modern era is the increasing annihilation of space and time through successive revolutions in information technologies. Telecommunications networks in particular carry uniquely expansive qualities. The number of possible connections increases as the square of the number of customers, while each network's value increases with the number of users; the net effect of this has been the rapid reduction in user costs of each subsequent telecommunications technology.[1] The European conquest of Africa was accompanied by its incorporation into global telegraph networks: North Africa in 1868, East and South Africa in 1879, and

West Africa in 1886. Britain invested heavily in telegraphs; France and Germany more quickly adopted radio networks following its invention in the early 1900s. Like road and railways, colonial telegraphs and radio linked provincial centres but were systematically extraverted through capital cities to metropolitan hubs. Africa developed sophisticated communications networks, but also ones so thoroughly organized around metropolitan hubs that communication between countries, particularly ones controlled by different empires, was absurdly difficult and expensive. Specific colonial legacies are important in this story, but it is the global diffusion of successive technologies that best orders the African experience of media production, distribution, and consumption.

Academic studies of Africa's media have been overwhelmingly synchronic, carried out within models of media studies, journalism studies, and other social science frameworks. The questions posed are thus typically presentist and normative in nature. What is the degree of press freedom within a given nation-state? To what extent do the media of a given country produce objective or interest-laden reporting? These are important questions for historians as well, but the best historical studies of African media have neither been framed in such terms nor have sought to offer a comprehensive overview. The best survey of the subject, Rosalynde Ainslie's *The Press in Africa*, remains valuable but it is now almost fifty years since its publication.[2] Instead, the prospective student of African media history must contend with a literature in which this subject is either only of partial interest to a wider historical study, or in which the question is phrased first—and perhaps most effectively—in anthropological terms. This chapter will survey both these approaches, as well as formulating wider questions for further historical research.

THE BIRTH OF A PUBLIC: LITERACY, THE PRESS, AND PRINT CULTURE IN AFRICA

While the written word thrived in Africa's mosques, mission stations, and coastal towns before the mid-nineteenth century, information elsewhere survived almost exclusively through oral transmission. Early studies of pre-colonial African media focused on the transmission of information across time through inter-generational oral tradition, and only secondarily on its transmission across space. Oral genres, as Karin Barber has argued, were generally 'premised on the assumption that society is segmented, that knowledge is by definition unequally distributed (otherwise it would not be knowledge)', and that interpretation required supplementary knowledge outside the texts themselves.[3] This relationship between segmented knowledge and segmented power stands as a massive yet indispensable generalization for understanding the cultural value of secrecy and generationally defined entitlements to rank and wealth. While the focus here is on modern-era technologies, it should be observed that the drum, an instrument that stands as a communicative centre in widespread practices of dance and public healing (*ngoma* in Swahili and many other Bantu languages), was itself a media technology that, like many of its aural successors, was both an instrument of entertainment as well as a transmitter of information, though its latter role was largely circumscribed by language difference.

The transformation of this generalized picture—from segmented knowledge to public debate—is perhaps the central question at stake regarding the growth of media across the globe. The most alluring model to theorize the significance of these changes has been Jürgen Habermas's *The Structural Transformation of the Public Sphere* (1962), which locates the specific conditions for rational-critical debates on public matters within a particular chapter of European history. Yet Habermas's specifically European model has pushed others to find creative ways to translate his general concerns to different contexts. The most productive approach to the question of media transformation for Africa has been the work of Karin Barber, who has argued that the most significant aspect of the spread of modernity across the globe has been 'the emergence and multiplication of publics', in which a public is an audience whose members 'are not known to the speaker/composer of the text, and not necessarily present, but still addressed simultaneously, and imagined as a collectivity'. Such a change in relationship between author/speaker and recipient requires a new form of address to meet the challenge of anonymity, while also striving to form 'a real, single, co-present collectivity'.[4] The shift from audience to public, therefore, is not merely a product of new media, but also reflects a fundamental shift in the relationship between power and knowledge in African society. Whereas previous audiences of African oral genres had to link texts to specific and non-inferable bodies of knowledge for them to make sense, the meaning of texts among new publics, as the term indicates, were no longer segmented but publicly available 'to anyone in command of the relevant language and conventions'.[5] Barber's model has the virtue of not imposing the European experience as normative, a defect that characterizes most Habermas-inspired studies. The readerships of Africa were not the products of preceding social and economic development as they had been in Europe, which fostered anonymity and interchangeability, but rather were hurriedly imposed, primarily by Christian missionaries, as a conscious effort to restructure the social and inner lives of Africans. The idea of the individual person participating in Europe's public sphere had been forged within long-developing structures of law and class. In nineteenth-century Africa, missionaries confronted multiple layers of belonging—family, clan, village, generation, and religious community—and the thin stratum of literate converts were primarily translators.

It is within this narrow band of translators that Africa's modern media history begins. Newspapers constituted Africa's earliest and most enduring public. The first newspapers began in Egypt in 1797, arrived in South Africa in 1800, and then in Sierra Leone in 1801 and Liberia in 1826.[6] They continued to flourish over the nineteenth century, primarily along or near the continent's coast and largely under the control of European settlers or missionaries. Among the latter was the Anglican Henry Townsend, who brought out Nigeria's first newspaper, *Iwe Irohin* (*News Sheet*), in 1859, likely the first vernacular newspaper in West Africa. Reading transmitted information and transformed consciousness. According to J. D. Y. Peel, the purpose of *Iwe Irohin* was not simply to foster literacy, but more deeply 'that sense of individual inwardness, of solitary self-motivated quest, so integral to the evangelical sensibility'.[7] This wider textual culture, best embodied by that 'mini-bible' of Protestant evangelicalism, Bunyan's *The Pilgrim's Progress*, saw texts as emanating from a divine source and print culture as a force that transcends human agency.

Exceptions to the rule of European control of early newspapers and print cultures did emerge. These included pioneering editors from the African diaspora: men such as Charles L. Force, John Brown Russwurm, Hilary Teage, and Edward Wilmot Blyden, all of whom, at different times, operated the *Liberia Herald* (*c*.1830–62); as well as independent African newspapers from the Gold Coast, such as Charles Bannerman's *West African Herald* (1859–73) and James Brew's hard-hitting *Gold Coast Times* (1874–85). Indeed, such rare but well-placed figures would loom large in the local propagation of Pan-Africanist arguments—from the foundational figure of Blyden himself, who edited Liberian and Sierra Leonean newspapers during the 1850s to the 1870s, to an ever-widening set of Nigerian thinkers engaged in defining the idea of 'Africa' towards the end of the century.[8]

Yet such literate elites did not form a culturally hegemonic class, but rather a porous group of writers characterized by lonely and eccentric odysseys that frequently failed to fulfil personal expectations. As Karin Barber notes, these figures 'always looked both ways, interpreting the colonial authorities to the native population, and native customs to the colonial authorities'.[9] While far more research remains to be done regarding the actual mechanics and economies of print distribution, what is generally known is that, beyond Africa's coastal towns, print culture began its rapid popularization during the interwar years, through both print and oral distribution. According to Andrew Roberts, the volume of post between 1920 and 1938 roughly tripled in the Belgian Congo, Kenya, Nigeria, Tanganyika, and Uganda, while doubling in Sudan, Southern Rhodesia, and South Africa. Furthermore, the generally low distribution figures for colonial African newspapers mask the actual rates of informational distribution—in Tanganyika during the 1930s, vernacular reading groups were often attended by one hundred or more listeners.[10] As Philip Zachernuk and Stephanie Newell have demonstrated in their studies of the colonial intelligentsias of Nigeria and the Gold Coast (Ghana), respectively, it was within the literary clubs, fraternal lodges, and other voluntary societies of the interwar years where the patronage and distribution networks emerged to support multiple and vibrant independent newspapers.[11] Yet the content and success of many independent newspapers proved overly dependent upon the outsized personalities of its publishers—be it Mohandas Gandhi's *Indian Opinion*, J. B. Danquah's *West African Times*, Nnamdi Azikiwe's *West African Pilot*, or Kwame Nkrumah's *Evening News*. When the press turned towards criticism of the colonial state, legal controls went into action.[12] While the 1930s were the golden age of independent African newspapers, such publications were overshadowed by the wartime regulations and scarcities of the Second World War, but more permanently displaced by subsequent concentration in newspaper ownership by the late 1950s and 1960s, either by larger corporations or by the state. Well-produced media targeted at Africa's narrow intelligentsia could thrive in this thrifty environment if it was done well—as with *Jeune Afrique*, the gorgeously produced weekly newsmagazine published since 1960 in Paris by a Tunisian for an African audience and consumed with alacrity across Francophone Africa.

In keeping with wider academic shifts towards the study of representation, African historians since the 1990s have understood writing as part of a wider cultural practice that sought to fix ambiguous truths or negotiable positions as written facts. In these accounts, literacy and print are not mere technologies of informational transmission, but wider systems of thought and power. To this end, the colonial state in Africa has been increasingly characterized by historians as an 'epistolary state', whose bureaucratic apparatus required that subjects acquire and often carry written documentation to express conformity to legal authority over taxation, land ownership, mobility, and public performance. Such injunctions fostered what has been termed 'tin trunk literacy', in which individuals hoarded precious documents not only to keep on the right side of colonial law but also to constitute a literary 'self' through the production of diaries and letters. Literacy enjoyed not only a powerful association with upward mobility, but also served as a means of self-projection that constituted a sphere of the 'private' that co-evolved with that of the 'public'.[13] The written word, as Derek Peterson and Sean Hawkins have argued, permeated colonial domination and was in turn appropriated by Africans who identified writing and its paraphernalia of letterheads, account books, and grammars with respectability, utilizing them as tools of both instrumental and creative power.[14]

The relationship between colonial literacy and nationalism has naturally attracted much attention. 'Nationalism was also a literary undertaking', Heather Sharkey has argued in her study of Sudan's colonial intelligentsia; 'much like empire itself, it was reliant on the power of the written word to affirm and eventually popularize its values'.[15] Yet, the argument of Benedict Anderson's *Imagined Communities* (1983), which traces nationalism as a product of print capitalism exported from Europe to the world beyond, has had, like Habermas, similar problems of translation to an African context. With the notable exceptions of Arabic in North Africa and Swahili in East Africa, vernacular print languages did not generally serve as vehicles to create 'imagined' nations in what were predominantly multilingual colonial states. Rather it was English, French, or Portuguese that provided the language of nationalism (or, as in Cameroon, languages of nationalism) and that subsequently became an official language of government after independence. The sources of information for nearly all newspapers were local, regional, and global, the latter often being transmitted through corporate or consulate bodies. Anti-colonial international press—be it pan-African, Indian, or Communist—could often bypass colonial post censors, but could not meet the daily or weekly news requirements of nationalist editors in the way that wire services such as Reuters and Agence France-Presse (AFP) could.[16] Despite the widespread existence of nationalist newspapers by the 1950s—far more richly in British colonies than in those of other powers—the building of nationalist movements across the continent was overwhelmingly oral work. Even in the most successful cases such as mainland Tanzania, party-building efforts to transform political consciousness could only contain and ameliorate—rather than eliminate—abiding divisions based on region, generation, class, and religion. Histories of the press that followed independence regularly asserted that the content and politics of Africa's independent or 'nationalist' press was a simple reflection of its larger readership, such as in the work of James Scotton, who repeatedly discovers linear nationalism in the media history of East Africa.[17]

The story of decolonization in more recent African historiography, however, has stressed the decline of political opposition and civil liberties. While circumstances varied tremendously from country to country, between the mid-1960s and the early 1990s newspapers—like radio and television—were effectively controlled, as Francis Nyamnjoh observes, 'either with draconian laws or by simply making them part of the civil service'.[18] Far too many postcolonial reporters resembled the 'true African journalist' extolled by Kwame Nkrumah:

> He does not need to peep through keyholes for scandals, or bribe underlings to divulge what should remain private and personal...The true African journalist very often works for the organ of the political party to which he himself belongs and in whose purpose he believes.[19]

William Hachten overstates the case when he argues that 'the young African press was strangled in its cradle' after independence, but correctly notes that many small independent presses 'disappeared along with political oppositions'.[20] Nkrumah again was the pioneer in closing down critical newspapers and arresting journalists on (often spurious) charges of sedition—many of whom later re-emerged to take immense glee in his overthrow in 1966.

Such patterns were not universal, however. Ethiopia's *dirigiste* press controls easily rivalled their Soviet counterparts, both before and after the overthrow of Haile Selassie. Apartheid South Africa presents a paradox—a highly 'unfree' media environment characterized by widespread publication bans and pervasive censorship of incoming material, yet also one in which newspapers were entirely private-owned, where there was no public television service or state news agency, where the continent's largest and best-resourced newspaper, the Johannesburg *Star*, was headquartered, and where journalists enjoyed at least nominal legal protection not found elsewhere on the continent.[21] Even within this tightly controlled environment, as Les Switzer and Mohamed Adhikari's collection demonstrates, an alternative press of trade union, student, and community newspapers not only survived but thrived, including, for a while at least, the inimitable *Drum*.[22] In South Africa, the existential threat came not only from the possibility of being shut down by government security services, but more prosaically from the inability to secure reliable revenue streams—although this latter factor is mentioned only in passing. The historiographical retreat from discrete categories of 'resisters' and 'collaborators', here as elsewhere, remains a slow one.

Fragile 'public spheres' across twentieth-century Africa found themselves closed down not just through heavy-handed press controls, but through the adoption of a non-negotiable vituperative political language, characterized, for example, by the widespread use of epithets such as 'sellouts' in Southern Rhodesia (Zimbabwe) in the 1960s. Cold War actors rushed in with cheap or free news service agreements and ample propaganda to fill up the foreign news and feature sections of many state and quasi-state newspapers. With a small handful of Marxist or determinedly non-aligned exceptions, the victors of this informational scramble for postcolonial Africa were Britain and France, whose respective news agencies—Reuters and AFP—continued to dominate not only international news content but often regional and national news within African countries, playing foundational roles in the creation of dozens of national news services.[23] There remains much research to be done on the production and control of postcolonial news, not only with respect to wire services, but more importantly with a focus on newsroom cultures and the business of journalism. Gerard Loughran's recent history of the Kenya-based, Aga Khan-owned *Daily Nation* demonstrates how politically significant such newspapers have been to the postcolonial histories of African nations.[24]

BETWEEN DISCIPLINE AND DELIBERATION: FILM AND THE ELECTRONIC MEDIA IN AFRICA

Africa's media landscape has been transformed by the global revolutions in communication technology. According to a 2004 study by the BBC, radio was easily Africa's main medium, used by 95 per cent of its population, followed by television at 65 per cent, and newspapers at 45 per cent.[25] Radio, television, and other electronic media have created what Barber describes as 'a vast intermediate zone which is both live and mediatized, both local and trans-local, and which absorbs models and elements from the formal, official, literate sphere without being subjugated to it'.[26] Only recently have historians begun systematically to research electronic media, and have found—despite their seemingly ephemeral nature and the generally low survival rates of actual broadcasts—that rich documentary and oral evidence survives, offering multiple paths of study.

Film

Several scholars have examined cinema as a medium of African artistic expression, but the social and cultural impact of film in colonial and postcolonial societies has only recently emerged as a topic of serious study. In his pioneering *Signal and Noise*, Brian Larkin approaches the subject by dividing colonial cinema into two categories—short didactical films, often displayed for free by roving vans, and feature-length commercial films, often shown in dedicated theatres to ticket-paying customers. Known in northern Nigeria as *majigi* (from 'magic lantern'), mobile cinema vans offered highly organized (and highly popular) presentations on health, agriculture, and other topics, sandwiched between rousing music and 'God Save the Queen'. *Majigi* stood as a bureaucratic state institution, as 'mental tractors' that broke hard ground to plant seeds of progress, and as a political ritual that advertised the infrastructural largesse bestowed upon Nigerians by Britain.[27] Commercial films, in contrast, offered commodities of entertainment in exchange for money. The films of Hollywood, Bombay, and Hong Kong regularly aggravated the protective sensibilities of colonial officials, although subsequent systems of censorship were often slapdash affairs that were surprisingly vulnerable to the racial and nationalist politics of colonial subjects.[28]

The richly documented anxieties of colonial officials have offered the most accessible portal to recapturing a history of African film-going, which has been carried out for Zimbabwe and Zambia by James Burns and Charles Ambler, respectively.[29] Yet there are limitations to this 'official mind' approach. Criticizing self-satisfied European accounts of African wonder, awe, and fear in the face of new technologies offers a useful corrective (if one is needed for African historians) to the racial fantasies of colonial officials. Scholar-activist zeal to repudiate such racism, however, also forecloses analysis of just what terror and other visceral processes may have been experienced and, as Brian Larkin argues, denies 'the autonomous properties of technologies—the way technologies fashion subjects rather than the other way around'. Cinema-going undoubtedly took habituation before the viewing of exciting screen phenomena—cowboys, criminals, phantasmata, and the rest—could be internalized and reproduced as natural.[30] There need not be a 'universal' film-goer any more than there need be an 'African' film-goer.

Anthropologists and historians have recently taken up the more arduous task of recapturing the urban social and mental life that went on in darkened theatres. The visceral qualities of cinema have understandably directed attention towards the emotional and interior dimensions of the film-goer. As Larkin has noted, the experience of going to a film is greater than the film itself, and it is 'this excess, the immaterial experience of cinema emerging from that assemblage of built space, film, and social practice' that not only piqued colonial anxieties but should stand at the centre of academic attempts to divine the significance of the medium. The movie theatre space of the city of Kano emerged out of the competition between Lebanese entrepreneurs seeking to maximize revenues and colonial officials seeking to maximize control and minimize potential risks. They emerged adjacent to the similarly cosmopolitan public forums of mosque and market, mimicking the symbolic and spatial qualities of markets.[31] In such spaces, patrons demonstrated a particular affection for Hindi films, which, in Larkin's evocative phrase, offered 'parallel modernities' to Hausa film-goers in Nigeria, who participated 'in the imagined realities of other cultures as part of their daily lives'.[32] Laura Fair has demonstrated that Hindi films also offered Tanzanian audiences a space to reimagine their relationship with the wider world, while furtively seeking out romance with future partners.[33]

Yet there remains a vital economic component to film-going that has yet to be explained. Fair demonstrates that Hindi films were in such high demand that theatres had to practise 'reeling', a system of showing the same film print in multiple theatres through a synchronized circulation of available reels. Such practices pose more basic questions about the business models and logics of theatres and distributors, as well as questions of class and patterns of discretionary income spending among what was a highly segmented film-going public. The only full-length work to consider the business side of African cinema is Thelma Gutsche's outstanding study of South Africa in the period 1895–1940, which shows that heated competition between the country's two major film distributors during the 1920s created the continent's best-developed cinema infrastructure. Following their amalgamation, a further round of competition ensued against expanding American giants, together with rising Afrikaner resentment against Anglophone domination.[34] Cinema was first a business, and cinema-going raised larger questions about the relationship between urban entertainment and national discipline, as well as between public investment and individual consumption. These remain early days for the sustained historical research into this most fascinating topic.

Radio

Film was employed as a medium of education and entertainment, but served little other practical function for governments or commerce. Radio, in sharp contrast, revolutionized the form and possibilities of all types of communications. The critical breakthrough was the creation of short-wave radio broadcasting in 1924. Cheaper and faster than long wave, let alone telegraph lines, and with near-instantaneous global reach, short wave proved a great fit for the enormous distances and shoestring government budgets of colonial Africa. Short wave was adopted—more quickly in French than British colonies—for encrypted government and commercial transactions, and more unevenly for public broadcasting. Interwar audiences were overwhelmingly European households with the ability to purchase and operate radio receivers. Traversing geographical and political borders with ease and not dependent upon literacy, radio was adopted across the continent during the 1950s and 1960s. As in the West, electronic media were hardly divorced from print culture—far from it, news broadcasts were largely replications, both at the national and international level, of newspaper and other print media. But radio (and television) did require significant capital investments, which often left the late colonial and postcolonial states as the only institutions positioned to establish such media, usually under the guise of development and national unity. Language became a critical issue. How would national broadcasters distribute vernacular broadcasts when singular territorial-cum-national identities were often its stated goals? How would languages become standardized through official guidance given to radio broadcasters?

The luxury to pose such questions only came after the creation of a durable broadcast infrastructure. Before independence, wealthy immigrant communities with access to mains electricity could enjoy radio within their homes; for most Africans, however, radio listening was a public experience within a crowded compound or restaurant or, far more often, gathered around outside loudspeakers. Owing to their favourable population densities, West African coastal cities such as Freetown, Accra, and Lagos adopted radio diffusion systems, consisting of wired relays to fixed speakers, until they were gradually abandoned in the 1950s for the wireless system adopted across the rest of the continent. The pioneering territory in cultivating a mass African listenership was Northern Rhodesia, where Harry Franklin famously helped to organize the invention and distribution in 1949 of the battery-operated 'Saucepan Special' at £5 per set. While hardly affordable to the average African household at the time, the Saucepan Special did mark a turning point for more prosperous Africans, few of whom had access to mains electricity. Battery power would remain the critical cost bottleneck in the diffusion of radio listening, although the invention of the low-energy transistor radio provided a breakthrough for mass marketing. As a result, the numbers of radios in sub-Saharan Africa (exclusive of South Africa) grew from an estimated 460,000 in 1955 to 4.8 million in 1965, 18.5 million in 1975, and 70.2 million by 1995. In mainland Tanzania alone, the number of receivers rose from about 1,000 in 1951 to 70,000 in 1960, and to 1.7 million in 1973. While some radios were distributed free of charge to favoured chiefs and other subjects, the larger project, as Debra Spitulnik has argued, was the gradual but sure adoption of this vital technology as part of a larger advertising project to situate Africans as modern consumers.[35]

Expanded radio service was part of the postwar commitment to African development by Britain and France. During the 1930s, local radio broadcasting in British colonies was often the pet project of ambitious officials who relied on BBC secondments to establish basic technical and programming systems. In French colonies, programming began as a centralized affair—relying entirely on stations based in Paris, Dakar, and Brazzaville—and became further centralized in 1956 with the establishment of the Société de Radiodiffusion de la France d'outre-mer (SORAFOM), which controlled station as well as network content. SORAFOM, however, quickly went the way of the French Union and transformed into the more modest Office de coopération radio-phonique (OCORA), in 1962, with the remit of technical assistance and recording of traditional African music.[36] In contrast, radio in Angola originated as an amateur endeavour among Portuguese hobbyists during the 1930s and 1940s, with the establishment of the state station Emissora Oficial de Angola (EOA) following only later in the mid-1950s. The South African Broadcasting Corporation (SABC) created a set of FM ethnic radio stations in the early 1960s as part of a wider plan to discourage short-wave listening, express the 'separate development' philosophy of Apartheid, and, crucially, to entice participation on the part of black middle-class intelligentsia whose presence helped to legitimate the stations. Despite these origins, such stations acquired significant vernacular listenerships and have not only survived the fall of Apartheid but have thrived within the post-Apartheid SABC system.[37]

Radio's most illustrious role in African history was as a propaganda tool for liberation movements. During the Second World War, radio broadcasts across Africa were swollen with the hostile invective of Axis powers challenging the legitimacy of British and French rule. The Free France movement of Charles de Gaulle offered the most sustained counter-attack on the continent through a high-wattage station in Brazzaville—wattage subsequently deployed by the Republic of Congo's President Marien Ngouabi for Marxist and liberationist propaganda during the 1960s and 1970s. The most influential anti-imperial broadcasts originated from Nasser's Egypt, which took aim at French ambitions in Algeria and, further afield, challenged colonial states through polemics produced in Swahili, Somali, and Hausa. Such broadcasts not only popularized anti-colonial invectives, but also strengthened funding applications to enlarge colonial capacities to counter Cairo and other hostile voices. Accra, Brazzaville, and Dar es

Salaam joined Cairo as broadcasting platforms for organizations such as the MPLA's Angola Combatente and the ANC's Radio Freedom to wage informational war against minority-ruled regimes in southern Africa.[38]

Having deeply imbibed the sensibility, if not the actual writings, of development media thinkers such as Wilbur Schramm and Daniel Lerner, postcolonial African leaders employed radio as a transformative tool of development, discipline, and didacticism in an effort to modernize tradition-bound listeners. State monopolies over radio broadcasting in British and French colonies remained largely in place during the first three decades of independence. In Cameroon, President Ahmadou Ahidjo announced in 1967 that all the media, but in particular radio, had been entrusted with the 'sacred task of nation-building', and thus would 'transform mentalities in order to accelerate development'.[39] As Marissa Moorman has shown for postcolonial Angola, artists who were not either transparently loyal to the ruling MPLA or producing explicitly nation-building music were informally censored by disc jockeys, while similarly self-censoring broadcasters heaped fawning praise upon MPLA leaders. Radio Tanzania Dar es Salaam (RTD) employed an official censorship committee that approved music only if it did not oppose 'national interests'; like its sister cinema censorship board, it was widely seen as both unaccountable and inconsistent.[40]

Radio multiplied African publics during the era of decolonization, yet historians have only begun to trace its social and intellectual ramifications. Dedicated listening clubs in particular grew during the late 1940s and 1950s, creating new spaces in which news, editorials, and music would be discussed by regular attendees. As Gregory Mann has shown, soldiers from French West Africa serving abroad in the 1950s could send and receive greetings or dedicate songs over Radio Hirondelle or Radio France-Asie, using French, Wolof, or Bamanankan; those stationed in Indochina were particularly avid listeners. For all its capacity to popularize deceit and misinformation, radio could also put older social facts to test. The long-standing alternative political discourse surrounding rain-making in north-eastern Tanzania, famously identified in Steven Feierman's *Peasant Intellectuals*, withered over the 1960s and 1970s as reliable meteorological information from national radio broadcasts grew increasingly accessible. Weather was now understood in national terms, challenging earlier explanatory frameworks in which local medicine makers could plausibly withhold rains. The result of this testable information, which came in greater detail and greater frequency than had earlier discussions about the weather, was not the simple abandonment of older practices, but rather a pragmatic down-grading of the understood efficacy of local medicines and, more importantly, the undermining of the power of rain-makers to demand tribute.[41]

Beyond academic analysis, general interest towards radio in Africa tends to focus on the medium's capacity to incite violence. In Rwanda, Radio-Télévision Libre des Mille Collines (RTLM) began broadcasting in 1993 as the country's first (nominally) private radio station, with the purpose to counter what Hutu extremist groups deemed the 'leftwing' and unduly pro-Tutsi programming of the state-owned Radio Rwanda. RTLM entered world-historical infamy for its role in fomenting and coordinating the country's genocide in 1994—although its degree of culpability remains open.[42] 'Hate radio' has certainly not been limited to Rwanda. Witness white supremacists on Radio Pretoria; state-owned Radio ELBC and HAM radio enthusiasts during Liberia's civil war; calls by Radio Candip in Bunia to kill Tutsis in eastern Congo in the late 1990s; and, more recently, vernacular broadcasts in Kenya by Kass FM (in Kalenjin), Radio Lake Victoria (Luo), and Kameme FM (Kikuyu) following the disputed 2008 presidential elections.

But how were broadcasts—be they 'hate radio' or anything else—received over time in Africa? Popular reception has long stood as both the Holy Grail and Achilles' heel of media studies. One starting place is to get a fuller sense of *how* people listen to radio. Listening patterns, as Debra Spitulnik has demonstrated for Zambia, are less dependent upon global forces than on local conditions. Where receivers and batteries are seen as expensive, a radio is a prized investment that often circulates between home, work, and recreation, making it vulnerable to theft. The desire to preserve batteries often leads to highly selective listening patterns.[43] Another starting place is to understand how vernacular language shapes listener engagement. The contemporary Malawian state broadcasting programme *Nkhani Zam'maboma* (News from the Districts) serves as one of Africa's often theorized—but less often realized—platforms for political accountability. As Harri Englund demonstrates, its listeners identify and debate abuses of power using Chichewa-language idioms concerning conduct of personal relationships, rather than through generic social categories or human rights discourse. The proliferation of new publics such as *Nkhani Zam'maboma* underlines the unexpected forums and content that Africa's media liberalization has brought about.[44]

Yet questions of broader political economy, in particular how radio has been financed by broadcasters, remain open. Until the early 1990s, commercial radio was largely the exception to the continental rule of state-controlled stations. Spot commercials took on an increasing role in some countries, but most systems were financed through licence fees. As the numbers of receivers expanded radically in the two decades surrounding independence, the percentage of license fee collections plummeted, leading most countries to abandon the system by the 1970s, severing the financial link between broadcaster and listener. Like certain newspapers, many African radio stations persist for cause rather than for profit, creating a modern media environment of far greater complexity than existed during the state-dominated decades from radio's beginning to the 1980s, in which market research only exacerbates existing patterns of listener segmentation.

Television and Other Media Technologies

Brian Larkin speaks with a conviction widely held among Africanists when he stresses that electronic media, like print media, do not represent a singular advance towards a universal modernity but rather the particular adaptation of globalized technologies to fit historically specific social formations. The range of gadgets, from tape recorders to videos to cell phones, have all undergone quick adoption when they finally became affordable, but are each utilized towards particular ends. Electronic media provided, as Karin Barber has noted, 'new means of learning and retaining oral genres'. Tape recordings of performances could be used for a variety of purposes—archival, commercial, or private enjoyment. Among Tupuri people in northern Cameroon, recordings served as *aide-mémoires* to replace painstaking memorization of *gurna* society songs, but were discarded after the composition of a new song.[45] Television, so dominant in much of the world from the 1950s, only achieved exponential growth in Africa after 1975. This was due not only to the greater expense and need for mains electricity for receivers, but also to the expense of creating programmes. Television production was far more reliant on foreign expertise and assistance than radio, with a heavier emphasis on sports and melodramas. The number of television sets on the continent lagged far behind all other regions of the globe, accounting for only 0.3 per cent of the world's total in 1965 and rising only to 2.6 per cent by 1989, when Africa had 21 million of the world's 797 million receivers. Access to television remained overwhelmingly urban until fairly recently, when affordable black-and-white Chinese sets costing US$50 became available in rural areas. Rising affordability in video technologies has ushered in a shift in continental programming: as recently as 2005, Kenyan television overwhelmingly consisted of Western productions, but by 2011, roughly 80 per cent of its programmes were produced in Africa.[46]

As with radio and film, ethnographically posed questions offer steep but rewarding challenges for historians of African media. Perhaps most significantly, technology has reconfigured religious observance and piety. In Ghana's liberalized media landscape, television and radio broadcasts, video recordings, and billboard advertising have filled media spaces previous controlled by state organizations. Pentecostal charismatic churches have utilized audiovisual mass media to project images of good living and God-sent miracles in the ongoing battle against traditional religion and occult forces.[47] As Charles Hirschkind has argued, religious media form not an idealized Habermasian 'public' in which deliberation can be immunized from the discipline of power, but instead a 'counterpublic' in which deliberation and discipline are thoroughly interdependent. Egypt's Islamic revival has profited from the portability of cassettes that circulate across the Arabic-speaking world, freeing religious messages from gatekeeping imams at mosques to range freely across public and private spaces of shops, cafés, taxis, and buses.[48] Right of access to national media more generally has long been a point of debate and even conflict among religious communities. The most vexing problems to emerge with the liberalization of Africa's media concern the regulation of religious pluralism. Small media, as Dorothea Schulz has argued, 'rather than unequivocally broadening access to public debate, exacerbate conflicts over participation and often feed into already existing strategies of exclusion'.[49] Competitive proselytization and other forms of mediated religion now fill the air of African towns as never before. Despite the profusion of new radio and television outlets, religious groups continue to covet national broadcasting. When SABC attempted to reduce its religious programming by 75 per cent in 1997, both Christian and Muslim broadcasters protested, each demanding a greater share of the remaining airtime.[50]

It would be overdramatic, but only slightly so, to characterize the transformations in media technologies over the last fifteen years as being greater than Africa has experienced over the past five hundred. The very name 'Nigeria' has become internationally synonymous with unsolicited emails that promise recipients a massive payout in exchange for an advance fee. The rapid spread of mobile phones and internet access in the past decade has raised sharp and seemingly intractable issues over state control of content. In 2004, a rumour that Cameroon's President Paul Biya had died spread rapidly across the world, putting its government—usually on the cutting edge of censorship strategy and tactics—on the back foot. Most recently, Facebook and other social media played an unquestionably important role in the popular overthrow of Egypt's President Hosni Mubarak. Yet the future of these innovative technologies is difficult to predict. International media developments since the 1990s have overwhelmingly been in the direction of deregulation and oligopolies, in which firms grow quickly out of fear of being swallowed up by competitors. Such stark patterns of ownership concentration in the West, however, have so far only been partially realized in Africa.

FUTURE DIRECTIONS

The history of communications and media in Africa has an undoubtedly bright future, not only because of strong academic interest in related topics of representation and modernity, but also because fundamental notions of community, ethnicity, and nation are inevitably constituted through historical media. The production, distribution, and reception of newspapers, pamphlets, radio and television broadcasts, films, and video is cultural work that not only produces the evidence upon which professional historians rely, but also form processes that are dependent upon global networks yet are also constantly domesticated within specific local contexts. Writing contemporary history, as Stephen Ellis has explained, not only requires greater use of newspapers and radio as historical sources, but also greater savvy as to how such sources mediate cultures of oral communication propelled by a mixture of truth-seeking and rumour-mongering, best captured by the fitting and now-ubiquitous phrase *radio trottoir* ('pavement radio').[51]

Popular reception has been the most important yet difficult aspect of media studies. Sparse qualitative data in the form of audience letters and official reports dominate what survives of the documentary record of sub-Saharan African media before the late 1950s, when quantitative surveys began in earnest across the continent. Yet the styles, situations, and structures of actual reading, listening, and watching often survive only in living oral memory or, more systematically, in the sort of foundational ethnographies conducted by Debra Spitulnik, Brian Larkin, and others since the 1990s. Creating ways to pose the questions they have raised to historical evidence will be a major challenge for future research on Africa's media history.

Notes

1. Daniel R. Headrick, *The Invisible Weapon: Telecommunications and International Politics, 1851–1945* (New York: OUP, 1991), 3–5.
2. Rosalynde Ainslie, *The Press in Africa: Communications Past and Present* (London: Victor Gollancz, 1966).
3. Karin Barber, 'Orality, the Media and New Popular Cultures in Africa', in Kimani Njogu and John Middleton, eds, *Media and Identity in Africa* (Edinburgh: Edinburgh University Press, 2009), 9.
4. Karin Barber, *The Anthropology of Texts, Persons and Publics* (Cambridge: CUP, 2007), 139–40.
5. Barber, *Anthropology of Texts*, 203.
6. Francis B. Nyamnjoh, *Africa's Media: Democracy and the Politics of Belonging* (London: Zed Books, 2005), 40.
7. J. D. Y. Peel, *Religious Encounter and the Making of the Yoruba* (Bloomington, Ind.: Indiana University Press, 2000), 131.
8. Isabel Hofmeyr, *The Portable Bunyan: A Transnational History of* The Pilgrim's Progress (Princeton: PUP, 2004); Carl Patrick Burrowes, *Power and Press Freedom in Liberia, 1830–1970: The Impact of Globalization and Civil Society on Media–Government Relations* (Trenton, NJ: Africa World Press, 2004), 17–49, 63–4; Philip Serge Zachernuk, *Colonial Subjects: An African Intelligentsia and Atlantic Ideas* (Charlottesville, Va.: University Press of Virginia, 2000).
9. Barber, *Anthropology of Texts*, 185.
10. Andrew Roberts, 'African Cross-Currents', in A. D. Roberts, ed., *Cambridge History of Africa, vii. From 1905 to 1940* (Cambridge: CUP, 1986), 231–3.
11. Zachernuk, *Colonial Subjects*, 90–4; Stephanie Newell, *Ghanaian Popular Fiction: 'Thrilling Discoveries in Conjugal Life' and Other Tales* (Oxford: James Currey, 2000), 53–9.
12. See Fred I. A. Omu, 'The Dilemma of Press Freedom in Colonial Africa: The West African Example', *Journal of African History*, 9/2 (1968); Stanley Shaloff, 'Press Controls and Sedition Proceedings in the Gold Coast, 1933–1939', *African Affairs*, 71/284 (1972).
13. See esp. Karin Barber, ed., *Africa's Hidden Histories: Everyday Literacy and Making the Self* (Bloomington, Ind.: Indiana University Press, 2006).
14. See Derek R. Peterson, *Creative Writing: Translation, Bookkeeping, and the Work of Imagination in Colonial Kenya* (Portsmouth, NH: Heinemann, 2004); and Sean Hawkins, *Writing and Colonialism in Northern Ghana: The Encounter between the LoDagaa and 'The World on Paper'* (Toronto: University of Toronto Press, 2002).
15. Heather Sharkey, *Living with Colonialism: Nationalism and Culture in the Anglo-Egyptian Sudan* (Berkeley, Calif.: University of California Press, 2003), 3.
16. James R. Brennan, 'Politics and Business in the Indian Newspapers of Colonial Tanganyika', *Africa*, 81 (2011).
17. James F. Scotton, 'The First African Press in East Africa: Protest and Nationalism in Uganda in the 1920s', *International Journal of African Historical Studies*, 6/2 (1973); James F. Scotton, 'Tanganyika's African Press, 1937–1960: A Nearly Forgotten Pre-Independence Forum', *African Studies Review*, 21/1 (1978).
18. Nyamnjoh, *Africa's Media*, 69.
19. Kwame Nkrumah, *The African Journalist* (Dar es Salaam: Tanzania Publishers, 1965), 10.
20. William A. Hachten, *The Growth of Media in the Third World: African Failures, Asian Successes* (Ames, Ia.: Iowa State University Press, 1993), pp. ix, 25.

21. William A. Hachten, *Muffled Drums: The News Media in Africa* (Ames, Ia.: Iowa State University Press, 1971), 237–48.

22. Les Switzer and Mohamed Adhikari, eds, *South Africa's Resistance Press: Alternative Voices in the Last Generation under Apartheid* (Athens, O.: Ohio University Press, 2000).

23. Timothy Scarnecchia, *The Urban Roots of Democracy and Political Violence in Zimbabwe: Harare and Highfield, 1940-1964* (Rochester, NY: University of Rochester Press, 2008), 161; Rosalynde Ainslie, *The Press in Africa: Communications Past and Present* (London: Victor Gollancz, 1966), 199–211; Jonathan Fenby, *The International News Services* (New York: Schocken Books, 1986), 185–9.

24. Gerard Loughran, *Birth of a Nation: The Story of a Newspaper in Kenya* (London: I. B. Tauris, 2010).

25. Kimani Njogu, 'Rekindling Efficacy: Storytelling for Health', in Njogu and Middleton, *Media and Identity*, 128.

26. Barber, 'Orality', 7.

27. Brian Larkin, *Signal and Noise: Media, Infrastructure, and Urban Culture in Nigeria* (Durham, NC: Duke University Press, 2008), 86–99, 105, 168.

28. James R. Brennan, 'Democratizing Cinema and Censorship in Tanzania, 1920–1980', *International Journal of African Historical Studies*, 38 (2005).

29. J. M. Burns, *Flickering Shadows: Cinema and Identity in Colonial Zimbabwe* (Athens, O.: Ohio University Press, 2002); Charles Ambler, 'Popular Films and Colonial Audiences: The Movies in Northern Rhodesia', *American Historical Review*, 106 (2001).

30. Larkin, *Signal and Noise*, 40, 116, 137.

31. Larkin, *Signal and Noise*, 2, 130–4.

32. Brian Larkin, 'Indian Films and Nigerian Lovers: Media and the Creation of Parallel Modernities', *Africa*, 67 (1997), 407.

33. Laura Fair, 'Making Love in the Indian Ocean: Hindi Films, Zanzibari Audiences, and the Construction of Romance in the 1950s and 1960s', in Jennifer Cole and Lynn M. Thomas, eds, *Love in Africa* (Chicago: University of Chicago Press, 2009); Laura Fair, '"They Stole the Show!": Indian Films in Coastal Tanzania, 1950s–1980s', *Journal of African Media Studies*, 2 (2010).

34. Thelma Gutsche, *The History and Social Significance of Motion Pictures in South Africa 1895-1940* (Cape Town: Howard Timmins, 1972).

35. Debra Spitulnik, 'Mediated Modernities: Encounters with the Electronic in Zambia', *Visual Anthropology Review*, 14 (1998/1999). For overviews of radio, see Graham Mytton, *Mass Communication in Africa* (London: Edward Arnold, 1983); and Graham Mytton, 'From Saucepan to Dish: Radio and TV in Africa', in Richard Fardon and Graham Furniss, eds, *African Broadcast Cultures: Radio in Transition* (Oxford: James Currey, 2000).

36. Ainslie, *Press in Africa*, 158–61; Nyamnjoh, *Africa's Media*, 127; Mytton, *Mass Communication*, 53–4.

37. Marissa J. Moorman, *Intonations: A Social History of Music and Nation in Luanda, Angola, from 1945 to Recent Times* (Athens, O.: Ohio University Press, 2008), 143–4; Sekibakiba Peter Lekgoathi, '"You are Listening to Radio Lebowa of the South African Broadcasting Corporation": Vernacular Radio, Bantustan Identity and Listenership, 1960–1994', *Journal of Southern African Studies*, 35/2 (2009).

38. James R. Brennan, 'Radio Cairo and the Decolonization of East Africa, 1953–1964', in Christopher J. Lee, ed., *Making a World After Empire: The Bandung Movement and its Political Afterlives* (Athens, O.: Ohio University Press, 2010), 173–95; Moorman, *Intonations*, 142; Sekibakiba Peter Lekgoathi, 'The African National Congress' Radio

Freedom and its Audiences in Apartheid South Africa, 1963–1991', *Journal of African Media Studies* 2 (2010).

39. Nyamnjoh, *Africa's Media*, 131.

40. Moorman, *Intonations*, 185–6; Kelly M. Askew, *Performing the Nation: Swahili Music and Cultural Politics in Tanzania* (Chicago: University of Chicago Press, 2002), 253–4.

41. Gregory Mann, *Native Sons: West African Veterans and France in the Twentieth Century* (Durham, NC: Duke University Press, 2006), 158–60; Steven Feierman, *Peasant Intellectuals: Anthropology and History in Tanzania* (Madison, Wis.: University of Wisconsin Press, 1990), 251–3.

42. Richard Carver, 'Rwanda and Beyond', in Fardon and Furniss, *African Broadcast Cultures*, 188–97.

43. Debra Spitulnik, 'Reception Studies and the Mobile Machine in Zambia', in Fardon and Furniss, *African Broadcast Cultures*.

44. Harri Englund, *Human Rights and African Airwaves: Mediating Equality on the Chichewa Radio* (Bloomington, Ind.: Indiana University Press, 2011).

45. Barber, 'Orality', 5.

46. Hachten, *Growth of Media*, 7; 'Digital Revolution', The *Economist*, 9 April 2011.

47. Birgit Meyer, 'Pentecostalism and Modern Audiovisual Media', in Njogu and Middleton, *Media and Identity*, 114–23.

48. Charles Hirschkind, *The Ethical Soundscape: Cassette Sermons and Islamic Counterpublics* (New York: Columbia University Press, 2006), 106.

49. Dorothea E. Schulz, 'Morality, Community, Publicness: Shifting Terms of Public Debate in Mali', in Birgit Meyer and Annelies Moors, eds, *Religion, Media and the Public Sphere* (Bloomington, Ind.: Indiana University Press, 2006), 145.

50. Rosalind I. J. Hackett, 'Mediated Religion in South Africa: Balancing Airtime and Rights Claims', in Meyer and Moors, *Religion, Media and the Public Sphere*, 171–2.

51. Stephen Ellis, 'Writing Histories of Contemporary Africa', *Journal of African History*, 43 (2002).

BIBLIOGRAPHY

Ainslie, Rosalynde, *The Press in Africa: Communication Past and Present* (London: Victor Gollancz, 1966).

Barber, Karin, *The Anthropology of Texts, Persons and Publics* (Cambridge: CUP, 2007).

Bourgault, Louise, *Mass Media in Sub-Saharan Africa* (Bloomington: Indiana University Press, 1995).

Burns, James, *Flickering Shadows: Cinema and Identity in Colonial Zimbabwe* (Athens, O.: Ohio University Pres, 2002).

Englund, Harri, *Human Rights and African Airwaves: Mediating Equality on the Chichewa Radio* (Bloomington, Ind.: Indiana University Press, 2011).

Fardon, Richard, and Graham Furniss, eds, *African Broadcast Cultures: Radio in Transition* (Oxford: James Currey, 2000).

Finnegan, Ruth, *Literacy and Orality: Studies in the Technology of Communication* (Oxford: Basil Blackwell, 1988).

Gutsche, Thelma, *The History and Social Significance of Motion Pictures in South Africa, 1895–1940* (Cape Town: Howard Timmins, 1972).

Hachten, William A., *Muffled Drums: The News Media in Africa* (Ames, Ia.: Iowa State University Press, 1971).

—— *The Growth of Media in the Third World: African Failures, Asian Successes* (Ames, Ia.: Iowa State University Press, 1993),

Larkin, Brian. *Signal and Noise: Media, Infrastructure and Urban Culture in Nigeria* (Durham, NC: Duke University Press, 2008).

Meyer, Birgit, and Annelies Moors, eds, *Religion, Media and the Public Sphere* (Bloomington, Ind.: Indiana University Press, 2006).

Moorman, Marissa J., *Intonations: A Social History of Music and Nation in Luanda, Angola, from 1945 to Recent Times* (Athens, O.: Ohio University Press, 2008.

Mytton, Graham, *Mass Communication in Africa* (London: Edward Arnold, 1983).

Njogu, Kimani, and John Middleton, eds, *Media and Identity in Africa* (Edinburgh: Edinburgh University Press, 2009).

Nyamnjoh, Francis, *Africa's Media, Democracy and the Politics of Belonging* (London: Zed Books, 2005).

Switzer, Les, and Mohamed Adhikari, eds, *South Africa's Resistance Press: Alternative Voices in the Last Generation under Apartheid* (Athens, O.: Ohio University Press, 2000).

Tudesq, André-Jean, *L'Afrique parle, l'Afrique écoute: Les Radios en Afrique subsaharienne* (Paris: Karthala, 2002).

Zachernuk, Philip Serge, *Colonial Subjects: An African Intelligentsia and Atlantic Ideas* (Charlottesville, Va.: University Press of Virginia, 2000).

Index

UK Ltd.

002B/5/P